Families

Joys, Conflicts, and Changes

Families
Joys, Conflicts, and Changes

Alex Liazos

Regis College

Paradigm Publishers
Boulder • London

Copyright © 2004 by Paradigm Publishers

Published in the United States by Paradigm Publishers, 3360 Mitchell Lane, Suite C, Boulder, Colorado 80301 USA.

Paradigm Publishers is the trade name of Birkenkamp & Company, LLC,
Dean Birkenkamp, President and Publisher.

Library of Congress Cataloging-in-Publication Data

Liazos, Alex, 1941–
    Families : joys, conflicts, and changes / Alex Liazos.
        p. cm.
Includes bibliographical references and index.
    ISBN 1–59451–016–4 (alk. paper)—ISBN 1–59451–017–2 (pbk. : alk. paper)
    1. Family—United States.   2. Family.   I. Title.
    HQ536.L53 2004
    306.85'0973—dc22

                                                                                2003022454

Printed and bound in the United States of America on acid free paper that meets the standards of the American National Standard for Permanence of Paper for Printed Library Materials.

Designed and Typeset by Straight Creek Bookmakers
12 11 10 09 08 07 06 05 04 1 2 3 4 5

Lovingly and longingly dedicated to
My aunt Sofia Liazos Stratis (1917–1994), a gentle and wise woman
Our long talks and her memory are with me always.

My daughters and their husbands,
Melissa and Rudd,
and Ariane and Tony,
for all the times we have enjoyed together

And the future of our family:
my grandnieces
Ariadne, Eftihia, Eleftheria, Georgia,
Natasha, Rachel, and Sofia;
and grandnephews
Christopher, Christos, and Thomas

Contents in Brief

PREFACE   xv

ACKNOWLEDGMENTS   xvii

Chapter 1

Setting the Scene   1

Chapter 2

Families in U.S. History   12

Chapter 3

Making Sense of Families   35

Chapter 4

Marriage, Cohabitation, and Same-Sex Marriage   50

Chapter 5

Parents and Children   71

Chapter 6

Living in Families   103

Chapter 7

Families, Kin, and Communities   116

Chapter 8

Economies, Migration, and Families   138

Chapter 9

Families and Gender   159

Chapter 10

Class, Race, and Families   177

Chapter 11

Families, Work, and Housework   195

Chapter 12

Divorce: A World Tradition   224

Chapter 13

Violence in Families   262

Chapter 14

Closing Reflections and Parting Comments   283

REFERENCES   287

INDEX   307

ABOUT THE AUTHOR   313

Detailed Contents

PREFACE   xv

ACKNOWLEDGMENTS   xvii

Chapter 1   Setting the Scene   1

Family Changes, Family Continuities   1

Seven Family Scenes   2

Plymouth Colony, 1680s / A Kentucky Mountain Family, 1887–1946 / An Italian Family, 1910s–1930s / A Lesbian Family, 1990s / African American Families Returning South / Working-Class English Families, 1950s / Polynesian Families, 1930s

What Are Families?   7

Major Themes of the Book   9

Appendix A: Data on U.S. Families   9

Appendix B: Some Terms to Understand   10

Chapter 2   Families in U.S. History   12

Introduction and Overview   12

Images and Fears of Family Decline   13

Colonial Families   14

Families under Industrialism   17

Families in the Twentieth Century   20
Companionate Families and Marriages

Muncie, Indiana, 1890s, 1920s, and 1970s   23

The 1950s, in Memory and Reality   25

Enslaved and "Free" African American Families   29

The African Heritage / African American Families after Emancipation / Northern Free Blacks, 1700–1860 / Sharecropping, the Journey North, and the 1950s

Conclusion   33

Chapter 3   Making Sense of Families   35

Ideals, Longings, and Realities   35

Perspectives on Families   35
The Decline and Demise of Families / Families Are Well and Healthy / Anxious, Distressed, and Enduring Families

Power, Feminism, and Families   43
Letty Cottin Pogrebin / Joan Walsh / Judy Aulette / Judith Stacey / Summary

Sociology, History, and Families   46

Difficulties in the Study of Families   46
"The Good Old Days" / The Nuclear Family as "Normal" and Universal / Family Secrets and Façades

Conclusion: Beyond Power Struggles and Conflicts   49

Chapter 4   Marriage, Cohabitation, and Same-Sex Marriage   50

Marriages   50
Why Marry? / Some Statistics on Marriage / Marriages in U.S. History

Good Marriages and the Benefits of Marriage   53
Research on Marriage / Characteristics of Good Marriages / The Benefits of Marriage

Marriages over Time   58

Debates on the State of Marriage   60
Feminist Critiques / Marriages in Muncie, Indiana, in the 1970s / The Decline of Marriage?

The Rise of Cohabitation   62
*What Is Cohabitation? / The Normalization of Cohabitation in Europe and the United States /
Why Do People Cohabit? / Cohabitation and Divorce / Cohabitation and the Law*

Same-Sex Couples—and Marriages?   65
*The Struggle for Same-Sex Marriages / Same-Sex Unions in Other Countries / Rights and Benefits /
Debates on Same-Sex Marriages*

Conclusion   70

Chapter 5   Parents and Children   71

The Joys of Childhood and Parenthood   71
"Me and My Dad" / Celebrating a Family's Good Times / Why Have Children?

Parents and Children in Earlier Times   76
*The Mundurucu of the Amazon in the 1950s / The Tikopia of Polynesia in the 1930s /
The Mbuti of Zaire / The Montagnais of the St. Lawrence Valley*

Our Babies, Ourselves: Some Lessons on Parenting   78
Bonding / Sleeping / Touching / Feeding

Parents and Children in African American Communities   82
All Our Kin / Call to Home

Historical Notes on Childhood and Parenting   84
Children / Parents

Children Today   85
*Busy Parents, Fear, Computers, and the Decline of Childhood? / "The Devaluation of the Work of
Raising Children?" / Child Care and Day Care / Class, Race, and Childhood*

Parents Today   93
Blaming Parents / Fatherless America? / One-Parent Families / Gay and Lesbian Parents

Conclusion   101

Chapter 6   Living in Families   103

Cooking and Eating Meals   103

Being Together and Having Fun   106

"Women, Families, and the Work of Kinship"   108

Caregiving   109
History / Caregiving Today / Call to Home *and Caregiving / Crisis in and Solutions
of Caregiviging / Experiences of Caregiving / The Stresses of Caregiving*

Homeless People and Their Families   113

Conclusion   115

Chapter 7 Families, Kin, and Communities 116

Kin and Community of Sofia Stratis 116

Extended Family and Kin 118
Gathering–Hunting Societies / Kinship in East London in the 1950s / The Abkhasians

Extended Families in U.S. History 120
Plymouth Plantation / Early Twentieth Century / Second Half of the Twentieth Century

Extended Families and Kin Today 122
Extended Families / Kin Ties of Elderly People / Personal Reflections

Grandparents and Grandchildren 126
Three Societies, 1930s–1960s / Grandparents in Recent U.S. History / U.S. Grandparents Today / The Importance and Benefits of Generational Ties / Raising Grandchildren

Families and Communities 130
Societies outside the United States / The United States through the 1800s / The United States in the Twentieth Century / Kin and Community Today: A Memory and a Wish?

Conclusion 136

Chapter 8 Economies, Migration, and Families 138

Migration and Families 138
Poverty, the Search for Work, and Migration / Migration to the United States / Migration within the United States / Reflections about Migration / Debates on the Effects of Migration / Migrants Who Return Home

The Changing U.S. Economy 149
The 1950s to mid-1970s / Economic Problems and Inequalities since the 1970s

Consequences for Families 153
Families Doing Well / Trials and Predicaments / Families before Economies

Conclusion 158

Chapter 9 Families and Gender 159

Sex and Gender 159

Socialization, Social Barriers, and Resistance 160

Gender in U.S. History 162

Families and Gender Today 163
Men as "Good Providers" / Work, Income, and Gender / Toward Equality and Sharing

Conclusion: Sharing Our Lives 175

Chapter 10 Class, Race, and Families 177

Classes and Families 177
What Are Classes? / How Classes Shape Family Life / Summary of Classes and Families

Race and Ethnicity 185
Trials and Strengths of African American Families / Economic and Social Statistics / Breakdown or Strengths of African American Families? / Summary of Race and Ethnicity

Chapter 11   Families, Work, and Housework   195

The Nature of Work   195

Work, Identity, and Gender   196

Interactions between Work and Family   198
How Work and Family Influence Each Other / Work and Types of Families / Negative Spillover from Work / A Theory of Family and Work

Recent Changes and the Time Bind Debates   203
Reversal of Home and Work? / Trends in Hours at Work / Why Do People Work Long Hours? / Chaotic Lives and Other Issues

What Are We to Do?   209
Individual Solutions / Social Policies and Political Struggles / Some Guiding Principles

Housework: Dust Wars and Stealing Our Lives   215
Reflections and Scenes / History and Nature of Housework / Why Do Women Do Most Housework? Part I / Why Do Women Do Most Housework? Part II / Farming out Family Chores and Responsibilities

Conclusion: Sharing It All   222

Chapter 12   Divorce: A World Tradition   224

Perspectives on Divorce   225
A Universal Experience / An American Tradition / Statistics on Divorce

Experiences, Attitudes, and Laws of Divorce   233
Experiences / Beliefs and Culture / The Debate over No-Fault Divorce

Women, Men, and Divorce   239
Women's Experiences / Men's Experiences / Custody of Children / Economic Issues / Gender Feuds

Why Do People Divorce?   241
Some Preliminary Observations / The Rise in Divorce / Other Conditions That May Contribute to Divorce / An Ethic of "Obligation to Self"?

Children and Divorce   246
Facing Parental Separation / Living Arrangements / Child-Support Payments / Divorced Fathers and Their Children / Does Divorce Damage Children? / What Do Children of Divorce Need?

Life after Divorce   257
"Divorce is never good, but good can come out of it" / New Families

Conclusion: The Meanings of Divorce   260

Chapter 13   Violence in Families   262

Introduction   262
Stories / What Does It all Mean? / Types of Violence

Violence in Intimate Relationships   264
Cultural Perspectives / History of Violence in the United States / How Much Violence? By Whom? / Experiences of Violence, Control, and Terror / Staying and Leaving / Shelters

The Reasons . . . ? Because He Could   275
Isolation, Control, and Economic Dependence / Other Explanations / Men Beat Their Wives and Partners Because They Can

What Should We Do? 278

Progress Made / An Anthropologist's View / Jane Doe, Inc. / Autonomy and Gender Equality / Men against Violence / Legal Strategies / The Limits of Therapy / Some Practical Advice

Conclusion 282

Chapter 14 Closing Reflections and Parting Comments 283

Recent and Ongoing Changes 283

Same-Sex Marriages / Divorce / Working Mothers

Perspectives on Families 284

Some Important Reminders 285

A Toast and a Wish: More Family Time 286

REFERENCES 287

INDEX 307

ABOUT THE AUTHOR 313

Preface

Writing this book has been a satisfying and challenging experience. It has been a journey of social discovery, and of self and family exploration. I present scenes of family joys and of playful times from many places and times. I hope it will be a voyage of discovery for you, too. In that spirit, you might try writing your family history, an assignment that students in my family course always find gratifying and informative. While they research that history, they often unearth new relatives and family events.

This is a selective text. I explore fewer family issues in depth rather than try to provide an encyclopedic review of all fields. For example, I discuss in depth the connections between families, kin, and communities, something few texts even mention. On the other hand, as important as marital communication is, I do not devote the space to it that some texts do.

I present a point of view on families, but I also try to be balanced and fair to other perspectives. For example, I provide extensive summaries and quotations of writers who worry that families are falling apart (see chapter 3 and elsewhere), although I disagree with them. I encourage you to reflect on and debate the various studies and interpretations I provide. I especially hope you will use this book to reflect on your family, other families you know, and families in general. Please question, debate, and discuss everything you read here—and in all books.

Data found in the book are, whenever possible, from the most recent U.S. Census in 2000. Most family studies I present are also recent, since the 1990s. But I also present studies from earlier years, both because they are well-established classics and because in important ways they still reflect the world today. They also tell us how we arrived where we are now. But the world changes constantly. You should bear this in mind and read this text—like all texts—critically and with a vigilant eye on the world, which both changes and stays the same.

This text has some distinct features and approaches.

1. It presents all three realities of family lives and family relationships:
   - the *joys* of being together and supporting each other
   - the *conflicts between* family members
   - the *changes that* have been happening in families throughout history
2. It explores the wide variety of families historically and across cultures and allows us to understand family changes, such as the gradual acceptance of same-sex marriage.
3. It offers two chapters not found in other texts:
   - "Family Living" explores the social value of caregiving, family meals, and other family activities.
   - "Kin and Community" shows how families are connected to their extended family kin and their communities.
4. Other coverage and features include:
   - Families and migration
   - Women, men, work, and housework
   - Social policies to support all kinds of families
   - New family forms and family changes emphasized throughout the book
   - Family changes and families in other cultures presented in all chapters
   - Extensive coverage and discussion of major research, scholars, and ethnographies (for examples, see the list in Acknowledgements)
5. I also present examples from my own family history: camping trips and other good times with my daughters; visits to my family in our ancestral village of Longo, Albania; the family, kin, and community history of my beloved Aunt Sofia, to whom I dedicate this book; and others.

Acknowledgments

For those of us who write textbooks, our first and foremost debt should be to the hundreds and thousands of people whose research and writing provide the information, inspiration, and explanations we use in our texts. I am deeply grateful to all of you.

I would like to acknowledge especially the following writers whose works have inspired, informed, and guided much of the thinking and writing that went into this book. (Publication information for each work is found in the reference list.)

Stephanie Coontz, *The Way We Really Are: Coming to Terms with America's Changing Families*
John Demos, *A Little Commonwealth: Family Life in Plymouth Colony*
Francine Deutsch, *Halving It All: How Equally Shared Parenting Works*
Arlie Russell Hochschild, *The Second Shift: Working Parents and the Revolution at Home* and *The Time Bind: When Work Becomes Home and Home Becomes Work*
Robert S. Lynd and Helen Merrell Lynd, *Middletown: A Study in Modern American Culture* and *Middletown in Transition*
Jerre Mangione, *Mount Allegro: A Memoir of Italian American Life*
Letty Cottin Pogrebin, *Family Politics: Love and Power on an Intimate Frontier*
Glenda Riley, *Divorce: An American Tradition*
Lillian B. Rubin, *Worlds of Pain: Life in the Working-Class Family;* and *Intimate Strangers: Men and Women Together;* and *Families on the Fault Line: America's Working Class Speaks About the Family, the Economy, Race, and Ethnicity*
Marjorie Shostak, *Nisa: The Life and Words of a !Kung Woman*
Carol Stack, *All Our Kin* and *Call to Home: African Americans Reclaim the Rural South*
Colin Turnbull, *The Forest People*

I am very grateful to Regis College for a paid sabbatical leave in the fall of 1999, which gave me time to write about half of the book without teaching responsibilities.

My friends and colleagues Barbara Dowds, Donna Huse, and Victoria Rader read parts or all of the first draft, and it was their encouragement and support that gave me the strength to continue writing for three years. I followed most but not all of their suggestions and they are responsible only for those I did.

As an outside reader, Deborah Merrill provided both support and very useful suggestions for improvement. I am very thankful to her; in some ways, she made the book possible.

Two Regis College students made major contributions. Lauren Kane once told a classmate that "sociology is good birth control" (see opening of chapter 5); I overheard that comment, and it confirmed my determination to write a family text that explores the joys of family life as well as the conflicts.

Erin Gettens read the entire first draft of the manuscript while she was taking my course "Changing Families." She made numerous, careful, and wise suggestions, most of which I was happy to follow. I am very indebted to her.

My brothers, sisters, and their spouses, and all my nieces and nephews, have been a constant and supportive presence in my life. It is a privilege and a joy to have them in my life, and to thank them here for the love and strength they have been giving me.

My daughter Melissa and her husband Rudd, and my daughter Ariane and her husband Tony, are my immediate family. Only they know what they have meant to me, and how much I love them and relish their company and love.

Mark Lewis, director of academic computing at Regis College, helped me each time I needed to e-mail different versions and parts of the text to Paradigm. His assistance was indispensable. My deepest thanks, Mark. I could never have done it without you.

Thank you to all of the anonymous families who shared their personal photographs as illustrations for this book.

Dianne Ewing was the ideal production editor and copyeditor. She appreciated the spirit of this book and gently helped me improve and clarify what I meant to say. She found many incomplete and missing references, found better words for what I wanted to say, spotted missing words, and improved the text in many other ways. And it was fun to chat about New England foliage and other topics while we conducted business by phone and e-mail. It was a pleasure to work with you, Dianne. I am very grateful and thankful for all you did.

The final thanks go to Dean Birkenkamp, founder of Paradigm Publishers, who took a chance to publish a different kind of text. I will always appreciate the support you provided in so many ways, Dean.

Other people, too many to mention here, played various roles in the creation of this book. I am also indebted to them.

1

Setting the Scene

FAMILY CHANGES, FAMILY CONTINUITIES

Families have always been changing.

Sometimes fast and at other times slowly, U.S. marriages, relationships to relatives, number of children, and other family matters have been transformed since Colonial days. In addition, history and anthropology tell us that family change has been a world reality. But there have been continuities, too. Family forms may have changed, but there has been a constant commitment to some form of family living.

Let us look at same-sex marriages. Since the late 1980s, some European nations have recognized a modified form of marriage for same-sex couples. They enjoy many, but not all of the legal rights and responsibilities of heterosexual married couples. During the first three years of this century, same-sex marriage became legal in the Netherlands and Belgium. Heterosexual and same-sex couples enjoy all the same rights and responsibilities. (For more details, see ch. 4.)

Meanwhile, in the U.S., it seemed during the 1990s that Hawaii would legalize same-sex marriage, but citizens voted against it in 1998. In 2000, Vermont became the first state to create "civil unions" for same-sex couples, which, like their European predecessors, grant them some, but not all, rights of heterosexual marriages. In late 2003, it seems that it's only a matter of time before same-sex marriage becomes a reality in the United States. In April, a Massachusetts poll showed that 50 percent of respondents favored it; 44 percent did not, 6 percent were unsure. Each time I take anonymous polls in my sociology classes, 90 percent or more of the students say they approve of it.

The impending arrival of same-sex marriage seems only fair and just to many people. Others, however, are filled with fear and dread. They think it will undermine and destroy traditional marriage. When a state or federal court, or state or national legislative body, approves same-sex marriage, the debate and the conflict over its meaning and consequences will be with us for decades. Few of us would have predicted, even ten years ago, that two men or two women would be granted the same social recognition and legal rights that a man and a woman have enjoyed for thousands of years. No doubt, millions of people are profoundly bewildered; others celebrate; and still others shudder at the coming of same-sex marriage.

But however we feel, let us remember that same-sex couples are seeking to enjoy the rights and responsibilities of marriage, one of the oldest human institutions. They value, honor, and long for marriage. They do not seek to abolish it. What could be more conventional than wanting to create a family, to have a home and children? Same-sex marriage shows both sweeping change in families and profound continuity.

But gay and lesbian families are already with us, even if not yet legally recognized. They have homes and some are raising children. They celebrate, have fun, and worry about their lives, just as traditional families do. In Provincetown, Massachusetts, family weeks for same-sex couples and their children have been celebrated for some years (Capps, 2002; Stacey, 2003).

Family changes are many. Some are problematic, others beneficial. We'll explore them throughout this book. For example, people are marrying later, and a few are not marrying at all; but most people marry at least once in their life, and many others cohabit for long periods. Women are having fewer children, and they are having them later, but about 90 percent of women do bear at least one child in their lives, and some others are adopting.

Those of us who are older (I was born in 1941) sometimes regret the loss of traditions and practices that were comfortable and enjoyable. But at least to some of us, other changes are welcome. For example, we would not to return to the days when abused women suffered in silence, because we ignored their existence and their plight.

SEVEN FAMILY SCENES

At this point, you may ask, what is a family if we come to define same-sex couples as families. If you know some history and anthropology, you may wonder what the many different group-ings people have called families in history share in common. Before we define family directly, we may benefit by looking at a few historical examples of families. I chose them because they cover a wide geographical and historical range. Reading them may enable us to appreciate the nature and variety of families. After you read these seven descriptions, I will make a few summary comments. But I hope that you read, appreciate, and reflect about them on your own first.

Plymouth Colony, 1680s

In *A Little Commonwealth: Family Life in Plymouth Colony* (1970), John Demos presents a detailed and rich portrait of families and family living in that colony during the 1680s.

Let us begin by dispelling the common belief that in the past the United States was populated by large, three-generation families, "a large assemblage of persons spanning sev-eral generations and a variety of kinship connections, all gathered under one roof." In fact, "small and essentially nuclear families" were the norm in Plymouth, and probably throughout the United States for all its history (Demos, 1970, p. 62). In Bristol in 1689, households aver-aged six people.

But in many other ways Plymouth families did differ from contemporary ones. Couples had many children; "eight to nine children apiece was pretty standard." These children were born over many years; for example, "the household of a man forty-five years old might well contain a full-grown son about to marry and begin his own farm, and an infant still at the breast, not to mention all of the children in-between" (Demos, 1970, pp. 68–69).

These households were often augmented for periods of time by non-family members living with the family. For example, men were hired to help with some tasks for a given period; children and adults from other families lived with a family while they learned a trade from the man of the house; and petty criminals "were obliged to become servants [to a family] as an act of discipline initiated by the community at large" (Demos, 1970, p. 70).

Some households decreased in size, while others increased, when illiterate parents would send their children to live with other families who taught them to read and write. Some poor families would send their young children to live as servants with wealthier ones. Family and household size was affected in other ways still. When they were old and unable to care for themselves, aged parents would go stay with their grown children. Adult single men and women would live with their parents or siblings. And finally, sick or homeless people without families were placed by the community to live with families.

All these people lived in fairly small homes, by contemporary standards, the equivalent of two to three room houses. The "hall," the main room, was the scene of many activities: "Cooking, eating, spinning, sewing, carpentry, prayer, schooling, entertaining, and even sleeping

. . . ; and each [activity] demanded its own props" (Demos, 1970, p. 39). (We shall return to Plymouth Colony in later chapters.)

A Kentucky Mountain Family, 1887–1946

In *What My Heart Wants to Tell* (1979), Verna Mae Slone tells the story of her family. Her parents were married in 1887 and had twelve children. Verna Mae, the youngest, was born in 1914.

They led a simple life. They worked hard, raising and making almost all they ate and used. But work was also fun, talking with family and friends while they worked, or with people as they passed by. Dinners were enjoyable occasions, often including passing neighbors; "when anyone passed the house he was asked to come in. . . . This was a very strict code of the hills. . . ." Storytelling by family and friends was the major entertainment. "There were many great storytellers. We had few books and listening to these stories was our only entertainment of this kind" (Slone, 1979, pp. 47, 95).

Men and women had many skills, learning them from parents, siblings, and neighbors. They built their own homes; made their furniture and tools; knew much about many plants and herbs; could tell time by the sun and the weather by the chimney smoke; and possessed much other knowledge they needed to survive, which they acquired in their families and communities.

In her loving tribute to her parents and family, Slone also presents conflicts, contradictions, and difficulties. But she primarily describes large families that worked together and cooperated with their neighbors; had fun in their work and socializing; shared memories of their times together; and were close to family, community, and nature.

An Italian Family, 1910s–1930s

In *Mount Allegro* (1942), Jerre Mangione presents a warm and loving account of his childhood years with his family in Rochester, New York.

His parents, Sicilian immigrants who spoke little English, had four children. But their family extended to uncles, aunts, cousins, other relatives, and some friends. They saw each other often, for long and large Sunday dinners and many weekday gatherings of cards and socializing.

Any excuse sufficed for a large family gathering. Parties, celebrations, and other occasions brought many relatives together for talk, food, and singing. His relatives had "a magnificent talent for gregariousness and a pathetic dread of being alone." They "seemed happiest when they were crowded in a stuffy room noisy with chatter and children" (Mangione, 1942, p. 23).

When Mangione decided to go away to college, his relatives were shocked. "When I broke the news that I was going to an out-of-town university—Syracuse—my relatives were plainly horrified. Could it be that I was becoming a calloused American? The idea that I could bear to leave them behind offended some of them. They began to regard me as a heretic. A good Sicilian son stuck near his family; the only time he left it was to marry, and even then he lived close by so that he could see his relatives often. Life, after all, was *being* with each other. You never left your flesh and blood of your own free will. You left only when it was impossible to earn a living near them, or when you died" (Mangione, 1942, p. 227).

On some Sunday nights, after his aunts and uncles had left following a big Sunday gathering and dinner cooked by his father, they would return late at night and serenade the Mangione household. "They stood under our bedroom windows and sang gently until some member of the household awoke; and when they saw a light go on, their singing became louder and more joyous, breaking into an uproarious crescendo as the door was opened to them" (Mangione, 1942, p. 21).

On one occasion, his parents gave a banquet for some relatives who were leaving for California. When they changed their minds and they stayed in Rochester, his parents gave another banquet to celebrate their staying.

Like Slone, Mangione remembers hours of telling long and elaborate stories, most of them by his uncle Nino.

The intense closeness and socializing sometimes led to angry family squabbles. For example, not all relatives could fit in at any one social gathering, and those who were not invited sometimes vocalized their discontent. The arguments would be bitter and people would not speak to each other for months and even years. Other relatives would set in motion elaborate plans to reconcile the disputing parties. And the frequent gatherings and intense socializing seemed suffocating and oppressive to some people.

A Lesbian Family, 1990s

In *Family Values: A Lesbian Mother's Fight for Her Son* (1993), Phyllis Burke tells the story of her partner Cheryl and their son Jesse. Burke had been unsure about bringing a child into a world unkind to gays and lesbians. "I was afraid. If I loved the baby as much as I might, I wouldn't be able to stand the pain if the world treated him cruelly" (pp. 7–8).

Cheryl, however, was absolutely certain she wanted a child because "I want the meaning in my life that only a child can give." In time Cheryl convinced Burke, and Cheryl became pregnant through "assisted conception, which is what donor insemination has come to be called." Burke continued to struggle with her feelings. How should she relate to the child? She would not be its mother or father. "I decided, Yes, I will help Cheryl raise the baby, but I would be his aunt. He would call me Aunt Phyllis . . ." (Burke, 1993, pp. 5–8).

This young girl has two legal mothers—her biological mother and her adopted mother. Although not identical, the story of this family is similar to that of Cheryl and Phyllis.

They attended Lamaze classes together, where the straight couples assumed Burke was Cheryl's friend, even though Cheryl introduced her as "my partner." Jesse was born and they instantly fell in love with him and raised him together. Jesse sabotaged Burke's plan to be "Aunt Phyllis" by calling her "Mama."

"Jesse looked at me and smiled.

"'Mama,' he said.

"I looked at him. . . . He smiled with satisfaction. He had never said this word. It sounded so sweet and alien to me.

"'No dear,' I corrected him. 'Auntie, Auntie. . . .'

"He tossed his head back and laughed. 'Mama. Mama'" (Burke, 1993, p. 33).

In time, Jesse called them "Mama Cher" and "Mama Phyllis."

As Burke realized she had no parental rights to Jesse, they launched a campaign for Burke to adopt him. After a long investigation the California Department of Social Services recommended against adoption. "A normal, affectionate, parental relationship is well established between petitioner [Burke] and child. However, the State Department of Social Services does not believe that this adoption is in the best interests of this minor. . . ." At the adoption hearing, however, the judge disagreed and allowed the adoption. "Each respectively shall have all the rights and be subject to all the duties of natural parent and child" (Burke, 1993, p. 229). They became a family. (As of 2003, a number of states allow the non-biological parent of a child in a lesbian or gay family to adopt the child.)

African American Families Returning South

In *Call to Home: African Americans Reclaim the Rural South* (1996), Carol Stack tells the stories of southern African American families whose members migrated north for work in the 1940s, 1950s, and 1960s, but who began to return home in the 1970s. They did so despite the persistent poverty and discrimination in the small southern towns where their families lived.

They came home primarily for family reasons, but also to escape the violence in northern cities. "People feel an obligation to help their kin or even a sense of mission, to redeem a lost community, . . . ailing grandparents, a dream of running a restaurant, a passion for the land, . . . homesickness, missionary vision, community redemption, fate, romance, politics, sex, religion" (Stack, 1996, pp, xv, 6).

Pearl and Samuel Bishop's family is one of the families whose story Stack narrates. Pearl was fourteen and Samuel twenty-two when they married in 1944. Together they had and raised ten children, plus nephews and nieces whose parents could not care for them. Since they were first married, Samuel always went north for work for part of every year. When he was home, he partook in raising the children; Pearl said that "with them children, he was just like a woman" (Stack, 1996, p. 83).

For some or many years, all of their ten children, and most of their friends, went north for work. But while up north, they kept their family ties, and children always sent money home. Grandchildren came south for summer visits, and sometimes even stayed year round, to be raised by Pearl and Samuel. Even more, during those years, their children "all came back, all the time—for holidays, weekends, two weeks in the summer, jobless seasons, times when their help was needed with crops in the field, times when their health wasn't up to the rigors of a life away from home in the meanest streets of some of America's meanest cities" (Stack, 1996, pp. 4–5).

In the 1970s, their children began to come home to stay, to help parents and siblings and neighbors and communities, and to root their families in familiar soil, people, and surroundings.

Working-Class English Families, 1950s

Michael Young and Peter Willmott, in *Family and Kinship in East London* (1957), describe families in the working-class neighborhood of East London, during the 1950s. Couples live close to their parents and siblings and spend time with each other several times a week. Indeed, family to them is more than parents and children. The son of one of the authors came home one day from the local East London school and told his parents: "The teacher asked us to draw a picture of our family. I did one of you and Mummy and Mickey and me, but isn't it funny, the others were putting in their Nanas [grandmothers] and aunties and uncles and all sorts of people like that" (p. 14).

The authors found out that, because of economic reasons, twenty-one of the forty-five couples in their sample began their marriage by living with their parents, sixteen with the wife's. But the ideal was to live *near* the parents, not *with* them. And they valued living near their parents. Daughters visited their mothers daily or almost daily, often stopping for afternoon tea or to go shopping together; after school, grandchildren dropped by their grandparents' homes for cookies; women turned to their mothers for advice on how to raise their children. For example, Mrs. Banton "goes around several times a day to see her mother and gets her shopping for her; her mother, although getting on in years and not so active as she was, is still able to look after her grandchildren whenever the need arises" (Young and Willmott, 1957, p. 39). And "when the time comes for the mother to need assistance, the daughter reciprocates, . . . by returning the care which she has herself received" (p. 56).

People live with and associate with relatives all their lives. Most unmarried adults (82 of 137 in the study) live with their parents. When the parents die, they often live with a sibling (usually a sister) (as they did in the West End of Boston in the late 1950s; see Gans, 1962).

Polynesian Families, 1930s

Raymond Firth, in *We, The Tikopia: Kinship in Primitive Polynesia* (1936), offers a detailed and often loving portrait of Tikopia families in the 1920s and 1930s.

Let us begin with his descriptions of "personnel of sample households."

"*Tatamoa.*—This may be described as a multiple family household. It is a large dwelling in the village of Potu sa Kafika, and is occupied by the eldest son of the Ariki Kafika, Pa Fenuatara, with his wife, two sons, and three daughters. . . . Pa Fenuafuri, third son of the chief, with his wife, son, and daughter live there also [and an adopted son]. . . . These two families share the house, each having its portion of floor space to itself. . . . The [members] of these two houses comprise a closely knit little group. They spend a considerable amount of time in each other's dwellings, taking meals there and joining in any work . . ." (Firth, 1936, pp. 108–109).

"*Raroakau.*—[This household] consists of Pa Taitai, his wife, son Tekila, and infant daughter, with his widowed mother Nau Raroakau, and his two unmarried sisters. An elder brother also lives there periodically whenever he is home from Anuta, where he normally resides as a mission teacher" (Firth, 1936, p. 111).

Husbands and wives, and relatives in general, spent much time with each other, cooking, working the fields, and running their households. "Men and women of the household share in the work of getting food ready . . . nothing is more common on public occasions than to see men and women together around the oven. So much is this co-operation regarded as a social norm that a bachelor without close kin or a widower lacking mature children will generally join forces with some elderly female relative similarly situated. . ." (Firth, 1936, p. 95).

Firth thinks that the essence of Tikopia family life may be best observed in "almost infinitesimal actions," in "caresses, food handed over without pretension, glances of eye, tone of voice, bodily protection sought and accorded, as when the baby runs to its father—in short, a multitude of small services . . ." (Firth, 1936, p. 115). (For a discussion of the gentle manner in which the Tikopia raise their children, see ch. 5.)

These seven families span centuries, thousands of miles, and very different cultures. They exhibit a variety of family arrangements. But except for the lesbian family in San Francisco, they include many more people within the family circle than do most families in the United States today (and the "nuclear" family is increasingly common in industrial societies today). Aunts and uncles, grandparents, cousins, and others are involved in daily family living in these sample families.

They generally led simpler lives materially than people do in the United States today. But there was joy, sharing, and cooperation in their lives. The joys and delights of family living exist everywhere, and they are a major theme of this book.

WHAT ARE FAMILIES?

What *are* families? The small sample of families I presented above exhibit a wide variation in membership and functions. Can they all be families? Do they have anything in common?

According to the U.S. Census Bureau, a family is "a group of two or more persons related by blood, marriage, or adoption and residing together in a household." A household "comprises all persons who occupy a 'housing unit,' that is, a house, an apartment or other group of rooms, or a single room that constitutes 'separate living quarters.'" Before we examine attempts at definition by anthropologists and sociologists, let us see what groupings of people living together a sample of Americans considers families (*Statistical Abstract,* 1998, p. 6).

According to a survey cited by Skolnick, the following percentages of Americans considered these groupings as families:

"A married couple living with their children"—98 percent (here and in the following cases, the missing percentages were people who said this grouping was not a family, or, they were not sure).

"An unwed (never married) mother living with her children"—81 percent.

"A man and a woman who live together for a long time, but are not married"—53 percent.

"A group of unrelated adults who live together and consider themselves a 'family'"—28 percent.

"Two lesbian women living with children they are raising together"—27 percent.

"Two gay men committed to each other and living together"—20 percent.

(Skolnick, 1996, p. 18; date and source of survey are not given, but the survey is probably from the early 1990s.)

The fact that 20 percent of Americans were willing to consider two gay men in a committed relationship a family is noteworthy. It shows that our understanding of family was going through some changes and debates; this becomes more evident as same-sex marriage is approaching reality.

Let us begin with a definition by Ember and Ember, two anthropologists. A family is "a social and economic unit consisting minimally of a parent and a child." It seems to exclude couples without children, siblings living together, and many others (1999, p. 351).

Macionis, a sociologist, also focuses on children as the essential aspect of families. To him, a family is "a social institution, found in all societies, that unites individuals into cooperative groups that oversee the bearing and raising of children" (1999, p. 653). Many gay and lesbian couples, who decide to raise children, might agree with these definitions.

To Benokraitis, a family is "any sexually expressive or parent-child relationships in which (1) people live together with a commitment in an interpersonal relationship; (2) the members see their identity as importantly attached to the group; and (3) the group has an identity of its own." By this definition, all the groups cited in the survey above would qualify as families (1996, p. 583).

From the discussion so far in this section, we see that how we define family, how we feel about our families, what we want governments and other institutions to do for families, all these and related issues have been debated for many years. The examples and definitions above only begin to hint at the controversies and debates and conflicting emotions.

Let us look at three recent periods during which there were intense debates on families. Pogrebin, in *Family Politics* (1983), explores some of the social and political debates of the late 1970s–early 1980s. A conservative political and social movement, which led to the election of Ronald Reagan as President in 1980, wanted to define "family" in what they considered a more traditional and beneficial direction. One controversy focused on the name for a 1980 White House conference. Would it be a "Conference on the Family," harking back to a perceived idyllic traditional family of father, mother, and children; or, would it be a "Conference on Families," embracing the variety of groups many people choose to consider their families: "single-parent families, extended families, grandparents raising their grandchildren, gay men and lesbian couples, and many others, in addition to heterosexual married couples and their biological children." It finally became the "Conference on Families" (Aulette, 1994, p. 9; see also Pogrebin, 1983, pp. 55–57).

The Moral Majority proposed a series of laws, first introduced in the U.S. Senate in 1979, that sought to restore their view of the traditional family. Among other items, they wanted to "give a $1,000 tax exemption for the birth or adoption of a child, but only for a married couple"; "require that marriage and motherhood be taught as the proper career for girls, and deny federal funds to schools whose textbooks show women in non-traditional roles"; and "provide tax incentives that discourage women's employment and promote wives' economic dependence on husbands" (Pogrebin, 1983, pp. 14–15).

By the early 1990s, the debate on those particular items had ended—none became law. But other fronts opened in the eternal debate on families. Skolnick (1996) refers to some of those issues, most centering on legal cases of what we consider a family, what rights parents and children have, and optimal conditions for raising children.

There is no end to the discussion, concerns, worries, struggles, commitment, contradictions, court cases, and political conflicts over the definition and conditions of families. (We shall return to them in ch. 3 and throughout the text.) Farrell refers to the "vast reservoir of social anxiety about contemporary family life that is . . . being tapped . . . from a variety of political and social perspectives: working mothers who are consumed by worry about child care; white Christian men who, by the tens of thousands in the late 1990s, attended Promise Keepers revivals that focused on renewing their traditional roles as husbands and fathers; adolescents seeking the emotional attachment of family ties among peers and in gangs when it is found lacking in their own homes; committed gay and lesbian couples fighting for inclusion in the legal definition of family even as they retain a skeptical stance toward this fundamentally heterosexual institution" (1999, p. 3).

So, what *are* families? I offer a tentative definition, one you need to consider and debate in light of your own experiences, the cases and experiences you read in this book, and other stories and discussions of families you encounter. I propose that a family is any group of two or more people, related or unrelated by birth, marriage, or adoption, who have a commitment to the group and (usually) live together. It's a description that includes all the families discussed in this and later chapters.

In conclusion, let me clarify that the word "family" has three different but related meanings; the context usually makes clear which one we mean.

1. The most restricted usage refers to the people with whom we share a home: couples with or without children; single parents and children; grandparents and grandchildren; two or more siblings living together; and so on.

2. Family has a larger meaning, referring to all relatives we feel close to and keep in some contact with. For example, my two brothers and my two sisters, and their spouses and children, in addition to my two adult daughters, are my family in this sense.

3. Often we use "family" to refer to all our relatives, including those we rarely see and even those we never met. For example, I have many first cousins; some I see occasionally, some I have met only two or three times, and some I have never seen. In some contexts, we can refer to such distant relatives as family.

MAJOR THEMES OF THE BOOK

1. There are conflicts and problems in most families, as we will see throughout this book, and as you surely know from your own experiences and observations. But there are also joys and good times. Much writing on families ignores the fun times, the cooperation, the gentle touch of a baby, the quiet delight of being together. (See ch. 6.)

2. Most people today do value their families. They say so in surveys, in class discussions, in family histories they write. They show it by giving care to family members, by traveling thousands of miles to be together, by taking a grandparent shopping. In chapter 7, I present some evidence that family ties may be weakening, certainly in comparison to the families discussed previously, but they are alive still (Thornton and Young-DeMarco, 2001; Loven, 2001).

3. Just as real, however, are the conflicts and disagreements of families today, as has always been the case. Disputes, different lives, and differing interests have been common in the relationships between women and men, as feminists have shown. For example, today women who hold full-time jobs are struggling to get their husbands to share the housework, as we'll see in chapter 11. Divorce and violence are other examples of family conflicts.

4. Families have always been changing. The opening discussion of same-sex marriage, all of chapter 2, and much of the text attest to the truth and importance of this statement. We may be able to understand better our families, and we may be less alarmed by today's changes, if we understand the long history of family changes.

5. Families everywhere provide love, support, and sustenance for their members, but they do so in many different forms and arrangements. We need to appreciate the wide variety of families, both within the United States and across history and cultures. The seven families presented earlier begin to attest to the diversity of families.

6. Change is always with us, but if we work together in groups we can direct the course of that change. For example, mothers who work and the relative absence of extended family present major problems for families with children. Who will raise them? Will it be day-care centers? Can we reduce the work hours of both parents so that women and men will share in raising the children? These and other issues that families confront can be, as they have been in the past, shaped by organized groups. The creation of the eight-hour day, social security, and the family leave act of 1993 (imperfect as it is) attest to collective and political work to create the family conditions we need and want.

APPENDIX A: SOME DATA ON U.S. FAMILIES

In 1970, there were 63.4 million households, with an average size of 3.14 persons. Of those, 51.5 million, or 81 percent, were family households. And of those, 87 percent were married couples, 10.6 percent with a "female householder," and 2.4 percent a "male householder." There were 12 million non-family households in 1970, of which 10.8 million were single-person ones.

By 2000, some significant changes had taken place. The average size of households had decreased from 3.14 persons to 2.62. Of the 104.7 million households, 69 percent were family ones (81 percent in 1970). And of family households, 76.8 percent were married couples (87 percent in 1970); 17.6 percent were female householder ones (10.6 percent in 1970), and 5.6 percent were male householder (2.4 percent in 1970).

There were 32.7 million non-family households in 2000, of which 26.7 million were persons living alone. We should note that these people were 9.5 percent of the population of 281.4 million. In the history of human societies, everyone lived with some family group, not alone, thus the number of single-person households represents a very significant change. At the same time, we should remember that some people listed as living alone, for example non-custodial divorced parents and their children who visit, do live with someone for part of the time (Statistical Abstract of the United States, 1998, pp. 60–62; 2002, pp. 48–50).

APPENDIX B: SOME TERMS TO UNDERSTAND

Clan. The broadest kinship term anthropologists use is clan. It refers to a group of people who believe they have a common ancestor or ancestress, but who may be unable to trace the links to that person. Clans are common to many societies all over the world. Clan members often feel allegiance and obligation to each other. In most societies, people cannot marry anyone from their clan.

Nuclear families. Such families are composed of two generations—parents and children—who reside in one household. They were typified in the TV families of the 1950s: *Father Knows Best, Leave It to Beaver, The Donna Reed Show,* and others. Today, they exist all over the world. Most of you probably live in nuclear families.

Extended families. They consist of three or more generations living together in one household, and often also include two or more married brothers or sisters with their spouses and children. My family had been extended for many years but is no longer. With my parents both dead, and my brother's three children living in Greece, their household has only two people, my brother and his wife. Extended families were common in many societies, but they are being gradually replaced by nuclear and modified extended ones.

Modified extended families. They are neither composed of three generations living under one roof, nor are they independent and often isolated households with only parents and children. Adult married children, and their children, live next to or near their parents, siblings, and other relatives. While they have their own separate households, they socialize with each other frequently. They help each other and share their daily lives. Contact is frequent. The East London families described previously are an excellent case of modified extended families, as are the Mangione family in *Mount Allegro* and many families in the United States today. Of course, there is no sharp dividing line between nuclear and modified extended families. As related nuclear families socialize more, and as they may live closer to each other, they become modified extended ones.

Indeed, these three family types only begin to describe the many varieties people create to meet their needs and wishes. The families I describe earlier in this chapter, and remember they are only a very small sample of families in human history, combine elements of the three forms and often go beyond them. Think of Pearl Bishop in *Call to Home.* At different times, she and her husband lived in nuclear, extended, and modified extended families, and, for much of her life, Pearl also raised nephews and nieces, grandchildren, and unrelated children (Stack, 1996).

Matrilineal, patrilineal, and bilateral descent. "A *descent group* is a permanent social unit whose members claim common ancestry. The group endures even though its membership changes as members are born and die, move in and out. Often, descent-group membership is determined at birth and is lifelong" (Kottak, 1999, p. 113). They are the relatives we relate to in our daily lives.

Anthropologists describe three forms of descent: *matrilineal*, where women and men affiliate with relatives through females only; *patrilineal*, through males only; and *bilateral*, equally through both sexes. Families in Greece, Albania, and the Balkans generally are patrilineal. In the United States, families are generally bilateral, even though in many families individuals may feel closer to their mother's or father's relatives. In many Native American and other societies, families have been matrilineal.

Patriarchy and matriarchy. In households, clans, and societies in general, authority and power may generally be held by men, by women, or equally by both. European peasant societies, from which many people came to the United States, China, and other places were patriarchal. In these families, authority was held by the oldest male, usually the father (but often the grandfather, as in my family for long periods).

In matriarchal families, the oldest woman held authority. There has been a long debate in anthropology whether matriarchal societies have ever existed, with most anthropologists taking the negative. (See Kottak, 1999; Chinas, 1992.) The Iroquois people of upper New York State are often given as an example of matriarchal societies.

I believe a third type has existed, where women and men shared authority. The Ju/'hoansi (!Kung) may be an example, as may be other gathering-hunting peoples. (See Liazos, 1989, ch. 12.)

2

Families in U.S. History

INTRODUCTION AND OVERVIEW

I will discuss three broad eras in the history of U.S. families: (1) Colonial times, when most white families were largely self-sufficient farming groups, where everyone worked and contributed; (2) the 1800s, when industrialism arose and transformed the economy and all institutions; the separation of work from family life began; and there were fewer families farming; (3) and the twentieth century, when families became smaller and more private, with more emphasis on personal fulfillment. As we describe and discuss these eras, please remember that they are at best approximations of the complex realities of family lives. Changes over time are gradual and overlap with previous conditions. Out of necessity we create categories in order to make some sense of history, of how families changed and why they did so. But individuals and families pay no attention to historians and sociologists and the periods they create. People live their lives to meet their needs and wishes; they respond to immediate conditions before them and they often go beyond what they inherited.

We begin with a few statistics on the size of households, number of children, and a look at farming families that may offer us an opening insight into some of the historical changes.

In 1689 in Plymouth Plantation, households averaged 6 people. By 1790, when the first U.S. census was taken, at 5.8 people per household, there had been little change. By 1900, however, households averaged 4.8 persons. They had decreased to 3.37 by 1950 and 2.62 in 2000 (Demos, 1970; Kobrin, 1976; *Statistical Abstract,* 2002, p.48).

Another indication of family change is the percentage of one-person households. In 1790, only 3.7 percent of households consisted of one person, and they increased to 5.1 percent by 1900. Then they grew to 10.9 percent in 1950, 17 percent in 1970, and 25.5 percent in 2000 (Kobrin, 1976; *Statistical Abstract,* 2002, p.49).

The percentage of women who have at least one child sometime in their life has remained fairly constant in our history, about 90 percent. But the *number of children* they average has decreased gradually, with some notable diversions, such as the 1950s. In 1800, and we can assume for decades before, "women gave birth to an average of 8.0 children; by 1900, that average had dropped to 3.7" (Gerstel and Gross, 1995, p. 95). That number has been decreasing further (with the exception of the 1950s, when it was 3.77 in 1957), reaching a low of 1.77 in 1976 and stabilizing at 2.00 for the 1990s, where it was in 1997 (Calhoun, Light, and Keller, 1997, p. 507; Cox, 1999, p. 362).

In Colonial times, and even during the beginning years of industrialism around 1800, at least three-quarters of American families farmed the land. As industrialism progressed, and as immigrants came to work in factories and construction during the 1800s, the percentage of farm families declined. But millions still worked the land, and as late as 1900, 25–30 percent of U.S. families still were farmers. Today the percentage is around 2 percent, and constantly decreasing, as large corporate farms are increasingly dominating the production of our food.

These are numbers and averages that need interpretation of their meaning and people's experiences. For example, when most families farmed in Colonial times, it meant that the

A family with five children was still fairly common in Massachusetts in the 1960s. There were several larger families in this family's neighborhood in 1966.

entire family worked together to support themselves. They were in or near each other's presence most of the day. Today, smaller and one-person households have many implications and meanings, among them fewer human contacts while in the home.

IMAGES AND FEARS OF FAMILY DECLINE

Many scholars, politicians, media people, and the public in general are bemoaning the condition of families today (see ch. 3 for an elaboration of the family decline perspective). They cite increasing divorce, latchkey children, working mothers, juvenile crimes, and other conditions and statistics to support their concerns. They hark back to some golden era when children always listened to their parents and all couples lived in harmony. Such longings ignore two issues. One, to which "traditional" family do they refer? The 1950s family differed significantly from the 1800s family, for example. Two, whenever families change, many contemporaries of those changes worry that the family is deteriorating and declining. The fear of family decline is not new.

In *The Way We Never Were,* Coontz (1992) shows that the students who long for "traditional" families hold very different visions of them. Historical families include very different relationships, expectations, and obligations. The extended families that some students imagine peopled the United States in the 1700s and 1800s, even in the early 1900s, refer to "extended families in which all members worked together; grandparents were an integral part of family life; children learned responsibility and the work ethic from their elders; and there were clear lines of authority based on respect for age" (p. 8). But these families worked very differently from the visions of "traditional" 1950s families as exemplified on TV (and partly in life). In eighteenth- and nineteenth-century families, "children who worked in family enterprises seldom had time for the extracurricular activities that Wally and the Beaver [in the TV show *Leave It to Beaver*] recounted to their parents over the dinner table; often, they did not even go to school full time. Mothers who did home production generally relegated child care to older children or servants; they did not suspend work to savor a baby's first steps or discuss with their husband how to improve a grade-schooler's 'self-esteem'" (p. 9).

The 1950s Cleaver TV family of *Leave It to Beaver,* composed of parents and their two children, is in some ways a rejection of another TV ideal family, the Waltons of the 1930s, where the grandparents lived with the family. During many past periods of ideal "traditional" families, for example, slave children and children who worked in factories co-existed in time with children of white middle-class families. Indeed, there are many past "traditional" families, and we cannot aspire to all of them since they differ so much from each other.

The fear of family decline is ancient. Around 1800, for example, industrialism arose and farming began its steady decline, with "the break in the web of connections between the family and the larger community; the dispersion of the household group, with the young increasingly inclined to seek their fortune in a new setting; the improvement in the status of women; the erosion of parental authority; and a growing permissiveness in the area of sex. These changes were experienced by many people at the time as a kind of decline" (Demos, 1975, p. 66).

Around 1900, as families were undergoing more changes, there were new concerns and worries about the fate of families. "An increase in premarital sex. A drop in the birthrate. A new youth culture rebelling against propriety, dressing outrageously, and indulging in indecent dance steps. And a rapidly rising divorce rate." They could be the concerns of parents and others since the 1960s, but they were in fact stated by people in the early 1900s, during years usually seen as the traditional good old days (Cherlin, 1999, p.62).

Looking back in time we can indulge in nostalgia, remember the good parts (real or imagined), and forget the real concerns of people who lived during those "golden days." For example, many people today cite divorce as a sign of family decline, but divorce has been a troubling issue for centuries, indeed, from the beginning of our history. (See Riley's *Divorce: An American Tradition,* 1991.)

COLONIAL FAMILIES

Historians have shown that colonial families were the center of most social activities. Each family produced most of the food, clothing, and other items it needed. Families bought very little from stores, but they did often turn to neighbors for help (Demos, 1970, 1975).

This description should not evoke images of harmonious and perfect families. Conflicts, disagreements, and problems did exist. People did not always act as they were expected to (see below). But most of life took place within families, one's own and neighboring ones.

The following concise statement by Demos shows precisely all the functions of Plymouth Plantation families in the 1680s:

> The Old Colony family was, first of all, a "business"—an absolutely central agency of economic production and exchange. Each household was more or less self-sufficient. . . . Work, indeed, was a wholly natural extension of family life and merged imperceptibly with all of its other activities.
>
> The family was also a "school." "Parents and masters" were charged by law to attend to the education of all the children in their immediate care. . . .
>
> The family was a "vocational institute." Mothers and fathers taught their children farming, cooking, making clothes, and all other skills they needed in their economy.
>
> The family was a "church." . . . Daily prayers and personal meditation formed an indispensable adjunct to the more formal devotions of a whole community.
>
> The family was a "house of correction." Idle and even criminal persons were "sentenced" by the Court to live as servants in the families of more reputable citizens. . . .
>
> The family was a "welfare institution"; in fact, it provided several kinds of welfare service.
> (Demos, 1970, pp. 183–184)

When too old to care for themselves, people lived with their children; orphans were placed to live with relatives or another family if no relatives were present; and sick people would stay with families where someone "was thought to have special medical knowledge" (Demos, 1970, p. 184).

Almost all of these functions are now performed by institutions outside the family. Much of what family members did for each other is now farmed out to outside institutions, including, lately, cleaning the house, organizing birthday parties, and walking the dog. (See ch. 11 for a discussion of this trend.)

It took three centuries to travel from the Colonial families described above to the families we know today. The changes over these centuries have been gradual, uneven, often resisted and regretted. But always individuals, families, and communities have struggled to keep a sense of family, even as people worried that the institution of the family was in danger of disintegration.

Let us examine Colonial families in some detail. They were not as large as we may imagine them; many children died; many adults died before reaching 50 or 60. But they were larger than today, as the statistics cited earlier in this chapter show, averaging 6 people per household.

With few exceptions, families were not extended. Three generations rarely resided in one household, not in the sense of the classic extended family of my Greek ancestors and many other societies. But in some significant ways families did differ from today's nuclear ones. Elderly parents who could no longer care for themselves were taken in by their children. Sick, elderly people without family were placed by the community to live with a family. Apprentices, hired help, sentenced criminals, children whose parents could not teach them, and others added to the size and composition of many families.

In addition, widowed men and women with young children usually remarried and created complex families (perhaps like today's families created after divorce). At times each spouse brought in children from their previous marriages, and then the couple had their own. Some people who lived to their sixties had two or three spouses. We can imagine that such large and crowded families were ripe for conflicts and disagreements on ways to raise children and other matters (Scott and Wishy, 1982, p. 4; Zinn and Eitzen, 1996, p. 43).

Colonial families lived in relatively small communities of a few hundred or a few thousand people, where no one was a stranger. There was a general lack of privacy (as we think of it) from neighbors and the community. According to Coontz, "City officials, social superiors, and prying neighbors regularly entered homes and told people whom to associate with, what to wear, and what to teach their children; families who did not comply were punished or forcibly separated" (1992, p. 126).

Colonial courts could "remove a child from the care of 'unseemly' parents and place it in some other family." Of course, today also state child protection agencies remove children from their parents for neglect or abuse. But no court, no other government agency, and very few neighboring families today would direct people living alone "to find families in which to locate themselves," which courts did do in Colonial times (Demos, 1975, pp. 60–61).

Let us now turn to the social position of women during pre-industrial times. According to Skolnick, most scholars think that women "occupied a very lowly status." (1996, p. 83) Certainly, pronouncements and writings from those years might indicate so. For example, Pilgrim pastor John Robinson thought that "the proper attitude of a wife towards her husband was 'a reverend subjection'" (Demos 1970, p. 83). In theory, women were the inferior sex, and married women spent most of their adult lives bearing and raising children. Patriarchal authority was the stated principal, but reality was more complex. The frequent invocation of the need for obedience by women and children hints that there were problems (Scott and Wishy, 1982, p. 7).

In daily life, women's lives were not sex typed. "Colonial women were never truly set apart. Women's lives and characters overlapped with men's at many points; a whole world of thought and feeling and practical circumstance was effectively shared. Their experience from day to day was too similar, their partnership too profound, to support the more radical forms of sex typing that would develop in a later era" (Demos, 1975, p. 63). Demos went on to observe that "There are, in the records of Colonial America, no grounds for inferring a pervasive system of deference based on sex" (1975, p. 65).

Some writers have argued that women's work and women's contributions to the survival and functioning of their families were indispensable. Men and women were partners in running a farm and a household. Men expected the women they married to be their partners, they did not expect to support them. Compared to England, Colonial women did less farmwork, but in both societies women were equal partners in the production of essential goods. For example, one woman "spun her own linen, grew her own cabbages, and raised enough turkeys to last from August to Thanksgiving." Another "made her own sausage and soap, manufactured textiles and candles." And both in England and America many women held jobs outside the home (Demos, 1975; Blau, 1976; Oakley, 1974; Ulrich, 1987,pp. 242–243).

And while women were involved in production, Colonial men were more active in raising their children and domestic life than were fathers in later industrial times. They "were active in all aspects of domestic life, from monitoring their wives' pregnancies to taking responsibility for the daily socialization of children" (Coontz, 1997, p. 62).

In regard to the reasons for marriage, most historians conclude that men and women married each other for practical considerations: they needed a partner to farm and survive. People did not earn money with which they could buy what they needed, there were no stores for most food and other necessities. Marriage and living in families were absolute essentials.

A common belief today is that in Colonial days parents chose their children's spouses. Certainly then, as now, most parents did want to influence their children's choice of mates, and most people also married within their social class. But practical necessity, parental wishes and influence, and social class did not preclude the existence of love, romance, and sexual attraction. "Affection took precedence—in the literal sense of coming first in time—and practical considerations followed. Life in these communities presented regular opportunities for courtship, and some for sexual dalliance (witness the long sequence of 'fornication' cases in the court records.)" (Demos, 1975, p. 62).

Premarital sex was also present. As some historians have shown, many new brides gave birth to children long before they reached the nine-month anniversary of their wedding day. By 1750, a third to a half of brides were pregnant on their wedding day. As the 1700s progressed, there was a growing acceptance of premarital sex, and "the main problem was the disposition of those illegitimate children brought into the world as a result of this tolerance" (Demos, 1975, p. 66). (Demos does not say what happened to these children, but they must have been raised by some family; there were no orphanages.)

And as we said, there were many children in Colonial days; they were everywhere. They were not consigned to any schools, for schooling did not become a reality for most children until the mid-1800s. Nor did they work in factories or other settings. They were in and around families, playing when very young and beginning to perform some useful tasks very early, from six or seven on. They dressed much like adults. Boys joined their fathers in planting or fencemending and girls their mothers in cooking, spinning, or candlemaking (Demos, 1970, p. 142).

As we saw, Colonial families lived in small communities, and neighbors and the community in general were involved in the lives of the other families. They also exchanged many goods and services. "Family subsistence in early America was achieved by hundreds of transactions with neighbors. . . . They traded goods and services . . . ; they engaged in labor transactions; and they joined in communal work." Women would trade cloth they had for seedlings they did not have; men would help each other with their farm work; and people would share abundant crops they gathered (Ulrich, 1987, p. 243).

We must avoid romanticizing and idealizing Colonial families. Out of necessity, husband, wife, and children worked together, and out of necessity they did cooperate with neighbors. But they, like we, had their own conflicts, disagreements, and problems within families and between neighbors. For example, court records include cases of husbands and wives complaining of the other's violent behavior, and adultery did exist (Demos, 1970, pp. 95–97).

FAMILIES UNDER INDUSTRIALISM

Industrialism began to appear in England in the mid-1700s, and in the U.S. toward the end of the 1700s. In both places, and in the entire world since then, it has caused profound changes in the economy, education, social classes, the environment, and most other areas of life. The family was no exception.

The most fundamental change industrialism caused for U.S. families was the separation of family members from each other during most of the day, and the dependence of women and children on husbands and fathers. In Colonial days, and for millions of families during most of the 1800s, men, women, and children worked together to provide for themselves. The labor of all three was essential for a family to support itself. As men left farms for work in factories, offices, stores, and construction sites, family members were no longer together, and men became the main or sole providers of their families. Men left their homes and women were increasingly consigned to stay in them, to become full-time housewives and to raise children (Oakley, 1974, p. 59).

This ideal of the husband providing for his wife and children, the wife keeping house and raising children, and the children attending school for some years, did not apply to millions of enslaved Africans, poor immigrants, working-class families, Native Americans, and others. Women worked in various settings and provided for their families. But this ideal of the husband providing for his wife and children *was* held up as the ideal for all families, and it created rigid gender roles for women, men, and children.

Before describing nineteenth century families in more detail, I want to explain that the consigning of women at home and men at work was created by specific historical and economic developments. In all societies before, such role restrictions never existed for the vast majority of people. Women had been equal providers with men. And as during the past thirty to forty years women are again providing for their families (not by producing material items but by earning an income); people are only returning to the lives women and men had led. *Today's families are returning to the traditions families had practiced before industrialism.*

But as the ways of life people had practiced for generations waned, many people were alarmed by the changes. Other people, however, embraced them. For example, sons who no longer had to wait for years to inherit their fathers' farms but could now get jobs in factories felt liberated.

As family farming gradually gave way to factories, offices, and stores, which took men out of the home (and initially some women and children, as whole families worked in factories during early industrialism), the home became the idealized place that gave people protection and security from the outside world. According to Demos, a new literature that romanticized families arose in the early 1800s. Its "simple message, endlessly repeated, was the transcendent importance of family life as the fount of all the tender virtues in life. Love, kindliness, altruism, self-sacrifice, peace, harmony, good order: all reposed here behind the sacred portals of home" (1975, p. 67).

Following Degler (1980), many historians and sociologists refer to these nineteenth century families as "the modern family." (Many people today see that family as the "traditional family".)

Three general characteristics may describe "modern" families of the 1800s.

1. They had fewer children, and parents, mostly mothers, focused more attention on them. In middle-class families, children no longer contributed to the family economy. Parents devoted resources, attention, education, and love to raising them. The nature of childhood began to change; children were seen not as "potential working members of the family group . . . [but] as dependent subjects of tender nurture and protection" (Hareven, 1982, p. 80).

2. Women became primarily housewives, devoting their lives to running the house, raising their children, and tending to their husbands' needs.

3. Marriage "came to be based on romantic love. Traditionally, husbands and wives had been expected to become affectionate companions over time, but romantic attachment did not rank high as a reason for marrying in the first place" (Skolnick, 1996, p. 103). (But as I indicated previously, some historians think romance before marriage did exist in Colonial times.)

Perhaps the dominant characteristic of nineteenth century middle-class families was the separation of the social worlds inhabited by women and men. The work and lives of women and men were separate. Men went to their jobs outside the home to support their wives and children, and women were confined to the home.

The partnership between wives and husbands that prevailed in Colonial days was disappearing. Instead, women were now idealized as the essence of morality and goodness, and "The Cult of True Womanhood" arose. "The attributes of True Womanhood, by which a woman judged herself and was judged by her husband, her neighbors, and society, could be divided into four cardinal virtues—piety, purity, submissiveness, and domesticity. Put them together and they spelled mother, daughter, sister, wife—woman. Without them, no matter whether there was fame, achievement, or wealth, all was ashes. With them, she was promised happiness and power" (Welter, 1966).

The social and physical separation of women and men extended beyond the house. There was a profusion of same-sex clubs, lodges, unions, and other organizations, where men and women found sociability with members of their own sex (Demos, 1975).

According to Demos, the early feminists despised women's restriction to the house, but the ideal and the tradition were entrenched and difficult to oppose. And because of women's economic dependence on men, and the difficulty of divorce (although it was becoming more common, it was still relatively rare), many women and men were trapped in unhappy marriages they could not leave.

While women were largely limited to the home, men too were typed and confined. The limits on and stereotypes of women automatically created men's limits and stereotypes. They were required to show "strength, cunning, inventiveness, endurance—a whole range of traits henceforth defined as exclusively 'masculine.' . . . He was now a more distant, less nurturant figure" (Demos, 1975, p. 70).

The creation of separate worlds was accompanied by the campaign for the "family wage." It called for companies to pay men wages that would allow them to support their families without any contribution from their wives or children. It was primarily a working class and union call to enable working-class men to support their families under the ideal of "true womanhood." It began as a strategy for working-class families to earn enough money to escape poverty, and this idea was supported by men and women. But in time, as the twentieth century approached and arrived, it became more of a gender issue and was used to keep women out of many jobs. For example, "In the 1920s the Baltimore and Ohio Railroad agreed with . . . [unions] to prohibit married women's work." Other unions excluded women entirely. Thus, what began as a worthy goal to provide a living wage for families, in time became a means to keep women in their place at home (May, 1985, p. 150).

Of course, "The Cult of True Womanhood" was an ideal that never applied to millions of African American, immigrant, and working-class families. The family wage campaign enabled many of these families to approach that ideal eventually, but for decades it was an impossible dream, and for millions it never materialized. It was, however, an ideal propagated for everyone and probably shaped most families' hopes and dreams. Traces of the ideal lingered on far into the twentieth century, as men would be proud to say they earned enough so that their wives could stay home, and ashamed if their wives had to work to enable the family to support itself. Traces probably survive today. (Rubin 1976, 1994; see ch. 9 for discussion of the "good provider role".)

Of course, for decades during the nineteenth and twentieth centuries millions of working-class women did much work to provide income for their families. Many worked at home, sewing clothes, or doing other people's laundry, or taking in boarders whose rent helped family finances. "By one estimate, 15 to 20 percent of all urban households contained board-ers at any given time." In addition, before child labor laws that passed around 1900 made it difficult, many families sent their children to work, at fairly young ages. All these sources of income barely enabled most working-class families to support themselves (Cherlin, 1999, p. 55).

Repressed sexuality, notably for women, is another characteristic of the ideology of True Womanhood. Women were to be pure and free of sexual desire. They were by nature asexual beings. Orgasms and sexual pleasures were unnatural. At most women were to con-sent to sex in order to have children and to satisfy their husbands, whose nature did allow for sexual pleasure. The ideology held not only that women should not enjoy sex, but that *by nature they did not.* But this perception of women's sexuality may say more about what men *wanted* to happen rather than what *did* take place.

Degler and others have shown that this view of women's sexuality was only one side of a debate that took place from the mid-1800s to the early 1900s. Some doctors and others wrote that women did not enjoy sex, but just as many doctors wrote that sexual pleasure is normal, desirable, and necessary for women. In 1870, one doctor wrote: "Passion [is] absolutely nec-essary in woman. . . . That female passion exists is as obvious as that the sun rises." Those arguing for the asexual nature of women were not reporting a reality, rather, they were trying to create reality. They were *prescribing* what women should do, not *describing* what women in fact did (Degler, 1974).

An unpublished survey on women's sexuality that was carried out in the late 1800s supports this conclusion. Forty-five middle-class married women took part. Most were born around 1870 and were married by 1900. Thirty-five of the forty-five "testified that they felt desire for sexual intercourse independent of their husbands' interest, while nine said they never or rarely felt any such desire." To the question, "Do you always have a venereal or-gasm?" two did not respond; five said "no" (possibly meaning they experienced orgasm some of the time); nine said "always"; seven said "usually"; eighteen said "sometimes," "not always," or "no" but noted exceptions; and four said "once" or "never". This is hardly a portrait of sexually repressed women (cited in Degler, 1974, p. 416).

How people behave and how they should behave are always matters of debate and conflict. It is rare that there is unanimity on behavior and values. Thus, we can imagine that many women were unhappy trapped in their corsets, layers of clothes, and housework during the height of the True Womanhood era.

Historians have written that another new feature of the 1800s was the gradual focus on individualism. There was a shift away from obligations people owed to their families to an emphasis on people's right to pursue their own happiness, which may at times require forego-ing obligations to the family. For example, the steady rise of divorce, and the intense debates over laws granting divorce and the increasing grounds for divorce, may be seen as one indication of the value of individualism. People's obligations to their spouses and children were no longer absolute. Physical abuse, emotional abuse, alcoholism, and other conditions that made life intolerable for women or men, which deprived them of happiness, were now grounds for leaving their spouse (May, 1980; Riley, 1991; Whitehead, 1997; Basch, 1999). (See also the history of divorce in ch. 12.)

But individualism did not destroy families. It did change them, but people still turned to their families for support and assistance. Relatives from different households kept close ties and socialized with each other. When people left U.S. farms or migrated from overseas to find work in American cities, it was to relatives they went for help to find jobs and housing. In new ways and under new conditions, families continued to be meaningful and useful in people's lives (Hareven, 1982).

I close the history of families in the 1800s with three conclusions:

1. Millions of families were still close to their colonial ancestors, practicing subsistence farming. Moreover, many urban families raised much of their own food.

2. The 1800s, which in the eyes of many people were the good old days for families and marriages, had their own problems. We cannot separate whatever desirable characteristics we find in those families from their total social context. Katha Pollitt reminds us that we would have to "Restore the cult of virginity and the double standard, ban birth control, restrict divorce, kick women out of decent jobs, force unwed pregnant women to put their babies up for adoption on pain of social death, make out-of-wedlock children legal nonpersons. That's not going to happen" (Pollitt, 1993, in Coontz, 1997, p. 95).

3. Industrial capitalism removed many functions from families and turned them over to profit-making corporate activities and products. As we shall see in later chapters, families participate in fewer activities as a group. Work, school, and mass entertainment leave little time for family members to be with each other (Braverman, 1974, p. 277; Hochschild, 1997).

FAMILIES IN THE TWENTIETH CENTURY

There were no sharp breaks, no dramatic changes, in families at the dawning of the twentieth century. Trends that began in the 1800s continued and accelerated in the 1900s, and by the end of the twentieth century families had changed considerably. But the changes were gradual and uneven. Millions of families were still largely farmers in 1900, millions of children worked to help their families, millions of women baked their bread and made their butter or had boarders in their homes.

But by the end of the twentieth century, families had come a long distance from the Colonial families Demos describes in *A Little Commonwealth: Family Life in Plymouth Colony* (1970). Most functions performed by those families, and also by nineteenth century families, were gradually transferred to other institutions: schools, hospitals, stores that sold products once made at home. Entertainment and socializing were largely taken over by the movie industry, television, and other media. Cars made it possible for young people to court each other, and to explore sexuality, away from their parents' watchful eyes. The changes were many, widespread, and deep.

The number of children couples had continued to decline; "husbands and wives are spending a relatively longer lifetime together; they invest a shorter segment of their lives in child rearing; and they more commonly survive to grandparenthood" (Hareven,1982, p. 84).

As the 1900s progressed, people lived longer. Women born in 1900 could expect to live an average of 48 years; in 1920, 54.65; in 1950, 71.1; in 1970, 74.8; and in 2000, 79.5 years. For men, the figures are: 1900, 46 years; 1920, 53.6; 1950, 65.6; 1970, 67.1; and 2000, 74.1 years (*Statistical Abstract,* 1982–83, p. 71; 2002, p. 71).

Such longer lives have many implications for families and family relations. Uhlenberg (1996) explores some of these new realities. As people live longer, it is more likely that children will have living grandparents, and that middle-age people will have living parents. (But whether and how often children see these grandparents is another matter; we are such a mobile society.) In 1900, "fewer than one fourth of all children began life with all four of their grandparents alive, and by age 30, only 21% had any surviving grandparent. By the end of the century, on the other hand, over two thirds will have begun life with all four grandparents still living and more than three fourths will have at least one grandparent alive when they reached age 30" (1996, p. 71).

Indeed, the longer life span means that for the first time in history, it is common for children to have great-grandparents, introducing a new family relationship. We are also more likely to have parents well into our late middle age. In 1900, at age 60, only 7.5 percent of people had at least one parent alive; by 2000, it is 44 percent—a significant increase, with ramifications for taking care of elder parents as we age ourselves.

Spouses live longer, making longer marriages possible—and allowing us more years for the escape of divorce. In 1900, 50 percent of 70–year-old husbands had living wives, but 85 percent did in 2000. For wives at 70, 33 percent had living husbands in 1900, but 60.6 percent did in 2000.

Our siblings also live longer, allowing us the possibility of more years being with them—or, being estranged from them. Today, "most persons will not experience the death of any particular sibling until they are well past 70 years of age." For example, the percentages of people having a younger brother alive were, at age 60, 48 percent in 1900 and 85.3 percent in 2000, and at age 80, 14.7 percent in 1900 and 47.9 percent in 2000 (Uhlenberg, 1996, p. 75).

Uhlenberg concludes with a promise and a qualification. We have "an unprecedented potential for persons at all stages of life to have kin relationships involving older persons. . . . [But] grandparents may be valued resources, or may be irrelevant. Old parents may be loved ones, or they may be burdens. Aging first spouses may be intimate companions, or they may be ex-spouses. Elderly siblings may be close friends, or they may be distant relatives" (1996 p. 70). Experience may show us that one set of possibilities blesses some of us, and the other may curse others—or, at different times, we may experience both alternatives.

The social conditions of children changed significantly during the twentieth century. Discussing the children of Plains families, McNall and McNall point out that whereas during the 1800s children were allies with their parents in providing for their families, "children of the [1930s] Depression often did not have this option, and so their identities came to be established in peer groups. As adolescence became a separate status, affirming one's identity means becoming like other adolescents, rebelling against parental norms and authority" (1983, p. 202).

Coontz makes a similar observation. She thinks that teen-parent conflicts are very old, probably as old as humanity itself, but in "preindustrial societies most kids were integrated into almost all adult activities, and right up until the twentieth century there were few separate standards or different laws for teens and adults. For centuries, youth and adults played the same games by the same rules. . . . From 'blind man's bluff' to 'follow the leader,' games we now leave to children were once played by adults as well. There were few special rules or restrictions that applied solely to teens." Today, however, teenagers are not as early or easily integrated into the culture and are segregated into a "youth culture" which is "actually [a product of] adult marketers seeking to commercially exploit youthful energy and rebellion" (1997, pp. 14–15).

Three major social developments around 1900 changed the lives of young people. "Compulsory education dictated how adolescents would spend their time; child labor legislation regulated their participation in the productive labor force; and the development of [the juvenile court] transformed them into a special class of citizens and provided a unique system of control over them" (Bortner, 1988, p. 18).

The laws and institutions that grew from these developments have been with us for so long that we may not realize they were created at a specific historical period. For example, laws prohibiting child labor came about for three reasons: humanitarian concerns over the dangerous and deadly conditions in factories where children worked; oversupply of workers as machines took over much production and immigrants streamed to America; and "unions seeking to establish better wages and working conditions for adult laborers" (Bortner, 1988, p. 18).

The conditions and status of children and teenagers in U.S. families underwent significant changes during the course of the twentieth century. Indeed, the very concept of adolescence and youth culture are creations of that century. As we saw, before and around 1900 young people worked in and with their families. The middle-class ideal of the nineteenth century that children need protection, education, and special nurturance became a reality for most of them only in the twentieth century.

I end with a note that as we enter the 21st century, some children in the United States, and millions of children throughout the world, are exploited as they work in awful factories and fields and are paid a pittance. The lives of these children are a long way from most family farms before 1900, where children contributed, according to their abilities, to their own and their families' sustenance.

Companionate Families and Marriages

Many historians consider the gradual rise of the "private" or "companionate" family to be the major twentieth century change in families and marriages. More than its nineteenth century predecessors, the characteristics of companionate families are "mutual affection [between spouses], sexual attraction, and equal rights, where husbands and wives [are] friends and lovers and parents and children [are] pals" (Aulette, 1994, p. 43; summarizing Mintz and Kellogg, 1988).

In his discussion of the private family, Cherlin cites the history of his family: "My grand-parents immigrated from Eastern Europe just after the turn of the [twentieth] century, started a grocery store, and raised 10 children. Had I been around to ask them whether their marriage was satisfying, they would have said of course—they were raising a big family. They would not have answered in terms of companionship, romance, sexual pleasure, excitement, or personal growth. Yet these were the ways in which more and more Americans came to define a successful marriage in the twentieth century" (1999, p. 63).

Increasingly, couples and families were to be held together by love, romance, affection, friendship, communication, personal growth of each person, and emotional satisfaction, rather than by economic necessity. In a study in the late 1990s, young women said that the most important parts of marriage were, in order of frequency, "'communication,' 'friendship,' 'equality,' 'honesty,' 'partnership,' 'compromise,' and 'openness'" (Kamen, 2000, p. 152).

I think the distinctions people draw between the companionate and private families of the twentieth century, and earlier families, are more matters of *degree* rather than *kind*. Certainly, families no longer are the largely self-sufficient, farming economic units they once were, but they still perform a number of economic functions. They earn money, cook, buy materials and products they need. It is in such economic units that most of us are raised, and it is such economic units we create later in our lives. They are different from earlier families, very different, but families still meet material, biological, and economic needs (of course, they do so in a very different economy).

Let me add two points about the emotional and romantic aspects of marriages and families. (1) Hardly all families today are ideal examples of love and romance, as divorce rates indicate. (2) Romance, affection, and friendship were present to some degree in most pre-twentieth century families, as we saw, for example, in the discussion of Colonial families. My close reading of families and marriages in pre-industrial, non-western societies convinces me that they were not solely, or primarily, economic and practical arrangements. Sexual desire, affection, companion-ship, and friendship could and did exist. That they were not expressed in ways we express them—romantic walks, holding hands, and so on—does not mean they were absent.

So too for pre-1900 families and marriages. We must not see them through our lenses. As with us, affection and sexual desire and friendship were present and wanted; and as with us, some people experienced them fully, some in part, and some very little.

Let me close with a comment on change and continuity in families. Without a doubt, compared to earlier families, men and women today do not need to marry for material and physical survival. "Before the advent of washing machines, frozen foods, wrinkle-resistant fabrics, and 24-hour one-stop shopping, Barbara Ehrenreich has remarked, 'the single life was far too strenuous for the average male.' Today, though, a man does not really need a woman to take care of cooking, cleaning, decorating, and making life comfortable. Many men still choose marriage for love and companionship." Similarly, women do not need men to provide for them. "Neither men nor women need marriage as much as they used to" (Coontz, 1997, p. 81).

But in other ways, women, men, and families have not changed. About as many women as ever have at least one child. Many do so at later ages, and most have fewer children. But they have at least one. In 1998, 87 percent of married women 35–39 had at least one child, and 86 percent of married women 40–44 had at least one (and at least some of the others had adopted a child). Even never-married women have children, almost 40 percent of those 30–39 had at least one in 1998, and 33 percent of those 40–44 did (*Statistical Abstract* 2002, p. 48).

And the vast majority of women and men marry at least once; "the proportion of women who remain single all their lives is *lower* today than at the turn of the [twentieth] century" (Coontz, 1997, p. 30). In 2000, of people 45 to 54, only 8.6 percent of women had never married, and 9.5 percent of men had not. These figures include millions of lesbians and gay men who have lived in committed relationships but do not have the option of legal marriage. Also, even in the past not everyone married. Thus, as many people as ever try marriage at some point in their lives (*Statistical Abstract of the United States,* 2002, p. 48).

MUNCIE, INDIANA, 1890s, 1920s, AND 1970s

Robert and Helen Lynd wrote two classic studies of Muncie, Indiana. *Middletown* (1929) discusses life in the 1890s and 1920s, and *Middletown in Transition* (1937) updates that study by focusing on the effects of the Great Depression (1930s) on the economy, family, education, and other institutions.

In 1890, Muncie was "a placid county-seat of 6,000 souls, [and] still retained some of the simplicity . . . of early pioneer life." People led a largely rural life, "relatively close to the earth and its products" (Lynd and Lynd, 1929, pp. 12, 87). When the Lynds arrived in 1925, Muncie had grown to 38,000 and had become an industrial center, especially of glass-making. Craftspeople and farmers had been replaced by factory production workers. Glass-making had been a craft that people learned over many years, in the process earning prestige and higher wages, but by the 1920s it was a factory process that took a few days to learn, and carried no prestige

Factories had introduced night shifts, and from several hundred to 3,000–4,000 men worked nights, thus disrupting the rhythms of living and community life. The "normal relations between husband and wife, children's customary noisy play around home, family leisure-time activities, lodge life, jury duty, civic interest, and other concerns are deranged. . . . 'I work nights, judge, and sleep during the day, and I haven't been able to keep in touch with George,' pled a father to the judge of the juvenile court in behalf of his son." (Lynd and Lynd, 1929, p. 55).

Having lived in and studied Muncie twice, the Lynds concluded that its citizens believed the following about the family:

> That the family is a sacred institution and the fundamental institution of our society.
> That sex was "given" to man for purposes of procreation, not for personal enjoyment.
> That sexual relations before or outside of marriage are immoral.
> That "men should behave like men, and women like women."
> That women are better ("purer") than men.
> That a married woman's place is first of all in the home, and any other activities should be secondary to "making a good home for her husband and children."
> That men are more practical and efficient than women. . . .
> That everybody loves children, and a woman who does not want children is "unnatural."
> That married people owe it to society to have children. . . .
> That parents should "give up things for their children," but "should maintain discipline and not spoil them."
> That it is pleasant and desirable to "do things as a family."
> That fathers do not understand children as well as mothers do. . . .
> That young people are often rebellious ("have queer ideas" but they "get over these things and settle down." (Lynd and Lynd, 1937, pp. 410–411)

In the 1890s, "the preparation of food . . . was one of woman's chief glories." In the 1920s, meal times were still important both for "nutrition and social intercourse." But the trend was "away from the earlier attention to elaborate food." A local butcher complained: "The modern housewife has lost the art of cooking. . . . Folks today want to eat in a hurry and get out in the car." People complained that families were having fewer leisurely meals together (Lynd and Lynd, 1929, pp. 153–154).

In contrast to the 1890s, in the 1920s "romantic love [is] the only valid basis for marriage. . . . [Muncie] adults appear to regard romance in marriage as something which, like their religion, must be believed in to hold society together. Children are assured by their elders that 'love' is an unanalyzable mystery that 'just happens'—'You'll know when the right one comes along,' they are told with a knowing smile" (Lynd and Lynd, 1929, pp. 114–115).

But even as romance reigned supreme, divorce was very present, as were abandonment and separation. "Loss of affection after marriage was not legally recognized as sufficient reason for dissolving a marriage until recent years, but in 1924 divorces were granted to couples who came into court frankly saying, 'We have no affection for each other and do not want to live together,' and 'She says she does not love me and does not want to live with me'" (Lynd and Lynd, 1929, p. 114).

Remembering that we are discussing the citizens of a small Indiana city in the 1920s, we read the comment that people then thought that women and men resorted to divorce far too quickly, almost nonchalantly. "'Anybody with $25 can get a divorce' is a commonly heard remark. Or as one recently divorced man phrased it, 'Any one with $10 can get a divorce in ten minutes if it isn't contested. All you got to do is to show non-support or cruelty and it's a cinch'" (Lynd and Lynd, 1929, p. 121).

And then, as now, people attributed divorce to changing times, such as women working outside the home. "With the spread of the habit of married women's working, women are less willing to continue an unsatisfactory marital arrangement. Said [a] lawyer . . . 'If a woman has ever worked at all she is much more likely to seek a divorce. It's the timid ones that never worked who grin and bear marriage'" (Lynd and Lynd, 1929, p 127).

And also then, as now, writers noted that, because of the value of individual happiness, people were less willing to stay in unhappy marriages. The Lynds quote Dorothy Dix, an Ann Landers of her day: "The reason there are more divorces is that people are demanding more of life than they used to. . . . In former times . . . they expected to settle down to a life of hard work . . . and to putting up with each other. . . . But now we view the matter differently. We see that no good purpose is achieved by keeping two people together who have come to hate each other" (Lynd and Lynd, 1929, p. 128).

In another footnote, the Lynds point out other changes in families and households. "Fewer 'old-maid' sisters live with married relatives now when [they] commonly work outside the home for pay, move about town freely at night unescorted, and live in small flats of their own. Smaller houses without 'spare' rooms are diminishing the custom . . . of having elderly parents live in the homes of married children. . . . [A government agency] suggested that 'there should be legislation to prevent the abandonment of parents by children who are able to support them'" (Lynd and Lynd, 1929, p. 110).

The movies were emerging as a major entertainment form, and people began to observe and complain about the changes they were causing. Parents complained that, away from parental supervision, young people would get in their cars and go to the movies. Families were in danger. Indeed then, as today, some people blamed the movies for causing crimes. A local juvenile court judge said that movies were one of the "big four" causes of local delinquency (Lynd and Lynd, 1929, p. 268).

If Muncie residents and the Lynds were alarmed that families were losing their strength and functions in the 1920s, the sociologists who studied Muncie again in the 1970s did not share that alarm. Indeed, they concluded that 1970s Muncie families were in "splendid" condition.

In *Middletown Families,* Caplow and his associates (1982) compare Muncie of the 1970s, then a city of 80,000, to Muncie in the 1920s. They offer some evidence presented by the Lynds that suggested that family interaction and contacts were lower in the 1920s than they had been in the 1890s. If that were so in the 1920s, Caplow and others find no evidence of weakening families in the 1970s. Indeed, they think that they discovered evidence of "kinship solidarity." "Although most of [Muncie's] families live in one-family dwellings where the family consists of a married couple, a married couple with children, or a single parent and children, the majority of these two-generation nuclear families are related to members of other families in [Muncie]. . . . When there are relatives living in town, especially close ones—parents, brothers and sisters, or grown children—they are seen, talked to, and visited more frequently than are friends or neighbors. When [Muncie] people need assistance or advice, they are apt to turn to their relatives" (Caplow and others, 1982, pp. 198–199).

From their study of Muncie, and from other evidence, Caplow and associates conclude that in the 1970s in urban U.S. areas "kinship ties are extremely important." They refer to a 1960s survey that found "as many as 85 percent of urban adults recognize an obligation to keep in touch with their parents," which included both face-to-face contact as well as telephone calling (Caplow and others, 1982, pp. 195, 196).

To further support their conclusions, they present survey evidence from Muncie in the 1970s. Relatives live close and are important to each other. "The odds are one in five that a [Muncie resident] has a sister or brother living in the city, one in three that one or both of his parents live there, and two in five that he or she has more distant relatives—grandparents, aunts, uncles, cousins—who live in [Muncie] too" (Caplow and others, pp. 200–201). (One can reverse these figures and show that 80 percent have no sibling, 67 percent have no parent, and 60 percent have no distant relative in Muncie.)

Other data show that "fifty-four percent of the grown children, 43 percent of the parents, and 31 percent of the brothers and sisters of our respondents lived right in [Muncie]." Also, "86 percent of the respondents . . . said that they recognized an obligation to maintain contact with their close relatives." And to some degree, they fulfill that obligation: "48 percent of [Muncie] adults with living parents see them at least weekly and about 80 percent see them at least monthly." In addition, people call their parents more than once a month and siblings half as often. When parents live more than 50 miles away, children see them much less, with letters substituting for visits (Caplow and others, 1982, pp. 203, 205, 209–211).

In the 1970s, Caplow and his associates celebrated families as close and vibrant. As you read through this book and discuss it with others, you may decide whether this optimistic statement on families in the United States is true in the 21st century, assuming it was true in the 1970s.

THE 1950s, IN MEMORY AND REALITY

Today, for many people of all ages, the 1950s represent the golden past of families and family living. They think of the 1950s as the days when mothers took care of homes and husbands, when children came home from school and found their mothers waiting with milk and cookies, when there were no drugs and no crime, when children played in the streets unafraid of strangers, and as a time when husbands and wives worked out their problems and did not resort to divorce so easily. We heard of no child abuse or incest or wife beating in the 1950s. The dominant TV shows were *Leave It to Beaver, Father Knows Best, The Donna Reed Show, and Ozzie and Harriet*—all lovely families with loving parents and well-behaving children, living in suburban homes of neat lawns and good neighbors. (The movie *Back to the Future,* which begins with November 12, 1955, is a good physical portrayal of those days.) I arrived in Worcester, Massachusetts, on October 5, 1955, at age 14, and lived through the second half of the 1950s there. I was an avid watcher of *Leave It to Beaver*. I remember some of the hopes and good feeling and optimism of those days.

Before we try to distinguish between facts and fantasies of the 1950s, let us first look at demographic data and the historical events that preceded those years.

Let us begin with births. The total fertility rate went down from 7.0 in 1800 to about 3.5 in 1900 and 3.2 in 1920. It then plummeted down to a little over 2 during the Great Depression of the 1930s, rose after World War II to a high of almost 4 during the 1950s, and after another steep decline during the 1960s and 1970s, it stabilized at around 2 in the 1980s and 1990s. Clearly, during the 1950s women had more children then they did before or after that decade (Aulette, 1994, p. 51; and sources cited earlier in this chapter).

More women and men married in the 1950s than did in earlier or later decades, and at younger ages. In 1900, the median age at first marriage was 22 for women and 26 for men. It stayed around 22 for women and 25 for men for decades, until it declined to 20.3 for women and 22.8 for men in 1950. It remained about the same for the 1960s, and increased since the 1980s, becoming about 25 for women and 27 for men in 2000. The increasing age of first marriage is also seen in the following statistics. In 1960, only 11.9 percent of men and 6.9 percent of women from 30 to 34 were still never married. By 2000, it was 30 percent for men and 21.9 percent for women (see ch. 4 for more details; Skolnick, 1996, p. 21; *Statistical Abstract, 1977*, pp. 40 and 76; *1999*, pp. 58 and 111; 2002, p. 48; Stockman, 2002a).

The 1950s divorce rate followed the long historical record of a gradual but steady increase. In 1860, there was a little over one divorce per 1000 marriages. It rose to 4 divorces in 1900 and 8 divorces through the 1920s, and declined to 6 during the 1930s (because of hard times, fewer people divorced during that decade, since it cost money to divorce; also, many spouses simply left without a formal divorce). The rate spiked to 18 in 1945–46 (partly because of delayed divorces during World War II). It then began to decline until it came to 8 divorces per 1000 marriages in 1960. Soon it began a steady and steep rise, reaching 23 around 1980 and stabilizing at 20 to 22 since then (Cherlin, 1999, p. 370).

The historical context of the 1950s is important. People in their twenties and older had just undergone two significant experiences: the Great Depression of the 1930s and World War II from 1941 to 1945. The economy almost collapsed in the 1930s: unemployment rose to 25 percent, many businesses failed, banks collapsed, millions of young people had no jobs and no hope, and birth, marriage, and divorce rates declined. Many men, without jobs and unable to support their families, left them; others committed suicide. Studs Terkel's aptly titled *Hard Times: An Oral History of the Great Depression* (1970) offers a vivid and thorough account of those years, as remembered by people who lived them. They tell of desperate times, of labor strikes and traveling to far places to find work, of help and indifference, of government work programs, of bitter memories of eating so many sardines that they can't stand the sight of them now.

The United States had hardly begun to recover from the 1930s Depression when it entered the war in 1941. The war created a demand for arms for the military, and with men fighting overseas, factories and other enterprises were forced to hire married women, African Americans, and others they had not employed before. Millions of women and children were separated from husbands and fathers, many becoming widows and orphans. During the war years, many marriages fell apart because of the long separation, and many of these couples divorced after the war (as we saw above). Because of the war, many economic needs and wants—cars, household products, houses—were postponed as the country worked to meet the needs of the U.S. and allied armies.

These are the times that preceded the 1950s, that shaped the lives of old families and newly created ones. Material possessions, hopes, and dreams had been postponed. Millions of people had sharp memories of deprivations during the 1930s, and of fighting, injuries, deaths, and separations from the war. It was time for people to marry and have children and buy houses, to have hope again.

The U.S. economy quickly began to provide the unmet material needs. Good jobs and good pay became available. Since the United States had been the only major country in the war on whose soil there was no fighting, killing, and destruction (except for the Pearl Harbor attack), it was in better shape to rebuild its economy than other countries were. And for over twenty years, while other countries sought to bring back to life their war-torn economies and facilities, the United States was the dominant economy of the world, exporting many more products than it imported.

In addition, after the war the government created programs to help veterans and others. For example, 40 percent of young men were eligible for benefits, among them college education. "The GI bill paid most tuition costs for vets who attended college, doubling the percentage of college students from prewar levels." When these men graduated, they, like millions of others, could buy homes with government mortgages at interest rates of about 4 percent. Because of such government assistance, and because of jobs in booming factories and offices, a typical thirty-year-old man in the 1950s could buy a median-priced house with 15–18 percent of his income—and it was only *his* income; most wives did not work (Coontz, 1997, pp. 41, 33).

Governments spent money on schools for children, the new interstate highway system, and on many other projects. Indeed, the economy and economic well-being of families during the 1950s were heavily shaped by such government spending. "Between 1950 and 1960, nonmilitary, nonresidential public construction rose by 58 percent. Construction expenditures for new schools (in dollar amounts adjusted for inflation) rose by 72 percent; funding on sewers and waterworks rose by 46 percent. Government paid 90 percent of the costs of building the new Interstate Highway System. These programs opened up suburbia to growing numbers of middle-class Americans and created secure, well-paying jobs for blue-collar workers." (Coontz, 1997, p. 41)

Taxes for the average taxpayer were also lower. The Federal government collected 23 percent of its revenue from corporations in the 1950s, but only 9.2 percent in 1991. After the 1950s income taxes paid by the average American worker rose to make up for what corporations did not pay.

The government programs and booming economy of the 1950s, in contrast to the 1930s and the war years, created a sense of hope. Parents could look forward to buying a home, to sending their children to college, to a steady job that paid a living wage. Unlike the practices of corporations since the 1970s, corporations in the 1950s did not usually move their plants to poor countries to find cheaper labor. Thus, American workers could plan with confidence for their future and their families. People look to the 1950s as a time "when there were fewer complicated choices for kids or parents to grapple with," as a chance to "*dream* of creating a secure oasis in their immediate nuclear families" (Coontz, 1997, pp. 33, 35).

During the 1950s, there was a total lack of media coverage, research, and discussion of child abuse, violence against women, incest, and other family problems. Coontz thinks this was "terribly hard" on the victims but "protected more fortunate families from knowledge and fear of many social ills" (Coontz, 1997, p. 39).

A large part of the hope and the media avoidance of family problems was the TV family shows of those days. I cannot recall now whether I ever looked at *Leave It to Beaver* critically, whether I reflected on how realistic a portrayal of families it was or on all that it ignored. I did feel good watching it, and it did leave me smiling. There were no serious family arguments; there were no problems that could not be solved by the end of the show. I'm not sure I agree with Coontz that "everyone knew" that these shows "were not the way families really were," but I do agree that we watched them "to see how families were *supposed* to live—and also to get a little reassurance that [we] were headed in the right direction" (1997, p. 38).

But discussions of 1950s TV shows tend to ignore *I Love Lucy,* another popular show of those years. I watched *Lucy* as regularly as I did *Beaver.* Looking back, *Lucy* seems to be a better vehicle for understanding the 1950s. In real life, Lucille Ball, one of the show's stars, was the wife of Desi Arnaz, another star (they were also married in the show). She was the majority owner and power behind the company that produced the show. But on the screen she was a housewife totally dependent on her husband for money. One repeated theme on *I Love Lucy* had Lucy trying to trick Ricky to allow her to work, but he always refused her. She was once spanked (he put her over his knees and hit her on the buttocks) because she had bought some furniture without his permission (he promptly returned the furniture). The real life of Lucille Ball and Desi Arnaz, and the family they portrayed on TV, show some of the realities, images, and contradictions of the 1950s.

So we see that despite the good and improving economic times, despite the hope and the smiles, despite the realities of and nostalgia for those years, there were serious problems and conflicts and contradictions. A letter sent to the *Boston Globe* in 1998 by a survivor of the 1950s speaks simply and eloquently:

> As a girl, I was told I didn't have to excel in school. I just needed to be pretty and sweet and my husband would support me. As a girl, the closest I could get to sports was to be a cheerleader for the boys. When I was raped by a date, our family doctor discreetly came to the house. Of course, no charges would be made, only the girl went on trial.
>
> When I held an entry-level job and my boss asked me out, the company asked me to leave. Sexual discrimination was rampant. I did not even have the language to express my indignation.
>
> Meanwhile, our government was testing bombs and polluting the atmosphere, large companies were polluting our water supplies, those 1950s Tailfin cars were polluting the air with leaded gasoline. Black citizens had to ride at the back of the bus, and gays were still in the closet. Senator Joseph McCarthy was ruining lives with his witch hunt for Communists, and my father (a federal employee) was asked to spy on his fellow employees.
>
> I thank God for the 1960s! My daughters have freedom I didn't even dream about. This is not utopia, but we have made great strides for the equality of the sexes and races. Our air, water, and land are slowly being cleaned up.
>
> I think only the white male can be nostalgic for the '50s decade. After all, it was the male driving those big cars with fins, and we girls were told to just look pretty in the passenger seat. (Cordima, 1998; used with permission of the author)

Child abuse victims, women whose husbands beat them, and many others could find no refuge. The shelters for battered women did not arise until the mid-1970s, the first ones created entirely by women of the feminist movement. Racism, violence, and discrimination against African Americans were widespread and legal. In 1996 I had a long talk with an African American coworker from a restaurant where we worked from 1956 to 1961. He told me of discrimination and beatings African Americans experienced in Worcester, Massachusetts, in the 1950s, things he never revealed to me when we worked together. He told me of an uncle who was mercilessly beaten by the police simply for being drunk, and of the time he took his mother to a restaurant for a birthday present and they were refused service.

Poverty and childhood poverty were widespread, especially for African Americans. For example, almost 50 percent of African American married-couple families were poor, "a figure far higher than today." Government agencies discriminated against African Americans. "The Federal Housing Authority, such a boon to white working-class families, refused to insure homes in all-black or in racially mixed neighborhoods." Women, African Americans, and many others did not thrive during the 1950s (Coontz, 1997, p. 44).

Of course, even in the middle of these conditions, hope did appear and flourish. The Civil Rights movement emerged, grew, and spread in the 1950s. It was the precursor, the spark, and the training ground for all the 1960s movements: peace and anti-war, feminist, gay rights, senior rights, children's and youth rights, and many others. We may be nostalgic for the 1950s as the ideal family time, but the 1950s also gave rise to the movements that would work to resolve the family contradictions and problems hidden behind *I Love Lucy* and *Leave It to Beaver.*

ENSLAVED AND "FREE" AFRICAN AMERICAN FAMILIES

One of the most enduring debates in the history of families concerns the effects of slavery, discrimination, and oppression since 1865, on African American families. Were they largely destroyed by those experiences, or, despite the horrors of slavery and post-1865 oppression, did African Americans manage to create and live in functioning families? (This section draws from Aulette, 1994; Billingsley, 1992; Douglass, 1855; Gutman, 1976; Horton and Horton, 1997; Jacobs, 1861; Sudarkasa, 1988; and Zinn and Eitzen, 1996.)

The African Heritage

Implicit in much past research on African Americans was the assumption that they were brought to the American shores with no culture, with no memories of family traditions. It is as if they forgot everything while on slave ships crossing the Atlantic. More recent research has begun to show that not only did they carry the cultures and memories with them, but also that these traditions and memories lived on, many were passed on to later generations, and survived for centuries.

So let us begin with a brief discussion of their African family heritage. The nuclear family was the tradition in the United States, but not in West Africa, the ancestral home of most enslaved Africans. "Upon marriage, Africans did not normally form new isolated households, but joined a compound in which the extended family of the groom, or that of the bride, was already domiciled." Obligations and interactions were not primarily with one's spouse and children, but also with many other people living in the same compound. All "the children within the compound regarded themselves as brothers and sisters," and adults assumed responsibility toward "nephews" and "nieces" as well as their own biological children. Indeed, in most African cultures children used the same word to refer to people we separate as "mother" and "aunt" or "father" and "uncle." There was a "commitment to the collectivity. The family offered a network of security, but it also imposed a burden of obligations" (Sudarkasa, 1988, pp. 94, 95, 97).

African American Families in Slavery. It was such experiences, values, and traditions that lived in the souls of enslaved Africans and shaped their socialization and outlook. These experiences, values, and traditions were what generations of people brought to the United States as slave ships carried them from the mid-1600s to 1808, when the slave trade ended.

There are many theories and interpretations of the effects of slavery on African American families. I will simplify the discussion considerably by describing only three major perspectives.

Slavery destroyed families. The following words, by Kardiner and Ovesey, may typify the perspective that slaves had no families: "The most rudimentary type of family organization was not permitted to survive, to say nothing of the extensions of the family. The mother-child family, with the father either unknown, absent, or, if present, incapable of wielding influence, was the only type of family that could survive" (cited in Gutman, 1976, p. xvii).

Gutman also summarizes parts of that perspective: "the alleged inadequacy of the slave father and husband, the absence of male 'models' for young children to emulate, . . . the insistence that slave marriage usually meant little more than successive polygyny, and the belief that the 'matrifocal' household (a 'natural' adaptation by most blacks to the 'realities' of slavery) prevailed among the mass of illiterate plantation field hands and laborers" (1976, p. 13).

According to this perspective, a number of slavery conditions made families impossible. Slaves could have no legal marriages; parents could be separated from each other when owners decided to sell one or both of them; children could be sold and separated from their parents and each other. In addition, enslaved women were often raped and otherwise sexually exploited by male slave owners, thus making marriages and families difficult to maintain. And the general brutality, exploitation, deprivation, and control that were the daily realities of slavery added to the burdens people faced if they tried to marry and have families.

Let us focus on one condition, the separation of children from their families. Frederick Douglass was separated from his African American mother when he was a young child. He came to believe that his father was a white plantation owner. His maternal grandmother raised him and other children in a hut some distance from the master's plantation. When he was seven or eight, he was brought to work on that plantation. For years his mother, who was a slave in a nearby plantation, would walk thirteen miles each way to see Frederick on Sundays. When she died, he was not allowed to attend her funeral (Douglass, 1855; Takaki, 1993, pp. 122–126).

While a slave, Harriet Jacobs witnessed the sale of children and the separation from their parents. To "the slave mother New Year's day comes laden with peculiar sorrows. She sits on her cold cabin floor, watching the children who may all be torn from her the next morning; and often does she wish that she and they might die before the day dawns. . . . [A mother] begged the trader to tell her where he intended to take them; this he refused to do. How *could* he, when he knew he would sell them, one by one, wherever he could command the highest price? I met that mother in the street, and her wild, haggard face lives to-day in my mind. She wrung her hands in anguish, and exclaimed, 'Gone! All gone! Why *don't* God kill me?'"(Jacobs, 1861, pp. 350–351)

Two-parent families under slavery. No one can deny the horrors and destruction slavery visited on enslaved Africans. Marriages and families were indeed made difficult to undertake, to nourish, to perpetuate. But according to some historians, marriages and families did exist, *despite* slavery. Parents, children, and siblings were committed to each other, longed for each other, despite forced separations.

The lived reality of such separations is found in a letter Hannah Grover, an old slave woman, wrote to her son, separated from her for 20 years, on June 3, 1805. "Now my dear son I pray you to come and see your dear old Mother—Or send me twenty dollars and I will come and see you in Philadelphia—And if you cant come to see your old Mother pray send me a letter and tell me where you live what family you have and what you do for a living—I am a poor old servant I long for freedom. . . . I love you Cato you love your Mother—You are my only son" (cited in Gutman, 1976, p. 4).

Gutman and other historians argue that whenever possible slaves did marry and they lived together as long as possible. He argues that despite the involuntary breakups of families, "most slaves lived in double-headed households" and plantation slave records show "long slave marriages." Furthermore, "common slave marital rules and intensive naming for slave blood kin are found in all plantations" (1976, pp. xxii–xxiii).

Adult slaves—women and men—who lived in long marriages became role models for younger ones, who then carried on marriage and family traditions. Some of the best evidence for the existence of long marriages and two-parent families is found in the numbers of couples who registered and legalized their marriages upon emancipation in 1865 and 1866 (see below for details).

A related debate centers on the roles enslaved African men could play as husbands and fathers. The traditional view has held that slavery completely denied them any such roles, and thus they were "emasculated" and destroyed. Unable to provide for their families, unable to protect women from being sold and raped, unable to prevent the sale of their children, how *could* they be husbands and fathers? No doubt that slavery did make it profoundly difficult for enslaved African men to be fathers and husbands, but men—like women—did struggle, with some success, to have family lives. The long marriages, cited above and below, attest to their success.

Slave marriages showed more gender equality than did white marriages. Strong women worked with their husbands to support their families. But men too found ways to provide for their children. Many of them "hunted and trapped animals to supplement the meager food supplied by plantation owners. . . . Even when a slave boy was growing up without a father in the house, he had as a model a tough, resourceful driver, a skilled mechanic or two, and other field hands. Some of these men . . . told them stories, taught them to fish and trap animals, and instructed them on ways of survival in a White world" (Zinn and Eitzen, 1996, p. 81).

Enslaved African women had very difficult lives. They were sexually exploited by their white owners. They worked incredibly long days. During most of the day they worked either in the fields or in the owner's home, doing all the cleaning and cooking and raising of white children. When they returned to their cabins in the evening, they had to cook, clean, and sew for their own families. A man describes the work of his mother, a house servant: "She would go to the house in the morning, take the pail upon her head, and go away to the cow-pen, and milk fourteen cows. She then put on the bread for the family breakfast. . . ." She also had the care of ten to fifteen children whose mothers worked in the fields. After she also got the breakfast for the slaves, she made beds, swept floors, cooked the family dinner, and in the evening milked the cows again. She then had to return to her cabin to take care of her family. "She would then be so tired that she could scarcely stand," but she still had clothes to sew, children's cuts to tend to, and so on. After a short sleep she would "hasten to the toil of the [next] day" (cited in Zinn and Eitzen, 1996, pp. 80–81)

Extended families in slavery. A third perspective agrees with the previous one that families did survive and function under slavery, but stresses the existence of large extended families, along the African traditions described previously. It focuses on large family groupings, which often included unrelated people, rather than on only mothers, fathers, and children.

To survive under the harsh and brutal conditions of slavery, enslaved Africans turned to family traditions they brought from Africa *and* created new roles and customs in reaction to slavery. They could not re-create the extended family compounds of West Africa, but they could and did turn to a variety of relatives and non-relatives so they could survive. For example, upon marriage young mothers did not establish their own households, but "continued to live in households headed by other adults." Relatives "assisted each other with child rearing, in life crisis events such as birth and death, in work groups, in efforts to obtain freedom, and so on" (Sudarkasa, 1988, pp. 98–99).

There was "a sharing of responsibility for food and shelter. . . . [M]uch of the domestic work of supporting the community was done communally by slave women. For example, 'most infants and toddlers spent the day in a children's house, where an elderly slave was in charge.'" Since "women were essential to the community's survival" they were "critical members of the community [and this allowed] them to emerge as important political leaders" (Davis, 1981, as summarized in Aulette, 1994, pp. 68–69).

African American Families after Emancipation

People who argue that slavery destroyed African American families carry that argument to the years after the 1865 emancipation and to the present.

E. Franklin Frazier, a family sociologist who wrote extensively on African American families, argued that after the end of slavery families found themselves with few family traditions. "What authority was there to take the place of the master's in regulating sex relations and maintaining the permanency of marital ties? Where could the Negro father look for sanctions of his authority in family relations which had scarcely existed in the past? Were the affectional bonds between mother and child and the solidarity of feeling and sentiment between man and wife strong enough to withstand the disorganizing effects of freedom?" As a result, "promiscuous sexual relations and constant changing of partners became the rule [among] demoralized black" (cited in Gutman, 1976, pp. 8–9).

But Gutman, Billingsley, and others cite extensive evidence—government records, letters, and more—which shows conclusively that immediately after the end of slavery, and for decades later, the great majority of African American families had two parents. In many cases where there was only one parent, the other one had died. "Upon their emancipation most Virginia ex-slave families had two parents, and most older couples had lived together in long-lasting marriages." An 1866 census in Nelson, Virginia, showed that 55 percent of marriages of former slaves were ten or more years old; 24 percent were ten to nineteen years, 16 percent were twenty to twenty-nine, 8 percent were thirty to thirty-nine, and 7 percent were forty and over (Gutman, 1976, pp. 9, 12).

Similar percentages of two-parent families and long-lasting marriages existed all over the South. In the North, most African American families also had two parents. A study in Buffalo, New York, showed that from 1855 to 1925, "the double-headed kin-related household always was the characteristic . . . Afro-American household, ranging from 82 to 92 percent of all households." In 1925 in New York City, 85 percent of "kin-related black households were double-headed" (Gutman, 1976, pp. xviii–xix). And in Chicago, "a 1930 study by sociologist Irene Graham showed that a smaller percentage of black children . . . lived in broken homes than their white peers. Ninety percent of black children lived with their own parents; and a portion of the remaining tenth lived with relatives" (Billingsley, 1992, p. 13).

In closing, it is clear that African American families faced enormous obstacles, exploitation, and other problems. But they struggled against these conditions to enable individuals and families to survive. Their heritage and their strength were powerful and contained "the seeds of their survival and rejuvenation" (Billingsley, 1992, p. 17).

Northern Free Blacks, 1700–1860

Horton and Horton, in *In Hope of Liberty: Culture, Community, and Protest among Northern Free Blacks, 1700–1860* (1997), devote an entire chapter to "the evolution of family and household." Evidence found in a small settlement of African American families in Plymouth, Massachusetts, shows that they "maintained cultural memories of the African past over many years." For example, "following African custom, the four families built their houses in a cluster in the center of the tract" (p. 78). At the same time, in some families there was a mixing of African American, white, and Native American members and cultures.

Forming families was also difficult for northern African Americans. Horton and Horton cite one case. "John Moranda gained his freedom late in 1795 when Samuel Jones, Jr., a New York lawyer and politician, paid his owner $200. A few months later he had managed to save the $50 necessary to purchase his four-year-old daughter from her owner in New Jersey, but it was another three years before he managed to save $160 to buy his wife and son and finally unite his small family in freedom" (1997, p. 84).

Horton and Horton too cite evidence which shows that throughout Northern cities, around 1820, most African American families had two parents. And most women who were single parents became so from their late thirties on, most of them because of their husbands' deaths.

In conclusion, they state: "As African Americans in the North moved from slavery into freedom, traditional family and household forms, many based in African cultures, were adapted to their needs, their new conditions, obstacles, and opportunities. . . . Generation after generation extended the family and household to shelter and nurture kin and nonkin. . . . [They] formed the basis for cooperative arrangements to meet the problems associated with poverty, hardship, illness, and prejudice" (Horton and Horton, 1997, p. 100).

Sharecropping, the Journey North, and the 1950s

Following emancipation, most freed slaves were economically destitute. Governments at all levels did nothing to provide them with land or jobs. Prejudice, discrimination, and oppression were fierce from the 1860s to the 1970s. (For two extraordinary accounts of the oppression African Americans faced, see Richard Wright's *Black Boy* (1945), which focuses on the 1920s and 1930s, and John Howard Griffin's *Black Like Me* (1961), for the 1950s.)

As a result, African Americans held the worst jobs. Women worked as maids for white families and many families became sharecroppers. Typically, sharecropping involved poor people (mostly blacks, but some whites too) who were allowed to cultivate a portion of a white landowner's farm in exchange for usually 50 percent of the crops they raised. Most sharecroppers barely managed to feed their families, and were often in debt to landowners and store owners. While in debt, they could not leave the owner's land—thus, they became virtual slaves again.

According to Aulette, African American families were still connected to their extended families and the larger community, but gradually became more nuclear, focusing largely on couples and their children (1994, p. 72). Others believe that both in the past and today most African Americans live in extended kin networks (Stack, 1974, 1996).

As the nineteenth century closed and the twentieth began, African Americans started to leave the rural South for Northern cities. They did so for three reasons. First, the mechanization of farming allowed and encouraged white landowners to dismiss sharecroppers since they were no longer needed to work the land. Second, there were more industrial jobs in Northern cities, creating a demand for workers, especially during World War I and World War II, when white men were overseas fighting. And third, the continued and intense violence and discrimination they faced in the South pushed African Americans to leave the region.

When they moved North, they continued to live in two-parent and extended families, as we saw earlier in this chapter. In addition, they kept close ties with their relatives in the South, visiting and writing them. The exodus continued after World War II, picking up speed in the 1950s. And up to 1960, 78 percent of African American families were still composed of two parents. In time, some began to return to the South (Stack, 1996).

(Space does not allow discussion of the family histories of other groups. See Gonzales, 1998; Benokraitis, 2002; and Taylor, 2002, for Native American, Mexican, Cuban, Haitian, African, Vietnamese, Chinese, Japanese, and other groups.)

CONCLUSION

Changes, worries, and struggles have characterized families throughout U.S. history (and surely the history of families of the world). As we proceed to discuss marriage, parents and children, work, and other areas of family life, we shall find changes, joys, worries, and struggles.

And we shall also find many continuities, despite the profound changes we have seen in this chapter. Most people still marry and have children. Most people live in families most of their lives. Even as same-sex marriage is becoming a reality, and some people see its coming as a threat to "traditional" marriage and the family, we should notice that most same-sex couples who wish to marry long for families with parents and children.

We have traveled a long way from Colonial families, from the families of enslaved Africans, from the family traditions of ethnic groups that migrated to the United States, from the families Native Americans formed over their long history. Much has changed, much has been lost, and much has been gained. In the chapters that follow, you are invited to ongoing discussion, debate, and reflection of families in the past and today. (For "historical perspectives on family studies," see Coontz, 2000.)

3

Making Sense of Families

IDEALS, LONGINGS, AND REALITIES

Our families inspire and create high hopes, warm memories, and close ties and relationships—and they also create pains, disappointments, confusions, and at times physical and mental violence. Almost all of us are raised in families, if not by our parents, then by aunts and uncles, grandparents, or other relatives, or even by nonrelatives who became our family. When we wish to describe close ties with friends we say they are "like family" to us. Families and our experiences in them touch us deeply, move us profoundly, and can wound us terribly.

People and experiences that are so very much part of our entire being can be difficult to understand precisely because they are so close to us. We have such high hopes for our families that it may be impossible to acknowledge hurt and pain when they arise. High expectations often lead to high disappointments.

The hopes we have for our families are evident everywhere. Every time I teach the course "Changing Families" I begin by asking students two questions. Anonymously, they write about "what my family means to me" and "the condition of families in the United States today."

In response to "what my family means to me," almost everyone offers positive, glowing, and moving comments. They cannot imagine life without their families.

"My family means my world to me. Without my family, I wouldn't be who I am today. I can't imagine my existence without them. My family is 'love.'"

"My family is security, love, understanding, and a sense of belonging. I know that no matter what I do, they'll always be there for me."

"To me my family means love, security, and protection. They mean understanding, comfort, and help to each other."

Later in the course, and in this book, we explore some of the dashed hopes, some of the insecurities and lost loves, when we discuss divorce, violence, and other conditions found in many families. But at the beginning of the course, over 90 percent of the students say that their families are havens of love and warmth. Most Americans think similarly of their families, as various surveys have shown through the years. (For examples, see Caplow and others, 1982; Glenn, 1992; Stacey, 1996, p. 9.)

On the other hand, the question "what is the condition of the family in the United States today?" elicits concerns and worries. Most students think that families are very troubled, that they are falling apart, that they do not provide the love and care families members need, especially children. They cite increasing divorce, parents too busy to spend time with their children, and working mothers as conditions leading to the decline and demise of families.

PERSPECTIVES ON FAMILIES

Each one of us looks at families, past and present, through our own experiences, perceptions, stories we hear, nostalgic memories of our own and those of others, hopes and dashed hopes, longings, and other realities that shape what we think and feel. None of us, no matter who we

Colorado, Texas, and Illinois families—all enjoy being together, and all deal with balancing the pressures of today's world.

are, can escape our past and our experiences when we try to make sense of what is happening to families. We look at them through our unique lenses, which are shaped to various degrees by the stories we read, watch on TV, see at the movies, and hear from relatives and friends.

Sociologists, historians, politicians, and groups like the Council on Families in America, the Christian Coalition, and the National Organization for Women have their own views and perspectives. In this chapter, I will discuss three such general perspectives. Be aware, however, that these *are* generalizations, and that any one person or group may in reality hold parts of each perspective, may fall somewhere between them, or may claim a perspective they consider different from these three.

Perhaps the most common view on families today is that they are in decline, have serious problems, and are falling apart. The opposite belief, that they are in fine condition, was held by some sociologists and historians in the 1970s and early 1980s, and may still be held, but we hear relatively little from this outlook today. A third view holds that families are changing, that they face problems and challenges, that they are beset by economic and social conditions which make it difficult for families to function well, but they are not falling apart. As in the past, crises and changing social conditions lead families to make adaptations, to change roles and functions. According to this view, families have always been changing. (This discussion and these categories draw from many writers, especially Skolnick, 1996; Stacey, 1996; Coontz, 1997. For a variation on these three categories, see Giele, 1996, and Benokraitis, 2000. I will present feminist views on families later in this chapter.)

The Decline and Demise of Families

The concern that families are weakening and not meeting the needs of their members has a long history. For centuries, writers have bemoaned what they have seen as the deterioration of families in their times.

Since the early 1970s, we can find such expressions and worries in the writings and politics of religious organizations, interest groups, politicians, sociologists, and historians. Most recently, the Council on Families in America, composed of sociologists, historians, and other writers, has joined the chorus. Whereas in the past the battle to restore more traditional families was led by the Moral Majority, parts of the Republican party, and other social and political organizations generally characterized as "conservative," the concerns expressed in the 1990s came from groups and individuals which consider themselves "moderate" and "centrist," even "liberal" (including President Clinton in 1994 and 1995). They have sought to undo family changes they see as negative and harmful. (See Stacey, 1996, for a detailed discussion.)

People who think that families are in danger express their concerns very clearly and directly. Illinois Governor Jim Edgar said in November 1995: "As governor, I can tell you that about 80 percent of the problems that hit my desk can trace back to the breakdown of the family structure in our society, and I think everyone who doesn't want to admit that is kidding themselves." And sociologist Amitai Etzioni predicted in 1977 that "by the mid-1990s not one American family will be left" (cited in Stacey, 1996, p. 1; and in Coontz, 1997, p. 3).

In the 1990s, media campaigns by some religious groups and the Council on Families led to an abundance of stories on the decline of the family and family values, which were blamed for most social problems. Coontz stated: "In a computer search of newspapers from March 1993 through January 1995, I found 263 articles attributing more than twenty distinct 'crises'—teenage drug use, urban violence, unemployment, America's declining international competitiveness, federal budget deficits, even individual 'narcissism'—to the 'collapse of family values' or abandonment of 'the two-parent paradigm.' As the American Enterprise Institute put it, 'The drug crisis, the education crisis, and the problems of teen pregnancy and juvenile crime' can all be traced 'to one source: broken families'" (1997, p. 6).

Let us go back in time to the 1970s, when religious groups like the Moral Majority joined forces with many politicians to undo family changes that they bemoaned. To some degree these groups led to the election of Ronald Reagan as president in 1980. They introduced a number of proposed laws in the U.S. Congress, collectively known as the Family Protection Act. According to Kain, a critic of those proposals, "the goal of the legislation was to reinforce what is defined as the traditional family—based upon a mythical vision of peaceful family life . . . in which the husband is the breadwinner and the wife is in the home raising children" (1990, p. 10). More recent writers on family decline, however, seem to have accepted the economic reality that most mothers must have jobs while their children are young.

Pogrebin outlines the specific details of the Family Protection Act, whose supporters wanted to:

> Protect the right of parents and other authorized individuals to use corporal punishment against children. . . .
>
> Require that marriage and motherhood be taught as the proper career for girls, and deny federal funds to schools whose textbooks show women in nontraditional roles. . . .
>
> Provide tax incentives that discourage women's employment and promote wives' economic dependence on husbands. . . .
>
> Give a $1,000 tax exemption for the birth or adoption of a child, but only to a married couple (1983).

In 1995, the Christian Coalition published a pamphlet entitled "Contract with the American Family: A Bold Plan to Strengthen the Family and Restore Common-Sense Values." It states that the Contract "emerged from a survey of Christian Coalition members and supporters conducted in March and April, 1995. . . . Each item in the Contract enjoys support from between 60 and 90 percent of the American people. More than half of the items in the Contract already have legislative sponsors, and several have already been passed by committee" (p. 34). (None had become law in 1995.)

The specific proposals aim to reverse "the breakup of the family" and to provide financial, political, and social supports for more traditional families. Among the proposals are:

"Protecting Parental Rights. Enactment of a Parental Rights Act and defeat of the U.N. Convention on the Rights of the Child." That convention said that, among other items, "No child shall be subjected to arbitrary or unlawful interference with his or her privacy, family home or correspondence. . . . The child has the right to the protection of the law against such interference or attacks" (pp. 14–15).

"Family-Friendly Tax Relief." Among other items, this includes legislation which would "allow homemakers to contribute up to $2,000 annually toward an IRA, thereby providing equitable treatment to spouses who work at home" (pp. 17–18).

Opposition to abortion (pp. 20–24).

"Restricting Pornography" (p. 27).

A more recent publication, using elements of the Christian Coalition's contract and drawing heavily from the Council on Families, is "The Crisis of Family Decline in Massachusetts," published by the Massachusetts Family Institute, which declares itself as "dedicated to strengthening the family" (Daniels, 1998). It finds the absence of fathers from their families as the basic cause of family decline.

> A growing number of scholars and commentators from across the political spectrum have concluded that America must confront the grave threat that fatherlessness and the decline of two-parent families pose to the health of our society. . . . Tragically, the percentage of fatherless families in [Massachusetts] has more than quadrupled since 1960 and has continued to rise dramatically over the past year. At present, a record level of over 29 percent of all families in Massachusetts are fatherless. . . .
>
> [S]tudies strongly suggest that there is a connection between the decline in the percentage of two-parent families in Massachusetts and the following disturbing statistics . . .
>
> The total crime rate has *more than tripled* since 1960.

The violent crime rate is *13 times* higher than in 1960.

A greater than 200 percent increase in the number of homicides has caused the homicide rate to *triple* since 1960.

The number of young people under age 17 entering the criminal justice system has increased by almost *90 percent* since 1979.

The adult prison population has *more than tripled* since 1980.

More than *39 percent* of children ages 12 and 13 report using illegal drugs.

The percentage of children living in poverty has almost *doubled* since 1970s. As a result, approximately 15 percent of all children in Massachusetts are currently living in poverty. (Daniels, 1998, pp. i, iii)

Daniels relies heavily on writings of the Council on Families, which is composed of twenty social scientists (see list in Glenn, 1997). Among them are David Blankenhorn, David Popenoe, Judith Wallerstein, and Barbara Dafoe Whitehead.

In the literature from the Council, divorce and divorced or never-married fathers who do not stay in their children's lives are seen as the major cause of family decline. Popenoe, in *Life Without Father,* says: "And according to a growing body of evidence, this massive erosion of fatherhood contributes mightily to many of the major social problems of our time, . . . [among them] crime and delinquency; premature sexuality and out-of-wedlock teen births; deteriorating educational achievement; depression, substance abuse, and alienation among teenagers; and the growing number of women and children in poverty" (1996, pp. 1, 3).

He cites the work of McLanahan and Sandefur (1994) which concludes, in Popenoe's summary, that fatherless children are "twice as likely to drop out of high school, 2.5 times as likely to become teen mothers, and 1.4 times as likely to be idle—out of school and out of work—as children who grow up with both parents." Later, he says: "What the decline of fatherhood and marriage in America really means . . . is that slowly, insidiously, and relentlessly our society has been moving in an ominous direction—toward the devaluation of children" (pp. 9, 14).

Whitehead also focuses on divorce as the major indicator of family decline. Indeed, she thinks we have become a "divorce culture," one that values individual happiness above responsibility to children and family. "Beginning in the late 1950s, Americans began to change their ideas about the individual's obligations to family and society. Broadly described, the change was away from an ethic of obligation to others and toward an obligation to self. I do not mean that people suddenly abandoned all responsibilities to others, but rather that they became more acutely conscious of their responsibility to attend to their own individual needs and interests. . . . People began to judge the strength and 'health' of family bonds according to their capacity to promote individual fulfillment and personal growth. . . . The family began to lose its separate place and distinctive identity as the realm of duty, service, and sacrifice. . . ." As individual happiness and divorce increased, the well-being of children declined. Whitehead presents and discusses statistics and studies—on school attendance, delinquency rates, poverty—to show that children have been the victims of the divorce culture (1997, pp. 4–6).

In *Marriage in America: A Report to the Nation* the Council on Families (1996) echoes Popenoe's and Whitehead's discussion and analysis. It ends by presenting recommendations to strengthen marriages and families. They propose "four broad goals":

1. Reclaim the ideal of marital permanence and affirm marriage as the preeminent environment for childrearing.

2. Decide unequivocally that out-of-wedlock childbearing is wrong, that our divorce rate is far too high, and that every child deserves a father.

3. Resolve in the next generation to increase the proportion of children who grow up with their two married parents and decrease the proportion who do not.

4. Resolve in the next generation to increase the time that parents spend raising their children. For married couples with children at home, aim for an overall commitment to paid employment that does not exceed sixty hours per week. (p. 308)

The Council also published a critical report of sociology texts on the family. Entitled *Closed Hearts, Closed Minds: The Textbook Story of Marriage* (Glenn, 1997), it concludes that these texts present a biased and pessimistic outlook of marriages. "Both by what they say and, sometimes even more importantly, by the information they omit, these books repeatedly suggest that marriage is more a problem than a solution. The potential costs of marriage to adults, particularly women, often receive exaggerated treatment, while the benefits of marriage, both to individuals and society, are frequently downplayed or ignored. Second, almost all of these textbooks shortchange children, devoting far more pages to adult problems and adult relationships than to issues concerning child well-being" (p. 3).

Since the early 1990s, the Council and people associated with it seem to have conducted a systematic campaign to present their arguments and recommendations in scholarly journals, books, and the popular media. (See Stacey, 1996, for a detailed account.) Whitehead's article "Dan Quayle Was Right" (1993), printed in the liberal magazine *The Atlantic Monthly,* was a major event in that campaign (she later expanded it to a book, *The Divorce Culture* [1997]).

More recently, Popenoe and Whitehead became co-directors of the National Marriage Project at Rutgers University. They continue their media campaign. For example, in July 1999, the *Boston Globe* published two articles on work of the project. The headlines were "Marriage not in blissful state, study says" and "Women down on marriage, study finds." A conclusion reported in one of the articles states: "The institution of marriage is in serious trouble," pointing to "an increasing number of young adults, particularly young women, [who] are pessimistic about finding a lasting marriage partner and are far more accepting than in the past of alternatives to marriage, including single parenthood and living together with a partner outside of marriage" (Fletcher, 1999; see also Ataiyero, 1999).

How many Americans share the above pessimistic perspective on families? It would seem that a majority does, when you ask them to comment on families in general. But the story changes when we see that most people say *their own family* is fine, and that they value their families above all else. (Popenoe, 1999, and Waite and Gallagher, 2000, are two recent statements of this perspective.)

Families Are Well and Healthy

Sociologists have shown that the fear of families falling apart has been present throughout U.S. history. Present warnings and discussions of family decline are but the latest version of that fear. Beginning with this realization, some sociologists and historians have argued that families are no worse than they have ever been; indeed, in some ways perhaps they may be better than ever.

Middletown Families by Caplow and others (1982) may be the clearest example of this perspective. Their study of Muncie, Indiana, in the 1970s updates families in that community first studied by Lynd and Lynd (1929, 1937). Their chapter on "the myth of the declining family" shows the long history of that belief, held by many sociologists and historians long before the Council on Families appeared.

Middletown Families tries to refute that myth. Theirs and other studies show "(1) that kinship ties are extremely important in contemporary urban society and (2) that the existence of a vital, all-embracing, extended family of 'the good old days' was mostly a myth." Families in Muncie were "in exceptionally good condition." In contrast to sociological generalizations that people are increasingly isolated from their relatives, Muncie families had many and deep ties with parents, uncles and aunts, siblings, and other relatives. They conclude that the "composite family . . . is in splendid condition" in Muncie. Discussing child and wife abuse, they praise the increased awareness of these problems and of the places and institutions that protect women and children, "but there is no evidence whatever that these ugly behaviors have been increasing" (Caplow and others, 1982, pp. 195, 323, 340, 336).

Wattenberg, in *The Good News Is the Bad News Is Wrong* (1985), presented a similarly positive portrait of families. According to Skolnick, "He made three points: There has been *less* change than was generally assumed; many of the changes that have occurred are for the *better;* to the extent that harmful changes have occurred, they are being corrected. . . . For example, with regard to premarital sex, he cited evidence to show that virginity was far from universal before the sexual revolution of the 1960s; Alfred Kinsey's data showed that 36 percent of American women born between 1900 and 1925 experienced premarital intercourse by the age of 25. Almost one out of five live births in the 1950s were conceived before marriage. . . . Finally, a variety of statistics indicate that casual or promiscuous sex has been decreasing in recent years" (1996, p. 8)

Mary Joe Bane, in *Here to Stay: American Families in the Twentieth Century* (1976), asserted that the claim of family decline was exaggerated and unwarranted. For example, contrary to the nostalgia of large and loving extended families living and working together, in the past and today only about 6 percent of the families have been extended. Mothers with outside jobs today spend no less time with their children than mothers did in the past; they were busy with cleaning, cooking, making clothes, and so on, and did not give constant direct attention to their children. Indeed, Bane thinks that the statistics she presents suggest that parental watchfulness over children may have increased compared to three to four generations ago. A recent study concluded that mothers today spend as much time with their children as mothers ever did.

Kain, in *The Myth of Family Decline* (1990), argues that because we idealize the past we tend to think that families are declining. He thinks that changes have been gradual and evolutionary, and many have improved families. Also, many things have not changed. For example, if we examine marriage over the entire U.S. history, and we do not consider the 1950s as typical, we find that the percent of people who ever marry has been about the same (pp. 7–8 and ch. 4).

These studies were published in the 1970s and 1980s. Would these authors hold the same views today? How many people think that families are in fine condition in the beginning of the 21st century?

One indicator of family living—divorce—is no higher today than it was in the 1970s. Contrary to Etzioni's prediction, there are families still and people still marry. And whatever people may say about families in general, most of them think their families are in good condition. Are we living in the midst of family decline, even disappearance, or, are families as alive, vibrant, and important as ever?

Anxious, Distressed, and Enduring Families

In *Brave New Families: Stories of Domestic Upheaval in Late Twentieth Century America* (1990), Judith Stacey narrates the family histories of two women, Pamela and Dotty, from the late 1950s to the late 1980s. In 1996, she wrote a summary and discussion of that book in *In the Name of the Family*. Here are some excerpts from that summary.

> In the summer of 1986 I attended a wedding ceremony in a small Christian Pentecostal church in the Silicon Valley. . . . Serving as the wedding photographer was the bride's [Pamela's] former husband accompanied by his live-in lover, a Jewish divorcee who hoped to become his third wife. All of the wedding attendants were stepkin or step-in-laws to the groom: two daughters from the bride's first marriage served as their mother's bride matrons; their brother joined one daughter's second husband as ushers for the groom; and the proud flower girl was a young granddaughter from the bride matron's first marriage. At least half the pews were filled with members of four generations from the confusing tangle of former, step-, dual, and in-law relatives of this . . . divorced-extended family. . . .
>
> [W]hile the national divorce rate was doubling after 1960, in Santa Clara County [where Pamela and Dotty lived] it nearly tripled. 'Non-family' and single-parent households grew faster

than in the rest of the nation. . . . The high marriage casualty rate among workaholic engineers was dubbed 'the silicon syndrome,' and many residents shared an alarmist view of family life . . . .

Pamela's first marriage in 1960 to Don Franklin, the father of her three children, lasted fifteen years, spanning the headiest days of Silicon Valley development [when the computer industry arose] and the period of Don's successful rise from telephone repairman to electronics packaging engineer. . . .

Pam and Dotty, like most white women of their generation, were young when they married in the 1950s and early 1960s. . . . For a significant period of time, they and their husbands conformed, as best they could, to the culturally prescribed pattern of male breadwinner and female homemaker. Assuming primary responsibility for rearing the children they began to bear immediately after marriage, Pam and Dotty supported their husbands' successful efforts to progress from working-class to middle-class and upper-middle class careers in the electronics industry. . . .

In the early 1970s, while their workaholic husbands were increasingly absent from their families, Pam and Dotty each joined friends taking women's reentry courses in local community colleges. There they encountered feminism, and their lives and their modern families were never the same. Feminism provided an analysis and rhetoric for their discontent, and it helped each develop the self-esteem she needed to exit or reform her unhappy modern marriage. Both women left their husbands, became welfare mothers and experimented with the single life. Pam divorced, pursued a college degree, and developed a social service career. Dotty, with lesser educational credentials and employment options, took her husband back, but on her own terms, after his disabling heart attack (and after a lover left her). . . .

[After her second marriage, Pamela] collaborated with her first husband's live-in . . . lover, Shirley Moskowitz, to build a remarkably harmonious and inclusive divorced-extended kin network whose constituent households swapped resources, labor, and lodgers in response to shifting family circumstances and needs." (Stacey, 1996, pp. 17–24)

Pam and Dotty underwent much conflict and many changes in their family lives. Many people would look at them and conclude they do not value families and their families are in decline. Instead, Stacey insists that they are adapting to new gender expectations and new economic conditions, and their (changed) families are the center of their lives, as we see in the previous paragraphs.

Stacey's writings, and those of others, represent examples of the third perspective on families. They fully acknowledge that families face serious problems: "Indisputably, family life in the United States today, as in most of the world, is deeply vulnerable and insecure." But they also insist that marriages and families are changing but not declining, that people want to and do find meaning in their families, that we are creating new families. Pam and Dotty are good examples of people committed to their families (Stacey, 1996, p. 2; Coontz, 1997, 2000; Cowan and Cowan, 2003).

Coontz outlines some of the stresses families face today. Millions of 5 to 14 year-old children are left alone after school, they are the "latchkey" kids who need monitoring that busy working parents cannot provide. "Parents with long commutes, evening shifts, or irregular hours face special problems finding consistent child care; they often patch together a 'crazy quilt' of multiple care combinations that cause stress for both parents and children." A related problem is "men's failure to change their domestic roles as much as women have changed their work ones [and this] is a major source of discord between men and women" (1997, pp. 68–69).

But Coontz, Stacey, Skolnick, and others attribute most of these problems to government policies and economic conditions that require both parents to work, not to declining family values and increasing individualism. The stress over caring for children, for example, is created by governments that do not provide quality and affordable day care, and by economic conditions that drive both parents to work long hours. In another area, children live in poverty not because of divorce or single parents, but because we have no policies and programs to provide for children, and most jobs do not pay enough to support a family. For example, Sweden and other countries have as high rates of divorce, single parents, and children born to unmarried women as the United States, but children's poverty rates are much lower. In single-mother households in the United States, 59.5 percent of children were poor in 1989–1991, whereas only 5.2 percent were in Sweden and 13.9 in Italy (Houseknecht and Sastry, 1996, p. 734; see also Coontz, 1997, pp. 151–153).

Popenoe and others insist that father absence causes childhood poverty, and Coontz responds that even if we were to reunite the biological parents of every child in the United States, "two thirds of the children who are poor today would *still* be poor." Governments do not provide adequate income support, and many jobs do not pay enough for parents to support their children. In 1993, half of African American and Hispanic men 25–34 years old held jobs whose pay could not support a family of four (Coontz, 1997, pp. 139–140).

Also, proponents of this perspective point to statistics which tend to show commitment to families is not as weak as the Council on Families claims. The vast majority of people still marry. Over 90 percent of Americans marry at least once in their lives, and many of the other ten percent are gay or lesbian couples who would marry if they could, or heterosexual couples in long-lasting or permanent cohabitation (Mason, Skolnick, and Sugarman, 2003, p. 2).

Statistics cited to show family decline present only part of the changing landscape. For example, whereas there are absentee fathers, other fathers are becoming increasingly involved in their children's lives. There are similar problems with data on single mothers. Statistics on never-married mothers in the past may underestimate their numbers. Many of them, to avoid social embarrassment, told census takers that they were separated or widowed rather than tell the truth (Gerson, 1993; Coontz, 1992, p. 16, and 1997, p. 29).

To the degree there is less commitment to marriage, it's the inevitable outcome of social changes we would not want to undo. For example, if women's access to well-paying, non-traditional jobs increases the chances of divorce, what should we do? Send women back to the kitchen and low-level jobs? Should we raise our daughters to have low or no ambitions? And in regard to the Council on Families' recommendation that people stay in "good enough" marriages, "what government agency or private morals committee will decide if a marriage is 'good enough' " (Coontz, 1997, pp. 80–82, 84)?

In short, families today do face serious and troubling challenges. Often, parents do not have much time for their children; there are millions of children in poverty; about half of the marriages end in divorce; other problems beset families. Coontz, Stacey, and others acknowledge and worry about them. But they respond that they exist because of, or are made worse by, government policies that ignore them. Moreover, most people are still very much committed to their families and work to adjust to changing social conditions. Finally, many changes are either desirable or not as negative as Popenoe and others claim, and most of us find joy and warmth in our families.

(For "conservative, centrist, liberal, and feminist perspectives" on families, see Benokraitis, *Feuds about Families*, 2000)

POWER, FEMINISM, AND FAMILIES

Many of the conditions that the Christian Coalition and the Council on Families bemoan have been changes in women's roles and functions in and out of families: women holding jobs outside families, having children outside marriage, leaving abusive and oppressive marriages. To return to the "good old days," a call either explicit or implied by those who assert families are declining, would necessitate considerable transformation in women's lives today, back to a patriarchal society. But from the earliest days of the modern women's movement many writers and social activists have argued that the families of the 1950s and before were oppressing women; they would never wish to return to those days. They and later writers developed a feminist critique of families in the United States.

There are, however, many feminist perspectives. Here I will present four women writing on feminism and families: Letty Cottin Pogrebin (1983), Joan Walsh (1986), Judy Aulette (1994, 2002) and Judith Stacey (1990, 1996)

Letty Cottin Pogrebin

Pogrebin thinks those who argue families are in decline pose false alternatives when they say we have only two choices: either we have families where the women cook, raise children, and stay at home to do the housework, while the husbands work to provide for their families, or, we have chaos and disorder and no families. But other alternatives are possible, and indeed most people today define, accept, and live in a variety of families.

Pogrebin raises a question students of families must address: *"Is the family an inherently oppressive institution,"* especially for women? Since the late 1960s, feminists have presented much evidence that shows that women are often oppressed by other family members. Pogrebin describes a situation found in millions of homes in the 1950s and 1960s (less common today, one hopes): "For the wife and mother, [the family] is not a happy place when she feels trapped in the role of the cook, cleaning woman, and child-caregiver—and taken for granted besides. It is not a happy place if she has to ask her husband's permission to go out in the evening, to spend $10, go to a meeting, or visit her friends. (Hundreds of women at the National Women's Conference in Houston testified that this was the case in their marriages.) It is surely not a happy place if it is the place where she is assaulted or raped by a husband who views the marriage license as a license to abuse his wife in the sacrosanct privacy of his home" (Pogrebin, 1983, p. 16).

But while Pogrebin does see considerable oppression in most families, she also thinks that most women also find satisfaction and nurturance in them. Speaking personally, she says that while she learned much from critiques of families as oppressive places, "I continue to feel privately gratified by romantic love, motherhood, and family life. . . . [F]or many women the family has been 'a source of power' as often as a 'tool of oppression.' I think it insulting, not to mention irresponsible, to overlook the psychological satisfactions many women find in marriage, motherhood, homemaking . . . What's more, in many black, white ethnic and poor communities, there is a great deal of pride in families' 'adaptive resilience and strength' and there is more confidence in the reliability of the family for support, succor and sheer survival than might be the case in more affluent, educated classes where the luxury of individualism can be indulged" (1983, pp. 24–25).

Also, "It is within the family that the sex/gender system can be broken by women who resist oppression and men who relinquish male privilege. It is the place where children, reared on shared parenthood or raised by one parent who chooses to transcend sex-role behaviors, can be empowered to control their own lives, rather than become addicted to power over others" (Pogrebin, 1983, p. 35).

Joan Walsh

Reviewing the feminist movement in 1986, Walsh concluded that feminists must also talk about the nurturing and emotional sustenance that families provide for women as well as men. She thought that "the vast majority of American women . . . still find comfort in the notion of family" (p. 23). Walsh applauded the women's movement for helping women to resist violence at home, work for equality in wages and jobs, work to change their husbands so they would share housework and childcare, and so on. But she also argued that while the movement fought for safe and legal abortions, and for the equal rights amendment, the demand for quality and affordable daycare "was generally a footnote" (p. 22). Feminists must work for higher family incomes, widely available and affordable daycare, and other policies that will support all families, all women and men and children.

Judy Aulette

In chapter one and throughout her text *Changing Families* (2002), Aulette develops a detailed feminist critique of families. I present only a small part of it.

Families are places of power relationships and conflicts. Some struggles are over "who should do the dishes, who should decide how money will be spent, or which family members can use violence against others in the family" (Aulette, 1994, p. 10). Families often "restrict women's opportunities" and may be a happy place for some family members but not for others" (pp. 18, 19). Aulette thinks that feminists have sought to understand if and how families function to oppress women, to benefit men more than women, to limit women's lives more than they do men's.

A principle of feminist research is "to replace the 'view from above' with the 'view from below.'. . . This means that we examine the lives of people who have often been invisible, such as working-class people, racial ethnic people, children, and women" (Aulette, 1994, p. 22).

Feminists have also engaged in long struggles to help women escape oppression. For example, it was women from the feminist movement who understood the need for shelters where women could escape from violent partners, and they worked to set them up. Later, other groups also founded shelters for abused women, but the idea and the first shelters were created by feminists (Schechter, 1982).

Judith Stacey

A long-time feminist and activist, Stacey warns against a limited view of the family. Violence, oppression, and incest are not all that characterize families. "Certainly, protecting women's rights to resist and exit unequal, hostile, dangerous marriages remains a crucial project, but one we cannot advance by denying that many women, many of them feminists, sustain desires for successful and legally protected relationships with men and children." (1996, p. 76) Later, she notes that in the 1970s and 1980s sociologists, women and men, feminists and others, wishing not to seem anti-women and anti-feminist, may have downplayed some of the negative aspects of divorce (especially for children), daycare, single parenthood, and so forth (pp. 90–92).

Stacey thinks we should seek to understand the obstacles, conflicts, and struggles women and men face in families; explore the social and economic conditions and changes families confront; and show in rich detail how women and men create and find meaning in their relationships and families. *Brave New Families* (1990) (the stories of Pam and Dotty from this study were summarized earlier in this chapter) is a fine example of this principle.

Summary

In short, feminists have insisted that we pay attention to the daily realities of families and their members, and that we focus on such seemingly mundane subjects as housework, which are arenas of power, conflict, and oppression. Early feminists had to overcome a long history of neglect of the limits, control, and violence women experienced in families. In their insistence that we pay attention to those conditions they may have ignored the love, nurturance, and support families also provide. All of us need to examine carefully, openly, and in detail all of the experiences and realities families provide for women, men, and children. (For a text of feminist perspectives, see Andersen, 2000; for a review of feminist research in the 1990s, see Fox and Murry, 2000.)

SOCIOLOGY, HISTORY, AND FAMILIES

Our family lives are intensely personal, individual, and private experiences. It is specific relatives who love us, who provide for us, and we provide for them, those who agree or disagree with us, those who hit us or we hit them. Because they are so private and so important, it may be difficult to see how our family lives are influenced by social, economic, and political conditions.

How we relate to our parents or children, our spouses, and other relatives seem to be decisions we can control. It is our own specific father and mother, our own brother or sister, that we are spending much or little or no time with, praising or punishing us, and so on. How can economic, social, and political events outside our family play any role? In my many years of teaching, I have found that most students do indeed focus on their own individual world of friends and relatives, on what sociologists call the *micro*-world.

As sociologists use it, *micro* (from the Greek for small or little) refers to our personal and immediate lives and experiences, to the private and individual world which we share directly with family and friends. They use *macro* (from the Greek for large or long) to refer to the social world around us, to economic, social, and political institutions and conditions in which we and our families and friends live.

Here is an example. Men and women hold jobs to earn money to support their families (micro). The office or store or factory in which we work is part of the economy (macro). But the money we earn there, and our experiences while we work, affect us and our families very directly (micro). A good or bad day at work shapes our mood and thus may affect how we relate to our spouse or children; an adequate or low pay we receive directly influences what we can or cannot buy for our family. And the loss of our job affects us and our family in material and social ways: we may be less patient with the children, we have less money to cover the expenses, and we may in time move to find another job, thus endangering ties with relatives, friends, and community.

But the macro world does not totally shape and dominate the micro-world. Rather, they interact in many ways, each influencing the other. A loving and supportive family enables people to do their work well, or gives them courage to struggle to improve working conditions by joining their co-workers to seek changes, or encourages them to get together with neighbors to remove polluting factories from their neighborhood. The examples could be many, but the principle is simple: we must avoid both a total focus on the micro-world of our private family lives, *and* also avoid the common sociological sin of saying or implying that the macro-world largely controls our lives. The micro and the macro constantly interact and influence each other. (For a good discussion and good examples of the relationship between the micro- and macro-worlds, see Coontz, 1997, chapter 1, and Rubin, 1976 and 1994.)

DIFFICULTIES IN THE STUDY OF FAMILIES

Each of us comes to the study of families with our own experiences, stories and images of families, and hopes and dreams. These pre-existing conditions surely influence how we think of and how we understand families in general. We need to examine our assumptions and perspectives carefully so that they will not cloud and prejudice our study of families.

"The Good Old Days"

Chapter 2 showed that we need a clear understanding of the history of families. But our tendency to romanticize the past, both the past in general and our own in particular, makes such an understanding profoundly difficult. We long for an easier and simpler world, and we tend to transform this longing into a belief that such a world did exist—whether in the 1950s, or in 1900, or in 1800, or even earlier.

Farrell provides a neat summary of the nostalgia for the past: In "the traditional American family children had a more protected life, adolescents were under stricter parental control, married adults made life-long commitments to each other and to their families, and older people were well integrated into family life and consequently less lonely and isolated" (1999, p. 13).

But historical periods we may now consider the good old days were often experienced and interpreted as difficult by many people who lived through them. We may idealize the 1950s now, but parents then worried that the new music of rock 'n' roll was ruining the morals of their children, and magazines like *Time* ran stories about rampant delinquents in the streets. It was so also in the 1920s, when the automobile and the movies were seen as the destroyers of morality and families. Our ancestors have always worried about family decline. If we appreciate that we are not the first generation to fear that families are disintegrating, we may lose some of our anxiety. As families survived the concerns of our ancestors, families today should survive the dire predictions of the Council on Families and others (Bernard, 1992).

In later chapters we shall explore in detail family living in the past and today. For example, we shall see that divorce has existed throughout American history, that many couples in the past were separated without a legal divorce, that there have always been tensions between parents and children.

Caryl Rivers, journalist and feminist, has long protested against romantic versions of the past and the longing for a simpler life that never existed.

> Well, I was there in the good old days. . . . Try telling some of my acquaintances how good they used to have it. For example:
>
> My friend whose father regularly beat her mother; the woman just put on more makeup and kept quiet.
>
> My friend with the alcoholic husband and four kids who found herself one day driving 70 miles per hour on a highway, wondering which of the telephone poles she should hit, ending her desperation. Fortunately, she chose none of the above, threw the bum out, went back to school, and got a good job—with the support of the women's movement.
>
> My friend whose workaholic father was a total stranger to his children. (Rivers, 1999)

In his seventies in 1992, Donald Murray wrote about "the good ol' days that never were." He begins with the myths about the old days before he presents the realities of those days:

> When I was a boy, father worked. Six days a week. He was grateful he could go to work early and stay late. On Sunday he went to church. Twice. . . .
>
> Mother happily scrubbed—remember the scrub board? remember the long waxtaper that lit the gas water heater?—and cleaned and cooked. She was grateful she could care for her invalid mother and was content to stay home and serve her menfolks. . . .
>
> There were no lesbians, no gays, no premarital sex, no AIDS [just good old-fashioned heterosexual syphilis], no rape, no funny positions in bed, no nudity. . . .
>
> There were no abortions, no illegitimate children, no unhappy homes, no divorce, no liberated wives, no insolent kids, no untrimmed lawns. . . .
>
> I am over 60. I, too, find myself nostalgic for a life I never had.
>
> My family history—and yours—was not as I described it. Not even close. . . .
>
> My father-in-law had a third grade education. He ran away from home in Kentucky as a child to escape the beatings of his father. . . .
>
> Bigotry controlled where you lived and worked: I can remember when "No Irish Need Apply" was a policy and my Scottish family thought that was just right. African Americans were not dark skinned. They were invisible. Things aren't good today, but we are trying.
>
> We spoke in whispers of battered wives, aunts locked away in attics, incest, marital rape, drunkenness, but there was no divorce in the good old days.

Selective memory may be necessary for the individual, but it is dangerous for a nation when political leaders announce a march backward to the days that never were. We face enormous social, medical, educational, economic problems, and we will not solve them by a return to the past. (Murray, 1992; used with permission of the author)

As we look at families in the past and today, we must try to separate wishes and misperceptions from facts. This is an almost impossible undertaking, but a necessary one.

Let me end on a personal note. At 62 I have my own memories, some sad and some nostalgic. I recall fondly a childhood free of cars on streets and free of the stress I see in many families today. I remember my own unhurried times with my daughters when they were young, and I worry about children today (as you will see in chapter 5). I say to myself that whereas there were many serious problems in families in the past, as I just noted, there were also some good things about those days. Thus, I think we should assume neither that all was good, nor that all was bad in the past. When people recall a golden past, we need to study each statement carefully before we accept, reject, or modify it. Some aspects of family life may have been better in the past, others may be better today.

The Nuclear Family as "Normal" and Universal

We know from history and from the study of other societies that there have been many types of families. But people often assume that the nuclear family, as shown in 1950s TV shows, is the best and ideal family for parents and children. Such an assumption prevents us from appreciating the diversity of families in human history, and it frightens us when families begin to change. People predict that families will cease to exist when they encounter Pamela in *Brave New Families,* instead of realizing that the Pamelas of our time value families deeply but are trying to create new families to survive in the social conditions of our times.

And the assumption that the nuclear family is the best one for all times and places prevents us from understanding other societies. Places where parents choose their children's spouses, where married children live with their parents, and where children are raised by many relatives, not just their parents, will seem strange. But these family practices are merely different from ours, neither right nor wrong.

Family Secrets and Facades

If families are where we become human, if they are our most important relationships and experiences, if life is impossible without families, then we are deeply invested in them. If our families do not function well, our very existence may be threatened. Failure and problems should not exist in our families, and thus we often decide that they do not.

Thus it is that most of the sixty-one divorced fathers I interviewed in 1992 told me that it was painful for them to admit to themselves that they had failed in their marriages. Many said, "I felt like a failure." And thus it is that many women whose husbands beat them cover the marks with make-up and tell no one; and many relatives are surprised when a couple reveals their divorce—they had no idea; and incest is hidden; and couples don't discuss sex and other problems they have. Problems and failures are very painful to expose when they happen at the very core of our lives, our families.

But in recent years there has been less secrecy about family experiences. We might even say that there is too much telling of our private lives on TV and in books. No doubt, compared to the 1950s and 1960s, the awful realities of incest, marital violence, child abuse, and much else have finally been exposed. Indeed, some people protest that they have been exaggerated.

I believe, however, that even today there is much about family life that is still hidden and untold. We want our families to love and protect us, to nurture and support us, and it is never easy to acknowledge problems and conflicts. We can never know the full truth of people's family lives. People cannot admit all that exists, and even more likely, they do not see and know the full reality of their families.

CONCLUSION: BEYOND POWER STRUGGLES AND CONFLICTS

Feminists taught us to look at families carefully and critically, to ask difficult questions, to pay attention to inequalities, conflicts, and oppression within them. Even more, they organized and provided avenues of escape from oppressive families. They have helped us to see families as they really are, in all their complexity and contradictions.

But Stacey, Walsh, and Pogrebin, among others, also taught us that part of the complexity is that families also love, protect, support, and nurture us. There are joys, there is goodness, in them. In this book, I hope to pay attention to both oppression and liberation, to joys and sadness, to the tenderness and violence we find in our relationships with our parents, children, grandparents, and other relatives.

Finally, there was no golden past, nor are families falling apart. Families are changing, struggling, adapting, as they always have.

4

Marriage, Cohabitation, and Same-Sex Marriage

MARRIAGES

Why Marry?

It may be that in many societies today marriage is an option. Although most people still marry, they may do so after considerable debate about whether they should. Also, the pity and stigma that often were visited on single people have diminished. For example, whereas a 1957 survey showed that 80 percent of the people thought that those who chose to stay single were "sick," "neurotic," and "immoral," by 1977 only 25 percent agreed with that judgment (Coontz, 1992, p. 186).

But in the past, marriage was a universal expectation. People could become full social adults only through marriage. It has been incomprehensible that anyone would choose to stay single. The only exceptions were people who could not marry because of physical or emotional problems, and they were pitied. Single anthropologists have baffled the people they went to study. Colin Turnbull, a single 6'2" Scotsman who lived with the Mbuti who averaged only 4'6", came to his hut one evening to find a tall woman from a neighboring non-Mbuti tribe waiting for him. Concerned for his well-being, his Mbuti friends sought to find him a wife. Turnbull tactfully vetoed the marriage (Turnbull, 1961).

Jules Henry, another single anthropologist, had a similar experience. "The women who did not want to interest me in themselves or in their children besought me to marry someone else—anyone. . . . 'Why? Why?' she kept repeating, 'why do you live alone thus without a wife? Get a wife.' 'Whom should I marry?' said I. 'Marry anybody. Why go around unmarried?' Even the children found it hard to understand that I was single and they used to ask me interminably: 'Have you a wife in your country?'. . . 'Do you intend to marry?'" (1941, p. 25).

Although in different forms, marriage has been the universal process that created couples within families in order to have and raise children. Couples in these families have provided the food, shelter, clothes, and other material necessities for themselves, their children, and often other family members.

Of course, many marriages have not been blissful. Within marriage, "some individuals find salvation, romance, or eternal validation; others find slavery, violence, or psychic death." It has been a blessing for some, a curse for others, and perhaps something in between for most people. In 1966, Cadwallader concluded that marriage was "a wretched institution." Is marriage an expectation and an obligation, something desirable, or a curse (Ward, 1999, p. 120; Cadwallader, 1966)?

50

This couple has just exchanged vows during their commitment ceremony in a Unitarian Universalist church. The local country club refused to rent space for the reception, because they are a same-sex couple. Since this ceremony a number of years ago, the couple has been married in Canada.

Some Statistics on Marriage

Statistics and studies show that about 90 percent of Americans want to and do marry at least once in their lives. People are more accepting of cohabitation and singlehood; their first marriages come later, at a median age of 25 for women and 27 for men (in 2000); and about half the marriages end in divorce. But marriage is still a goal and an experience for most Americans, and it will soon include same-sex couples (Thornton and Young-DeMarco, 2001; Armas, 2002; Dedman, 2002, Stacey, 2003).

Table 4.1 shows the percentages of people in the United States who have never married, classified by sex and age, in 1960 and 2000. These statistics show both that marriages are later and the fact that the vast majority of Americans try marriage at least once.

Remember, again, that a large number of those never married are or have been in long-lasting gay or lesbian relationships, and many heterosexuals are living or have lived as cohab-

Table 4.1 Percentages of Never Married U.S. Citizens

		Ages 20–24	Ages 45–54
Women			
	1960	28.4 percent	7.0 percent
	2000	72.8 percent	8.6 percent
Men			
	1960	53.1 percent	7.4 percent
	2000	83.7 percent	9.5 percent

Source: Statistical Abstract, 1977, p. 40; 2002, p. 48

iting couples. Marriage and coupling, at least for some years of our lives, seem to be still almost universal.

But economic and political changes do shape when and if people marry. Finding a well-paying job now requires more years of education than ever; thus most people postpone marriage until they finish school. Increased cohabitation and women working for their own financial independence have also raised the marriage age.

Marriages in U.S. History

Traditional tales of marriage in Europe and the United States, according to Ucko, echo the somber view of many anthropologists. These stories show that "for centuries incompatible expectations, psychological tensions, and troubled marriage relationships have been the norm. Marital difficulties have endangered positive emotional ties and enjoyable shared experiences over the centuries, and have left a heritage of unsatisfactory marriage models" (1995, p. 5).

Whatever the quality of most marriages, during Colonial days there were three general expectations of married couples (Demos, 1970). First, they were expected to live together. "No married person was permitted to live apart from his spouse except in very unusual and temporary circumstances (as when a sailor goes to sea)." When necessary, courts would force couples to live together. Indeed, desertion was grounds for divorce (very few divorces were sought or granted). A second expectation was that a couple's "relationship must be relatively peaceful and harmonious." Husbands and wives were admonished by the courts for abusing the other, for example. And a third expectation was "a moral and exclusive sexual union." Impotence by the man and adultery by the woman (but not the man) were other grounds for divorce. Demos concludes that most couples never experienced court interference in their relationships; they met the expectations of the community and of each other (Demos, 1970, pp. 92, 95, 98).

In the 1800s, marriages gradually became more companionate, according to historians. Love, intimacy, friendship, and sexuality were increasingly seen as the goals couples should achieve with each other.

By the early 1900s, companionship in marriage was even more stressed. To the duties spouses traditionally had in marriage were added the goals of personal happiness, fun, and excitement. "Matrimony was intended to promote the happiness of the spouses. . . . Women wanted their mates to be good providers as well as fun-loving pals; men desired wives who were exciting as well as virtuous." Because of these higher expectations of marriage, divorce was increasing, but it did not reflect a rejection of marriage, but rather the rising expectations of it. "The desperation of [the women seeking divorce] reflects the high stakes placed on marriage" (May, 1980, pp. 67, 90, 161).

Also, a mutually satisfying sex life became a requisite of all good marriages. "The 'glorification of sex' was an aspect of the 'sexualization of marriage.'. . . [T]he sexual side of marriage [became part] of a more intimate personal relationship between husband and wife" (Skolnick, 1991, p. 46).

At least one contemporary study of the 1920s concluded that for most couples these new expectations were largely unmet ideals. There was little communication, sharing, or intimacy in the large majority of marriages in Muncie, Indiana. They were dreary and disappointing; men and women lived in almost separate social worlds. Lack of birth control, fear of more pregnancies, and physical exhaustion from work made for troubled sexual relations. Affection "between the two is regarded as the basis of marriage, but sometimes in the day-after-day struggle this seems to be a memory rather than a present help. Not one of the sixty-eight working class wives mentioned her husband in answering the question as to the things that give her 'courage to go on when thoroughly discouraged.'. . . To many husbands their wives have become associated with weariness, too many children, and other people's washings"

(Lynd and Lynd, 1929, p. 129). (See also Caplow and others, 1982, pp. 116–119 for a summary of Lynd and Lynd.)

What are we to believe? Was companionate marriage mostly an ideal that approached reality for only a few couples? Did the Lynds focus so much on problems couples faced and thus they missed moments of sharing and love? Or have writers of the 1920s and future historians and sociologists written about what couples hoped to achieve in their youth but rarely achieved when faced with making a living, running a home, and raising children?

Whatever the explanation for unhappy and dreary marriages in Muncie in the 1920s, the sociologists who studied Muncie again in the 1970s came to very different conclusions than the Lynds did. They stated unequivocally that most married couples were happy and communicated well with each other. (Given that in 1975 there were 1,300 marriages and 661 divorces in Muncie's county, one may disagree with their conclusion; Caplow and others, 1982, p. 348.) (For more on Muncie, see debates on marriage later in this chapter.)

Where is marriage as we enter the 21st century? Despite all the changes and concerns that marriage is withering away (from many social, religious, and political perspectives), as many people as ever enter it (perhaps foolishly). People marry later; there is a high divorce rate; more women are having children outside marriage; there are gay, lesbian, and heterosexual cohabiting couples; same-sex marriage is becoming a reality; and people no longer need marriage for material survival. Yet the vast majority of us are, have been, or hope to be in an intimate, loving, and sexual relationship.

Given so many obstacles, you may wonder why people still marry. Men do not need women to cook and clean for them, they can do their own cooking and cleaning or buy these and other services. And more and more women can support themselves, at least at a minimal level. But marriage and intimate relationships may be absolutely vital, indispensable, and desirable for social and emotional health and survival. Skolnick summarizes what many people think: "[M]odern society generates intense needs for psychological support. The more complex, impersonal, and large-scale the public world, the more intense the need for a small-scale, intimate, private world rich in the very qualities lacking in the world at large—love, concern, tenderness, nurturance" (1991, pp. 195–196).

Marriage may now be an option. We can postpone it, or assume it for a while, but leave it if we find it unsatisfactory or oppressive. Or we can avoid it entirely. Certainly, the stable and lifelong marriage to one partner some people long for existed and was possible in a world they might not wish for. In that world, there was a sexual double standard; restricted birth control; job discrimination against women, African Americans, and others; forcing of single pregnant women to have the baby and give it up for adoption; and much more. Lifelong marriage did not exist in a social vacuum. As much as we may long for it, it cannot happen under our social and economic conditions, under the values we espouse (Coontz, 1997, p. 95).

And yet, we still marry, we still hope to marry, we still want and need love, intimacy, nurturance, and companionship. And to some degree, many people, perhaps most, do find them.

GOOD MARRIAGES AND THE BENEFITS OF MARRIAGE

All of us reflect at least occasionally on the nature and meaning of marriage. Novelists, philosophers, sociologists, playwrights, and many others have written extensively on marriage, and today much research focuses on it.

Research on Marriage

Let me begin with a warning that research on marriages may not report what actually happens in them; indeed, it may mislead us. It "has been based largely on self-reports, interviews, therapy sessions, surveys, responses to vignettes, and other similar methods. These sources tell us what people say or what they want us to think, but not necessarily what they do. How many men will say, 'I frequently punch my wife to get my own way'? Yet we know how prevalent wife abuse is. How many wives will say, 'I nag and nag and nag till I get what I want'? Yet men will tell you how often they see and how much they dislike this behavior" (Ucko, 1995, p. 3).

Given the serious possibility that social science research on marriage may not accurately report what really happens in marriages, what has it told us? After years of reading studies on the topic and marriage chapters in family texts, I agree with Pogrebin that they report few happy marriages. Many feminists joined in this negative assessment, seeing love and marriage as an oppressive illusion (Pogrebin, 1983, pp. 217–219).

Recently, as wives began to work outside the home, new possibilities for and new tensions in marriages have arisen. On the other hand, the extra income women earn provides more for the family, making for a happier life and improving marriages. Also, working wives and mothers tend to feel better about themselves (Barnett and Rivers, 1996).

At the same time, however, the rise of two-job marriages has created new conflicts and disagreements about the sharing of housework and childrearing, as Hochschild has shown in *The Second Shift* (1989) and *The Time Bind* (1997, 2000). Since most husbands will not share housework equally, women are often burdened with a second shift. Starving for time and energy, women cut back on "'what needs to be done' for the welfare of the house, the child, the marriage, or oneself." Men's resistance to sharing becomes a source of tension in marriages. Women who do most of the housework often feel angry at their husbands and "cannot afford the luxury of unambivalent love" for them. Tension and resentment abound. But marriages where husbands do share housework and child care are happier than those where husbands resist sharing. "Sharing the second shift improved a marriage *regardless* of what ideas either had about men's and women's roles" (1989, pp. 196, 260, 211).

When couples are in conflict over the second shift, divorce is a frequent result. The rise of divorce has created new tensions, conflicts, and possibilities in marriages. Most of my students think that these days it is impossible to plan for and enter marriage without the reality of divorce somehow entering their consciousness.

In "Wives' Marital Work in a Culture of Divorce," Hackstaff shows how the existence of divorce outside the marriage affects the relationships between husbands and wives. The divorce culture of our age includes three premises: "Marrying is an option, marriage is contingent, and divorce is a gateway." Marital work is essential to avoid divorce and create a satisfying marriage. With divorce as a real option, husband and wife need to talk with each other, to be aware of the other's needs, to take care of the marriage. But it's women who are "more likely to initiate the work," who insist that problems be addressed and conflicts resolved, and they want men to share this marital work. They threaten divorce if men don't share, and making the threat credible "requires them to have financial independence, egalitarian ideals, and accessible divorce" (1998, pp. 460, 463).

People believe that it takes work to maintain marriages. Twenty-eight of the thirty-four spouses Hackstaff interviewed talked about "the need to work on marriage" and of spouses "working harder today" to make for good marriages. They see a need for "adjusting," "communicating," and other necessary skills and activities (1998, p. 462).

Characteristics of Good Marriages

Through the years, social scientists have sought to understand and describe long-lasting and happy marriages. First we will look at two studies of good marriages.

Jeanette and Robert Lauer gave a questionnaire to 351 couples married for fifteen years or longer. It included "39 statements and questions about marriage—ranging from agreement about sex, money and goals in life to attitudes toward spouses and marriage in general. We asked couples to select from their answers the ones that best explained why their marriages had lasted." Of the 351 couples, 300 reported they were happily married, 19 unhappily, and in 32 marriages, one partner was unhappy (1985, p. 22).

Listed in order of frequency, women and men chose the following reasons why their marriage had lasted (in the same sequence):

1. My spouse is my best friend.
2. I like my spouse as a person.
3. Marriage is a long-term commitment.
4. Marriage is sacred.
5. We agree on aims and goals.
6. My spouse has grown more interesting.
7. I want the relationship to succeed. (Lauer and Lauer, 1985, p. 23)

In their discussion, Lauer and Lauer emphasize the following:

1. Liking the other person, having him or her as best friend, and confiding in them was essential and most frequently mentioned.

2. As we see in items 3, 4, and 7, the spouses made a commitment that they would do their utmost to make the marriage work. "Commitment means a willingness to be unhappy for a while," according to one man.

3. Most couples had a satisfying sex life, but they did not see it as a major contributor to their happiness. Indeed, some said they were happily married "despite a less-than-ideal sex life" (Lauer and Lauer, 1985, p. 24, 26).

Some years later, Pepper Schwartz studied couples in "peer marriages." She found couples who shared housework, childrearing, and control of the money, and who "considered themselves to have 'equal status or standing in the relationship'" (1994b, p. 57).

Echoing the historical development of companionship as a core value and condition of marriage, peer couples focused "their relationship on *intense companionship*. To be sure, they shared child raising, chores, and decision making more or less equally and almost always equitably, but for most of them, this was just part of a plan for a true companionship marriage." They wanted to avoid the pain of divorce, and they "believe that the only way to maintain a lifetime together is to create an irreplaceable, and interdependent, union of equals" (Schwartz, 1994a p. 2).

For many men, their peer marriage was a vehicle for a closer relationship with their children. "My main objective in having an equal relationship was not to be the kind of father I had. I want my kids to know me before they are adults. I want them to be able to talk to me." To do that, some men had to leave careers that required long workdays, so they could share the raising of their children (Schwartz, 1994b, p. 58).

Peer marriages require careful monitoring to avoid what happens in many marriages: one partner, usually the woman, gradually assumes most of the housework and childcare while the other partner increasingly devotes more time to his career. It often happens, for example, that the laundry, the cleaning, the cooking, and so on become the woman's responsibility. It takes conscious effort to avoid such an outcome.

According to Schwartz, peer marriages have benefits and costs. Among the benefits are the "primacy of the relationship" between the spouses, the strong, intense, and satisfying bonds which are a priority over all other relationships the two could have; "intimacy," which they develop as they spend much time sharing their lives, housework, and children; and "commitment," which is the inevitable outcome of their shared lives. Costs include "treason against tradition," people's disapproval of their non-traditional marriage; "career costs," an outcome of the commitment to their relationship and children, which often requires leaving well-paying jobs that demand too much time; and "exclusion of others," a result of the intense relationship with each other (Schwartz, 1994a, pp. 13–15). (Excellent examples of egalitarian marriages are found in Hochschild's *The Second Shift,* 1989, chapter 12, and Deutsch's *Halving It All,* 1999). (Egalitarian marriages are not a modern invention. They existed in many pre-industrial societies. See Leacock, 1981; Liazos, 1989, chapter 12; and Bacdayan, 1977.)

What can we conclude from studies of good marriages? Assuming some validity of marriage studies, and remembering Ucko's warning that such studies may not tell us what actually happens in marriages, they seem to point to the following conclusions.

1. *Fun.* A couple should have fun—with each other, with their children, with friends and relatives. They should play and laugh together and enjoy each other. Fun does not guarantee a good marriage, nor does it erase conflicts and problems, but it enables them to weather tough times and to reduce conflicts.

2. *Change.* They should learn to adjust to changes through their years together. Change is inevitable—in each of them, in their relationship with each other, in their families and friends, in their community and the world. What worked and was good when they were young newlyweds may not apply when they are in their thirties and raising children. At that time, they need to find new ways for spending time with each other, while also spending time with their children. They must create a balance between time for each of them alone, time for each other, time for their children, time for family and friends, time for their community.

3. *Friendship.* By all accounts, friendship is essential, at all stages of their lives together. Bell even insists that friendship is the foundation of love and marriage. It includes sharing emotions, thoughts, and experiences, and trusting each other to be open and honest without fear of being hurt by the other (Bell, 1999).

4. *Commitment.* Writers used different words, but all agree that commitment to the marriage and to each other is another foundation of good marriages. Of course, for most people these days there are limits to commitment, for example, if the partner is violent. But short of extreme conditions, people who have long and happy marriages have vowed to work through and weather tough times. Some people may think that the increase in divorce indicates we are less committed to our marriages. Others think that divorce means a commitment to a certain kind of marriage, but not to this marriage at any cost (May, 1980).

5. *Equality.* Equality and the sharing of housework, child care, and all major decisions are becoming increasingly necessary for many couples. We cannot say that no marriage can be good without sharing, but sharing becomes necessary as both partners work. Refusal to share has become a major strain in many marriages. (See Deutsch, *Halving It All,* 1999.)

6. *Sex.* There is some disagreement on the role of good sex in happy marriages. To Wallerstein, it is "the heart of the [marriage] contract." To others, it's not as vital; marriages can be happy with a modest sex life, and marriages with great sex can be unhappy. But clearly, when free and enjoyable, sex enhances the love, friendship, and intimacy two people share (Wallerstein, 1995).

(The previous discussion is based on Lauer and Lauer, 1985; Klagsbrun, 1985; Wallerstein, 1995; Kahn, 1995; Kantrowitz and Wingert, 1999; and Schwartz, 1994a and 1994b.)

I end with a personal reflection. Some writers, Schwartz for example, describe such an intense and total relationship between the two partners that they seem isolated from the world around them. There is such a focus on their relationship that there is no room for others. Perhaps such a private relationship can exist and can survive over time. But I wonder how a couple can live in splendid isolation. What about children, relatives, friends, and community? Are they peripheral and almost a hindrance to the couple?

I suspect that few such couples exist, if any. We need to remember that the descriptions of these couples may reflect the nature of the interviews where they are asked to focus on their relationship, and not the actual conduct of their lives. In fact, for all of us, marriage and life in general is an ongoing process to find a balance between time for our own self, time to be with our partner, and time for our children, friends, relatives, and community. Perhaps too often we lose that balance, and we may need to work to regain it. For even these days when our extended families and communities may be weaker, we cannot exist in a private social world of two people.

The Benefits of Marriage

Some writers claim that marriage is stressful, especially for women. The routines of life, the responsibility of raising children, and conflicts and disagreements cause psychic tension (Bernard, 1972). But whatever the perceived unhappiness of married people, other writers argue that generally marriage is good for people, for our physical and mental health, and for society in general.

Let us first look at physical health. Caplow says that Americans are "healthiest when married." Christensen cited a variety of studies that support Caplow's conclusion. For example, "The lung-cancer rate for divorced men is twice that for married men, while the rates for some [other] forms of cancer . . . are three to four times as high among the divorced. The pattern among divorced women, while not quite so stark, is similar. Among both men and women, the single and divorced die from hypertensive heart disease at rates between two-and-a-half and three-and-a-half times those among the married." And for these same diseases, unmarried people have longer hospital stays (Caplow and others, 1982, p. 124; Christensen, 1988, p. 60).

A 1987 survey of 47,240 households (with 96 percent response), the National Health Inventory Survey, conducted by the National Center for Health Statistics, contains similar findings. The authors concluded: "Marital status differentials persist despite changes in American marriage patterns [more divorce, older age at first marriage, more single people and cohabitation]. . . . Chronic conditions are still more prevalent among the unmarried and . . . the differences generally increase with age. . . . [U]nmarried people pay a significant monetary, psychological, and social cost for their marital status." For example, the percentages of men who said they were "limited in activity due to chronic conditions" were 15.1 percent for married people, 18.8 percent for widowed, 19.7 percent for divorced, and 20.1 percent for single. For women, they were 14.5 percent for married, 20.2 percent for single, 20.8 percent for divorced, and 27.8 percent for widowed (Schoenborn and Wilson, 1998, pp. 15–17).

What about mental health? Are married people happier? Studies of marriages over time conclude that most married people are dissatisfied and unhappy in various ways (see discussion that follows). Moreover, some recent studies note that marriage has more mental health benefits for men than for women. In short, there is no evidence in these studies that marriage provides emotional benefits.

Two recent studies, however, disagree and report better mental health for married people. Using data from telephone interviews conducted between 1979 and 1981 in New Jersey, Horwitz and others explored the mental health of married and single young adults. They concluded: "In general, our findings indicate that marriage still benefits mental health. . . . Married people are less depressed and have fewer alcohol problems than people who remain single" (1996, p. 904).

Stack and Eshleman studied marital happiness in seventeen countries (most in Europe, plus Australia, Canada, and Japan). During 1981–83, 18,000 people were interviewed. They conclude that married people have a "significantly higher level of happiness" than unmarried ones, even after we take into account income and other differences. The difference is "remarkably consistent across nations." "Marriage is also associated with a relatively high level of perceived health, which, in turn, elevates happiness" (1998, p. 534).

I interpret these findings with some caution. When we see actual numbers, the differences between married and unmarried people are relatively small. For example, we saw that about 14.5 percent of married people reported they were "limited in activity due to chronic conditions" compared to about 20 percent of unmarried ones. At most, these figures indicate that unmarried people were *somewhat more likely* to report chronic conditions. In fact, the vast majority of both married and unmarried people did not suffer chronically. It would be a great overstatement to say that married people are healthier than unmarried ones.

The same caution applies to the cancer rates that were given as two to three times higher for unmarried people. The vast majority of married and unmarried people do not get any of these cancers. Thus, the health benefits of marriage are real, but they are limited to a few people.

MARRIAGES OVER TIME

Many studies tell us that marriages change over time. For many writers the ability to adapt to and understand these changes is an essential quality of good marriages.

Couples often worry about whether the changes mean a decline in love and commitment. Traditional folk stories reflect these worries: "Folklore has long recognized the contradiction between romantic expectations and the harsh realities of marriage." A saying holds that "marriage is the sunset of love" (Ucko, 1995, p. 41).

Recent studies conclude that the realities of work, money, children, and routines gradually take over and couples have little time for each other and romance. Hochschild cites a 1980s survey in a large U.S. corporation that reports that 50 percent of the workers said that their marriages suffered "from the effects of time pressures" (1997, p. 154).

In the early 1990s, Rubin interviewed working-class families about their lives, work, and marriage. Alesha and Daryl Adams worked opposite shifts in order for one of them to be home with their children at all times. This financially necessary arrangement, however, took a toll on their marriage. Alesha told Rubin:

> Daryl leaves a few minutes after I get home, and the rest of the night is like a blur—Shona's homework, getting the kids fed and down for the night, cleaning up, getting everything ready for tomorrow. I don't know; there's always something I'm running around doing. . . .
>
> Then on the weekends, you sort of want to make things nice for the kids—and for us, too. It's the only time we're together, like a real family, so we always eat with the kids. . . .
>
> I don't mean to complain; we're lucky in a lot of ways. We've got two great kids, and we're a pretty good team, Daryl and me. But I worry sometimes. When you live on this kind of schedule, communication's not so good.(Rubin, 1994, pp. 95–96)

These realities of life vary from time to time and from place to place, but it seems that they are ever-present in some form. Sociological studies over the last few decades differ in their assessment of how the passage of time shapes marriages. Some see decline, corrosion, and disappointment.

One often cited study is Blood and Wolfe's *Husbands and Wives*. (1960). They interviewed wives in the Detroit area in the mid-1950s. The following passage summarizes their conclusions; it has been printed in a number of texts.

> The first few years of marriage are a honeymoon period which continues the romance of courtship. With the birth of the first baby, satisfaction with the standard of living and companionship decline. In subsequent years, love and understanding lag. . . .
>
> These trends do not involve all couples, but affect a very large proportion of the total. In the first two years of marriage, 52 percent of the wives are very satisfied with their marriages, and none notably dissatisfied. Twenty years later, only 6 percent are still satisfied, while 21 percent are conspicuously dissatisfied. These figures suggest that a majority of wives become significantly less satisfied in later marriage than they were at the beginning.
>
> Some of this decline involves the calming of enthusiasm into satisfaction as a result of getting used to the partner, no matter how fine he may be. . . . However, much of this decline in satisfaction reflects observable decreases in the number of things husbands and wives do with

and for each other. Hence, corrosion is not too harsh a term for what happens to the average marriage over the course of time. (Blood and Wolfe, 1960, pp. 87–88; as cited in Skolnick, 1996, pp. 194–195)

I first read this passage in 1980, and *corrosion* has stayed with me. It's a harsh and critical word, and it may reflect the writers' values about what a marriage should be as much as it says about the marriages of the women they interviewed (Melville, 1980, p. 307).

Other studies of marriage find a more cyclical development. The arrival of children and the demands of work do mean dissatisfaction and diminished time for the couple. But as the children grow older and leave, and as financial pressures ease, wives and husbands have more time with each other. They may travel more, be together more, and they often rekindle the romance of their youth. For many other couples, however, the distance that grew between them becomes permanent. Some adjust to the distance by leading semi-independent lives from each other; others divorce (Skolnick, 1996, pp. 294–298; Bird and Melville, 1994, pp. 192–193).

Still other studies have concluded that marital satisfaction "drops markedly over the first ten years of marriage on average and then drops more gradually in the ensuing decades" (Bradbury, Fincham, and Beach, 2000, p. 965; for other studies on the decline of marital satisfaction over time, see Cowan and Cowan, 2003).

Even with the rising divorce rate since the 1960s, millions of couples have long marriages. A few may stubbornly stay together in very unhappy, even violent, marriages. Many more, however, have long marriages that may no longer exhibit the spark, excitement, and romance of their youth, but, despite Cuber and Harroff (1965), are not "devitalized." There is contentment, trust, caring, comfort, and love. Barrow refers to "recent studies [which] find . . . an increasing enchantment with each other in the later years" (Barrow notes that in some cases, health and other problems do cause stress and unhappiness in the marriage). Married elders are happier than widowed, divorced, and single ones. They are a "source of great comfort and support to one another" (1996, pp. 98, 96).

In October 1999, the city of Boston gave a party for 60 couples married for fifty or more years. They told Negri why they had such long and happy marriages.

All of the couples interviewed said that it was love, simple love, that kept them together— that and being adept at the fine art of compromise. . . .

The answer to a successful marriage, Edith said, is in "taking care of each other." Joe said the secret was to "agree on everything" and agreed with Edith, adding, "especially on finances." . . .

"You've got to respect each other's point of view and compromise," Joe said, "'and never go to bed mad." . . .

Most said their love is stronger today than it was on the day they were wed. . . .

"You know the song, 'Sunrise, Sunset,' from *Fiddler on the Roof?*" he asked. "Well, marriage is like that. One day following another" (Negri, 1999, p. B3).

Their words remind us of the studies of good marriages I discuss above. They speak of friendship, commitment, caring, compromise, and love as the qualities that make for a long and happy marriage.

Donald Murray often writes about his long marriage to his second wife. In his 70s, he writes a weekly essay on aging for the *Boston Globe*. In "Comfortable silence gilds their golden years," he shows a couple who have grown closer with time, who now feel comfortable in silence together. It's not the intense romance of youth (most people think it cannot exist in old age); it is commitment, trust, respect, memories, and comfort.

I find myself comfortable with silence. Not as comfortable as Minnie Mae, but at ease. We are the old couple who sit in the restaurant and do not speak. Our evenings are often filled with silence. . . .

I relish the privacy of our marriage. Minnie Mae's silence gives me room for fantasy, for remembering, for wondering, for becoming lost in a book, for doing the most important writing, that writing that is done in the daydreaming state away from the writing desk. . . .

Perhaps the good marriage can be defined by the distances we allow each other. . . .

I have discovered how important it is that we live alone while we live together, how good an evening can be when we have sat within touching distance, not spoken for hours, and been 'comfortably off' in our shared silence. (Murray, 1999, p. C3)

DEBATES ON THE STATE OF MARRIAGE

Debates on the condition of marriage have been going on for a long time. What goes on in marriages; how happy or unhappy those within them are; whether marriage oppresses women; the effects of the "declining" commitment to marriage in the society in general—on these and related issues there is intense debate. Recently in the United States, the social and political changes that began in the 1960s have rekindled the discussion, which included a major critique of marriage by the feminist movement.

Feminist Critiques

Traditionally, social scientists studied families and marriages as units, as one experience. They wanted to understand how they worked in order to help societies run smoothly. Feminists forced us to see that men and women in marriages had different experiences. Bernard (1972) wrote of his and her marriage. Other writers went further and focused on *power inequalities,* which exist in most marriages. Jobs, money, positions of authority, laws, and traditions have allowed men to control their wives. Violence has been another means of control some men have used. (Aulette, 1994, pp. 258–262; Thorne and Yalom, 1982).

It became common to criticize marriage as oppressive for women. Many argued that "the legal, economic, and psychological costs of marriage often exceed the benefits" for women (Skolnick, 1996, p. 259). Some compared it to slavery; "[T]he institution of marriage 'protects' women in the same way that the institution of slavery was said to 'protect' blacks—that is, the word 'protection' in this case is simply a euphemism for oppression. . . . [T]he marriage relationship is so physically and emotionally draining for women that we must extricate ourselves if for no other reason than to have the time and energy to devote ourselves to building a feminist revolution" (Cronan, 1971, p. 329; in Aulette, 1994, p. 27).

The women's movement also demanded that we pay attention to violence in families: incest, child abuse, and violence against women. Marital rape is one form of violence. Some studies have argued that about 10 percent of married women have been raped by their husbands (Aulette, 1994, p. 318).

Various writers, including some feminists, have argued that early feminist critiques of marriage were overly negative and ignored the benefits to women (as well as men), and created the myth of the "sad, mad, and miserable wife" (Skolnick, 1996, p. 273).No doubt we must pay attention to the benefits of marriages and families, but we cannot forget that before the women's movement there was silence and ignorance of the quiet desperation many wives (and many husbands) lived daily. As a college student in the 1960s, I remember not one reference in my courses to child abuse, incest, or violence against women. Their existence was hidden in total denial and pretense. We owe a great debt to those early feminist critics of marriage; perhaps in their desire to describe the actual realities of marriage for women, they may have overlooked all that is good in it. We can now balance the portrait of married life.

Marriages in Muncie, Indiana, in the 1970s

Just as feminists were beginning their critique of marriage, Caplow and others wrote *Middletown Families,* where they came to a very different conclusion about marriage in Muncie, Indiana. "The claims in the mass media that modern marriage is an oppressive yoke borne by many . . .

appear absurd in [Muncie], where a happy marriage is the common experience." Communication between most spouses had improved compared to the 1920s and made for satisfying marriages. In one survey, 57 percent of the people said they were "very satisfied" with their marriages, 38 percent were "satisfied," and 5 percent were neutral or dissatisfied (1982, pp. 127, 126). (I do wonder how they would explain an estimated 50 percent divorce rate in a community where 95 percent of the couples are satisfied or very satisfied with their marriages.)

The Decline of Marriage?

Since the late 1970s, some religious-political organizations have warned that families, marriages, and commitment to marriages are in decline. They were joined in the 1980s and 1990s by some social scientists, notably the Council on Families (Blankenhorn, 1995; Popenoe, 1996; Whitehead, 1997; Waite and Gallagher, 2000; Whyte, 2000; Whitehead and Popenoe, 2002).

Let us look at two documents produced by the Council. *Marriage in America: A Report to the Nation* asserts unequivocally that Americans no longer value marriage, that their commitment to the search for individual happiness overshadows their commitment to marriage. We value "individualism, choice, and unrestricted personal liberty" (1996, p. 300). To support their claim of marriage decline, they cite statistics of shorter marriages, more divorces, millions of children born outside of marriages, and so on (1996, p. 300).

Indifference, hostility, and disrepute are the messages on marriage propagated by our culture. Fewer people marry each year. Thus, in the 1970s, 72 percent of adults were married, but only 62 percent were in 1990. In 1960, 5.3 percent of children were born to unmarried women, whereas 30 percent were in the early 1990s. And whereas in a 1960 survey 50 percent of respondents said they would stay in an unhappy marriage for the sake of the children, only 18 percent said so in 1985. All of these statistics, and many more, are offered to support the contention that there has been a decline and devaluing of marriage (Council on Families, 1996, p. 299).

The Council on Families also sponsored and published a scathing review of family textbooks: *Closed Hearts, Closed Minds: The Textbook Story of Marriage*. Glenn reviewed twenty books published in 1994 and later. He concluded that individually and as a group they portray marriage as a dismal and oppressive institution. In all of them, there is the assumption that it is bad for women. He observes that if marriages are as presented in these books, no one should want to marry. Glenn often presents statistics on the positive aspects of marriage, which he says are entirely missing from the texts. He concludes that the three chapters in Aulette (1994) that discuss marriage do not have "a single mention of any beneficial consequences of marriage to individuals and society" (Glenn, 1997, p. 6; Aulette, 1994).

Here are some of his other comments and criticisms. The texts present marriage in America as "just one of many equally acceptable and equally productive adult relationships. These various relationships include cohabiting couples, divorced non-couples, stepfamilies, and gay and lesbian families. In fact, if anything, marriage as a lifelong child-rearing bond holds special dangers, particularly for women, who, if they don't find marriage physically threatening, will very likely find it psychologically stifling" (Glenn, 1997, p. 5).

Influenced by this perspective, various groups argue that we should create programs to "promote marriage." For example, in 2002 the Bush administration urged Congress to allocate $300 million a year toward that goal. They cited West Virginia as an example, where "married couples [on welfare] get an extra $100 in welfare benefits." In other states, the money could be used for programs to reduce divorce, such as Utah's, where "couples who apply for marriage licenses get a free video with tips for a strong relationship" (Meckler, 2002; see also Whitehead and Popenoe, 2002).

Some people do not share the government's enthusiasm to promote marriage. Polls show that 86 percent of respondents think the money should be spend to "help people get good jobs rather than programs that encourage marriage." Even more, critics think that monetary incentives might encourage people in troubled relationships to marry, and such marriages can only be troublesome for everyone, children included (Meckler, 2002; Cowan and Cowan, 2002).

In response to the Council on Families, Coontz, Stacey, Skolnick, and others note that marriages today differ from those in the 1950s and before. We cannot return to those days; we live in a very different economy and society. Would we want to live in times when women were forced to stay home, when men dominated, when family violence was hidden? The lifelong marriages that the Council longs for co-existed and were made possible by conditions we would never accept. Today, we need to create our own marriages and other couple arrangements. The women in *Brave New Families* were very committed to their children and to their families, but they would not accept domination and inferiority. Most of us today, whatever our marital or non-marital arrangement, are committed to relationships, family, and relatives (Stacey, 1990).

A personal reflection: Although I do not share the Council on Families' view that marriage is in decline, I do have my own concern that texts present few or no positive aspects of marriage. In order to honor non-marital arrangements, such as gay, lesbian, and cohabiting heterosexual couples, we need not dismiss or denigrate married heterosexuals. We should study, honor, and respect all couple relationships people create that give them joy and fulfillment.

THE RISE OF COHABITATION

When I began college in the fall of 1960, my sociology teacher often spoke of people "shacking up." That old expression, referring to poor people who lived together unmarried in rundown housing, is used no longer. We now speak of "living together" and of "cohabitation" if we're sociologists. But "shacking up" reminds us that long before unmarried living together became common among college students and middle-class people, it was a prevalent arrangement among the poor who could not afford to marry legally. It remains more common among lower-income people (Seltzer, 2000, p. 1250).

What Is Cohabitation?

Most of us understand it as two unrelated people in a sexually intimate relationship, living together in one household for an indefinite period. They can be a man and a woman, or two women, or two men.

There are four general types: for convenience, as a trial marriage, as the first household of a couple engaged to marry, and instead of marriage.

1. Many people who date spend much time together. They gradually have more overnight stays in each other's apartment and at some point decide it would be less expensive and more convenient to live together in one apartment.

2. Many couples who are in a relationship think that living together for a while will allow them to see if they are compatible with each other. They hope that as they share space and more time together they will learn more about the other's personality and about their ability to live with the other. If they find they are suitable partners, they will marry; otherwise, they will go their separate ways and avoid a bad marriage. Some surveys have shown that about 60 percent of cohabiting couples go on to marry. Another survey showed that 50 percent of cohabiting relationships end within a year, when the couple either marry or end the relationship (Benokraitis, 2002, p. 205; Seltzer, 2000, p. 1252).

3. I know many people who first decide they will marry each other, many actually becoming engaged, and then live together before the actual wedding. They differ from couples in (2) because they are not testing their relationship. Living together seems practical and logical.

4. Some couples who are committed to each other choose not to marry. I asked friends who have been together 24 years and have two daughters why they do not marry. "It's none of the government's business what we do in our private lives," they told me. In the early 1990s, 15 percent of cohabiting couples had children. And we read that a third of cohabiting households included children, many of the individuals having children from previous marriages or relationships (Seltzer, 2000, p. 1250; Rauch, 2002, p. 24).

But some long-time cohabitants finally decide to marry when they have, or plan to have, children. They say they do so "for the sake of the children," meaning that the children will have an easier time with friends and in school if their parents are married. Also, many retired people who cohabit do not marry because they think they might or would receive lower Social Security benefits as a married couple than they do as two single people. There are many other reasons and explanations for permanent cohabitation.

Not all cohabiting couples fit these categories. Some couples, for example, may have almost decided to marry but they are still somewhat uncertain. You may know people who live together and fit none of the four groups.

The Normalization of Cohabitation in Europe and the United States

Cohabitation has been socially disapproved of, and usually illegal, for decades and centuries. In Greece during the 1950s, it was incomprehensible and unheard of. I now know that it existed in the United States in the 1950s, but we never talked about it then. In 1987, the Massachusetts legislature finally legalized it. But in 2003, the North Dakota legislature voted 26 to 21 not to repeal its law against cohabitation, even though the law is "almost never enforced" (Arnold, 1987; Boldt, 2003).

In the United States in the early 1990s, 4 percent of people 19 and over were cohabiting, and about 25 percent had cohabited at some time. In 1995, almost 40 percent of women 19–24 had cohabited for some period of their lives. It may be safe to predict that at least 50 percent of young people today will cohabit at some point in their lives. It has become socially accepted, if not expected, especially for younger people. In 1995, I gave out a survey to 23 college-age women. Three had already cohabited and seven more said they would consider it. Only three said they knew of no close relatives or friends who had cohabited. In terms of social approval, none said they thought it was "largely disapproved of." All 23 thought approval ranged from almost half the population to a majority. I see parents my age who led a conservative and religious life now publicly accepting their children's cohabitation (perhaps grudgingly) (Seltzer, 2000; Thornton and Young-DeMarco, 2001).

Various statistics on the number of cohabiting couples show significant increases over time.

1960	425,000 couples
1970	523,000 couples
1980	1,589,000 couples
1990	2,856,000 couples
1998	4,236,000 couples
2000	5,476,000 couples (594,000 were listed as same-sex couples)

(*Statistical Abstract,* 1987, p. 42; 1999, p. 60; 2002, p. 48)

Most people who have studied cohabitation think there are many more cohabiting couples than official statistics show. Many people refuse to reveal their living arrangements to government statisticians or sociologists. A 2002 news story reported 11 million heterosexual and same-sex couples (Wen, 2002c).

Cohabitation shows similar increases and acceptance in many other countries. In Ireland, a poll showed that "a staggering 89% of those between the ages of 18 and 25 believe it is acceptable to live with a partner before marriage." In Sweden, cohabitation is almost universal, with 99 percent of the couples living together before marriage. The rate is 80 percent in Denmark, and in France it is somewhere between the U.S. and Swedish rates. And in Sweden, "about two-thirds of first children are born to cohabiting, not married, couples," and divorced people are far more likely to cohabit than to remarry (Dwyer, 1999; Cherlin, 1999; Jones, and others, 1995, p. 71).

Why Do People Cohabit?

In some places, cohabitation seems to have replaced marriage for many people. Cohabiting arrangements last longer than in the United States and many cohabiting couples never marry. In the United States, few couples live in permanent cohabitation; 60 percent eventually marry and 40 percent end it.

The types of cohabitation presented reveal the reasons couples choose to live unmarried: for a testing of their relationship, or in place of marriage, or for convenience. The Council on Families and some religious organizations worry that cohabitation signals a vast cultural shift, a devaluing and diminishing of marriage, a decline in our commitment to lifelong partnerships. It may have such a meaning in Sweden, but it certainly does not in the United States, where 80 percent of cohabiting couples plan to marry or are thinking of marrying. But clearly marriage no longer has the compelling necessity it once had. Men do not need to marry for someone to take care of their home, and women can support themselves economically. Without that necessity, women and men now have a conscious choice to make. We do, however, still need social contact, friendship, love, and companionship. So, whether we have a legal ceremony or live together without one, *we are still living together.* And at least according to one study, cohabitants who plan to marry are "involved in unions that are not significantly different from marriages" (Cherlin, 1999, p. 259; Brown and Booth, 1996, p. 677).

Cohabitation and Divorce

For some years, some people thought that if they lived together before they decided to marry, they would have better marriages and less divorce. It seemed logical that if they shared a home with their partner, they would find out if they are compatible, and if not, they would not marry each other. The result would be better marriages.

But studies since the late 1980s have not supported that logical assumption. A 1987–1988 survey found that within a decade after they married, 38 percent of couples who had cohabited first had divorced, compared to 27 percent of those who had not cohabited. Ten years later, another study concluded that couples who cohabit before marriage are 46 percent more likely to divorce than those who do not. It also says that cohabitants "are less committed to the institution of marriage and more open to the possibility of divorce" (Sege, 1989; Associated Press, 1999a; see also Seltzer, 2000).

Larry Bumpass, who has studied cohabitation for some years, doubts the claim that the increase in cohabitation has led to an increase in divorce. Cohabitation has almost tripled from 1980 to 1998, but the divorce rate has remained stable in that period. He said: "To lay everything on the doorstep of cohabitation is to fail to recognize the dramatic change that is occurring in the way marriage is viewed." The same changes in social conditions and values have led to more cohabitation, more divorce, and later marriages. "The data argue that people who are willing to cohabit are also willing to divorce." Expectations of marriage have steadily increased; we want romance, friendship, companionship, and sexual fulfillment. It may be that cohabitants who later marry held these expectations to a higher degree than other people do, and thus will not stay in unhappy or even "good enough" marriages. On the other hand, people who do not cohabit may be the same people who believe you should stay in a marriage, no matter how happy or unhappy you are (probably short of violence and abuse) (Bumpass is cited in Associated Press, 1999a; other discussions of the topic are found in Jones and others, 1995, p. 74; Seltzer, 2000; Thornton and Young-DeMarco, 2001).

Cohabitation and the Law

When cohabiting couples eventually marry, there are no legal complications. But for those who break up, and those who make cohabitation permanent, legal problems may arise. Unlike married people, cohabiting couples cannot provide health insurance and other work benefits for their partners. Only a few municipal governments, the state of Vermont, and some corporations provide such benefits to unmarried couples (gay, lesbian, and heterosexual).

If partners have no will and one dies while they're still unmarried, the other inherits nothing legally. But the most common legal issue may be the division of property when a couple ends their relationship. There are no laws yet guiding such division. For now, many couples are drafting legal documents that state financial arrangements should their relationship end. Others create "health-care proxies and power-of-attorney papers, that appoint their life partners as their stand-ins in case of sickness or incapacitation." In 2002, there was the Alternatives to Marriage Project, with 4,000 members (a third of them same-sex couples) in 50 states. It is an organization devoted to advocating and lobbying for the legal rights of unmarried couples (Wen, 2002c; Stockman, 2002a).

In time, laws may be passed by legislators and rulings made by judges which may make cohabitation the legal equivalent of marriage. Graff argues that in previous centuries long-time cohabitants were recognized and treated as married (as they still are in 13 states). It may be "back to the future" if we come to accept cohabitation as the social and legal equivalent of marriage. Cohabitation is no longer the practice of people in a few social circles. Millions practice it as a convenience, trial marriage, or marriage alternative (Graff, 1999b).

SAME-SEX COUPLES—AND MARRIAGES?

On February 14, 1991—Valentine's Day—a domestic-partner law, which had been approved by the voters, took effect in San Francisco. Under it, "any committed couple, regardless of sexual preference, could be legally recognized by the city of San Francisco. . . . [But it] held no legal weight whatsoever in terms of health insurance, child custody, inheritance, or taxes" It was primarily a symbolic and public expression of love and commitment, a social recognition of same-sex and heterosexual couples.

On that day, many such couples came to City Hall to register as domestic partners. In the crowd outside, a truckload of white men in their thirties shouted "Faggots! Dykes!" Inside, couples were announcing their love for each other.

> The couples emerged and formed a line as a string-and-keyboard ensemble began to play "The Shadow of Your Smile." Just like a real wedding, I thought, down to the bad music. As they descended the stairs, Kurt and Jean took turns announcing the couples' names. . . . Down they came, the variety of human beings unbelievable, dressed in tuxedoes, dresses, leather, ACT UP and Queer Nation outfits. . . .
>
> Two old fellows in their sixties, with rumpled baggy pants and John Deere hats, walked carefully down the stairs, their work-battered hands entwined, their eyes on their feet. They looked like they had just come off the farm. . . .
>
> "Gail Brown, Lucinda Young, and their daughter, Mara Young." Mara was a teenager. It is difficult for a teenager to be different from her peers in any way, yet she walked down the stairs with her mothers. . . .

> Most of the people who descended those steps never have done and never will go into the streets [to demonstrate for gay rights]. . . . They are our silent majority, and it was only in this way, only to express their love for each other, that they would perform such a public act.
> (Burke, 1993, pp. 104, 111–113)

Same-sex unions are also gaining recognition in the wedding announcement pages of some newspapers. Papers in small cities and towns in Maine, New Hampshire, and Massachusetts now list announcements of same-sex unions. The *New York Times* joined them in August 2002. Newspapers in other cities are selling space for ads announcing such unions. So far, few same-sex couples have taken advantage of the ads or the wedding announcements (Chinlund, 2002; Jurkowitz, 2002).

The Struggle for Same-Sex Marriages

On the other side of the United States, the citizens and courts of the state of Hawaii debated whether to legalize same-sex marriages. In 1990, three same-sex couples who were denied marriage licenses sued the state, arguing that it was unconstitutional for the state to limit marriage to heterosexual couples.

The case was in courts for some years. In 1996, Judge Chang ruled that there was no compelling social interest in prohibiting same-sex marriages; there was no evidence that such marriages would harm society. The state government appealed the case to the Hawaii Supreme Court. Before the court could rule, however, on November 4, 1998, the voters approved a referendum that prohibits same-sex marriages. That ended the hopes of some people and the fears of others that Hawaii would be the first state in the United States to legalize same-sex marriages. And on that same day, Alaska voters approved their own constitutional amendment limiting marriage to heterosexual couples only.

In April 2000, the Vermont legislature and governor did enact legislation that created "civil unions." After three same-sex couples sued the state for denying them marriage licenses, the state's Supreme Court had ruled in 1999 that the state had discriminated against gay and lesbian couples, and it ordered the legislature to write a law that would end such discrimination.

Holly Puterbaugh and Lois Farnham were one of the couples that sued the state. They said that

> [T]heir lives have been intertwined as those of any married couple.
> They share a mortgage, eat breakfast together, nurse one another through the flu. Together, they run a Christmas tree farm. They share vacations, health-care benefits, job victories, and car trouble. They finish one another's sentences.
> They are raising a daughter adopted four years ago.
> Puterbaugh and Farnnam consider themselves one another's next of kin.

But the state did not. The state argued that "Vermont has an interest in maintaining marriage as a union between the sexes. Among their arguments is that the purpose of Vermont's marriage laws is to further the link between procreation and child rearing. Therefore, marriage is limited to couples most likely to procreate—heterosexuals. . . . [Law professor] Tribe called the procreation argument 'insane.'. . . 'That means that sterile people shouldn't be able to marry, that two octogenarians should not be able to marry. It's just ridiculous" (Shea, 1998, pp. B1, B8).

The "civil unions" law passed in April 2000, grants same-sex couples many rights but falls short of full marriage rights. "The benefits will be manifold, from state tax breaks to family leave, to legal acknowledgments of partner rights in the event of sickness or death. Same-sex couples choosing to dissolve their civil unions would have to go through a 'dissolution' in family court in the same way that heterosexual divorces are handled.

"The unions will not be automatically transferable to other states, and there are no commensurate federal benefits" (MacQuarrie, 2000a, p. A18).

The debate in Vermont was intense, both before and after the law was enacted. It is too early to tell the social consequences of civil unions. Most of the couples that took advantage of the law were from outside Vermont, and they would not receive any of the legal benefits outlined above unless they lived in Vermont. But just as the couples did in San Francisco in 1991, they wanted to make a public declaration of their love and to partake in a historic event, the first state recognition of same-sex relationships. Meantime, during the fall 2000 elections the debate continued. Governor Dean, who signed the law, faced intense opposition when he ran for re-election. Most of the money for his and his opponent's campaign came from out of state, from people who believed the civil union law will have national consequences, and they wanted to support their side. Dean was re-elected, even though some polls showed 40 percent of Vermont voters opposed the law and 37 percent approved of it (MacQuarrie, 2000a, 2000b; Good, 2000).

Before Vermont, Alaska, Hawaii, and other states passed laws for or against same-sex unions or marriages, in 1996 the United States Congress passed a law, signed by President Clinton, that allows states to ignore the legalization of same-sex marriage any other state might pass. Under what is known as the Full Faith and Credit clause of the U.S. legal system, states are required to honor each other's laws because not to do so would create chaos. For example, if one state allows married couples to divorce only for adultery (as New York did for decades), while other states allow more grounds (such as abuse), couples' divorces would be legal in some states but not in others. You can imagine the complications.

Under the 1996 congressional act, states do not have to recognize Vermont's civil unions. And indeed, soon after Clinton signed the law, 29 states promptly passed laws against recognizing same-sex marriages from other states (Graff, 1999e).

In Massachusetts, in 2002 the state legislature leadership stopped a referendum against same-sex marriage from going to the voters. Had it come to the voters, it would have likely been approved. A 2003 poll of 400 Massachusetts residents showed that 50 percent thought same-sex marriage should be legalized, 44 percent thought it should not, and 6 percent were unsure. In 2000 and 2001, national polls had shown 35–40 percent support for same-sex marriage. Civil unions, similar to the Vermont one, were supported by 47 percent of those polled nationally (42 percent against) and 58 percent in the Massachusetts poll (35 percent against). In the Spring of 2003, six of the eight people running to be the presidential candidate of the Democratic party supported same-sex unions; two supported same-sex marriage. And in 2001, nationally 58 percent of college freshmen supported same-sex marriage (Phillips, 2003; Milligan, 2003; Rauch, 2002),

In the absence of same-sex marriages or unions in 49 states, and in the absence of domestic partner laws in most of the United States, many couples still wish to announce, honor, and celebrate their relationships. To that end, they hold "commitment ceremonies." Friends and relatives join the couple for a ceremony, usually written by the couple, which declares their love and commitment to each other. In a few cases, clergy people bless these unions. As of early 2001, however, only Unitarian Universalists and Reform Jews allowed their clergy to perform the ceremony. The Episcopal Church voted in February 2000 not to take an official stand for or against same-sex ceremonies, allowing individual dioceses to make their own decision (Paulson, 2000; Lieblich, 2000). (For a review of research on same-sex relationships and marriages, see Patterson, 2000.)

Same-Sex Unions in Other Countries

With or without religious or social blessing, same-sex couples have lived together in many societies. But some countries are moving toward legalizing such unions. Canada, Holland, France, the Czech Republic, Switzerland, South Africa, Brazil, Spain, and others have created or will soon create the equivalent of Vermont's civil unions. Same-sex couples will have most of the benefits and rights married people do.

Let us look at France. In 1999, it passed a law to legalize unmarried unions (same-sex and heterosexual), "via passage of legislation creating 'civil solidarity pacts.' As a result of the vote in the National Assembly, unmarried French couples, including homosexuals, will be able to register unions at courthouses for the first time next year [2000] and get most of the rights of traditional married couples. . . . Under the legislation, after three years of stated fidelity, unmarried couples may file tax forms jointly and claim rights of married couples such as simultaneous vacation time from employers and lighter inheritance taxes" (Trueheart, 1999).

Thus, as of September 2000, seven European countries legally recognized same-sex unions, granting them most of the rights of married couples, as France did. Besides France, they were: Denmark, 1989; Norway, 1993; Greenland, 1994; Sweden, 1995; Iceland, 1996; and the Netherlands, 1998. And in the United States., the state of Vermont joined these countries in 2000, as discussed previously (Deutsch, 2000).

In 2001, the Netherlands became the first country in the world to legalize same-sex marriage, with all the rights and responsibilities of heterosexual marriage. In 2003, Belgium became the second country. And in 2003, after a court decision, parts of Canada became the third one. (But the situation in Canada is fluid, with court challenges and controversies).

According to E. J. Graff, same-sex unions, like those in France and Vermont, have spread throughout the world. "In most of the developed [industrial] world, lesbian and gay couples have been getting partnership rights under some other name. More than 318 million world citizens live under national family law systems that treat lesbian and gay couples equally [to heterosexual ones], or very close to it. By the end of 2005, that roll call will include the Netherlands, Belgium, Sweden, Denmark, Finland, Iceland, Greenland, Germany, Hungary, Switzerland, France, Canada, Australia, New Zealand, Portugal, and South Africa." And in places where national governments have not moved to grant rights to same-sex couples, many local governments are doing so (private communication from E. J. Graff 2003; used with permission). (Graff writes extensively on these issues and is author of *What Is Marriage For? Our Most Intimate Institution,* published by Beacon Press, 1999c.)

Rights and Benefits

Groups seeking same-sex unions and marriages want both the social recognition such unions imply and the rights and benefits bestowed upon married people. These benefits are considerable.

According to Winfield, "there are 170–plus rights and responsibilities that go with legal marriage." Among these rights are: to collect your spouse's pension and Social Security; to swap frequent flier miles; upon death of your spouse, to automatically receive all their possessions; to be covered under your spouse's family health insurance policy. Married people can adopt children together. If married people divorce, both are entitled to their children's custody or visitation. Also, married people "are jointly responsible for their children, and each can give legal permission to schools, doctors, and the like, for trips, operations, and so forth." Finally, when married people are ill and cannot make decisions for their care, the spouse has automatic rights to make them. Unmarried couples have no such rights (Winfield, 1996; Cherlin, 1999, p. 284). (See also Stoddard, 1989; Rubenstein, 1993.).

But in Vermont and in some municipalities and corporations, same-sex and heterosexual couples are gaining some of these rights. A common benefit is health insurance that covers the worker and his or her partner. In Cambridge, Massachusetts, the city's domestic partner ordinance grants partners "bereavement leave, the right to visit partners in Cambridge jails and city-run hospitals, and access to the records of partners' children who attend Cambridge schools" (Chafetz, 1992, p. 21).

In 1998, New York City passed a similar law that applies to all city residents, not just municipal employees. "It allows bereavement leave for city employees, visitation rights in city-run facilities, tenancy succession rights, and permits partners to be buried together in a city-owned cemetery (Reuters, 1998; for a very detailed list of other benefits for same-sex couples, see Rubenstein, 1993, pp. 431–474).

In all states but Florida, same-sex couples can adopt children and can be foster parents. And in some states, Massachusetts, Vermont, and California among them, courts have ruled that lesbians can adopt the biological children of their partners. By doing so, the non-biological parent can cover the child under her health insurance, and has parental rights should the couple separate (Associated Press, 1999c). (See Burke, 1993, for the successful court case she and her partner fought for Burke to adopt her partner's son.)

Debates on Same-Sex Marriages

As societies are gradually moving toward the inevitable recognition of same-sex marriage, there is intense debate and disagreement on its desirability and consequences.

Some groups argue that social catastrophe will follow if same-sex unions and marriages are socially and legally blessed. For example, Knight states that same-sex marriages would "deny the procreative imperative that underlies society's traditional protection of marriage and family as the best environment in which to raise children; seek to legitimize same-sex activity and homosexuals' claim that they should be able to adopt children, despite the clear danger this poses for children's development of healthy sexual identities; . . . mock the idea of commitment, since most domestic partner laws allow for easy dissolution of the relationship and the registry of several partners (consecutively) a year" (1994, p. 52).

Bennett also fears for the children. He says that "it is far better for a child to be raised by a mother and a father than by, say, two male homosexuals." He adds two more objections: one, that "marriage is almost universally recognized as an act meant to unite a man and a woman." Two, he fears that if we allow same-sex marriages, we would also have to allow other types of nontraditional unions. Could we deny marriage licenses to two brothers who wish to marry each other, or "to a bisexual who wants to marry two people?" (1996).

Neither Knight nor Bennett provides any evidence or cites studies in support of their assertions and fears. In the next chapter, I will discuss studies that show children who grow up in same-sex households do as well as children raised in traditional marriages. Stacey's review of studies of children raised by same-sex couples shows no evidence of harm to these children (2003).

As we saw, the state of Vermont argued in court that marriage must be connected to procreation. But of course states give marriage licenses to people who cannot have children (such as two elderly people marrying), and they do not take them away from couples who choose not to have children. In addition, many same-sex couples do have children, either by biological birth (lesbian couples) or by adoption.

Some lesbian and gay writers have also objected to same-sex marriage. They see marriage as an oppressive institution, very much in the spirit of some early feminist critiques of marriage. They wonder why they should embrace a practice that limits personal growth and freedom. The following comments may typify those objections. "Marriage runs contrary to two of the primary goals of the lesbian and gay movement: the affirmation of gay identity and culture; and the validation of many forms of relationships. . . . Marriage, as it exists today, is antithetical to my liberation as a lesbian and as a woman because it mainstreams my life and my voice. I do not want to be known as 'Mrs. Attached-to-Somebody-Else.' Nor do I want to give the state the power to regulate my primary relationship." Also, marriage might give same-sex couples benefits such as family health coverage, but it would not help women and men whose jobs provide no health insurance (Ettelbrick, 1989, pp. 482–484; see also Stacey, 2003; Weston, 1991).

Most supporters of same-sex marriage probably do not see it as an ideal institution. They understand that in many societies and during many periods marriage has been oppressive to women, and to men to some degree. There has been a "general absence of edifying examples of modern heterosexual marriage" (Stoddard, 1989, p. 476).

But they still advocate marriage for a variety of reasons. Some are practical benefits, as we saw above. Others are political, giving social equality to gay and lesbian couples. And others are philosophical, giving people the option and the right to marry, which they may or may not exercise. Same-sex marriages would help many people, making "lesbians and gay men . . . become visible as partners, families, and kin" (Pierce, 1995, p. 50).

There is also the argument that same-sex marriages would undermine the institution of marriage. But as Winfield points out, heterosexual marriages have problems now: about half end in divorce, many are plagued by violence, and half a million children live in foster homes. All these conditions exist today, before any legalization of same-sex marriages (1996).

There are no convincing arguments against same-sex marriages. The gradual but steady social recognition of same-sex couples and marriage shows that more people are coming to that conclusion. Even the U.S. Census now officially counts same-sex cohabiting couples, reporting 594,000 of them in the 2000 census (*Statistical Abstract,* 2002, p. 48). (That number is surely a vast undercount; most same-sex couples are probably still reluctant to report their relationship to the government.)

How can we object to relationships that bring people joy, love, and fulfillment? How can we object if couples who cannot now marry, could find meaning and love for themselves and their children in same-sex unions or marriages? Or how can we object if people who are trapped in unhappy heterosexual marriages (as millions have been, trying to lead "normal" lives) could find meaning and love in a same-sex union or marriage? How can love and commitment and caring for each other be wrong? How can long-lasting loving relationships, ever be wrong? (See Rauch, 2002, for a social conservative's argument in support of same-sex marriage.)

CONCLUSION

Many writers have observed that we place heavy demands and high expectations on marriages. We want love, sexual excitement, friendship, companionship, and constant communication, in addition to childrearing and other social functions. No one institution or relationship may be able to provide all of them. And the problems families and marriages face—work and money worries, divorce, violence in and out of the home, and so many more—are very real. (All discussed in later chapters.)

Despite these complexities and problems, despite probably unrealistic expectations, most heterosexuals still marry, millions of others are living together in long-term committed relationships, and gays, lesbians, and heterosexuals are working for the legal recognition of same-sex marriage. Marriages are changing in many ways. Same-sex marriage has arrived and is spreading. Millions of people are embracing cohabitation for short or long periods. But by their actions, people in all three relationships are attesting to the importance of intimate, loving, and caring relationships. Marriage is changing and expanding, and some people are avoiding it (at least temporarily), but marriage as an institution is not about to disappear. As Farrell (1999) said, there is a "powerful pull toward" marriage.

5

Parents and Children

As we waited to start the class, Lauren Kane, one of the students, turned to a classmate and said: "Sociology is good birth control." We all laughed, but I realized she had made a wise and serious comment on the nature and consequences of sociological writing on families.

It was the spring of 1999 at Regis College, in my "Changing Families" class. The topic for the day was parents and children. Lauren Kane went on to explain, "Who would want to have children after reading about the many problems parents face in raising them?"

A few days earlier we had finished discussing Hochschild's (1997) *The Time Bind*, which documents the rushed lives of working parents, the little time they have for each other and their children. For this class, they had read two chapters of Aulette's (1994) *Changing Families*, one on parents and the other on children. In over sixty pages of text, there were only two pages on the joys of parenthood and childhood (394–396). There were also chapters from Blankenhorn's (1995) *Fatherless America* and Popenoe's (1996) *Life Without Father*, which argue that absent fathers are the major cause of juvenile delinquency, poor school performance, and other problems. There was also a chapter from Coontz's (1997) *The Way We Really Are*, a response to Blankenhorn and Popenoe, and some other writings. The clear and overwhelming message of these readings concerned the problems and conflicts of raising children. So let us open this chapter with stories about the joys parents and children share together.

THE JOYS OF CHILDHOOD AND PARENTHOOD

"Me and My Dad"

Deborah Silverstein, who grew up near Johnstown, Pennsylvania in the 1950s, remembers times with her father in the following song.

"Me and My Dad"

Day is over, supper's done,
we're doing the dishes in the kitchen
Sun is slipping behind the hills,
my eyes light up, I got a reason

Cause me and my dad,
we're gonna take our walk
We're gonna hold hands
and stroll around the block
He's gonna buy his cigar,
I'll get my ice cream cone
Just me and my dad
till we get home

We head out for the corner store,
I'm already asking my questions
Maybe I asked a million times before,
but I love to hear answers in the evening

Yea me and my dad,
we're gonna take our walk. . . .

I got to tell him what went on today,
got to hear what he's got to say
About my big ideas and my fancy plans,
I can count on him to understand

Cause me and my dad,
we're gonna take our walk. . . .

The sun has settled and evening's come,
cigar smoke drifting in the twilight,
My eyes are drooping, we're almost home,
tonight I know I'm gonna sleep tight

Cause me and my dad,
we're gonna take our walk. . . .
(Used with permission of the author)

Celebrating a Family's Good Times

In May 1990, I wrote a column for my local paper about some of the good and happy times
my daughters and I had had. I reprint some of it here.

It was May 1974; Melissa was just three weeks old, when she awoke at 4:30 one morning. As
I was rocking her back to sleep, the birds began their morning songs. Melissa immediately
became alert, stood straight in my arms, and moved her head to listen to the birds. If I close my
eyes I can still see her startled and alert and alive, and so taken by the new experience entering
her consciousness.

One evening about three and a half years later, when Ariane was 15 months old, and just
beginning to say her first words, I was lying next to her trying to help her fall asleep. She
looked at my nose, touched it with her finger, and haltingly said "no." For the next ten or so
minutes we went back and forth: she would touch my nose and say "no," I would touch hers
and say "nose," until she came close to saying "nose." The wonder of language and of discovery
made her so excited and so happy, and each time she said "no" it was fresh and wonderful.

I recall the many times I rocked them to sleep, lasting from 15 minutes to over an hour. It
was such a warm and gentle and peaceful feeling. Not only were they slowly lulled to sleep, I
too was transformed by the experience. I was as peaceful as they were, and soon felt free
enough to make up songs and sing them.

When Melissa was two and a half years old, one day, as we were having tea, we had the
following conversation. As she took a knife, I asked, "why do you want the knife?" "I want to
cut the table in half." "Why do you want to cut the table in half?" "Because I want to cut my tea
in half." "Why do you want to cut the tea in half?" "Because I like it blue." She was having a
great time playing with words, trying out meanings and sentences.

And one day, in October 1982, when Ariane had just started first grade and could only write
a few words, she wanted to write me a special message. But she could not spell most of the
words, so, as she asked me to spell each word, she wrote it, and then "surprised" me with her
note: "Dear Daddy, I love you for a thousand reasons."

By the time they were five or six, we had developed rituals and routines, and had found
favorite places to visit. At Drumlin Farm, we have watched spring lambs and piglets nursing, a

dozen at a time; watched sunsets from the top of the drumlin; walked on frozen ponds; taken sleigh and hay rides; had pancake breakfasts with fresh maple syrup immediately after we saw the making of the syrup; eaten grapes off vines as we waited on lines during fall harvests; and always enjoyed the tranquillity and gentleness of the place.

Since 1983, we have taken an annual June trip to a rocky beach in Rockport. It is our initial summer outing. We eat our lunch on top of the rocks, we walk on rocks and walls, we watch the waves as they wash ashore, and we gaze at sea gulls and lobster boats and the clouds. The sun is warm but not hot, and the relative solitude of the beach is restful. As we walk around we examine the puddles of sea water that collect on the rocks and watch all sizes of creatures swimming about. On the way back to Watertown, we usually stop at Wingaersheek Beach where we spend an hour or two watching the sunset with a few other people still lingering on the beach and with the sea gulls. It is a cool, tranquil, and unhurried time.

Every August, we camp for a week at Wellfleet, near the national seashore. We walk the endless miles of clean beach, approach and run away from the waves, collect stones, eat soft ice-cream three to four times a day, watch the millions of stars in the brilliant night sky, and take walks around the Massachusetts Audubon Society reservation. The summer of 1988 is especially memorable. Every evening around seven, when very few people were still at the beach, we would have a picnic supper there. Then we would lie down on the sand, listen to the waters washing on the shore, watch the stars, and listen to the Red Sox baseball game on the radio.

In 1989 we went to Longo, Albania, where I was born, to visit the rest of my family. My brother from Worcester (Massachusetts) and his two sons also came, and, for the first time ever, all of us were together [it turned out to be the first and only time]. We will talk about those ten days for many years.

The sweetest moments were the times Melissa and Ariane and all their cousins played and talked (limited by the fact that they talked only a few words of each other's language, so my brother and I did much translating). They played cards and other games, climbed mountains, listened to local and "American" music, and watched American soap operas from the Greek television station. For the last five evenings of our stay, in the early evening they would dance in our yard.

My older nieces taught Melissa and Ariane traditional Greek dances, and Melissa and Ariane taught them "rock" dancing. One evening, the two of them put on traditional wedding dresses from the region (very bright, cherry red) and did the slow circle dance. As I watched them, and as I listen to that music now, I feel the special flavor of tradition, of family reunion, of cousins finally meeting, of fun and play. (*Watertown Sun,* May 30, 1990, used with permission)

Barely a month after I wrote the above column, came another experience with my daughters. In late June we were camping under the trees on Cape Cod in Massachusetts. About ten o'clock on a Sunday evening we went for a walk through a grassy field. We noticed fireflies near a clearing and we stopped to watch them. Soon there were hundreds of them, lighting up the darkness (there was no moon that night). As we watched the fireflies in silence occasionally we looked up at the clear sky and saw countless stars. From a pond nearby came the sounds of bullfrogs, loud yet gentle. For an hour we were surrounded by fireflies, stars, and bullfrogs singing.

I cite my family's good times only as examples of what most families also experience.

Why Have Children?

There are three decisions married couples (and others) face in relation to children: whether and when to have them, and how many to have.

Ask some people who have children why they had them. Think why you may want them. In surveys I have taken through the years in my classes at Regis College (a women's college in Massachusetts), each time over 90 percent said they planned to have children—and each time, one or two said they intended to have none. Surveys taken in the 1980s and 1990s

Author Alex Liazos with his young daughters, Melissa (left) and Ariane (right) on an outing to Walden Pond in Massachusetts in 1983. *(Photo by Richard Quinnly)*

also reveal that the great majority of young women and men intend to have children. Also, a survey of professional women showed that two-thirds of them had children, although they did so in later life. On the other hand, about a quarter of women born from 1946 to 1964 have remained childless (Thornton and Young-DeMarco, 2001, p. 1028; Barnett and Rivers, 2002; Vissing, 2002).

I once wrote my parents in Albania that I planned to have no children. My father replied with a question: "What are you going to do when you get old?" In my parents' and all other societies, children were expected to take care of their parents in their old age. Almost all did, although some less willingly and happily than others. Some writers claim that these days we surely don't have children to take care of us in our old age, that we get no tangible return from our children, that indeed they are an economic burden. At most, we get love and emotional and social satisfaction (LeVine and White, 1987; Zelizer,1985, p. 4).

Such statements are very wrong, for three good reasons. (1) Unless most people have children, who will grow the food and make the goods and provide the services we all need, and who will staff the institutions that will take care of us in our middle and later years? As members of society, we must have children for it to function, to our and everyone's benefit. (2) Indeed, in many tangible ways children do care for their parents (see section on caregiving in the next chapter). Logan and Spitze show this in *Family Ties* (1996), and Stack's *Call to Home* (1996) presents children who return to the South to take care of elderly parents. (3) The social and emotional satisfactions that our children (as well as nephews and nieces, and children of our friends and neighbors) provide from their birth to our old age are indispensable and invaluable. (This is not to deny that parents and children sometimes disappoint each other, and that there are conflicts.)

But it is also true that some people do debate whether for *them* it makes sense to have children, given their lives, choices, abilities, and temperaments. And in all societies, some women did not have children; often because they could not, sometimes because they chose not to. Women and men have questioned whether they should become parents (Vissing, 2002).

It may be that childlessness has become acceptable today. Through various routes, some couples decide not to have children. Some start marriage with the clear decision not to have any. Others keep postponing them until the "right" time (finish school, make more money, etc.) but then gradually realize they like their lives free of children. Some feel they would not make good parents. Others conclude there are already plenty of children in the world and they take an active part in the lives of other people's children. Other people, whose careers are very important to them, believe children would interfere with their jobs. For some people, children seem a financial burden. There are indeed some benefits to childlessness: time and energy for work, fun, and community involvement; time to devote to one's marriage; and others (Veevers, 1980; Newman, 1993, pp. 118–122; Farrell, 1999, pp. 124–125).

The great majority of women still have children. In 1998, 86 percent of women 40–44 who had ever married had had at least one child. We can assume that at least some of the other 12 percent adopted children. In addition, 33 percent of women 40–44 who had never married had also given birth to at least one child. Of course, women generally have children later in life than in the past. For example, in 1998 almost 30 percent of married women 25–29 had no children yet. People marry and have children later these days (*Statistical Abstract*, 1999, p. 84).

And they are having fewer children, as we saw in chapter 2: about 8 in Colonial times, 3.7 in 1900, fewer in the following decades, up again in the 1950s to 3.77 in 1957, 1.77 in 1976, and around 2 through the 1990s and into the twenty-first century. In Muncie, Indiana, in the 1890s families had 6–14 children, but by the 1920s 2–4 was more common, and having children was still "a moral obligation." In 1940, in Plainville the ideal was two children, but many couples had more (Lynd and Lynd, 1929, p. 131; West 1945, p. 170).

Births have declined throughout the industrial world. In 2001, of countries of 10 million and more people, Spain had the lowest birth rate in the world, an average of 1.15 children per woman (see below for some more examples). The costs of raising them, the demands of work, and lack of childcare are among the reasons parents cite for having none, one, or two children (Ball, 1997; Jolivet, 1997).

Birth rates in some countries of the world, 2001, listed alphabetically, were as follows:

Brazil	2.09
Canada	1.60
China	1.82
Egypt	3.07
France	1.75
India	3.04
Italy	1.18
Japan	1.41
Mexico	2.62
Nigeria	5.57
Russia	1.27
Spain	1.15
United States	2.06

(*Statistical Abstract*, 2002, p. 829)

A personal reflection: I am very aware of the conflicts, financial problems, time pressures, and violence which are all too present in the lives of many parents and children. We will explore them in this and later chapters. But children also—indeed, first and foremost—enrich our lives as we enrich theirs. We cannot forget the simple reality of our existence, that life *is* having children. Life would end without children. In our endless discussions of the problems we confront raising children we may forget this obvious reality. It is a reality echoed lately by the many lesbian and gay couples who decide to raise children.

PARENTS AND CHILDREN IN EARLIER TIMES

We risk a deep misunderstanding of families, of parents and children, if we ignore the delights and pleasures of parenthood and childhood. Similarly, our understanding of parents and children will be incomplete unless we explore their situations and conditions in non-industrial societies, which include almost all of the history of humanity. The examples below do not represent all human societies. Rather, they are examples of gentle and communal childrearing.

The Mundurucu of the Amazon in the 1950s

During their infancy and early childhood, Mundurucu children receive constant care, feeding, and holding. The mother provides this attention at first, but soon others in the community join in.

> During the first three months or so after birth, [the mother] is rarely absent from her baby. If she is working in the house, the infant either rests in her arms or is put to sleep in a small hammock next to her. . . . The baby is not only near her, but in physical contact with her body. The position of the child in the sling is such that its face is no more than a couple of inches from the mother's breast. . . . Feeding is wholly scheduled by the baby's demands, and infants are breast-fed whenever they show signs of hunger. No attempt is made to wean children until about three years of age, and, even then, the process is slow and gentle. (Murphy and Murphy, 1985, p. 193)

> For the first few months after the baby's birth, the mother is responsible for almost all the care of the baby. However, as it emerges from early infancy other women of the house increasingly share the burden. . . . By the time the baby is six months old, the little girls of the household are pressed into service, and seven-year-old girls are often given the care of their year-old siblings or cousins for hours on end. (Murphy and Murphy, 1985, p. 195)

> The lack of any strict training regimen is also characteristic of the Mundurucu attitude toward children, which is indulgent and nonauthoritarian. In keeping with this laissez-faire orientation, children are not strongly encouraged to walk and are allowed to proceed at their own pace. When a little one does struggle to his feet and makes his first tentative steps, however, adults and older children guide him and save him from tumbles. But he is not urged, goaded, or pushed to walk, or for that matter, to do anything else. In the same vein, children are almost never given corporal punishment. An irritated parent may swat a child gently to stop it from doing something, but punishment as such or severe thrashings never occurred during our fieldwork. (Murphy and Murphy, 1985, pp. 197–198)

Because of their culture and life, parents are not overwhelmed by the tasks of raising children. Life is simpler than in industrial societies, and children are raised more communally.

> Mundurucu women, quite simply, do not spend as much time looking after children as American women do, nor are they as pre-occupied with their welfare. The reasons for this have less to do with devotion than with the circumstances of life. Mundurucu mothers do not have to prepare their children for school and supervise their studies because there are no schools. Mothers do not watch their children cross streets or caution them against traffic because there are neither streets nor cars. Women do not warn the young about "strange men" because there are no strangers. They are not obsessed by the life chances of their children because the course of life is predetermined. Piano lessons, orthodontia, Little League, and all the other means by which the modern mother bedevils both herself and her children are absent. By the time a child is six or so, the burden of its protection and socialization shifts to the household, the peer group, and the community-at-large. Mundurucu women are not 'eaten up' by their young, as are

American women, and child rearing is less work. Moreover, those children they do tend to are often not their own. (Murphy and Murphy, 1985, p. 250)

The Tikopia of Polynesia in the 1930s

When Tikopia baby cries,

"[I]t is rocked very gently to and fro, with its face pressed against the woman's cheek, while she makes soft pulsating little 'br-r-r-r' noises with the lips to soothe it. . . . (Firth, 1936, p. 126)

[T]he care of the child is essentially a household affair, in which both parents play their part, but in which other persons who live there also assist. . . . As far as one can judge, the child's parents appear to have charge of it more constantly than other people—it usually sleeps between them, for example—but in a large household with several unmarried young folk they are relieved of their duties to a much greater extent than in a small household where they are the only adults. . . . Natives, as a whole, are fond of taking children around, and it is common to find a child, on the beach or with a group in the shade of the trees, in the arms of someone not of its house-hold or immediate circle of kin. . . . (Firth, 1936, pp. 129–130)

Young children are frequently taken by their parents to the scene of their work in the garden or orchard and are set down to sleep or play. . . . This early association with the economic life acts as a very important educational mechanism, since the child comes gradually to participate in the task of the moment, and is almost imperceptibly inducted into one of the major spheres of its future activity. There is also in consequence little real breach in the tenor of life. The infant play period, the childhood and adolescent educational period, and the adult working period are not sharply demarcated as in modern urban communities. (Firth, 1936, p. 131)

Small demonstrations of affection are exceedingly common in the contacts of everyday life, especially when the child is young. Coming round the corner of a house near mine one day, I was able to watch unnoticed the wife of one of my neighbors as she sat playing with her babe. She held it on her knees and looked at it with fond smiling eyes, then caught it up to her with a sudden movement, and began to press her nose in a greeting of affection to its nose, its cheeks, its ears, its breast and hollow of its neck and limbs, with swift but soft caresses in an abandon of obvious pleasure. (Firth, 1936, pp. 150–151)

In all cultures, including our own, such tender and playful moments create our humanity. Parents, relatives, and neighbors partook in them in earlier times. To the extent we have less time to enjoy them today, we are the poorer for it.

The Mbuti of Zaire

In *The Human Cycle,* Turnbull tells us that Mbuti mothers begin caring for their children even before birth.

In the last few months she takes to going off on her own, to her favorite spot in the forest, and singing to the child in her womb.

The lullaby that she sings is special in several ways. It is the only form of song that can be sung as a solo and it is composed by the mother for that particular child within her womb. It is sung for no other, it is sung by no other. The young mother sings it quietly, reassuringly, rocking herself, sometimes with her hands on her belly, or gently splashing her hands or feet in the water of her favorite stream or river, or rustling them through leaves, or warming herself at a fire. (Turnbull, 1983, p. 33)

During infancy and childhood, mothers carry their children everywhere, even while they gather food with other women or help the men with the hunt. They carry them "on the hip, not on the back, so every child had ready access to the breast and a full view of the adult world ahead of it, as seen by its mother" (Turnbull, 1983, p. 52)

In his earlier book, *The Forest People,* Turnbull depicts the communal childrearing of the Mbuti. All children are raised by everyone in the group (they live in groups of forty to fifty people). A child "calls everyone in the same age group as his parents 'father' or 'mother'; those still older are called 'grandparent.' Those of the same age as himself he refers to by a term which could be translated as either 'brother' or 'sister,' and anyone younger is 'child,' although more often they are just called by name" (1961, pp. 126–127).

If a little one is in possible danger, for example, he or she gets near a bed of hot ashes, anyone and everyone jumps into action. "In a moment he [or she] will be surrounded by angry adults and given a sound slapping, then carried unceremoniously back to the safety of a hut. It does not matter much which hut, because as far as the child is concerned all adults are his parents or grandparents. They are all equally likely to slap him for doing wrong, or fondle him and feed him with delicacies if he is quiet and gives them no trouble. He knows his real mother and father, of course, and has a special affection for them and they for him, but from an early age he learns that he is the child of them all, for they are all children of the forest" (Turnbull, 1961, pp. 127–128).

The Montagnais of the St. Lawrence Valley

In the 1600s, French Jesuits came to what is now eastern Canada, to convert the Montagnais and other peoples to Christianity. In the process, they were in frequent conflict with local cultures and strongly disapproved of their traditions. They were especially critical of how the Montagnais raised their children. They rarely hit them, comforted them whenever they cried, and raised them communally—all in contrast to French ways. When a Jesuit taunted a man that he could not be sure if his wife's son was his or another man's, the man replied: "You French love only your own children; but we all love all the children of our tribe" (Leacock, 1981, p. 50).

When Leacock lived with the Montagnais in the early 1950s, over three hundred years later, they still practiced the gentle and communal raising of their children. Fathers

> participated in the care and socialization of children with an ease and spontaneity deemed "feminine" in our culture. They were assured even with tiny infants. One day a father cradled a sick and fussing infant in his arms, and crooned over it for hours while his wife worked at smoking a deer hide. In a Montagnais camp, toddlers wander around, casually watched by older children or parents or other adults who happen to be near, and they gradually extend their range farther and farther from their own tents. . . .
>
> Men were patient with the interruptions of children, even when engaged in important tasks essential to the group. A man was planing planks for a canoe when his small grandson toddled over to him. The man pulled the boy to him, with the gentle tentativeness that bespeaks the Montagnais attitude of not forcing a decision on anyone, even a child. He showed the boy how to hold the planing tool, and allowed the child to play with it until the child himself became bored and chose to move on. . . .
>
> A man with whom I was working one afternoon took out his handkerchief to wipe the nose of a little boy who wandered by. After the session I scurried to my genealogical charts, remembering no son, grandson, or nephew of that age. Nor was there one, a fact I double checked; the boy was simply a child who needed his nose wiped. (Leacock, 1981, pp. 227–228)

OUR BABIES, OURSELVES: SOME LESSONS ON PARENTING

The preceding review of parents and children in some pre-industrial societies may give you a glimpse at some differences in childrearing between the United States today and those societies. For example, in most of them the surrounding community was more involved in raising the children than most of us are in the United States today.

In *Our Babies, Ourselves: How Biology and Culture Shape the Way We Parent,* Meredith Small explores in detail how parents in various cultures have raised their children. She begins

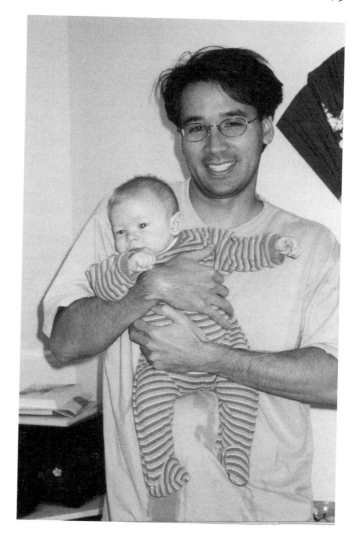

A Maryland father and his new son are enjoying getting to know each other.

by telling us that in some societies babies are carried in slings by their mothers all day, sleep in between their parents in the same bed, nurse for years, and cry much less than babies do in the United States and other societies (1998, p. xii).

Bonding

In the past twenty to thirty years, there has been some debate on the importance of "bonding" between parents, especially the mother, and the newborn. But except for Western societies since 1900, there has been no such debate and no such "need." "During most of human history and pre-history, immediately after birth babies have been placed on their mothers' bodies. In most cultures today, babies are still born this way." The separation of babies from their mothers after birth has only been practice in Western cultures during the last hundred years, and has been the standard until very recently. Doctors and hospitals have now returned to the practice common throughout human history, and babies and mothers stay together from birth. "Western culture has now returned to accepting that babies and mothers are a natural pair" (Small, 1998, pp. 19, 22).

Bonding is not only or mostly biological, and not with the mother only. For example, among the Efe of the Ituri forest of Central Africa, "infants are cared for by a number of adults, and this infant-adult relationship can be more communal. An Efe infant will spend 50 percent of its time with some other adult than its mother during the first four months of life, and interact with five or more adults per hour. A baby is also nursed by several women who are lactating." Children know who their natural parents are, but they are cared for and bond with other adults in the community (Small, 1998, p. 25).

Sleeping

As recently as around 1940, in some U.S. communities (such as "Plainville," a small town in the Midwest) babies slept with their parents. Small claims that the United States is almost alone in having babies sleep apart from their parents, but even in some U.S. communities co-sleeping is still practiced (or being reintroduced). In 2002, an estimated 25 percent of parents brought their babies to bed with them (West, 1945, p. 172; Small, 1998; Meltz, 2002).

The fear that parents may suffocate the babies next to them is unwarranted. There is no evidence for that fear. Indeed, Small and others argue that co-sleeping lowers the death rate by SIDS (sudden infant death syndrome), which is highest in the United States, 2 per 1,000 live births. (Small, pp. xiii, 132). (For a possible explanation of how co-sleeping lowers SIDS, see pp. 131–136.)

Co-sleeping has many advantages, among them the mother's ability to nurse the hungry child without leaving the bed, and the babies' "need to be in contact, connected, and part of an adult biological system while they develop and mature at their own biological pace." Babies are not optimally ready to be entirely on their own immediately after birth. Sleeping with their parents provides them security and helps them learn how to sleep and adjust to their environment (Small, pp. 130–131).

Touching

In varying degrees, American children are held by their parents and others. In some societies there is limited touching and holding of children. In others, however, children are almost constantly held and touched from the day they are born. Among the Arapesh of New Guinea, "During its first months the child is never far from someone's arms. When the mother walks about she carries the baby suspended from her forehead in its special small net bag, or suspended under one breast in a bark-cloth sling." Sleeping or awake, children are in constant physical contact with the mother or another adult. Mead thinks that the constant holding, touching, and affection lead to a "warm and maternal temperament of both men and women" in Arapesh society (Mead, 1935, p. 40).

Ju/'hoansi children of southwest Africa are also held and touched constantly. They "spend their first few years in almost constant close contact with their mothers. The . . . infant has continual access to the mother's breast, day and night, usually for at least three years, and nurses on demand several times an hour. The child sleeps beside the mother at night, and during the day is carried in a sling, skin-to-skin on the mother's hip, wherever the mother goes, at work or at play. (This position is an ideal height for older children, who love to entertain babies.) When the child is not in the sling, the mother may be amusing her— bouncing, singing, or talking. If they are physically separated, it is usually for short periods, when the father, siblings, cousins, grandparents, aunts, uncles, or friends of the family are playing with the baby while the mother sits close by" (Shostak, 1981, p. 45)

Ju/'hoansi babies, according to Small, live in a "dense" social environment—they are never alone; they are surrounded, held, and carried by older children and adults (1998, pp. 82–83).

Small reviewed ten recent studies of gathering and hunting societies and found that in all ten the babies were carried more than 50 percent of the time. In 56 percent of other non-industrial societies, babies were also carried that often. In contrast, in the United States, "babies are typically in physical contact with their parents 25 percent of the day" (Small, 1998, p. 174).

Feeding

For 99 percent of human history, mother's milk was the sole or primary food for the baby's first two years, and in many societies babies continued to breast feed beyond two years. As we have seen, in the Ju/'hoansi and other pre-industrial societies babies nurse whenever they want, "in short intervals all day long and at night as well." Ju/'hoansi children resisted being weaned (Small, 1998, p. 202). Nisa recalls vividly her continued attempts at nursing when her mother was breast-feeding Nisa's newborn brother. Ju/'hoansi mothers would allow their last child to nurse until the age of five (Shostak, 1981, p. 47).

In the 1800s in the United States, 95 percent of babies were nursed until the ages of two to four years. In Plainville, in the early 1900s babies were nursed whenever they wanted, and West heard stories that some children were still nursing at six. By 1940, when he lived there, babies typically stopped nursing at 12 to 24 months (1945, pp. 172–173).

For many decades in the twentieth century in the United States and other industrial societies, mothers were persuaded to give up breast-feeding and use formula. Manufacturers produced

> a plethora of baby formulas—evaporated, condensed, and powdered, and all easily transport-able. Artificial food was readily accepted by the public and also endorsed by the medical profession (some say in collusion with the corporations). Even the name "formula" has the aura of science, offered and seen as something better, more modern, and healthier for baby. Advised by their doctors, swayed by advertising, and pushed by the thought of convenience, mothers made bottle-feeding the norm. In the United States, for example, only about 20 to 30 percent of babies were breast-fed in the 1940s. Wet nursing was already out of fashion, and during the post-World War II baby boom, breast-feeding itself became unfashionable—out of date, even—and so uncommon that women who chose to breast-feed were considered odd. (Small, 1998, pp. 206–207)

Since the 1960s, more mothers have begun to breast-feed their babies. In the 1970s, about 25 percent did so. Today, about 60 percent nurse in the United States (rates are higher in other industrial societies), but only for a few months. In 1998, only 29 percent of mothers were still nursing by the time babies were six months old (Foreman, 1998; Weiss, 2001).

Today, when most mothers hold jobs outside the home, it is difficult for them to breast-feed beyond a few months. Using survey data collected between 1980 and 1986, Lindberg concluded that "significantly more women who are employed part-time are likely to breastfeed and for longer durations than women employed full-time," and they were more likely to stop nursing when they returned to work than women who did not work. Other studies and experiences make it clear that most working women who wish to breast-feed face a conflict between that wish and the time realities of their jobs. (Lindberg, 1996, p. 239)

But workplaces and societies can and do make accommodations for mothers of infants and young children. Sweden gave mothers up to 18 months paid leaves from work. China and some other societies gave working mothers two extra breaks during each work day so they could breast-feed their babies (who were in day care facilities in or near their workplaces) (Liazos, 1982, p. 206). Foreman reports that some U.S. companies provide a "mother's room" where nursing mothers can use an electric breast milk pump to express and then refrigerate their milk. Their children's caretakers feed it to the babies next day. This is a considerable improvement over the hassles mothers face who express their milk in bathrooms and boiler rooms. With healthier babies and happier mothers, lactation rooms also decrease worker absenteeism, 27 percent in one study (Foreman, 1998; Weiss, 2001).

After a century-long detour, we are now "discovering" the health and social benefits of mother's milk. Groups are working to make nursing more public and more acceptable. And Foreman reports that in 1998 the American Academy of Pediatrics declared: "Human milk is the preferred feeding for all infants, including premature and sick newborns with rare exceptions." Nutritionally, it is the best food for babies. It also decreases the incidence and severity of many diseases, including various infections (Weiss, 2001; Foreman, 1998, p. C4).

Personal reflection: I do not mean to say that parents in pre-industrial societies raised perfect and always happy children. Problems, conflicts, and diseases did exist; in some of those societies (notably peasant ones in Europe and Asia) they were common. In her autobiography, Nisa recalls many conflicts with her parents over her refusal to share and cooperate (sharing is essential and valued among the Ju/'hoansi) (Shostak, 1981). Nevertheless, people in industrial societies can learn from pre-industrial ones. Indeed, in some areas—such as breast-feeding—we are returning to the wisdom and practices of parents and communities of earlier times. Sleeping with parents, being in frequent physical touch with parents and others, breast-feeding, always being consoled when crying, and being raised by parents together with relatives and the larger community—all seem desirable. They make life easier and more pleasant for babies and children, for parents, for everyone.

PARENTS AND CHILDREN IN AFRICAN AMERICAN COMMUNITIES

In the United States today, most children are raised solely or primarily by their parents. When both parents work, they turn to various forms of child care during their working hours (discussed later in this chapter). But in some communities extended family members help the parents raise the children.

Carol Stack, a white anthropologist, lived in two such African American communities. In two remarkable books—*All Our Kin* (1974) and *Call to Home* (1996)—she describes the people, extended families, and economies of these communities. Prominent in her accounts were the children and how parents and relatives raised them.

All Our Kin

In the mid-1960s, Stack lived for three years in a poor black neighborhood, "The Flats," in the city of Jackson Harbor (the fictional name of a midwestern city). Stack shows how poor families manage to make a living and a home primarily by creating and living in an extensive network of relatives who continually share and cooperate. They share "food stamps, rent money, a TV, hats, dice, a car, a nickel here, a cigarette there, food, milk, grits, and children" (1974, p. 32).

Children are highly valued. "Men and women in The Flats regard child-begetting and childbearing as a natural and highly desirable phenomenon" (Stack, 1974, p. 46).

Because at different times parents may have no money or job, or may have no place to live, or need child care while they work, children live with grandparents, aunts, uncles, or other relatives for various periods of time. The "size of the dwelling, employment, and many other factors determine where children sleep." One man recalls his childhood: "My brother stayed with my aunt, my mother's sister, and her husband until he was ten, 'cause he was the oldest in our family and we didn't have enough room—but he stayed with us most every weekend. Finally my aunt moved into the house behind ours with her husband, her brother, and my brother; my sisters and brothers and I lived up front with my mother and her old man" (Stack, 1974, p. 63, 93).

"Loretta Smart, a forty-year-old Flats resident was raised by her great-grandmother for the first five years of her life. 'When I became five years old,' Loretta told me, 'my daddy just got too old to care for me. My mother was living in The Flats at the time, but my daddy asked my mother's brother and his wife to take me 'cause he really trusted them with me. I stayed with them and their three kids, but my mother came by and took care of us kids lots of times. When I was about nine years old my mother got married and from then on I stayed with her and her husband and he gave me his name'" (Stack, 1974, p. 64).

As need arises, various relatives provide shelter, food, clothing, and child care. Another example of the sharing and giving is the $1500 inheritance Magnolia and Calvin Waters received in 1971. They had hoped to use it for a down payment for a house. Instead, they spent the money for their children's, grandchildren's, and other relatives' needs. They bought "coats, hats, and shoes for all of the children (at least fifteen)" who had been forced to miss some school days during very cold weather. In addition, they bought train tickets for relatives to attend a family funeral in the South, paid overdue rent for a sister so she would not be evicted, and so on (Stack, pp. 106–107).

These living situations and child care arrangements may seen chaotic to some middle-class people. But as these examples indicate, and as Stack explains, there is order, organization, and expectations to share and cooperate. Children know many relatives, and they know they will be taken care of by someone if their own parents are unable to provide. When parents have no money for winter clothes, an uncle, an aunt, a grandparent, or even at times a friend will provide them. Children do experience stress and conflict during these family crises and emergencies, but they also learn to expect—and later to give—help from relatives in the larger family. (For similar findings on African American families in New York City in the 1990s, see Newman, 1999.)

Call to Home

From the 1930s to the 1960s, African Americans left the South and went North to escape poverty and racism. Since the 1970s, they started returning South to be with family, and to escape the violence and drugs of northern cities. During all the years they lived North they kept in touch with families down South, including many visits. They also sent children to the South for a month, for a summer, and sometimes for years to stay with relatives.

In addition to their ten children, Pearl and Samuel Bishop also raised grandchildren and nephews and nieces who were orphaned or whose parents were up North. Eula, the Bishop's daughter, told Stack: "People knew, if there was a child that needed a mother, Miss Pearl was somebody they could count on." To raise so many children, every room—including the living room and the kitchen—was a bedroom. When he wasn't up North working, Samuel helped raise them. Pearl said: " with them children, he was just like a woman." He washed them and played with them and fed them, and "he had a certain patience with children" (Stack , 1996, pp. 85, 83).

Raising so many children wasn't easy for Pearl and Samuel; and in her adult years at least one of the children they raised thought that she had received little attention or affection. Also, other people's children that Pearl raised often missed their parents who were North, and cried for them. But when these children joined their parents in the North, they missed Miss Pearl and called her almost daily. When they grew up, most of them sent her money (Stack, 1996, pp. 85, 105).

Pearl and Samuel Bishop may have been unusual in the number of other people's children they raised, but, whether up North or in the South, many black children have been raised, for at least parts of their lives, by grandparents, aunts and uncles, and other relatives. Even while living with their parents, many children received care, clothes, and food from other relatives. If we think about how children all over the world have lived, we find many places where, for many reasons, people other than natural parents supplement or replace parents.

From 1947 to 1955, for complex political reasons, my brother Chris (age 10 in 1947) and I (6) were living in Greece, being raised by our father's mother (age 67 in 1947), while our parents and three younger siblings lived thirty miles away in Albania, on the other side of the border with Greece. All over the world, in Mexico, South Africa, Greece, the United States, India, and hundreds of other places, in the past and today, children live without one or both parents who are away, usually in order to find work in faraway places to support their children. Then other relatives step in to raise the children.

HISTORICAL NOTES ON CHILDHOOD AND PARENTING

Children

In Colonial times, childhood as we know it today was briefer and different. As in most pre-industrial societies, at around six to eight years children began to play less and to perform useful and necessary tasks around the farm, the shop, or the store. They were not full adults, by any means, but they did become part of the adult world. Ideally, they were totally obedient to their parents; corporal and other punishments were common. But in every society about which I have read a detailed account of life, there has never been total obedience to parents. Contemporaries and historians tell us how children *should* have behaved, but reality differs from these ideals.

The coming of industrialism did begin to change childhood. As families ceased farming, children had fewer tasks to perform. Gradually, children became *future* producers, especially for middle-class parents. Parents focused on educating them for later life, protecting them from the outside world. More and more children began attending public schools, and by the end of the 1800s schooling was mandatory in every state.

Historians Laurel Ulrich and Julia Grant discuss the changes in childhood and childrearing by comparing eighteenth-century "extensive" mothering with nineteenth-century "intensive" mothering." For Colonial period women,

> child rearing was only one of a multitude of tasks shared by neighbors and kin. With the help of older children, mothers supervised numerous offspring—their own and those of neighbors and relatives—while attending to household needs—sewing, washing, preparing food, and caring for the sick. Historian Laurel Ulrich defines seventeenth-century mothering as "extensive," explaining that "mothering meant generalized responsibility for an assembly of youngsters rather than concentrated devotion to a few." . . . During the colonial period mothers raised an average of seven or eight children to adulthood, but during the nineteenth century women's fertility rates declined dramatically. . . . With fewer children to share their resources of care and affection, middle-class mothers of the nineteenth and twentieth centuries increasingly engaged in "intensive" parenting—that is, they concentrated their attention on the physical and emotional nurture of individual children. Certain mothers, however, continued to engage in extensive mothering: those who were living in slavery, raising large numbers of children, struggling to make ends meet, caring for children alone, or working for wages inside or outside the home. (Grant, 1998, p. 15)

Around 1900, three important social changes were happening or had happened: (1) Mandatory education kept children out of the labor force. (2) Child labor laws limited and postponed their entrance into the labor market. (3) Juvenile courts separated children from adults.

Parents

As we saw in chapter 2 and other places, families have changed over time, and so have mothers' and fathers' roles. Pleck proposes four historical periods of the relationship between parents and their children.

1. In the 1700s and early 1800s, mothers carried out most child care for infants and young children, but fathers "had far greater responsibility for, and influence on, their children. Prescriptions for parents were addressed almost entirely to fathers; the responsibilities of motherhood were rarely mentioned." It was fathers who taught reading and moral and religious lessons to the children. Mothers were suspected to be too soft, so fathers were to provide the "vigorous supervision" which children needed. For these and other reasons, in the few divorces which took place, fathers were usually given custody of the children. As many historians and sociologists have noted, in the farming economy of the Colonial era, work and childrearing were carried out around the same places and times, thus allowing fathers to be with their children (Pleck, 1987, p. 351).

2. From about 1850 to about 1940, there was a gradual decrease in the father's relationship with the children, and an increase in the mother's. The change was largely related to the industrial economy, which took fathers away from home. Fathers were now absent from the family for most of the day, and lost touch with much of daily life. Some fathers complained that they did not know how to "chum up" with their children when they saw them (Lynd and Lynd, 1929, pp. 148–149).

As fathers lost much of their role with their children, the mothers' role increased. There was more emphasis on the importance of infancy and early childhood, where the mother's maternal influence could be best exercised. Because of this belief, mothers were now given custody of the children when couples divorced.

3. From about 1940 to about 1965, as the mother's importance in childrearing became more established, some writers were concerned that fathers were losing their parental role entirely, and children, boys especially, were being harmed. For example, some people linked the "perceived epidemic of juvenile delinquency" to fathers who spent hardly any time with their sons. Various psychologists argued that boys needed to be with their fathers and to model themselves after them in order to develop properly (Pleck, 1987, p. 357). (Note: These are perceptions and theories. We need observations and survey data from those years to determine how much time fathers in fact spent with their boys and girls.)

4. What has happened to fathers and mothers since the 1960s, especially as more mothers began working outside the home, and as the feminist movement challenged the culture and traditions that confined women to the home and limited the time fathers had with their children? Many changes have indeed taken place. Compared to the 1950s and 1960s, when fathers, for example, would hide behind the newspaper even when they were home, many fathers are spending more time with their children, and women are no longer raising the children alone (Ford, 1994; Gerson, 1993; Aldous, Mulligan, and Bjarnason, 1998).

But some writers claim that most fathers have changed relatively little, and it is still mothers who do most of the childrearing. Fathers wish to, hope to, or think they spend more time with their children than their fathers did with them, but in fact they do not. As LaRossa aptly expressed it, the *culture* has changed but not the *conduct*. For example, one study examined how much time parents spent alone with their children. Mothers spent 19.5 hours a week and fathers 5.5 hours, a ratio of 3.6 to 1 (LaRossa, 1988). (See chapters 9 and 11 for more details on parenting.)

CHILDREN TODAY

Psychologists, sociologists, historians, and others talk, worry, and theorize about children. They blame parents or they absolve parents for what they see as problems in children's lives. They endorse or criticize a variety of proposed actions and policies for children. Lately, in many states, children and their teachers are blamed for not learning enough, or not learning certain material. Increasingly, we are told that it is "harder and riskier to be a child today than it was in the past," that "contemporary children do face more obstacles in the process of growing up" than children did in earlier times (Farrell, 1999, pp. 54–55).

Textbooks—this one no exception—drown us with long discussions about poverty, child abuse, absent and busy parents, and many other problems. These conditions *do exist*. What seem missing, however, are descriptions of the experiences of children *as children* know and feel them. In a quick search through studies and texts I found very little that tells us how our children experience the world around them. Mostly, we read the worries and concerns of parents and other adults.

Busy Parents, Fear, Computers, and the Decline of Childhood?

In 1995, the *Boston Globe* ran a four-part series on children. In its May/June 1997 issue, *Sanctuary* (the journal of the Massachusetts Audubon Society) included five essays on "the loss of free play." Between them, they portray modern children's lives as restricted by fear of crime so they don't go outside to play, and dominated by scheduled activities and television, and more recently by computers. The seven writers, and the people they interviewed, hark back to more carefree, exploring, playful, and free of the fear of crime days (real and imagined, I assume). While they see the economic and social need for mothers to work, they bemoan what they see as the loss of adult presence in the children's lives. Even as a survey of 400 parents around Boston showed that 72 percent (67 percent of mothers with full-time jobs) said they were "able to balance parenting and work" to their satisfaction, the predominant theme was that parents and children lead busy, hectic, over-scheduled lives, with little time for each other (Matchan, 1995a, 1995b; Lakshmanan, 1995a, 1995b; Mitchell, 1997; van Dam, 1997; Fenton, 1997; Hecker, 1997, Sobel, 1997).

I cannot tell whether the writers engage in romantic nostalgia of carefree days that never existed, or whether they exaggerate when they talk of children with no free time and of parents with no time for their children. But they do raise some important questions about childhood today, so I present some of their worries and memories in their own words (all from *Sanctuary*, May/June 1997).

John Mitchell grew up in the late 1940s and early 1950s in a suburb outside New York City, near the Hudson River:

> We found nests, we caught frogs and put them into our mouths on a dare, we collected salamanders and put them in fish tanks to watch them grow; we pulled clumps of onion grass from the moist earth and showered one another; we scaled the peaked roofs of a large nearby church. We rescued poor pigeons and English sparrows whom we brought home to nurse, along with baby rabbits, moles and mice the cats brought in, squirrels, and Oscar the crow, whom my brother rescued and who lived with us for years and always fixed me with his glinty eye if ever I came near him when by brother was not around.
>
> There were no Boy Scouts in this tribe. There were no after-school programs. Saturday-morning television held no attraction, and personal computers, to my eternal gratitude, had yet to be invented. We were bounded only by the wilderness of our own imaginations. But, there are times when, staring in the child-empty fields and woods around the town in which I now live, I wonder in what fields the children of this lost generation of wanderers play. (Mitchell, 1997, p. 2; used with permission of the author)

Laura van Dam worries about children without free time.

> The trouble . . . is that today's children—whether urban, suburban, or rural—are spending far less time outdoors doing whatever they might dream up. . . . [Children] clamor for the multitude of organized activities their friends are in, beseech parents to take them to "pay-for-play" centers, and pull out calendars to write in play dates. . . .
>
> Experts repeatedly note the loss of community. Factors range from, they say, the drop in corner shops and the concomitant rise in automobile use to go to larger, distant stores, to the growing number of children in magnet and private schools and the subsequent decline in neighborhood schools. . . .

[W]e should encourage kids to go outside whenever possible. This past winter, a little nudging on my part one weekend resulted in my son and a friend cooking up the idea to dye snow with vegetable color. For days my child felt compelled to go outdoors to check what was happening to the very bright green and blue spots in our yard. (van Dam, 1997, pp. 3, 4, 5)

The parents of first-graders in a small school in California were anxious that the school get them computers. Sobel comments:

They couldn't really articulate why they thought computers were important for young children, but they were anxious to have their kids jump on the bandwagon so they wouldn't get left behind. . . . [D]oes the computer really make your preschooler smarter, happier, and healthier? Or does it numb her brain and make her just another contributor to the globalization of a consumer-oriented, ecologically destructive culture? . . . [Sobel's children] ride bikes, make forts and pretend they are lost children, smell the wet dog trilliums, play baseball, knock on neighbors' doors and hide in the bushes. . . . [C]omputers should follow, not lead. Dynamic, real-life engagements that build skills, self-confidence, and a sense of purpose in life are the motivational forces in education. The computer has a role to play in this drama, but it should be a supporting cast member, not the star. . . . The old Sufi saying, "If you only have a hammer, everything looks like a nail," has relevance. Technology enthusiasts want us to believe that all educational problems are nails and that we can solve them by giving everyone a computer hammer. . . . I say we start a new movement called Take Back the Afternoon that advocates for good, old-fashioned real play. (Sobel, pp. 10, 12, 13) (For studies and discussion of how computers may affect children, see Weltner, 2000 and Wen, 2000.)

Because of overscheduled and busy lives, groups in some suburban communities have begun to organize community-wide "family nights." For one night, parents, children, and schools schedule no outside activities, school assigns no homework, and families stay home to spend the entire evening together. It's unclear from the stories how many families participated, but those that did said they appreciated the leisurely evening meal, followed by games and other time together (Parry, 2002; Sherrill, 2002; Tauchert, 2002).

"The Devaluation of the Work of Raising Children"?

The Amerco parents Hochschild studied in *The Time Bind* led hectic lives. Far too often, they would rather work extra hours in the office or on the assembly line than go home and face children and housework. Some parents seemed to engage in a "gender war for time" as they struggled to meet the demands of work, housework, children, and time for each other. "Implicit in this war was the devaluation of the work of raising children. Deb and Mario Escalla surely wouldn't have struggled so to escape their children were the work of raising them more valued. Hunter's crisis with the zwieback, Gordon's messy diaper, and the children's loud screams were, in themselves, no more reason to avoid parenting than a difficult equation was a reason to avoid a career in mathematics. 'Women's work' has always been devalued, however, and under the pressure of the new time-math of corporate America its value is sinking lower still." Parents and children are rushed and parenting is devalued because the American culture and economy pressure and require both parents to work more hours. As a result, combined weekly parental time with children decreased 22 hours from 1969 to 1996 (Hochschild, 1997, pp. 191–192; Rankin, 2002a, p. 4).

I witnessed a student discussion in an anthropology class in 1993, which also reflected a fear that we devalue the raising of children. Five or six students who took that course worked as baby-sitters and nannies for wealthy families who lived in towns near Regis College. On the day we began discussing Shostak's *Nisa* (1981), one student opened by saying that she thought Nisa's childhood had been carefree, happy, free of an over-scheduled life, and surrounded by loving parents who spent much time caring for their children. Her comment began an hour-long conversation that went around the circle of chairs spontaneously and without any contribution from me. The five to six students who worked as nannies, and eventually others, insisted that these parents neglected their children, that they spent no time with them, that they hired people to do all the child care, that feeling guilty they bought their children too many and too expensive toys and games, that the fathers were too busy with and committed to their careers and the mothers were busy with tennis and lunches, that they did not value their children. Some students said they wondered why these people had children, given how little time and care they gave them.

Toward the end of the class, I asked whether they thought these parents were typical of most American parents. They were unsure, they said, but they insisted that these and many other parents could not love their children much given how little time they were with them. That discussion is probably the most spontaneous and deeply felt one I have heard in my thirty years of teaching. The students expressed a fear, concern, and worry that we devalue children.

Child Care and Day Care

As we have seen in chapter 2, and in previous sections of this chapter, in earlier times and other societies fathers and mothers mostly took care of their children while they worked. Relatives and neighbors also partook in raising children. Child care was not the sole or primary province of mothers. All this was possible in economies where parents worked in or near their homes, and they lived in smaller communities with no strangers and with everyone looking out for children.

History. As mothers in industrial societies have gradually taken jobs outside their homes, and as most people no longer live in small communities, parents have needed to find others to tend to their children while they both worked. Baxandall outlines "the history and development of day care in the United States." One lesson we learn from that history is that the U.S. government and other institutions encourage parents to place their children in day-care centers when the society and economy require mothers to leave their homes for factories and offices. Thus, while men fought in World War II in the early 1940s, and while women were encouraged to hold the jobs the men had left when they went to war, the U.S. government created an extensive day-care system. By July 1945 it was "responsible for 3,100 day-care centers serving 130,000 children, and about 1,600,000 children were receiving care financed largely by federal funds." But when the war ended, the government withdrew the funds and most of the centers closed. Mothers were now told it was best for their children if they went back home (Baxandall, 1976, p. 491).

But after a short interval of a decline in women's employment in the late 1940s, women gradually began to return to work (see chapter 9), and parents began anew the search for people and settings to tend to their children while they worked. In 1960, 18.6 percent of married mothers with children under 6 worked, and 40.5 percent of widowed, divorced, and separated such mothers worked. By 2001, the figures were 62.5 percent and 76.2 percent. Also in 2001, 69.7 percent of single mothers with children under 6 held jobs (*Statistical Abstract,* 1998, p. 409; 2002, p. 373).

Child-care settings. Before we examine the costs, effects, and other issues of day care, let us see how many children are cared for in what settings. See table 5.1.

Using table 5.1, if we add all settings in which a relative tends to children, we see that 43.7 percent of children under six whose mothers work are cared for by relatives, and another 5.5 percent by their mothers. Thus, in these statistics, almost half are cared for by a relative.

Parents often cannot arrange for the childcare they prefer. One study of 247 mothers who returned to work within a year of their child's birth found that 53 percent of them

Table 5.1 Child-Care Arrangements for Children under 6 Whose Mothers Work

Child-Care Site/Care Giver	Percent
Organized child-care facility	**29.4**
Day-care center	21.6
Nursery-preschool	7.8
Child's home	**32.9**
Father	18.4
Grandparent	5.9
Other relative	3.5
Non-relative[a]	5.1
Another home	**31.3**
Grandparent	10.4
Other relative	5.5
Non-relative[b]	15.4
Mother's work site	**5.5**
(mother cares for child while at work)	
Other	**1.0**

[a]Includes a variety of nannies and others who either live with the family, or come for part of the day, to care for the children.
[b]Refers to people, mostly women, who care for up to six children in their own homes.
Source: Macionis, 1999, p. 465; from U.S. Bureau of the Census data.

preferred the father to be the primary caretaker for their child while they worked, but only 23 percent were able to do so. Also, 78 percent of mothers were "not using the type of child care at 6 months post-partum that they most wanted" (Riley and Glass, 2002, p. 14).

Indeed, parents often need to use two or more caretakers for their children while they work. A survey of 44,000 households found "about 30 percent of parents have two child-care arrangements . . . and another 8 percent are using at least three. . . ." They turn to relatives, friends, and neighbors after their day-care center hours end (Gullo, 2000).

Child care remains an issue even after children enter school. Most parents work long after school hours end. Younger children need some supervision before parents come home, but according to two surveys 20 percent of children ages 6–12 have no adult supervision when they come home. Cost, few after-school programs, and lack of nearby relatives are some explanations (McQueen, 2000; Gomstyn, 2002).

Experiences of child care. How do children experience child care outside their homes? Little has been written about family day care (see below), but there has been some research on centers providing child care. Arlie Hochschild, in *The Time Bind: When Work Becomes Home and Home Becomes Work* (1997), studied Amerco, a U.S. manufacturing corporation in the Midwest. She found that both for economic reasons, and because the corporate culture rewarded people for long work days, most people worked many more than 40 hours. By necessity, most of them brought their children to child-care centers.

Hochschild opens the book with parents on their way to work dropping off their children at a center. A mother has just brought her twins. "Car keys in hand, she pours out Cheerios and milk, consulting each twin about the amount. She watches them eat for a few minutes. Then, glancing at her watch, she bends down, offers long hugs, leaves the child-care room, and reappears outside. She feigns surprise at the first window, makes a funny face at the second, races to the third, and gives a big wave at the fourth. Finally, out of sight, she breaks into a run for her car" (1997, p. 4).

Gwen brings her daughter Cassie into the center, who pleads, "'Pleeese, can't you take me with you?' . . . 'You know I can't take you to work,' Gwen replies in a tone that suggests she's heard this request before. Cassie's shoulders droop in defeat. . . . Aware of her mother's unease about her long day at childcare, however, she's struck a hard bargain. Every so often she gets a morning fudge bar. . . . Like other parents at the center, Gwen sometimes finds herself indulging her child with treats or softened rules in exchange for missed time together" (Hochschild, 1997, p. 4–5).

Cassie and the twins, however, attend an excellent child-care center. It "works on 'child time.' Its rhythms are child-paced, flexible, mainly slow. Teachers patiently oversee the laborious task of tying a shoelace, a prolonged sit on the potty, the scrambled telling of a tall tale." It was one of a dozen similar centers near Amerco. (Hochschild, 1997, p. 5).

The director of Cassie's center told Hochschild: "Most of our Amerco parents work from 8 a.m. to 5 p.m. They bring their children in half an hour ahead of time and pick them up a half hour after they leave work. It's longer if they have a late meeting, or try to fit in errands or exercise. It's a nine- or ten-hour day for most of the children." When Hochschild asked her "what kind of a day at the center she thought would most benefit a child, she replied that on average most three- and four-year olds should have 'an active morning, lunch, a nap and go home after their nap—ideally six or seven hours.' Though she . . . felt that most children did well under her care, nine hours, she remained convinced, was generally 'too long'" (1997, p. 10).

From these and other observations and comments, Hochschild concluded that "Everywhere in Amerco's factories parents were working long hours while their children put in long hours at day care. Everywhere parents were having . . . problems meshing schedules" (Hochschild, 1997, p. 190–191).

As we saw in the comments by the director of a day-care center, some people who believe and work in such centers think some children spend too many hours in them and cannot receive much attention. Dorothy Conniff, former head of the municipal day-care assistance program in Madison, Wisconsin, who worked in the field for sixteen years, thinks that day care for infants poses impossible demands on the caretakers. A person attending to four infants who must feed each of them 3–4 times in an eight-hour day, change their diapers, and wash her or his hands after each diaper change is left with little or no time or energy to play with them and attend to their social and emotional needs. As she feeds or changes one infant, the other three are left mostly unattended. And "if a child is deprived of language stimulation for eight to ten hours a day, how much compensation—how much 'quality time'—can concerned parents provide in the baby's few other waking hours at home?" (Conniff, 1988, p. 22; see also Polsgrove, 1988).

Studies of the effects of day care. A multi-year study of 400 day-care centers in California, Colorado, Connecticut, and North Carolina, by a team of researchers from four universities, concluded, in the words of a reporter, "the vast majority of the 5 million children who spend their days in child-care centers are receiving mediocre care, and one in eight are in poor-quality settings where their health and safety are threatened. . . . [It] rated just one in seven centers as good quality, where children enjoyed close relationships with adults and teachers focused on the individual needs of the children." It seems that parents did not agree, however, since the study reports that 90 percent of them "rated their children's programs as very good" (*Washington Post,* 1994, p. 3).

Quality clearly varies. There are some excellent centers, providing warmth, love, stimulation, and learning. But they are few, small, and expensive.

To determine the long-term effects of day care, 29 investigators undertook a $10 million study of 1,300 children in day care. Their initial conclusions were mixed and controversial. On the one hand, they found that "those who were in day care at least ten hours a week had better cognitive and language skills." On the other hand, a newspaper story on the study featured the bold headline that "Study links child care to aggression." According to Jay Belsky, one of the investigators, the more time children spent in day care, "the more aggressive and disobedient" they were. They argued, lied, and cheated more (cited in Fitzgerald, 2001).

Alarming conclusions, until we read that "five percent of children who spent 10 [hours per week] or less in child care scored at the high end for behavior problems, compared to 17 percent of children who spent 30 or more hours in child care." The better conclusion would seem to be that some children exhibit problems, but that the vast majority—83 percent—who spent 30 or more hours exhibited normal behavior (Barry, 2002; Fitzgerald, 2001).

Other research disagrees with the above studies. A study of families and day care, released in 1996, conducted by "25 researchers who began their work with sharp disagreements about child care," followed 1,300 children since 1991. "The results show that children's attachment to their mothers is not affected by whether or not they are in day care, what age they enter, or how many hours they spend there, . . . so long as the parents are responsive and sensitive to their children's needs while they are at home," and provide adequate parenting. A later study, by Elizabeth Harvey, followed families with 12,000 people until some of the children reached 12. It concluded, in Dolores Kong's words, that "mothers who work outside of the home during the first three years of their children's lives do not harm their youngsters' behavior, mental development, or self-esteem" (Coontz, 1997, p. 67, summarizing Chira, 1996; Kong, 1999a, p. A1).

What are we to do? Cost, availability, quality, and effects on children are the major issues of non-relative child care. But if we truly consider the future and well-being of our children (and thus, ourselves), we can provide quality affordable care for all children who need it. Many countries do. For example, in France, "99 percent of 3-, 4- and 5-year olds attend preschool at no or minimal charge. . . . Poor families pay $390 per year, middle-class families pay about $3,200, and the rich pay $5,300." A U.S. study of child care in France concluded that most programs are as good as the best American ones, and what few American children receive is what most French children have (Greenhouse, 1993).

In the United States, parents and communities are always searching and working for better and more affordable child care. For example, some parents in the Jamaica Plain section of Boston have created "child-care co-ops." If one working parent from each couple has a flexible working schedule, four households with pre-school children join and together hire a caregiver for 20–30 hours a week. They rotate meeting in the four houses and each day one parent stays with the children and caregiver. The children receive attention from two adults, the parents pay a reasonable $3 an hour ($60 to $90 a week), and caregivers receive $12 an hour (Brennan and Collins, 1998).

But if we are to have affordable and quality child care for all children who need it, the federal, state, and local governments will need to finance most of the costs (Helburn and Bergmann, 2002).

My personal conclusion is that day care of various types is beneficial to children if they attend for fewer than the 8–10 hours many now attend, if all settings were high quality, and if workers were paid a living wage. My experience with my two daughters, the stories I hear and read from child-care workers, and other evidence convince me of the following:

1. Infants are best cared for by parents, with the help of family and friends. Paid leaves, for both parents, which exist in many countries, allow parents to enjoy their newborns and to have time for each other, their family, and their community.

2. Beginning around one, children (and parents) benefit if they are with other children and adults 3–5 hours a day. As they get older, they can tolerate and benefit from more hours, but 8–10 hour days in family- and center-care settings are simply too long, as child-care workers testify. This can be done if we change our priorities and allow parents to work shorter days, perhaps 6 hours. (For more details, see Liazos, 1991, and chapters 9 and 11 in this volume).

Class, Race, and Childhood

When one of my daughters was six and talking with some of her friends, one of them said: "*When* I go to college . . ." Lafeyette, a ten-year-old African American boy living in a poor section of Chicago in 1985, said: "If I grow up, I'd like to be a bus driver." Kotlowitz adds, "*If,* not *when.*" (1991, p. x). These casual comments by two children living in the different worlds of their parents illustrate sharply the effects of parental class and race on their children. Middle-class children, as young as six, assume they will attend college. Children growing in the midst of poverty and violence cannot be certain they will grow up, no matter what their parents' efforts and hopes.

Children acquire their parents' status and conditions. All around them they see and feel what their parents endure to make a living, they see where they choose or must live, they see how others treat their parents. Their opportunities in life are shaped by these realities (MacLeod, 1995; Elkin and Handel, 1989, pp. 139–160).

Two news stories illustrate how the parents' class and race affect children.

Poor children's health is affected by the rising cost of housing, which forces parents to live in crowded and run-down apartments. In the Boston area in 1999,

> Children are showing up at hospitals and doctors' offices with rat bites, lead poisoning, or asthma from exposure to cockroaches and other pests. . . . Or they are going hungry as more family income has to go to rent, rather than to nutritious food. Or they are failing in school because their family has to move repeatedly in search of affordable housing.
>
> Across the United States, an estimated 14 million young children live in housing with lead paint, and 10,000 children between ages 4 and 9 are hospitalized for asthma attacks each year because of cockroach infestation. (Kong, 1999b)

In Massachusetts, the highest rate of childhood asthma is in Roxbury, a poor section of Boston. Doctors suspect that the living conditions trigger the asthma attacks. Roxbury has "the highest number of dumpster lots, trash transfer stations, junkyards, and recycling plants in the city." Old buildings, unrepaired by landlords, create dust and mildew. These and other living conditions cause breathing problems in children (Rodriguez, 1998).

Children have the highest poverty rate of any group. In 2000, 11,018,000 persons 17 and under were listed as poor by U.S. government definitions and statistics. Table 5.2 provides poverty percentages of different groups.

The percentage of children in poverty, and problems such as hunger that accompany poverty, decreased in the years from 1990 to 2000. But as the years of economic boom were over by 2000, we can expect a rise in poverty in the early 2000s (Pertman, 2000).

Generally, children are poor because their parents are. In the booming economy of the 1990s, a few people had huge income increases, many only modest ones, and many others had none or lost ground. (See chapter 8). Studies tracking poor children from the 1950s on concluded that over 50 percent escaped poverty when they reached adulthood. One study concluded that two-thirds did better than their parents when they reached adulthood (Lakshmanan, 1995b, p. 10).

Table 5.2 Persons below Poverty Line (in percent)

	1970	1990	1996	2000
All persons	12.6	13.5	13.7	11.3
All children	14.9	19.9	19.8	15.6
White children	10.5	15.1	15.5	12.3
Black children	41.5	44.2	39.5	30.4
Hispanic children	not available	37.7	39.9	27.3

Source: Statistical Abstract, 1998, p. 477; 2002, p. 441.

Two comments: (1) When many children overcome poverty (most only modestly so, I think), they are replaced by as many and more new children. (2) Poverty in childhood, even when overcome later, often leaves permanent memories, resentments, and regrets. In a land of great material wealth, there is no excuse for childhood poverty. (For more on children and poverty, see Coles, *Migrants, Sharecroppers, Mountaineers,* 1976; Kotlowitz, *There Are No Children Here,* 1991; Kozol, *Savage Inequalities,* 1991, and *Amazing Grace,* 1995; MacLeod, *Ain't No Makin' It,* 1995.)

I do not mean that all poor children are hungry and miserable all the time. Most find some joy and have some good times. In the late 1980s, in the middle of poverty, discrimination, housing that the Chicago Housing Authority allowed to deteriorate, and frequent violence, children found joys. While walking along railroad tracks, Pharoah and his friends chased butterflies, and after a rainstorm they ran after a rainbow. Pharoah also found a quiet, secluded courtyard, which he kept secret from everyone, where "he retreated regularly to the comfort of the lush lawns that circled the buildings. . . . Pharoah found a shady place in the lawn and shot marbles or read a *Captain America* or *Superman* comic. Or, if the mood fit him, he just sat and daydreamed. He thought about school and next year's spelling bee. He urged on the Chicago Cubs and imagined himself a professional wrestler. . . . He wanted a place . . . where he didn't have to worry about gunshots or fire bombings. . . . In later weeks, he finally confided to his mother about his discovery. 'My mind be cleared of everything there,' he told her" (Kotlowitz, 1991, pp. 142, 143, 145).

(Gender will be discussed in chapter 9.)

PARENTS TODAY

Every person ever born has had parents, although some parents had little or nothing to do with raising their children. All of us have been or have known parents.

Earlier in this chapter we came across a variety of ways of raising children, each involving parents and usually other relatives. Social and economic conditions make parenting possible, pleasant, easy, or, difficult, harsh, and at times painful. Parents often watch helplessly as their children are hungry, or sick, or suffer other misfortunes. They are helpless because wars kill children, or needless poverty deprives them of food and clothes and shelter, or for many other reasons. For example, throughout the 1990s, the United Nations estimated that 30,000 children died each day in the world, from hunger or diseases caused by malnutrition and poverty.

On the other hand, in many other societies (such as the Tikopia, earlier in this chapter) parenting is a delight. The pace of life, the values of the society, the communal life, and the guarantee of the essentials of life to all people make parenting relatively easy and joyful. I imagine that for most parents today, raising their children is somewhere between the almost idyllic Tikopia conditions, on the one hand, and the grinding poverty which sickens and kills children, on the other.

(Various aspects of the roles of fathers and mothers are discussed in chapters 9, 10, 11, and 12. See also the reviews of research on motherhood and fatherhood in Arendell, 2000 and Marsiglio and others, 2000.)

Blaming Parents

For the past few decades, many people have written that mothers and fathers are failing in their parental duties. Sometimes mothers are criticized, sometimes fathers, and often both. We are told that parents care primarily about their own happiness and fulfillment, resort to divorce, and ignore their children's needs. Or, we read that parents are preoccupied with their careers and have little time for their sons and daughters. Generally, some historians, sociologists, and others have portrayed children as ignored, neglected, and even abandoned by their parents. (In chapters 8 and 11, I will argue that work and economic conditions require both parents to be away from their children for long hours.)

Parents are criticized from many sides. Some people blame them for abandoning their authority over children, while others think they punish children harshly. Sometimes mothers and fathers are told to be close to their children, but at other times, they (especially mothers) are criticized for being overinvolved, overprotective, and suffocating. There is no end to blaming parents. "If you stayed too long in the Jacuzzi or took a couple of drinks during pregnancy, your baby is 'at risk' for learning disabilities. . . . If you are divorced, your kids are 'at risk.' If you and your spouse stayed together for the sake of the kids and couldn't hide the tension, then they are still 'at risk'" (Coontz, 1992, pp. 208–209).

At least some parents dispute the conclusion that parents today are less involved with their children. Bane examined a variety of data on parent-children relations and concluded that "parental watchfulness has [not] decreased over the span of three generations; much [data] suggest that it has increased." For example, despite increasing divorce, more children today "live with at least one of their parents rather than with relatives, with foster parents, or in institutions" (1976, pp. 105, 99).

Demo reviewed many recent studies on parent-child relations and came to a somewhat similar conclusion as Bane. American parents, he thinks, show "supportive detachment" toward their children.

> Most parents . . . are highly supportive in that they love their children, consider their children to be important, invest years of nurturance, protection, and guidance in rearing and disciplining their children, and typically succeed quite well in transmitting norms and values from one generation to the next, especially values regarding important issues. On the other hand, however, parents also tend to be detached from their children in the sense that direct interaction is severely restricted by the substantial periods of time children spend in day-care settings, schools, before- and after-school programs, and camps; the time children spend with peers and babysitters and the countless hours they spend simply watching television (or playing video games); and by the physical absence of parents (most often fathers). The result is that although parents typically support their children, both emotionally and financially, for extended periods of the life course, the child-rearing years are characterized by low levels of face-to-face participation in shared activities. (Demo, 1992, pp. 306–307)

Demo seems to regret that schools, camps, and other settings keep children away from parents. Two comments: (1) Some of these are activities and conditions over which individual parents have little or no control. Children are required to attend school. (2) Beyond infancy and early childhood, I doubt that in any society children have been constantly with their parents or watched by them. By the time they are 5 and older, they have often played away from parental eyes. In other societies, after 7 or 8 children began performing some tasks alongside their parents. But outside of some decades during the nineteenth and twentieth centuries in the United States and other industrial societies (and even here mostly for middle-class and upper-class families), mothers have not devoted exclusive attention and time to full-time parenting (see chapter 2).

Parents today *do* face problems. Perhaps foremost is the stress they experience as they both work, often long hours, but receive few or no supports from employers and governments. Finding quality and affordable day care is especially troubling, and "they often patch together a 'crazy quilt' of multiple care combinations that cause stress for both parents and children" (Coontz, 1997, p. 69). (See ch. 11, on work.)

LeMasters and DeFrain wrote about the condemnation and problems parents face. "They take all the blame and get precious little praise for their efforts on behalf of the young." They mention social conditions and recent social changes which they think make parenting difficult, such as higher standards and judgments by teachers, doctors, and social workers (1989, pp. 2–9).

As a whole, LeMasters and DeFrain insist that raising children today is much more difficult than it was in the past. I'm not sure how much I agree with them, but I would remind all of us that always in the past parents argued that it was easier to raise children in *their* childhood. Specifically, fifty years before 1989 were the 1920s, and we know from *Middletown,* that parents then bemoaned the movies, the cars, and other cultural changes of that decade, which seemed to them to have created rebellious youth and to have made their jobs as parents miserable. Parenthood has always seemed difficult. (For a recent statement on problems middle-class parents face, see Cowan and Cowan, 2003.)

Fatherless America?

During the 1980s and 1990s, two opposing views of American fathers appeared: "the deadbeat dad and the nurturant father. . . . Good old dad is both castigated and celebrated." For example, while many studies describe the emergence of men who consciously choose to spend more time with their children, who challenge careers that keep men away from them, other writers warn of divorced or never-married fathers who give little or no time, or no financial support, to their children (Seelow, 1999).

Let us first present the argument for "fatherless America" and its consequences. According to Blankenhorn, divorced and never-married fathers are "the leading cause of declining child well-being in our society" and "the engine driving our most urgent social problems, from crime to adolescent pregnancy to child sexual abuse to domestic violence against women." Popenoe agrees: "[A]ccording to a growing body of evidence, this massive erosion of fatherhood contributes mightily to many of the major social problems of our time." Absent fathers are the "major force" behind "crime and delinquency; premature sexuality and out-of-wedlock teen births; deteriorating educational achievement; depression, substance abuse, and alienation among teenagers; and the growing number of women and children in poverty" (Blankenhorn, 1995, p. 1; Popenoe, 1996, pp. 1, 3).

Fewer children are living with both parents: 80.6 percent did so in 1960, whereas 57.7 percent did in 1990. Popenoe gives comparable figures: 17 percent of children lived apart from their biological fathers in 1960 and 36 percent did in 1990 (1996, pp. 2–3). He says that fathers are essential not only for the money they provide for the family, but also because they challenge their children, urge them to strive and compete, and develop their physical and activity levels (whereas mothers comfort and nurture children in other ways) (Blankenhorn, 1995, p. 18; Popenoe, 1996, pp. 2–3, 10–12).

Absent fathers also mean lower income and poverty for their children. Seventy-three percent of single-parent families are poor at some period before children reach 18 (and 22 percent for seven or more years), whereas only 20 percent of two-parent families are poor (2 percent for seven or more years). Popenoe concludes: "But children need more than a father's money. They need a father's attention, care, and love" (1996, pp. 55, 70).

For children six and under, in the early 1990s, 59 percent of those who lived only with their mother were classified poor by the U.S. government, whereas only 13 percent were poor if they lived with a married couple (Henslin, 1998 p. 202).

The result of absent fathers, according to Popenoe, has been "the human carnage of fatherlessness." (Carnage: "slaughter; great destruction of men, especially in battle; massacre; bloodshed.") Some of the statistics he offers: Children in one-parent families (almost all mothers) are twice as likely to drop out of high school than do children of two-parent families, and girls [are] 2.5 times more likely to become teen mothers. From 1960 to 1992, when fatherlessness increased, "teen suicide has tripled," "SAT scores have declined nearly eighty points," and "juvenile crime has increased sixfold." Popenoe quotes a study which concluded that "young people from single families or step families were 2 to 3 times more likely to have had emotional or behavioral problems than those who had both of their biological parents present in the home" (1996, pp. 9, 52–53, 57).

Focusing on children whose parents divorced, Popenoe cites another study which concluded that they performed "more poorly [no statistics given] on a wide range of assessments, such as: . . . (2) teachers' ratings of school-related behavior and mental health, including dependency, anxiety, aggression, withdrawal, inattention, peer popularity, and self-control; (3) scores in reading, spelling, and math; . . . (5) physical health ratings; and (6) referral to the school psychologists" (1996, p. 57–58).

Many other problems are attributed to divorced and never-married fathers. What are we to make of these claims? Are almost all major social problems caused by absent fathers? Would poverty, crime, and school problems disappear if all children had their father living with them?

Let us first acknowledge that single-parent families (the vast majority women) *are* poorer. In 2000, the median income for married-couple families was $59,184, and for those without husbands was $25,794. Two incomes are better than one, and women make much less money than men. Also, poor families and children live in poor neighborhoods, where schools provide lower quality education, and thus it should be no surprise that the children have lower academic achievement (*Statistical Abstract,* 2002, p. 437; Kozol, 1991; Coontz, 1997, chapter 8).

As for crime figures, they are higher in areas where single-parent families predominate than in suburban areas, but at least some of the difference is the result of more police activity (see below).

Would it help children to live with their poorly paid or unemployed fathers? Coontz cites a government study which concluded (in her words) that "even if we could reunite every child in America with both biological parents . . . two-thirds of the children who are poor today would *still* be poor" (1997, p. 140).

Thus, poor families have problems mostly because they are poor, and less because the father is absent. In Sweden and other countries, with similar divorced and never-married fathers, children do not have the school and other problems that similar children in the United States have. Houseknecht and Sastry compared the United States, Sweden, Italy, and the former West Germany on six indicators of child well-being: "educational performance . . . , percent of children in poverty by family type . . . , deaths of infants from presumed abuse . . . , juvenile delinquency rates . . . , and juvenile drug rates." They also rated the countries on "family decline" (divorce rates, percent of single-parent families, and so on). They concluded that Sweden, with the highest family decline scores, also had higher rates of child well-being (less delinquency, etc.) (1996, pp. 729, 736).

Why? Primarily because Sweden supported *all* children—no matter what the family type—with income and other benefits. For example, half of Swedish and 25 percent of French children are born to unmarried women, but both countries provide adequate income support to children. Once families do not suffer from poverty, father absence is much less of a problem (Coontz, 1997, p. 89). (A recent study of Swedish single-parent families did conclude, however, that children growing up in such families are "twice as likely as their counterparts [in two-parent families] to develop serious psychiatric illnesses and addictions later in life" [Ross, 2003]).

Stacey makes a similar observation when she summarizes research on family types: "[M]ost children from both kinds of families turn out reasonably all right, and when other parental resources—like income, education, self-esteem and a supportive social environment—are roughly similar, signs of two-parent privilege largely disappear. Most research indicates that a stable, intimate relationship with one responsible, nurturant adult is a child's surest route to becoming the same kind of adult" (1996, p. 60).

The income disadvantages of fatherless families, which Popenoe and others stress, would diminish if government provided income support to children, if more divorced fathers who are financially able paid child support, and if women's pay were equal to men's (remember that women head most single-parent families). In 2000, full-time working women averaged $32,641, which was 65 percent of men's average of $50,557. It is social policies which do not support all our children, and gender inequality, more than absent fathers, that explain most of the economic and social disadvantages of many children (*Statistical Abstract,* 2002, p. 440).

Many men never marry their children's mothers because they do not earn enough to support a family. From 1973 to 1994, the real earnings (what money can buy after inflation) of 25–year-old men declined by 31 percent (and even more for black men). In 1993, almost half of African American and Hispanic men, 35–44, did not earn adequate incomes to support a family of four (Coontz, 1997, pp. 127, 139).

Crime and other statistics offered by Popenoe and Blankenhorn are also misleading. First, if single parenthood caused crime, Sweden and Denmark would have higher delinquency rates than the United States, which they do not. Second, crime and drug statistics are created by the police and the courts. We know from various surveys, for example, that drug *use* is about the same for blacks and whites. But African Americans, who make up 13 percent of drug users, make up "35 percent of the arrests, 55 percent of the convictions and 74 percent of the sentences for drug charges." It is clear that police and courts are arresting and sentencing African Americans more than whites. William Chambliss and his students rode with police cars in Washington, D.C. "He points out that the 'intensive surveillance of black neighborhoods' leads to arrest and sentencing disparities that actually help *create* the single-parent families" (Coontz, 1997, pp. 151, 153; Jackson, 1996; Chambliss, 1994).

Thus, young men who are in prison cannot support families, and the children of poor, single-parent families have high arrest rates. Popenoe attributes these higher crime rates to absent fathers, when in fact they are largely created by policy decisions to police intensively poor areas (where more single-parent families live), and they largely leave alone areas where wealthier people live. Another study showed that children from two-parent families are more likely to get probation (and not jail) than are children from one-parent families, *when the two groups commit the same offenses* (Coontz, 1997, p. 153).

And it is a stereotype that most divorced and unmarried fathers are absent from their children's lives, even for those who do not or cannot pay child support. Two recent studies question the stereotype.

Way and Stauber interviewed forty-five adolescent girls, ages 15–19, who lived in a U.S. northeastern city. All came from poor and working class families. Nineteen lived with their fathers; of the twenty-six who did not, seven had frequent contact with them (daily to weekly), ten had occasional contact, and nine were entirely absent (three of them were dead). They concluded that their "fathers are typically very much present in their daughters' lives. . . . [T]he majority offered accounts of complex, multilayered relationships with their fathers." Twelve of the thirty-six who had contact with their fathers voiced conflicted feelings of "outrage, hurt, appreciation, and attachment." Thirteen had "open and warm relationships" with their fathers (and seven of these thirteen did not live with them) (1996, pp. 299, 304).

One girl, who does not live with her father, said about him: "We get along good. He's like—I can talk to him about—I, I think I could talk to him more than I could talk to my mother. . . . Since he's not with me all the time, he like wants to know everything I'm doing so he's always like, 'What are you doing?' and—so he gets to know more about what I do than my mother does. And my mother's there so she thinks she sees everything. Sometimes she asks. But my father asks all the time" (Way and Stauber, 1996, p. 306).

I call your attention to the seven fathers who did not live with their daughters—absentee fathers, according to some writers—who were close and important to them. We should not look at official statistics of who lives with whom and make assumptions about how these people relate to each other.

Stier and Tienda studied 811 poor fathers in Chicago in the late 1980s. Most fathers reported providing some economic support for their children. Most also gave in-kind support, such as clothes and toys. A quarter of the men said that their relatives gave some financial support to their children (such as buying a coat for a nephew or niece, as noted previously). Those who held jobs were "almost three times more likely to support their non-resident children as compared to fathers who [were] not working." Most stayed close to their nonresident children. One-third saw them daily, one-third once to twice a month, and one-third had no contact. The authors concluded that these fathers made "great efforts to maintain ties with their children," and when they had no money, they solicited support from other relatives and spent time with their children (1993, p. 198).

Newman shows that fathers and other men were very much present in their children's and families' lives in Harlem, New York City. Although officially "absent," they "often provide regular infusions of cash, food, and time to the mothers of their children with whom they do not live." A more recent review of research on "low-income, unmarried, and minority fathers" came to conclusions similar to Way and Stauber and Stier and Tienda (Newman, 1999, p. 119; Coley, 2001).

I cannot discuss all statistics and conclusions reported by Blankenhorn and Popenoe. I offered some of what they present, much of it in their own words, and I tried to show some weaknesses in their argument. They neglect other countries with similar father and family arrangements that are not plagued by crime and other problems; they ignore the social origins of some statistics, which reflect more the work of police and courts rather than differences in criminal behavior; they underestimate the role of poverty in poor school performance and other problems; they pay little attention to economic conditions which make fatherhood difficult for many men; and they wrongly assume that because fathers do not live with their children they must be absent from their lives.

One-Parent Families

The rise in one-parent families is one of the conditions Popenoe and others cite as an indication of family decline and problems for children. Let us examine some statistics, reasons for one-parent families, and situations of such parents.

In 2000, one-parent families were 27 percent of all family households with children under 18, compared to 20 percent in 1980. The trend is global. "The number of one-parent families increased from England to Australia during the 1990s" (*Statistical Abstract,* 2002, p. 53; Armas, 2001).

According to Sugarman, there are many types of single-parent families. In his words, they are "mother-headed" and "father-headed"; "unmarried," "divorced," and "widowed"; "cohabitants"; "working" and "not working"; "poor" and "nonpoor"; and "white" and "nonwhite" (2003).

Much of the focus is on births to unmarried women. Unmarried motherhood has become generally more socially acceptable, if not desirable. Surveys in the 1990s, for example, showed that only 35 percent each of women and men considered nonmarital childbearing "immoral or destructive to society." This acceptance is part of the general acceptance of more and new personal and family choices and behaviors since the 1960s, such as cohabitation and same-sex couples (Thornton and Young-DeMarco, 2001, pp. 1025–1026).

Let us look at some statistics. In 1940, only about 4.5 percent of all children born that year were born to unmarried women. It was about the same in 1950, about 7 percent in 1960, 11 percent in 1970, 19 percent in 1980, 26.6 percent in 1990, and 33.2 percent in 2000 (Ludtke, 1997, pp. 411, 412; *Statistical Abstract,* 1998, p. 76; 2002, p. 63).

Today, however, there are societies with higher rates: in 1998, 54 percent in Sweden, 45 percent in Denmark, 38 percent in France, 38 percent in the United Kingdom. Canada's rate was 28 percent, Italy's 9 percent, and Japan's 1 percent. All of these rates, except for Japan's, represent significant increases from 1980 (*Statistical Abstract,* 2001, p. 836).

Many of the children in single-parent families have considerable contact with the nonresident parent (usually the father), and with grandparents and other relatives. And if children live in one-parent families at one time, their living situations change over the years. According to one study, "Only 1 in 5 [children born to unmarried mothers] spent their entire childhood in a single-parent family, and nearly half coresided with grandparents or relatives while growing up." For example, in 1997, 3.9 million children lived with their grandparents. Of this total, in 14.2 percent of the cases, the parents also lived there; in 6.4 percent, the father only there; in 45.8 percent, the mother only there; and in 33.6 percent, neither parent did. Thus, over half of these children of one-parent families lived with grandparents (Aquilino, 1996, p. 293; *Statistical Abstract,* 1998, p. 70).

The great majority of single parents, whether never married or divorced, are women, and most discussions of single parents focus on them. (I will discuss divorced parents in chapter 12.)

Most never-married mothers fall into two large categories: (1) teenagers and young women who are poor; and (2) older women in their thirties and forties, many professional, who decide to have (or adopt) a child.

Why so many unmarried mothers? Over the last few decades sexual standards have changed, and it has become more acceptable for unmarried mothers to raise children, as we saw above. In addition, although most are poor or barely managing, unmarried women have more money and jobs than in previous years, and they can survive. Finally, especially for younger women, the fathers of their children are unable to support families (as we noted above). The largest increase in unmarried births began in 1975, which was two years after the beginning of the steady decline in young men's incomes (Coontz, 1997, p. 86).

After talking with 130 poor mothers in the Philadelphia area, Edin came to similar conclusions. The women said "they were willing and even eager to wed if the marriage represents substantial economic mobility and their husband doesn't beat them, abuse their children, insist on making all decisions, or 'fool around' with other women. If they cannot find such a man, most would rather remain single" (2000, p. 164).

But there are also personal, emotional, and social reasons why young women get pregnant and decide to keep their children.

> Many young girls who have babies—primarily the girls who are already failing in school and feeling battered by an unsupportive environment—are wrestling, too, with a sense of incompleteness in their lives. In their eyes, a baby can seem like the one person capable of making fuller and more meaningful their lives, which seem, in the disquieting moments of adolescence, to be dismal, empty, and devoid of embracing love. "You have a baby because you think it will make things different," one teenage mother said. Psychologist Judith Musick writes that "Motherhood offers these girls a ready-made role with ready-made functions, what to be, what to do." Motherhood can become a seductive route by which girls become women. . . . From a teenager's perspective, having a baby suggests the welcome possibility of gaining a new measure of control over her undirected life even if her view is illusionary. Motherhood can appear to offer her the chance to define herself anew. To get married suggests the opposite; marriage seems to offer the likelihood of being defined by someone else, of ceding control to the baby's father, and of surrendering the opportunity of self-redefinition. Marriage will come later, the girls say." (Ludtke, 1997, pp. 416–417, 419–420) (For "families started by teenagers," see Mauldon, 2003.)

For older women, the decision to have a baby and parent alone is a long and difficult one. Ludtke insists that they would prefer to have a partner, but after years of not marrying (for many reasons) they decide to have a child alone.

> Many older women who are single and aren't mothers talk about how their lives, professionally accomplished as they might be, feel sadly incomplete. Marriage, while desired by many, does not evoke the intense longing for children. A child is regarded by many as a connecting wire to the charge of emotional energy they want to give. . . . [T]he desire to give something of themselves to another compels many of these women to want a baby. But as we've learned from mothers in this book, having and raising a child on her own is not usually a woman's first choice. Rather, it's what some decide to do after years and years of anguished consideration. As

one unwed mother said, describing her perspective after she finally abandoned her lifelong hope of starting a family in the conventional way, "The nuclear family's relevance should be respected, but not necessarily idealized." (Ludtke, 1997, p. 416)

Today, single motherhood for older women has become more common and more acceptable. In 2000, there were 64,523 children born to single mothers 35–39—six times the 1965 figure. (Rodriguez, 2002a; Kantrowitz and Wingert, 2001)

Despite the support many women get from relatives, however, raising children alone is difficult, for both young and older mothers. Older single mothers "describe the immense responsibility they have assumed, and how time-consuming, difficult, and exhausting being a single parent can be." A 41-year-old single mother noted that even though, in 1993, it was easier and more acceptable to be a single parent, "I'd counsel my [11-year-old] daughter long and hard before I'd recommend the same path to her" (Ludke, 1997, p. 433; Mashberg, 1993, p. 23).

For example, since they have limited energy and time, single parents cannot supervise their children's homework or meet their teachers as often as married ones. "A teacher who has met a parent, for example, is more likely to work with the family in helping a child get past any temporary academic or behavior difficulties" (Coontz, 1997, p. 163).

Single mothers, especially younger ones, face severe economic problems. Their greatest needs are affordable housing and jobs that pay a living wage (Mulroy, 1995). As we saw earlier in this chapter, their income is less than half of two-parent families' income. (See also Sugarman, 2003 and Hays, 2003.)

There are also families with single fathers, 690 thousand in 1980 and two million in 2000. But even though such families have increased dramatically, 82.5 percent of single-parent families (9.7 million) were still headed by women in 2000 (compared to 90 percent in 1980). Most men became single parents through getting custody after divorce or separation, widowerhood, and their children's unmarried mothers giving up custody (*Statistical Abstract,* 2002, p. 51; Wong, 1999b).

They face many of the same challenges single mothers do: "juggling work and family, tight finances, arranging child care, finding time for themselves. But single fathers also said they wrestle with stereotypes of either being wonderful saviors at one extreme or bumbling incompetents at the other." Because men are raised to be independent and self-reliant, many say they find it difficult to ask for help. Others do, as did most of the ten divorced single fathers in my 1992 study (Wong, 1999b; Rodriguez, 2001b; Liazos, 1995).

Single fathers have more income than single mothers do, but less than married couples. In 2000, married couples with both spouses working had a median income of $69,463, and $39,735 if the wife had no job. Male householders with no wife had a median income of $37,529, and female householder families with no husband present, $25,704 (some of these families, however, had no children under 18.) (*Statistical Abstract,* 2002, p. 438).

But most single parents, like other parents, also report joys. For most of them, their lives are richer and more fulfilled, despite the problems I describe above, than they would have been without children. We find evidence of joy and satisfaction in many books about poor people (Stack, 1974 and 1996; Kotlowitz, 1991; Newman, 1999).

Gay and Lesbian Parents

Throughout history gays and lesbians have become parents through children they conceived in heterosexual unions before they left those relationships. More recently, lesbians have been adopting or conceiving children (through alternative insemination), and gay men have begun to adopt children or have them through a surrogate parent. In 1999, only Florida prohibited gay and lesbian people from adopting, but in reality it is often difficult for them to do so (Jacobs, 1992; Stacey, 1996, 2003; Associated Press, 1999c).

Until recently, the vast majority of gay and lesbian parents had children in heterosexual marriages. After divorce, many former husbands agreed to custody of the children by the now openly lesbian mother (in rare cases, gay fathers were given custody by their former wives). But when divorcing parents did not agree on child custody, newly open lesbian and gay parents simply gave up in the past. Before 1969, we know of only six such parents who sued for child custody. Fifty more did so in the 1970s, and many more have since. According to Stacey, they all lost, but some received shared custody (1996, p. 109–110).

Why do lesbians want to become parents? "For the same reasons heterosexual women do. They love children. For lesbians wanting to become mothers, . . . the process is much more deliberate. There is a lot to think through." It's the same for men: "You know, I grew up expecting to fall in love, to mate for life and to raise a family. Just because it was a man I fell in love with doesn't mean I have to change that" (Longcope, 1992, p. 42; Jacobs, 1992, p. 1.).

There seems to be more acceptance of gay and lesbian parents today compared to decades ago. Children's books present families with two mothers or two fathers, for example. Sooner or later, most relatives and friends accept the families and the children. But gay and lesbian parenthood is a long way from full acceptance. In a recent survey, only about 25 percent of the respondents said they would consider "two lesbian women (or two gay men) living with children they are raising together" a family (11 percent were not sure, and about 63 percent would not) (cited in Skolnick, 1996, p. 18; no date of survey is given).

A few gay parents report name-calling, and for many more "there is no escaping the glances of disapproval." And when the children become teens, they are likely to meet some harassment and disapproval from their peers, since the adolescent culture remains "mercilessly homophobic." But the increasing social and legal acceptance of same-sex marriage should mean same-sex families with children will also become more acceptabale. In a study of lesbian families in England, the authors concluded that the children "were no more likely than their counterparts from heterosexual single-parent families to experience peer stigma during adolescence, and most were able to integrate close friends with family life" (Jacobs, 1992, p. 5; Stacey, 1996, p. 133; Tasker and Golombok, 1997, pp. 100–101).

What happens to the children? Some writers insist they will suffer emotionally from the social disapproval they will meet, they will grow up confused about their gender identity, and they may become themselves gay or lesbian. But considerable research has shown that these children do as well as children of heterosexual couples. In their study of lesbian mothers in England, Tasker and Golombok showed that the children were positive about their family life, got along with other children, showed no more anxiety or depression than other children, were clear about their gender identity, and were no more likely to become gay or lesbian. And in 2002, the American Academy of Pediatrics stated that same-sex couples "can provide the loving, stable, and emotionally healthy family life that children need" (Tanner, 2002; see also Patterson, 2000, and Stacey, 2003).

Stacey's review of research on children of gay and lesbian parents came to the same conclusion. Children who are loved by their parents—any parents—and who are given guidance, care, and their basic needs, do well. And when gay or lesbian *couples* raise children, they receive the benefits of two parents. They also receive support from extended kin communities that the parents create from their relatives and friends (1996, pp. 128–144).

CONCLUSION

We traveled a long way in this chapter. We began with the joys of parenthood and childhood, to remind ourselves that joys do exist despite problems and conflicts. We read about childhood in a variety of non-industrial societies and explored the feeding, sleeping, holding, and general raising of children in those societies. We also looked at parents and children in African American communities around 1970 and 1990. After a brief history of parenthood and childhood in the United States, we explored a variety of issues and conditions of children and parents today. We closed with gay and lesbian parents, who are struggling to create their own families in which to raise children.

For societies to survive, for older people to live in functioning communities that will provide for their needs, children must be born and raised. The societies and economies in which we live shape and guide how we live together as parents and children—who cares for the children and in what settings. That is a lesson we learn when we examine childhood through time and across cultures. We cannot return to olden times and non-industrial societies, but we might learn from their experiences and change our communities and workplaces to meet our own needs and values.

I end with a simple conclusion: Both children and parents benefit when we raise children in extended families and communities, with parents, relatives, grandparents, neighbors, and friends all involved. Workplaces, schools, child-care institutions, governments, and communities all need to understand and practice that principle.

6

Living in Families

As we discuss conflicts, historical changes, roles, and other conditions and problems that families face, we may forget that what gives reality to families are the times people spend with each other, and the memories of those times. Without these experiences, and the relishing of them in memory, families cannot exist.

Family members share a wide variety of activities: eating meals, taking walks, telling and sharing stories, watching TV and movies, catching up on each other's news, working together (especially in older days), driving someone to the doctor or the store, baking cookies, reading bedtime stories, picnicking, fishing, planning and holding family reunions, writing letters, talking on the phone, baby sitting for a relative's children, exchanging presents on religious holidays and birthdays and other occasions, giving advice, sitting quietly by a fireplace. The list could on for pages.

When my students write their family histories, they describe such experiences and activities, which they recall fondly. As we get older, we laugh or cry as we retell and share them again and again with each other, and as we tell them to friends.

These daily realities of our lives, which are the substance of our families, are largely missing from family texts. We need to pay attention to them, and to understand what may seem too obvious to state: families *are* these shared experiences and memories.

I will discuss five areas of family living: sharing meals, having fun, the work of kinship, caregiving, and being homeless.

COOKING AND EATING MEALS

Everett Hughes, who taught sociology at Brandeis University in the 1960s, once told us that a meal is more than eating. It is a meaningful social occasion when people share news, hopes, plans, experiences, worries, laughs, stories, and memories. Sometimes anger, conflict, and even violence also take place.

Eating together has even wider social significance. Throughout the world, families and friends share food during weddings, funerals, and other happy or sad occasions. At parties we offer food, as we also do to visitors and guests. Poor people often borrow money so they can cook a meal for relatives. Everywhere, family gatherings of all types become occasions for elaborate meals. Mangione's parents gave a banquet for relatives who were leaving for California, but when the relatives changed their minds and stayed in Rochester, his parents gave another meal to celebrate their staying (Mangione, 1942, p. 127)..

Strangely, family textbooks seem to ignore the importance of food for families. I examined ten of them, all published in 2000 and later, looking through the tables of contents and for index entries for cooking, dinner, eating, food, feeding the family, and meals. There is no mention at all of meals and cooking in seven of them, and two make passing references to food in relation to other topics (such as class). The only exception is the section on "feeding the family" in Aulette (2002, pp. 176–78).

Families around the world enjoy meals together. It is a time to nurture the body and to share each other's lives. *(Photo by Anna Piller.)*

Before I discuss family meals today and their meaning, I present a few examples from U.S. history.

Verna Mae Slone's *What My Heart Wants to Tell*, first discussed in chapter 1, tells her family's history in the Appalachian mountains from the 1860s to the 1970s. In the olden days, people raised almost all their food and cooked all meals. Meals were shared with family, of course, but also with neighbors who passed by at mealtimes, and with everyone who came together for a "workin" (to help a neighbor with a building project). "The men were fed first, then the women and children, but there was always enough for everyone and a lot of jokes and plenty of laughter. They worked together, ate together, and loved each other as neighbors were intended to since time began" (1979, p. 40).

Mangione's Italian family gathered regularly every Sunday. His parents, siblings, aunts, uncles, cousins, and as many relatives as could crowd into the house came together to eat, talk, play cards, and tell stories. In addition, there were banquets to celebrate holidays, baptisms, and other occasions. "There was a banquet for as many occasions as my father could imagine, and his imagination was fertile." His mother cooked meals during the week and his father on Sunday. "His meals had an extravagance about them that was far out of proportion to his salary. To finance them he often had to borrow money. But for him that was less important than sharing the joy and warmth that good food and gay company created" (1942, pp. 127, 131).

As among Italians in Rochester in the 1920s, relatives also shared meals in Plainville around 1940. "People are criticized for not 'eating a meal' with kin folks. . . . People say, 'it's about time we eat at John's, to show 'em we're still kin'" (West, 1945, pp. 67–68).

Poor black people in a midwestern city in the late 1960s also celebrated family gatherings with food. "Viola and Leo frequently see their relatives who are residing in The Flats, in neighboring counties, and in Chicago and St. Louis. . . . When relatives come unexpectedly . . . it is the occasion for a big and festive meal. The women devote all day to preparing it" (Stack, 1974, p. 7).

Thus, daily meals, Sunday dinners, banquets for special occasions, holiday family gatherings, and planned and unplanned visits from relatives all become opportunities to affirm, create, and renew family ties. Cooking for our relatives and sharing food help to form and generate families.

Meals are social events we create consciously. Generally, it is women who produce them. To ensure that all family members can be present, meals take planning. DeVault cites a mother who organized meals and meal times to include her infant daughter and husband returning from work: "I'll pull her high chair up so that she can be part of the family. . . . I think she was six months old when she started eating as part of the family—breakfast, lunch and dinner. We adjusted our schedule a little bit to her schedule. And it worked out really well. Now, everything is as a family. . . . If it's real ugly outside and I know my husband's going to want a hot meal—which is all the time—and I want the house to warm up and smell good, I'll make stew. Or I'll bake a cake." DeVault comments: "As she thinks ahead toward the evening meal, she plans to produce an experience: the return to a warm and pleasant house" (1991, p. 60).

It takes thought and planning to arrange meals to accommodate everyone's schedules. But by eating at the same time, parents and children share more than food. Jean, one of the women DeVault interviewed, recalls her childhood meals: "We'd sit down and everybody would tell what they had done that day. And my father, when the main meal was over, you know, like if there was dessert or something, that was time for Daddy to give us quizzes, on world capitals or something like that." Now a mother, Jean struggles to create similar times for her family (DeVault, 1991, p. 63).

Women, and some men, who plan, organize, and cook daily meals, Sunday gatherings, and special banquets produce and re-produce families; "[T]hey organize their cooking so as to produce a group life for their families. . . . Their efforts are directed toward creating patterns of joint activity out of the otherwise separate lives of family members" (DeVault, 1991, p. 64).

It may be that family mealtimes are fewer, shorter, and more difficult to arrange than in the past. Indeed, as long ago as the 1920s people bemoaned the perceived decline of family meals, attributing it to the arrival of the automobile and other developments. People began going for long Sunday drives, thus reducing the time left for "the leisurely Sunday noon dinner of a generation ago at which extra leaves had to be put in the table for the company of relatives and friends who sat down to the great Sunday roast." Even the daily evening meal was reduced to "an informal 'bite'" as people took evening drives (Lynd and Lynd, 1929, p. 153).

Modern families, especially with most mothers now holding jobs, may be further stressed to find time for long meals, or even any meals. In *The Time Bind*, Hochschild presents a dark and gloomy portrait of family meals and family times. Families have little time to be together as both parents work long hours. Breakfasts are rushed for everyone to get out the door; evening meals are no less rushed, as parents strive to cook and then get children to bed. Parents rush through cooking and eating, and "they ignore the contribution that a leisurely pace can make to fulfillment, so that a rapid dinner, followed by a speedy bath and bedtime story—if part of 'quality time'—is counted as 'worth the same' as a slower version of the same events." According to Hochschild, many children resisted and protested against this speed up (1997, p. 212).

Almost echoing the Lynds (see above), Hochschild laments the modern working conditions that are making family meals a memory. Long ago, when industrialism made it impossible for family members to work together, to "plant . . . the corn, harvest . . . the wheat, shear . . . the sheep," family meals became the times for families to be together. Now with parents working long hours, "the family gathering is slowly losing its actuality and becoming like a phantom limb, there only in memory or fantasy" (1997, p. 237).

Preparation and cooking are a major part of the enjoyment and social importance of meals. And cooking with our children becomes another occasion for being with them. For example, as they get older we may bake cookies with them. Increasingly, however, families do less cooking, going out to quick meals or having more take-out meals, frozen dinners, and instant mixes. And many rushed parents who mean to spend time cooking with their children find that work intrudes. "One ad features a portable phone to show that the working mother can make business calls while baking cookies with her daughter" (Hochschild, 1997, p. 214).

Instead of cooking *with* their parents, many children today seem to need to cook *for* themselves and their parents. In 1999, "among children ages 9 to 17, almost half regularly prepare meals for themselves, up from 15 percent in 1988." Much of what these children do is heating prepared meals, of course, or pouring milk on cereal. In these hectic days, some parents create family time by having their children assist them while they prepare meals. "We can talk about the day while we're doing this stuff" (Sege, 1999, p. A10).

And according to a 1990 *New York Times*/CBS News poll, 80 percent of parents "typically" had week-night meals with their children. "Sixty-six percent said . . . that everyone in the family had dinner the previous night." However, meals were short. Thirty-one percent spent more than half an hour at the dinner table, 48 percent half an hour, and 20 percent less than half an hour. Some of the meals were at fast-food restaurants. Most reported that they talked while they ate, but 42 percent watched TV. Short as they often were, family dinners were seen as "the linchpin of the day, a respite from the chaos and separation in daily life" (Kleiman, 1990).

We may conclude that family meals remain important, that families strive to have them, but that they are often short and rushed (See also Daly, 2001.).

BEING TOGETHER AND HAVING FUN

In the last chapter, I described some of the restful and joyous times with my daughters. These warm memories bring a smile to my face. All families have similar experiences: vacations and trips, stories we read to our children and stories we tell later, shopping, cooking and eating meals, and so much more. And as important as any activity is "boring time": just being together, doing nothing in particular, even being silent near each other. (A divorced father told me about boring time in 1992; see Liazos, 1995).

More in the past than today, families would tell stories with relatives, and often with neighbors. All over the world, people told stories. Less family time and the various media—beginning with movies in the 1920s—have reduced drastically this ancient tradition (Turnbull, 1961; Lynd and Lynd, 1929; Ewen, 1985, ch. 8; Hochschild 1997).

Slone describes vividly the setting of storytelling with her neighboring Appalachian families: "We'd gather around the fire, if it was winter, or on the porch, around a 'gnat' smoke made by burning rags, if it was summer. The older folks would sit in chairs with the young children in their laps, or huddled around their feet. That's when we would hear all these scary . . . tales" (1979, p. 99).

In addition to their long and elaborate meals, Mangione's family—especially his uncle Nino—devoted hours to telling, retelling, and embellishing a variety of stories. About 15–20 years later, when Mangione wrote *Mount Allegro,* he described the large family gatherings with warmth and humor, and retold the stories in minute detail.

Uncle Nino "had a flair for making the most ordinary situations absorbing and if he was sometimes suspected of stretching a narrative into the realm of fancy, he was forgiven on the grounds that he was only doing what Dante might have done. . . . His most effective trick was to introduce a climax every few minutes, piling one on top of the other, and giving the impression all the while he told the story that each climax was the final one. He punctuated his stories with long, tantalizing pauses and a versatile set of facial expressions, which included a diabolically suggestive leer and the raising of either his left or right redhaired eyebrow" (Mangione,1942, p. 141).

More recently, some families still told stories. Billie and Hank had lived in the North for many years, but eventually Billie tired of life there and returned South with the children. (Hank stayed in the North for a few more years). They lived very simply, but the first "two years were

. . . the best. They had no electricity. They had three rooms and a well—no running water, no kitchen, no bathroom. They cooked outside. . . . After it got dark, they would go inside on top of the bed and tell stories. The way Billie remembered it, every night a different one of them would tell stories. They had not TV, of course, so they played games" (Stack, 1996, pp. 24–25).

In addition to storytelling, relatives do many other things with each other. In neighborhoods where adult children and their parents live near each other, where extended families are alive, contact is constant. Young and Willmott describe a working-class neighborhood in London in the 1950s: "Mrs. Wilkins is in and out of her mother's all day. She shops with her in the morning and goes round there for a cup of tea in the afternoon. 'Then any time during the day, if I want a bit of salt or something like that, I go round to Mum to get it and have a bit of chat while I'm there.' If the children have anything wrong with them, 'I usually go round to my Mum and have a little chat. If she thinks it's serious enough I'll take him to the doctor.' Her mother looked after Marilyn, the oldest child, for nearly three years" (1957, p. 44).

Families, in addition to practicing cultural traditions such as Thanksgiving and Christmas, also develop individual and special ones. For example, one of my students once wrote about parties held by her grandparents every Friday evening "for the adults, teenage children, and their friends." Other students write of weekly or monthly shopping trips with their grandparents, regular vacations with extended families, and so on. After my divorce, in addition to every other weekend and school vacations, my daughters stayed with me every Wednesday evening, and I would take them to school Thursday morning. Fairly soon I began baking muffins for breakfast and it became a tradition. Now that they visit as adults, I still bake muffins, and the warm kitchen and steaming muffins remind me of their childhood and the mornings we drove to their school, and some of the conversations we had on the way.

Family time became increasingly hard to find as the twentieth century progressed. Families struggled to have time together in the late 1970s, and some working-class parents turned to family camping to recapture or create the close and intimate family life they felt missing in their lives. Cerullo and Ewen went camping with some of these families near Worcester, Massachusetts. They saw and were told that camping was an escape from all the conditions that made family life difficult. While camping, parents and children were freed from work, housework, and school demands, and all time became family time. "Many people turned to camping in response to wanting some time to 'be together' and to 'be a family.' 'Camping is a way to keep the family together.' 'This is the only time to really be a family. At home everybody's off in their own direction'" (1982, p. 32).

One wonders how much time families have for each other today. Hochschild's *The Time Bind* is a sobering and worrisome account of families struggling to find hours, even minutes, to be together.

> Working parents exhibit an understandable desire to build sanctuaries of family time, free from pressure, in which they can devote themselves to only one activity or one relationship. So, for instance, the time between 8 and 8:45 p.m. may be cordoned off as 'quality time' for parents and child, and that between 9:15 and 10 p.m. as quality time for a couple (once the children are in bed). Such time boundaries must then be guarded against other time demands—calls from the office, from a neighbor to arrange tomorrow's car pool, from a child's friend about homework. Yet these brief respites of "relaxed time" themselves come to look more and more like little segments of job time, with parents punching in and out as if on a time clock. When Denise Hampton read *The Narnia Chronicles* to her two sons at night, for instance, she made a special effort not to think about the e-mail piling up for her in cyberspace and the memos she might soon have to compose and e-mail back. Thus, for her, "relaxed" quality time actually took discipline, focus, and energy, just like work (Hochschild, 1997, pp. 211–212). (For a study of rushed family time, see Daly, 2001.)

We seem to have come a long way from the family gatherings described by Slone and Mangione.

"WOMEN, FAMILIES, AND THE WORK OF KINSHIP"

Women do most of the planning, cooking, and organizing of meals, as well as planning most other family activities like shopping and vacations. These and similar activities help constitute families. They are examples of what Micaela di Leonardo calls "the work of kinship," kin work for short (1987).

"By kin work I refer to the conception, maintenance, and ritual celebration of cross-household kin ties, including visits, letters, telephone calls, presents, and cards to kin; the organization of holiday gatherings; the creation and maintenance of quasi-kin relations; decisions to neglect or to intensify particular ties; the mental work of reflection about all these activities; and the creation and communication of altering images of family and kin vis-à-vis the images of others, both folk and mass media" (p. 420).

Before we continue with a summary and discussion of di Leonardo's paper, let us look at two examples of kin work.

Avoiding family conflicts, resolving them if they occur, and keeping and making peace, are necessary in most families. In the 1960s, Chinas studied women in a Mexican community. They played many important roles: organized fiestas and family gatherings, sold in the market to support their families, cooperated to prevent male violence in public places, and avoided and resolved family conflicts. Chinas found that "women elders are the keepers of peace and order in fiestas. They also have great authority within the extended kin network as arbiters of kin disputes and as enforcers of kin obligations." For example, when Cata was angry at his wife Chica, he broke some windows in their house. Ramon, Chica's brother, was irate when he learned what Cata did and was likely to attack him. A number of women stepped in and arranged to have Cata jailed for two days and get him out of harm's way. They then had the glass panes replaced (paid mostly by Cata's relatives) while Ramon stayed away. "By now I had observed at least a dozen instances, most of them less dramatic than the window case, in which San Juan women, both relatives and neighbors, cooperated to avert confrontations between men" (1992, p. 102; 1993, p. 124).

Mangione's mother and other female relatives were also peacekeepers in their Italian community in the 1920s. Family feuds came about, for example, because a relative felt insulted that he was not invited for a family dinner. (Their small homes could not accommodate everyone.) After a fight between his father and uncle Nino, Mangione's mother and aunt (Nino's wife) "could not see each other every day as they had. . . . The sisters met secretly at the home of relatives, at first to console each other, then to plot a peace offensive. It was not an easy peace to plot." After some plotting, preparation, and setbacks, peace was restored (1942, pp. 32–37).

Older women also become the centers of their family's social life. An example were the 'Mums' in Bethnal Green, a working-class community in East London in the 1950s. Speaking of her family, Mrs. Powers said: "[I]f anyone wants to know what's going on [with our family], they always go round to Mum's." When Mum died, relatives saw less of each other. "Of the 162 married, widowed, and divorced women in the general sample with their mothers alive, 35 per cent had seen a sister in the previous day, against 16 per cent of the 242 whose mothers were dead. 'It all broke up when Mum died,' said one woman." The mother's death also usually meant less contact with aunts, uncles, and cousins. "'You lose track of your cousins,' said Mrs. Jeffreys, 'once your aunts have gone'" (Young and Willmott, 1957, pp. 77, 78, 84).

From the 1950s to the early 1990s, my two aunts in Worcester, Massachusetts, were Mums, too, as are older women in many societies. Their children went to their homes for Sunday dinner, and whenever I visited my aunts on Sundays I also saw my cousins. Now that my aunts are dead, I rarely see or talk with my cousins, except for funerals and weddings. As we see from the examples above, the kin work women do crosses households to bring together extended family members; and "maintaining these contacts, this sense of family, takes time, intention, and skill." It also involves knowing and telling family history. In talking with women, di Leonardo found that they knew not only their own family's history but often also knew more of their husband's. And women wrote cards and letters to, bought presents for, and called both their own and their husband's relatives (di Leonardo, 1987, p. 420).

Di Leonardo maintains that women of all classes, ethnic groups, and races do kin work. And it is primarily women who perform it. "American men in general do not take on these tasks [holiday card lists, gift buying, etc.] any more than they do housework and child care—and probably less, as these tasks have not yet been the subject of intense public debate" (p. 423).

We shall see that women still do most housework and child care, but men are doing more of both than they did in the past. Thus it may come about that men will also gradually begin to share in kin work, or it will not get done. A few younger couples I spoke with, where both parents have jobs outside the home, told me that, for example, if the man does not send out Christmas cards to his relatives, it simply goes undone.

When women die, move, divorce, take time-consuming jobs, or want more time for themselves, "Christmas card lists, organized holiday gatherings, multifamily dinners, letters, visits, and phone calls" usually wane or disappear (but sometimes another woman assumes the work). Much of the kin work di Leonardo and others describe was women's domain when they were full-time housewives. As most women now have jobs, unless men learn to share kin work, families will lose some of their vitality, connections, and history. We shall all be poorer (di Leonardo, 1987, p. 423).

CAREGIVING

Caregiving is another essential experience of family living. Family members provide care for each other, at all stages of life: parents raise children and tend to them when they are ill; spouses nurse each other when they are sick; and adult children take care of their ill and frail elderly parents. (The following discussion focuses on caregiving to elderly people either by spouses or adult children.)

History

As we have seen, in Plymouth Plantation of the 1680s there were no hospitals or nursing homes. By necessity, family members tended to the needs of ill, frail, and elderly people. And the community placed those few without children, spouses, or siblings in a family. Over a hundred years later, it was still family members, mostly women, who nursed the sick and cared for parents. Ulrich points out, however, that neighbors often helped each other with births and illnesses. In mid-1800s New England, we find that family members, with much help from neighbors, still provided almost all care for ill and elderly relatives. Nursing family members was largely women's duty, but men "often cared for the sick." Men farmers and artisans took time off from their work to provide this care. Men, however, cared only for other men, with the exception of married men who nursed their ill wives (Demos, 1970; Ulrich, 1987; Hansen, 1994).

Caregiving Today

With the major exception of when older parents are very ill and are in hospitals or nursing homes, families still provide most care. And as in earlier days, women do most of the caregiving. All of the studies I discuss below provide data to support these conclusions. It is women, "in the home, as mothers, daughters, and wives; in the workplace, as nurses and child-care workers . . . who do the work of caregiving" (Hansen and Garey, 1998, p. 521). (For a study of men giving care, see Harris and Bichler, 1997.)

What do adult children do for their parents? They "offer help with the following activities: getting out of bed and going to the bathroom, shopping for food, traveling, doing laundry, preparing meals, doing housework, bathing, taking medicine, dressing, getting around the house, and providing personal, supportive communication" (Barrow, 1996, p. 271).

Abel says that families provided 70–80 percent of long-term care in the late 1980s. In 1998, the National Alliance for Caregiving estimated that "family caregiving saves society from $113 billion to $286 billion a year," with the care provided by 15 million caregivers. A 1997 study concluded that "at least 22 million Americans provide care to an older friend or relative, and one quarter of caregivers help two people" (Abel, 1989; Jackson, 2003; Knox, 1999).

Forty percent of caregiving is provided by spouses (26 percent wives, 14 percent husbands), 30 percent by daughters, and 10 percent by sons. Some elders have no available relatives, however. "Studies show that approximately 25 percent of elders have no surviving children or siblings residing close enough to provide regular assistance." In a study of people with AIDS, Schiller found that 74 percent lived with family (mostly mothers and sisters) and the rest were in regular contact with their families (Barrow, 1996, pp. 269–271; Schiller, 1993).

Data are consistent that caregiving is primarily women's work. In Abel's study, women were 77 percent of adult children caregivers and 64 percent of spousal ones; in Merrill's study, 42 of the 50 were women; and in Piercy's, 14 of the 17 were women. In "The invisible women: Caregiving and AIDS," Schiller explains that "women family members [mothers and sisters are] the major source of care for people with AIDS in the United States." She also points out that people who write about health care for AIDS patients ignore the overwhelming care provided by families and women (Abel, 1989; Merrill, 1997; Piercy, 1998; Schiller, 1993, p. 540).

Men are beginning to provide more care to elderly relatives, however. Various surveys show that men are 30–40 percent of caregivers. "Men are just as likely as women to help an elder with . . . dressing, bathing, transportation, and housework" (Jackson, 2003).

Call to Home and Caregiving

Among the many reasons African Americans had for returning to the South during the 1970s and 1980s was an ailing parent or grandparent back home who needed care. Chapter 5 of *Call to Home,* "Clyde's Dilemma," explores their motives, reflections, emotions, and experiences.

"Clyde's 'letter' is a research construct designed to elicit discussion of tensions between personal agendas and family pressures. . . . [T]he vast majority of people who spoke with me about Clyde's dilemma recounted personal experience caring for older family members."

This is the "letter" Stack's respondents read:

> Dear Abby:
> I am an unmarried man who lives in Washington, D.C. I work part-time as a security guard. My parents live back home in Rosedale, which is a small town out in the country, about 250 miles south of D.C. My mother has been bedridden for a couple of years, and my father has sugar and recently lost a leg, so he can't take care of her anymore. My two sisters in New Jersey have both had a turn taking care of them and hope to move back home eventually, but right now the older one has a good job and the younger one just got married. Both of my sisters think I am the one who should go back home and take care of my parents. What do you think I should do? (Stack, 1996, p. 108)

Most respondents had some concern about a man bathing, dressing, and otherwise caring for a woman, even if he is a son, although some concluded he had to do it. Others wanted to know why the sisters could not move back home. All struggled with the dilemma and spoke about their lives. Let us listen to some of them.

Ralph, age 33, asked for a leave of absence from his job to care for an ailing grandfather; "but they didn't grant it to me, so I just gave my job up and came home. My mother came home from the hospital and died four months later. I stayed on to take care of my grandfather. He seemed more like my father—I've never known my father" (Stack, 1996, p. 109).

Clayton, age 42: "If it were me instead of Clyde? Oh Lord. I guess I would come home and take care of her. Somebody has to do it. You wouldn't want to put them in a nursing home. I think families should take care of families. Getting old is no disgrace. It's a cycle. They had to feed us and wipe our butt. We just do the same for them. That's the way I feel about it" (Stack, 1996, p. 112).

Marlene, age 35: "I think Clyde should make arrangements for somebody to stay with his mother or have her placed in a nursing home. That way, it won't impose so many hardships and disrupt their children's lives. They won't have to give up their jobs. All three should chip in to pay for help."

But for her own father, "Of course, we didn't put him anywhere. When my father was sick, we rotated the care between the three of us. We were all back here [South] by that time. He didn't have to go to a nursing home" (Stack, 1996, p. 112, 114).

And finally Wilma, age 42: "My mother lived in the house for two years before she died in 1982. My father has been bedridden for the past two years. Because of that, I'm not working. I just can't. There have been days when I wanted to shove Papa into a rest home, but I promised him I never would as long as I was breathing" (Stack, 1996, p. 121).

Caregiving has been more common in African American, Hispanic, and Asian families. Cultural values and traditions oblige adult children to care for their elderly parents. But the traditions may be weakening. For example, as Asian families become more "Americanized," more elders turn to assisted living and nursing home facilities in their last years (Radina, 2001; Kong, 2002).

Crisis in and Solutions of Caregiving

As most of us live longer than our ancestors did, there are more of us who need care, and for more years. At the same time, people are having fewer children and most women have jobs outside the home. Thus, "the need for care is growing while the supply is declining." Hochschild fears that like time with children and for family is diminishing, care for our parents may also be the victim of less time, unless we change our economy, jobs, and values (1995, p. 532).

She thinks we have four options:

1. We may want to return to the 1950s and earlier times by sending most women back home. They could become full-time housewives and attend to their children's, husbands', and parents' needs. For economic and other reasons, this is impossible for most women and families.

2. A second solution is to "rid ourselves of the image of mother-and-child, replace it with nothing, and claim that everyone is happy anyway. . . . [W]e leave matters much as they are—with women in the labor force and men doing little at home. We *legitimate* the care deficit by reducing the range of ideas about what a child, wife, husband, aged parent, or home 'really needs' to thrive." We could deny the need for human contact and care by declaring that living alone and self-care are good for our parents (Hochschild, 1995, p. 533).

3. We could expand institutional care to provide all caregiving: from paid people who visit elders at home to clean, cook, etc.; to the recently arising "assisted living" facilities where older people have their meals, laundry, and other needs met; to nursing homes and hospitals where sick elders are cared for—these services and other settings would relieve children of most or all caregiving responsibilities.

4. The fourth solution is what many families today try to fashion: care for their parents, with some assistance from relatives and institutions. It would require a number of changes if we wish to make it widely practiced: "male participation at home, time schedules in the work place, and the value placed on care." In short, women *and* men would need to work fewer

hours, and workplaces should change to encourage shorter days, so men and women would have more time to care for their parents (and time for each other, their children, their extended families, their friends and communities) (Hochschild, 1995, p. 535).

Experiences of Caregiving

As we saw in the discussion of "Clyde's dilemma," most children clearly feel a responsibility to care for their parents. Reviewing research on adult children and their parents, Barrow concluded that they "feel a strong moral obligation to provide care for disabled parents." In many ways, it is a rewarding loving experience (1996, p. 267).

But there are stresses, dilemmas, and conflicts. Adult children have jobs, usually their own children and spouses, and friends. It is often almost impossible to care adequately for elderly parents in the midst of our own jobs, obligations to others, and our own needs and limits.

Abel's study describes well the experience of caregiving, and her findings typify those of other studies. Summarizing other studies and her own, she tells us that most instances of caregiving "fall disproportionately on a single individual. Spouses are the most common caregivers, followed by adult children, then other relatives, then finally friends and neighbors." Many of the forty women she interviewed "claimed that they found caregiving rewarding and fulfilling, but virtually all also insisted that it was a source of strain." Most had not anticipated it and "had little warning that they would be called upon to provide care." Several were proud of the quality care they provided and "derived emotional benefits from the experience" (Abel, 1989, pp. 557–562).

Caregiving competed with their work and many sought to reduce work hours and responsibilities. These forty women reduced drastically their leisure, time with friends, and community work. I have known women who left their jobs for full-time caring of their parents, and Stack's and other studies tell similar stories.

The emotional impact was strong.

> Caregiving brought women into intimate contact with their parents, often for the first time since they had been adolescents. Issues they assumed had been fully resolved suddenly reemerged. Several women were shocked by the intensity of the feelings this experience provoked. Old resentments suddenly had renewed force. Many women also acknowledged that they found themselves once again looking to their parents for approval and striving to please them. . . .
>
> Many women spoke about how difficult it was for them to assume responsibility for their parents' lives. Many were acutely aware that their parents resented their assertions of authority. These caregivers saw themselves wounding their parents further by taking action. . . .
>
> In short, parent care involves constant tensions between attachment and loss, pleasing and caring, seeking to preserve an older person's dignity and exerting unaccustomed authority, overcoming resistance to care and fulfilling extravagant demands, reviving a relationship and transforming it. (Abel, 1989, p. 561)

Abel's respondents did want siblings to support them in the decisions they made along the way of caring for the parents, they wanted help with chores, and they wanted some time off. All studies I read stress that caregivers should receive assistance from relatives, friends, and professionals in all three areas. Without that assistance, caregiving becomes overwhelming. The forty women Abel interviewed, however, reported little help from siblings, children, and friends. Indeed, they spent less time with their friends than they had in the past, because they had less time and they were reluctant to ask too much from them.

They did turn to support groups of adult children taking care of parents. There they found advice, information, some perspective, and understanding listeners. They were encouraged to express their emotions and find some relief by seeking outside help. Abel concluded:

"Certainly, caring for elderly parents encroached on various aspects of the lives of the women I interviewed and produced serious emotional difficulties. Nevertheless, it also was a profound human experience which could not be neatly subsumed under the terms stress and burden" (Abel, 1989, p. 570).

In her study, Piercy found that the women caregivers were "sensitive to the needs and desires of older family members. . . . [They showed] concern for maintaining the older person's autonomy for as long as possible, . . . meeting the care recipient's emotional needs, and respecting or deferring to the wishes of the older person. . . . A 40–year-old grandson described his efforts to cheer up his grandmother in this manner: 'One of the things I try to do when I go by is not so much talk about the present because a lot of times the present is not a very positive thing. . . . So I try to focus on the past, and what I try to do is just talk about things that provoke memories and, hopefully, good memories—times she visited when we were young, things they did for us when we were young, talk about my grandfather, you know, the way things used to be'" (Piercy, 1998, p. 113; see also Merrill, 1997).

The Stresses of Caregiving

Caregiving is necessary and rewarding; it is what family members owe to each other. But it also entails painful decisions and strains.

Carol Stack's reflections and observations paint some of the dilemmas we face. "Many of us have been pressed into service or have anticipated situations in which we might be called upon for help. Rich people can sometimes buy their way out of the family draft by hiring help of various kinds; poor people must work as their own best help. Many of us, rich and poor, bitterly resent being asked to defer our own dreams, interrupt our own lives, forget about our own plans, so we might attend, on a permanent or long-term basis, to somebody else's needs" (1996, p. 102).

Jimmy, a widower, had his leg amputated and would need care for many years. "Tonesha, his oldest daughter, lives at home with her father while she goes to junior college, and takes good care of him. . . . [But Jimmy] is wondering how long she will be willing to serve. After she finishes school, won't she want a good job somewhere? Will she marry someone who wants to move away, or have so many children of her own that she no longer has time for her invalid father? And what if she, too, becomes a diabetic? . . . Who will he call on after Tonesha has helped as much as she can help?" (Stack, 1996, pp. 100, 103).

Stack's observations and other studies make us aware of the stress caregivers undergo, often for years. A recent study quantified some of the effects stress brings about. Comparing older people who took care of their spouses with a control group of elderly people who did not, the study found that "elderly caregivers who reported feeling stressed by attending to a disabled spouse were 63 percent more likely to die over the next four years, compared to elders without such a burden." Depression, anxiety, more heart disease, and other illnesses were significantly higher among caregivers. They were especially higher for caregivers who received little support from others (Knox, 1999).

But as Abel reminds us, we should not end by focusing on the stress of caregiving, very real though it may be. Caregiving is what all of us need at some point in our lives; it is what we owe to each other; it is an essential aspect of family living.

(For two recent studies of caregiving and social policies on caregiving, see Meyer, 2000, and Gallagher and Gerstel, 2001.)

HOMELESS PEOPLE AND THEIR FAMILIES

Even though many homeless people and some writers attribute homelessness to family abuse and lack of family support (see below), the major cause is economic—not mental illness, not drug abuse, not "dysfunctional" families. People afflicted with one or more of these conditions but who have money are not homeless. Liebow stated it well: "[M]ost physically disabled people, most mentally ill people, most alcoholics and drug addicts, and most unemployed persons do have places to live. Moreover, when [all these people] do get a place to live, they are no longer homeless but they remain, as they were before, physically or mentally disabled, drug addicts, or whatever. . . . Homeless people are homeless because they do not have a place to live. . . . *Homelessness today is a social class phenomenon, the direct result of a steady, across-the-board lowering of the standard of living of the American working class and the lower class"* (1993, p. 224).

Most homeless people do not have a place to live because housing is expensive, governments do not provide as much affordable housing as in the past, many jobs do not pay enough so people can rent or buy housing (Wright, Rubin, and Devine, 1998).

Family conflicts and histories do play some role in the lives of some homeless people, however. According to many homeless people, they choose to live on the streets or in shelters rather than stay with families they claim abused them physically or emotionally. Wagner's interviews with homeless people in "North City," a city in northern New England, "revealed an astounding amount and degree of child abuse." Brad told Wagner: "You have to understand, man, we're all from dysfunctional families here. Been abused, thrown away, dumped. No, we're not family people." Given these realities, Wagner concluded that the people who talked with him "*consciously* avoided contact with [their] families . . . because of abuse, violence, and strife that characterized" them. Each year, thousands of teens are kicked out of their homes, for many reasons, and many become homeless (Wagner,1993, pp. 47, 45–46; Elsner, 2002).

Many North City homeless people, according to Wagner, never had families. Separated from their parents early in life, because of neglect, abuse, and other reasons, they were raised in a series of foster homes and institutions. They reported mistreatment and abuse in these settings and ran away from them as soon as they could. They effectively had no families to turn to.

Even when offered assistance from their families—in the form of money or invitations to stay with them—many homeless people rejected it so that they could keep their independence and avoid the abuse they remembered. They found human contact and support in each other and in some institutions. Contacts with families were few, brief, or non-existent.

Wagner's portrait of many North City homeless people is unequivocal: they prefer street life, with all its problems, for the freedom and independence it offers them, over their abusive, dysfunctional, and often absent families. Other studies present somewhat similar family situations for homeless people. According to Wright, Rubin, and Devine, most homeless people, beginning early in life, have steadily grown apart and away from their families; "a remarkably high percentage of homeless adults report having been reared in 'broken homes,' by single parents, by stepparents, in foster homes, or in institutional settings. . . ; reports of physical, sexual, and emotional abuse as children are widespread, especially among homeless women. . . . Familial estrangement is less a disability that befalls young adults than a process of family dysfunction and isolation that can be traced to early childhood in many cases" (1998, p. 99).

Snow and Anderson's account points to a more complex portrait of homeless people and their families than the one presented by Wagner for North City. According to Wright, Rubin, and Devine, "The process of familial estrangement is a two-way street, that is, some homeless adults are estranged because of things they have done to family members but many are estranged by things that family members have done to them" (1998, p. 103).

Liebow concludes that "just as some women are homeless because their families can no longer support them, other women have little or no family support because they are homeless. Some of the families break off relationships with the women because they are ashamed of them, because they can no longer support them, or because they feel guilty for failing to do so. The result is that homelessness can cause the loss of family support as well as be caused by it" (1993, p. 114).

It may seem that a discussion of homeless people does not belong in a chapter on family living. But even in the lives of adults who never had a family because they were raised in foster homes and institutions; or who fled emotional or physical abuse; or who were thrown out for a variety of reasons; or who were trying to rebuild or save family relationships; or who were escaping abusive husbands; or who embarrassed their families by their homelessness; or who were homeless and away from family for so many reasons—the importance and the memory and the meaning of families were very much present in their lives. Whether in defiance and rejection of their families, or whether in sorrow for being rejected, or whether in shame for being homeless, their families were present in their thoughts, hopes, and sorrows.

CONCLUSION

Family textbooks largely ignore family living, the experiences and memories of parents, children, and other relatives that make up our families. By discussing cooking and mealtimes, having fun, kin work, caregiving, and homeless people, I have tried to fill that gap. As we study all the problems families face and cause for themselves—all too real—we should remember also the joys and good times and warm memories of our family lives. Families and family lives *are* composed of such experiences. We revel in them while we live them, we remember them fondly, and we miss them when we cannot have them.

7

Families, Kin, and Communities

An enduring nostalgia about American families recalls "the extended family of a century ago [which] had aunts, uncles, parents, grandparents, and children all living under one roof." We are told that these families were more or less self-sufficient, taking care of each other in health and sickness, from birth to death. We also read that long ago families were close to their neighbors and communities, relying on them for assistance and cooperation. People watched out for each other (Landis, 1995, p. 230; Demos, 1975; Ulrich, 1987).

In contrast, we are presented families today, nuclear and isolated from the community. Our families no longer care for us throughout our lives. "One of the most telling facts about the family today is that it is no longer called upon to perform certain family caregiving functions. Most of us, for example, will never be expected to take care of a cousin who is temporarily unemployed, an autistic brother, or a grandfather who has Alzheimer's disease. These traditionally family responsibilities are increasingly given over to outside institutions" (Bird and Melville, 1994, p. 267).

Are today's nuclear families largely independent of and isolated from grandparents, aunts and uncles, brothers and sisters, cousins, neighbors, and communities? Let us note that the extended families Landis describes were never the norm in U.S. history. Families have always been mostly nuclear, with no aunts and uncles and grandparents living under the same roof. Colonial families did, however, meet most of their families' needs. But as we just saw in chapter 6, the caregiving we need today still comes mostly from family members, from spouses and children, and sometimes siblings and grandchildren. In order to function, most families still require and involve more than children and parents in many ways; they reach out to a wider circle of relatives.

It is more difficult to find connections today between families and their neighbors and communities. I will explore such connections, however, in earlier U.S. history and in other societies. First, I will discuss families and their kin both in the past and today.

KIN AND COMMUNITY OF SOFIA STRATIS

Sofia Stratis was born in 1917 in Longo, Albania. She was my father's youngest sister. She married in 1935 and soon had a son and daughter. After surviving the ravages of World War II, she and her family lived under communism for most of their lives. When I met her in 1980, we had long talks; she told me how she appreciated the benefits communism had provided—low-cost food, free medical care, and general social equality—but she detested the repressive control and lack of freedom of speech.

Mostly, however, we talked about her family. Her husband had been bedridden for many years and she became a widow in the late 1960s. She continued living with her children but they soon moved to nearby towns to find work, where they also married and settled

116

Great-grandmother meets her new great-granddaughter and delights in time with her granddaughter and her son. It is difficult for this family to be together often. Great-grandmother lives in Louisiana; her son and his wife and their younger children live in Colorado. The granddaughter and her husband and baby live in California.

down. Always, however, they came to visit and for long stays, especially in the summer. Grandchildren stayed with Sofia for their entire summer vacations. For two years, a grandson lived with her in Longo. In addition, for three years she stayed with her son and his wife to take care of their young twins while her son and his wife worked.

For all those years she was close to her brother (my father) and his family, her sister and her family, her husband's relatives, and her neighbors. She knew everyone in Longo, a village of about 600 people. Every day she talked with neighbors and relatives. Her life was rich with people, visiting them in their homes, talking with them as they met on paths, exchanging news when shopping in village stores.

When communism fell in 1991 and most of the people of Longo (all Greek) left for Greece, her son, daughter, and their families went to Athens. Sofia, however, wanted to stay on in Longo, in her house and near her neighbors and other relatives. Her kin and community were her life.

Her failing health, however, forced her to move to Athens to live with her children, alternating between their homes. But happy as she was to be with her children and grandchildren, she missed her home and her garden and the people she had lived with all her life. She felt almost imprisoned in a big city, with no neighbors to meet and talk with.

She did return to Longo once, but continuing health problems forced her to return to Athens in a month. Before she died in May 1994, we wrote a few letters. In all of them she told me of her deep longing for her home and her garden, for Longo and the people she knew.

She also wrote of visits from my sister and other relatives also living in Athens, noting that people were busy with their jobs and lives and could not come often. She always asked for news of her two sisters in the United States, my daughters (whom she had met), and other relatives.

Following are a few excerpts from the letters she wrote between August 1993 and March 1994.

She had left Longo for Athens because "I was sick and had no one in the house with me and all my neighbors had left" for Greece. But in Athens, "there is no one here during the day, everyone is at work, and I read and re-read your letters. . . . You write me, Alex, about our village. Everyone is gone. I ache for the people there and for my home that I worked to my bones to build, and all is in ruins. I have my children here but for me, at my age, it's no time to be in a foreign place. . . . The ache and longing are deep for everyone, for those who died and for those who live, and we can't see each other."

She was sick and sadly reflected, "Alex, I won't be able to go to my house one more time and see everyone." "The village is empty, only the old people and a few young ones are left. . . . I always ache for my place and for the people who are there."

She died in May 1994, before she could return to her neighbors, her home, her family, her village. Her children took her body to Longo and buried her next to her husband, and her relatives, friends, and neighbors. It was in that Longo cemetery that I visited her in 1994, 1997, 1999, and 2003. Each time I thought of our long talks, of her letters, of her love for her home and Longo and its people. My Aunt Sofia and my memories of those talks and letters make kin and community very real for me.

EXTENDED FAMILIES AND KIN

The reality, need, and value of kin and extended family have been present at all times and in all societies.

Gathering-Hunting Societies

Let us first look at the Ju/'hoansi (formerly !Kung). As among the Mbuti and other such societies, the game the hunters captured was carefully distributed and shared with relatives beyond one's spouse and children, indeed, with the entire community. Gatherers-hunters lived in groups of 25–100 people (Lee, 1993; Shostak, 1981).

According to Shostak, the nuclear family remains close to elderly parents and other relatives. "!Kung culture encourages strong bonds between parents and children, and between spouses. . . Husband, wife, and children form the basic living unit, with a variable number of other people joining from each spouse's extended family. Adults remain closely attached to their parents; in contrast to our own society, in which such closeness is often viewed as unhealthy, the !Kung consider these feelings natural and express them freely. When any member of such a close group dies, a major adjustment is required for everyone remaining" (1981, p. 202).

As we saw in earlier chapters, people in all gathering-hunting societies live in families where parents and their young children are deeply intertwined with grandparents, other relatives, and the entire group. Raising children, gathering and hunting for food, religious activities, and all of life's activities involved everyone around them.

Kinship in East London in the 1950s

As noted in chapter 1, the young son of a sociologist who studied Bethnal Green (in East London) one day told his parents that the teacher asked the students to draw pictures of their families. He drew his parents, his brother, and himself, but all the other students had also included grandparents, aunts and uncles, and other relatives in their drawings. The sociologist was also surprised to "discover that the wider [extended] family, far from having disappeared, was still very much alive in the middle of London" (Young and Willmott, 1957, p. 12).

Most adults wanted to and did live near their parents. In their sample, Young and Willmott found that two-thirds lived within two to three miles of their parents' home. Many daughters saw their mothers several times a day, and over half saw them at least once a day. They went shopping together, had tea in the afternoon, the grandmother watched her grand-children, the daughter sought advice about her pregnancy, and so on. For example, Young and Willmott quote one woman, Mrs. Cole, who discribes her day:

> After breakfast I bath the baby and sweep the kitchen, and wash up. Then I go up the road shopping with Mum, Greta (one of . . . [her] married sisters who also has a child), and the three children. After dinner I clean up and then round about 2 o'clock I go out for a walk if it's fine with Mum and Greta and the children. I come back at about a quarter to four to be in time for Janice when she gets back from school. She calls in at Mum's on her way home just to see if I'm there. This is an ordinary day. If anything goes wrong and I'm in trouble I always go running round to Mum's.(1957, p. 47)

Fifty-eight percent of the women had seen their mothers in the last 24 hours, and 48 percent had seen their fathers. Of the men, 31 percent had seen their mothers and 30 percent their fathers. Almost all the rest had seen their parents a few times in the last week. Of the 23 women who lived on the same street with their parents, all had seen their mothers in the previous 24 hours. Children lived close to parents partly because the parents found nearby apartments for them. Indeed, rental agents understood the code that you give preference to children of tenants and neighbors (Yount and Willmott, 1957, pp. 46, 48, 41).

Close associations were not limited to parents and children. Siblings also kept in touch and helped each other. Fifty-one percent of women had seen their sisters in the previous week, and 42 percent had seen their brothers. For men, 27 percent had seen their brothers and 35 percent their sisters. Most unmarried adults—83 of 117—lived with their parents. After parents died, most lived with a sister or brother.

Most people in Bethnal Green were surrounded by relatives. Of a sample of 45 couples, 4 had no relatives (other than parents) in Bethnal Green; 8 had 1–4; 12 had 5–9; 9 had 10–19; 8 had 20–29; and 5 had 30 and over, for a total of 1691. Relatives included "siblings, siblings' spouses, uncles and aunts, nephews and nieces, and grandparents, but not cousins or more remote kin" (Young and Willmott, 1957, p. 87).

These close family ties with many relatives, especially of adults with their parents, existed in a traditional and close-knit community, where people lived close to relatives and worked near their homes. When housing shortages forced some Bethnal Green residents to move some miles away to the new community of Greenleigh, the extended family connections became fewer. Before leaving Bethnal Green, husbands had averaged 15 "contacts per week with own and spouse's parents and siblings." In 1955, the contacts were reduced to 3.3 per week. For wives, they decreased from 17.2 to 2.4. Daughters saw their mothers "on average just under once a fortnight." Compare these numbers to earlier contacts in Bethnal Green. After the move to Greenleigh there were more contacts by phone, but clearly there was a drastic reduction, and both parents and children bemoaned the loss (Young and Willmott, 1957, p. 131).

Thus, to Young and Willmott's surprise, extended family relations were frequent and valued in Bethnal Green in the 1950s.

The Abkhasians

Sula Benet's study of the Abkhasian people in the Georgia Republic of the USSR (1970–1973) focused on its older people, renown for long lives. She found a number of reasons for their longevity.

They ate moderately and drank a glass of wine each day, no more and no less. In addition, they walked everywhere and breathed clean mountain air. They worked all their lives, reducing their work hours as they aged but continuing to work into their eighties and nineties. Their work provided them with exercise, a routine in their life, and a feeling of being useful. Their families were close and supportive, as was their community. They did not dread aging because they were respected and cared for as they aged. They lived in extended families and communities that provided them with respect and security.

All Abkhasians lived in families of "possibly forty or fifty persons in one homestead, three or four generations of great-grandparents, grandparents, uncles and their wives, cousins, and, almost incidentally, parents." In these families and communities, "The elders preside at important ceremonial occasions, they mediate disputes, and their experience with local ecology is invaluable, as is their knowledge of medicinal herbs" (Benet, 1974, p. 27).

Everyone was involved in family matters. "In times of crisis, sickness, or death, all kinsmen are informed. Immediately they converge on the homestead of an afflicted relative, offering help, taking over necessary responsibilities and acting together with the family" (Benet, 1974, p. 49).

People have strong obligations to their relatives, who number in the hundreds. In a meeting with students Benet asked how many relatives they had. "The first student said that according to his grandfather . . . they numbered 500. Another student said that her family was not such a large one, and only numbered around 350. Other people also responded with, seemingly to my ears, large numbers. They, in turn, asked me how many relatives I had in the United States. When I mentioned just a few, they looked at me with great sympathy. As one expression of their concern, they asked me whether I would like to be adopted into some large lineage, as is the custom for people as forlorn as I looked to them" (p. 60).

The Ju/'hoansi, East Londoners, and Abkhasians, each with their own family organization, generally represent family social conditions found in most human societies. Family extended beyond the nuclear unit of parents and their young children. People had ties, responsibilities, and interactions with a large circle of relatives. The details varied from society to society, but the basic principle was that of a familial social world peopled with siblings and their spouses, grandparents, uncles and aunts, cousins of various degrees, and others. In Africa, Asia, Europe, Australia, North and South America, various forms of strong extended families existed.

EXTENDED FAMILIES IN U.S. HISTORY

I doubt that the United States ever had the pervasive and large extended families found in places like Abkhasia. But the history and examples presented in earlier chapters show that nuclear families in the past were not detached units unto themselves.

Plymouth Plantation

Demos concluded that in Plymouth Plantation in the 1680s, despite the basic nuclear structure of families, there was "a considerable degree of interconnection among kin." Some relatives lived next door to each other. When children were orphaned, they lived with relatives, usually uncles and aunts, and sometimes grandparents (1970, p. 118).

In his summary of kin relations, Demos points to ties beyond the immediate nuclear family (but they were not nearly as extensive as those of the Abkhasians). A "man was involved, first of all, with his wife and children, and then with his grandchildren. Somewhat less intense was the relation to his own brothers and sisters, and to their children." Demos presents no information on how often, for what reasons, and on what occasions, kin met; such information may not exist (1970, p. 124).

Early Twentieth Century

In the more recent past, early twentieth century, we find that people still recognized kin relations and obligations. In early 1940s Plainville, West refers to kin expectations and relations. "For all the looseness in family obligations beyond the immediate family, there is always an emotional line on a blood relative. A place to sleep and a seat at the table can be expected from a kinsman anywhere, unless there is 'bad blood' or 'trouble' in the family. . . . People are criticized for not 'eating a meal' with kin folks, or for not staying at the houses of kin, when traveling, just as they are criticized for unwillingness to entertain and feed their kin. People say, 'It's about time we eat at John's, to show 'em we're still kin'" (West, 1945, pp. 67–68).

Many groups, especially ethnic ones, had and valued extensive kin relations. An example were some Italian people who lived in Rochester, New York, in the early 1900s. They were typical of other Italians and other ethnic groups. Grandparents were missing, because it was the parents who came from Italy. But the parents of Mangione's generation soon became grandparents, and they lived in extended families very similar to those that existed in East London (see above). People were intensely involved with parents and grandparents, siblings, uncles and aunts, cousins, and some close friends. They met constantly: for Sunday and weekday meals, for parties, for other gatherings, for card playing. Their lives were intertwined and interconnected (Mangione, 1942; see descriptions of Mangione's family in chapters 1, 2, and 6).

Second Half of the Twentieth Century

At least in some parts of the United States, kin relations were strong in the 1950s, 1960s, and 1970s.

In the late 1950s, before it was torn down for urban renewal, the West End of Boston had a thriving working-class Italian community, where family relations very much resembled those in Rochester, New York, in the 1920s and East London in the 1950s. "Married daughters often retain close ties with their mothers and try to settle near them. . . . Some households take in those relations who would otherwise be alone, especially unmarried brothers, sisters, or even cousins, because of feelings of obligation, love, and the desire to reduce the loneliness of the single person." Even unmarried adults living alone spent much of their time "with married brothers or sisters, and they often participated in child-rearing as quasi-parental aunts and uncles." Generally, extended family members spent much time together in long Sunday dinners, card playing, and so on. Kin also provided aid and advice for each other. When people needed care, they looked to relatives and neighbors (Gans, 1962, pp. 45–46, 159–160).

In *All Our Kin,* Stack reports an extensive kin network she found among poor black families in the late 1960s (described in chapters 1, 5, and 6). Adult children, and their children, often lived with their parents; children were frequently taken in by aunts and uncles for various periods; people who lost their apartments because they could not pay rent were taken in by parents, siblings, cousins, uncles, and aunts; money and goods were shared as needed; rides were offered to those without cars (Stack, 1974).

For all the above groups, and many others, during the second half of the twentieth century, family life included extended kin. What was happening to other working-class and middle-class families in other parts of the United States during those years?

In Muncie, Indiana, during the 1970s, the family was "in exceptionally good condition" and was "*not* isolated." People said in surveys that they felt obligated to keep in touch with relatives: 73 percent with parents, 58 percent with siblings, 36 percent with cousins, and 60 percent with grown children. In addition, "most Middletown people feel good about their parents, love them, and make sacrifices for them when necessary. They see them often and enjoy doing so" (Caplow and others, 1982, pp. 340, 220).

How often did relatives see each other, and what did they do when they did? Adults said that 48 percent of them saw their parents at least weekly and 80 percent at least monthly. Brothers and sisters saw each other half as frequently. The closer people lived to relatives, the more frequently they saw them. Of adults whose parents lived in Muncie, 83 percent visited them weekly; of those whose parents lived 50 to 100 miles away, only 6 percent saw them weekly.

What did they do together? Men and women said that 66 percent of them paid "brief drop-in visits for conversation" with their parents, 55 percent of the women and 47 percent of the men played cards and went on picnics with them, and 22 percent of the men and 51 percent of the women shopped together with them. Also, parents helped their children and (less often) children helped their parents.

To quote the authors: "Take any resident of the city at random. The odds are one in five that he or she has a brother or sister living in the city, one in three that one or both of his or her parents live there, and two in five that he or she has more distant relatives—grandparents, aunts, uncles, cousins—who live in Middletown, also" (Caplow and other, 1982, pp. 200–201).

What do these findings mean? To the authors, they are unambiguous evidence that the family—including adult parents and siblings—was vibrant, alive, and well in 1970s Muncie. But compared to other kin relations we have just seen—in Bethnal Green and Abkhasia, in the Italian communities of Rochester and Boston, in African American families in the South and Midwest—kin ties in Muncie were fewer and less intense. For example, in East London and the West End of Boston daughters saw their mothers several times a day, or daily, or at least several times a week. Compare that to "48 percent of the Middletown adults with living parents see them at least weekly and about 80 percent see them at least monthly" (Caplow and others, 1982, p. 209).

EXTENDED FAMILIES AND KIN TODAY

Let us now examine various studies and conclusions on kin relations in the very recent past and today. Family textbooks conclude that extended family ties continue to be strong in poor, working class, ethnic, and racial communities.

Extended Families

Beyond parents and children, kin ties in most middle-class families seem fairly weak. For example, Cherlin writes: "Typically, the middle-class conjugal family is more independent of kin than the working-class version. The married couple is expected to spend their income on their children and themselves rather than to provide financial assistance to siblings or other relatives. Any assets or savings are passed from parents to children, rather than being spread throughout a kin network." He then summarizes a 1984–85 survey carried out in Boston, which posed hypothetical situations where relatives "were experiencing crises that might require 'some financial help' or 'comfort and emotional support.'" Respondents expressed feelings of strong obligation only toward parents or children and weak obligation toward uncles and aunts, nephews and nieces (1999, pp. 124–126).

Logan and Spitze, in their study based on short interviews with 1,200 people in Albany, New York, in 1988–89, focused on ties between parents and their grown children. They concluded that "the bonds between generations are strong, founded on mutual caring. . . ." Parents help their children much more than children help parents. Occasional financial assistance, babysitting of grandchildren, some housekeeping, and running errands were common. Ties between adult children and their parents were central in the lives of these Albany residents: "Our analyses are remarkable for the apparent resilience of parent–child ties in later life. . . . Whether measured as contact, visiting, help given, or help received, these family ties are at the very core of people's networks outside the home. . . . Rather than being displaced by secondary associations, by friends or coworkers living at a distance or by paid helpers or public services, we find that family ties—when they are present—are people's preferred source of routine assistance. Others play distinctly subordinate roles" (1996, pp. xxiv, 156).

Other studies have also shown that adult children receive much more financial assistance from their parents than they give to them. For example, a 1992 Harris survey "showed that four times as many older parents said they contributed substantially toward their children's household income as vice-versa." And a 1990 survey of 1,500 adults, ages 18–90, found that "48 percent of Americans with adult children [said that they] give large gifts to them, usually money . . . [and] such things as large appliances, audio–visual equipment or checks of about $5,000." Some studies report limited giving: "In a national survey of adults with living parents, only 17 percent of the adults reported getting $200 or more from their parents" (Foreman, 1993, p. 26; Cherlin, 1999, p. 481).

Bird and Melville conclude that although kin ties today are not as strong as in the past, they remain important and valued for most people. Despite considerable geographical mobility in America, kin stay in touch with each other. And when they do migrate, people often move close to relatives and receive help from them in finding work and a place to live. Middle-class people are less likely to move near relatives than are working-class people, but even they "still consider kinship to be part of their lives. Air transportation and phone calls enable kin to keep in touch despite the wide distances separating them. Both emotional attachment and certain patterns of assistance can be maintained even though the amount of direct contact is reduced" (1994, p. 276).

Bird and Melville also note that in times of emergency, people turn to relatives, especially parents. In addition, parents often provide loans, assistance with a down-payment for a house, and presents on various occasions. As Logan and Spitze also found, help is mostly from parents to their adult children, until late in life when parents need care from them.

Many poor and working-class African American families continue to show strong kin ties. Stack describes such ties among Southern blacks who had migrated North and who began to return South in the 1960s. Families were composed of grandparents and grandchildren, brothers and sisters, uncles and aunts, nephews and nieces—and often neighbors and friends who became fictive kin. To repeat one example, Pearl and Samuel Bishop raised their own ten children, and for various periods also raised grandchildren, nephews and nieces, and even some unrelated children. Also, recall the discussion of caregiving, where children felt obligated and wanted to take care of their ailing parents (Stack, 1996).

Other studies support Stack's findings of close kin ties among poor and working-class African Americans. For example, custodial fathers "relied on [kin] networks to help them negotiate between parenting and work schedules." Relatives taught them how to raise their children and constantly supported them (Hamer and Marchioro, 2002, p. 127).

And there were similar kin ties in Harlem, New York City, in the mid-1990s. "In Carmen's building there are five households linked together by kinship connections. Their members move freely between them, opening the refrigerator door in one to see whether there's anything good to eat, watching television in another because it has a cable hookup, using the one phone that hasn't been cut off for nonpayment. Carmen's grandmother watches her grandchildren, a half-dozen in all now, so that their parents can go to work" (Newman, 1999, p. 116).

Kin Ties of Elderly People

As we age in the United States, our closest kin relations are our spouses, siblings, and children. "Most elders have a living sibling," and they are usually close to them. The closest relationship is sister to sister, then sister to brother, then brother to brother. These sibling ties, especially sister to sister, are often very significant and meaningful; sometimes they are closer than those to a spouse (Barrow, 1996, p. 105).

Treas disputes the portrait of lonely old people: "The everyday lives of many older people are closely entwined with those of their relatives. Family members are people to think about, to socialize with, and to help in one way or another" (1995, p. 29)

As we saw in chapter 6, most caregiving is provided by family members. Spouses, usually women, are the most common caregivers, followed by children. For example, Barrow points out that "for every disabled person who resides in a nursing home, two or more equally impaired aged live with and are cared for by their families" (Barrow, 1996, p. 265). Along these lines, Treas reports a study showing that "in 1984, fully 84 percent of noninstitutionalized persons ages 65 and older who received help with activities such as bathing or housework were assisted by relatives" (1995, p. 29). But there is a significant minority of elders with no close relative near them; twenty-five percent "have no surviving children or siblings residing close enough to provide regular assistance" (Barrow, 1996, p. 271).

In future years, there will probably be more elderly people without family assistance. As we have fewer or no children, we will have fewer supports in old age. And as more women hold jobs outside the home, fewer will be as available to provide care for elders. Generally, although it may be a stereotype to think of older people as socially isolated, many of us, as we age, and as our children and families move to new jobs and new communities, do face some isolation and loneliness. This isolation increases as we become frail, can no longer drive, and so on (Barrow, 1996, p. 114).

Of course, isolation in old age is not inevitable. As Jacobs shows in *Be an Outrageous Older Woman,* we can create an active life for ourselves by reaching out to our friends, neighbors, and communities. We can start new hobbies and new lives, we can join social and political groups, and we can create new social ties. For example, "Four women I know bought a four-apartment building, and, although each has her own quarters, they leave their doors open, eat together frequently, and enjoy knowing friends are nearby." Others get together for lunch or dinner, "each bringing a dish, or taking turns cooking" (1993, pp. 81, 82).

Another creative solution Jacobs reports involved an "older woman I know who has solved her housing and finance problem in one creative swoop. She saw an ad on a bulletin board offering free room and board in exchange for fifteen hours a week of being available to keep an eye on three school-aged children. The ad said the hours were late afternoon and evening. The woman, who loves children, applied for the job. Now, instead of living alone expensively, she lives freely with a nice young family who give her plenty of privacy but also companionship" (Jacobs, 1993, p. 84).

Such solutions to social isolation, necessary and creative as they are, may reflect the weakening of, and our ambivalence toward, family obligations. Whereas older people may expect aid from their children and other relatives, they also prefer not to live with them. Indeed, there has been a dramatic shift in the living arrangements of older people.

In 1900, only about 8 percent of persons over age sixty lived outside the family: with nonkin, as a boarder in a lodging house, or in an institutional setting. The vast majority—70 percent— headed households of their own that included both unmarried and married children or other kin. These older couples typically lived with unmarried children, often the youngest child, whose role was defined as the caretaker of the aging parents. The remaining 22 percent lived in the households of relatives. . . . A widowed woman who was no longer able to maintain her own household would likely move into the home of her married children. An elderly person who had never married would live with siblings or other kin. . . . [But by 1996,] among Americans aged sixty-five and older, 73 percent of men and 40 percent of women were living on their own in households with a spouse present. Another 17 percent of men and 41 percent of women lived alone. Only 9 percent of men and 19 percent of women in this age group lived with other relatives or nonrelatives. (Farrell, 1999, pp. 152–153)

Farrell thinks that now that they can afford it, older people want to live alone and prefer "intimacy at a distance." But it may be more a case of "I like what I get" rather than "I get what

I like" (from *Alice in Wonderland*). It may be that, as we have become a mobile society, with family members moving away for various reasons, older people realize that it would be difficult for them to live with their children and other non-spousal relatives. As our values on family obligations may have changed, we now value more individual autonomy. Older people may say they prefer what they know to be their only choice.

Evidence for "I like what I get" is found in the very pages where Farrell says that older people prefer "intimacy at a distance." She cites "age-integrated cohousing projects [and] suburban houses and city apartment complexes where elderly residents live together and share meals, communal activities, and opportunities for social interaction." Above, we read of a woman who lived with a family and cared for their children in the afternoons. There are many other examples of people creating ties and social contacts, including living together, with non-family people. But what are these arrangements but efforts to re-create what families used to provide? The need to be with people, to share meals, to chat, to do things together, is the same need whether met by living with children or non-relatives. I am not convinced that older people prefer living alone (1999, p. 155).

Perhaps an indication of weakening family ties may be how we die. According to Barrow, today most of us die in hospitals, our death observed by few if any family members. In contrast, throughout history people died at home, surrounded by family members and friends; their bodies were prepared for burial by the family, who then dug the grave, placed the body inside it, and covered it with soil. This was the case with my father and mother, it was the case throughout history.

And it may be an indication of re-creating family ties that more American are choosing to die at home, surrounded by family, through hospice and other arrangements. The two people whose funerals I attended in Watertown, Massachusetts, in December 2000 and January 2001 died at home with children and spouses all around them. (Turnbull, 1961, chapter 2; Chinas, 1992).

Personal Reflections

You probably noticed that my observations on kin relations in the United States today are tentative and uncertain. I am struggling to make sense of what I see, read, and experience.

Certainly, there is a wish and a longing for close family ties. Surveys repeatedly show that people say they value their families—their parents, grandparents, brothers and sisters, aunts and uncles, nephews and nieces (cousins are rarely mentioned). There is also considerable reality to these wishes. As we saw in chapter 6, family members provide most caregiving. That is surely not evidence for the disappearance of family ties.

As I write the first draft of this chapter, I have just finished reading sixteen family histories from the sixteen women students in the "Changing Families" course I teach. Almost all of them (most in their early twenties) wrote warmly about their families and how much they mean to them. They told of regularly babysitting for their nephews and nieces; going shopping with grandparents; and large family gatherings. All this is in addition to reports of frequent visits to their parents' homes and regular contact by phone, and increasingly by email. Not only did my students report "enduring relations between parents and their grown children," they also told of ties to grandparents, aunts and uncles, nephews and nieces (Logan and Spitze, 1996).

But ever-present in my thoughts and my consciousness are Mangione's family in *Mount Allegro,* the working-class families of Bethnal Green in *Family and Kinship in East London,* the Abkhasian families of up to 500 relatives, the African American families in Stack's *All Our Kin* and *Call to Home,* and of course my own family in Longo, Albania, before most people left for Greece in the early 1990s.

The 1989 Liazos family reunion in Longo, Albania

I stayed in Longo for a month each in 1980 and 1985, and for two weeks in 1989. Grown married sons lived with their parents from the day they married, and married daughters who lived in Longo went by their parents' houses daily. They exchanged food, did errands for each other, told news, asked for advice, made plans for trips. In their walks to and from work or visits, people met cousins, uncles and aunts, nephews and nieces, and more distant relatives. Everyone was surrounded by many relatives, everyone interacted with them. Even people living alone for a while, as my Aunt Sofia did, had daily contact with relatives. People were shocked when I told them that most old people in America do not live with their adult children. It seemed unnatural to them. They kept asking why Americans are so cruel to their parents.

And even now, as so few people are left in Longo, relatives and neighbors are constantly interacting. For example, my brother and his wife visit and are visited by our sister's mother-in-law, who lives alone, and they buy her food and other necessities.

What I see and read about kin relations in the United States does not seem to approach the intense family living of those places. People may value their relatives, but they focus mostly on their spouses and their young children. I can find no statistics similar to those for Bethnal Green, but it's difficult to believe that most American families experience the pervasive and frequent social contacts that existed in that community in the 1950s.

Did such kin relations ever exist in the United States? They certainly did for some groups, such as for Mangione's Italian family in 1920s Rochester. But were they ever widespread in the United States? They may have been, if we are to believe the statistics for 1900 that Farrell presents (see above). As for today, I don't think we can say with certainty.

The *wish* for family ties is evident, but does it extend beyond the immediate circle of parents and their young children, and how often does the wish become a reality?

(For an argument that "multigenerational bonds" in U.S. families are becoming increasingly important, see Bengston, 2001.)

GRANDPARENTS AND GRANDCHILDREN

The kin tie between grandparents and grandchildren is a special one. It has existed in all societies. Every society I have read about recognized and celebrated grandparents.

Three Societies, 1930s–1960s

In many societies, the Ju/'hoansi among them, grandchildren often stay with their grandparents. "Personal and intimate topics not discussed with parents are taken up freely with grandparents, and grandparents often represent a child's interests at the expense of those of the parent. Also . . . [grandparents] have more time to play with grandchildren. It is not surprising that children are willing to live with them or with other relatives, especially during times of conflict with parents" (Shostak, 1981, p. 50).

Indulging grandchildren is reported widely. For example, "a considerable degree of affection for a grandchild is displayed by the Tikopia. They treat it with indulgence, caress it and make it little gifts of food and the like" (Firth, 1936, p. 194).

Young and Willmott found similar indulgence in Bethnal Green, and they quote Radcliffe-Brown's statement that "in Africa as elsewhere, grandparents are much more indulgent towards their grandchildren than are parent to their children." In all societies, grandparents have played a special role in their grandchildren's lives (Young and Willmott, 1957, p. 58).

Grandparents in Recent U.S. History

Around 1940, in Plainville, a small midwestern town, grandparents generally acted as they have all over the world.

> Grandparents and grandchildren treat each other "with the same affection" that exists between parents and children, but more familiarly. The same restrictions on obedience, respect, and mutual care theoretically obtain, but they are actually relaxed greatly. The child "does not really have to mind" its grandparent; he can be "sassy" with a grandparent, and such "sassiness" is considered very "cute" (charming and laughable) in a child. . . . Grandparents love grandchildren dearly and are proud of them. They often "spoil the child" with leniency, gifts, and candy. The grandparental home is always open to grandchildren, who visit there, not only with parents, but alone, to "spend the night" or stay for a week or two. It is sometimes used as a threat of sympathetic refuge or as an actual refuge from stern parents. Parents with several children sometimes let one child live permanently with their grandparents, or send children in turn to "stay with" them. (West, 1945, pp. 62–63)

Sharon Curtin, in *Nobody Ever Died of Old Age,* wrote fondly and warmly of her grandparents in the 1930s and 1940s. They were fun and fascinating people to know. Since "I grew up in a small town, my childhood had more of a nineteenth-century flavor. I knew a lot of old people, and considered some of them my friends. There was no culturally defined way for me to 'relate' to old people, except the rules of courtesy which applied to all adults" (1972, p. 36).

> My Grandfather Curtin used to refer to old age as "a hell of a long sentence, with no time off for good behavior." It was his habit to wander in and out of rooms and in and out of conversations, providing what his wife Carrie regarded as a perpetually disruptive presence. . . . He would tell us stories, and Carrie would tell him to remember to go to confession on Saturday for being such an outrageous liar. Every morning Carrie would go to Mass to pray for Willy's soul; every afternoon he would go down to the local hall to sit and smoke his pipe and swap lies with the other old men. . . . When I was very young, they still had a small farm and we spent some time there, especially the times when my mother was having another baby. Carrie would refer to it as a "blessed event, a little gift from God," and Willy would take us out to the barn to see a litter of kittens being born." (Curtin 1972, pp. 3, 4, 5)

Reflecting on the old people she had known, Curtin writes: "Most of all, they seemed to have time for me. The very young and the very old reach quick understanding; both groups recognize their dependence on the middle generation—for food, clothing, shelter—and have an ability to escape from these kinds of everyday concerns into the world of the imagination." And she laments that "Traditional roles for the aged have vanished. There are no quiet, warm spaces by the fireplace to sit and watch grandchildren play; no cracker barrels to sit upon and speak of times past. There is no security in old age" (Curtin, 1972, pp. 45, 194).

Some old people that Cherlin and Furstenberg interviewed in the late 1980s, however, have recollections of grandparents different from West's 1945 descriptions and Curtin's 1972 memories. They "heard stories of their childhood that differed from the idyllic *Waltons* image. Their grandparents, we were told, were respected, admired figures who often assisted other family members. But again and again, we heard them talk about the emotional distance between themselves and their grandparents. [Interviewer: What was it like, having your grandmother live with you?] 'Terrible [laughter]. She was old, she was strict. . . . We weren't allowed to sass her. I guess that was the whole trouble. No matter what she did to you, you had to take it. . . . She was good, though. . . . She used to do all the patching of the pants, and she was helpful. But, oh, she was strict. You weren't allowed to do anything, she'd tell on you right away.'" Cherlin argues that in older days grandparents were "emotionally distant," but now there is more affection between them and their grandchildren (Cherlin, 1999, pp. 478–479).

United States Grandparents Today

It is true that children in the United States today have more grandparents, for more years, than children did in 1900. But what is the nature and quality of the relationship between the two? "Grandparents may be valued resources, or they may be irrelevant." They may be indulging and loving friends, some may even raise grandchildren, or they may live thousands of miles away and see the grandchildren once or twice a year (Uhlenberg, 1996, p. 77).

Cherlin (1999) and Barrow (1996) provide somewhat different portraits of grandparenthood today. Cherlin concludes that there is much contact between the two groups, much more than people assume. In a survey Furstenberg and Cherlin carried out, they found that half the grandparents "had seen at least one grandchild that day or the day before, and 70 percent had seen a grandchild within the last week. Just one in six had not seen a grandchild within the previous month." Distances made a difference; if they lived within a mile of the grandchildren, they saw them twice a week; one to ten miles, once a week; "and at further distances, the number of visits fell off rapidly." For Cherlin, these and similar data reveal a close and meaningful relationship between the two generations (Cherlin and Furstenberg, 1992, cited in Cherlin, 1999, pp. 477–478).

Barrow, in her text on aging, provides a more qualified account. She concludes that most grandparents never develop "close intimate relationships with their grandchildren." They do, however, gain "pride and pleasure" from them. There is great variation in the relationship. Some grandparents are distant, others are formal, some indulge the grandchildren, and some play and have fun with them. As we shall see, some get to raise their grandchildren, while millions of others provide child care for them. For example, 16.4 percent of children under six whose mothers worked were cared for by grandparents in the mid-1990s (see chapter 5). As we have seen, African American and other ethnic grandparents are generally more involved with their grandchildren, because they live in extended kin networks (Barrow, 1996, pp. 107–109; Stack, 1974, 1996).

Today, for some grandparents divorce weakens their ties to their children and grandchildren. Although "the influence of divorce on grandparenting should not be overstated," King concluded that "divorced grandparents have less contact with grandchildren and participate in fewer activities with them." This is largely because they "live farther away from children and grandchildren, and they report weaker bonds to their adult children than do never-divorced grandparents" (King, 2003, p. 179).

In short, Cherlin, Barrow, and others might agree that many, if not most, grandparents are present in their grandchildren's lives, and most of them value and enjoy time with them. The frequency and depth of involvement vary, however.

The Importance and Benefits of Generational Ties

We have seen that grandparents provide special ties and times for their children's children. They may have time for them, they may indulge them, they may provide relief from the parents' strictness, and they may tell them family stories. Most accounts show that grandparents are a warm and positive presence.

The benefit is mutual, however, as Young and Willmott point out. In 1950s East London, grandparents, "as old age draws on, are even more likely to be lonely than their daughters, and oppressed by their uselessness. If they have children and grandchildren around them, they can not only be of some value to youth, they can also enjoy the reward of being appreciated; and, as they watch over their grandchildren, they can perhaps find some comfort in this evidence of the continuity of life. In their declining years they can call on their descendants to complete the circle of care by easing the strain of infirmity, illness, and bereavement" (1957, p. 192).

In 1990, Meltz wrote of "the magic of grandparent relationships."

> Children and their grandparents make up the largest mutual admiration society going. It's no wonder, for each offers the other a special gift. Children give their grandparents a sense of immortality; in return, they receive unconditional love. . . . by far, what makes this relationship so special is the ability to indulge, not in material ways, but in emotional ones. Grandparents' love is unconditional; they are less judgmental than parents. . . . having a young child regard [grandparents] as wise, is the most important aspect of their role. . . . Such unwavering love gives a child a sense of affirmation. "They see they are wonderful in that grandparent's eye, no matter what. That kind of love validates them. It builds self-esteem," Bengston says. Every child needs it, Guerney adds.
>
> This doesn't mean grandparents can do no wrong. There are plenty of times when they are a destructive influence—they butt in where they shouldn't, ignore rules parents have struggled to establish or criticize parents in front of a child. (Meltz, 1990, pp. 57, 61)

Raising Grandchildren

Millions of children are raised by their grandparents, mostly by grandmothers. In 1998, of 71.4 million children under 18, 3.9 million (5.5 percent) were living at their grandparents' home. For 2.6 million of them, one or both parents also lived there, but 1.4 million were being raised by grandparents alone. The 2000 census "found 2.4 million grandparents who are responsible for grandchildren who live with them." Children are raised by grandparents because their parents "are dead, abusive or neglectful, in jail, coping with alcohol or drug addiction, or roaming the country looking for jobs." Some of the parents have died from AIDS (*Statistical Abstract*, 1999, p. 69; Davis, 2000; Dedman, 2002; Foreman, 1994; Joslin, 2001).

Families headed by grandparents have special problems and needs. To respond to these needs, Boston built GrandFamilies House, the first public housing in the United States only for these families.

> The resident grandparents range in age from 50 to 74, the 49 children from 1 to 17. Grandparent friendly features include an elevator, wheelchair ramps, grab bars in bathrooms, and a ground-floor common room for socializing. To protect the children, there are window guards, child-proof electrical outlets, and secure storage areas for toxic household products. There is also a supervised playground, a day-care area, and an in-house enrichment program that includes computer training.
>
> But for the grandparents, all but three of whom are women, the thing that makes Grand-Families House really special is the opportunity to be with one another. One of the ways she battles her blues, Parker says, is to "hang out with Vera Sanders; she's like a sister to me. (Davis, 2000, p. F8).

How do the two generations experience this family arrangement? Little seems to have been written about it (at least I have not seen it). My brother and I were raised by our grandmother since he was 10 and I was 6. It was in a different culture and long ago (1947–1955 in Greece, and 1955–1964 in Worcester, Massachusetts). It was difficult, financially and emotionally. I can't remember how I understood the separation from my parents, but I do remember crying periodically. On the other hand, our grandmother took care of us and loved us, she did the best she could in an almost impossible situation. I imagine that grandchildren raised by grandparents in the United States today must undergo some combination of similar experiences and emotions.

No doubt, for many grandparents and grandchildren, there is a magic in their relationship, a warm indulgence in time and presents and story telling. For many others, there is something less. And for others, the relationship is but a distant reality, perhaps a wish and a longing for people who live far away and are rarely seen. Even then, we can't assume that the relationship means little. Often, it surely does. But if we dig a little deeper, we may find that even rare contacts between the generations may have deep meaning. For example, my daughters saw my mother four times only, during visits to Greece in 1987 and Albania in 1989, and my parents' visit to the U.S. in 1991 and my mother's visit in 1994 (they saw my father in 1989 and 1991 only). In between, they exchanged letters twice a year, which I translated. Then in 1997, Ariane, 21, visited Greece to see aunts, uncles, and cousins. Against everyone's advice, she and her cousin Orestis decided to cross the border into Albania, despite the near civil war, anarchy, violence, and danger that prevailed in that country. They wanted to see my mother (my father had died in 1995). They were there for only three days, but until the day she died two years later, my mother spoke warmly about that visit each time we talked. She had been ailing for months when Ariane and Orestis arrived in June 1997, and she told me time and again that their visit lifted her spirits and helped her regain her health. As I write, I look at a 1997 photograph of Ariane and my mother in the courtyard of our house in Longo, holding hands and smiling. That moment and those days were magic, for the two of them and for the rest of us.

FAMILIES AND COMMUNITIES

Traditionally, people have lived not only in networks of extended family and kin, but also these kin have been closely connected with and supported by the surrounding community. In small communities, everyone knew everyone else, and families related to other families in a variety of ways. They shared the hunt, helped each other with the gardening and other tasks, and watched out for all the children. There were no sharp boundaries between family and community.

That was then. How do families relate to their surrounding communities today? Are families largely independent of and isolated from communities, or are there still some connections?

Societies outside the United States

Before we attempt to answer that question, let us first look at some earlier societies.

For most of human history, people lived in gathering–hunting societies, which were organized in groups of 25–100 people. In these communities, families did exist, children knew who their parents and other relatives were, and everyone recognized family relationships and obligations. But families were deeply intertwined with all other families and individuals in the group. For example, as we saw in chapter 5, in all societies, as soon as they could walk, children were raised by the entire community. An old man wiped a child's runny nose even though there was no family connection.

Among the Mbuti, everyone cooperated during the hunt and they all shared the meat they caught. "Hunting . . . is a cooperative affair—net-hunting particularly. . . . For the net hunters it is impossible to hunt alone. Men, women and children all have to co-operate if the hunt is to be successful." Children make noises to direct animals toward the nets. "In a small and tightly knit hunting band, survival can be achieved only by the closest co-operation and by an elaborate system of reciprocal obligations which insures that everyone has some share of the day's catch. Some days one gets more than others, but nobody ever goes without" (Turnbull, 1961, pp. 97, 107. See also Shostak, 1981, p. 85).

Also, among the Mbuti, everyone knew every family's disputes, and when such disputes became serious, the entire group intervened to resolve them. "Co-operation is the key to [Mbuti] society; you can expect it and you can demand it, and you have to give it. If your wife nags you at night so that you cannot sleep, you merely have to raise your voice and call on your friends and relatives to help you. Your wife will do the same, so whether you like it or not the whole camp becomes involved. At this point someone—very often an older person with too many relatives and friends to be accused of being partisan—steps in with the familiar remark that everyone is making too much noise, or else diverts the issue onto a totally different track so that people forget the origin of the argument and give it up" (Turnbull, 1961, p. 124; see chapter 6 for details).

In societies where people cultivated plants, cooperation with people outside one's relatives was also needed. In earlier chapters, I presented the Mundurucu of Brazil. The Murphys lived with them in the early 1950s, and they wrote: "In a sense, the village is an extension of the household, from the female's point of view. . . . [T]he other women may be persons with whom she has been raised, with whom she played as a child, and whom she has known intimately throughout most of her life. In her adult years, these are also the women with whom she makes farinha [flour made from manioc], washes clothes, bathes, and amuses herself. . . . When women help in farinha making, they are always given a share of the product. And if a household runs short, others will give it enough farinha to tide its women over until they can make more. If a garden fails and a house is left short of food for the season, they will be allowed to harvest from the gardens of others" (1985, p. 157).

Women worked together to process manioc into flour. They needed to do so because no household had enough women to do the work alone, but they also enjoyed working together. Almost daily, women worked with and along other women outside their household. "Except for minor household chores, women's work is always done in cooperation, or in companionship, with other women. . . . Mundurucu women enjoy each other's company, and the congregation of women in the farinha shed turns the tedium of a grinding chore into a chatty sort of sewing circle. They switch tasks, allowing each other to rest or wander off, and keep the workers amused with constant conversation." They talked about their children, husbands, and friends (Murphy and Murphy, 1985, p. 156).

In these and other societies, even in illness and death people were surrounded by their family and community. Chinas, who lived in a Mexican village in the late 1960s, provides a vivid example. For a while, she stayed with Dona Lucia, who was bedridden most of the time. But she was still very much part of the family and community. There was "a conscious effort to include the gravely ill member in all household affairs by placing her in a central spot where she can observe and hear everything." Dona Lucia "was anything but isolated from community life. There was a daily flow of persons coming and going. First, in a community without telephones, messages had to be carried by people. Early mornings and evenings after dark were the hours people came on business; to buy an ox team or a pig, to pay for milk they bought yesterday, to solicit orders for tomorrow's tortillas, to deliver a huipil Dona Lucia had ordered a month earlier, to buy maize, or to borrow against a pair of gold earrings" (1992, p. 56; 1993, p. 128).

Before we turn to the U.S., let us look at family and community in a Western society. As we saw, Young and Willmott found that extended families in Bethnal Green (East London) were thriving and strong. But these families were not isolated from their community. Indeed, they acted "as an important means of promoting" ties to the wider community. A person's "friends and acquaintances also have their families in the district, so that when he gets to know an individual person, he is also likely to know at least some of his relatives. The Bethnal Greener is therefore surrounded not only by his own relatives and their acquaintances, but also by his own acquaintances and their relatives." As people walked down the street, they saw and talked with relatives, friends, and relatives of friends. They also met in neighborhood pubs. They knew most people, they felt comfortable in a friendly place. A Bethnal Greener said, "familiarity breeds content" (1957, pp. 105, 116).

But those who left Bethnal Green for housing in a new development found themselves isolated from both kin and community. People there "kept themselves to themselves." Without the many shops and pubs that abounded in Bethnal Green, it was difficult to meet neighbors. "Their lives outside the family are no longer centred on people; their lives are centred on the house" (p. 154).

These are but a few examples that show that kin and communities touched each other, that families existed in, depended upon, and related to friends and neighbors.

The United States through the 1800s

According to some accounts, families were very much connected to and controlled by the community in Colonial Massachusetts. Neighbors and courts, ideally representing the community as a whole, felt free to, and did, intervene in family life. For example, "colonial magistrates might remove a child from the care of 'unseemly' parents and place it in some other family. Or . . . a local court could order the reunion of a husband and wife who had decided to live apart." Courts did so to insure what they considered the proper functioning of families and the preservation of social order (Demos, 1975, p. 60).

We may also assume that those 17th century Massachusetts families assisted each other, that they shared and cooperated, that they socialized with friends and neighbors. Certainly such cooperation did exist in late 1700s New England. As we saw in chapter 2, colonial families were largely self-sufficient. They made and grew most of what they used, they provided all care for ill family members, and they taught their children. But Ulrich argues that in 18th century New England "self-sufficiency was sustained by neighborliness." They traded and exchanged goods and services; there were "hundreds of transactions with neighbors." For example, "The interweaving of home production and trade is apparent in a brief entry in Martha Ballard's diary. 'Mr. Woodward & his wife here at Evening,' she wrote on December 18, 1789. 'I let her have 1lb. of Cotten for Combing worsted.' Although the Ballards raised flax, they did not own sheep, nor does cotton grow in Kennebec. . . . Once Mrs. Woodward had finished carding the worsted, Martha Ballard's daughter Dolly did the spinning and weaving, though Polly Savage, another neighbor, warped the loom" (Ulrich, 1987, pp. 242–244).

Women and men also exchanged labor with neighbors. "Berrying, nutting, breaking wool, fishing, husking, house or barn raising, and quilting joined work with sociability." We can find many similar accounts throughout colonial and U.S. history, and not only among the Amish. Slone describes the "workings" when her Appalachian neighbors came together to build someone's cabin, for example (Ulrich, 1987, p. 246; Slone, 1979, pp. 39–41).

Out of both necessity and choice, and for enjoyment, families in 18th century New England turned to each other. Almost all of life was communal. Ulrich concludes that this was "a world neither of free-floating individuals nor of self-sufficient households. . . . birth, illness, and death were all group events: friends even accompanied newly married couples on their wedding journeys" (pp. 248, 247).

Ulrich says that some of the ties with neighbors and communities loosened with the coming of industrialism in the nineteenth century. But they did not disappear entirely. For example, in mid-1800s New England, there was "community responsibility for the sick. When patients had to be watched around the clock, community members would rotate the responsibility. In one example, Samantha Barrett, a farmer, recorded the visitors and watchers at her side for the last twenty-one days of her life. Seventeen neighbors, friends, and kin watched her (in addition to her doctor) during that final period" (Hansen, 1994, p. 576).

As Americans moved from the East to the Midwest during the nineteenth century, they did so mostly alone or in nuclear families. Most left other relatives behind. These nuclear families faced hardships and challenges, and needed to turn to their new neighbors around them for help. Even though most of the time "people lived in individual, often isolated family units," they did often cooperate in "raising barns, plowing fields for a sick farmer, helping with chores, and sharing equipment." When a cow was stuck in a hole, "Henry ran off to get Mr. Perkins to help dig her out." And in 1889, Lucy Martin wrote in her diary that a pregnant neighbor, Mary Turner, whose husband was away, came to stay with the Martins when the roof of her house collapsed. The next day, Lucy helped Mary deliver her baby (McNall and McNall, 1983, pp. 71, 57–58, 64–66).

The United States in the Twentieth Century

Many sociologists and historians have argued that beginning in the nineteenth century, and accelerating in the twentieth, both the sense of community and communities themselves have declined. Muncie residents who talked with the Lynds in 1925 certainly bemoaned what they saw as the decrease of neighborly ties. Remembering the 1890s, they said: "Neighbors used to be in each other's house much more than they are now. . . . Mother couldn't understand when she came to live with us why people didn't run in more and neighbor as they used to. . . . People ain't so friendly as they used to be. There's less neighborly visiting." Some people attributed this change to telephones and radios. "Instead of going to see a person as folks used to, you just telephone nowadays" (Lynd and Lynd, 1929, pp. 274–275; see also Stein, *The Eclipse of Community,* 1960).

But in other places during the twentieth century, in small towns and ethnic neighborhoods, families were still very much enmeshed with neighbors and friends. Let us look at some examples.

In *What My Heart Wants to Tell,* Slone describes her Kentucky community from about 1870 to 1946. Families were close to their neighbors in many ways. For example, if a family were at the dinner table and neighbors passed by, you asked them to join you. Generally, "when two mountain people met, they always asked each other to go home with them, and when anyone passed the house he was asked to come in. The one who was passing also asked the other folks to go home with him. This was a very strict code of the hills, and it was very bad manners if you did not observe them." When you met a neighbor working on her garden, "you lean against the fence and discuss with her the wisdom of doing the cabbage first, waiting until the sun dries the dew from the leaves of the tomatoes and cucumbers." People ate fruits and vegetables from each other's garden, and it was not considered stealing. When someone died, it was the neighbors who dug the grave, made the coffin, and took care of all other needed tasks (1979, pp. 47, 118).

At about the same time, even as Muncie residents and other Americans bemoaned the decline of community, Italian and Jewish families in New York had close ties with their neighbors. They helped each other in times of need. When people were sick, neighbors would drop in to see how they were. Since they were poor, people needed help often. One woman recalled: "How often have I seen my mother help families who were evicted because they could not pay the rent. She wrapped herself in her old shawl, and went begging through the tenements for pennies. Puffing with bronchitis, she dragged herself up and down the steep landings of a hundred tenements, telling the sad tale with new emotion each time and begging for pennies" (Ewen, 1985, p. 119).

They were new to America, and neighbors helped them learn the new culture. Women socialized, watched each other's children, and taught newcomers how to shop and wash clothes. A woman who grew up in the Lower East Side recalled: "If someone got sick, the neighbors took care of them. My mother went for an operation and the neighbor took the younger children. They would shop and cook. Neighbors gathered in the halls, brought out their chairs, and chatted. If someone was bad off, they made a collection" (Ewen, 1985, p. 162).

Let us close this section with Buffalo Creek, West Virginia, in the early 1970s. Towns were destroyed and at least 200 people died when an unsafe dam created by coal companies burst on February 26, 1972, and accumulated sludge and water poured downstream. Former residents told Erikson that before that day they had lived in close communities and families. Neighbors treated each other as part of each other's immediate family. Everyone was concerned for everyone. They spoke with simplicity and eloquence.

> What's a neighbor? Well, when I went to my neighbor's house on Saturday or Sunday, if I wanted a cup of coffee I never waited until the lady of the house asked me. I just went into the dish cabinet and got me a cup of coffee or a glass of juice just like it was my own home. They come to my house, they done the same. See? . . . .
>
> If my car wouldn't start, all I'd have to do is call my neighbors and they would take me to work. If I was there by myself or something, if my husband was out late, the neighbors would come over and check if everything was okay. So it was just a rare thing. It was just a certain type of relationship that you just knew from people growing up together and sharing the same experiences. (Erikson, 1976, pp. 187–188, 190).

So, whatever may have been happening in other places in the United States during the twentieth century, at least in some places families were embedded in communities. Neighbors socialized and helped each other, families were supported by their communities. To be sure, there were conflicts, and not all neighbors helped or were friendly. And like caregiving within families, supporting neighbors can become burdensome. But at least in these places, people felt the need to give and to receive, and they enjoyed being with their neighbors. These ties to the community and to neighbors made families stronger.

Kin and Community Today: A Memory and a Wish?

It may be that for us today, ties between kin and community are mostly a memory and a wish, and only occasionally a reality. It we are to judge by the silence of family texts, families are largely separate from communities. Does their silence reflect a reality, or are they missing something? Bird and Melville do discuss communities and conclude that "it is common for today's families to be relatively isolated from their neighbors and the surrounding community. . . . [F]amily life has become a more private affair." Ties with neighbors have "eroded" and "walls of privacy" have been erected around families. Spouses depend largely on each other (1994, pp. 268, 277).

The disappearance of the front porch may symbolize the separation of the family from the community. "The relatively public front porch gave way to the more private screened back porch, sun room, or deck. In most suburban middle-class communities today, the front lawn . . . is mainly for ceremonial display. Not much of family life is visible from the street. Outdoor activities take place in the backyard, which is far more private than the front porch was in our grandparents' generation" (Bird and Melville, 1994, p. 278).

In the 1970s, my neighbors in Lexington, Massachusetts, recalled the 1920s and 1930s, when they would sit on the front porch of their house and watch neighbors walk by on their way to or from a store, who would stop and chat, often for hours. In the 1970s, hardly anyone sat on the front porch and almost all people drove by. Porch visiting was a sweet memory.

Can the nuclear family, with some ties to other relatives, fulfill the needs once met by neighbors and community? Indeed, without outside supports and checks, nuclear families may be less able to meet their members' needs. Parents without neighbors to help watch their children may be more stressed and less patient with them, for example.

But the memory, the longing, and some reality of kin and community links are alive. Isolated as most families may be, here and there we find old and new forms of kin and community connections. The reality and the memory of Buffalo Creek neighborliness may be missing for most of us, but traces survive in some places. You will need to think about your city or town and your neighborhood, you will need to read more and talk with other people, before you can conclude how many and how strong are the ties between families and communities.

Let me close with three examples.

The first example comes from Los Angeles. In the late 1980s, government agencies proposed to build a prison and a toxic waste incinerator in the middle of a poor and working class Hispanic neighborhood. Many mothers organized to oppose both of those projects. In their traditional roles as mothers, they had been "overseeing [their children's] progress in school, interacting with school staff, and supporting school activities." Along the way, they had created networks of friendships (Pardo, 1990, p. 254).

They summoned those relationships and networks to organize to stop the prison and the incinerator, which they saw as threats to the health and safety of their communities, their families, their children. They spoke of their "communities and their activism as extensions of their family and their household responsibility." They added to their work as mothers "militant political opposition" to outside threats. They linked "family and community as one entity." In doing so, they emulated, revived, and added to the historical connections between family and community. Women, and some men, worked with relatives, neighbors, and friends to shield and defend their families (Pardo 1990, pp. 251, 255–256).

The second example I learned just the day before I wrote these words. In my role as the local town councilor, and because I know many of the people involved, I was invited to attend a dinner honoring volunteers in a Watertown program called "Faith in Action." A number of churches created a board to run the program. They find people who need help shopping, going to a doctor, and for other daily activities, and they recruit volunteers to meet those needs.

Cohousing is a third example of people searching for community, for ties beyond their families. It is a concept and a reality that began in Denmark in the early 1970s. A number of families get together and plan housing which will allow "private dwellings for individual households and public spaces for community use" such as dining and play areas and laundry rooms. Each family has its own home but the common spaces encourage them to spend time with each other. In a Copenhagen cohousing community, "A common house is shared by all residents and includes a darkroom, couches surrounding a large-screen TV, a walk-in freezer, guest accommodations, a music room, and a computer area. On any given evening, 50% of the residents eat dinner together. Two adults, assisted by one child, plan each day's menu, shop, prepare and serve the food, and do the required clean-up. Each adult cooks one dinner a month; the diners then divide the cost at the end of the meal" (Bader, 1999, p. 22).

People are attracted to cohousing because it seems to create the community living that existed in places like Buffalo Creek. One resident said: "I've always wanted to live in a place where people drop in on one another. I never wanted to live in isolation." Another said: "Kids run around the open courtyard and I'd say about half the residents don't even lock their doors. People mingle." Still another resident refers to neighbors helping neighbors: "I want to live in a place where I know people will watch my back, watch my kids' backs, and who trust I'll do the same" (Bader, 1999, pp. 23, 25, 41).

According to Bader, there are still other attractions: "Some find cohousing appealing because of its ecologically sound emphasis on shared commodities, from snow blowers to cars, sports equipment, and washing machines. Others find the notion of group meals—even if they occur only once a week—a particular lure. Still others like the mix of residents, young and old, toddlers to retirees" (1999, p. 22).

In Denmark, there are about 200 cohousing groups, varying from 6 to 80 families. In the United States 20 already exist and 150 more are "in the planning or construction stages." Six other countries also have cohousing communities. All seek to emulate and re-create the bonds between family and community, between neighbors, that were people's daily experiences among the Mbuti, New Englanders in the 1700s, Appalachian communities, working-class families in East London, immigrants in New York, and people everywhere (Bader, 1999, p. 22).

CONCLUSION

The nuclear units of parents and children have always been embedded in networks of extended kin that related to the communities around them. Husband and wife and their young children have lived in contexts that included grandparents, siblings, aunts and uncles, cousins, neighbors, and communities at large.

Let me close with the recent history and present conditions of my ancestral village of Longo, Albania (presented in earlier places). Up to 1990, Longo had for centuries had close extended families that lived in a village fairly similar to the communities I describe in this chapter. Adult siblings, cousins, grandparents, and uncles and aunts were very much present in people's lives. For example, my sister Niki and her family lived about a mile away from our parents' home. She came by the house daily, as did her children. On various occasions Niki and our mother worked together, such as on the days they went to the local spring to do the laundry.

Families were also close to their neighbors (there were some arguments and disagreements, of course). For example, every family had a donkey to carry supplies up and down the steep paths of the village. On many occasions a family would need more than one for a particular task, so they would use their neighbors' for the day. I witnessed much such cooperation when I first returned to Longo in 1980.

Now that Longo has declined from 600 to 63 people (people have migrated to Greece and other places to find work), what's left of extended families and the village community? Most children and grandchildren return for visits two to three times a year, some more frequently (and those who came to the United States much less often). The arrival of cell phones enables people to keep in touch, some calling two to three times a week. The old people visit their children in Greece, and it's becoming common that when they can no longer live alone in their homes in Longo, they stay in Greece with their children; but always they are buried in Longo when they die. Some older parents stay in Greece for months and years to take care of their grandchildren while their children work. A cousin and her husband stayed in Athens for about a year tending to their grandchildren, but in February 2001 they returned to Longo; life in Athens was too fast and impersonal for them, and they missed their home and their neighbors. My brother and his wife were delighted to see them again; they had been close friends and neighbors.

In a few cases, grandchildren are left in Longo for months, especially during the summer. My niece Anthoula left her two-year-old daughter with her parents for two months in June and July of 2000, and then she came to Longo also to stay for August, to take care of the house and animals, while her parents came to my daughter's wedding in the United States.

There are many similar ties and ongoing relationships between kin. But the ancient tradition of parents living the rest of their lives with an adult son and his wife and children is now gone and impossible. Their children are in Greece and they want to stay in Longo, in the home and the land and the village where their lives have history and meaning. Only when they need caretaking do they leave, and, as we saw in my Aunt Sofia's case, they miss their home and neighbors intensely.

Despite the economic devastation and wholesale migration of people, Longo struggles on as a community. Indeed, with children and most relatives now gone, neighbors need each other more than ever. They seem to have responded so far. There is constant borrowing, sharing, and cooperation (and still some arguments) with the neighbors and the few remaining relatives (mostly older siblings and cousins). Here are some examples. When thieves stole my brother's fourteen sheep, relatives and neighbors gave him a lamb each so he could rebuild his flock. The only stores in the village are a steep walk down and up a rocky road, so people buy bread and other necessities for neighbors and friends who can't go or don't have the time. Finally, many homes don't have telephones yet, so people arrange for their relatives in Greece to call them in neighbors' houses, and they call from those homes. But of course the telephone is a very poor substitute for the daily personal contacts people once lived. "Cars, telephones, telegrams, and letters represent not so much a new and higher standard of life [but are] a means of clinging to something of the old" (Young and Willmott, 1957, p. 159).

And clinging *is* what my family and their neighbors are doing—clinging to kin and community under new and unexpected conditions. In 1999, time and again I heard cousins and neighbors tell me how they never expected, or even imagined, that they would spend the last few years of their lives without their children and grandchildren, and without most of their neighbors, and that when they need caretaking they will have to leave Longo.

And I imagine many Americans are clinging to the memory, and sometimes even the reality, of kin and community.

8

Economies, Migration, and Families

In gathering and hunting societies, people lived in communities of 25–100 members; they experienced their families and their communities as one. A few families composed the entire community. But as societies became larger, outside political, social, and economic conditions began to intrude on both family and community.

In the most recent past, beginning around 1800, industrialism and capitalism changed societies, and therefore families. They destroyed the farming economy, they created factories and cities, and gradually forced people to move to cities to find jobs to support their families. (See chapter 2.)

As capitalism developed, corporations built or moved plants to find cheap labor (which they continue to do, as we will see later in this chapter). These corporate actions always affected families. When they built new plants, people moved there to find jobs, leaving families behind or moving their families to these sites. When corporations closed plants, families were left without jobs to support themselves, and often they were forced to relocate to new communities to find work. Family lives changed. Grandparents, parents, aunts and uncles, cousins, and friends were left behind.

Thus, social, political, and economic changes have shaped family lives throughout history, and they still do so today. In this chapter, I present a very short history of migration of individuals and families. Almost all of us are in the United States today because our ancestors migrated to these shores, or were brought forcibly as slaves, because of many social and economic conditions. We have relatives and ancestors in other countries and continents. And those ancestors, in Europe, Africa, Asia, and Latin America, at some point came to that land from some other place. All these migrations to and from places were the result of many social conditions, and all shaped families.

Before we look at economic conditions in the United States today, and their influences on families, let us first explore migration and families, in the past and today, and throughout the world and in the United States.

MIGRATION AND FAMILIES

Archaeological and historical evidence tells us that people have always moved. More recently, migration has been the central historical event in all continents, whether to escape poverty in China, Mexico, southern Europe, and many other places; famine in Ireland and other nations; political and religious persecution throughout the world; and whether people came on their own because of these conditions, or were brought to the Americas from Africa in chains and slave ships. Separations from home, family, and community have forever shaped the lives of millions. Parents, children, friends, and neighbors were left behind, for most people forever. (Some migrants did return to their communities, as we will see later in this chapter.)

Poverty, the Search for Work, and Migration

Before we explore migration to the United States and internal migration within the United States, I present a few recent examples of migration in other parts of the world. They are but a few randomly selected cases; migration has been universal and extensive.

In many countries of the world today, you will find people whose ancestors came from China and India, among others. The Chinese left to escape poverty, partly caused by imperialist exploitation visited on them by Britain, other European nations, and the United States. People from India also left, or were forcibly moved, because of poverty and political instability, mostly caused during British occupation. Historically, Britain moved people from one part of their empire to another, primarily because they wanted them to perform some work in the new place. In the process, millions of families were separated. Today, you will find Chinese and Indian families in parts of Africa, throughout Asia, in parts of Europe, in the Caribbean, and of course in the United States.

Much migration was forced by colonial powers to serve their economic interests. For example, during the nineteenth century the Belgian government ruled the Belgian Congo (now the Democratic Republic of Congo) and often relocated people hundreds of miles from their homes. "Africans were forced to leave their villages to work the mines, cultivate and harvest the crops, and live alongside the roads and maintain them. . . . [F]amily members . . . endured prolonged separation as a result of the migrant labor system. . . . [There were] 'serious physical and psychological repercussions for all concerned'" (Ferrante, 1998, pp. 165–167).

More recently, in South Africa millions of people were separated from their families because of the white government's apartheid policies. It had forced most black Africans to live in areas within South Africa called "homelands," which were fictitious nations recognized by no country. These lands are barren, little or nothing can grow on them. About 87 percent of the farmable land in South Africa was (most of it probably still is) owned by whites. There were few jobs in these homelands, and most people got work permits for jobs in mines, factories, and other workplaces outside the homelands, often very far away. But the workers, mostly men, were not allowed to bring their families with them. Most visited home three to four times a year. The rest were gradually separated from their families. Families were devastated. Wives and husbands rarely saw each other; children and fathers became strangers.

Traditionally, most people moved to the United States and other places intending to settle there, although many did return to their homelands. For some decades now, many governments have created a new form of migrants, usually called "guest workers." For example, in addition to legal and illegal Mexican migration to the United States at certain times the U.S. government and U.S. corporations invited Mexicans to come to the United States as individual workers and not as families, to work here for some years and then return to Mexico. From 1942 to 1964, under the Bracero program, thousands came to the United States to grow and harvest fruits and vegetables, work on trains, and perform other work. About a quarter million came from 1942 to 1945 alone. The program began because of labor shortages during World War II, but U.S. employers extended it because it provided them with cheap workers. It introduced migration as an escape from poverty to many Mexican families, and many of them migrated illegally to the United States in later years (Chavez, 1992, pp. 22–23; Takaki, 1993, pp. 311–312).

A more recent and more extensive instance of supposedly temporary labor migration are the guest-worker programs begun by western and northern European countries in the 1950s and 1960s. They attracted workers mostly from southern and southeastern Europe, North Africa, and Turkey. Following World War II, as their economies expanded, Germany, France, England, and other European societies experienced severe labor shortages. They invited workers from poorer nations, who were to return home after some years. Most did, but many did not. They waited on tables, made cars, worked in mines, cleaned streets.

During the 1960s and 1970s, up to half a million Greeks, mostly men from their twenties to forties, left Greece as guest workers in Germany and elsewhere. In a population of ten million, these men may have been almost half the men in their age groups. Thousands of families were without children, husbands, fathers. Many husbands and wives grew apart; many children grew up without fathers. Some of the men married German women and stayed in Germany, including one of my cousins. He also owns a house in Athens and visits during the summers to see his siblings and their families.

Turkey had an even larger migration, also mostly to Germany. In the mid-1990s, of the 5.3 million foreigners in Germany, Turkish people were the largest group, almost all with relatives in Turkey. Some of them married German people and have children who have never been in Turkey. But they are not allowed to become German citizens, thus leading an uncertain life, neither German nor Turkish (Ferrante, 1998).

Also because of labor shortages, and because most Japanese people shunned dirty and dangerous jobs, Japanese companies began to invite guest workers (legal and illegal) from Iran, Malaysia, Pakistan, South Korea, and other nations. And oil-producing Arab countries, also short of workers, hired Egyptian, Palestinian, and other workers (Bryjak and Soroka, 1997 pp. 203–204; Calhoun, Light, and Keller, 1997, p. 484). (For migration from Armenia during the 1990s, see Filipov, 2001.)

In effect, for decades and centuries we have lived in an international labor market. For many economic, social, and political reasons, some countries and some companies in the world needed workers, and other places had people who needed work. In addition, some governments forcibly moved people to places where they wanted certain work done. For all these and many other reasons, people left families behind. The consequences, most negative but some positive, have been enormous, as we will see when we examine the histories of Irish, Mexican, and other migrants.

Migration to the United States

The English and other Europeans forcibly took lands away from Native Americans and started their own nation. In 1790, the United States was composed of 48.3 percent English people, 19 percent Africans, 1.8 percent Native Americans, and the rest were other northern Europeans. Migration to the United States never stopped. From the 1820s to the 1990s almost 60 million people came to the United States. From the 1880s to the 1920s, 27.5 million left southern and eastern Europe to escape poverty and oppression. Industrialism dislocated peasants all over Europe, and they came to the United States where industrialism created jobs building railroads, digging canals, and working in factories and mines. Most recently, 9 million arrived in the 1990s, and 3.3 million in 2000 and 2001 (Parrillo, 2000, pp. 130,171; *Statistical Abstract*, 1998, p. 20, 2002, p. 10; Rodriguez, 2002b).

Enslaved Africans. Let us begin with people from Africa. It is likely that the first Africans who arrived in North America in 1619 came as indentured servants, not as slaves. But the conditions Africans met later changed gradually and slavery developed by the late 1600s (Takaki, 1993).

No one knows how many people were forced onto slave ships in Africa for colonial America or the United States, and no one knows how many died on the way to these shores. Conditions aboard slave ships were horrendous and very crowded, and many died. "Estimates of the number of Africans brought alive into the Western Hemisphere [from the mid-1600s to the 1860s] are in the range of 10 to 15 million." About half a million were brought to the United States. Millions were thus enslaved for the profit of plantation owners and other capitalists (Feagin and Feagin, 1999, p. 237; Williams, 1944).

They were violently taken away from their families and communities. Almost none ever saw their families in Africa again. Imagine the devastation these separations caused to millions of families, both in Africa and the Americas. Imagine yourself living with such separation and you may be able to understand the pain and suffering of these families.

Irish Immigrants. Different in some ways but substantially similar was the experience of Irish people. Ireland was colonized by England from around 1200 to the 1920s. Irish people were forbidden to speak Irish; Catholicism was repressed; all the best lands were taken by English people. The Irish peasants were almost enslaved. The potato famine of the 1840s was the direct result of the English stealing the best land. The Irish were forced to cultivate the least productive pieces of land, usually on steep hills, and to raise potatoes, the one crop that grew best and gave them the most nutrition per acre. But the continued intensive cultivation of only potatoes led to potato blight, a disease that ruined crops for some years. A terrible famine followed. Somewhere between one and two million died from starvation. Migration had begun around 1820, but the famine caused a stampede to leave. Millions left for England, the United States, Canada, and Australia, decimating families and communities. Over five million came to the United States alone between 1815 and 1920, 1.2 million just from 1847 to 1854, immediately after the famine. (For descriptions and explanations of the famine, see Gallagher, 1982; Fallows, 1979; Takaki, 1993; Newsinger, 1996; Parrillo, 2000, p. 151.)

There was a massive splitting of families. It did take the calamitous and gruesome famine for people to leave their families, "for most of them were people with deep roots in the familiar soil, and bound by the web of family and religious ties." The Africans were taken by force, and the Irish were forced to leave, in the face of millions starving around them, to escape certain death (Fallows, 1979, p. 23).

Leaving was gloomy and mournful, for people knew they would never see each other again. For most of the 1800s, ships from Ireland took weeks to arrive to the United States, and many people died on the seas. Few people would hazard another trip to visit home, and even fewer wanted to live under English occupation again. Everyone knew that the day your daughter or son left was the last time you would ever see him or her again. Thus, families held what became known as "American wakes." Gallagher provides a detailed, vivid, and heart-rending account of the last few days and hours families shared with their departing sons and daughters.

> On the night before the departing one was scheduled to make the trip to port and board ship, the family held what later became known as an "American wake," a custom unique to Ireland. . . . Since departure was a kind of death, especially during sailing-ship days when the voyage across the ocean lasted two to three months and the prospect of a return voyage was beyond imagining, the emigration ceremony was inevitably associated with waking the dead. . . .
>
> During the week preceding his departure, the emigrant would make calls throughout the parish and beyond to inform his friends and neighbors of his intentions. In every cabin, cottage, or farmhouse visited, there would be a minor tempest of regrets, blessings, and good wishes. . . . Sandwiched in all this talk and hubbub was an invitation to attend the American wake at the home of the emigrant's parents on the night before he was scheduled to leave. Those invited were not obliged to attend, but almost all did, just as they attended funerals. . . . As one old Irishman remarked, "In those days, people made very little difference between going to America and going to the grave.". . .
>
> The basic elements necessary for a successful American wake were those that had for generations enmeshed the participants in their parish and village way of life—neighborliness, friendship, respect, warmth, reminiscence, dancing, singing, food, liquor, and a shared feeling of loss and regret at the permanent departure of a loved one. . . .
>
> The older guests could see that Ireland was on its way to becoming "one vast American Wake.". . .
>
> Finally, at three or four in the morning, as if concentrating in one act the love, sorrow, and loss everyone was feeling, the emigrant's father would stand and say, "Get up here, son, and face me in a step, for likely it will be the last step ever we'll dance."

This sculpture shows a mother and her son as he leaves Ireland for a new life in the United States at the time of the great famine. According to Maurice Harron, the sculptor, it shows "the aged mother with a dead child in Ireland and her grown-up son with a young sister who survived to make a new life in America." The scene bears witness to the pain of separation felt by all emigrants and the families they leave behind. The sculpture is on the Common in Cambridge, Massachusetts. *(Photo by Alex Liazos, and printed here by permission of Maurice Harron.)*

> As father and son faced each other, arms akimbo, legs springing in triple rhythm, each one trying as never before to make it a jig to remember, there would not be a dry eye in the house. . . .
>
> [At dawn, the guests left parents and child alone.] The parents did not want to embarrass their son; they tried, in fact, to appear calm, but this was the end of the American wake, the closing of the coffin, and as the seconds passed, a kind of family torment webbed the air and made it hard to breathe.
>
> "Be sure and write, lad, as soon as you can," the father would say, rather than wait speechless for the inevitable.
>
> "I will, Da. You can rest on that.". . .
>
> "[H]is mother] told everyone present, in a language as true as the emotion it expressed, that . . . [s]he and her husband would retain their full consciousness of loss and their full strength to suffer, knowing as they would that their son was still alive but forever gone, never to be seen, touched, or spoken to again. (Gallagher, 1982, pp. 121–134)

Other emigrants probably did not hold such wakes, but they surely felt similar emotions upon departure from their relatives. Before modern travel and communications, separations were permanent, and letters took months each way. Families in Africa, China, India, Greece, and everywhere mourned the loss of their children, parents, brothers, and sisters. Whether they left in chains or to escape famine, or to find work unavailable at home, or for a "better life," departure was and is always sad and awful.

Chinese Immigrants. Chinese people left their homeland to escape local poverty and foreign exploitation. Soon after they began arriving in the 1850s, they faced considerable discrimination and some violence. After 1882, the U.S. government severely limited Chinese immigration (Takaki, 1993, ch. 8).

Most Chinese immigrants were men who had left their wives and families in China. They had intended to save some money and return to their families, but about half of the 400,000 who had come by 1930 never made it home. Married men with "widows" still in China received "'letters of love, soaked with tears' that complained about their long absence." With time, "as they built their businesses and developed personal and social ties to their new community, they came to feel detached from their homeland and their families." Many store owners, missing their children back home, gave "candy, oranges and other goods" to white children in the neighborhood. Most remained bachelors all their lives (Takaki, 1993, pp. 219–220). (For Chinese women who left China for the United States since the 1960s, see Louie, 2001.)

Mexican iImmigrants. The relationships of Mexicans and Mexican Americans with the United States is a long and complicated one. Many Mexicans in the United States today are the descendants of people who lived on the lands the United States captured from Mexico in the 1848 war. These lands comprise most of present California, Texas, and the Southwest.

But through the years, other people from present Mexico crossed the border to find work. They did so legally and illegally, for a few years or permanently. The Bracero program of 1942–1964 is but one period in the long history of migration. For example, in the early 1900s, at least half a million Mexicans migrated to the U.S. Southwest. Factory owners, large farmers, and other employers encouraged them to migrate because they wanted them as cheap workers. As one person said, he worked "on the railroad, in the cotton fields or beet fields, in the hotels as a waiter, as an elevator man, or in the asphalt" (Takaki, 1993, p. 317).

Poor Mexicans are still crossing the border into the United States . They continue a long tradition of seeking work here, whether they are openly invited, or secretly enticed by employers, or chased when they cross the border illegally. In *Shadowed Lives: Undocumented Immigrants in American Society,* Leo Chavez (1992) explores their histories, families and communities in Mexico, their experiences of crossing the border, and their lives in the United States. (He focuses on people crossing the California border.)

"Mexican workers and U.S. employers are part of one international market." This labor market has existed for centuries. Today, Mexicans perform work most Americans will not do at the wages employers offer. Even though the U.S. government formally prohibits their crossing the border, Mexican workers are wanted and needed by hotels, restaurants, large farmers, and many others (Chavez, 1992, p. 39).

So people leave family, friends, and community to find work in the United States. But the migration of individuals is often part of a family history, of parents and others who worked in the United States in the past. For example, Enrique's father had been a Bracero worker in the United States. Enrique began his migration by leaving his village for Mexico City. After seven years there, he was earning very little money, so he decided to seek work in the United States, despite his father's warning that he would face many difficulties across the border. Another example is Andrea, who entered the United States in the late 1960s. But "five generations of Andrea's family, spanning over most of the twentieth century, have lived and worked in the U.S." (Chavez, 1992, p. 25).

Thus, a family history of going to America for work encourages many Mexicans to cross the border. But they, and others, have other reasons for leaving. They migrate, primarily, because of poverty. (Chavez reminds us, however, that most poor Mexicans stay home and manage to survive somehow.) Many leave to earn enough to build a house, or for another reason, and return. Some come because they dream of becoming wealthy some day. Others leave to escape conflicts with parents or spouses. And some seek adventure. Almost all have sent some money to relatives in Mexico, an estimated $10 billion in 2002 alone, often to their parents who are taking care of their children. Most return to Mexico after a season in the United States, but some stay and become long-term and permanent residents (Rodriguez, 2002b).

While they live and work in the United States, almost all have families back in Mexico, who are affected by their relatives' migration. Wives miss their husbands, and worry they may become involved with women in the United States and forget their families in Mexico. Parents miss their young children still in Mexico. For five years, while Hector worked in the United States, once a year he would visit his family back home for two to four weeks. During those visits, he noticed that his children had no affection for him; they hardly knew him. Felicia, his wife, raised the children alone, doing all the hard work, such as cutting wood.

Sometimes mothers migrate to the United States and leave the children with their husbands. Andrea was one of these mothers. But after her husband lost his job in Mexico, he too came to the United States. And other relatives were left to raise the children. Andrea and her husband worried about their children constantly, and they eventually brought the children to San Diego. "My life was very difficult. Sometimes, in fact, I would go see them and the little one would be sick and I'd think, Well, I'll stop working [in the U.S.] and try to find work here because my children are sick and unattended. Then I'd start working in [Mexico], but we just couldn't make it" (Chavez, 1992, p. 122).

Another mother had not seen her children for three years. "Estela, 35 years old, worked as a live-in maid [in the United States. She left her three children with her parents in [Mexico] after her husband abandoned her. 'Life in Mexico is hard and I am taking advantage now that my children are young to earn money.' When I spoke with her, it had been three years since she left her family, and she intended to return soon. At that point she did not intend to stay in San Diego. When she reunites with her family, it will be back home in Mexico" (Chavez, 1992, p. 123).

While in the United States, Mexican workers live outdoors in canyons, camps, garages, apartments, or houses. "They live alone as live-in maids, in nuclear families, in single-parent households, and in extended families" (Chavez, 1992, p. 129).Some share apartments with friends; sometimes two families share an apartment or a house. The low wages they earn, the need to save money for families in Mexico and to take back with them necessitate the sharing of housing. They also need to find work and to reduce the loneliness of living away from family and friends. They turn to relatives, neighbors, friends, and other Mexicans for assistance and companionship. (For living conditions, see chs. 4, 5, and 6; for problems in finding work, see ch. 8.)

Many eventually stay in the United States permanently. After they have lived in San Diego for some years, and if they have their family with them, they are less likely to return to Mexico. They do often express the desire to go home, but time and their children and grandchildren in the United States diminish that possibility. Their children, raised or born here, know and prefer U.S. culture, and they have friends here. To them, Mexico is not home. Thus, their children's links to the United States become a major reason to stay here. Also, parents want a better material life for their children, which they see as more possible in the United States. So they stay. For most, however, the memories of home and family and friends in Mexico live on in story and song.

Current economic conditions in Mexico seem to ensure more migration to the United States. From 1984 to 1994, the income of 90 percent of Mexican households decreased, for most 15 percent and more, while it increased for the richest 10 percent. Besides creating more political conflict within Mexico, this poverty will increase "the incentive for people to migrate to the U.S., the traditional safety valve for Mexico's economic problems." In addition, others are losing their jobs because U.S. corporations are shutting down their factories in Mexico and moving to China, where they pay workers only 25 percent of what they paid in Mexico. More families will be uprooted and separated (Russell, 1997, p. 33; Landau, 2002).

Immigrant Women Workers. Since the 1960s, millions of women have "trekked across mountains, rivers, oceans, and borders" to find work in the United States. They "sew our clothes; grow, cook, and serve our food; . . . care for us when we are sick; and clean up our messes." Most of them left families behind. They are usually paid below minimum wages, work long hours, and are exposed to unhealthy and unsafe working conditions. But beginning in the 1980s, they organized for better wages and safer work, as other immigrants did in the past (Louie, 2001, p. 3; see also Takaki, 1993).

Migration Today. Migration continues unabated, to the United States and most of the world. People have been arriving on the U.S. shores from Vietnam and Southeast Asia, from Haiti and Cuba and other Caribbean islands, from Mexico and Central America and other Latin America countries, from Russia and the Philippines and Albania and Korea, and many other places. People move to Europe and Japan and Saudi Arabia to find work. As some Greeks come to the United States for better economic opportunities, thousands of Albanians, Poles, Russians, Filipinos, and others go to Greece for work in the fields, to raise children, to clean homes.

As in the past, millions are on the move.

Each person's move touches one or more families. Old families are left behind, often permanently. New ones are created. In the process, millions of children are separated from one or both parents for years. One study found that 85 percent of children in migrating families had "been separated from at least one parent during the family's migration to the United States . . . [and] 35 percent of the children studied had been separated from their fathers for more than five years." Many were depressed, "feeling sad, worrying a lot," and not eating (Rodriguez, 2001a; see also Guendelman, 2003).

Today, telephones and airplanes allow these separated families to stay in touch. Such connections are a vast improvement over permanent breaks, such as those symbolized by the "American wakes" of the Irish. But telephone calls and periodic visits are still a distant substitute to living with or near each other, to being together daily.

Migration within the United States

Once in the United States many people in time moved from one region to another. They did so to cultivate new lands, to escape poverty and racism, to find better jobs, and for many other personal and social reasons. But always, to some extent, work and economic conditions played a role.

A few examples may illustrate the general history of internal migration. During most of the 1800s people left the eastern United States for the Midwest, which was then sparsely populated by white people (but very much populated by Native Americans, who were displaced by the whites). People were separated from their families and lived often lonely lives, often miles away from other families. "Life was particularly hard for the frontier women. Taken away from friends, family, and community, they were dropped on the prairie, as one woman put it, 'without even a tree to hide behind.' They were left alone in crude dwellings built as shelter from the fierce winds that blew across the plains. The loneliness was often unbearable. Food was often scarce, and feeding a family was difficult. It was impossible to keep clean in the blowing dust. Childbearing was especially hazardous." Some returned home; others moved on to more hospitable places (McNall and McNall, 1983, p. 6).

Another great migration was that of African Americans out of the South, beginning around 1900. They left to escape grinding poverty and violent racism. Also, new farm machinery was displacing them from farm work. And northern industry needed workers, especially during World War I; foreign immigration to the United States was severely limited after 1922 and 1924 because of new legislation; and there was another labor shortage when millions of men went overseas to fight World War II. (Many jobs, of course, were still not available to black people.) Factory managers often sent labor recruiters to the South. People migrated to the North even though they faced much discrimination there too. For despite its problems, the North was seen as the Promised Land, the escape from poverty and violence (Takaki, 1993, p. 342).

In North Carolina and particular southern counties that Carol Stack studied for *Call to Home* , since the 1920s three-quarters of each generation left upon high school graduation. After they found jobs up north, they would send money to their parents, and for their children, who were being raised back home. Young people continued to leave into the 1950s and 1960s. About then, however, many began returning to the South. The first generations of migrants to northern cities had found jobs in factories, but since the early 1970s many factory jobs left the United States. Facing poverty, urban violence, and discrimination, many returned to the South (Stack, 1996).

The effects of migration on families are many. Stack's description is of African American families whose members moved to the North, but it may be universal for all separated families. "Rootlessness is but one of the many costs of migration. Marriages are strained beyond endurance, children are torn repeatedly from their friends and their nest, generations are scattered, never to meet again. The community of trust supporting civil society is undermined; social capital is squandered. Efforts to maintain love and friendship and ordinary neighborliness must be started all over again from scratch. The toll is paid in the old homeplace as well as in the new town up the road, and individuals and families and communities continue to pay the toll for many years—probably even after scores of years" (1996, p. 197).

Debates on the Effects of Migration

Most of what I say on migration and families points to undesirable and painful consequences for these families. This is especially so for the families left behind, as we see in the tradition of the "American wake" in Ireland. To be sure, people who left parents and others behind often sent them money; they did so even as they usually lived under harsh conditions and poverty in their new country. But does such assistance (not universal by any means) compensate for the separation, for the longing to see people you love?

There is relatively little research and writing on the home countries of migrants. We read about the migrants' living conditions and the work in their new country, and the longing for their homes, but we know little about happened to those left behind. Mangione and Morreale's *La Storia ,* through letters and other documents, offers some information about families left behind in Italy.

> Women were especially affected by family separations. When their men left for America, mothers and wives wept bitterly. Some went into mourning. America, they said, was like a *mala femmina* —a bad woman—who lures men away from their families.
>
> For the women left behind, America was perceived as a *terra maledetta* (cursed land) where their husbands, sons, and fiancés were at the mercy of an infected atmosphere that made them forget their Italian past. "There must be something in the American air they breathe that shortens their memory," was the lament of many a wife. Especially disturbing was the departure of the father, who always promised to return in a few years. Those "few years" would often stretch into five and ten; for months at a time there would be neither letters nor remittances—only silence. . . .
>
> An early Italian feminist, Irene DeBonis, described the "sad odyssey" of the women she interviewed who, when a husband, father, or brother left, remained alone, obliged to assume not only the hard field work of the men but also the debts incurred by the emigrants before they left. The typical woman left behind was "young, strong, healthy, married only a few years and often only a few months at the time of her husband's departure. Frequently, she was pregnant or with small children, and invariably prey to the malice of village gossips.". . .
>
> Not all women summoned to America by their husbands were willing to go. Their reluctance usually derived from the realization that they might never see their parents again. A common

tactic was to repeatedly invent excuses that would postpone the departure to some future unnamed date. In many such instances the husband would eventually lose patience and threaten to stop sending maintenance money for his wife and children unless they joined him by a given date. When there were no children, the husband, feeling abandoned himself, threatened to discard the wife altogether.

Abandonment is one of the darkest aspects of the emigrant story; it usually befell young married women whose husbands left for America shortly after their first child was born and were never heard from again. (Mangione and Morreale, 1992, pp. 92–94)

As for the migrants in their new homes, it seems that until recently writers argued that migration had led to family breakdown for most people. Poverty, crowded living conditions, a new culture, and separation from families created disorganization and "families and kin groups broke down under the impact of migration to urban industrial centers and under the pressures of industrial work" (Hareven, 2000, p. 21; Hareven summarizes a view she does not share).

Since the 1970s, there has been much research on the history of families. Many of these historians have disputed the argument that migration destroyed families. Perhaps foremost among them has been Tamara Hareven. She shows in detail that when people migrated to the United States they usually came with their family, or lived near relatives and friends from their former communities, or both. They stayed connected with families. Relatives found jobs and housing for each other, and they sometimes took in relatives. The Irish, Italians, Jews, African Americans moving to the North, and many others did so (Hareven, 2000; Fallows, 1979; Ewen, 1985; Stack, 1996).

Migrants still move near relatives and friends and settle down in ethnic neighborhoods. Family and community assist individuals and families in their new lives. At Regis College, where I teach, almost all custodial staff migrated to the Boston area from one area of Colombia. They told others of job openings at Regis.

Hareven has called this migration experience "chain migration." She quotes a Canadian woman who went to the United States: "So when my neighbors went to the U.S., I decided to go with them. It cost [my parents] a little to let me go (not money cost, but feeling cost) but they knew the people well and they had faith in me. . . . I didn't know anyone when we arrived. . . . Then I met a woman who had taught me in school in Canada when I was small. She worked in the mills here. She helped me, found me a job in the mills. . . . My mother came up later with my little brother and my little sister. . . . As time went on, we'd have another person come up, and another, and finally the whole family was here" (2000, p. 38).

And families back home have often played important roles in the lives of those in the United States. For example, the people who left Quebec for jobs in Manchester, New Hampshire, relied on relatives back home to take care of "the property and family responsibilities. . . . A backup system in the community of origin was especially important, because French-Canadian immigrants in New England industrial towns during the early part of the century did not consider their migrations final. Ties with the relatives remaining behind had to be maintained to ensure that elderly parents would be taken care of and that the property or the farm (often still functioning) would be tended to while the owners migrated on a provisional basis." The migrants' lives were shaped by family and friends both in Manchester and in Quebec (Hareven, 2000, p. 39).

Similarly, African Americans who left the South for work in the North never broke ties with relatives still in the South. "Ella, the Bishops' oldest daughter, was the first of the children to come back. Strictly speaking, of course, they all came back, all the time—for holidays, weekends, two weeks in the summer, jobless seasons, times when their help was needed with crops in the field, times when their health wasn't up to the rigors of life away from home on the meanest streets of some of America's meanest cities. Almost always, they sent money home, and from time to time they sent the grandchildren home to Miss Pearl [their grandmother], sometimes for a summer, sometimes for part of a school year, sometimes for most of a childhood.

Unless they died or something died in them, they all came back to Burdy's Bend, all the time" (Stack, 1996, pp. 4–5).

Hareven and other researchers help us see that migration does not destroy families, that most immigrants have stayed connected to family and community, both in the United States and back home. But I know from other readings, stories I was told, people I know, and my own life, that the reality Hareven describes does not apply to all migrants, and it cannot erase the loneliness, sadness, and loss members of separated families experience. Many people never or rarely communicate with parents and siblings left behind, and they will not, or cannot, send them money. When I visited Albania in 1980, many people came to see me and asked me to help them understand why a brother, a sister, a child had not written for years, and to try to locate them when I returned to the United States.

Migrants Who Return Home

Many migrants have meant to return home after they had saved some money. Many did, but others stayed on in their new homes. Many others had meant to make their migration permanent, but some returned home: they were unhappy in the new land, they missed their families and communities, or both.

Millions who came to America, whether intending to stay or return, did go back. Among Italians, of the 4.5 million who came to the United States between 1880 and 1924, over half went back to Italy. The numbers were especially high when the economy was depressed. For example, 57,000 arrived but 170,000 left for Italy in 1908. Between 1908 and 1914, 2 million people left the United States to return to Europe. The majority were Greeks, Italians, and Slavic males who had come to the United States to earn money to buy land, for dowries for their daughters, and other needs (Mangione and Morreale, 1992, pp. 118–119; Parrillo, 2000, p. 183). Among them was my mother's father, who returned to Albania sometime in the 1920s. His son, however, stayed on in Detroit, and my grandparents never saw their son again.

Return rates have been high for other groups, too. But for some others, few wanted to relive the conditions they escaped. Most Irish could not imagine living again under English occupation and the poverty and starvation they endured, so only about ten percent left America. Jews had escaped centuries of religious persecution and oppression, and only three percent went back to Europe.

With the notable exception of Carol Stack's *Call to Home,* little has been written on return migration. Why, and with what dreams and hopes, do people go home again? Why did African Americans leave the "Promised Land" of the North to return to the South? "Why did they come back?. . . There were a million stories. . . . : ailing grandparents, a dream of running a restaurant, a passion for land, a midnight epiphany, rumors and lies, weariness, homesickness, missionary vision, community redemption, fate, romance, politics, sex, religion. Often people tell their stories in terms of pushes and pulls, disequilibriums, both personal and historical that perturbed the heart until the feet hit the road. They speak of problems up north pushing them out of the city, and problems down south pulling them home to help their folks" (Stack, 1996, pp. 6–7). (We don't know how many may regret the move to the South, and for what reasons. Nor do we know if any may go to the North again.)

Reflections about Migration

It is obvious that migration separates families. But people usually migrate *for* their families. They have little or no land, they have no jobs or jobs that do not enable them to support families. So they leave, hoping to find work in distant lands; work that will enable them to send money to their families, to save money to take with them if they return, or to send money to bring their families to their new homes.

Many do save enough and they buy land, build a home, open a business, and otherwise help their families after they return. Others, however, go home with little or no money, and broken in spirit and in body. Millions of migrants to the United States, whether they stayed or left, barely survived and were never able to save for their families (Chavez, 1992; Mangione and Morreale, 1992, p. 88).

The migrants who came to America may have missed relatives in the old country, may have lived in crowded urban neighborhoods, may have worked under harsh conditions for little pay, may have faced discrimination. But in time, most of them, and especially their children and grandchildren, did lead good lives. They founded new families and new traditions. The ties to Ireland, Italy, China, Mexico, and everywhere else gradually became distant, but still warm, memories. Perhaps the same experience awaits the recent migrants from Haiti, Vietnam, Russia, Central America, and all the other lands of origin.

But at least one generation had their families uprooted and often devastated. I imagine most of the new migrants to the United States, Europe, and Japan will experience the same separation and loneliness. Families everywhere are scattered. Some forget each other, and ties are broken. Even ties kept are fragile. Parents spend their last few years without their children and grandchildren near them; siblings gradually grow apart as telephones cannot bridge the miles between them; children only hear about grandparents they rarely or never see.

Families separate for long periods, often forever. New families are begun. In time, many of these new families also separate. Migration has been a universal human condition, affecting families everywhere. It will probably continue into the foreseeable future.

Can we change social, economic, and political conditions that usually necessitate migration? Perhaps. If England had not colonized and exploited Ireland and caused the poverty and famine; if Europeans and Americans had not enslaved millions of Africans; if poverty everywhere were not created by governments and elites—millions of families would not have been split. There would have been less suffering, and less need for migration by millions of people.

THE CHANGING U.S. ECONOMY

We have just seen that millions of individuals and families have migrated, and are migrating, largely because of economic conditions. Poverty and oppression in their own lands force people to seek work in other places. Economic conditions always affect families, providing the material conditions for people to support their families, or making such support difficult. They shape families in many ways (see "Consequences for Families," later in this chapter). Let us look at the recent history of the U.S. economy.

Note: The incomes, costs of living, housing prices, and economic conditions that follow are national averages. They vary, often widely, from region to region, and even within one state. For example, in 2003, housing prices in the Boston area were at least twice as high as they were in Worcester, just forty miles west of Boston. Also, the 2000 and 2001 economic figures from government publications were at the height of the late 1990s economic boom. Since then, increasing unemployment, government cutbacks, and other economic changes mean hard times for many families.

The 1950s to Mid-1970s

In the period after World War II to the mid-1970s, the average paycheck, in real dollars (what money can buy after inflation) doubled. This economic gain was created by the following conditions. (1) The government gave money to veterans who attended college, gave low-interest mortgages, spent to build roads, schools, and other structures, and provided other economic supports. (2) Unions were relatively strong and negotiated higher wages for workers. (3) Men with only a high-school education were able to find factory and other jobs that provided adequate incomes to buy a home and support a family (most wives stayed home). *There were* problems in the 1950s, as we saw in chapter 2, but the economy was growing and providing income and jobs for most families.

Economic Problems and Inequalities since the 1970s

The following statistics show that since the 1970s, the rich and upper-middle class have become considerably richer, the middle class has lost ground, and there are many more working poor. In that time, we have seen the first "generation-long decline in the average worker's wages in American history, and the stresses on kids and families have been ferocious." The economy has grown, to be sure, especially during the 1990s, but almost all the new wealth has gone to the top 15–20 percent of families. As you read the statistics, remember these conclusions (Finnegan, 1998, pp. 343–345).

A number of economic changes took place over the last three decades of the twentieth century.

1. Generally, there is less job security, with many corporations moving their operations outside the United States. Millions of manufacturing jobs (such as making cars and televisions) have disappeared, thus millions of young people without a college education can no longer find work that pays a living wage. Service industry jobs pay much lower wages (see below). And even 20 percent of college graduates have jobs that do not require a college degree (Newman, 1993, p. 49).

2. Unions, which once fought for good wages for industrial workers, have lost membership and power. In the 1950s, over 30 percent of U.S. wage and salary workers were union members, and the percentage was close to one hundred in some industries, such as auto makers. By 2001, only 13.5 percent were union members; 37.4 percent in the public sector and 9.0 in the private.

3. Service sector jobs, which pay much lower wages than manufacturing ones, have grown rapidly, replacing industrial jobs. "For every doctor in the country there are scores of hospital orderlies; for every stockbroker there is a fleet of clerical workers." Fewer people produce goods and more people work "in offices, banking, insurance, retailing, health care, education, custodial work, restaurant work, security, and transportation." The greatest growth in jobs in the first decade of the twenty-first century will be for cashiers, janitors, retail salespeople, waiters, registered nurses, general managers, system analysts, home health aides, security guards, and nursing aides/orderlies/attendants. Seven of these ten jobs pay relatively low wages (Newman, 1993, p. 46; Zinn and Eitzen, 1999, pp. 96–97).

In 2001, the average weekly earnings of full-time wage and salary workers were:

   All workers: women—$511; men—$672

   Service workers: women—$331; men—$438

   Machine operators, assemblers, and inspectors: women—$369; men—$512

   Professional and managerial workers: women—$732; men $1038

   (*Statistical Abstract,* 2002, p. 403)

4. The rise of automation, the export of many U.S. jobs to countries with cheap labor, and the decrease in the real value of the minimum wage have made it difficult for most workers to ask for raises, and so their real pay has remained steady or even decreased. In *2000 dollars,* the minimum wage has fallen from $7.92 in 1968 to $4.80 in 1995, $5.53 in 1997, and $5.15 in 2000 (*Statistical Abstract,* 2002, p. 405).

Declining Earnings. Millions of workers make lower wages. "In 1973, the real (inflation adjusted) hourly earnings for production and nonsupervisory workers averaged $14.19 [in 1998 dollars]. By 1998, that wage had fallen to $12.77" (Sanders, 2000, p. A15).

The decline has been more dramatic for young workers. First, three-quarters of workers 19–35 have no college degree, and, given the jobs available to them, they do not need one. In 1994, 25-year-old men were earning 31 percent less than comparable men did in 1973. In 1996, "young skilled or semi-skilled factory workers [made] one-fourth less, compared to the late 1970s, and laborers [made] about 30 percent less." One 25-year-old college dropout "has moved from one part-time service job to another—from Java Central to Borders Books to Havajara Bagel, never making more than $7 an hour, with few or no benefits." Children were victimized. From 1996 to 1998, 27 percent of children lived with "parents who [did] not have full-time, year-round employment" (Coontz, 1997, p. 127; Moberg, 1999, p. A21; Portman, 2000, p. B5).

Income and Wealth Inequalities. The economy may have grown in the 1990s, and unemployment may have stayed low at around 4–5 percent, but most of the income and wealth went to a few people. Robert Reich, former Secretary of Labor, describes the low incomes of millions of Americans who do necessary work. "More than 2 million Americans work in nursing homes—bathing and feeding frail elderly people, cleaning their bed sores, lifting them out of bed and into wheelchairs and changing their diapers. They earn, on average, between $7 and $8 an hour, about the same as janitors. Some 700,000 people . . . work as home health care aides, attending to the elderly, sick, or disabled at home. Their pay averages between $8 and $10 an hour—less than $20,000 a year. Another 1.3 million Americans work in hospitals as orderlies and attendants at about the same rate. Adjusted for inflation, most of them also are earning less than they did 15 years ago" (Reich, 2000).

Given these wages, there is considerable poverty. Thirty percent of American workers earn poverty or near-poverty wages. As a result, 11 million children lived in poverty in 2000, even under the very low and unrealistic poverty income of $17,600 for a family of four (Sanders, 2000; Portman, 2000; Bergmann, 2000; *Statistical Abstract,* 2002, pp. 441–442).

Let us next look at *family* incomes. In 2000, 72.4 million families had a median income of $50,890. About 21 percent made under $25,000; 49 percent under $50,000; 29.6 percent over $75,000; and 17 percent over $100,000. Where wealth and comfort begin for any family vary widely because of many circumstances: region of the country, number of people in the family, age, whether the house is all paid up, and so on. But assuming $75,000 as the bare minimum of a middle-class life, we see that 29.6 percent reach that level. And assuming $100,000 allows an upper-middle class lifestyle, 17 percent reach that (*Statistical Abstract,* 2002, p. 436).

The distribution of the income families earn each year has always been unequal, but it grew more so in the late 1900s. Dividing the total number of households in fifths, we see the following increases from 1979 to 1999.

Richest fifth	up 115 percent
Second fifth	up 43 percent
Middle fifth	up 14 percent
Fourth fifth	up 1 percent
Poorest fifth	down 9 percent
(Miller, 2000, p. 42)	

Thus, while the richest twenty percent more than doubled their income in that period, the poorest twenty percent actually saw a decline in their income.

Looking at how much of the total income each fifth made in 1975 and 2000, again we find increasing inequality. The share of the total income earned during each year increased for the richest fifth, from 43.2 percent to 49.6; for the middle fifth, it went from 17.1 percent to 14.8; and for the poorest fifth, it decreased from 4.5 percent to 3.6. Thus, in 2000 the richest 20 percent of households made almost as much as the other 80 percent combined. In dollar amounts, in 2000 the richest 5 percent of families had an average income of $252,582; for the poorest 40 percent it was $21,520—less than a tenth of what the richest 5 percent had (*Statistical Abstract,* 2002, p. 437; Caplow, Hicks, and Wattenberg, 2001, p. 173; Kerbo, 2003, p. 23).

Income inequality is even sharper when we look at the salaries of the richest Americans. In 1990, corporation presidents averaged a salary of $1.8 million. In 2002, just twelve years later, the average had grown to $14.9 million—that's $7,452 an hour. They made 450 times as much as the average of the salaries of their workers (Reich, 2000; Sanders, 2000; Hightower, 2003).

And wealth—the money and property families have accumulated over the years—is even more unequal. Unequal annual incomes create the wealth inequality. "The richest 1 percent of the population now owns as much wealth as the bottom 95 percent of all Americans combined." To repeat: 1 percent own as much as 95 percent do (Sanders, 2000).

The conclusion is simple and obvious: every year,

- a few people make much more income than most people
- a very few families have most of the wealth
- and these inequalities have only become wider since the mid-1970s

How Families Manage. The first, and most significant, adjustment families have made to the lower real earnings of most workers has been to have more members work. Mostly, that has meant that wives and women hold jobs (see next chapter). Indeed, in many cases, the combined incomes of husband and wife today do not equal the earning power of the husband's sole income in the 1950s (Newman, 1993, p. 19).

Families with one earner thus face severe economic problems. Their income is considerably lower than that of two-earner families. In 2000, married-couple families with both spouses working had a median income of $69,463; with only the husband working, it was $39,735. In single-parent families, the median income in 2000 was $37,529 for those headed by men, and only $25,794 for those headed by women (*Statistical Abstract,* 2002, p. 438).

A second adjustment families have made is to borrow more money. In 1949, the average household's debt burden was 32 percent of personal income. By 1999, it had grown to 103 percent. As a result, there were five times as many bankruptcies in 1998 as in the middle 1970s (Aulette, 2002, p. 90; Caplow, Hicks, and Wattenberg, 2001, p. 171).

Many families struggle to pay their bills and meet their needs. Two stories summarize these problems.

> Eight million Americans in families earning more than $45,000 a year say they've had trouble paying rent, medical bills, or for other basic daily needs, a U.S. Census Bureau report shows. Nationwide, about 20 percent of Americans reported problems paying bills. The poorest were the most likely to have trouble. But even some families with significantly higher incomes reported financial instability. . . . [M]any families with healthy incomes are still living close to the financial edge, without enough saved for emergencies. . . . Overall, about 49 million Americans said there was at least one time in 1995 when they had trouble paying an important bill: rent, mortgage, utilities, food or medical care. Most were poor or near poor, but some were earning higher incomes, including 2.9 million families earning over $68,000 (Meckler, 1999).

The Women's Educational and Industrial Union created a "sufficiency" standard of living for Massachusetts families, which ranges from "$15,888 a year for a single adult living in Boston to nearly $43,000 for a Boston family with one toddler and one child in school." A fourth of the families did not meet this standard in 2000. "'I spend two-thirds of my income just on housing and food,' said Maria Andrade of Dorchester, a single mother who is raising three children, 5, 12, and 16, on her $30,000 annual salary" (Blanton, 2000).

Housing. Housing costs and conditions vary enormously across the U.S. Generally, the cost of housing, as a percentage of a family's income, has increased dramatically. In the 1950s, "the average 30-year-old man could buy a median-priced home on only 15–18 percent of his salary." That was on only *one* salary. Today, most families need two salaries to afford a home, and they pay considerable more than 18 percent of their combined income. Housing costs rose dramatically in the 1990s, and millions of families faced a housing squeeze (Coontz, 1997, p. 33; Newman, 1993, p. 40; Barry, 1998; Ebbert, 1999; Wright, Rubin, and Devine, 1998).

There was a surplus of affordable housing units in 1970, but by 2000 there was a shortage of four million. Families have to wait up to five years for public housing. The guideline is that families should spend about 30 percent of their income on housing, but the typical poor renter pays 50–60 percent. "In nearly every county in the United States at least one-third of renters earning the median renter income for their area cannot afford a typical rent." They pay it because they must, but they cut back on food, heat, and other essentials (Pitcoff, 2000).

CONSEQUENCES FOR FAMILIES

Where we live and the work we do shape our family lives: when and who we marry, or, if we marry; if and how many children we have, when we have them, and how we raise them; the quality of our marriage; our relationships with our parents and other relatives, including how far from them we live. The ending of the 1950s-1970s economy, and the rise of the new service economy with its higher concentration of income and wealth in a few families, have affected family lives.

Families Doing Well

For many families, the U.S. economy provides adequate incomes for good housing, for vacations, for sending the children to good schools, and for various amenities. Many of my students describe such family lives, free of stress and major worries. These days, families lead satisfied and happy lives when both husband and wife work, like their jobs, and provide quality care for their children. Barnett and Rivers, in *She Works, He Works: How Two-Income Families Are Happy, Healthy, and Thriving*, make that argument (1996).

Now that most mothers work, families face new problems and conflicts (see chs. 9 and 11). But despite the conflicts and ambivalence, most women, working class and middle class, like working and are happy doing so. They like earning money, for it gives them independence, pays for their family's needs, and connects them to the outside world. The working-class mothers and wives who talked with Rubin in the early 1990s testified to these conclusions. They all recognized that for their families to manage they needed to work. The 1950s economy had disappeared. They liked the freedom their income provided them, they felt better about themselves, and would not leave their jobs. Phyllis Kilson told Rubin: "Gary always made all the big decisions, and I never felt like I had a right to my say. I mean, I tried sometimes, but if he said no, I figured I didn't have a right to contradict him. Now I make money, too, so it's different. I go out and buy something for the grandchildren, or even for me, without asking, and he can't say anything" (1994, p. 83).

There was also ambivalence, however. The reality and the myth of the 1950s families have left a powerful hold on our imaginations. We think that if a mother is not constantly with the children, "their future is in jeopardy." Mothers feel guilty. They told Rubin: " 'It's hard to be away at work all day and be a good mother.' 'Every day I leave my kids at day care, I think to myself: *What kind of mother am I?* It's like I'm not raising my own children. . . What if something happens with one of the kids I'd never forgive myself. . . . When one of my kids got in trouble, even my mother said it was because I was working'" (Rubin, 1994, p. 79).

Before we explore some of the problems many families face in the present U.S. economy, we need to remind ourselves that some or many families do not face these problems, and that despite these problems, most families manage to create good lives for themselves. Many or most families experience the joys I describe in earlier chapters. At times, of course, many families are overwhelmed by unemployment, or housing costs, or jobs that pay poorly, or other conditions. But we cannot forget that joys are as real as problems for most families.

Trials and Predicaments

The new economy since the 1970s has affected marriages and births in the United States. We saw in earlier chapters that people are marrying later, having fewer children, and having them later in life. Even though as many people as ever marry at least once, they are in marriages for fewer years because they marry later and more are getting divorced. "According to the 1990 census, married couples make up a smaller percentage of the nation's households than at any other time in the last two centuries." The 2000 census showed that the percentage of married couples is even smaller than in 1990 (Newman, 1993, p. 52; *Statistical Abstract, 2002,* p. 48).

Young men's incomes have declined dramatically. With less or no income, they have been unable, and thus unwilling, to marry and support families. The fall in real wages for young men began in 1973 and was soon followed by an increase in single motherhood. By 1993, half of African American men did not earn enough to support a family of four. From 1979 to 1984, half of black men working in durable goods manufacturing (cars, refrigerators, and so on) lost their jobs. These jobs had paid wages adequate to support families (Coontz, 1997, pp. 86, 134, 139).

MacLeod's study documents Coontz's conclusions. In *Ain't No Makin' It,* he talked with two groups of poor and working-class young men, first in the mid-1980s, when they were in their mid- and late teens, and again in 1991. Both groups lived in the same low-income housing project in Cambridge, Massachusetts. When in school in the mid-1980s, the eight Hallway Hangers (six were white) did not study and were barely passing. They had concluded that there was no hope for them, that no matter how much they devoted themselves to their studies, they would not find good jobs. They were utterly hopeless. One of them imagined that twenty years later he would have "shitty jobs. Picking up trash, cleaning the streets." They drank, used drugs, hung around, stole, and committed other petty crimes (1995, p. 69).

On the other hand, the seven Brothers (six of them black) were committed to their studies, did moderately well, and finished high school. They stayed away from drugs and crime. They believed and hoped that with determination and hard work they would find good jobs and make a good living. One Brother thought that in twenty years, "I'll have a house, a nice car, . . a good job, too" (MacLeod, 1995, p. 74).

MacLeod visited them in 1991 to find out about their lives and work. He concluded that neither group had succeeded in the new economy, although the Brothers were doing marginally better. Almost all 15 young men were failing occupationally, both in their eyes and in the eyes of the larger society.

The Hallway Hangers were working sporadically, unemployed, in prison, or selling drugs (usually more than one). "They have been employed as janitors, garbage collectors, cooks, caterers, couriers, cleaners, carpet layers, landscapers, inventory keepers, movers, packers, plumbers' assistants, groundsmen, soldiers, and store clerks. They have worked as car washers, and at junkyards, hotels, and restaurants. . . . [These jobs tend] to pay low wages, offer few opportunities for promotion, and encourage high turnover" (MacLeod, 1995, p. 161).

Chris had been in prison, sold drugs, and was homeless in 1991. He and his girlfriend often stayed with friends. He told MacLeod: "I wanna have a normal life so bad. You don't know how bad I'm aching inside. I just want so bad to have a normal life." Frankie was doing better. With the help of AA, he settled down. He also turned to religion. In 1991, he was living with his girlfriend and son, but he was unemployed (MacLeod, 1995, p. 157).

In the older manufacturing economy, most of the Hallway Hangers would have found steady union jobs and settled down. They would have married and lived in working-class communities near their families. But in 1991, none of them led such a life. Marriage and a stable life were difficult to establish with the jobs available to them, where "wages are lower, raises are infrequent, training is minimal, advancement is rare, and turnover is high" (MacLeod, 1995, p. 169).

What about the Brothers in 1991? Had their aspirations been realized? Did staying in school and out of trouble reward them? Four of the seven had attended college, but only one of them had graduated. They had "certainly fared better than the Hallway Hangers," but they had also "stumbled economically in the transition to adulthood" (MacLeod, 1995, p. 196).

What jobs had they found?

> Even more than the Hallway Hangers, the Brothers have been employed in the service sector of the economy. They have bagged groceries, stocked shelves, flipped hamburgers, delivered pizzas, repaired cars, serviced airplanes, cleaned buildings, moved furniture, driven tow trucks, pumped gas, delivered auto parts, and washed dishes. They have also worked as mail carriers, cooks, clerks, computer operators, bank tellers, busboys, models, office photocopiers, laborers, soldiers, baggage handlers, security guards, and custom service agents. Only Mike, as a postal service employee, holds a unionized position. . . . [Mostly] they have been stuck in low-wage, high-turnover jobs. (MacLeod, 1995, p. 196)

What about families? "Most of the Brothers are involved in stable relationships with women. And yet Mike, Craig, James, Mokey, and Super do not have children. Juan does have children—two baby daughters [with two different women] born five months apart. . . . Juan tries to be buoyant, but he is struggling to stay afloat. Under the combined weight of a job he hates and family responsibilities he can not properly fulfill, Juan seems to be slowly sinking. Hope is the only thing he can hold onto" (McLeod, 1995, p. 234–235).

Thus, both the Hallway Hangers' and the Brothers' lives were shaped by the relative scarcity of good jobs for working-class youth. Most Brothers were still living with their parents, and only two had their own homes. Only two had jobs with health insurance. Without it, how can people support families? Living by the rules did not seem to pay for the Brothers. (For similar stories of young people in four states, see Finnegan, 1998.)

Single Motherhood. But even though young men do not marry, many still father children. Most of the mothers, however, raise the children without husbands and with limited economic support from the fathers. "A man who can barely support himself isn't likely to look forward to taking the responsibilities of a wife and children" (Rubin, 1994, p. 53). (But as we saw in earlier chapters, most provide some support for their children.)

Young women who cannot find men to join them and raise a family still want children and a family. Althea Peterson, 18 years old, told Rubin: "The papers and the TV keep saying about how black girls are always having babies without being married and how we should wait and get married. But who are we supposed to marry, tell me, huh? It's not like there's some great guys sitting around just waiting for us. Most of the guys around here, they're hanging on the corner talking big talk, but they're never going to amount to anything. When I see white people on the TV telling us we should get married, I just want to tell them to shut up because they don't know what they're talking about. What black girl wouldn't want to be married instead of raising her kids alone?" (Rubin, 1994, pp. 54–55).

Another reality is that even if we were to reunite every child now being raised by one parent (usually the mother) with both biological parents, "two-thirds of the children who are poor today would *still* be poor." Some would be less poor, of course, but poor still, because the missing fathers have no jobs, or ones that pay low wages (Coontz, 1997, p. 140).

The Quality of Married Life. Even though many families thrive with both parents working, others do not. Often, as Hochschild points out in *The Second Shift* (1989) and *The Time Bind* (1997) jobs consume most of the parents' time and energy. After coming home from work and taking care of the children and housework (mostly women's work, still), there is little time left for the marriage. Also, childcare is often uneven; it is too expensive for most parents and often causes strains.

The tensions may be especially present in working-class families. They have less money to afford quality childcare and other services. Many couples work opposite shifts so one of them can always be with the children, and they hardly see each other. Alesha Adams told Rubin: "Daryl leaves a few minutes after I get home, and the rest of the night is like a blur—Shona's homework, getting the kids fed and down for the night, cleaning up, getting everything ready for tomorrow. I don't know; there's always something I'm running around doing. . . . Then on the weekends, you sort of want to make things nice for the kids—and for us, too. It's the only time we're here together, like a real family, so we always eat with the kids. And we try to take them someplace nice one of the days, like the park or something. But sometimes we're too tired, or there's too many other catch-up things you have to do. . . . I don't mean to complain; we're lucky in a lot of ways. We've got two great kids, and we're a pretty good team, Daryl and me. But I worry sometimes. When you live on this kind of schedule, communication's not so good" (1994, p. 95–96).

Drinking, Violence, and Other Problems. For many years, sociologists and economists have argued that worsening economic conditions, especially unemployment, increase the rates of mental illness, suicide, drinking, violence, and other family problems (Brenner, 1973).

Rubin's interviews uncovered some of these problems. When men lose their jobs, many feel lost and angry when they are not providing for their families (see next chapter). Men define themselves primarily as the providers for their families. For many of these men, the combination of unemployment and alcohol abuse contributes to violence against their wives and children. Inez Reynoso told Rubin: "I guess he tries to drink away his troubles, but it only makes more trouble. I tell him, but he doesn't listen. He has a fiery temper, always has. But since he lost his job, it's real bad, and his drinking doesn't help it none." Rubin asked if he hit Inez. "He did a couple of times lately, but only when he had too many beers. He didn't mean it. It's just that he's so upset about being out of work" (1994, pp. 118–119).

Children are also victimized. "Researchers in the 1970s found that the rate of physical abuse to children in homes with an employed husband was 14 percent; in homes with an unemployed husband, it rose to 22 percent" (Coontz, 1997, p. 129).

In their review of studies on "economic circumstances and family outcomes," White and Rogers state that these studies show "economic pressure increases husband's hostility and wife's depression and, through these paths, reduces both husband's and wife's marital happiness" (2000, p. 1044).

Moving Away from Family. Higher rents and more expensive homes often drive people away from their communities and families. It is happening in Watertown, Massachusetts, where I live. Housing costs have more than doubled in the last five years (1998–2003). Watertown, next to Boston, had been mostly a working-class community. As people with higher incomes have moved to town and driven prices up, many children of the older residents can no longer afford to live here. In Boston, where housing costs are also skyrocketing, Stephanie King told a reporter: "They say that people are flocking to [Boston], that's why rents are going up so high. But I don't think you should be driven out of your hometown" (Babson, 1999).

The same conditions developed in the New Jersey suburb of Pleasanton (fictional name). Working-class families moved there in the 1950s. But as housing prices increased steeply in the 1980s, most of their children could no longer buy homes there. Young couples moved tens and hundreds of miles away. Family and community ties were weakened. The grandparents still in Pleasanton could not see their grandchildren growing. In turn, aging parents could not receive help from adult children. Two such parents told Newman:

Amy: The house my son has in Madison, Wisconsin, is probably a nicer house than our home in Pleasanton. It's much larger. But they've had to go a long way from home to have that housing. While we think that it's wonderful for them to have it, we find it painful for them to be so far away and for our grandchildren to be that far away. We would like to have a close relationship with them, but a twenty-hour drive is not my idea of fun.
George: It's an emotional burden." (Newman, 1993, pp. 128–129)

Families before Economies

What can we do to control the harmful consequences of economic conditions and changes? Do we—as individuals, families, communities, nations—have any opportunity and power to shape economies so they will not hurt our families, indeed, so they will enhance them?

Families. As we have seen throughout previous chapters, families help each other cope with economic difficulties. Stack's *All Our Kin* and *Call to Home* document how poor and working-class African American families share food, help with the rent, raise grandchildren and nephews and nieces, care for elderly parents, and help each other in many ways to survive poverty and unemployment. While probably less so than in the past, most families still turn to kin when they need support and assistance.

Communities. In the last chapter, we saw how families live in communities, how neighbors enable families to live and meet their needs. Beyond such assistance to individual families, groups often organize to address conditions that affect many families in their communities. If you examine your own community, you will find such groups.

A recent example is the Greater Boston Interfaith Organization. More than sixty churches, and ten community development corporations, got together to create more affordable housing units in and around Boston. As a beginning they circulated a petition which stated the following goals:

1. Double local, state, and federal budget to create affordable housing.
2. Corporations and Universities commit their fair share of money and/or land for affordable housing.
3. Use appropriate public land for affordable housing.
4. Protect and increase affordable housing for renters and homeowners. (*Source:* flier distributed by the Greater Boston Interfaith Coalition)

The Coalition pressured local and state governments and institutions to commit resources for more affordable housing. They are also working to help families find housing in their communities. This organization and other groups were instrumental in getting the Massachusetts legislature to allocate $500 million dollars over some years to increase the supply of affordable housing.

National Social Policies. The United States is a rich country. We have enough resources for all families to live decent lives, with affordable housing, good schools, jobs with adequate pay, medical care for all, quality childcare for all children who need it. But as the economy was booming in the 1990s, many families were falling behind. This unequal distribution of goods and services is not dictated by any law of nature or society. It is a consequence of our political and economic institutions, which are dominated by a few wealthy families and corporations (Collins and Yeskel, 2000).

Many people are working to undo the injustice of suffering in the midst of plenty. One of them is Vermont U.S. Representative Bernie Sanders. He made the following proposals:

Establish a tax on wealth so that billionaires begin paying their fair share in taxes, and reform our tax system to make it more progressive. There is no moral excuse for some people having billions of dollars in wealth while children go hungry.

Raise the minimum wage to a living wage. The minimum wage today would have to be $7.33 an hour to have the same purchasing power it had in 1968. At a time of exploding technology and increasing productivity, no American working 40 hours a week should live in poverty. . . .

Enact a single-payer, state-administered, national health care program guaranteeing health care for all Americans. Our current system, at 14 percent of GDP [gross domestic product], is the most costly and wasteful in the world and leaves 80 million Americans uninsured or under-insured. (Sanders, 2000, p. A15).

United for a Fair Economy is one of many groups working to create a more just economy. They seek to reduce the vast income inequalities we saw earlier in the chapter. For a detailed description of proposals to achieve this equality, and a list of groups working toward that goal, see Collins and Yeskel, *Economic Apartheid in America* (2000).

Such economic policy changes are necessary if we are to help most families. For example, a national health insurance plan (such as exists in Canada, Europe, and other places) would assist the millions of parents whose jobs provide no health insurance. The quality of their family lives would improve if they did not have to worry about medical care for their children and themselves. For example, at present few part-time jobs provide medical insurance, but if there were a national plan that covered everyone, then both parents could work part-time and have more time for their children and themselves.

(In chapter 11, we will discuss work and how it shapes family lives. There I will present some proposed changes to address problems which work creates for families. They include: fewer hours for both parents; longer and paid family leaves to raise young children and care for elderly parents; and income support for families, especially single-parent ones.)

CONCLUSION

Our family lives are shaped by the economies of our societies. What we do to make our living—whether we work together to gather or raise our food, or whether we need to be away at our jobs for hours or days, or whether we migrate for work and are separated for months, years, decades, or forever—each affects how we relate to our family.

Migration has been a necessity for many family members, or even entire families, for centuries. It continues today. It usually provides a solution to poverty and enables families to improve their economic condition, but it also splits families, for at least the first migrant generation.

Economic conditions also shape the lives of families that do not migrate. Adequate or low income, work or unemployment, shorter or longer work days—these and other conditions touch our lives for better or worse.

9

Families and Gender

In addition to the economy, many other social conditions shape families. Among them are gender, class, and race. Every person and every family are touched by them. In our daily living, we experience all three simultaneously. At each moment of our lives, we are men or women; rich, poor, or somewhere in between; and black, white, Asian, or any one of a variety of "races." Gender, class, and race are *social* realities that always affect our lives. We discuss gender in this chapter and class and race in the next. Gender is the oldest and most pervasive social division.

SEX AND GENDER

Sex refers to our primary sex characteristics; it is a biological concept. Although almost all of us are born either female or male, some people do enter the world intersexed. They possess "some mixture of male and female biological characteristics." But societies today recognize only male and female, and intersexed people are assigned to one of these two groups. Often, operations are performed to change these people's biology so they can become male or female. And about 25,000 people have changed their sex as adults. But at least some societies have recognized more than two sexes (Ferrante, 2000, pp. 328–330; Money and Erhardt, 1972; Ward, 1999; Nanda and Warms, 1998).

Gender refers to the emotions, behaviors, appearance, expectations, and roles societies assign to boys and girls, women and men. As little children, we are taught what is appropriate and expected from boys and girls. The Mundurucu (discussed in earlier chapters) are an example of the creation of different gender identities. "By the age of five or six, the watershed between boys and girls is reached. The little girls maintain a focus on the household, but the boys begin to range throughout the village and out into the nearby savannahs. This is the start of the classic pattern in primitive societies, which sees the sexes divide into separate play groups, the boys striking out from the home and the girls staying behind." Boys start following their fathers, and at around twelve they join the men in the men's house. Girls, on the other hand, while playing with other girls, stay closer to the house and their mothers. They begin helping raise babies and perform various chores. Thus Mundurucu families, like families in many other societies, direct girls and boys to different lives and relationships within the family (Murphy and Murphy, 1985, pp. 199–201).

Some other societies place less emphasis on gender differences. The Ju/'hoansi, for example, minimize differences between girls and boys. They are not segregated by sex, and neither is raised to be submissive or fierce. Girls are as free as boys, as active as boys, and children play in mixed age and sex groups. Boys are somewhat "more physically aggressive than girls" (Shostak, 1981, p. 109).

During the last three decades of the twentieth century there was a lively and intense debate over whether there has been equality or inequality between women and men. All anthropologists agreed that men and women are socialized, treated, and behave differently.

159

Most of them also concluded that men have been more powerful than women, that men's roles and lives have had more prestige. These differences were much smaller in gathering-hunting societies, but even there they did exist, according to most anthropologists (Mead, 1935; Shostak, 1981; Nanda and Warms, 1998; Ward, 1999; Kottak, 2000; Liazos, 1989, ch. 12).

But some anthropologists disagreed and concluded that at least in some societies women have held equal social positions with men, especially in gathering-hunting societies. There is a debate on what conditions create this equality. One position holds that where women contribute equally to the material needs of the group, and they control the use of what they produce or earn, equality prevails. (Leacock, 1981, makes that argument eloquently. See also Liazos, 1989, ch. 12.)

Even writers who think that there has been social equality, however, agree that women and men live and behave differently. These differences in behavior have coexisted with social equality. (For two examples, see Murphy and Murphy, 1985; Chinas, 1992). We do know of at least one society, however, where men's and women's roles have been very similar. Among the Western Bontoc in the Philippines, men and women share 81 percent of the tasks in their society, among them cooking and feeding the children. The 19 percent they do not share are mostly seasonal tasks (Bacdayan, 1977).

We men and women are much more alike than we are different. Gayle Rubin, an anthropologist, concludes that "far from being an expression of natural differences, exclusive gender identity is the suppression of natural similarities." We are different, of course, but not "as different as night and day, earth and sky, yin and yang, life and death. In fact, from the standpoint of nature, men and women are closer to each other than either is to anything else" (Rubin, 1975, p. 180). (See also Burke, 1996; Vannoy, 2001, chs. 5–11, "learning to do gender.")

SOCIALIZATION, SOCIAL BARRIERS, AND RESISTANCE

Let us see briefly how gender differences have been created in the United States. Training for these socially created differences begins at birth and becomes well developed by age five. Children are taught that women and men "differ in the levels of independence, aggression, activity, strength, fearlessness, dominance, obedience, expressiveness, concern with physical appearance, nurturance, intellectual ability, and mechanical competence" (Hesse-Biber and Carter, 2000, pp. 95–96).

Most children learn early, and learn well, to follow the gender script. Some do not, however, and their parents and others worry about them. In a few cases, some children were "treated" so they would conform to gender expectations. Boys and girls were brought to clinics and were given behavior and other therapies. What transgressions did they commit? Burke provides case studies of such children. In 1978, Becky was eight, and the following behaviors convinced her parents to send her for "experimental behavior treatment" (funded by the U.S. Public Health Service and the National Institute of Mental Health) (Burke, 1996).

"Becky liked to stomp around with her pants tucked into her cowboy boots, and she refused to wear dresses. She liked basketball, and climbing, and if she wore a dress, she didn't like the idea that the boys might see her underwear. She liked 'rough-and-tumble play' which, in psychological terminology, is the hallmark of the male child. She liked to play with her toy walkie-talkies, rifle, dart game and marbles. She stood with her hands on her hips, fingers facing forward. She swung her arms, and took big, surefooted strides when she walked. Becky's mother told her, 'I'm taking you to a doctor because you act too much like a boy. I don't want you to be like a boy when you grow up'" (Burke, 1996, p. 5).

What did boys do to earn "treatment"? When he was almost five, one night Kraig "was putting his infant sister's clothing on her stuffed animals" and his father "became furious and spanked him while his mother stood by, watching." The doctor who "treated" him wrote that Kraig "continually displayed pronounced feminine mannerisms, gestures, and gait, as well as exaggerated feminine inflection content of speech. He had a remarkable ability to mimic all the subtle feminine behaviors of an adult woman" (Burke, 1996, pp. 33, 35).

Training begins at birth. Girls are perceived as softer and weaker. Parents tend to handle boys more vigorously and encourage more physical activity with them. In one experiment, five young mothers were given Beth, "a six-month-old in a pink frilly dress for a period of observed interaction; five others were given Adam, a six-month-old in blue overalls. Compared to Adam, Beth was smiled at more, offered a doll to play with more often and described as 'sweet' with a 'soft cry.' Adam and Beth were the same child" (Lake, 1975, as summarized in Oakley, 1981, p. 96).

Another study found that day-care teachers reacted differently to 12–month-old boys and girls, even though the children communicated similarly by "gestures, gentle touches, whining, crying, and screaming." But the teachers "tended to ignore assertive acts by girls and to respond to assertive acts by boys. Thus, by the time these toddlers reached two years of age, their communication styles showed dramatic differences." These were created, not natural, differences (Ferrante, 2000, p. 347).

Probably unconsciously, parents subtly give different messages to their children. When her son fell from his bike, a mother told him "Up and at 'em, Tiger" and urged him to get back on his bike. But when her twin daughter fell, she told her, "Honey, are you sure you're all right? Come and sit with me a minute." No fourteen-month-old girl likes to wear jewelry on her own. Parents put it on her and praise her for looking pretty. In time, little girls learn to like wearing it, but it is something they were taught to like. Boys, too, are taught by their families and others what later seems natural. It begins with infant boys and continues unabated. Boys who are not athletic and physical are ridiculed and called sissies and other names. Some, as we saw, were even sent to therapy where they were taught appropriate boy behavior (Sadker and Sadker, 1994, p. 254; Townsend, 1998, p. 368; Burke, 1996).

We use many ways to create male and female gender identities. For example, we discourage strength in women. Also, we exaggerate sex differences when teenage girls are taught to shave body hair. (For a fascinating discussion and more examples, see Ferrante, 2000, ch. 11).

Most gender training, especially in the early years, takes place in the family. But schools soon come to play an important role, also. Gender identities are created even as children are taught seemingly neutral lessons. For example, when a textbook teaches children about silent letters, it may give as examples "plumber" and "knit." If pictures accompany the lesson, the book would show a man plumber and a woman who knits—teaching children what men and women should do. One text reversed those images and showed a boy knitting and a girl working as a plumber. (Sadker and Sadker, in *Failing at Fairness,* 1994, document thoroughly and analyze how schools indoctrinate boys and girls with gender expectations.)

But socialization, pervasive and powerful as it is, cannot fully explain why women do most child care, why fathers become providers, and why men and women generally hold different jobs and careers. Often, schools, companies, governments, and the culture in general have rules and practices that force women into gender roles. For example, women have been going into nursing partly because as girls they played nurse, but also because medical schools did not accept them as students or discouraged them from applying.

Let us look at two examples. Management openings at Lucky Stores were never posted and women never knew to apply, and they were filled with men. When women found this out and sued for discrimination, the company argued that women were not interested in these positions. It lost in court and began posting openings, and soon "the percentage of women in entry-level management positions jumped from 12 to 58 percent. . . . [I]f we improve structural barriers to advancement, women will seek to improve their position" (Ferrante, 1995, p. 408).

During World War II, with men fighting overseas, women began to enter previously male occupations, such as bartending. After the war, male bartender unions "mobilized to drive . . . women from the trade." Soon there were very few women bartenders. But after the women's movement of the 1960s and 1970s, and after anti-discrimination laws were enacted, women began tending bar once again. By 2001, 51 percent of bartenders were women, up from 48.4 percent in 1983 (Brenner, 1998, p. 9; *Statistical Abstract,* 2002, p. 383). (See also Walshok's *Blue-Collar Women: Pioneers on the Male Frontier,* 1981.)

Thus, gender roles—in families, in schools, at work, and in marriages—are the products both of socialization and social barriers erected by institutions. Nothing biological or natural decrees that men tend bars and women wait on tables, that men are managers and women sales people, that men cut the grass and women do the laundry. (See Andersen, 2000, pp. 46–47 Ferrante, 2000, pp. 348–349; Vannoy, 2001.)

Indeed, people often choose what childhood lessons they will practice as adults. For example, Evan Holt argued that he avoided housework because he was brought up that way. But "Evan didn't do many other things he was brought up to do, like go to church, avoid using credit cards, or wait to have sex until after marriage. In these areas of life he was his own man. But around the house, he said he was just doing what his mother taught him." Nancy Holt was burdened with the housework because Evan created a barrier by refusing to do it, not because Evan was taught it was women's work (Hochschild, 1989, p. 218).

Socialization and social barriers are indeed powerful, but people often resist and struggle against them. Sometimes the resistance fails, as it did for Nancy Holt, who eventually resigned herself to Evan's refusal and did the housework he refused to share. In other cases, women's resistance to housework leads to men sharing it, as we will see below (Hochschild, 1989, ch. 12).

Gender roles, like all roles, are not scripts that we must follow as actors who play roles on stage. Even when people comply, we cannot assume they do so happily and willingly. Various forms of coercion are often used to ensure compliance. And history clearly shows that people have resisted, despite threats and penalties. Individually and in groups, women and men have defied gender and other roles. Along the way, many have suffered for their resistance. Nevertheless, they marched, defied parents and other relatives, organized, rebelled, and spread visions of different lives. For example, women in the 1970s organized to create shelters for abused women. (For details, see Schechter, 1982; and ch. 13. See also Ferrante, 2000, for different reactions to gender expectations.)

Ferrante concludes that "human beings do not passively accept gender ideals regarding masculinity and femininity. In fact, most people find ways to subvert these ideals through deception, secret agreements with others, impression management, or outright challenges to the ideals. . . . We might argue that resistance, compliance, and the strain of simultaneously complying yet resisting speak to the importance of gender ideals in shaping our lives" (2000, pp. 339–340).

GENDER IN U.S. HISTORY

In brief summary: In Colonial America, women and men supported their families by raising and producing together all the essential goods they needed. Most women and men worked in and around their families. Mothers and fathers were near their children. Colonial fathers "were active in all aspects of domestic life, from monitoring their wives' pregnancies to taking responsibility for the daily socialization of children." Industrialism took fathers out of the family environment and transformed mothers into non-producing housewives. During the 1800s, the partnership between husbands and wives gradually disappeared. Most women were not allowed to work and the house became their life: they cooked, cleaned, and raised the children. Gender typing became extreme for women and men, for men were removed from the home and became "good providers" (discussed later in this chapter). By 1900, most women were out of the labor force and housebound. Various social, economic, and political changes since 1900 (outlined in previous chapters) have gradually brought women out of the house. By 2001, 73.9 percent of women were in the labor force, as were 87.4 percent of men.

This compares to 20 percent of women and 85.7 percent of men in 1900. However, women still do most of the housework and child care (Coontz, 1997, p. 62;*Statistical Abstract,* 2002, p. 369; Liazos, 1989, p. 480).

Let us look briefly at Muncie, Indiana (Middletown). In 1890, respectable women were to stay home, but 10 percent did hold jobs. By 1925, almost 25 percent did. Interestingly, a 1924 survey of 446 high school girls showed that 89 percent said "they were planning to work after graduation." Most would stop upon marriage, but many would continue because their families needed the money. In 1928, 28 percent of working women were married (Lynd and Lynd, 1929, pp. 25–27).

There was indeed an ideology of male dominance in Colonial America. In theory, women were the inferior sex; "the proper attitude of a wife towards her husband was 'a reverent subjection.'" But Demos and some other historians argue that in daily living their roles were not sex typed. Because they worked as partners in each other's presence, because husbands needed their wives' work as much as wives needed their husbands', women were essentially equal to men. Most historians, however, do not agree. They believe that Colonial gender roles prescribed different work for the sexes and created a system of male dominance (Demos, 1970, p. 83; 1975, p. 63; Hesse-Biber and Carter, 2000, p. 19).

By the 1800s, here is some evidence that gender roles were not sharply different. For example, men were not exclusively practical-minded family providers. In the mid-1800s, New England men (farmers and artisans) "often cared for the sick"—other men and their wives. There was a "capacity for intimacy" in men of all classes. In "battlefields, the workplace, the wild western frontier and fraternal societies" men revealed feelings for each other and they developed friendships (Hansen, 1994, pp. 576, 579).

In conclusion, the gender division that consigned women to home and full-time motherhood was a creation of the 19th and early 20th centuries. Industrialism produced it. In almost all societies, women were not full-time housewives and did not raise children alone (see ch. 5). The 1950s were almost a parody of the ideals of men as providers, distant from children and housework, and women confined to housework and children. Even in the 1950s, of course, a large minority of women did work, 25 percent in 1950 and 32 percent in 1960.

FAMILIES AND GENDER TODAY

Are men's and women's gender roles as rigid as they were decades ago, or are they changing? Have men begun sharing child care and housework, now that their wives are holding jobs? Is the man's "good provider role" diminishing? What is changing, and how much, in gender roles? How are families affected by these changes?

The conflict between motherhood and work, and fatherhood and work, too, is not inevitable. In all societies, fathers and mothers have both worked and parented, although usually differently. Men have cared for their children, and women have provided for their families. Among the Mbuti, for example, sometime in the second year children became closer to their father. He "begins to fondle the child as its mother does. He takes it to his breast and holds it there. With everything else so familiar, the child explores for milk, but instead of milk is given its first solid food. This person offers everything the mother has always given; however, the food he offers comes not from the breast but from his own mouth or his fingers. The child thus learns to distinguish between *ema* and *eba,* mother and father. At the same time, it learns to equate them" (Turnbull, 1983, p. 40).

Men as "Good Providers"

In her 1981 paper "The Good-Provider Role," Jessie Bernard proclaimed the demise of the male provider. That may have been more a hope than a prediction. Even though most wives are providing a significant portion of their families' income, most men are struggling with this change and still feel the need to be their families' providers.

The husband as the sole financial and material provider of his family was a product of the industrial revolution. In Colonial times, when "husbands and wives ran farms, shops, or businesses together, a man might be a good, steady worker, but the idea that he was *the* provider would hardly ring true . . . [women] were still viewed as performing a providing role, and they pursued a variety of occupations." Industrialism gradually removed men from their homes and sent them to factories, shops, and offices, and made most women into housewives who earned no money and produced no food, clothing, or other material goods. Men earned all the income to provide for their wives and children, their dependents (Bernard, 1981, pp. 276–277).

A man's worth, his social standing, was entirely judged by his ability to provide for his family; a woman's worth was judged by her housework and childrearing. A woman was to be grateful if her husband was a good provider, and expect no more. "If in addition to being a good provider, a man was kind, gentle, generous, and not a heavy drinker or gambler, that was frosting on the cake. Loving attention and emotional involvement in the family were not part of a woman's implicit bargain with the good provider." Thus emerged the roles of men as practical, unemotional workers and women as nurturers. Thus, in the early 1970s, a woman whose husband was the stereotypical provider told Rubin: "I guess I can't complain. He's a steady worker; he doesn't drink; he doesn't hit me" (Bernard, 1981, p. 277; Rubin, 1976, p. 93).

This role had its rewards. A man derived satisfaction from supporting his family and status in the eyes of his neighbors. In addition, his wife cooked for him, washed his clothes, raised his children. A man's entire purpose in life, his identity as a human being, revolved around his being a good provider. Bob Ford describes such a marriage,

> Betty was an excellent cook, a very neat housekeeper, a good mother, equipped with a sense of humor. Many of the tedious tasks she seemed to perform so willingly were devoted to make life as smooth as possible for husband Ed.
> This included cooking his favorite meals, shopping for his suits, shirts, ties, socks, shining his shoes, and doing all the laundry, in the day before drip-dry. Many hours were spent at the ironing board, getting starched collars just so, ironing sheets and pillowcases. What amazed me most was a special way she had of folding his socks, carefully mated, so that all Ed had to do was stick a toe in and the sock would kind of slide on. Ed's part of the marital bargain, one he did well, was to make a darn good living, providing many of the luxuries both he and Betty were deprived of growing up. (Ford, 1994; used with permission of the author) (As we'll see later, men like Ed and Bob were also strangers to their children.)

But there was also a danger and a cost. It was "an all-or-nothing game." Nothing could compensate if a man were not a good provider. Being loving, gentle, kind, friendly might be good qualities, but you were still a failure if you did not earn enough money for your family to live by the material standards of your community. Thus men's emotions were gradually repressed. Men gained respect by being tough, practical, and successful in the work world, not by nurturing their children and wives. "Sometimes it looked like a no-win game." If you worked hard at a job you did not like, but provided for your family, you gained status but no satisfaction. If you worked at a job you liked, but for less money, you had satisfaction, but no status.

In Muncie, Indiana, in the 1920s, "as in 1890 a healthy adult male, whether married or unmarried, loses caste [status] sharply by not engaging with the rest of the group in the traditional male activity of getting a living." It was thus in Pleasanton, a New Jersey suburb, in the 1950s: "the most important, overriding concern for men of this generation was to pay the bills. To this end everything else—all forms of personal satisfaction—had to be subordinated. Hence, many took jobs in insurance or sales that were . . . respectable but not nourishing for the soul. The meaning of work was first and foremost instrumental, to provide for the family" (Lynd and Lynd, 1929, p. 25; Newman, 1993, p. 82).

This preoccupation with providing for their families alienated fathers from their children. In the same column cited above, "Stealing the children," Bob Ford, who raised his children from the late 1950s to the early 1970s, regretted his relative absence from their lives. The theft of his children took place while he was working to provide.

It was cloaked in such actions as "keeping the kids out of dad's hair when he came home from a hard day's work." It was followed by getting the children all ready for bed, with a quick kiss from dad, momentarily diverted from his newspaper, or a quick visit to the kids' bedrooms to say good-night. There were generations of men who never changed a diaper, men who proudly stated—in regard to cooking—that they didn't even know how to boil water. . . .

In most of my years as "Pop" to four children, the old rules were in effect. In the evening I'd flop into a comfortable chair, prop my arms on the armrests, and spread out the full-sized paper, an effective shield from little people. [Then something happened.] My third child, Mike, began the habit of quietly moving into position to give the paper a sudden whack, scaring the hell out of me—every time. For years, I put this in the category of a prank, just a bugging of Pop. . . . To my shame, it has only occurred to me recently that both Mike and Chris were probably . . . asking me to come out from my hiding place, to interact with them, to be more of a father.

Looking around at the young families . . . and the roles . . . young fathers are taking in the loving care of their children, I sometimes have tears of regret for opportunities lost. (Ford, 1994; used with permission of the author)

These were the costs borne by good providers.

As women began to help provide for their families, especially since the 1970s, some men felt relief in being free from the responsibility of being the sole provider. Many more were ambivalent, feeling degraded because they thought they failed in their main duty in life. Meantime, women began making new demands on their husbands, to be more than providers. They wanted intimacy and nurturance from them, and for men to share housework and child care now that women worked (For two excellent discussions of the changes and new demands, see Lillian Rubin's *Worlds of Pain,* 1976, and *Intimate Strangers,* 1983.)

Does the good provider role persist, or did Bernard's prediction of its demise come true? Clearly, most married women work and provide, and most people approve of women working, 83 percent in 1996 (versus 18 percent in 1936). In 2001, 64.1 percent of married women 20–24 were in the labor force, as were 70.2 of those 25–34, and 74.5 of those 35–44. If we look at married women with children in 2001, 62.5 percent of those with children under 6 worked, as did 76.7 with children 6–13 (Caplow, Hicks, and Wattenberg, 2001, pp. 39, 41; *Statistical Abstract,* 2002, pp. 372–373).

Most two-parent families would not live nearly as well as they do without the mothers' income. Women are now co-providers (see next section on work and income). How do men feel about this? It seems that most are struggling to reconcile the traditional expectations with the new realities. They understand, even appreciate, the need for their wives' work; many are even working to share child care and housework (discussed later in this chapter and ch. 11). But it is a struggle, and though diminished, the good provider role lives on in the lives and emotions of most men, and even in the expectations of many wives who want men to be the providers.

Let us look at what some writers say about the state of men as providers.

During the 1970s and early 1980s, Rubin asked men, "Who are you?" "Almost invariably, a man will respond by saying what kind of work he does. 'I'm a lawyer,' 'I'm a carpenter,' 'I'm a writer,' 'I'm a teacher,' 'I'm an electrician.'. . . Only then, if at all, will he speak about being a husband, a father, a son, a lover." Work and the money it affords to provide were a man's primary identity (1983, p. 162).

The powerful hold of work and success on men is shown in a case Rubin presented. Laura and Michael were very much in love (not yet married), living on the West Coast, and both had very satisfying jobs. A problem arose, however, when Michael was offered an even better job in Philadelphia, which he wanted to take. But Laura did not want to leave her friends and job. Would Michael take the new job if Laura did not move with him? "I don't have a choice; I have to take this job." When Rubin reminded him that he *did* have a choice, he replied: "I suppose that's true; I hadn't thought about it that way. But it doesn't *feel like* a choice. If I don't take this opportunity, I'll never know what I could have done and how far I could go. I can't pass it up; I can't. I love her desperately, and I need her, but I have to go." He was willing to risk losing a woman he loved very much because, as a man, his life and identity were focused on work and success (Rubin, 1983, pp. 180–183). (Rubin does not say what Michael finally did.)

In the early 1990s, Rubin interviewed working-class people about their families, work, and related matters. Most of the men appreciated their wives' income, understood their need to work, and found them more interesting as people because they worked. "At the same time, they can't fully shake the feeling that they've failed at their primary task. . . . Doug says, shaking his head morosely, 'A guy should be able to support his wife and kids. But that's not the way it is these days, is it? I don't know anybody who can support a family anymore'" (1994, p. 78).

Most men were shaken when they were laid off and without an income. As one man told Rubin, "[W]hen you get laid off, it's like you lose a part of yourself." It shakes the core of their existence. Women are upset too when they are laid off, but they are also mothers, wives, friends, daughters, sisters (1994, p. 104).

When men lost their jobs, their wives became sole supporters for a while and the men did more housework. Both men and women felt uneasy about this situation, however. First the husband: "'Don't get me wrong; I'm glad she has her job. I don't know what we'd do if she wasn't working,' says Jim. 'It's just that . . . ,' he hesitates, trying to frame his thoughts clearly. 'I know this is going to sound pretty male, but it's my job to take care of this family. I mean, it's great that she can help out, but the responsibility is mine, not hers. She won't say so, but I know she feels the same way, and I don't blame her'" (Rubin, 1994, p. 109).

And she does feel the same way: "'I'm not sure what I think anymore. I mean, I don't think it's fair that men always have to be the support for the family; it's too hard for them sometimes. And I don't mind working; I really don't. In fact, I like it a lot better than being home with the house and the kids all the time. But I guess deep down I still have the old-fashioned idea that it's a man's job to support his family.'" She added that she did not mind the present arrangement, but she would probably lose "respect" for her husband if he remained unemployed and could not provide "for a real long time like with some men" (Rubin, 1994, p. 109).

Another father, who had been unemployed for a while, said: "I had no self-esteem. I felt terrible about myself." So, even in the 1990s, many men and women (perhaps most of them) still considered it a man's primary role to provide for his family (Deutsch, 1999, p. 185).

In the mid-1990s, Susan Faludi, after talking with men all over the United States, wrote *Stiffed: The Betrayal of the American Man*. This study reports the personal experiences of many men who lost their jobs in the 1990s. From 1995 to 1997, eight million people were laid off because of "economic restructuring, plant closings, and economic dislocation." Some never found new jobs, and some found work at lower pay (1999, p. 153).

Men who lost their jobs were shaken, embarrassed, confused, and threatened. They felt they had failed to provide for their families. Some took a long time to tell their wives that they had lost their jobs. "At one time, three former McDonnell Douglas [it built airplanes] men pooled their money, bought a motor home, and parked it in the lot. 'We have men here,' . . . Shirley Judd said, 'who have not told their families. They get dressed and come in here every day.' One man had been engaged in that charade for five months'" (Faludi, 1999, p. 63).

These workers had assumed that they were assured of providing for their families. Everything changed when they lost their jobs. Don Motta told Faludi: "There is no way you can feel like a man. You can't. It's the fact that I'm not capable of supporting my family. . . .

When you've been very successful in buying a house, a car, and could pay for your daughter to go to college, . . . you have a sense of success and people see it." (1999, p. 65). Now he felt like a failure because he could no longer pay for these items.

James Lawrence blamed his divorce on the loss of his job. "All of a sudden, my wife became—I don't want to say the breadwinner, but the focal point of earning our living. And all of a sudden I'm trying to justify what my purpose is—and I couldn't. I'm trekking down this traditional path and she is taking a divergent path. . . . And she just found it easier to file for divorce" (Faludi, 1999, p. 90).

At least some older men regret the costs of the provider role that ruled their lives, and many younger men are working to move away from it and partake in parenting (as we'll see below). But most men—and perhaps as many women—are still struggling to overcome the long history and expectation that men could only be men by being the sole supporters of their families. Bernard's prediction of the demise of the male provider remains to be fulfilled, but we have moved in that direction considerably.

Work, Income, and Gender

Whether parents work, what work they do, and how much they earn affect their families. It guides where they live, what necessities and wants they can meet, how much time they have for each other and their children, and much else.

We have seen that men have been the economic providers, but increasingly women have also worked. In 1890, 18 percent did, 3 percent of those married and 40 percent of those single. By 1940, 22 percent did, 15 percent married and 48 single. By 1975, 47 percent married and 60 single. And by 2001, 68.1 percent single and 61.4 married. By now, most women— single, married, divorced, with or without children—do work. Table 9.1 reveals that reality (Hesse-Biber and Carter, 2000, p. 28; *Statistical Abstract,* 2002, p. 372).

Although most jobs are still predominantly male or female, there has been some change. Women are entering traditionally male fields in greater numbers. For example, women were 15.8 percent of physicians in 1983, and 29.3 in 2001. But registered nurses were still almost all women, 95.8 percent in 1983 and 93.1 in 2001. And generally speaking higher-paying administrative positions are mostly male, and support positions mostly female. "Administrative support, including clerical" workers were 80 percent women in 1983 and 79 percent in 2001. About 25 percent of all women workers hold clerical jobs. Historically, as employers have needed more clerical workers, they hired mostly women because they could pay them less than men. Clerking was a male occupation in the mid-1800s, but in time women replaced men (*Statistical Abstract,* 2002, pp. 381–383; Hesse-Biber and Carter, 2000, pp. 114–117).

Women have been making significant gains in education.

We see from table 9.2 that by 2000, women earned most degrees, except for PhDs. But many fields were primarily male or female. For example, men earned 72 percent of computer and information science bachelor degrees, and women 75.8 percent of education bachelor degrees. Few fields were equally divided. Many fields have changed over time. For example, women received 40.6 percent of psychology master's degrees in 1971, but 75.4 in 2000. For

Table 9.1 Labor force participation for wives with husband present, by age of youngest child (percent)

	1975	2001
Child 1 or under	30.8	58.0
Child under 6	36.7	62.5
Child 6–13	51.8	76.7
Child 14–17	53.5	80.0

Source: Statistical Abstract, 1999, p. 417; 2002, p. 373

Table 9.2 Earned degrees conferred on women, by level 1960, 1980, 2000 (percent of degrees)

	All degrees	Associates	BAs	MAs	PhDs
1960	34.2	NA	35	32	10
1980	48.9	54	49	49	30
2000	57.4	60	57	58	44

NA = not available
Source: Statistical Abstract, 2002, p. 175

doctorates in psychology, the percentage of women increased from 24 percent in 1971 to 67.4 in 2000 (*Statistical Abstract,* 2002, pp. 176–177; see also Hesse-Biber and Carter, 2000, p. 108).

In terms of income earnings, women have also made significant gains, but considerable differences remain between women and men. If we examine the *median weekly earnings of full-time workers,* we find that in 1970 women earned 62 percent of what men did; 68 percent in 1985; and 76 in 2001 (*Statistical Abstract,* 1977, p. 412; 2002, p. 403).

The earnings gap is worse for married women. "While the hourly wages of women without children are roughly 90 percent of men's, the comparable figure for women with children is 70 percent." Mothers devote considerable time to child care and housework (futher discussion follows in this chapter and ch. 11), and this works against them in time. They are able to save less money, they accrue lower Social Security credits, and upon retirement will receive lower benefits (Barnett and Rivers, 2000).

The differences exist even within the same job categories. (Remember that we are comparing earnings of full-time workers; women working part-time are excluded from these comparisons.) In 2001, managerial and professional women workers had median weekly earnings of $732—70.5 percent of men's $1038. In service occupations, it was $335 for women, $438 for men—76 percent. And in technical, sales, and administrative support, women $473 and men $667—71 percent (*Statistical Abstract,* 2002, p. 403).

Even at the very top positions, men earn much more. "Of the top 2,267 [executive] earners in the Fortune 500, 83 are women [that's 3.6 percent] whose median annual compensation is $518,596, compared to $765,000 for men in similar positions." That's 68 percent (Lewis, 1998).

Thus, women have made gains in education, employment, and earnings, but significant inequalities remain in earnings. Also, many occupations remain mostly male or female, with women concentrated in some of the lower-paying jobs, such as service and clerical areas. Indeed, this concentration may partly explain the 76 percent that full-time women workers earn compared to what full-time men workers earn.

But despite the lower earnings, women contribute a significant amount of their families' incomes. In 2000, families with husband and wife working (and many wives worked part-time) had an annual median income of $69,463; those with only the husband's income, $39,735; male single-parent families, $37,529; and female single-parent ones, $25,794. There is no doubt that families with two earners have considerably higher incomes. And in many families, women earn more than men. In 1980, about 20 percent of wives did, compared to 30 percent in 1999 (*Statistical Abstract,* 2002, p. 438; Goldstein, 2000).

To overcome the lower wages women earn in "female" occupations, "labor and women push[ed] for equal pay for equivalent work." The principle of *comparable worth* in jobs argues that when men and women hold jobs with comparable skills, education, and responsibilities they should receive equal wages. How do you establish comparable worth between an auto mechanic and a secretary, for example? There are means to do just that, as Minnesota did with its pay-equity law in 1982. "A state bureaucracy helps evaluate jobs based on what knowledge, skill, effort, and responsibility they require. . . . [T]he wage gap between men and women in Minnesota is 9 percent" (Leonard, 1999, p. A22).

Toward Equality and Sharing

Mothers, wives, and all women have become a significant and permanent part of the labor force. Problems remain, as we saw, but most women work for most of their adult lives. Meantime, what is happening back at home? If women share in earning their families' income, are men sharing child care and housework? We shall see that there has been considerable change on that front, too, but there is no equal sharing in most families (see also ch. 11).

History. A brief review of the recent history of child care and housework will support the conclusion that there is no equal sharing in most families. As the momentous social changes were to begin in the 1960s, "husbands contributed only about two hours a week to the combined tasks of cooking, meal clean-up, housecleaning and laundry . . . , compared to an average of 25 hours a week for wives" (Coltrane, 1996, p. 43).

Slowly, changes began in the late 1960s, parallel with the increasing entry of women in the labor force, from fewer than 20 percent in 1950 to 45 percent in 1975. Men did some housework and child care, but women did at least two-thirds of the total, even when they worked. "Studies of domestic life in the 1970s and 1980s showed that men whose wives worked outside the home didn't seem to be doing any more at home than men whose wives were still full-time homemakers." Most women did not complain. "Most wives had low expectations for help and did not necessarily think that their husbands should do more around the house. In part, this was because it was not socially acceptable for men to do 'women's' work" (Deutsch, 1999, pp. 3–4; Coltrane, 1996, p. 46–49).

But by the 1980s, women and men believed that men should participate in housework, and even more in child care. Even though there was little change in practice from 1976 to 1988, "more couples wanted to share and imagined that they did." As LaRossa said, the *culture* of fatherhood had changed, but not its *conduct*. Men believed that they should, and they did, contribute meaningfully to raising their children, but careful observation showed that they did not contribute equally. According to one study, in the 1980s fathers spent 5.5 hours a week interacting with their children, while mothers spent 19.5 hours (Hochschild, 1989, p. 20; La Rossa, 1988).

In her study of 60 California couples in the late 1980s, where both spouses worked, Hochschild concluded that in ten percent the wives did almost all housework; in 70 percent, they did about two-thirds; and they shared in the other 20 percent. A review of six studies of housework concluded that wives, even those with jobs, spent two to four times as much time in housework and child care, and they performed three-quarters of domestic tasks. In addition, full-time housewives devoted about 50 hours a week to household tasks, compared to 26–33 hours for employed wives (Hochschild, 1989; Coverman, 1989).

By the 1990s, some men had begun to share or almost share housework and child care equally, and almost all fathers did some. A 1998 survey concluded that in the mid-1970s "men spent 30 percent as much time as women on workday chores; by 1998, this percentage rose to 75." A 1997 study of children's time with fathers in two-parent families concluded that "the relative time fathers . . . were directly engaged with children was 67% of mothers' on weekdays and 87% of mothers' on weekends" (Hesse-Biber and Carter, 2000, p. 192; Yeung and others, 2001, p. 148).

Sharing. In 1999, Francine Deutsch published *Halving It All: How Equally Shared Parenting Works.* It is a thorough, detailed, and revealing study of couples who share parenting, couples who do not, and the reasons they do or do not. She interviewed 150 couples, husbands and wives separately, in western Massachusetts in the mid-1990s. They were predominantly middle and upper-middle class, and some were working class. Ninety-six percent were white, reflecting the population of the region. Thirty couples came from each of five categories: "equal sharers; potential equal sharers; 60-40 couples; 75-25 couples [women doing the 60 and 75 percent]; and alternating shift couples." (For more details of the study, see pp. 239–249).

What does equality mean? "Families were classified as equal sharers if husband and wife agreed that, overall, when everything that went into the care of children in a typical week was taken into account, the work was split 50-50. Equality takes many forms. This definition included parents who split each task down the middle, alternating who cooked the kids' dinners, who took them to daycare, and who got them dressed in the morning, as well as families who split the work into separate but equal spheres. . . . fathers were more than playmates, more than helpers, and more than substitutes for mothers. Just like their wives, they were primary in their children's lives." Couples need to work out who will buy clothes, make appointments for the children, get up at night for a crying child, and many other details. And whatever child-care arrangements they make, they must continually change and negotiate as children get older and conditions change (Deutsch, 1999, pp. 5–6, 12).

Daniel and Janet are college teachers who explained to Deutsch how they raise Noah together. They share all tasks. "Daniel cooks Noah's dinner, gives him baths, feeds him, gets him ready to go in the mornings, and picks up his toys just as often as Janet does." Janet and Daniel insist that it is a 50-50 split. Daniel can't understand why most fathers do not share in parenting. "I don't understand why they don't want to be in this . . . from eighteen months on they're a gas . . . it's not that he's easy; he's exhausting, but he's really a blast!" (1999, pp. 16, 21).

Mary and Paul have five children. She's a medical secretary and he's a fire inspector, and they work opposite shifts. They describe their typical day: Paul says, "I get up at four, make lunches for the four oldest kids, get to work at five, work until one-thirty, come home,

These two Colorado engineers attempt to divide child-care and household tasks evenly. Dad cooks dinner four times a week and mom three times. They alternate giving the children baths, for example.

basically, pick up from what's left from breakfast, (finish the) dishes, do a load of wash, pick up Crystal at the babysitter at a quarter of three. . . ." He drives their children to afternoon activities, does more laundry, and cooks supper. Now Mary talks: "We eat supper, and I usually do some laundry. Paul usually does the dishes or we'll do them together and by then, seven at night, he's had it so he collapses. I get the kids to get into the tub and one of us will go upstairs or read them a story. Often nights we're just so busy that we're all in bed by nine or nine-thirty." Even though they share the physical labor of child care and housework, there are some gender differences: "She's the confidante, he's the playmate" (Deutsch, 1999, pp. 24–25).

They share not because of any preceding ideological commitments, rather, because they love each other and their children. Also, it seemed only fair to Paul since they both work. The commitment is to "each other and their marriage" (Deutsch, 1999, p. 27).

Equal sharers do not all begin their marriages committed to sharing; they are not all feminists. They are "ordinary people simply inventing and reinventing solutions to the dilemmas of modern life" (Deutsch, 1999, p. 11). Couples have different explanations for sharing. Some believe in individual rights for men and women; others love their spouses and think it only fair that they share parenting if they both work. Other studies report that some are committed feminists; some think it's best for the children; and others come to sharing as the husbands no longer find satisfaction in work (Gerson, 1993; Glass, 1998).

Often there is a long period of conflict before husbands agree to share (a third of the couples in Deutsch's study share). Wives threaten to divorce, or refuse to have another child, if husbands do not share. They insist that "family work be valued as strongly as paid work." Husbands must partake in parenting when they come home, not read the newspaper, watch TV, or engage in hobbies. Couples realize that traditional family roles cannot work while they both have jobs, and they have no option but to change (1999, pp. 35–37, 64).

The women who share "feel entitled to equality. But sometimes they had to convince their husbands. By embracing equality unambiguously, they . . . were steadfast in their demands." On the other hand, unequal women "ask for less and ask less directly." This is a major finding in Deutsch's study: in couples that share, the women believe that sharing is fair and right; they insist on it; and they assert themselves. Equally important is that husbands also come to agree to the fairness of sharing (1999, pp. 61–62, 81).

But sharers live in a sea of mostly non-sharing couples. They need to protect, defend, and justify what they do. They largely create their own social world, surrounding themselves with people who share and support the choices they made. They openly challenge traditional norms, and they often find sympathizers and allies (Deutsch, 1999, pp. 100–102).

Change is rarely total, however. Remnants of traditions and past roles hang on. Even in fully sharing couples, it is women who mostly perform some tasks. Mothers do much more of the management and arrangement of child care. They keep track of permission slips for social functions, buy their children's clothes, and arrange play dates for them.

Others have found men who share parenting. In her study of couples in the New York City area, *No Man's Land: Men's Changing Commitments to Family and Work,* Kathleen Gerson found that one-third of the men "had developed, or planned to develop, significant involvement as a father." They became more involved with their families, held an egalitarian outlook, and had fulfilling experiences with their children (1993, pp. 142, 172–177). (For two other studies of egalitarian marriages, see Schwartz, 1994a, 1994b; Coltrane, 1996.)

Women and men have been working to change power inequalities. Women are winning more power and freedom as they are earning more money. Phyllis Kilson is an excellent example. At 46, she had been working for four years. "Gary always made all the big decisions, and I never felt like I had a right to my say. I mean, I tried sometimes, but if he said no, I figured I didn't have a right to contradict him. Now I make money, too, so it's different. I go out and buy something for the grandchildren, or even for me, without asking him, and he can't say anything" (Rubin, 1994, p. 83). Many writers and researchers have noted that wives gain more power in marriages as they work for their own money (Coontz, 1997, pp. 58–60).

Women in Deutsch's study had power and used it. "The equally sharing mothers . . . are not afraid to use power, and the language of power. . . . Simply communicating one's expectations in a clear and direct way doesn't always work; it may take the exercise of power to change the division of labor at home." The strongest use of power is the threat of divorce. In *The Second Shift,* Hochschild reports that the fear of divorce ended many women's long struggles with their husbands over sharing. But some women in *Halving It All* felt confident and committed to sharing, and used the threat of divorce to gain equality. They had power, were willing to use it, and did use it, and were able to create egalitarian and sharing marriages (Deutsch, 1999, pp. 65–66). (Most women in Deutsch's study, however, did not exercise power to change their marriages.)

There are still many obstacles to egalitarian and sharing marriages. Before we explore the reasons for persisting inequality, let us first look at types of unequal marriages.

Deutsch found two patterns: the wife reduces her work hours and does most parenting; or, she works as many hours as her husband but he still does much less parenting than she does. Denise and Eric are an example of the first pattern. Eric is very committed to his job and "fits parenting around his work life." She works part-time and "fits her work life around parenting" because parenting is her primary role. As a result, she does the "bulk of childcare and almost all housework." Perhaps feeling guilty, Eric is pushing her to use more child-care help. Deutsch concludes that they seemed happy with their arrangement, despite some conflicts (1999, pp. 39–44).

In the second pattern, after a futile struggle to change their husbands, many women resign themselves to doing almost all of the work. They come to compare their husbands to men who did nothing, not to the ideal of equal sharing. But worn out, they periodically explode in anger and frustration. Many, whose careers are important to them, are forced to reduce their work hours, since full-time work and sole parenting are exhausting. Nancy Hold, in *The Second Shift* (Hochschild, 1989), is an example. But equality was so important to her that she defined her situation as a sharing one, even though what Hochschild describes is obviously and painfully very unequal. Nancy does most of the parenting and housework.

Other obstacles to equality are persistent emotions, old roles, ambivalence, and reluctance to give up "secondary gains" of those roles. Men, having been providers for so long, fear giving up the privileges of that role, even as they see the benefits of parenting their children. Women, even as they enjoy work and the power of earning money, find it difficult to give up control of parenting and the house.

In their early days of parenting, Daniel and Janet confronted the dilemma of Janet truly sharing the parenting (as men find it difficult to give up their provider role). He was frustrated because she kept checking up on him. She would check the lunch box he had made for their child, adjust the tapes on the diaper he had just put on the baby, and so on. He told her that her checking up on him made him feel "like I'm not doing a good job." "Because mothers in the past have been in charge of the care of their children, equally sharing mothers potentially face a loss of control and authority at home." They discussed her actions and his feelings and in time came to an understanding (Deutsch, 1999, pp. 18–19).

As important as control and secondary gains are women's feelings of guilt and obligation. For many, it somehow "doesn't feel right" not to be the primary parent. Their ideas of what they should do or feel as mothers, their very self-worth, make it difficult to focus on work and to share parenting. For some women, motherhood overrules career goals (Deutsch, 1999, pp. 154–155; see also Newman, 1993, ch. 4; Arendell, 2000).

Various surveys show that most men and women worry about balancing work and family, even as they realize that both of them need to work. Men *say* their family is more important than their work, but in fact the job and the provider role are primary in their lives.

Fathers do not feel guilty about working, but mothers do. "Fathers take it for granted that after becoming parents they will continue to work. Unlike mothers, who believe that they are choosing to work rather than to be with their children, fathers who are involved believe that they are choosing their children over work and leisure. Women who have invested in their work lives are left feeling that they have chosen to be there less for their children, chosen in some sense against their children" (Deutsch, 1999, pp. 98–99).

And because mothers feel torn and guilty, many strive to avoid or limit day care, and change their work so they will provide most of the child care. Deutsch writes: "As much as some couples believed in equality, the fear of day care, the desire to be home after school, and the worry about having enough time with children weighed more heavily on women than on men" and led many women to work part time. The ideal of the "moral mother" of the 1950s entrenched itself deeply in our minds; it has been passed on to millions of women and men, and it lives on. It has a powerful hold on our emotions, and thus on our actions. Women feel guilty and are blamed for not being full-time mothers (Deutsch, 1999, p. 161; Doten, 1996; Newman, 1993, ch. 4; Rubin, 1994, p. 79).

Perhaps as much as emotions and gender roles, however, there are the practical difficulties of managing two jobs *and* raising children (often jobs of over 40 hours each). People have only so much energy, and something gets lost, often the children, as Hochschild worries in both *The Second Shift* and *The Time Bind*. Equal parenting, two time-demanding careers, enough time for the children, and some time for the parents are impossible to attain. As a result, one parent, almost always the mother, reduces work hours.

Comments and criticisms by family, friends, and co-workers often add to the problems parents face. Praising men for sharing, for example, while meant as a compliment, creates an insidious double standard, according to Deutsch. It assumes that women should be the primary parents, for which they get no praise, but they should be thankful to their husbands who share. "You're lucky your husband shares" conveys the message that women are not entitled to equality, that it's a gift. And women are not praised equally for sharing in earning the family income. Bernice told Deutsch: "Why should I appreciate him any more than he appreciates me? . . . Often it would come down to that, that I should be grateful that he does half and I would say, 'Look, why should I be grateful, are you grateful that I do half?'"(1999, p. 102; for a similar "praising" of fathers, see Coltrane, 1996, p. 11).

Couples also face direct criticisms if they share parenting. Fathers are criticized by other men for vacuuming or grocery shopping, and for doing too much child care. Mothers are told they are neglecting their children, and such comments "stir up their deepest fears." But we should not exaggerate these criticisms. For example, 65 percent of fathers who work alternate shifts with their wives, and who average 28 hours a week of solo child care, told Deutsch "they have never received any criticism for their unusual involvement at home" (1999, pp. 91, 93).

Finally, a very serious obstacle to shared parenting is located outside parents and their families and friends. It is the social organization of work, which makes it difficult for parents to change parenting arrangements. With jobs that demand 40 and more hours a week, with men earning more than women, with men still feeling the pressures of the provider role and women of motherhood, with very limited work leaves for new parents, and with many other pressures, it is no wonder that shared parenting loses out to the two other alternatives Deutsch discusses. These alternatives are that mothers cut back on their jobs while fathers increase their hours; or mothers do most child care and housework even as they work full time. Both sabotage shared parenting. The social organization of work is a primary obstacle to shared parenting.

Working Women. Victoria Segunda, a thirty-year-old mother of three and assistant manager of a children's clothing store, told Rubin: "I didn't imagine how much I'd enjoy going to work in the morning. I mean, I love my kids and all that, but let's face it, being mom can get pretty stale. . . . The kids are great. But going to work, that's like, hmmmmm, that's like another reason to live. Since I went to work I'm more interested in life, and life's more interested in me" (Rubin, 1994, p. 81).

Sue told Deutsch: "I love my job. I love my job, I really do. I'm probably one of the only people in the world who loves their job as much as I do . . . It's the people I work with . . . They all have young children. We all have the same types of problems. It's more like a counseling session every night for six hours" (1999, p. 189).

The women in *The Second Shift* also loved their work, even when their beliefs told them that as good mothers they should not. Ann, vice-president of a consulting firm, enjoyed her job and it was essential to her identity. But "caring for two small children and working full-time [became] an unbearable strain," and she left her job. She also convinced herself that her husband's work "has always been more important than mine, because he's more talented and more interesting than I am" (Hochschild clearly disagrees with this assessment) (1989, pp. 96, 105).

Alternate Shift Couples. Millions of parents work alternate shifts as the number of nonday workers has increased. In 51 percent of couples with children 14 years and younger, "at least one parent is working a nonday shift." Fathers are the primary caretakers for "28 percent of preschoolers whose mothers work a nonday shift" (Deutsch, 1999, p. 170).

Let us look at one such family. Stan is a construction worker and Maureen a retail worker. He rushes home at three so she can get to her job. From four until ten, Stan is the sole parent with their two young daughters. He plays with them, feeds them, bathes them, and at eight-thirty puts them to bed. "In his wildest imagination, Stan never pictured himself as the father he is today, doing all the tasks that used to be Mom's: diapering babies, giving baths, even taking his four-year-old daughter to ballet lessons" (Deutsch, 1999, pp. 169–170).

In most cases, these working-class men worked many more hours for pay, and they did fewer hours of child care and housework, than their wives. Yet they still spent an average of 28.5 hours parenting alone, compared to the 14.5 hours average of the middle-class men Deutsch interviewed. Out of necessity, they also did more cleaning and other housework than middle-class men did.

They worked alternate shifts for three reasons: they needed the money and could not afford to pay for day care; they believed only family members should care for children and did not trust outsiders; and they wanted to teach their own values to their children (Deutsch, pp. 170–181).

A father said that, since he was alone with his children, he *learned* to listen to them and how to cook. He and others gained respect for the family work that women do. They also came to know and feel close to their children. "Fathers were thrilled to be admitted to a relationship they previously thought was reserved for mothers. One father, who thoroughly enjoyed bath time with his kids, said: . . . 'Like when it's bath time. They love bubbles and they're always calling me in there'" (Deutsch, p. 182).

Deutsch thinks the change is limited and not deep. Men help with the children and housework because they must, but when the children are older, they may return to traditional roles. Even now, the mothers are ultimately responsible for parenting and the house. The couples "cling" to beliefs about gender roles: the father is the major provider, and the mother is the primary parent for whom work is not a major part of her identity. One mother said: "Somewhere in my head, I think that she (her daughter) should depend on me more." They lead "nontraditional lives" while holding onto "traditional ideologies" (1999, pp. 191, 193). (For other couples who worked alternate shifts, and the problems they faced, see Rubin, 1994, pp. 94–97.)

CONCLUSION: SHARING OUR LIVES

1. *Creating Equality, Creating Inequality.* Sharing and equality are possible. Couples can create them in their marriage. Couples can also create inequality. And they do *create* it—it is not foreordained by nature. To be sure, all couples operate within a long history and a culture that encourages men to be providers and women to be housewives and mothers; within an economy that assumes these roles; within social constraints. Increasingly, however, women and men can choose to create sharing or inequality. Equality does involve a conscious struggle, and people face many obstacles, as we saw, but equality can and does happen. Equality is possible, it exists, and it benefits men, women, and children.

Most men work more hours to ensure that they are the primary providers. Although it is true that men's jobs pay more money, that is not always the case. At early points in many marriages, women did earn or could have earned as much as their husbands. If we look at their *hourly* rates, many women make as much or more, but men work more hours to increase their income. If both worked the same number of hours, their income would be equal, and they would have an equal number of free hours for parenting. Tammy and Thomas tell Deutsch that he had a greater earning potential than she did, so they decided he would work more hours. But when they made that decision "the two of them were earning approximately the same salary. They both ignored that she might have had a lucrative career in management, possibly with a higher earning potential than his in sales" (1999, pp. 130–134).

But other couples chose to have equal work hours and equal parenting time, usually after much struggle against traditional gender roles. Deutsch presents two men college teachers who shaped their careers differently: one to allow time for a sharing marriage, the other not. Same careers, same conditions, different choices. One reduced the demands of his job, the other worked longer hours for higher professional success. Both men made a choice (Deutsch, 1999, p. 141).

2. *Consequences of Inequality.* Traditional marriages usually create a hierarchy where the provider men dominate the housewife women, and where both are incomplete human beings: he does not parent and she does not provide. Men and women lead limited and distorted lives. (See earlier discussion on the provider role; also Schwartz, 1994a, pp. 115–125.)

3. *Beyond Good Providers and Housewives.* To avoid these and other negative consequences, men and women need to relinquish sole control of their domains. As we have seen, men still contest and obstruct changes to their provider role, women to their control of the house and parenting. Men's identities still reside largely with work and income, women's identities with mothering and home. But both can change and each have their identities connected with work *and* home. Schwartz recommends that spouses both control their incomes together and also keep some separate money each, to ensure autonomy and independence. They should also share such "mundane activities as doing the marketing, or taking the children for shoes" (1994a, p. 138).

4. *The Benefits of Sharing.* Women and men may relinquish parts of their traditional roles, but sharing marriages provide benefits for each of them, and their children. Men get to share the burden of providing for their families, instead of bearing it alone. They get to know their children and have fun with them. Various studies present fathers who speak with deep emotion about the joys of raising their children (Deutsch, 1999, p. 230; Gerson, 1993; Coltrane, 1996).

Mothers benefit by gaining respect, independence, and a life beyond the home. They too get someone else to share their traditional work, the raising of children, instead of bearing it alone. The happiest women (men, too) are those who balance family and work. And women and men fashion happier marriages, with more honest and fulfilling relationships, based on equality, respect, and sharing. There is more money for the family; women are healthier and less depressed; children do as well as, or better than, children of traditional marriages in school, and they are more responsible and independent (Coontz, 1997, pp. 64–67, 98).

5. *Backsliding, Overwork, and Oppression of Other Women.* There are many dangers to avoid on the way to equality and sharing. Backsliding is one of them. Couples may begin their marriage by sharing, but when children arrive they may slowly and subtly revert to traditional roles. *Halving It All* offers many examples. Women and men must be always alert to and resist such tendencies. A second danger is if *both* men and women focus more on their work than the home. Hochschild found that for some men and women "work becomes home and home becomes work." Marriages suffer and child care becomes devalued. All examples of successful sharing and of happy families in *Halving It All* required both women and men to moderate career and work demands. You cannot have two highly successful, highly demanding careers in one family. (See discussion on work, ch. 11.)

Or rather, you can if you are willing to exploit other people and neglect your children. And that is the third danger. Some couples farm out most or all child care and housework to others (usually women) whom they pay low wages. In the process, they exploit those women and spend very little time with their children (Hesse-Biber and Carter, 2000, p. 15).

6. *Changes in the Economy, Social Policies, and Culture.* Deutsch rightly insists that couples choose to make sharing or non-sharing marriages. People can choose and can shape their lives. But Deutsch does not stress the other side of choice, the social, economic, and cultural conditions that form the world within which we make our choices.

We need to change the world outside our own families and marriages, too. We need to make it more possible for people to fashion sharing marriages. The women's movement and other groups have been working for changes that allow women and men to focus on both work and home.

- Equal pay and equal work opportunities for women
- Various income supports for low-income families
- Affordable and quality child care
- Reduction of work hours, especially in some very demanding careers, and especially for parents of young children
- Flexible work schedules, so parents can spend more time with their children
- Longer, and paid, parental leaves for parents of newborns (See Hochschild, 1997; Hesse-Biber and Carter, 2000; Coontz, 1997. In chapter 11, I discuss some of these proposals.)

7. *A Better Future, A Traditional Present?* Deutsch shows us that equality works and is good for everyone. Coltrane predicts more sharing in the future, when even more mothers will work, at more equal pay and in less traditionally female occupations, and when men will invest more of their time and identities in child care and housework (1996, ch. 8).

Meantime, our attitudes on gender roles seem to be contradictory. In 1994–1996 surveys, we read that on the one hand men and women approve of non-traditional roles. For example, 81.9 percent of women and 82.7 percent of men said that they approved of a woman working even "if she has a husband capable of supporting her." At the same time, however, 87 percent of men and 78.1 percent of women also thought that "women are biologically better-suited to care for children" (Hesse-Biber and Carter, 2000, pp. 198–199).

Which *do* we believe? Deutsch says that the choice is ours. Various surveys in the 1980s and 1990s showed that significant majorities of men and women said that they believed in gender equality. Many of us are struggling to give reality to our beliefs, to make the dream come to life.

10

Class, Race, and Families

In the introduction to chapter 9, I noted that gender, class, and ethnicity/race shape family lives. They do so simultaneously. For an African American mother supporting her family on income from making beds in a hotel, both her life with her children and her relationship to her kin are influenced by the low wages she earns (class). At the same time, her life and relationships are also influenced by the jobs that are more available to her as a woman (gender), and by the history of her group (race). A rich white man's family life is also shaped by his class, gender, and race; by his inherited wealth, privileges, and occupations open to him as a white male. The money, hours, prestige, and other conditions of his work and life will mold his family life in many ways.

For all of us, whatever the combination of our class, gender, and race/ethnicity, it shapes and limits, or enhances, what we do for a living, who we marry, what we can do for our children, and how we relate to our kin. Let us now turn to class.

CLASSES AND FAMILIES

What Are Classes?

A short and simple definition from a sociology text tells us that a social class "is a group of people who share a similar economic position in a society, based on their wealth and income." A stratification text states that a class is "a grouping of individuals with similar positions and similar political and economic interests." Our class is determined by whether and how much property we own, and also by what we do for a living. And to Zweig, "class is about the power some people have over the lives of others, and the powerlessness most people experience as a result." It is the great power of the few people who own and control corporations and politics, the smaller power of managers and others in the middle, and the relative powerlessness of factory workers, service people, and others (David Newman, 1999, p. 593; Kerbo, 2000, p. 519; Zweig, 2000, p. 11).

Most sociologists, following the first two definitions, think there are five classes: the upper, upper-middle, lower-middle, working, and the poor. Zweig says there are the capitalist, middle, working, and poor classes, and he concludes that about 62 percent of Americans belong to the working class.

The data on the U.S. economy, some presented in chapter 8, support the preceding discussion of classes. There are a very few people, about 1 percent of the population, who own most of the wealth and make a very disproportionate share of the annual income. For example, in 2002 corporation CEOs averaged $7,500 an hour, or about $15.6 million a year. Also, in 1998, the richest 5 percent of families averaged $252,582. Then about 15–20 percent of the population, the managerial class, earned good annual salaries (the upper fifth in the data in ch. 8), with an average household income of $127,529 in 1998. At the other end, the poor (the bottom 20 percent) are those with an average income of $9,223 in 1998. In the middle stand the people I consider the working class: the second fifth, at $60,266; third, at $38,967; and fourth, at $23,288 (U.S. Census Bureau, 1999, p. xv).

How Classes Shape Family Life

To some degree, our social class affects almost all areas of our lives: where we live (in a crowded city near dangerous chemical factories, a pleasant suburb, or a country estate), our education, whom we marry, wealth and income we inherit or do not, our job or career, how we think of ourselves, how we speak, our health care, treatment by police and courts, and in general the quality of our lives.

All these differences affect our families, the families into which we are born and those we create. I will look at six specific areas shaped by class: whom we marry, how we raise our children, relationships between husbands and wives (with a focus on gender roles), relationships with kin and extended families, daily experiences, and the primacy of class and the economy.

Whom We Marry. It may seem obvious that most people marry someone from the same or neighboring class. But because it seems obvious, researchers have gathered very few statistics on the topic.

Warner reports that in Newburyport, Massachusetts, during the 1930s, most people married within their own class. (Despite considerable social pressure to marry within ones' own class, however, some people married above or below their class.) Class endogamy (marriage within the same class) is especially important to the rich. To keep and increase their wealth, ruling class and managerial families encourage and guide their children to marry each other. "Elite families are nationally connected by a web of institutions they control. Families in various sections of the country are linked by boarding schools, exclusive colleges, exclusive clubs, and fashionable vacations resorts." Young people meet and fall in love in these settings, and later marry (Warner, 1963, p. 47; Zinn and Eitzen, 1999, p. 147).

Gilbert reports two studies, in the Detroit area (1980s) and in Massachusetts (1960s), that also show strong class endogamy. A Massachusetts woman from the upper-middle class said: "What sort of husband would a carpenter be? What sort of education would he have? My viewpoint would not jibe with a carpenter. Marriage is based on equals. I would want my daughter to marry in her own class. She would go to college and would want her husband to be educated. I would want to be able to mix with in-laws and converse with them" (Gilbert, 1998, p. 123).

A female college student (in one of my classes), whose father was a doctor, told the class that she once dated a high-school dropout who was a mechanic. When he came to pick her up, her father did not shake his outstretched hand. When she returned from the date, he told her never to date him again. She never did. When I take class surveys on class and marriage, however, most students write that a potential husband's class does not matter to them.

Parents, especially those from the upper classes, ensure class endogamy. Through choice or lack of choice, they live in neighborhoods with people from the same class, and their children mostly meet children of the same class in their play, school, sports, dances, and so on.

Childhood. There are many class differences in childhood experiences and in what parents may do for their children. Professional, middle-class parents worry about *which* college their children will attend, whereas working-class parents worry *whether* theirs will attend any college or even finish high school. Some families and their children live on the streets or in cars; other homeless families live temporarily in a hotel room, where children have no place to

These children are thriving with a loving extended family surrounding them.

play. Working-class children share bedrooms with siblings, middle-class children have their own private rooms, and rich children whose parents own many homes have many rooms in each of these homes. Depending on their class and location, children attend vastly different schools, from run-down urban ones, to well-provided suburban ones, to private academies (Rubin, 1976; Kozol, 1988, 1991; Mantsios, 1994).

Whereas, on the rich end, children have private tutors, attend summer camps, and go on vacations to Europe; on the poor end, parents struggle to provide for their children. One poor mother said: "In the winter we don't go anywhere [with the children]. Because it's very hard without a car. I always had a car until last winter. It was very hard. Because we had to wait there sometimes twenty minutes for the bus. And with the kids and the very cold days, it's very hard. I only took them out last winter once, besides the Saturday afternoons that we go to church" (Rank, 1994, p. 114).

Upper-class children, on the other hand, often grow up with a sense of entitlement. They expect, much in the same manner we all expect the sun to rise and set, high social position, wealth, and servants to care for them. They reflect what they see, hear, experience. They hear their parents talking about making important decisions; they are surrounded by people who attend to their every need and desire; they are raised by governesses while their parents are out having fun; so they expect to do the same later. Opportunities and activities for most children vary between these two extremes (Coles, 1977).

Many books have been written on the effects of class on children, most of them on poor children. They leave no doubt that it is poverty—the lack of money and opportunities—not the parents' values, discipline, or language that shape the children's lives. For example, lead paint has been very prevalent in houses in many urban neighborhoods, where poor parents are forced to live with their children. Lead is very harmful to children who ingest it or breathe it as dust. A 1996 study of 800 boys in Pittsburgh found that "boys with higher lead levels were more likely than other boys to engage in antisocial acts, regardless of their parents' marital status or intelligence, and aside from any differences in income, medical problems, race, or ethnicity." Other studies report similar findings. But it is the children of poor parents who are far more likely to be exposed to lead (Coontz, 1997, p. 148; see also Seccombe, 2000, 2002).

I close this discussion of class and childhood with a cautionary note. Not all children of rich and professional parents lead ecstatically happy lives, nor do all poor and working-class children live miserable ones. There can be, there is, some sadness, unhappiness, and conflict in the lives of most children of all classes. And even the poorest children experience some joy. I was raised in half a room during very hard times in Greece, but there was joy and fun in my life.

I do not mean to diminish the profoundly shaping consequences of class on our families, childhoods, and lives. But we may dehumanize poor and working-class people when we stress only the problems of their childhoods. Few people could survive such relentlessly unhappy childhoods as those Rubin describes in *Worlds of Pain*. Even children in the poorest housing projects see rainbows, play with friends, and have fun. I do not in any way diminish, dismiss, or excuse the awful consequences of poverty caused by the U.S. capitalist economy. But people are not only victims, they manage to find joy and friendship and sharing. (See Stack, *All Our Kin,* 1974, and *Call to Home,* 1996; Kotlowitz, *There Are No Children Here,* 1991.)

Relationships with Extended Families. According to most sociology texts, poor and working-class families tend to be close to their kin, to see them often and share resources; middle-class and upper-middle-class families may be close to their kin but do not see them as often nor do they share as much as poor and working-class ones; and upper-class families, because of their wealth, power, and many residences are in frequent contact with extended family members.

Let us begin with poor families. As we have seen in earlier chapters, poor families can survive only by sharing resources and by cooperation. They help a relative to pay the rent; take in nephews, nieces, and grandchildren when their parents are unable to provide for them; and they spend considerable time with each other. Carol Stack's *All Our Kin* describes such African American families around 1970. Newman found that African American extended family members in Harlem, New York, helped each other constantly during the 1990s. Other studies of poor people, black, white, and of other groups, show similar ties in extended families. On the other hand, Roschelle suggests that worsening economic conditions may have made it more difficult to share resources (Katherine Newman, 1999; David Harvey, 1993; Roschelle, 1997).

Stack also points out, however, that while these kin networks may help poor families manage their lives by sharing limited resources, they may also make it difficult for individuals to escape poverty. People may accumulate some money, but if they must share it with needy relatives, they cannot buy a house, for example. Of course, they were probably recipients of such assistance at some point.

Working-class families may have a few more resources than poor ones, but they too share and socialize extensively with extended kin. Two pioneering studies from the 1950s focused on such families: Young and Willmott's *Family and Kinship in East London* and Gans's *Urban Villagers* (an Italian neighborhood in Boston, torn down in the late 1950s). After marriage, couples lived near, and sometimes with, their parents and saw them frequently. Grandchildren stopped at grandparents' homes after school, daughters went shopping with mothers a few times a week, and generally people socialized often with parents, grandparents, aunts and uncles, and cousins (Young and Willmott, 1957; Gans, 1962, 1982).

Later studies have generally supported the descriptions and conclusions by Young and Willmott and by Gans. For example, working-class families are more likely to care for elderly parents themselves than middle-class ones, as are poor people and women. Reciprocal aid and socializing with family have been characteristics of working-class families (Merrill, 1997; Stack, 1996; Rubin, 1976).

It may be that working-class families have changed since the 1950s. New introductions in the books by Gans, Young and Willmott, and Rubin "report that the distinctiveness of the working-class family has faded somewhat. The family circle is not as central to the sons and daughters of the Italian Americans Gans studied, he concluded in 1982, because greater affluence has reduced the need for mutual assistance . . . because migration to the suburbs has spread relatives apart, and because resistance has grown to the conformity that the family circle demands" (Cherlin, 1999, p. 123).

Whatever the conditions of extended family relations in the working class, sociologists seem to agree that there is less reciprocal assistance and socializing in middle-class and upper-middle-class families than in working-class ones. When they need assistance they turn to various institutions outside the family. (Although even middle-class families provide considerable caregiving; see ch. 6.) Because they move away from relatives when they relocate in their search of professional jobs, these families cannot stay in touch with relatives as often as working-class people who live in the same communities, even same streets, with their relatives. They socialize with friends from work and other places, not with relatives.

A cautionary comment: These distinctions between the working class and the middle class are not total. I present them because some research suggests them and they are almost assumed by sociologists. But in their family histories, however, many of my middle-class students report family ties that remind me of East London and Boston's West End families.

Also, when sociologists observe that poor and working-class families share and socialize with their kin more than middle-class ones do, they state or imply that they do so only out of necessity. If only they had more money, as good Americans they would focus on their nuclear families instead of siblings, grandparents, parents, and others. And it seems, as Cherlin notes, that this is what they do when they move to suburbia, away from relatives. But isn't it possible that necessity is only one reason for kin networks? Where is the dividing line between necessity and choice? Perhaps people enjoy and value time with adult parents and other relatives. As we saw in chapter 7, families throughout the world have been connected to kin and the wider community. Are relatively isolated nuclear families preferable? Isn't there something cherished in close ties between grandparents and grandchildren?

I close with a comment Rubin's mother made. Rubin grew up poor, with a widowed mother who struggled to support her family. Rubin herself in time became a very successful professional. When "in hurt and exasperation, I once asked her why she'd never told me she was proud of what I had achieved, she answered angrily: 'Proud? What do I get out of it? It's like I don't have a daughter. I see my friends' daughters taking care of them; they go to lunch; they take them shopping. What do I have? You live three thousand miles away, and even if you didn't, what would I have? You're too busy.'" (1994, p. 151).

Marriages and Gender Roles. To manage the discussion of husband-wife relationships, I will compare only working-class marriages with upper-middle class marriages. Most writing on marriages focuses on these two classes.

Working-class marriages have been described as limited and unsatisfactory, especially to the wives. Spouses don't say very much to each other and share relatively few experiences. What may be called an assault on working-class couples has a long history, but this assault accelerated with a number of studies in the 1960s, especially Mirra Komarovsky's *Blue-Collar Marriage*. Komarovsky and her research assistants interviewed 58 couples in a community somewhere near New York City. Her conclusions were unambiguous: there was little depth and reflection in working-class marriages. The "conceptualization of the marital relationship is primitive. The days may be full of joy and resentment, pity and pride, anger and love, but these emotions are not named, distinguished or reflected upon to anything like the degree characteristic of better-educated respondents." Gender roles led husbands and wives to live in two separate worlds. Komarovsky noted that in all classes men and women resided "in different psychological worlds," but the "gulf" was wider in working-class marriages (Komarovsky, 1962, pp. 17, 32–33).

Working-class couples socialized almost entirely with their families. Women turned almost exclusively to their mothers for advice on their marriages and children, unlike middle-class women who turned to professional counselors. "The fact is that working-class life is more restricted. . . . There are no books to be finished or current magazines to be read." They socialize only with relatives, and their children partake in no organized activities like dancing classes. "In comparison with college-educated women, then, the lives of these homemakers are narrow in range of activities and interests." Wives seemed unhappy with their husbands, who often preferred to spend time with their friends in the local bars (Komarovsky, 1962, pp. 36, 59).

This unflattering portrait pervades the book. I would like to modify it with two comments. One woman "interrupted her description of her husband with 'Gosh, I make him sound like a dud. He is really a lot of fun.'" Perhaps the interview situation accentuates problems and we tend to forget that couples also have good times together (Komarovsky, 1962, p. 14).

A later section in the book is headed with the question, "Are the husbands and wives friends?" "For almost one-third of these men and women the answer to this question is clearly in the negative. If it is one of the functions of modern marriage to share one's hurts, worries and dreams with another person—a large number of couples fail to find such fulfillment" (Komarovsky, 1962, p. 140). But turning that statement around, it would seem that over two-thirds were friends. How can a minority response describe a group of people? Why focus on the one-third who fail and ignore the two-thirds who are friends?

Rubin's *Worlds of Pain* continued with a similar sketch of working-class marriages. They married young, in their late teens and early twenties, to escape unhappy homes. Forty-four percent of the women were pregnant when they married. Unlike middle-class couples who came to know each other and grew together before children arrived, these couples were overwhelmed with the demands of the newborn and with financial problems. One woman told Rubin: "One day I woke up and there I was, married and with a baby. And I thought, 'I can't stand it! I can't stand to have my life over when I'm so young.'" The constant shortage of money added to the tensions of the marriage. Unlike middle-class couples, they could not leave the children for an evening of entertainment for the two of them (1976, pp. 81, 189–190).

By the early 1970s, working-class wives began looking for more companionate marriages, such as those enjoyed by professional couples. They wanted greater intimacy, communication, and sharing with their husbands, who often preferred to socialize with their work friends, away from their wives. Expectations were changing, but they were still burdened with the routine and financial problems of marriage, with segregated gender roles that made for somewhat separate lives for men and women (Rubin, 1976, chs. 5 and 6).

By implication and by statement, professional couples enjoyed good marriages. They were friends who could talk with each other, they shared their lives and were social equals. They were the opposite of the "primitive" and unreflective marriages Komarovsky described.

Changes had occurred by the 1990s. Certainly people married later than they did in the 1950s and 1960s. Neither men nor women were rushing to marry, and in the early 1990s parents were not anxious for their children to marry early. Many unmarried adult children were still living at home. Gender roles were also changing. As we saw in the last chapter, they were less segregated and distinct in all classes. For example, if we are to believe those earlier studies, no working-class husbands in the early 1970s and before would have taken care of children and done housework, which the men Deutsch describes did. Wives and husbands of the 1990s led less segregated lives, as women assumed more of the provider role and men more of the parenting role (Rubin, 1994; Gilbert, 1998, pp. 129–131; Cherlin, 1999, pp. 123–124).

As we saw in chapter 8, most wives of all classes expect to and do work, they like working, and the money they earn gives them more power in the marriage. No wife in the 1990s would have said that her husband "won't let me" attend school or hold a job. Indeed, working-class wives often earn a greater ratio of the family income than middle-class wives do. "Moreover, upper-middle-class men do not have to acknowledge that they couldn't make it without their wives' incomes; blue-collar [working-class] men do." (Rubin, 1976, pp. 96–97; Deutsch, 1999, p. 181).

Despite these changes, not all is well with the marriages of working-class couples. For example, as we saw in chapter 8, when wives and husbands work alternate shifts, they have less time for each other. Communication and their sex lives may suffer. And whereas divorce, lack of family time (see next chapter), worries about child care, and other issues are problems for all marriages, working-class couples have fewer resources to address them. As in 1976, they have less money for an evening out without the children, for "a family vacation, for tickets to a concert, a play, or a movie" (Rubin, 1994, p. 98; see also White and Rogers, 2000).

Daily Living. Class and economic realities profoundly affect family lives. Rich professional families have many amenities and opportunities, although their lives are not free of conflicts, such as overly long workdays for parents who then have little time for their children. On the other hand, poor and working-class families struggle. These struggles do not completely devastate them, but they do live on the edge.

Let us look at poor people first. Families on welfare are among the poorest. Rank depicts their lives. They have "difficulties paying monthly bills, not having enough food, worrying about health care costs, and so on." For example in 1994, a divorced mother with two teenage daughters received $544 from Aid to Families with Dependent Children (AFDC) and $106 in food stamps a month. They paid $280 for rent, and were left with $370, which came to $4 a day per person. She said: "You can't make a move. You can't buy anything that you want for your home. You can't go on vacation. You can't take a weekend off and go and see things because it costs too much. And it's just such a waste of life." It was tough leading a normal life. But there were some simple pleasures, such as walks, visits with friends and relatives, reading, and watching TV. Usually by the end of the month they were out of cash. Then they would turn to relatives for help, go to food pantries for supplies, even go hungry (Rank, 1994, pp. 113, 115).

The negative consequences of poverty are many. Tasks most Americans take for granted are difficult or impossible: "Being unable to afford to go to the dentist even though the pain is excruciating; not purchasing a simple meal at a restaurant for fear it will disrupt the budget; never being able to go to a movie; having no credit, which in turn makes getting a future credit rating difficult; lacking a typewriter or personal computer on which to improve secretarial skills for a job interview. The list could go on an on" (Rank, 1994, p. 119).

Higher on the income scale, deprivation and consequences are less severe. Working-class families still struggle, however. Sheehan describes the income, work, and lifestyle of Bonita and Kenny Merten and their two sons. In 1994, both worked full-time and earned $32,428. After tax and other deductions, they were left with $26,417. They spent almost $6,000 shopping in food stores, and $2,000 more on snacks and occasional dinner out, mostly at places like McDonald's. For mortgage payments and property taxes, they paid $4,000. Clothing, occasional nights out, and visits to relatives and short vacations consumed the rest of their income. Indeed, they were in debt, for which they went to a consumer counselor. He made many suggestions, such as buying powdered milk, stopping eating out, and no more vacations, which had cost them $1,500 to $2,500. They resisted most of these suggestions, for to follow them would have meant foregoing activities that were important to them as a family. Using powdered milk would have made them feel poor (Sheehan, 1995).

The Primacy of Class. Much has been written about the (wrong) values of poor and working-class families, and families in general. We read that parents have low education or are depressed and do not properly motivate their children to study and achieve. People on welfare are said to develop a "culture of poverty" that emphasizes gratification, does not motivate people to work, leads to unwed motherhood, and so on (Mayer, 1997).

Let me first stress that most poor people *do* work, but the low wages they are paid do not even reach up to poverty income (nationally, $18,104 for a family of four in 2001). But the service economy jobs available to them offer low wages and few promotion opportunities. They barely survive, and often they do not, since the jobs they hold usually offer no medical coverage or other benefits. They live in the same neighborhoods with families on welfare and other non-working poor people. Indeed, families often alternate between work and welfare, or, at times, supplement welfare benefits with jobs that pay under the table, in order to survive (Newman, 1999; Edin and Fein, 1997; Associated Press, 1999b; Hill, 1999; Seccombe, 2002).

In 1999 and 2000, Barbara Ehrenreich, a sociologist and writer, set out to learn how people manage to survive on low wages. *Nickeled and Dimed: On (Not) Getting By in America* shows how hard and stressful such survival is. In Florida, Maine, and Minnesota she worked, at slightly above minimum wages, as a waitress, aide in nursing homes, cleaning lady, and salesperson at Wal-Mart. She found that "all of those jobs were physically demanding, some of them even damaging if performed month after month." She usually worked two jobs in order to live very sparsely and to pay her bills, which did not include health insurance. Working to support only herself, she barely managed, and only because she had brought a car and some money from her professional life (2001, p. 195).

Contrary to popular beliefs and many social science statements, few people remain poor and on welfare for decades. According to a study that has followed families for two decades, only 12 percent of the people were on welfare for five or more years. The median stay on welfare was 23 months (Zinn and Eitzen, 1999; Seccombe, James, and Walters, 1998, p. 850).

People move in and out of poverty and welfare because of many reasons, none of them related to their motivation to work. Divorce (mostly for women), death of a family member, loss of a job, the birth of a child (which usually means a mother cannot work for a while), and other events explain changes in family income and well being. And as divorce often means a fall into poverty for women, a marriage can mean moving out of it.

None of these conditions are connected to values, "culture of poverty," motivation, or childrearing practices. They result from jobs that do not pay enough to support families, from unequal distributions of income and wealth, from government policies that do not devote enough money to child care, income support, and other services that would support families. Indeed, national and state governments have reduced drastically even the traditionally meager welfare payments. In 1996, the Congress and the president changed the law, and now people can receive welfare benefits for a total of five years over their lifetime, and never for a continuous period of over two years. The assumption is that people stay on welfare rather than work, and this law would force them to find jobs and move out of poverty. Theory (or, rather, prejudice) ignored reality, however. Welfare rolls did decline from 12.2 million people in 1996 to 5.5 million in 2001, but the number of people living in poverty only declined by 15 percent (Hays, 2003, pp. 221, 224; see also Albelda, 1999).

In chapter 8, I referred to MacLeod's *Ain't No Makin' It,* a study of two groups of youths in Cambridge, Massachusetts. In the mid-1980s, the Brothers (six of seven black) were ambitious, believed in working, and stayed out of trouble. The Hallway Hangers (six of eight white) were in frequent trouble with the police, did not study, and saw no hope in the future.

When he visited them again in 1991, MacLeod found that most members of both groups had not succeeded in finding good jobs and in settling down.

Let us examine their families. The Hallway Hangers' families had lived in low-income housing (the despised "projects") for a long time, 13 to 30 years for six of them. Only two of their parents had finished high school. They were sporadically employed in "menial, low-paying, and unstable jobs." Fathers were often absent, families were large, and had "numerous encounters with the law." They resembled the stereotypical poor (MacLeod, 1995, p. 53).

Not so the Brothers' families. Most of their fathers were living with them, worked, and had finished high school. Most Brothers had older siblings with significant educational achievement. Only two of the families had lived in the projects for more than six years. The Brothers' parents exercised "a good deal of authority over them," insisting on early curfews, school attendance, avoidance of drugs, and so on. They had high educational and occupational hopes for them. Thus, the Brothers' limited achievement by 1991 could not be attributed to their parents or any "culture of poverty." MacLeod insists that it was the economy of the times, not parental attitudes, that largely shaped the Brothers' and their families' work and lives (1995).

And the hopelessness of the Hallway Hangers was also largely the product of the class and economic systems. They were intelligent observers of the world around them. Their families "are not people who are slothful or slow-witted; rather, they are generally industrious, intelligent, and very willing to work." But the parents' and the Hangers' "occupational histories can only be viewed as sad and disillusioning by the Hallway Hangers" (MacLeod, 1995, p. 71).

For both groups, willingness to work was not the problem. It was the economy and the jobs and pay available to them.

Summary of Classes and Families

Classes do influence, mold, and shape our families. The choice of a partner; the lives of our children; relationships with our kin; the marriages we experience; and our daily family lives are all affected by our class.

Sociologists, the media, and popular perceptions often exaggerate class differences. Values, motivations, and behaviors are attributed to poor and working-class families to explain their economic conditions, when in fact it is the economy and the class system that create those conditions. Families don't have enough money because the jobs available to them pay low wages, because they have few opportunities, because there are few social programs to assist families, not because they are lazy or they do not raise their children properly.

Let us return to gender issues. Poor and working-class families will benefit when men and fathers find work that pays enough to support families (see ch. 8). But women also need jobs that pay living wages. They need them to share the provider role with husbands, but also because many women are the sole providers of their families. Most poor families are headed by single women, and they need good jobs to raise their children. All families of all classes need affordable, quality day care; a free national health care system that will free all of us from the worry and burden of providing medical care for our families; and decent, affordable housing and schools. (For single-parent and poor families, see Seccombe, 2000, 2002; Sugarman, 2003.)

RACE AND ETHNICITY

"Race" and "ethnicity" are social creations, not biological realities. But because we came to believe that they are real, they have real consequences in our lives, including our family lives. The conditions and traditions of race and ethnic groups influence who we marry, the family traditions we inherit, where we live with our families, and other family aspects. In chapter 2, I discussed the history of African American families. Here I focus on African American families today. (For excellent discussions on the social construction of race, and the continued existence of racism and discrimination, see Takaki, 1993; Shanklin,1994; Ferrante and Browne, 2001; Williams, 1944; Kottak, 2000; Barnes, 2000; Steinhorn and Diggs-Brown, 2000; Feagin and McKinney, 2003; Bonilla-Silva, 2003; and especially Van Ausdale and Feagin, 2001. For useful discussions of the families of all major ethnic and race groups in the United States, see Gonzalez, 1998; Taylor, 2002; Parrillo, 2000; Benokraitis, 2002).

Trials and Strengths of African American Families

Throughout American history, both popular perceptions and social scientists have portrayed African American families as disintegrating and failing. "In almost every decade, for 200 years, someone has 'discovered' that the black family is falling apart." It was true in the twentieth century. In the 1930s, Frazier argued that slavery had destroyed black families. In 1965, Moynihan, following Frazier, wrote that black families were caught in a "tangle of pathology." And in 1986, Bill Moyers told TV audiences that black families were "vanishing" (Coontz, 1992, pp. 235–236; for more references to original sources, see p. 356, notes 11 and 12, of Coontz).

In chapter 2, we saw that African Americans have struggled mightily against oppression and discrimination and have created and maintained strong families. The obstacles were immense, during and since slavery, but people drew on their African traditions of strong extended families and shaped them to fit the conditions they were forced to endure.

Social science writing and research on African Americans during the last four decades of the twentieth century focused mostly on perceived weaknesses and failings. They studied the minority who did not work, not the majority who did. They paid little attention to extended families and cultural traditions that helped people lead good lives, despite poverty and many forms of discrimination. Many writers insist that we look at these families as they have really been, as they really are, at their weaknesses and strengths, and their trials and triumphs (Billingsley, 1992; Hill, 1999; Logan, 2001).

According to Hill (in his words), these strengths are: "Strong achievement orientation; strong work orientation; flexible family roles; strong kinship bonds (especially extended families); strong religious orientation." All three writers take note of and address problems within African American families. But they argue that black people would not have survived these many centuries without functioning families. And most of the problems they face today are caused by economic conditions and continuing discrimination, not by their families and family values.

Economic and Social Statistics

Income and Employment. For the last four decades of the twentieth century, the official unemployment rate for African Americans has been twice that of whites. It was 12.4 percent versus 6 percent in 1992, 7.3 versus 3.5 in 1998, and 8.7 versus 4.2 in 2001. That, of course, is the *official* rate. Millions of people, however, stop looking for work after years of not finding any, and they are not included in the official statistics. According to one study, for every black man officially unemployed in 1982, there were two more discouraged workers, out of the work force and not being counted (*Statistical Abstract,* 1999, p. 432; 2002, p. 368; Center for the Study of Social Policy, 1984; see also Hill, 1999, pp. 16–17).

A major reason many black men cannot find work is the criminal records they have. Years of discrimination by police and courts have taken their toll. First, as Chambliss has shown, police are much more likely to patrol urban areas populated by poor blacks than they are to patrol suburban communities. Thus, African American drug users have a much greater chance of being caught. The result is that even though blacks are no more likely than whites to use drugs, as many surveys have shown, they constitute the majority of those in prison for drug use. African Americans, 12 percent of the American populations and 13 percent of drug users, "make up 35 percent of the arrests, 55 percent of the convictions and 74 percent of the sentences for drug charges" (Chambliss, 1994; Jackson, 1996).

Studies in the 1990s showed catastrophic results for black men. In 1995, one-third of black men in their twenties were on probation, in jail or prison, or on parole; that is, under the control of the criminal justice system. That was an increase from one-quarter in 1989. In 1994, 6.7 percent of white men in their twenties were in the criminal justice system, compared to 12.3 percent of Hispanics and 30.2 for blacks. That year 211,205 black men in their twenties were in prisons, 95,114 in jails, 351,368 on probation, and 130,005 on parole, for a total of 787,692. Most of these men were unable to marry and support families. Their limited education and skills, and their criminal records, cripple their chances of finding jobs that pay well, or any jobs, in the new economy (Mauer and Huling, 1995; see also ch. 8).

African American men who do work full time earn less than white workers. In 2001, the median weekly earnings of full-time male African American workers were $518; that is 74.6 percent of the $694 earned by white men. For black women, their $451 was 86.5 percent of white women's $521. The reasons for the differences are many, but the primary one is the various forms of discrimination that force workers to hold lower-paying jobs (*Statistical Abstract*, 2002, p. 403).

The earnings just quoted are those of individual workers who work full-time. Family incomes, however, include all types of families: those with no, one, two, or more earners; those with full-time and part-time workers; and families with many sources of incomes. In 2000, the median income of all black families was 64 percent of white families' median. We see in table 10.1 that when black families have both spouses working, they earn a median income 84.5 percent of similar white couples. On the other hand, female-headed black families earn only 69.5 percent of similar white families. But the most important conclusion from that table is that both gender *and* race affect family income. Single-parent families—black, white, and Hispanic—with a *man* receiving the income earn considerably more than single-parent families with the woman receiving the income. But race and ethnicity matter, as African American and Hispanic families of all types earn less income than white families do (*Statistical Abstract*, 2002, p. 41).

The disadvantage of black families is that a much greater percent are female-headed compared to white families. In 2000, 55 percent of black families with children were maintained by mothers, compared to 28 percent for Hispanics and 21 percent for whites. These families have increased for all three groups since 1980 (*Statistical Abstract*, 2002, p. 51). (I will explain below the reasons for and meaning of this increase.)

One consequence of these family compositions and incomes is that many black children live in poverty. In 2000, 12.3 percent of white children, 30.4 percent of black children, and 27.3 percent of Hispanic children lived in families with incomes below the poverty level, as defined by the U.S. government (which is unrealistically low). But it is the children of families maintained by single women who suffer the greatest poverty. A table published in the 1994 *Statistical Abstract* (no similar table exists in later editions) shows that 69 percent of these Hispanic and African American children, six years and younger, were poor in 1993. And

Table 10.1 Median family income in 2000

	White	Black	Hispanic
Married-couple families	$60,080	$50,729	$41,116
Male householder, no wife	44,020	37,015	39,015
Female householder, no husband	31,230	21,698	23,671

Source:*Statistical Abstract*, 2002, p. 435

again, we see the combined effects of gender and race/ethnicity. In 1993, almost half (46 percent) of the children of white mothers were also poor (*Statistical Abstract,* 2002, p. 441; Henslin, 1998, p. 202).

Poverty has deep and extensive consequences. For example, poor African Americans live in neighborhoods that are dangerous to their health. Studies have shown that "inner-city black communities were selected disproportionately as sites for landfills, garbage dumps, waste disposal facilities, and incinerators." They poison air, water, and earth, and cause many health problems. Poor health is the result. Childhood asthma is much more common in these communities. In 1997, there was a U.S. hospitalization rate for asthma of 179 cases per 100,000 people; but for African Americans, it was 360 cases. The long-term consequence is that in 2000 the average life expectancy was 77.4 years for whites but 71.7 years for African Americans (Hill, 1999, p. 24; Rodriguez, 1998; Kong, 1999b; Meckler, 1998).

Marriages, Births, and Children. From 1980 to 2000, for black, white, and Hispanic women and men, the percentage of people 18 and over who have never married has increased, the percentage of married has decreased, and the percentage of divorced has increased. All these figures are higher for African Americans. For example, never married white people increased from 18.9 percent to 21.4; black, from 30.5 to 39.6 percent. For married, white decreased from 67.2 to 62 percent; black from 51.4 to 42.1 percent. And divorced, white went from 6.0 percent to 9.8, black from 8.4 to 11.7 percent. These statistics show both that people are marrying at older ages and more people are getting divorced. Also, probably, that more couples are living together unmarried, doing so for longer periods, and doing so instead of marrying (*Statistical Abstract,* 2002, p. 47; Tucker and Mitchell-Kernan, 1995).

The percentage of children born to unmarried women has been increasing all over the world, as we saw in chapter 5. The percentage was in the 40s and 50s in some European countries in 1998. So, too, the percentage of children born to unmarried women in the U.S. increased. It went from 10.7 percent in 1970, to 17.8 in 1980, 26.6 percent in 1990, and 33.2 in 2000. For white women, the increase was from 5.6 percent in 1970 to 20.1 in 2000; for black women, from 37.5 to 68.5 (Cox, 1999, p. 326; *Statistical Abstract,* 2002, p. 59).

But the birth *rate* for unmarried black women has not been rising. Rather, the rate for *married* black women has declined sharply. From 1970 to 1990, the "birth rates for unmarried black women . . . [fell] by 13 percent," but the rates for married black women fell by 38 percent during that same period. Thus, since the contribution of married women to the total of births has declined, it makes the contribution of unmarried black mothers larger (Coontz, 1992, p. 236; 1997, p. 29; for later comparable data, see *Statistical Abstract,* 2002, p. 59).

Finally, because of increases in divorce and of women who never marry, many African American children live only with their mothers, according to statistics. In 1998, 51 percent did so (but only 18 percent for whites, 27 percent for Hispanics). Thirty-six percent lived with both parents (74 percent of whites, 64 percent of Hispanics). But statistics do not tell us much about people's daily lives. Various studies have shown that black children who are listed as living with only their mothers live in extended family networks where grandparents, aunts and uncles, and others support them in various ways. In addition, many of the fathers and their extended families are involved in the children's lives (*Statistical Abstract,* 1999, p. 67). (See discussions in earlier chapters, especially of Stack, 1974, 1996.)

What do these statistics on marriage, birth, and children's living arrangements mean? Do they indicate the breakdown of families in African American communities?

Breakdown or Strengths of African American Families?

As we saw in the opening paragraphs of this discussion on black families, people have been announcing their breakdown for centuries. In the twentieth century, the most well-known proponents of this theory were E. Franklin Frazier (in the 1930s) and Daniel Patrick Moynihan (in the 1960s and later).

"Frazier argued that slavery destroyed African familial structures and cultures and gave rise to a host of dysfunctional family features that continued to undermine the stability and well-being of black families well into the twentieth century. Foremost among these features was the emergence of the black 'matriarchal,' or maternal, family system. According to Frazier, the matriarchal unit was a product of slavery and the conditions of rural Southern life, which weakened the economic position of black men and their authority in the family. Moreover, this family form was inherently unstable and productive of pathological outcomes within the family unit, including high rates of poverty, illegitimacy, crime, delinquency, and other problems associated with the socialization of black children" (Taylor, 2002, pp. 19–20).

In the 1960s, while working for the U.S. Department of Labor, Moynihan wrote a fifty-page report, *The Negro Family*. In it, he cites Frazier as a source of his argument. He argued that most of the problems blacks faced were caused by "matriarchal" families and the "breakdown" of black families. In bold letters, he wrote: " . . . the family structure of lower class Negroes is highly unstable, and in many urban centers is approaching complete breakdown." He referred to high separation and divorce rates (25 percent in 1960), and "illegitimate" birth rates of black women eight times those of white women, and children not living with both parents. "It has been estimated that only a minority of Negro children reach the age of 18 having lived all their lives with both their parents." One graph showed that "almost a fourth of nonwhite families are headed by a woman" in 1962 (23 percent for black families, 8 percent for white ones). Moynihan concluded that these conditions caused the high unemployment, poor school achievement, delinquency, and most other problems black people were facing (Moynihan, 1965, pp. 5–11).

Divorce, single-parent families, children living with mothers only, births to unmarried women, and other conditions have increased considerably since Moynihan wrote his report in 1965, for blacks, whites, Hispanics, and other groups (see statistics above). Since 1965, the report has dominated the discussion on African American families; the report has had its critics and supporters. Some writers have concluded that Moynihan was prophetic is his description of African American families, and the breakdown is more devastating today than it was in the 1960s. (For a variation of Moynihan's report, see Popenoe, *Life Without Father*, 1996.)

All these conditions—divorce, children born to unmarried women, children living with one parent only (usually the mother), and others—have increased also for white families, at similar or higher rates. Since the 1960s, there have been significant family changes in the entire society, affecting all people. These changes have been higher, however, for African American families, because of historical and economic conditions and cultural traditions. (See ch. 2, on the history of black families, where I show that two-parent families were the majority of families from the end of slavery until the 1960s. It was social changes since the 1960s, not slavery, that have changed black families.)

The family lives of many black people are seriously affected by daily discrimination and racism, which are very much alive today. For example, studies and personal accounts have shown that many black families are steered away from renting or buying homes in quality neighborhoods. Thus, their children's education suffers because of the schools they attend in poorer areas, as does their ability to build up housing equity. When black families do move into white neighborhoods, they often meet silent ostracism and isolation. And discrimination of many kinds exists at work. In one survey of 187 black corporate managers, all said that racism existed in their companies (Feagin and McKinney, 2003, ch. 4).

Such experiences in the neighborhood and at work take their toll on families. Couples must deal with this extra stress in their lives. Discrimination and anxiety at work sap parents' energy and they have less time for their children; or, it "detracts from the quality of interaction with children." Thus, couple and parent-child relationships suffer (Feagin and McKinney, 2003, ch. 4; Steinhorn and Diggs-Brown, 2000).

Robert Hill, in *The Strengths of African American Families* (1999), directly and indirectly responds to Moynihan. Here I will present some of his major observations and analyses, and supplement them with evidence from other sources and writers.

Focus on the Positive. Hill says that African American families do face serious problems. "Over the past two decades, increasing numbers of black families have experienced rising levels of unemployment, poverty, divorce, separation, out-of-wedlock births, crime, delinquency, spousal abuse, child abuse, alcoholism, drug abuse, poor health, and AIDS." Media stories and much social science writing focus only on these problems, however. Little is said about the 8 out of 10 black families who received no welfare in the 1990s, or the 9 out of 10 unmarried teenage women who had no children, or the two-thirds of the women in single-parent families who have jobs, or the two-thirds of men in their twenties who had no contact with the criminal justice system (despite considerable provocation and discrimination). Even in poor areas, 60 percent of the families have income from work. Hill concludes that "the overwhelming major- ity of African American families are making positive contributions to the society in spite of racism and other social and economic constraints" (1999, pp. 15, 63, preface).

The Economy and Classes. Economic changes during the second half of the twentieth century, especially since the mid-1970s, have devastated many black communities, despite the ac- claimed economic "success" of the 1990s. In brief, there are many fewer industrial jobs that had enabled young men and women to marry and support families. They have been replaced with "service" jobs that pay much lower wages. These changes have affected black Americans much more than white Americans. (See ch. 8 for details and statistics.)

After black people began holding industrial jobs in the 1960s and 1970s, these jobs began to disappear. For example, in the Great Lakes region, from 1979 to 1984 half of the black workers in durable goods industries lost their jobs. As we saw earlier, the incomes of young black men in the 1990s were about half of the incomes of young black men in the 1970s (Coontz, 1992, p. 245; Hill, 1999, p. 28; Wilson, 1996).

In his study of gangs in Milwaukee in the 1980s, Hagedorn shows in *People and Folks* (1988) that after the city lost many jobs (beer breweries closed down, for example), there was considerable increase in unemployment. From 1980 to 1985, "the Milwaukee area lost 35,000 manufacturing jobs." One of the results was that young black men, unable to find the kinds of jobs their parents had had, stayed in gangs longer than earlier generations had stayed. They "will not have an industrial ladder to step on in order to 'mature out' of the gang." Unemployed young black men who started gangs in their early teens were still "hanging out on the same corners where they began the gang five to eight years before." Of those without jobs, 70.3 percent were still in the gang, compared to 9.7 percent of those with full-time jobs and 14.3 percent of those with part-time jobs. Unemployment, gangs, police surveillance, and time on their hands made for criminal records, which made future employment, and marriage, more difficult to achieve. Most of these young men came from working two-parent families, but the parents' example could not provide their children with jobs that did not exist (Hagedorn, 1988, pp. 42, 124).

The 1970s and 1980s recessions increased poverty and female-headed families, from 28 percent in 1969 to 42 percent in 1983. These families are much more likely to be poor when the women are unemployed (70 percent) than when they work (29 percent). Changes in the black class structure from 1969 to 1989 bear these conclusions (Hill, 1999, pp. 16, 18).

Table 10.2 shows an increase in non-working poor (from 13 to 19 percent), an increase in the two higher classes (from 23 to 30 percent), and a significant decrease in what Hill calls the working class (the working poor and working near poor) from 64 to 51 percent. (For somewhat comparable income statistics in 2000, see *Statistical Abstract,* 2002, p. 436.)

Achievement and Work Orientation of African American Families. No doubt the long history of discrimination and oppression has been harmful to black Americans. Stories of slavery and

Table 10.2 Class structure of African American families in 1969 and 1989 (percent)

	1969	1989
Upper class	2	5
Middle class	21	25
Near poor	42	32
Working poor	22	19
Non-working poor	13	19

Source: Hill, 1999, p. 78

life after emancipation offer detailed portraits of daily life. They all show much pain and suffering (Douglass, 1855; Jacobs, 1861; Wright, 1945; Gwaltney, 1993; Takaki, 1993).

But in large part through their strong families, African Americans have minimized and survived that history. Part of that family heritage Hill calls "achievement orientation." People knew that only through sustained and hard work would they survive. They taught their children the importance of education. Research studies that "have actually measured the academic orientation of black parents have found them to be equal to or higher than the orientation of white parents." In addition, Hill discusses educational aspirations of young people, peer approval of achievement, self-esteem and racial identity, and the work of black colleges and programs to educate and assist African Americans (1999, p. 82; for references to studies, see pp. 84–85; see also ch. 4).

Hill notes that it was hard-working families who raised the children who became professionals and now constitute the African American middle class. That generation of maids, cooks, and farm workers spoke eloquently about their lives, their families, and race relations when Gwaltney, a black anthropologist, interviewed them in the 1970s. *Drylongso: A Self-Portrait of Black America* is an extraordinary story. "Drylongso" means "ordinary," and the book presents the lives and stories of ordinary black Americans, who are "working members of stable families in pursuit of much the same kinds of happinesses that preoccupy the rest of American society," not star athletes or street criminals. A careful reading will dispel many stereotypes and much ignorance about black Americans (first published in 1980, and reprinted with an afterword in 1993).

Table 10.3 allows for three conclusions: the higher working rate for black women compared to white women, although the difference is decreasing; the increasing rate for both black and white women; and the significant drop in the rate of black men, from 76.5 percent in 1970 to 68.5 in 2001. The last change indicates the number of black men who have dropped out of the labor force because they are discouraged for various reasons (as I have explained in earlier chapters and in this chapter).

Flexible Family Roles. From slavery days, African Americans have generally lived in larger family groupings than white families have. As we saw, they brought that tradition from their African cultures and adapted it to slavery conditions.

That tradition has included family and community acceptance of children born to unmarried women. Living in larger family groups of parents and other relatives, young black

Table 10.3 Labor force participation rates in 1970 and 2001 (age 16 and over)

		1970	2001
White			
	Male	80.0	75.0
	Female	40.6	59.7
Black			
	Male	76.5	68.5
	Female	49.5	62.9

Source: Statistical Abstract, 2002, p. 367

women are not forced to marry the fathers of their children in order to survive. And given the worsening job prospects of young men, and the increasing employment opportunities and earnings of young women, unmarried black mothers have fewer incentives to marry (Taylor, 2002, p. 38).

Surrounded by larger family networks, single-parent families are resilient. They often do as well or better than two-parent families. We cannot automatically assume that a single parent (usually a mother) must fail as a parent. Her strength and love, and the support of relatives, can and do create a caring and effective environment. For example, if we control for income, single-parent families are "somewhat *more* likely to have children in college than two-parent families" (Hill, 1999, p. 112).

Billingsley also shows that single-parent families can and do function. In the 1980s "black teenage, unwed mothers and their households became synonymous with the black family." But people forget some facts. "Most single parents are adults, not teenagers. Most are white, not black. . . . teen parenting among white girls in America—leaving aside black girls altogether—is higher than in any of the other industrialized Western countries. Not all black teens succumb to the worst features of this predicament. Once pregnancy and childbirth occur, they need not wreak havoc." He then discusses the lives of seven women who were single parents. "They defy the dysfunctional stereotypes. . . . Each demonstrates that the obstacles commonly faced by single parents can be overcome with timely and appropriate social support" (1992, p. 334).

These seven women raised their children, went to school, and earned good incomes. Most single mothers, however, live closer to poverty, and we must not underestimate the financial struggles they face. Yet "the vast majority of these women, even the very poor ones, are self-supporting through their own labor. This is far from the stereotype of the 'typical' black female head" (Billingsley, 1992, p. 346).

Ever since Moynihan, writers have worried that the boys of these mothers lack proper male "role models." (To find such role models, Moynihan suggested that black teenage boys enter the armed forces.) They assume, however, that mothers are raising their boys alone. In fact, they seek out "responsible men—and women—to assist them in raising their sons—and daughters." In addition, fathers who do not live with their children are not necessarily absent from their lives. Studies show that many unmarried fathers are active in their children's lives (Hill, 1999, p. 115; see Stier and Tienda, 1993; Way and Stauber, 1996; Newman, 1999; Coley, 2001).

Finally, we should note that the higher the income and class, the lower the percentage of single-parent families; the lower the income, the higher the percentage. For example, in 1986, only 17 percent of middle-class black families were single-parent ones, but 67 percent of the working poor, and 75 percent of the non-working poor, families were single parent. Men who cannot find jobs that pay well, or any jobs, are less likely to marry (Billingsley, 1992, p. 57).

Some writers cite statistics to show that sons raised by single mothers are two to three times more likely to become delinquent, drop out of school, and meet other misfortunes than are sons raised by couples. But they forget that it is black single mothers who "raise the majority of [black] males who complete high school, who graduate from college, who work every day in legitimate occupations, who are responsible fathers, and who are productive citizens of this society." Secondly, they forget that the criminal justice system creates much of this criminality by patrolling the neighborhoods where young black men live. As we saw earlier, for example, adolescent drug use is not greater among blacks than it is among whites, but the criminal justice system catches and sentences more of them than it does white teens (Hill, 1999, pp. 114–115, 117–119).

Also, by most accounts, African American families have practiced more egalitarian gender roles than white families have. Most black women have shared the provider role throughout U.S. history. Women are not fully equal, and many black men may feel ambivalent about housework and child care, but they have been performing them at greater rates than white men. But according to Billingsley, black working wives still do most child care and housework, and feel overworked and tired. And as with white couples, many black men think they do more housework than their wives think they do (Hill, 1999, p. 109; Taylor, 2002; Billingsley, 1992; Landry, 2000).

Kinship Bonds. A number of studies have argued that from their earlier days in the United States, African Americans have been much more likely to live in extended families and have closer and more supportive relationships with their kin than white families have. Aschenbrenner concluded that African American families held five values: "(1) a high value placed on children; (2) the approval of strong, protective mothers; (3) the emphasis on strict discipline and respect for elders; (4) the strength of family bonds; and (5) the ideal of an independent spirit" (1975, p. 137).

In chapter 2, I summarized Sudarkasa's thesis that in Africa the core of the family was not the husband-wife couple. Families consisted of various groups of relatives who lived and worked together. In addition, in Africa, as in much of the world, people were close to relatives outside their residential group. Such extended families continue to this day. A 1980 study showed that *at all income levels,* from 25 to 30 percent of black families were extended, compared to 8 to 11 percent of white family households. According to another study, in 1991 "22 percent of black households were extended, in contrast to 10 percent of white households." And in 1992, "according to the National Survey of Family Households, one out of three (34 percent) of black households were three-generational" (Farley and Allen, 1987; Taylor, 2002, p. 25; Hill, 1999, p. 125).

Extended families have provided much support to unmarried parents. According to Hill, "Nine out of ten babies born to black teenagers live with their mother in the homes of their grandparents or other relatives. . . . [K]in provide a wide range of support to young single mothers, often enabling them to complete their education or to obtain a job." More recently, however, grandmothers have been younger and more likely to work, and thus unavailable to help raise grandchildren. Also, the deepening poverty of many families makes it more difficult for them to support relatives (Hill, 1999, p. 125).

In contrast to Stack's and other studies, some recent surveys claim that black respondents did not report more assistance from kin than white respondents did. Cherlin thinks that there are three possible explanations for the different findings between surveys and field studies like Stack's. First, perhaps "statistical analyses of survey data just aren't rich enough in detail to substantiate the difference" between black and white families. Second, field studies have very small samples compared to surveys, and do not compare blacks to whites, so they may have "overstated the differences between black and white families." Third, as Hill notes, poor blacks may have less money and other resources to share today, compared to the 1970s, when Stack and others carried out their studies (Cherlin, 1999, p. 147).

Having read and analyzed Stack's two studies carefully, I think the first explanation is the most likely one for the 1970s. Stack was fully accepted by the families, she was able to see their lives as they truly lived them. On the other hand, an interviewer who talks with people for an hour or even less can never see, experience, and understand people's lives as they really see them. But it may also well be that worsening economic and living conditions, and more grandmothers holding jobs, have made it more difficult for family members to assist each other. But at least one study showed that African American families in the 1990s in New York lived in kin networks similar to those Stack described (Newman, 1999).

Despite possible changing conditions, African American families continue to support their kin. For example, in the 1980s, 40 percent of working mothers relied on relatives, mostly grandmothers, for day care. In 1999, 18.8 percent of non-Hispanic white parents used relatives to care for their children, compared to 36 percent of non-Hispanic black parents. And children whose parents cannot care for them are usually taken in by relatives. "Of the one million black children living in the households of relatives without either parent, 80 percent are adopted by kin" (Hill, 1999, pp. 125—126; *Statistical Abstract, 2002*, p. 359).

Poor African American families do face serious problems. Money is very limited, housing crowded and unhealthy, streets often unsafe, children tempted by gangs. Life is often hard and mean. Many individuals and families crumble. A third of black men in their twenties (probably a higher percentage in some poor areas) are trapped in the criminal justice system and face limited job prospects because of their criminal records. In addition, even though people do help, when you are poor you have few possessions and often have limited energy to share. People share to survive, they help ill relatives, for example. But their resources, time, and energy are often stretched thin (Stack, 1974, 1996).

But we cannot allow these problems to blind us to the larger truths we find in Hill and other researchers. Most people and most families hold jobs, help each other, and function. They deserve as much attention, if not more, as the problem families. Field studies transcend statistics and surface appearances and allow us to see the strengths of even the poorest people, people who may not resemble the idealized middle-class white family. But they have their histories, traditions, toughness, and resilience.

Carol Stack was a white single mother, and anthropology graduate student, when she went to learn about black families in The Flats (around 1970). She became close friends with Ruby Banks, a poor black single mother. They helped each other with their children. One day, on a cab ride home, after she had swapped "some hot corn bread and greens for diapers and milk" with her baby's aunt, Ruby talked about her life and her philosophy. "I don't believe in putting myself on nobody, but I know I need help every day. . . . I don't believe in begging, but I believe that people should help one another. I used to wish for lots of things like a living room suite, clothes, nice clothes, stylish clothes—I'm sick of wearing the same pieces. But I can't, I can't help myself because I have my children and I love them and I have my mother and all our kin. Sometimes I don't have a damn dime in my pocket, not a crying penny to get a box of paper diapers, milk, a loaf of bread. But you have to have help from everybody and anybody, so don't turn no one down when they come round for help" (1974, p. 32).

Summary of Race and Ethnicity

African American families have a long tradition of strong kinship bonds. Such bonds have allowed most of them to mitigate poverty, discrimination, and oppression. Family values and family traditions have given them strength.

But for decades now, many writers have argued the reverse: that it has been the values of black families, especially poor families, that have trapped them in poverty. For example, programs have sought to teach people the value of work, assuming that they did not value work. They did this instead of trying to create an economy that provides people well-paying jobs. For when jobs have existed—during labor shortages in World War II, during the 1960s, and at other times—black people found them and they provided for their families. During these times they held the same "values" they always have. But when jobs disappeared, more women and men have been unable to find work to support their families.

And when single-parent families earn high incomes, as some do, they can live in better housing and their children can attend good schools. "The disadvantages for children often associated with one-parent or female-headed households are obliterated in high-income single-parent families, both black and white, indicating that family structure per se is not critical to the economic well-being of family members but rather that economic opportunity is" (Taylor, 2002, p. 34).

What we need is social policies to create jobs that pay enough for people to support their families, not lectures on "family values." History supports that conclusion, as do various recent studies. In addition, the daily discrimination directed against African Americans and other people must end (Seccombe, 2000, 2002; Feagin and McKinney, 2003).

11

Families, Work, and Housework

Before industrialism, people worked in family settings. There was no separation of family time from work time. Food was gathered or grown, cooking was done, and children were raised with family and neighbors. The many references to other societies and earlier America show that family and work were one experience.

Chapter 8, on migration and the economy, outlines economic developments since 1500, and discusses more specifically the rise of capitalism and industrialism in the late 1700s and how this development shaped families by causing the separation of work time from family time. Whether people have jobs, what kind of work they do, and the income they earn from their work either enable people or make it difficult for people to form and support their families. Chapter 8 shows that millions of people without land or job were forced to migrate to other lands to find land or work and that they were separated from many family members for years, often forever.

In this chapter, I examine more closely how work and family relate to each other, how one affects the other. We shall look at recent changes in work, the increasing numbers of women entering the labor force, and the positive and negative consequences our jobs have on our families. Then, we shall examine in depth the issues Hochschild raised in *The Time Bind: When Work Becomes Home and Home Becomes Work* (1997), specifically the argument that time and other demands of jobs create profound stresses for modern families.

One of these stresses is housework. In two-worker families or single-parent families—that is, families without a full-time housewife at home—there is not enough time for cooking, cleaning, laundry, shopping, and raising the children.

I end the discussion of work and housework by examining possible solutions to the problems and stresses we face in balancing the demands of work and family, and in doing housework and raising children.

THE NATURE OF WORK

Work is more than mere survival. It can also enrich us with a sense of accomplishment and fulfillment; it can be as much play as it is work; it can satisfy our creativity and imagination. Rip Torn, the actor, said: "You work out of necessity, but in your work, you gotta have a little artistry, too" (in Terkel, 1974, p. 127).

Traditionally, people worked in and with their families. Camara Ley describes his boyhood experiences in an African village, working the fields with his uncles and other relatives and neighbors:

> My young uncle was wonderful at rice-cutting, the very best. I followed him proudly, step by step, he handing me the bundles of stalks as he cut them. I tore off the leaves, trimmed the stalks, and piled them. . . .

"'Sing with us,' my uncle would command.

"The tom-toms, which followed us as we advanced into the field, kept time with our voices. We sang as a chorus, now very high-pitched with great bursts of song, and then very low, so low we could scarcely be heard. Our fatigue vanished, and the heat became less oppressive. (Ley, 1954, p. 56)

The Tikopia also worked in families and with relatives and friends:

Pa Nukunefu and the women share the work fairly among them, he doing most of the clearing of vegetation and the digging, they some of the digging and replanting, and nearly all the cleaning and sorting. There is no strict division of labour, and the tempo of the work is an easy one. From time to time members of the party drop out for a rest, and to chew betel. . . . About mid-morning the customary refreshment is provided in the shape of green coconuts. . . .

As the turmeric is being cleaned the young people pick out and chew an occasional root; the small girl takes a special delight in . . . the sight of the bright yellow saliva which she dribbles into a little cup made from a roll of banana leaf. The whole atmosphere is one of labour diversified by recreation at will. . . . Thus Pa Nukunefu as he digs the turmeric clears away the weeds before him and throws them to the side of the plot. Suddenly he takes a handful and tosses it out into the trees on the slope below him, so that the dirt from the roots sprinkles through the foliage on to the heads of his wife and daughter, who are working a little way down. They look up in some astonishment, see him grinning, and laugh too. (Firth, 1936, pp. 93–94)

Life was not hurried and not harried. People integrated work with raising children, with visiting, with stopping to talk to a neighbor or relative, with cooking. (See descriptions of the Tikopia and other societies in earlier chapters.)

WORK, IDENTITY, AND GENDER

As discussed in chapter 9, under industrialism men have seen themselves primarily as the providers for their families. Sharing the raising of their children and the housework are very recent possibilities (or problems, for many people). Deutsch shows that even men and women who want to change traditional roles find the change difficult. Deep within themselves, men want to be the providers and women feel uneasy not having the primary responsibility for their children.

As recently as the 1950s to the 1970s, the lives of most of the mothers of the baby-boomer generation revolved completely around their homes and their children. Middle-class mothers did not hold jobs, and working-class mothers worked (usually part time) for the "extras." They were judged by other people, and they judged themselves, by how well their children did in life and how well they kept their homes (Rubin, 1976; Newman, 1993).

But the daughters of these women came of age in a different economy (see ch. 8), an economy where most men's incomes did not suffice to support a family in the manner most people expected. Also, the women's movement and other social changes began to create new gender expectations. Women were increasingly unhappy being solely housewives. For example, Karen was born in 1962. Her only image of a mother is that of her mother, who stayed home. But Karen works, she likes her job, and wants to be the best salesperson. Even more, however, when she marries, if she stays home, she couldn't possibly afford the lifestyle she wants. And many daughters saw their stay-at-home mothers as isolated and unhappy, as having sacrificed too much. These daughters do not want to emulate their mothers (Newman, 1993, p. 94).

Thus, beginning as early as the 1950s, increasingly more women have entered the labor force. In 1960, 28.8 percent of married women ages 25–34 held jobs, compared to 70.2 percent in 2001. For married women ages 35–44, the rate increased from 37.2 percent to 74.5. From 1950 to 2001, the percentage of women with children ages 5 and under in the labor force increased from 11.9 to 62.5 percent. For women with children ages 6–17, the percentage working increased from 28.3 to 77.7 percent (*Statistical Abstract,* 1979, p. 401; 1999, pp. 416–417; 2002, pp. 372–373).

Women work for various reasons, largely the same ones that motivate men.

1. They and their families need the money. Most men no longer earn a "family wage" to support their families (see chs. 2 and 8). Millions of other women support themselves, or, if single parents, themselves and their children. In 2000, the median income of families where both spouses worked was $69,463, compared to the $39,735 where the wife was not in the labor force. In short, single-earner families had only 57 percent of the income of two-earner families. In comparison, the median income of male single-parent families was $37,529 and female single-parent families was $25,794 (*Statistical Abstract,* 2002, p. 438).

2. Many women want and need to get out of the house, to have contact with other adults. A working-class wife working in a routine, dull job still appreciated it, for "it gets me away from home" (Rubin, 1976, p. 170).

3. Like men, women appreciate the fulfillment and status people derive from their jobs. They may enjoy the work itself, their co-workers, and the prestige men traditionally earned from holding a job (Rothman, 1998, p. 211).

4. In addition, the service economy that blossomed in the second half of the 1900s needed more and new workers in offices, stores, schools, and other workplaces. "Since 1980, women have taken 80 percent of the new jobs created in the economy." Without them, most of these positions would have been unfilled (Zinn and Eitzen, 1999, p. 180).

A 1993 survey by the Women's Bureau of the U.S. Department of Labor asked women why they worked. These are the responses they gave:

> 32 percent—support family
> 24 percent—support self
> 21 percent—extra money
> 12 percent—interesting
> 11 percent—combination
> (Zinn and Eitzen, 1999, p. 181)

But if we were to talk in depth with these women, probably most of them would give two to three reasons, the same reasons men have for working.

By now, relatively few women, especially younger ones, want or expect to be full-time housewives most of their lives. At most, many want to stay home for a few years while their children are young. Women told Deutsch that they worked only to supplement their husbands' incomes, and their husbands believed so. But they also said: "I look forward to (going to work) every night, I really do . . . taking off in the car by myself. . . . I really enjoy it. . . . I love it, I love my job. . . . I feel very successful." Another woman said: "I wanted to work. I wanted to get out of the house" (Deutsch, 1999, p. 187). (Deutsch concludes, however, that work is not their *primary* identity.)

Most research shows that generally women with jobs, especially jobs they like, are happier and more satisfied than are full-time housewives. This is so even though employed women have less leisure and more stress in their lives, because they still do most housework and child care, in addition to their jobs (see discussion on housework, that follows). The money they earn gives them more independence; they have higher self-esteem, and they enjoy friendships at work (Chafetz, 1997; Coontz, 1997; Barnett and Hyde, 2001).

In the discussion of housework, however, we shall see that women with jobs who also perform most housework and child care are generally very tired, drained, and stressed. Their lives, especially as described in Hochschild's *The Second Shift* and *The Time Bind ,* hardly seem satisfying. You need to consider which description is an accurate account of mothers with jobs, or, perhaps, whether in some way both might be true.

Most writers do conclude, however, that women with families and jobs are torn between work and family. They struggle to balance them. The women Hochschild interviewed in the 1980s were "far more deeply torn between the demands of work and family than were their husbands." Indeed, even when they very much enjoy their work, and even when some have husbands who share child care and housework, many feel guilty that they may be neglecting their children. "Fathers take it for granted that after becoming parents they will continue to work. Unlike mothers, who believe that they are choosing to work rather than to be with their children, fathers who are involved believe that they are choosing their children over work or leisure. Women who have invested in their work lives are left feeling that they have chosen to be there less for their children, chosen in some sense against their children. . . . Women . . . must grapple with the moral issue of whether they are doing right by their children." Unless they are the primary parent for their children, many mothers feel guilty that they have failed as mothers (Hochschild, 1989, p. 6; Deutsch, 1999, pp. 98–99, 210).

INTERACTIONS BETWEEN WORK AND FAMILY

According to most accounts of the history of the sociology of the family, until the 1970s sociologists seemed to believe that the family and the world of work were two separate realities. The private world of the family was a haven, an escape from the stresses and problems of the public world of work. When they returned to their homes and families in the evening, men would leave behind them the pressures, the drudgery, or the physical demands of their jobs.

Sociologists who believed in the "separate spheres" of work and family must have ignored the research and writings of other sociologists, and must not have talked with working people. Many studies have shown that indeed people do bring home their work problems. And ordinary working people have been eloquently perceptive on the subject. Around 1970, a steelworker told Terkel: "When I come home, know what I do for the first twenty minutes? Fake it. I put on a smile. . . . If I feel bad, I can't take it out on the kids. . . . You can't take it out on your wife either. This is why you go to a tavern. You want to release it there rather than do it at home." But as we know from various studies, many men do take out their frustrations on their family, or, too tired for anything else, sit in front of the TV and ignore them (Terkel, 1974, p. 7; see also Komarovsky, 1962 and Rubin, 1976).

How Work and Family Influence Each Other

There is a wide variety of interactions between work and family.

Income. The money people earn enables them to support their families, if the pay is sufficient. Families can live in comfortable homes, eat well, have fun, and take vacations when the parents earn adequate incomes. Millions of families, however, struggle with lower incomes; for them, the economy and work have a negative influence (see ch. 8 for income data). We did see in earlier chapters that poor families turn to each other for material and social support. But low income still takes its toll on poor people. Among other consequences is the inability of poor and unemployed men to support families, and many never marry. On the other hand, whereas a very high income does allow a family many material goods and comforts, it can often also cause problems, because to earn that income people devote enormous amounts of time and energy to their jobs, time and energy they do not have for their families.

Satisfaction. There are four possible combinations of satisfaction and happiness between family and work.

1. *Satisfied with both.* We enjoy the tasks and our co-workers at our jobs, and relationships at home are fulfilling and free of major conflicts.
2. *Unsatisfied with both.*
3. *Satisfied with work, unsatisfied with family.*
4. *Satisfied with family, unsatisfied with work.*

Most writing on family and work seems to focus on (4), on the negative spillover from unsatisfied work into family life (explored below). But there can be positive spillover into work or family when people have positive experiences with the other. Indeed, often there are rewards when we play multiple roles. "A supportive family can . . . help to overcome difficulties and disappointments at work. In a very real sense, it is the good experiences in one role that allow people to survive and flourish in others." It is possible to balance work and family and gain satisfaction from both (Rothman, 1998, pp. 214–215; see also Voydanoff, 1987).

Time and Energy. Both family and work are "greedy institutions"—our job and our family each demand our primary time and energy commitments. Most of us experience a role conflict between work and family. We are both a family member and a worker, and the time obligations of one make it difficult, if not impossible, to meet the time obligations of the other (Rothman, 1998, p. 212; see discussion on the "time bind" below).

The discussion here usually focuses on the time demands of our jobs, time they take away from our families, or, time we may have free for our families. Working 20, or 30, or 40, or 50, or 60 or more hours a week allows for radically different relationships with our families. If we devote fewer hours to our job, we may take our child for an evening stroll, prepare and eat an unrushed meal, and so on. Conversely, heavy demands at home, especially for women who do most or all housework and child care, allow much less energy for work. Indeed, many women change to part-time work because of family demands.

Other Work Conditions. Many other work conditions make for a happier and smoother family life, or create stress and misery. Commuting to work may be short and pleasant, or long and stressful. Jobs may never require people to travel, may necessitate either a few or frequent trips, or may involve constant travel. Each condition allows for or reduces family time. Schedules vary: some may be rigid 9–5 or longer days, some may allow a late arrival or early departure for doctor appointments, visits to children's schools, or a walk through the woods on a lovely fall afternoon. (College teachers have flexible schedules, so on many afternoons I went home early to be with my daughters.)

Finally, management and co-workers may cooperate to help each other meet family needs, or, they may frown upon making allowances. In Amerco, in the early 1990s, "the coworkers of a single father . . . covered for him each night during fifteen minute extensions of his thirty-minute break so that he could drive to his house and put his ten-year-old daughter, home alone, to bed. On discovering the arrangement, his supervisor stopped the practice. The supervisor in [another] case threatened to fire a mother who left work to care for a daughter with a dangerously high fever" (Hochschild, 1997, p. 170).

The women of a payroll office in a community college in the early 1970s were constantly helping each other to accommodate their family needs. Sylvia Klein sometimes brought her four-year-old granddaughter to the office while her daughter worked. The women covered for each other while one of them went shopping or attended to other family needs during work hours. They liked working with each other, the payroll was always on time, and their family lives were more pleasant and less hurried (Garson, 1975, pp. 157–176).

Family Influence on Work. The women of the payroll office remind us that in many ways families and their needs affect work. At the most elementary level, parents and others may decide to limit their work hours so they will have time for their families. When people do so, companies need to either accommodate these workers' reduced time, or find new workers. More generally, it is families who raise and socialize the people who will later become workers. And it is individuals, families, communities, labor unions, and others who often struggle to change the workweek, the pay, and the working conditions so that they can support and be with their families. At the moment, unfortunately, it is probably true that "people generally have less control over the conditions at work than at home and thus work tends to be the dominant institution." But the dominance of corporations and work is not inevitable, as history shows. After decades of struggles by labor unions, for example, they forced companies and the government to reduce the working day from ten or twelve hours to the eight-hour day that became the standard (Rothman, 1998, p. 212). (See discussion of solutions in the next section.)

Work and Types of Families

In the last few decades, there have been four general types of families with workers: traditional families with the father-provider and mother-housewife; two-earner families; single-parent and single-earner families; and families with no earners.

Table 11.1 gives us the employment status of families with children in 2001. All four types of families are found in that table.

Male-Provider Families. These families are becoming fewer, but they are still a significant number of the families with children. In 2001, there were over 7.3 million of them, 29.5 percent of all married-couple families with children. They average a considerably lower income than do two-earner families (as we saw previously), although in some of them the husband earns a high income. Through choice, values, persuasion, or some compulsion, the mothers stay home to raise the children and do the housework.

Two-Earner Families. We see in table 11.1 that 63.2 percent of married-couple families have both parents employed. In most of these families, the mothers have full-time jobs along with the fathers, but in many others the mothers reduce their hours to part time. And in a few families, both parents reduce their hours to less than full time. Despite the decreased income, they do so in order for both parents to partake in raising their children and doing the housework.

Most writers have concluded that in today's economy and society the two-earner arrangement is the healthiest and best for the family, including the mother, despite the stress

Table 11.1 Employment status of parents of families with children, 2001

	Percent of total
Married-couple families: 24,810,000	72.2
Both parents employed	63.2
Father employed, not mother	29.5
Mother employed, not father	4.5
Neither parent employed	2.9
Families maintained by women: 7,665,000	22.3
mother employed	74.5
mother not employed	25.5
Families maintained by men: 1,890,000	5.5
father employed	85.2
father not employed	14.8
Total families: 34,365	100.0

Source: Statistical Abstract, 2002, p. 374

and other problems working women face when they still do most of the child care and housework. First and foremost, the greater income of two-earner families allows them to provide best for the entire family's needs. Second, "women who work, including mothers, are consistently found to be healthier, less depressed, and less frustrated than women who do not." Third, when working mothers are satisfied with their work, their children, on average, do better in school, and are more responsible and independent, than children whose mothers stay at home. Fourth, fathers are more encouraged to, and do, participate more in their children's lives and in raising them. Thus, two-earner families benefit in many ways from the mother's working (Coontz, 1997, pp. 64–67; Barnett and Hyde, 2001).

Single-Parent and Single-Earner Families. We see in table 11.1 that 27.8 percent of all families with children in 2001 were single-parent ones. Of the more than 9.5 million such families, the single parent was a woman in 80 percent of them. Their income was considerably lower than the income of two-earner families, especially where the earner was a woman. In addition, in these families the one parent is also responsible for all housework and child care.

No-Earner Families. Finally, of the 34.36 million families with children in 2001, about 9 percent of them had no earner. The issues they face are primarily economic (and they usually are very severe) since work takes no time away from the family.

Negative Spillover from Work

Most writers on the effects of work on family find mainly negative and harmful consequences. Unemployment, stress at work, long hours, and other work conditions are said to lead to more family violence, less time with children, weaker marriages, and other problems.

Many marriages suffer from long hours at work by one or both partners, many ending in divorce. Let us look at two cases. Seth Stein was a successful lawyer who worked long, hard hours, and felt he had no option but to do so. In time, he no longer enjoyed the work, but still felt he had no choice. While at work, he often shared tips with other lawyers on ways to avoid spending more time at home. He certainly had little time for his family; he gradually withdrew from them and paid little attention to his children. As he resisted sharing child care and housework, his wife Jessica (who also had a full-time job) "gradually began to detach her feelings from Seth." She withdrew from the marriage. Since they were earning a high income, she hired people to clean the house, take care of the yard, play with their sons, and do whatever other work was left. Their marriage became empty; neither provided love and nurturance for the other. The children felt cheated, were angry, and became hard to control (they stayed up late, and so on) (Hochschild, 1989, p. 112 and ch. 8).

Other men, however, saw the consequences of long hours and reduced them to save their marriages. For example "Ernie, a physical therapist, resigned from a managerial position in a large private firm when he discovered his job was damaging his family relationships. 'I was working from six-thirty in the morning to seven at night without breaks. I wasn't eating. I was irritable. I couldn't deal with anybody. I was fighting with my wife all the time. We were breaking apart. I wasn't communicating anymore. The job took control of me. I was possessed. I didn't feel patient with my daughter anymore. It was taking a big toll on me, and I didn't like it at all. I decided it wasn't worth it and the only way to stop it was to leave.'" (Gerson, 1993, p. 145).

More generally, Hochschild reports 1980s surveys that showed "half of hourly employees—factory and maintenance workers covered by union contracts—agreed that their marriages were suffering from the effects of time pressures" (1997, pp. 21–22).

Child care is perhaps the most painful tension in seeking this balance. Who will take care of the children while both parents work? Some couples decide to work opposite shifts so that one of them is always home. For them, the problem becomes time with each other. There are other costs to opposite shifts arrangements. Lewis reports a study that showed men who work at night and are "married less than five years are six times more likely to divorce and separate within the next five years than are men in traditional, 9–5 jobs" (Lewis, 1999b, p. A6).

Parents may simply have less time with their children. Hochschild cites a study that concluded that parents' time with their children decreased about 22 hours per week from 1969 to 1996. But a recent study disagrees, concluding that mothers spent as much time with their children in 1998 as they did in 1965. Based on a 1998 survey of 300 mothers across the United States, Suzane Bianchi "reported that mothers said they spent 5.8 hours a day with their children . . . compared to 5.6 hours in 1965." Since most mothers held jobs in 1998, compared to most 1965 mothers who stayed home, where did the 1998 mothers find the time? Bianchi thinks they sleep less, have less time to themselves, vacuum less, and are "busy rushing their children from one event to another, with little quiet time as a family" (Hochschild, 2000; Salmon, 2000).

Thus, whether parents (mostly mothers) spend as much or less time with their children today compared to the 1960s and before, everyone seems to agree that they and their children are rushed. Parents also complain that they miss their children's activities. In a 1980s survey of hourly workers, one-quarter of the parents said they "had 'a great deal of difficulty' leaving work to take part in a child's social activity or a parent-teacher conference, or simply to care for a sick child." Later in *The Time Bind,* Hochschild describes the problems Connie, a support staff at Amerco, faced in the early 1990s. Since she had to stay in the office until 5, her children missed many activities that took place before 5: Boy Scouts, ballet lessons, sports, and more. When she wanted to take her son to his weekly mid-day appointment for asthma shots, her boss denied her permission, and only relented, grudgingly, after Connie waged a long struggle (1997, pp. 22, 134–140).

In her studies of working-class families, *Worlds of Pain* (1976) and *Families on the Fault Line* (1994), Rubin explores in detail the effects that low pay, unemployment, and harsh and dangerous working conditions have on families. In "Work and Its Meaning," Rubin argues that for most of the working-class men she interviewed, work provided no intrinsic satisfaction. For them, "work is something to do, but not to talk about." As one of them said, "what's there to talk about?" Indeed, their jobs were becoming more mindless, routine, and degrading. They found no relief when they went home—the job and its deadening routine came home with them. To try to forget about work, they would plunge into projects around the house that might have given them some satisfaction; or they would collapse into a stupor by drinking and watching TV. Either way, family life suffered. Rubin further argued that because they had no authority or power at work, since they simply followed orders, they were authoritarian and strict at home, desperately seeking the power they lacked at work (Rubin, 1976, ch. 9).

In chapter 6, "When You Get Laid Off, It's Like You Lose Part of Yourself," from *Families on the Fault Line,* Rubin focused on the effects of unemployment. She interviewed 162 working-class families in the early 1990s. At the time of the interview, 15 percent of the men were unemployed and 20 percent more had had "episodic bouts with unemployment." Rubin argued that the loss of a job was more devastating for the men than it was for women. Women's family roles were more important to them, and their identity was not threatened when they lost a job, but for men work and being providers were primary in their lives. Without work, they were lost and aimless. They were embarrassed to be on the unemployment line with "dead beats" (1994, p. 103).

Rubin tells of the rage a father felt when, without the medical benefits of his job and unable to pay himself, he could not take his daughter to the hospital. Men like him were afraid and lost, covering their fear by keeping busy, or with angry outbursts at their wives and children. As the weeks of joblessness wore on, husbands and wives became more testy. The men felt helpless, then angry—often, angry enough to hit their wives and children. It was the teenage children who reported the violence to Rubin; the parents were ashamed to speak about it (1994).

Unable to make payments, a family lost its home. The teenage daughter complained about the consequences:

> "We can't afford anything anymore; and I mean *anything*" [15–year-old Tina] announces dramatically. "I don't even go to the mall with the other kids because they've got money to buy things and I don't. I haven't bought a new record since we moved here. Now my mom says I can't get new clothes this year; I have to wear my cousin's hand-me-downs. How am I going to go to school in those ugly things? It's bad enough being in this new school, but now . . . ," she stops, unable to find the words to express her misery.
>
> Worst of all for the children of the Materie family, the move from house to apartment took them to a new school in a distant neighborhood, far from the friends who had been at the center of their lives. (Rubin, 1994, pp. 123–124)

For a few families, unemployment became an opportunity. Some men used the time off to train for a new career (such as cook). But most families didn't have enough money saved to finance such an undertaking. Finally, for many families there was an initial relief from the hurried life. Fathers had more time with their children, who were delighted with the novelty of a father at home. But soon financial worries took over.

A Theory of Family and Work

In 2001, Barnett and Hyde proposed a theory on the relationship between family and work. Looking at recent developments in work, such as the data cited previously, they concluded that present theories of family and work have not taken these changes into account. Their theory has four principles.

1. "First, multiple roles [at home and work] are, in general, beneficial for both women and men, as reflected in mental health, physical health, and relationship health."

2. "Second, a number of processes contribute to the beneficial effects of multiple roles, including . . . added income, social support, opportunities to experience success," and opportunities for women to be income earners and men to be caregivers.

3. "[T]here are certain conditions under which multiple roles are beneficial," such as satisfying work. On the other hand, overly long hours at work (a problem explored in the next section), or time demands from too many people, diminish the benefits of multiple roles.

4. "[P]sychological gender differences are not, in general, large or immutable. The natures of women and of men need not force them into highly differentiated roles" (Barnett and Hyde, 2001, p. 784).

RECENT CHANGES AND THE TIME BIND DEBATES

Reversal of Home and Work?

In *The Second Shift,* Hochschild concluded that in families where both spouses held jobs, only about 20 percent of men shared equally the housework and child care. In the conclusion to that book, she called for corporations and governments to create policies that would encourage men to share the second shift. Looking for a corporation that embodied such policies, she undertook a study of Amerco (fictional name), a Fortune 500 company, which claimed to have family friendly policies (Hochschild, 1997, pp. 5–9).

In *The Time Bind: When Work Becomes Home and Home Becomes Work* (1997) Hochschild reports that Amerco's professions were not a reality. Few people took advantage of those policies: part-time work, flextime, and so on. Indeed, people from top management to factory workers felt compelled to, and did, work long hours. Furthermore, Hochschild argues that life at home was so hectic, rushed, and tense that people preferred to be and stay at work, where life was more orderly and less hectic, and they felt valued and appreciated.

Linda's life and words seem to exemplify this reversal: "My husband's a great help watching our baby. But as far as doing housework or even taking the baby when I'm at home, no. He figures he works five days a week; *he's* not going to come home and clean. But he doesn't stop to think that I work *seven* days a week. Why should I have to come home and do the housework without help from anybody else? My husband and I have been through this over and over again. Even if he would just pick up from the kitchen table and stack the dishes for me, that would make a big difference. He does nothing. On his weekends off, I have to provide a sitter for the baby so he can go fishing. When I have a day off, I have the baby all day long without a break. He'll help out if I'm not here, but the minute I am, all the work at home is mine. So I take a lot of overtime. The more I get out of the house, the better I am. It's a terrible thing to say, but that's the way I feel." Other Amerco workers also prefer staying at work and away from family conflicts and housework (Hochschild, p. 38).

Speaking of an assembly-line worker, Hochschild says that for "Becky and her friends, work was a more predictable, safer, more emotionally supportive and relaxing place to be than home." Whereas in older days people confided their worries to and sought advice from families and neighbors, Amerco workers turned to co-workers. In a world of more divorce and other family problems, "for many, work seemed to function as a backup system to a destabilizing family." Corporations make the workplace friendlier than the home. For example, they offer chess clubs, support groups, bank services, dating services, and other amenities (1997, pp. 152, 201).

How widespread is this reversal of home and work? At Amerco, "some people find in work a respite from the emotional tangles at home. Others virtually marry their work, investing it with an emotional significance once reserved for family. . . . Overall, this 'reversal' was a predominant pattern in about a fifth of Amerco families and an important theme in over half of them." Hochschild found a similar trend in a survey of 1,446 responses of "mainly middle- or upper-middle-class parents in their early thirties," who worked for various large corporations and whose children attended company-based child-care centers. "I asked, 'does it sometimes feel to you like home is a "workplace"?' Eighty-five percent said yes (57 percent 'very often'; 28 percent 'fairly often'). Women were far more likely to agree than men. I asked this question the other way around as well: 'Is it sometimes true that work feels like home should feel?' Twenty-five percent answered 'very often' or 'quite often,' and 33 percent answered 'occasionally.' Only 37 percent answered 'very rarely.'" (Pp. 44–45,199–200).

What do these numbers tell us? How deep is the disaffection from family life? What causes that disaffection? What does Hochschild's phrase "an important theme" mean? Even if true at Amerco and for parents for children in those child-care centers, how widespread is this reversal? Does it perhaps foretell increasing trends in American homes and workplaces? And can it possibly be also true for millions who work in sweatshop factories, make beds and clean hotel rooms, wash dishes, and work in other service and "dirty" occupations? Can *their* work be a respite from home for these men and women?

Some studies do not report the stress and the unhappiness Hochschild describes. In their study of working couples with children, Barnett and Rivers found no major stresses in their lives, and certainly no reversal of work and home. Although they did find some problems and conflicts, they clearly conclude that two-worker couples and their children are in fine shape. A news story of their study summarized it thus: "[T]oday's working women are in excellent health and do not suffer from stress; couples are cooperating to make the family work; working moms are not destroying their children; fatherhood is more important in men's lives; work is just as important to women's health and well-being as it is to men's; and marriage is as central to men's identity and sense of well-being as it is to women's" (Rosencrance, 1996, summarizing Barnett and Rivers, 1996).

Kiecolt also disagrees with Hochschild's conclusion that home has become work, and work has become home. After an analysis of the 1973–1994 General Social Surveys, she concluded that the reverse is more likely, that working women find home a "haven." "A cultural reversal has not occurred; work has not become more satisfying than home" (2003, p. 33). (Note: the analysis of the survey data is too complex to summarize here.)

Why the sharp difference between Hochschild's *The Time Bind* and studies that do not share her conclusion? There are four possible answers.

1. Each may be an accurate description of the people they discuss. Hochschild studied the workers of a corporation somewhere between the two coasts; Barnett and Rivers *interviewed* 300 working-class and middle-class couples in two Boston area communities. What the authors report may have been accurate for the people in those families, workplaces, and communities. Something about Amerco may have created the reversal of home and work; something about the Boston couples and their lives may have created the satisfactory balance between work and family.

2. The methods of the two studies differed, which may account for the opposing conclusions. Barnett and Rivers and Kiecolt *talked* with people. Generally, most of us are not the best and most accurate reporters of our actions, thoughts, and feelings. We may consciously want to hide them; we may be embarrassed to admit, for example, that we prefer to be at work rather than at home. Or, we may not even know that we have these feelings.

Hochschild, on the other hand, came to know the people at Amerco much better than survey interviewers ever can. She observed them at work, had long talks with them at their jobs, and went to the homes of some of them to see how they lived as families. It was while at their homes that she saw and felt the reversal of home and work. "Following weary workers home in the evenings, I also watched them cope with cranky children, makeshift dinners, unfed pets, and broken appliances. . . . I began to see how the friction-laden environments people found at home could be losing out to the sense of purpose, accomplishment, and camaraderie offered by the well-oiled social machinery of the workplace" (Hochschild, 2000, p. xx). Seeing the tense homes, and talking with workers in their more relaxed work sites, she picked up emotions and actions not usually visible during interviews.

3. It may be that the authors of one or both studies had or soon developed a bias, a predisposition, toward the conclusions they presented, and they soon began to focus mostly on evidence that supported their conclusions.

4. Or, the reality may be some combination of the three previous possibilities.

Let us look at some other studies and evidence on the debate over the balance between family and work.

A 1995 poll investigated family and work. It asked: "Generally, do you have enough time to do what you want these days, or not?" Fifty percent of men and 46 percent of women said yes. Only 30 percent of people with minor children said yes, as did 35 percent of employed people. Clearly, a good majority of employed people with minor children, men and women, said they did not have enough time for what they need to do outside work (Saad, 1995; as cited in Lamanna and Riedmann, 2000, p. 423).

Most Americans do in fact prefer to spend more time with their families and wish for fewer hours at work, but they fear they may jeopardize their careers if they "complain too loudly about the tensions between work and family schedules." A national survey in 2000 makes that wish clear. A thousand women and men, 21 and over, said the following. Eighty-three percent said they wanted distinct lines "between work and nonwork time." In addition, 64 percent "would prefer more time to more money." Of men ages 31–39, 71 percent "said they would give up pay for more time with their families." But most also seemed to share their employers' views on work; 62 percent "said they viewed working long hours as a sign of commitment." And another national survey concluded that 80 percent of "American adults would like to spend more time with their families" (Auster, 1996, p. 354; Quinn and Cintron, 2000; Cobb, 2000).

Let us look at Amerco. In 1990 Jimmy very much wanted to avoid becoming an ob-sessed worker, but by 1993 he had turned into "a rushed, rising executive . . . a manager without much of a life." Later on, Hochschild concludes: "Everywhere in Amerco's factories parents were working long hours while their children put in long hours in at daycare. Every-where parents were having the same problems meshing schedules" (1997, pp. 130, 190–191).

In conclusion, all surveys reviewed here report that most people want a better balance between family and work, and want to work fewer hours to achieve that balance. Some surveys conclude that most people think they have achieved that balance, but more surveys tell us that the balance people long for eludes them. It is more a wish than a reality.

Trends in Hours at Work

How many hours do Americans work? How do these hours compare to the long-ago past and the recent past? How do people decide that they work too many, too few, or the desired number of hours?

Let us first make a distinction between the total hours *individuals* work, and the total that *couples or families* work. When in the 1940s the average husband worked 45 hours a week and his wife stayed home, the individual and family totals were both 45 hours. If today husbands average 40 hours but wives average, say, 30 hours, men's total has decreased but the family total has increased from 45 to 70 hours. Thus, the parental time available for family work has decreased radically.

And this hypothetical case is the reality in most two-worker families today. In 1950, only 11.9 percent of married women with children under 6 were in the labor force, as were 38.3 percent of those with children ages 6–17. Most married mothers with children now work, and the comparable figures for 2001 were 62.5 percent of married women with children under 6 and 77.7 percent with children ages 6–17. Thus, the millions more women in the labor force today compared to fifty years ago indicate a clear reduction in family time. Together, the two parents have much less time for housework and child care.

Let us look at the hours of Amerco workers. Full-time employees averaged 47 hours a week. Parents worked as many hours as non-parents, and only 4 percent of fathers and 13 percent of mothers worked fewer than 40 hours. Fifty-six percent of parents worked on weekends, and 65 percent of women and 73 percent of men regularly worked overtime. Very few worked part time, and in reality even their "part time" often meant they worked forty or more hours. For example, a secretary who was scheduled to work until 3 in the afternoon rarely was able to leave at that time. About a third of the workers did work "flextime" (a policy that allows workers some flexibility in when they start or end the workday), the only benefit used widely. But over time the total number of hours people worked had increased (Hochschild, 1997, pp. 26–27, 93–100, 177).

There is considerable debate on whether people work more hours today. Methods and findings are contradictory. Some studies conclude that total work hours increased in the 1980s and 1990s. "Among two-parent families, annual hours increased by 497 hours [of total work hours for both parents] (or 18 percent) between 1969 and 1997; for single-parent households the increase was 297 (28 percent)" (Schor, 2002, p. 92; see also Schor, 1991 and 1999).

A 2000 survey of 1,000 people 21 and over revealed similar trends. Almost half of the workers "said they worked more than 40 hours a week, and one in five work more than 50." Two stories about Boston area lawyers in 1999 and 2000 report 60-hour weeks—12 hours a day—as typical. When some people reduced their hours, they felt devalued, were not pro-moted, and so on. When people went "part time" they were often given work to take home over the weekend. Under such conditions, 43 percent of newly hired lawyers had left within the first three years, "largely because they felt they had to choose between a career and a family" (Quinn and Cintron, 2000; Wilmsen, 1999; Lewis, 2000).

Robinson and Godbey, on the other hand, argue that most Americans overestimate the hours they work. When they compared what people wrote in time-diaries with their estimates of how many hours they worked in a week, they say that they found men overestimate their hours by 17 percent and women by 35 percent. In addition, they underestimated their free time by 50 percent and overestimated their family work time by 60 percent. But at least some of the data they dispute are not based on people's subjective reports. They are based on objective records of hours people actually work. Also, they may not consider the distinction between individual and family hours (Robinson and Godbey, 1997; see also Schor, 2002).

Everyone does agree that many people report time pressures in their lives. A 1997 survey showed that, on average, mothers said they wanted to work 11 fewer hours a week and fathers 12 fewer hours (Schor, 2002, p. 93).

Why *Do* People Work Long Hours?

There are many possible answers to this question. Any one person may work long hours for one or more reasons. But generally, most people have long workweeks because the economy and the culture demand and require them to do so.

1. First, millions of Americans work long hours at a job, and many hold two jobs, simply to pay for life's necessities as defined in modern America. Also, since many people fear they may not have a job because of plant closings and other conditions, they work overtime in order to save for that day. In the spring of 2001, in the Changing Families class I teach, some students told me that each of their parents held two jobs, some two full-time ones, others a full-time and a part-time one. Given the low pay of the service occupations they held, they needed to work all these hours in order to pay their bills and help a daughter attend college, who herself held a job.

2. Some people, of course, like working long hours. They may enjoy the work itself, the friends at work, the prestige that accompanies their position. At Amerco, "senior managers and professionals generally said they devoted long hours to work because they loved their jobs; assembly-line workers said they worked double shifts because they needed the money" (Hochschild, 2000, p. xxii).

3. In various ways, corporations and the capitalist economy and culture compel people to work long hours, either to hold their jobs (professional and managerial ones) or to pay their bills (assembly line, service, sales, and other workers). To maximize profits, management wants people to devote most of their time and energy to their jobs. As we have seen, people who don't make that commitment are not promoted, may lose their jobs, and/or cannot pay their bills. In reality, family-friendly policies are never meant to be taken seriously or used.

Meiksins shows us that corporations compel employees to work long hours by referring to Eileen's struggles at Amerco to reduce her hours. She chose to work part time, but she "experienced significant conflicts with her boss, who believed in time as a measure of commitment to work. Eventually she was laid off in a reorganization, in part because her part-time status made her vulnerable." Later she found a full-time job at Amerco, even though she had preferred part time all along (1998, p. 6).

4. A sub-category of (3) may explore greed, materialism, and a selfish preoccupation with people's own careers, happiness, and fulfillment over their families (traditional for men, now spreading to women). To the degree people hold these values, they are expressions of capitalist culture socialization and compulsions.

Chaotic Lives and Other Issues

When I first read *The Time Bind,* I felt an overwhelming sense that Amerco workers led hectic, rushed, tense, and unhappy family lives. That feeling appears each time I read the book. It was after she read *The Time Bind* that Lauren Kane, one of my students, said "sociology is good birth control," meaning, who would want to have children and lead such frantic lives?

In the spring of 2001 I taught a sociology seminar on work. Part of the course focused on family and work, and we had animated and anxious discussions. The students, all graduating seniors, gave numerous examples of their rushed lives, of boyfriends who were reluctant to share housework, of anxiety over how they would balance work they wanted with families they wanted equally. One class took on a life of its own, as they poured out their hopes, plans, anger, and worries that their careers would consume their lives.

They worried about living like Denise at Amerco. Her day began at 6 a.m. "My goal is to have showered and washed my hair by six-thirty. Then I go downstairs and get things organized and get the kids up by quarter to seven." Her workday ended at five, but "I can't get out of work at five. I accept that now. It's always six o'clock, at least. And then I have to pick up the kids, grocery shop, race home, and cook." After dinner, there are dishes to be done, children's homework to supervise, baths and bedtime stories (Hochschild, 1997, pp. 105–106).

The Speedup of Family Lives. Amerco workers, faced with a time starvation, resorted to a speedup. To manage, many women and men undertook two or more activities at one time. Instead of a leisurely bath for their children, they were rushing through it as their minds were elsewhere. For example, Gwen "sometimes . . . brought the cellular phone into the bathroom while Cassie splashed in the tub." Ads encourage parents to make business calls while baking cookies with their children, or when they take them to the beach. And parents prepare fast-cooking meals and rush through them as they think ahead of business calls, baths to give, and so on (Hochschild, 1997, pp. 49, 124).

People sleep less. In one survey of 1,000 adults, 72 percent said they sleep fewer than 8 hours on weekdays, and 44 percent said six or fewer hours. When seven *Boston Globe* reporters followed seven people through their entire day, they discovered that six of them arose at 6:30 a.m. or earlier, and five ate little or no breakfast. Another poll found that a third of Americans "regularly skip a meal simply to save time" (Cobb, 2000; Quinn and Cintron, 2000).

At least some of these disruptions are imposed on us by our employers. The parents who conduct business on the cell phone while at the beach with the children, or while giving them a bath, do so because of pressures to produce at work, not because they want to ignore their children.

The Lives of Children. Children are the primary victims of the family speedup, of the imbalance between family and work, of employer demands. Most studies conclude that parents have less time with their children, and the time they have together often feels rushed. A 1999 report by the Council of Economic Advisors in Washington found that "between 1969 and 1996 the increase of mothers leaving home to work combined with a shift toward single-parent families has led to an average decrease of 22 hours a week of parental time available to spend with children" (Hochschild, 2000, pp. xxi, 268).

For reasons mostly beyond their control, parents have less time with their children. The only way to manage everything they need to do is to speed up their and their children's lives. Hochschild describes the dilemma, the results, and children's frequent rebellion: "Parents are becoming supervisors with stopwatches, monitoring meals and bedtimes and putting real effort into eliminating 'wasted' time. . . . Of course, some children adapt quietly to the reversal of home and work, as do adults. But many children want more time with their parents than they get, and they protest the pace, the deadlines, the irrationality of 'efficient' family life. Parents are then obliged to hear their children's protests, to experience their resentment, resistance, passive acquiescence, to try to assuage their frustrations, to respond to their stubborn demands or whining requests, and in general to control the damage done by a reversal of worlds" (1997, p. 218).

Most parents feel guilty that they have so little time with their children. Aware of this emerging reality, Hallmark produced cards for busy parents. One says, "Sorry I can't be there to tuck you in," and another "Sorry I can't say good morning to you." And even when they are with their children, many parents feel rushed, preoccupied, guilty. They cannot enjoy their times together (Hochschild, 1997, p. 228; Daly, 2001).

While they speed up their and their children's lives, parents, mostly mothers, want and strive to spend as much time as possible with them. They do so, in large part, by depriving themselves of sleep, leisure time, and times for friends, relatives, and the community (Hochschild, 1989, 1997; Salmon, 2000).

Family, Friends, and Community. Thus, other victims of the time famine are our extended family, our friends, and the larger community, for whom we have little energy and time. Churches, civic associations, Boy and Girl Scouts, disabled and elderly people—these and others are left wanting for the time and care they need. Whereas in 1973, 22 percent of Americans reported that they had "attended a public meeting on town or school affairs in the previous year," only 13 percent said so in 1993 (Voydanoff, 1987, p. 16; Hochschild, 1997, p. 243).

In conclusion, economic, corporate, and cultural demands compel parents to devote more hours to work. In this dilemma, parents have little choice but to downsize family life and time, since corporations make it very difficult to reduce work hours. At Amerco, "parents didn't challenge the company; they stole time from their children. . . . They made do with less time, less attention, less fun, less relaxation, less understanding, and less support at home than they once imagined possible. They emotionally downsized life" (Hochschild, 1997, pp. 192, 221).

WHAT ARE WE TO DO?

In 1999, Andy Epstein left the twelve-hour days of a law firm for a job with fewer hours. Afterwards, he reflected: "You realize your life doesn't have to be your work and your work doesn't have to be your life." The longing for a balance between family and work is deep. And whereas women do experience the conflict between the two more than men do, many men are increasingly joining them. What are we to do, what *can* we do, as individuals, families, businesses, various government bodies, and as a whole society? (In Wilmsen, 1999, p. D1).

Whether we focus on individual or on social and collective solutions, first and foremost they must involve women and men equally. Now, many policies and programs allow or ask women to juggle the demands of work and family. Women reduce their hours, women take leaves, women are responsible for child-care arrangements while both parents work. That is not shared parenting, it is not balancing *family* and work needs.

Individual Solutions

Compared to other industrial societies, the United States generally has few social policies and programs to help families balance their family and work lives. For example, we were the last major industrial society to pass a family leave law, in 1993, and unlike all others, the leave is unpaid. Under the law, workers in organizations of fifty or more workers are guaranteed a twelve-week leave to care for a new child or give care to an ailing relative. Some companies formally have "family-friendly" policies, such as part-time and flextime hours, but workers are not encouraged to use them. For example, at Amerco Latesha worked part time, while her husband Sam took no work home when he left the office. But he felt that his superiors were watching him. "Sam and Latesha were still resisting the press of work but without allies" (Hochschild, 1997, pp. 119–120).

As a result, most parents, couples and single parents, are left to craft their own solutions. Sam and Latesha struggled mightily, on their own. We don't know how successful they have been over the years. Michael and Adrienne Sherman, both academics, both managed to reduce their work hours and share housework and child care. (This after Adrienne left the marriage because Michael would not reduce his work commitments and would not share housework, and returned only after he agreed to change both.) But this was an arrangement they worked out after a protracted struggle with the university. There was no university *policy* encouraging the reduction of work commitments without repercussions to people's careers (Hochschild, 1989, ch. 12).

Chafetz lists five strategies individual families may use.

1. "Reducing standards of domestic work." I still remember the student (a mother in her thirties) who had returned to college in 1967, who told me she had decided to tolerate more dust around her house so she could have time to study.

2. "Purchasing domestic and child-care services." Babysitters, nannies, daycare centers, housecleaning services and maids, and other services can be bought. But many families cannot afford them, and at least in some cases maids and other low-paid workers may mean the exploitation of some women for the benefit of one's career and family (Hertz, 1986).

3. "Having other family members (e.g., husbands, children, parents) perform more domestic work." The problem may be husbands who will not share (see housework discussion) and unavailable relatives. Also, we saw that 20 percent of couples resort to opposite shifts so one is always with the children. Others may have retired parents and other relatives who may help.

4. "Refusing to comply with the demands or requests of greedy employers (with a cost to one's career success, probably most often the woman's)." *The Time Bind* (Hochschild, 1997) and other studies provide ample evidence for this observation.

5. "Choosing an occupation (e.g., school teaching) which allows more time for the family (with a cost to one's income, usually the woman's)." People may choose positions with definite work hours—a 9–5 job—rather then "greedy" ones of twelve-hour days. Also, parents may both work part time, as we have seen, with or without the encouragement of employers (Chafetz, 1997, p. 120).

Other individual strategies may involve postponing having children and having fewer children, both to allow more time to develop one's career and to reduce the amount and years of child care. Also, many mothers manage by depriving themselves of sleep and time for hobbies and friends. (For a detailed discussion of individualistic strategies, see Hesse-Biber and Carter, 2000, pp. 184–186.)

Social Policies and Political Struggles

While it will always be necessary for individuals, couples, and families to craft their own work-family balance, their search will be much more successful if organizations, employers, governments, and the entire society create policies and programs that enable people to make that search successful, policies that value families.

Fewer Hours at Work. For parents to have more time for their children, for each other, for themselves, for other relatives, for friends and community, they need to reduce their work hours. This is an old issue and struggle. It was fought successfully in the past, when labor unions and others organized for decades to reduce the workday from 10–12 to 8 hours. While for millions, in the past and now, the problem has been not having a job or not having enough hours to support themselves, most people want and need to work fewer hours.

This is not an impossible dream. In the twentieth century, there was the successful campaign to make the workday eight hours. In the recent past, many European unions committed to and worked toward a shorter week of 30–35 hours "as a means of creating jobs, improving working conditions, and allowing workers more leisure and family time. In many industries, the week is already 35 hours. In addition, Europeans generally receive 4–6 weeks of paid vacation, compared to the 2–3 weeks common in the U.S" (Moody and Sagovac, 1995, pp. 9, 52–55; see also Liazos, 1991; Hochschild, 1997; Schor, 2002).

There have been some experiments of a shorter workweek in the United States. When business declined, one corporation allowed the workers to choose between some people losing their jobs or everyone working 32 hours. They voted for the shorter week. But productivity did not decline, and when business increased, no one wanted to return to longer hours (Hochschild, 1997, p. 253; for reports of other efforts to reduce work hours, see Mutari and Figart, 2001; Barnett and Rivers, 2002; Meiksins and Whalley, 2002).

We need to redefine what full-time work means. Just as we moved from 10–12 hours a day to 8, we can move to 6 or 7. This should not be some people working 8 or more hours a day and others having part-time jobs of 6–7 hours. Rather, full-time work would be 6–7 hours for everyone. In addition, parents of newborns would have family leave for a few months, followed by reduced hours for a few years, before they return to the full-time status of 6–7 hours. This is not a fantasy. Such policies have existed in various countries. These new policies must apply to, and be used by, *both women and men*. It will not help children and mothers if the mother works 20–30 hours a week but the father works 50–60. He will do little parenting (Deutsch, 1999).

Finally, these policies, in order to apply and be used widely, must be accompanied by two others: job security and income security. People will work longer hours, and try to save some money, when they fear they might or will lose their jobs. Also, we cannot expect people to work 30–35 hours a week at a minimum wage. Indeed, under those conditions people often work two jobs. Workers have shown that they will eagerly work fewer hours if they are guaranteed a job and if they receive a living salary or wage.

Reduced Consumption. But these reduced-hour jobs cannot pay for most people to live luxuriously. At the same time that we increase many people's incomes so they can afford life's necessities, many or most others must reduce their consumption of goods, must redefine what they consider "necessities." We cannot aspire to "Mountains o' Things" (Tracy Chapman's title of one of her songs). As a bumper sticker urged, "live simply so that other may simply live."

The cultural and capitalist imperative to amass and consume goods harms the environment, our families, and our communities. The big cars and endless gadgets consume gas and electricity, which pollute the environment and use up limited resources. And to buy all these material possessions we need to work long hours, to underpay the workers who produce them, to have less time for our families and ourselves. Many Amerco workers bought boats, campers, and other items to enjoy in their leisure, but they rarely use them since they have no free time because of all the hours they work (Hochschild, 1997, p. 14).

If we consume less, if we long for fewer possessions, we then need to work fewer hours, and we have time for our children and partners, for the community, for leisurely walks through the woods and along shoreline. (On consumption, see Schor, *The Overspent American,* 1999.)

National Policies. The major reason people work long hours, however, is economic necessity. Housing, daycare costs, health care, food, clothing, and other needs must be paid for. Government programs can meet these needs, as they have in many industrial societies.

The United States remains the only major industrial society without national health insurance. Most of us get medical coverage through our employers, but the amount we must contribute, the coverage we receive, and the quality vary widely. Also, millions of people (ages about 40–45) have jobs that provide no medical insurance. Many people who would prefer part-time jobs stay in full-time ones because part-time positions usually offer no health insurance. Universal free health coverage would allow people more work options and would remove a major expense and worry for millions of families.

Housing costs vary widely. Millions of families work long hours to pay rent or make mortgage payments. Many other families become homeless for some time. There is a great shortage of affordable housing. More such housing would lower the cost of housing generally and would remove another compulsion for working long hours.

Quality and affordable daycare, preferably at people's work sites, is a necessity. Most people cannot afford to pay for good child care. France, some Canadian provinces, and many other places subsidize daycare for all children. Government subsidies are also important so that daycare workers will be paid a living wage, while keeping the cost low for parents. (For proposed policies on child care and daycare, see Hartmann, 2002; Helburn and Bergmann, 2002.)

Family leaves are rarely taken because most parents cannot afford them. In countries where such leaves are paid, and longer, parents do use them. We need a national policy that would make family leaves paid for all parents. Various attempts to institute paid family leaves have failed; California may be adopting one (Russakof, 2000; Chavez, 2002; Lewis, 2003a).

You may ask, how can we afford all these government programs? They are affordable, since so many other countries, all less wealthy than the United States, do have them. If we reduce the military budget, and if wealthy people pay higher (instead of lower) taxes, we could afford them. If families indeed are our priority, we will find ways to reduce unnecessary spending and pay for national health insurance, affordable housing, quality daycare, and family leaves. That way, people will need to work fewer hours and have more family time. Rankin proposes that parents draw Social Security benefits while they have young children, so they can reduce their work hours (2002b).

But these and other changes will not come soon or easily. The eight-hour day became a reality after decades of strikes and other actions by labor unions, after decades of working to persuade politicians. Corporations warned and predicted that the eight-hour day would ruin them and the country. They were not willing participants in the change.

So too now for the above policies and those I describe below. It will take much organizing, much political participation, by many groups, organizations, and movements before we can have national health insurance, for example. Many groups, including many physician groups, are working to that end. Movements to reduce the workweek, and for all other changes, will have to take place outside corporations, and against them. They will not change willingly. Millions of us, in many settings, organizations, and campaigns will have to work together for a shorter week and the other changes (Skocpol, 2002).

Workplace Policies. Most of us still work for corporations, organizations, and other employers. Through national laws, through programs we work to install in our own workplaces, we can make changes there that will allow us to balance family and work, to enjoy both, and to earn a living.

Such worksite programs are usually called "family friendly." *Flextime* is a common one. It allows workers to adjust their working hours to suit family needs. For example, in offices where most people work 9–5, a person could start work any time between 7 and 11 and leave eight hours later. Flextime may be the most common family-friendly policy. Before discussing some other policies, I want to mention two cautions found in research on such policies.

1. Most employers do not in fact want workers to use the family-friendly policies they may have. Studies show that workers who use them in fact suffer the consequences: they are not promoted, they may be laid off, and they are devalued and discouraged. People using, or wanting to use, such policies are seen as not committed to their job and the company. The

promotions usually go to those who log the longest hours. An Amerco manager bluntly stated that nobody gets to the top by leading a balanced life (Hochschild, 1997; Kiser, 1998; Lewis, 1999c, 2000).

In fact, in time Amerco dismantled its Work-Life Balance program and folded it into its benefits department. Former balance advocates were working long hours, work was speeded up, employees were laid off, and those remaining worked more overtime to save for the day they might lose their jobs. Thus, family-friendly policies must be a real, long-term commitment, otherwise they are public relations games. The task employees face is double: to institute these policies, then to continue the struggle to implement them, and to enable workers to use them without being penalized.

2. In places where family-friendly policies are instituted, as in many European societies, they tend to reinforce gender inequalities. They are primarily directed to women. For example, it is mostly women who work part time so they will have more time for housework and child care. Few men use these policies. "Almost one of three working women in the European Union works part-time, compared with only one in 20 men." As a result, women do most of the family work and men earn most of the income. In Sweden, with the longest and best paid family leave, "despite the gender-neutral wording of the law and efforts encouraging men to take advantage of it, only 6% of leave-takers are men, a figure that has remained unchanged for 15 years." Full sharing and equality—in the workplace and at home—do not exist. Family-friendly policies must be used equally by women and men (Figart and Mutari, 1998, pp. 31, 29; see also Bergmann, 1998; Rosenberg, 1999; Mutari and Figart, 2001).

Let us now look at daycare at worksites, alternative work schedules, and social programs.

1. It makes perfect sense for parents to be able to take their children to daycare based on where they work. It reduces commuting time, enables the parents to see their children

Good day care can be a positive experience for children.

quickly if they need to see them during lunch, and generally to feel more at ease about their children's condition while they work. Some large employers and universities have developed such facilities.

2. Besides flextime and part time, flexible work schedules include work-at-home and compressed workweek (working four, ten-hour days, or three, twelve-hour days, for example). Computers enable more people to perform their duties from home, but that is possible only for some office workers, and deprives people of the social contacts available at work. Thus, these arrangements may be possible and desirable for some workers and employers, but "they are not feasible in all situations." For example, waiters and cooks must perform their duties when people show up to eat (Rothman, 1998, pp. 221–222).

Some organizations have instituted successful part-time programs, among them banks, such as Wells Fargo, and the federal government, where 63 percent of such part-time managers were women and 37 percent men in the mid-1990s. When interviewed, they said they were committed to work and family. Eighty-six percent said they had more time for family and personal life, "85 percent . . . asserted that they accomplish as much work as full-time managers," and 65 percent claimed their mental health had improved (Raabe, 1998, p. 185).

3. According to Chafetz, schools also can help families by providing more services for children. "Some local districts have begun to offer pre-school for 3–4-year-old children and extended or after-school programs for elementary school-aged children, which help to alleviate child-care problems for employed parents." In addition, schools might house clinics and special rooms for "moderately ill children," thus "minimizing the burden on parents to get such attention for their children" (Chafetz, 1997, pp. 121–122).

Workers and managers can conceive and implement many other policies to help people balance family and work. Real commitment to that principle, cooperation, and imagination could create many arrangements.

Gerson thinks employers should implement family-friendly policies for three reasons: (1) Practical and moral obligations. Most jobs no longer pay enough for families to survive on the income of one earner. (2) Such policies make for happier, more reliable, and productive workers. (3) They rely on a well-run society for their employees and customers. They must help to raise the next generation of their workers (1998, p. 20).

(For reviews of family-work issues and policies, see Perry-Jenkins, Repetti, and Crouter, 2000; Fredriksen-Goldsen and Scharlach, 2001; Wallen, 2002).

Some Guiding Principles

1. The causes of family-work imbalance are social, found in the economy, culture, and corporations where we work. When fathers and mothers are at work at 6 p.m. instead of being home preparing meals with their spouses and children, when they are on the cell phone while their children take a bath, their actions are mandated by the corporate search for ever-greater profits, and by an economic culture that values material possessions.

2. All companies and organizations should have policies that assume most workers have children. The government should require all companies to have family-friendly policies. They should be included in the cost of doing business. And if all companies have such policies, no company will be at a disadvantage for assuming the extra cost of such policies. Governments, workplaces, and the entire society should assume responsibility for balancing work and family, as we have done for the public education of all children.

3. Any significant changes that will help most of us can only come about if we work together with others to change laws and workplace practices. A few of us may, through considerable pressure and ingenuity, reduce our own week to 30 hours, but for most of us to work a six-hour day will only happen if unions, politicians, and many other groups wage a protracted and committed campaign to legally mandate that shorter workweek.

HOUSEWORK: DUST WARS AND STEALING OUR LIVES

Reflections and Scenes

"Both doing and remembering housework take one away from other things, therefore housework is not trivial; it steals one's life" (Pogrebin, 1983, p. 148).

Eric Bogle's song "Leaving the Land" tells the story of an old Australian couple closing down and leaving their farm. The storyteller says to Jenny, his wife: "You and the dust have been at war for far too many years."

"There is, perhaps, no greater testimony to the deadening and deadly quality of the tasks of the housewife than the fact that so many women find pleasure in working at . . . low-status, low-paying work made up of dull, routine tasks" (Rubin, 1976, p. 169).

In her study of two-worker families and of housework, Hochschild concluded that in most families women do most of the "second shift" and are left exhausted. "These women talked about sleep the way a hungry person talks about food" (1989, p. 9).

From 1957 to 1964, I lived with my brother and our grandmother. As she grew older and my brother was busy, and unwilling, to do housework, I came to do most of the shopping, cleaning, and cooking. One day a visiting friend told my grandmother, "lucky the woman who will marry Alex." Instantly I replied: "I won't do any of the housework when I marry, my wife will."

In a seminar on work I taught in the Spring of 2001, the women students repeatedly expressed frustration, anger, concern, and worry about boyfriends and future husbands who will probably not share the housework and child care.

In her classic 1970 pamphlet "The Politics of Housework," Pat Mainardi said that all men "recognize the essential fact of housework from the very beginning. Which is that it stinks" (1970, p. 516).

"The routine activities that provide food, clothing, shelter, and care for both children and adults are vital for survival. In fact, domestic work is just as important to maintaining society as is the productive work occurring in the formal market economy" (Coltrane and Adams, 2001, p. 148).

What do all these reflections and stories tell us about housework? People have seen it as women's destiny, or a curse. It has been debated, condemned, praised. Cooking, cleaning, and raising the children are necessities. All over the world people are struggling to meet them, as most women no longer are full-time housewives. In the United States and everywhere, women still perform most housework, what Hochschild has aptly called "the second shift." Let us examine the history of housework, some statistics and conflicts over who does it, the beginnings of men sharing it, some explanations of why women are still burdened with most of it, and ways for men and women to share it equally.

History and Nature of Housework

Housework was simpler and different in pre-industrial times. In gathering and hunting (the earliest) societies, people moved every few months to new sites for the animal and plant life they sought for sustenance. They owned few possessions and built small huts that they abandoned when they moved. Thus, house cleaning was minimal, there was little clothing to wash, and cooking was simple. Among the Ju/'hoansi, women devoted an estimated average (based on observation by the anthropologist Richard Lee) 22.4 hours a week to household tasks, compared to 15.4 for men. The total of gathering and hunting, making and fixing tools, and housework was 44.5 hours a week for men, 40 for women. Today, estimated totals for all kinds of work range from 70 to 90 hours a week. At Amerco in 1990, men totaled 75 hours a week for work and housework, women 96 (Lee, 1993, p. 58; Hochschild, 1997, p. 76).

In our own pre-industrial days, housework was also different. People lived in smaller houses, there was less cleaning, clothing was changed less often, and meals were simpler. Industrialism gradually created the full-time housewife (see ch. 2). Technology both reduced and made more work. Washing machines made it easier to wash clothes, but people began to change them more often, so women today spend as much or more time with the laundry as women did in olden days (Rothman, 1998, pp. 216–218; Ewen, 1985; and for a history of housework, see Horsfield, *Biting the Dust: The Joys of Housework,* 1998).

The role of the full-time housewife developed gradually, and was in full bloom from the middle 1800s to the 1960s. How were the lives of these women? In *The Sociology of Housework,* written at the end of this historical period, Oakley concluded that most women were dissatisfied with housework and found it monotonous and lonely. It had low social prestige and long hours, an average of 77 a week. Autonomy, "being one's boss" and in control of the pace of the work, was an advantage (Oakley, 1975).

In Muncie, Indiana, in the 1920s, people were observing and worrying that housework was changing compared to the 1890s. Women were said to be cooking less elaborate meals, not baking their own bread, and so on. Electricity and new laborsaving devices were changing the nature of housework; washboards were replaced by washing machines, for example. And the struggle for men to do some housework had already begun in the 1920s. "In the growing number of working class families in which the wife helps to earn the family living, the husband is beginning to share directly in housework" (Lynd and Lynd, 1929, pp. 167–68).

The Lynds probably exaggerated when they wrote of "sharing" housework; "helping with" was more accurate, and only in some working-class families. Housework remained women's domain for decades after. In the 1950s, most women's lives still revolved around home and children. In a study of working-class families, Komarovsky concluded that "the wives do not normally expect assistance [with housework and child care] from their husbands." Even the "one fifth of women who express a strong dislike for housework often feel guilty about their dislike of this normal feminine responsibility." But "when circumstances require it [such as a wife's illness], the husband expects and is expected to pitch in without worrying about doing 'women's work'" (1962, pp. 52, 55).

Change had begun by the 1970s. Two studies from those years show that women wanted their husbands to participate more, and cleanliness became less important to them. The working-class women Rubin talked with in the early 1970s still thought that housework and child care were their responsibility, but they wanted their husbands to "help" and to do so without being asked. And with few exceptions, men did only do some "helping her" and "almost always at the wife's instigation." Some women resented carrying the entire load of housework and kin work while they also worked (Rubin, 1976, pp. 102, 105).

In the late 1970s in Muncie, Indiana, women were still burdened with most of the housework, and men earned most of the income. In almost half the homes, wives did all the housework; in 40 percent, they did most of it, with husbands making "a recognized contribution"; and in 8 percent, they reported an equal sharing of housework. Women accepted the reality that housework was their domain, but most did not like it. They were not obsessed with cleaning and cooking and saw no prestige or status in being housewives. They were relaxed about it, and there were no proclamations of "cleanliness is next to godliness." One woman said: "If it gets done, it gets done; if it doesn't, it doesn't" (Caplow and others, 1982, pp. 74–75, 113).

Some women hated it. "I hate it. It's the most disgusting thing I've ever had to do in my life. Cleaning the toilet is not my idea of a good trip. . . . Unfortunately, I do most of it and bitching the whole time, really mad about it." According to the authors, however, the following woman's comments were more typical: "I'm not a person who likes the role of housewife as far as dusting everything and waiting for the dust to pile up again and again. I have never liked staying home and doing housework. That's just not me" (Caplow and others, 1982, pp. 76–77).

In summary, despite some changes during the twentieth century, by the early 1980s women were performing 80–90 percent of cleaning, cooking, child care, and other tasks. More men were helping, and a very few (5–10 percent) were sharing. All this when in 1980, 45 percent of married women with children under six were in the labor force, as were 62 percent of women with children ages 6–17 (Pogrebin, 1983, p. 146; *Statistical Abstract,* 1999, p. 417). (For a longer history of housework, see Coltrane, 1996, chs. 1 and 2.)

Why *Do* Women Do Most Housework? Part I

Despite some recent changes, housework has been women's duty, burden, and domain. There are three possible explanations for this condition: Women and men are socialized to see it as women's role; it makes economic sense to assign it to women; men use their power to force it upon women. Let us look at socialization here, and the other two explanations later.

According to Goldscheider and Waite: "Mothers teach teenage daughters to cook, but not their sons; sons learn, usually from their fathers, skills needed for traditionally male chores. As a result, at an early age girls and boys learn separate skills and become generally more efficient at them. Hence they feel more satisfaction and less frustration with their sex-linked tasks. . . . The traditional tastes and preferences normally created in the parental home are further reinforced by the responses of friends, family, and neighbors." The mass media add to and perpetuate the assumption that housework is women's chore. Coltrane and Adams think that image persists. "With few exceptions, comic strips, television shows, and movies show how inept men are when they attempt to perform 'women's work'" (Goldscheider and Waite, 1991, p. 110; Coltrane and Adams, 2001, p. 148).

Socialization and men's claimed inability to cook and clean are rationalizations, not explanations. Men can cook and clean; they have been chefs and cooks; and there is no deep dark secret to dusting and vacuuming. Men *choose* to avoid housework. Evan Holt attributed his aversion to housework to his upbringing. "Evan didn't do many other things he was brought up to do, like go to church, avoid using credit cards, or wait to have sex until after marriage. In these areas he was his own man. But around the house, he said he was just doing what his mother taught him." Men whose wives work evenings learn to cook, clean, bathe the children, and listen to them; they have to. One of them said: "you gain a lot more respect" for what women do (Hochschild, 1989, p. 218; Deutsch, 1999, p. 181).

I think we sociologists attribute too much behavior and motivation to socialization. The way we were raised does influence us, heavily. But it does not totally control and determine all we do as adults. Men can, and have changed. Many have quickly learned to clean, cook, change diapers, feed children.

Housework Today

For *The Second Shift: Working Parents and the Revolution at Home,* Hochschild "interviewed fifty couples very intensively, and . . . observed in a dozen homes." She concluded that "Twenty percent of the men in my study shared housework equally. Seventy percent of men did a substantial amount (less than half but more than a third), and 10 percent did less than a third" (1989, pp. 4, 8).

Her book is a detailed, intensive, sophisticated, and passionate study of working parents and housework. It shows no full sharing by most men, but considerable progress compared to earlier decades. It is limited to one area in California. Some recent national studies show even more sharing by men; some show less. No study has yet concluded that most men with working wives share equally. Before I summarize studies of who does what, and how much, housework, let me present some cautions.

1. Most studies are based on "self-reported retrospective estimates." People are asked to remember who did what, and when. Memories are unreliable. Consciously and unconsciously we distort, exaggerate, forget, and are embarrassed to admit actions (Rothman, 1998, p. 218).

We often observe and remember what we want and need. We create "myths." Hochschild concluded that many of the women in her study, deeply committed to equality and liberation, convinced themselves that their husbands performed half the housework, even though all evidence she gathered clearly showed the wives did most of it (The most obvious case, painful to read, was that of Nancy and Evan Holt, in chapters 4 and 7). In short, men and women may overreport the actual housework men do.

2. Also, "[A]ll generalizations mask wide variations among families, meaning that in some families a great deal of work is shared, and in others little or none is" (Rothman, 1998, p. 218).

3. Attitudes and emotions about men doing housework are often confused and contra-dictory. While most Americans say they want fathers to share family work, "[M]ost still feel uncomfortable if a father takes time off work 'just' to be with his kids or if a husband does most of the cooking and housekeeping." It seems that we still want men to be primarily providers, and not share that role with their wives (Coltrane and Adams, 2001, p. 152). (For excellent discussions of this uneasiness, see Rubin, 1994; Hochschild, 1989; Deutsch, 1999.)

Working-Class Men. In the early 1990s, Lillian Rubin conducted long interviews with 162 working-class families (*Families on the Fault Line,* 1994). Housework was one of the topics she explored. (Other studies I have read convince me that her comments and findings apply to couples of all classes.)

Unlike the women Rubin interviewed in the early 1970s (*Worlds of Pain,* 1976), these working women in the 1990s clearly and unequivocally wanted their husbands to share. The men's reactions to this appeal varied. Some were sympathetic, some ambivalent, and others resentful and hostile. One said: "I try to do as much as I can for Sue, and when I can't, I feel bad about it." Another was less sympathetic: "I'm damn tired of women griping all the time; it's nothing but nags and complaints. . . . What does she want? It's not like I don't do anything to help her out, but it's never enough." Generally, they were "slow to accept reciprocal respon-sibilities." (1994, pp. 86–87).

Rubin found that younger men were more likely to "grant legitimacy" to their wives' demands; they felt guilty if they did not share the housework. These feelings often made some difference, and men performed more housework. But even when men "helped" or "shared," women still had to ask and remind them, still had to plan and organize what needed to be done. A wife who worked as many hours as her husband, and shared equally in providing the family income, angrily told Rubin: "Sure, he helps me out. He'll give the kids a bath or help with the dishes. But only when I ask him. He doesn't have to *ask* me to go to work every day, does he? Why should I have to ask him?" (1994, p.86).

Rubin concluded that 16 percent of white men "shared the family work relatively equally." Almost all were unemployed or worked different shifts from their wives (1994, p. 91).

Statistics on Housework. Women clearly do less housework today, at least in Muncie, Indiana (see table 11.2). The explanation may be that people have reduced standards of cleanliness and other tasks, cook less and eat more ready food, use more time-saving devices, and so on.

In the 1990s, men were doing more of it than in previous decades. As women were reducing their hours of housework, given the paid jobs they held, and as men were increasing their contributions, men's percentage of total family work increased. But still, in the late 1990s, women spent "roughly twice as much time on routine household tasks as men." Women were also still responsible for organizing and monitoring the tasks men and children performed. And married women with children were responsible for "a greater proportion of housework

Table 11.2 Daily hours of housework by married women, by percent, in Muncie, Indiana

	1924	1977	1999
4+ hours	87	43	14
2–3 hours	13	45	53
1 hour or less	0	12	33

Source: Caplow, Hicks, and Wattenberg, 2001, p. 37.

than single women and those without children." Men were performing better in some tasks, less in others. "They have begun to take on at least a portion of grocery shopping, cooking, and meal clean-up. But there have been only modest increases in men's share of house cleaning, laundry, and other repetitive indoor housekeeping tasks" (Coltrane and Adams, 2001, pp. 145–146, 147, 150).

Studies of who carries out specific tasks support these conclusions. They showed that around 1990, wives did 90 percent of cooking, 94 percent of bedmaking, 92 percent of dishwashing, and 90 percent of vacuuming. In the typically male tasks, men did "86 percent of household repairs, 75 percent of lawn mowing, and 77 percent of snow shoveling." Generally, husbands are more likely to share child care (especially of older children) than housework (Coltrane and Adams, 2001, p. 147; Goldscheider and Waite, 1991, p. 113).

Coltrane and Adams conclude that men are more likely to approach sharing housework and child care when "they are employed fewer hours, when their wives work longer hours or earn more money, . . . when both spouses believe in gender equity," and when wives "actively bargain for it" (2001, p. 150).

Other studies also reveal that most tasks are still gender typed, but also that there has been some change. For example, one study showed that around 1990, women did 34 hours of housework a week: 26 hours of traditionally women's tasks, 2 hours of men's, and 6 hours gender-neutral work. Men's 18 hours consisted of 7 hours of traditionally male tasks, 7 hours of traditionally female work, and 4 hours gender-neutral tasks (Rothman, 1998, p. 218; Wen, 2002b).

Even though totally equal sharing may be decades away (pessimists insist it will never happen), we have made considerable progress. Many couples do share. In the mid-1970s, "men spent 30 percent as much time as women on workday chores; by 1998, this percentage rose to 75" (according to a Families and Work Institute survey in 1998, cited in Hesse-Biber and Carter, 2000, p. 192).

Parenthetically, most writers on housework have concluded that African American men have traditionally performed more of it than white men have, and their marriages have been more egalitarian. At the same time, many men have been ambivalent about the housework they do. And in African American families, too, women have done more of it, and they have felt overworked (Billingsley, 1992; Taylor, 2002; Hesse-Biber and Carter, 2000; Rubin, 1994; Landry, 2000).

Finally, single parents face even more tensions over work and housework. In 2001, three quarters of single mothers with children 17 and under were in the labor force. Some writers suspect that single mothers may have less housework than married ones because they do not have to cook and clean for husbands. But they do carry alone the entire burden of earning an income, performing all tasks at home, and caring for the children. The responsibilities of their jobs leave little time and energy for family work (*Statistical Abstract,* 2002, p. 373). (Some do receive help with child care from relatives and friends.)

Two studies published in 2002 show that cohabitation may create more sharing of housework. In one study, married women performed about 71 percent of housework, compared to 67 percent for cohabiting women. The other study, a cross-national one, concluded that married couples who had cohabited before marriage showed "greater equality in the sharing of housework" when they married than did couples who had not cohabited before marriage. But in both studies, the differences in sharing were small, and women in both groups still did most of the housework (Wen, 2002b; Balalova and Cohen, 2002, p. 753).

Some Consequences. There are no easy solutions to the burden of the second shift two-worker families face. There is not enough time for two full-time careers, for the many household tasks, for time with the children and each other. Many studies and the lives of family and friends amply support that conclusion. The strain affects women more, but the men do not escape it. "If men share the second shift it affects them directly. If they don't share, it affects them through their wives" (Hochschild, 1989, p. 189).

The women in *The Second Shift* resorted to different strategies. Some tried to be supermoms and to cope without imposing on their husbands, and they were exhausted. Some eventually reduced their career aspirations and their work hours. Others cut back on time for housework, the marriage, themselves, their children. A few reduced their notions of "what a baby needs" which "takes a great deal of denial and has drastic consequences." But "most women cut back on their personal needs, [giving up] reading, hobbies, television, visits with friends, exercise, time alone" (Hochschild, 1989, pp. 198, 199).

Where men resisted sharing, their resistance became a source of tension in the relationship. Marriages deteriorated. Some ended in divorce, and in others women abandoned their struggles to convince their husbands to share, and they cut back on their careers. When women were responsible for most of the second shift, they could not "afford unambivalent love for their husbands." Deutsch came to a similar conclusion in her study. When both spouses worked full time, but she was responsible for most of the parenting, "free and easy happiness never emerged" during the interviews (Hochschild, 1989, p. 260; Deutsch, 1999, p. 8).

Why *Do* Women Do Most Housework? Part II

Socialization. It does play a role, of course. But it cannot be the sole or the major explanation (See the previous discussion on socialization.)

Rational Economic Decision. Some writers have argued that it makes economic sense for women to work fewer hours and be responsible for most of the housework. Since their husbands earn more money, the family unit benefits by his working more hours and earning a greater income, and her working fewer hours and taking care of the house. This argument ignores two realities.

1. As Deutsch has shown, men often earn more income than their wives because they fought to create that reality. If we examine the history of a marriage, we often find a time when the wife did or could have earned as much as her husband. But decisions made by the couple, usually forced by the man, created unequal earnings. Thus, his greater earnings were first created, then used to justify why she should work fewer hours and do most housework.

> Thomas and Tammy's relative shares of the parenting have become unequal over time. . . . When asked, each attributes it to money. Tammy says: "It was money. . . . How could I get ahead?. . . His salary plus the company car plus the bonuses they get every year based on the amount of business they bring in. There's a potential for a lot more." . . . Thomas concurs: "My potential for earning power in a sales position would have been more than hers in mostly an administrative position." . . . Nevertheless, at the time they made this important decision the two of them were earning approximately the same salary. They both ignored that she might have had a lucrative future in management, possibly with a higher earning potential than his in sales. Although we can't know for sure, they probably wouldn't have ended up with such disparate salaries had each been able to invest equally in career. . . . Tammy did not push to change the balance in their work and family roles; Thomas did. Although neither has ever said so, his desire

to have the central breadwinning role may have been critical in how they now divide childcare, (1999, pp. 130–131)

But other couples chose to invest equally in both their careers and ended up with equal incomes and shared child care and housework.

2). The economic argument also accepts women's unequal earnings as inevitable and natural. But that assumption ignores women's struggles to remedy that inequality. Women's earnings have increased over time, from 60 percent of those of men to in 1960 to 76 percent in 2001 (comparing only women and men who work full time) (*Statistical Abstract,* 2002, p. 403).

Power. Women are burdened with most of the housework because of gender and power inequality. Since housework stinks and steals our lives, most men avoid it and resist women's struggles to have men share it. A recent study of Williams College students starkly shows what most men really want. "Women at Williams have overwhelmingly seen as ideal a marriage in which both partners worked part time and shared family commitments. The men's ideal pictured the wives at home, the men working full time. As Crittenden writes, 'A few years down the road, when many of these girls marry, become mothers, take on most of the costs of child-rearing, and watch their independence slip away, someone is sure to say, "well, it was her choice"'" (Overholser, 2001, p. A21; referring to Ann Crittenden, *The Price of Motherhood,* 2001).

Thus, who does housework, and who does not, is related to men's choices, privileges, and economic power. Most men believe they benefit by having women be responsible for and do their laundry, clean their house, cook for them, and raise their children. The extra hours they gain by devoting fewer hours to household chores than women do (see details above) they have available for their jobs and careers, and for leisure. The greater income they earn by working more hours gives them more power in their relationships with their wives, for many studies have shown that the more money women earn, the more equal their marriages. Consciously or unconsciously, men want to prevent women from gaining equality, because women would have more leverage for demanding that men share housework. Men are more likely to do more housework when they "are employed fewer hours [thus earning less money], when their wives work longer hours or earn more money, . . . when both spouses believe in gender equity," and when wives "actively bargain for it" (Coltrane and Adams, 2001, p. 201; see also Pogrebin, 1983, ch. 7; Hesse-Biber and Carter, 2000, pp. 182–184).

But like all privileged groups, most men are reluctant to give up their privileges, so they tend to resist their wives' efforts to convince them to share. Evan Holt resorted to similar tactics to sabotage Nancy's efforts to have him share. She worked out a schedule where she would cook dinner on Monday, Wednesday, and Friday, and he on Tuesday, Thursday, and Saturday (they would go out on Sunday). During the first week of the schedule, he "forgot" to shop and cook dinner on Tuesday and Saturday, and cooked hamburgers and french fries on Thursday. Nancy soon abandoned the schedule (Hochschild, 1989, p. 38).

Evan kept resisting. Nancy, fearing he would leave if she persisted, eventually reduced her work to half time, even though she loved her work more than Evan did his. She continued to do most of the housework. Adrienne, on the other hand, left Michael when he refused to share, and only returned when he agreed to share housework and for both of them to reduce their career commitments when they eventually had children (Hochschild, 1989, chs. 4, 9, and 12).

Faced with men's resistance, women need to persist and use whatever power and persuasion they possess. Nancy ceased her struggle fearing Evan would leave. But Deutsch found that women who *threaten* to leave the marriage may have better luck than Nancy. "Men succumb to the threat of divorce by agreeing to carry [their] load at home. . . . The equal sharers in my study have bet successfully [as did Adrienne in *The Second Shift*] that their husbands' love for them is strong enough to withstand their exercise of power." Most women whose husbands share were steadfast and insistent in their demand for sharing, and willing to "strike" to gain it (Deutsch, 1999, p. 66).

Men exercise their power to avoid household tasks, to perpetuate that power by having more time to earn a greater income than their wives, to have more leisure. Women need to oppose men's power by using *their* strength, and by committing to the struggle for equal sharing.

Farming Out Family Chores and Responsibilities

Another solution, available only to wealthier families, is to farm out family chores and responsibilities. But what becomes of family time if we pay others to clean our homes, cook our food, organize our children's birthday parties, and so on?

For centuries, many household tasks have been farmed out. It has been a long time since most families have raised their own food, baked their bread, or made their clothes. Already in the 1920s, people were bemoaning this trend. Few families today bake cookies or prepare elaborate meals. "Instant mixes, frozen dinners, and take-out meals have replaced Mother's recipes. Daycare for children, retirement homes for the elderly, wilderness camps for delinquent children, even psychotherapy are, in a way, commercial substitutes for jobs a mother once did at home." There is nothing new to the farming out of family functions. Still, when families hire an outsider to organize, plan, and carry out their children's birthday parties, it does seem that we may have reduced the functioning family to very little (Hochschild, 1997, p. 209).

Let us look at some family functions that some people hire others to perform. Streamline, a Boston suburban service company, will "pick up and deliver your dry cleaning every week, repair broken shoes, bring specially prepared meals from Legal Seafoods and the Uptown Gourmet, set up and replenish a Poland Spring water cooler, deliver . . . videos, leave groceries in a company-owned refrigerator and freezer in your garage." Busy parents could also hire Local Motion, which in 1995 was "shuttling Newton-area [next to Boston] children to and from school, and afternoon activities such as swim lessons and hockey games. More and more people hire companies to clean their homes regularly. One company will cook, freeze, and deliver all your meals for a week" (McGrory, 1999; Matchan, 1995a). For more examples, see Hochschild, 1997, p. 230). (Of course, very wealthy families have always hired nannies, housekeepers, groundskeepers, and others to relieve them of all household tasks and childrearing.)

Thus, there is a legitimate question: What *is* left of the family when every service, task, and product is purchased? What does it mean when parents don't have time to bake cakes and organize activities for their children's birthdays? When breakfasts come ready made? When we barely see our children and others drive them everywhere? Is the solution to stressed-out and time-starved families for both parents to work long hours and ship out all family functions and chores? Or, is the solution for both parents to reduce their work hours, to live a simpler life, and to do—equally—most of their own cooking, cleaning, cookie baking, organizing of birthday parties, and to spend time with their children and each other?

CONCLUSION: SHARING IT ALL

I close with five principles and conclusions.

1. We must begin with fewer work hours for everyone, especially parents of young children. Men and women will also need to work equal hours. Fewer work hours allows for the rest of life; equal hours will make equal sharing of that life more probable. And we must simply accept that, as in pre-industrial days, men and women provide equally for their fami-

lies. Nostalgia cannot, will not, and should not return us to the 1950s and full-time house-wives.

2. When we accept the necessity of equal work by men and women, in time it will only seem fair that men share housework and child care. Paul shared because he loved Mary and his children, and because it seemed fair. "You have to help out. How can you not help out?" Deutsch points out that many equally sharing men in her study did not start their marriages believing in sharing. They were "ordinary people simply inventing and reinventing solutions to the dilemmas of modern life." Sharing was the fair and the necessary solution (Deutsch, 1999, pp. 11, 26).

Parents and children will benefit if the parents share the work and the pleasures of child care with quality daycare workers, with neighbors and friends, and especially with grandparents and other relatives. As for housework, some assistance from outsiders may be occasionally necessary, but farming it out is not the solution.

3. Living simpler lives, in smaller homes and with fewer possessions, will make for far less housework. It will also require fewer hours at work, since we'll need less income for our simpler lifestyle.

4. Hochschild, Deutsch, and our daily experiences show that sharing housework and reducing work hours will make for happier marriages and families. Women will not be burdened with long hours of household chores and raising the children; men will not be burdened with long hours at work. By sharing, men will appreciate their wives' contributions; their wives will not resent them for not sharing. Children will spend time with and get to know their fathers and mothers. All will have time for relatives, friends, and community participation.

5. This is not a fantasy. It can be done, it has been done, it is being done. Many studies show beyond doubt that it is possible. The social policies of many societies show it can be done. Bacdayan's study of a horticultural village in the Philippines in the 1970s documents a generally equal sharing of all household tasks (Risman and Johnson-Sumerford, 1998; Bacdayan, 1977).

12

Divorce: A World Tradition

Divorce did not appear suddenly in the 1960s and 1970s. It is not a new or uniquely U.S. experience, nor does it mean the end of marriage and the family. But it is a subject of ongoing debate and concern, of proposals to make it more difficult to obtain, of groups seeking to prevent it, of other groups arguing that divorce is an inevitable and necessary expression of who we are and what we value. Groups like the Council on Families insist that most problems faced by children in the United States are caused by divorce, while others believe it is the U.S. economy and our political institutions that consign children to poverty and misery (Popenoe, 1996; Ahrons, 1994; Coontz, 1997).

Prevalent though it may be, divorce is still a painful, troublesome, transforming, yet often-positive experience. Let us hear from divorced women and men.

Meg Campbell wrote sixty-one poems about her divorce. *Solo Crossing* is a memoir of separation and divorce, the new life beyond, and the whole range of emotions in between." Matchan wrote: "After Campbell and her husband separated, she was consumed by 'shame, guilt, and failure. I had been a very proud person. This whole experience was very humbling. I cried every day for the first year.'. . . She is happier now than she has been in years, having discovered the support of a 'large, wonderful extended family who was totally there for me'" (Matchan, 2000, p. C8).

On a summer day in 1992, George Caldwell sat in my office and talked about a divorce he had not wanted, and about how it had changed him (he had custody of their two daughters). "It took a lot for me to go from being a macho cop in the military . . . to baking pies for school bake sales. . . . Now work is a secondary thing in my life. Career has to be second. My kids need me. . . . I'm a lot more sensitive than I used to be; to other people's feelings, to situations. I had to learn to be a mother and a father. . . . I had to learn what does a mother do, what does she contribute to the children. . . . I had to admit to myself that men can cry and that men can be homemakers and it doesn't make them any less of a man . . . , to reevaluate my entire thinking of what a man really is. [My father's teaching that] a man never cries doesn't hold water." Thus, despite the pain he had experienced, George thought he had also become a better parent and a better person (in Liazos, 1997, pp. 353–354).

For many women, divorce is "freedom from subordination." One woman said after her divorce: "I feel like I'm living again. I feel like I was dying a slow death in that relationship. There's joy in my life. . . . I feel energized and liberated. I feel a real emotional release" (Riessman, 1990, p. 165).

I should also note that I separated from my then wife in 1981, when our daughters were 7 and 5, and we divorced in 1984. Also, in 1992, I interviewed 61 divorced fathers. Finally, from 1990 to 2003, I taught a sociology seminar on divorce. (For details of my study of divorced fathers, see "Fathers still: Parenting after divorce," 1995; "Grieving and growing: Experiences of divorced fathers," 1997.)

PERSPECTIVES ON DIVORCE

Social catastrophe or an inevitable consequence of who we are, painful parting or liberation, divorce has been part of the human experience.

A Universal Experience

When they bemoan what they consider the catastrophe of divorce, writers often say the U.S. divorce rate is a unique event in history. They are mistaken. Divorce was common in gathering-hunting and in horticultural societies, where women were generally equal to men. It became fairly uncommon in patriarchal peasant societies (European, Chinese, and others), where women were socially subordinate to men and unable to leave oppressive marriages. Divorce is now common and increasing in industrial societies outside the United States, including Japan. It is being considered and debated in societies with no or limited divorce, such as Chile and Iran (Gallardo, 2002; Reuters, 2002).

Pre-industrial Societies. Divorce was easy and simple in gathering-hunting and horticultural societies, such as those found in North America. People owned few possessions, so there was little arguing over the division of property when the marriage failed. Men and women contributed equally to the material needs of families, and they lived in small groups where family and community supported all people. Thus, it was little hardship for people to divorce. Moreover, individual freedom and autonomy were basic in those cultures, and people saw no need for anyone to stay in miserable marriages.

When French Jesuits (Christians from a peasant society) came to the Northeast around 1600 to convert Native Americans to Christianity, they repeatedly commented in their annual reports about the ease of divorce. They reported that marriages had no stability, "and are broken more easily than the promises which children make to one another in France." Among the Huron, "the freedom of leaving one another on the slightest pretext is so generally admitted as a fundamental law of these peoples" (*Jesuit Relations*, 1896–1901, cited in Liazos, 1986, pp. 117–118).

The Native peoples were puzzled by the Jesuits' opposition to divorce. To them, it made no sense for unhappy couples to stay together. When husbands and wives were unhappy, "they separate from one another in order to seek elsewhere the peace and union which they cannot find together." They saw no reason to spend the rest of their lives together in misery. They could not believe Europeans allowed no divorce. "They look upon it as a monstrous thing to be tied to one another without any hopes of being able to untie or break the knot" (cited in Liazos, 1986, pp. 118–119; for divorce among the Iroquois, Zuni, and other Native American societies, see Leacock, 1981, pp. 150–227).

Among the Mundurucu of the Amazon in the early 1950s (see discussions in earlier chapters), most people divorced at least once, with divorces occurring mostly in the first two years of marriage. After children arrived, affection grew between spouses and there was no divorce in most marriages. Divorce was a "simple matter." Men left the women's households, where the children continued to live with their other relatives. There was little economic dislocation, since the living compounds of the Mundurucu—consisting of an older woman, her daughters, and their husbands and children—were production groups that supported everyone in the household (so too among the Iroquois and other peoples). In short, children, women, and men did not suffer economically (Murphy and Murphy, 1985, pp. 180–181).

Thus, divorce has been common in most societies. It even approached 100 percent in some, such as the Kanuri in Africa, where people still married and valued marriage, and where there was social stability (Skolnick, 1996, p. 300).

Reasons for Divorce. Grounds for divorce vary. Among the Mundurucu, "Divorces happen for a variety of reasons. The new husband may turn out to be lazy or inept and sufficiently irritating to his in-laws to be sent off. Or he may experience personal difficulties in the household, leaving him with the alternative of taking his wife away with him or divorcing her; the kin ties of the wife in such cases usually turn out to be stronger than the conjugal bond. The man may leave a woman because she is lazy, or he may discover her in an adulterous relationship and walk out in outrage. Similarly, the wife may become angered with the extra-marital affairs of her husband and seek backing from her housemates to divorce him" (Murphy and Murphy, 1985, p. 180).

In summary, "nagging, quarreling, cruelty, stinginess, or adultery may be cited as causes of divorce. In almost all societies, childlessness is grounds for divorce." As we'll see below, these explanations are very similar to those Americans give for ending their marriages (Schultz and Lavenda, 2001, p. 278).

Experiences of Divorce. To say divorce is common and simple is not to deny the pain, anger, sadness, and disappointment people feel. Nisa experienced all these emotions during her divorces, and as we saw above there were long arguments and discussions as people contemplated divorce. Among the Mundurucu, "ex-wives are commonly bitter and cynical about men." They were distrustful and reluctant to remarry (Shostak, 1981; Murphy and Murphy, 1985, p. 181).

Divorce in Modern Industrial Societies. We will see below that divorce is common in industrial societies today. It is not uniquely American. Even in Japan, often cited as a contrast of marital stability, divorce doubled from 1968 to 1998, and stood at about the same rate as Germany and France. Moshavi tells the story of 54-year-old Fusako, who had been unhappy in her marriage for a long time. She searched for a job to support herself and leave her empty marriage, but found nothing and was trapped. Meantime, younger women were attending workshops to learn about their legal rights as they considered divorce. They wanted "more personal happiness and fulfillment from their marriages." But Fusako had "resigned herself to her fate [a loveless marriage], and she's got advice for any young Japanese woman: If the marriage isn't working, get out fast" (Moshavi, 2000, p. A11).

An American Tradition

In *Divorce: An American Tradition,* Riley (1991) shows that:

1. Divorce appeared in the very beginning of U.S. history and has been steadily increasing through the decades and centuries.

2. Ongoing debates and conflicts over divorce have been constant.

3. The grounds for divorce expanded fairly soon, and people and the law have recognized many justifications for it.

4. The number of recorded divorces, especially before the twentieth century, have always undercounted the numbers of broken marriages, as many people left their spouses and never were officially divorced.

5. There are various explanations for the steady increase in divorce, foremost among them the high value of love in marriages, and women's growing ability to support themselves, enabling them to leave oppressive marriages.

Increasing Divorce. Divorce appeared in Colonial America. People had to petition the legislature for permission to divorce, and it was not always granted. In Colonial Massachusetts, for example, from 1692 to 1786, there were 229 petitions, 128 by women and 101 by men, with 143 granted (Cott, 1978).

As divorce increased during the eighteenth century, so it did during the nineteenth. In the 25 years from 1867 to 1881, there were 211,405 divorces; and in the 20 years from 1887 to 1906, 798,672 were granted. (As a comparison, there were 1,135,000 divorces in 1998.) Even given the population increase through immigration, this is a dramatic increase, and is reflected in the divorce rate. Divorces granted per year, per thousand people, went from .3 per thousand in 1860 to .4 in 1880; .7 in 1900; 1.6 in 1920; 2.0 in 1940; 2.2 in 1960; 3.5 in 1970; 5.2 in 1980; 4.7 in 1990; and 4.0 in 2001 (Riley, 1991, pp. 79, 124; Ahrons, 1994, p. 366; *Statistical Abstract,* 2002, p. 59).

Broadly speaking, "between 1867 and 1929, the population of the US increased 300%, the number of marriages 400%, and the divorce rate 2,000%." (May, 1980, p. 2). Today, and during the last two decades of the twentieth century, about 40–50 percent of marriages end in divorce. In the 1880s, about one in fifteen marriages did, which was a significant increase from the 1700s. (For more divorce statistics, see below.)

All during this time, many people left their marriages without ever bothering to divorce, especially in states where divorce was difficult or illegal, as it was in some southern states in the eighteenth and nineteenth centuries. For centuries, divorce statistics undercounted the number of broken marriages because people could not or would not divorce legally. Referring to the second half of the twentieth century, Riley notes: "Partings that would have gone unrecorded are now divorce statistics, which expands the divorce incidence and makes it seem considerably higher [compared to the past]." And many women, fearing the stigma of divorce, reported themselves as widows rather than divorced women, thus undercounting divorce in the past (Riley, 1991, pp. 159, 173).

Debates and Conflicts. Since the late 1970s, there has been an ongoing and often bitter debate about the meaning and consequences of divorce. But this is not a new phenomenon. Such debates have raged for centuries. "Opponents of divorce believed that the spread of divorce revealed decay in American society and breakdown in the American family. . . . In 1788, Yale President Timothy Dwight [said] . . . 'the progress of this evil' was 'alarming and terrible.'" At that time in Connecticut, about one in a hundred couples was divorcing. Others responded that divorce allowed people, especially women, to escape miserable and oppressive marriages. On July 4, 1826, Robert Owen declared that "no one should be forced to remain in a distressing marriage." Many others agreed with him. By the middle 1800s, novelists were passionately writing stories that presented divorce as an escape from empty and angry marriages, or, as hasty action that led to social catastrophe (Riley, 1991, pp. 59–60).

The heated debate continued. In 1852, Horace Greeley of the *New York Tribune* denounced divorce as a sign "that individualism was running amok. . . . In his view, divorce would soon result in 'a general profligacy and corruption such as this country has never known.'" This was 1852, a century and a half ago. The debate continued with reports that Indiana and other states were becoming "divorce mills," where people from other states went to obtain easy divorces. (Divorce had become easier to get, as we will see, but Riley provides statistics to show that most people divorcing in Indiana were from that state [Riley, 1991, pp. 62–63]).

From 1850 to 1880, there was a strong movement to make divorce more difficult to obtain. These people argued that "American society must return to the traditional view of marriage and divorce." (Today, many people long for the "traditional marriage" of the late 1800s, the very same period critics of divorce denounced then.) During that same period, Elizabeth Cady Stanton and others supported the availability of divorce as a means for women to leave oppressive marriages and alcoholic husbands. For them, "*marriage* was a social problem" (Riley, 1991, pp. 71, 73).

During the late 1800s to early 1900s the attack continued against laws some people thought made divorce easy. Delegates to a 1906 national convention in Washington, D.C., sought to decrease divorce. They recommended a waiting period of a year before divorced people could remarry, a requirement that people live in a state two years before they could divorce there (to avoid "divorce mills"), and so on. "After a long and often bitter debate, a majority vote endorsed six grounds for divorce: adultery, bigamy, conviction for a felony, intolerable cruelty, willful desertion for two years, and habitual drunkenness" (Riley, 1991, p. 117).

From 1896 to 1906, as the divorce rate increased, many states, especially in the East, "enacted more than one hundred pieces of restrictive marriage and divorce legislation in an effort to stem the tide." But at the same time, "many reformers and feminists . . . hailed divorce as a new advance in freeing victimized women from the shackles of marital bondage" (May, 1980, pp. 4, 3).

Divorce is an American tradition, and so is the debate over its meaning and social consequences.

Laws and Grounds for Divorce. Until the rise of no-fault divorce in the 1970s, divorce was only possible when one spouse sued the other and cited legally acceptable reasons for the petition. (Of course, legislatures and judges often had considerable discretion in deciding whether the facts fit the law, for example, deciding what constituted "cruelty.") Generally, acceptable reasons for divorce have been expanded. During some periods legislatures limited those grounds, hoping to reduce the numbers of divorced people, but this proved unsuccessful in the long run.

From 1639 to 1692, there were 40 known petitions for divorce in Massachusetts. Authorities "annulled marriages on grounds of consanguinity, bigamy, and sexual incapacity, and dissolved them for long absence and for adultery alone [only against women] or in combination with desertion, neglect, or cruelty." From 1692 to 1796, the following are some of the reasons petitioners cited for seeking divorce:

1. sexual incapacity (3 male, 4 female)
2. bigamous or fraudulent marriage (3 m, 12 f)
3. adultery (50 m, 6 f)
4. adultery and desertion or nonsupport (16 m, 12 f)
5. adultery, desertion, and cohabitation with another (10 m, 16 f)
6. desertion and remarriage (i.e., adultery) (3 m, 19 f)
7. adultery and cruelty (4 m, 3 f)
8. interracial adultery (4 m, 3 f)
9. desertion (8 m, 10 f)
10. cruelty (0 m, 23 f)
11. unknown (2 m, 4 f)

Not all of these petitions were granted. For example, none of the 23 women who cited cruelty as their only grounds were allowed to divorce (Cott, 1978, pp. 117, 121).

Allowable grounds were somewhat similar in North Carolina in the early 1800s. White people submitted 266 applications to the legislature (African Americans could not divorce legally). Over a third cited desertion; 8 percent accused their spouses "with committing adultery with African Americans. Other accusations . . . included adultery with a white person, cruelty, bigamy, impotence, incompatibility, non-support, ill temper, indecent conduct, and 'bringing another into house'" (Riley, 1991, p. 35).

In the West of the late 1800s, desertion was the most common grounds, with cruelty the fastest growing (cruelty included "mental suffering," which was a common complaint of divorces before the no-fault laws of the 1970s). In the nation as a whole, by the 1880s, forty of forty-seven states "allowed the inclusive, flexible ground of cruelty. Numerous other grounds were available" (Riley, 1991, p. 94).

For example, of the almost 800,000 divorces granted nationally from 1887 to 1906, 367,502 were for desertion; 206,225 for cruelty; 153,759 for adultery; 36,516 for drunkenness;

and 34,670 for neglect to provide. Of the total, 64.5 percent were women's divorces, and 35.5 percent were men's. These trends continued into the early twentieth century. In 1928, "women received 71 percent of all divorces granted. And in that year, 47 percent of divorces were granted on the increasingly popular ground of cruelty, a charge women continued to use more than men" (Riley, 1991, pp. 124, 133).

In an era when love was the only reason to marry and stay married, couples increasingly were divorcing because love had left their relationship. But falling out of love (what we now call no-fault divorce) was an unacceptable reason to end a marriage. Thus, couples manufactured the grounds. In New York State, where adultery was the only grounds until 1966, couples who agreed to part would create the "evidence" for adultery by hiring an agency to provide it. "Companies sprang up that supplied a hotel room, a phony partner, a private detective, and a photographer." The picture taken by the photographer was introduced as evidence of adultery during the trial (Riley, 1991, p. 144). (One of the few things I remember still from my sociology class in the fall of 1960 is stories of this practice from our sociology professor, who had practiced law in New York.)

Such deception and dishonesty, and the often-bitter conflict created when one spouse accused the other of misconduct in order to obtain a divorce, were among the reasons given for enacting no-fault divorce, beginning with California in 1970. Between 1970 and 1985, "essentially all states enacted divorce laws similar to those in California." Fault charges such as cruelty and adultery are still available in many states, but in essence people no longer have to prove that their spouse is at fault in order to receive a divorce. They can admit that the relationship between them has deteriorated, and there is no love and harmony. According to Weitzman, no-fault means that "one spouse can decide unilaterally to get a divorce without the consent or agreement of the other spouse" (Parkman, 2000, p. 71; Weitzman, 1985, p. 16).

But elements of no-fault were found in many laws before 1970, even as early as the mid-1800s. "According to some states' omnibus clauses, a petitioner had only to prove marital breakdown." In Iowa, an 1845 law "permitted judges to grant divorces 'when it shall be made fully apparent to the satisfaction of the court that the parties cannot live in peace or happiness together, and that their welfare requires a separation between them.'" (Riley, 1991, pp. 44, 47–48).

In summary, we have traveled a long distance from the 40 Massachusetts petitions of 1639 to 1692, which cited bigamy, neglect, cruelty, desertion, and adultery. But as the Colonial era progressed, as the new nation grew, and as love, companionship, and friendship became essential to marriages, the culture changed. New grounds for divorce were added to allow loveless marriages to end. Behind the cruelty, desertion, adultery, and other reasons people had cited, there were essentially empty and unhappy marriages. By 1970, it was time to state explicitly what had been implicit in many divorce laws of the 1800s.

Causes and Explanations. The Council on Families and other critics of marriage and divorce argue that U.S. citizens no longer value what benefits the family, children, and the community; rather, they place their own individual happiness and fulfillment over those larger social benefits. Any unhappiness and discontent within marriage drives them to divorce.

But what they see as a recent shift to the individual over the family is but the latest expression of social, economic, gender, and other changes that began with the very arrival of Europeans to these shores; indeed, divorce existed before they arrived. Divorce increased as marriages began to change, as people were having different and newer expectations. Historical studies of divorce lead to that conclusion. (The following account is based on Cott, 1978; May, 1980; and especially Riley, 1991. See also Basch, 1999.)

Historians of marriage and the family maintain that the rise of industrialism led to changes in marriage and the family (see chs. 2 and 4). Indeed, the changes may have begun even earlier. In Massachusetts, women filed 47 petitions, out of 97, in the 72 years from 1692 to 1764. But in the 21 years from 1765 to 1786, they filed 82 petitions, 62 percent of the total of 132. Cott thinks "women were becoming less resigned to their circumstances and were taking more initiative to end unsatisfactory marriages" (1978, p. 125).

Let us briefly examine the social changes that began around 1800 and have grown steadily and intensified since then.

1. Even before 1800, records of divorce indicate that people were beginning to expect love, affection, and happiness in their marriages. These expectations became more prominent with the passage of time. "Respect, reciprocity, and romance" were seen as essential to a good marriage, and thus to individual happiness. Indeed, May insists that the rise of divorce is the best indication of these new expectations. People were leaving unhappy marriages in search of love, romance, and respect in new ones. They were renouncing a particular marriage, not marriage itself. "The desperation of these wives [seen in their divorce papers] reflects the high stakes placed on marriage." Rather than a rejection of marriage, divorce "reflected the increased personal desires that matrimony was expected to satisfy, especially for women" (Riley, 1991, p. 55; May, 1980, pp. 161–162).

Somewhat ironically, Europeans in America were finally seeing the wisdom of Native Americans, who were shocked that in the early 1600s Europeans were totally opposed to divorce. Thus, gradually people became less willing to stay in unhappy marriages.

2. Gender roles have also been changing, especially in the twentieth century. In the nineteenth century, women argued passionately that divorce must exist to allow women to escape oppressive marriages and controlling husbands. Elizabeth Cady Stanton and others insisted that women could not gain equality if they were forced to remain in abusive and cruel marriages. The best indication that divorce is a gender issue is the fact that since the early 1700s women have filed 65–70 percent of divorce petitions. Also, divorce rates increased even more as women began to work outside the home. Able to support themselves (even if only in poverty), they left marriages they could not have escaped when they had no means at all to support themselves. Recall Fusako, the Japanese wife in 2000 who was forced to stay in an unhappy marriage because at 54 she could find no job.

3. Riley discusses other social changes that have also contributed to the increase in divorce. Together with the political revolution against England, people began to emphasize individualism and citizens' rights in a democratic society. "Life, liberty, and the pursuit of happiness," incomplete as they were, still encouraged people to value their own happiness together with the social and family good. In various places, Riley also mentions industrialism, urbanization, the labor movement and labor strikes, the women's movement in its various stages since 1848, economic developments in the twentieth century that drew women into the labor force, and other social developments.

In short, divorce has not been the cause of marriage and family breakdown. Rather, changes in marital expectations, gender roles, and the economy have made divorce an inevitable and necessary choice and response.

Divorce in Muncie, Indiana. In the middle 1920s, women were 75 percent of people seeking divorce in Muncie, with two-thirds citing "non-support" as their reason. The Lynds state that since many women could and did hold jobs, they could support themselves and were unwilling to stay in unhappy unions. Dorothy Dix, the Ann Landers of those years, wrote in the local Muncie paper: "Probably men are just as good husbands now as they ever were, but grandmother had to stand grandpa, for he was her meal ticket. . . . A divorced woman was a disgraced woman. . . . But now we view the matter differently. We see that no good purpose is achieved by keeping two people together who have come to hate each other" (Lynd and Lynd, 1929, p. 128).

Many people thought divorces were easy to obtain. "'Anybody with $25 can get a divorce' is a commonly heard remark. Or as one recently divorced man phrased it, 'Any one with $10 can get a divorce in ten minutes if it isn't contested. All you got to do is to show non-support or cruelty and it's a cinch.'" Essentially, there was no-fault divorce in Muncie in the 1920s. Couples who said "We have no affection for each other and do not want to live together" and "She says she does not love me and does not want to live with me" were granted divorces, according to the Lynds (1929, pp. 121, 114).

Fifty years later, in 1977, Muncie residents were still both accepting and critical of divorce. Some people complained that everyone was getting a divorce, that it was rampant, "contagious," and an epidemic. But even though it was detested and "condemned in the abstract," there was little disapproval of those who did divorce. People believed both that people should try harder to save their marriages, *and* they should not stay in unhappy ones. Committed as they were to marriage, they accepted divorce as a necessary remedy for people in a "sincerely unsatisfactory marriage" (Caplow, and others, 1982, pp. 49, 55, 129–133).

In the late 1970s, Muncie residents also thought of divorce as a woman's rescue from misery, as "part of a bundle of women's rights associated with economic independence." Residents told the authors: "Women don't have to put up with their [husbands'] crap—they can support themselves. They are free to end an unhappy marriage." "A lot of it has to do with the freedom women are gaining. Now a woman has rights. A woman is a person, not a chattel" (Caplow, and others, 1982, p. 131).

Let us close our discussion of divorce in Muncie by looking at statistics from 1920 to 1975. In 1920, the divorce/marriage ratio was 0.33 in Muncie and 0.13 in the United States. In 1930, it was 0.47 for Muncie and 0.17 for the United States,; in 1950, 0.34 and 0.23; and in 1975, 0.51 and 0.48 (Lynd and Lynd, 1937, pp. 544–545; Caplow and others, 1982, p. 348; *Statistical Abstract,* 1987, p. 58).

Statistics on Divorce

Divorces are difficult to count. In the past, many people left their marriages without ever divorcing their spouses. Even today, when most people who end their marriages do go to court, divorces are still difficult to count. (Of course, some people live apart from their spouses while they remain formally married to them. I have seen no figures on such marriages.)

Following People over Their Lifetime. Of couples who marry for the first time in any given year, 2003 for example, we could ask:

1. How many will stay married to each other for their entire lives?
2. How many will divorce?
3. How many will remarry?
4. How many who remarry will divorce again?
5. How many people who marry for the first time will marry a divorced person?

We could raise these and many other related questions. Based on recent experience, we may even offer some estimates. But we can never know the actual answers until all the people who first married in 2003 have died (and even this assumes accurate counting). The statements you may read that 40, 50, or 60 percent of marriages end (or, will end) in divorce are not actual statistics; they are statements of probability based on the following methods of counting divorce. It would be enormously expensive and time-consuming to count divorces by following people over their lifetimes, and so far as I know no one has done it on any large scale.

Divorce/Marriage Ratio. People who say that about half of U.S. marriages end in divorce most commonly cite this ratio. It simply divides the number of divorces granted during a year by the number of marriages that took place in that same year.

It has been the one divorce per two marriages since 1980 that people use to conclude that fifty percent of marriages end in divorce. (See table 12.1.) There are some serious problems

Table 12.1 U.S. divorces and marriages, in thousands and ratio, 1910–1998

	Divorces	Marriages	D/M ratio
1910	83	948	0.09
1930	196	1,127	0.17
1950	385	1,667	0.23
1970	798	2,159	0.37
1980	1,189	2,390	0.50
1990	1,182	2,443	0.48
1998*	1,135	2,256	0.50

Sources: Statistical Abstract, 1987, p. 58; 2002, p. 59
*For 1998, California, Colorado, Indiana, and Louisiana are not included.

with this measure, however. When the population is mostly young, there are more people eligible to marry and fewer people eligible to divorce, and the rate may be lower. When the reverse is true, with more older people eligible to divorce, the rate will be higher. Thus, if the number of divorces remains constant but the number of marriages decreases for various reasons, the *ratio* increases even as the *number* of divorces stays the same. The reverse can also happen.

In addition, the rate counts *marriages,* not *individuals* and their marital history. In any given year, many people marry for the second, third, or even fourth time, and many others get their second, third, or more divorce. (Some people do both in the same year.) Thus, these numbers do not tell us how many people remain married to one person all their lives, with their spouses also being married to them only. Nor do they tell us how many people will divorce one or more times.

Divorces per Thousand Married Women 15 Years and Older. Many sociologists consider this the best measurement of divorce. It focuses only on those who are eligible to marry or divorce in any given year.

1900	4
1920	8
1940	10
1960	10
1970	14.9
1980	22.6
1990	20.9
1998	19.5

(*Statistical Abstract,* 1999, p. 110; Cherlin, 2002, p. 420; Caplow, Hicks, and Wattenberg, 2001, p. 79)

But it, like all other measures, cannot predict what will happen in the future; people may change their behavior, as they have in the past. For example, looking at the doubling of this ratio between 1960 and 1980, we might have predicted a continuing rise in the rate of divorce, but we see that the ratio in 1998 was lower than in 1980.

Twenty per 1,000 means 2 percent, and that seems a low rate. But each year a married woman has another 2 percent chance of divorce, and over her lifetime that may add to 40–60 percent, depending on how long she lives and on social changes that may encourage or discourage divorce. For example, if women find it more difficult to find jobs, fewer of them may leave unhappy marriages.

Divorces per Thousand People. The number of divorces and the population have been counted since at least 1860, and this measure gives us a historical perspective. But it cannot account for changes in population over time, and it includes children, unmarried people, divorced people, and so on.

1860	.3
1900	.7
1940	2.0
1960	2.2
1980	5.2
1990	4.7
2001	4.0

(Ahrons, 1994, p. 366; *Statistical Abstract,* 1999, p. 110; 2002, p. 59)

Race and Divorce. Since in the past enslaved African Americans could not marry legally, neither could they divorce legally, so we have few historical statistics on them. After slavery, discrimination continued to keep many African Americans away from legal marriages and divorces (Riley, 1991).

Recent statistics indicate that African Americans have higher divorce rates than whites. For example, in 1990, 8.1 percent of whites, 10.6 percent of African Americans, and 7 percent of Latinos were divorced. For 2000, Henslin estimated these figures at 10 percent for whites, 12 percent for African Americans, and 7.8 percent for Latinos (Henslin, 2002, p. 321; Benokraitis, 2002, p. 307; Cose, 2003).

Divorce around the World. Contrary to frequent statements that divorce is uniquely American ("the American disease," as a cousin calls it), it is common and increasing throughout most of the world, especially in industrial societies. We saw previously that it is rising in Japan, having doubled from 1968 to 1998, from .87 to 1.66 divorces per thousand people (Moshavi, 2000). (This compares to 4.2 per thousand people in the United States in 1998.)

The following ratio of divorces to marriages existed in various countries.

Sweden	.64
Britain	.53
United States	.49
Canada	.45
Germany	.41
Greece	.18
Italy	.12

The source for these numbers (Kirn, 2000, p. 76) does not cite the years to which they refer. They probably are from the 1990s.

Conclusion. Whatever statistics we examine, they seem to point to two obvious conclusions: (1) Divorce has been rising steadily since 1860, and even earlier. (2) After doubling from 1960 to 1980, divorce has stabilized, even decreased somewhat, since 1980. And divorce numbers from the past do not include the marriages that had ended but couples had not divorced formally. And for our times, people who end cohabiting relationships, especially long-term ones, are also uncounted in divorce statistics. (For discussions on divorce statistics, see Kain, 1990, pp. 69–73; Sernau, 1997, pp. 165–167.)

EXPERIENCES, ATTITUDES, AND LAWS OF DIVORCE

Experiences

Discussions of divorce in my classes typically begin with student comments that people in the United States resort to divorce too easily and quickly. They reflect a belief held by Americans for centuries, as we saw previously in the historical overview. Many people today think that divorce is a casual, careless, simple, and easy undertaking. It may be for some people. But everything I have read and experienced tells me that it is a difficult, painful, confusing, and profoundly changing experience. In time, it can also become a growing and positive stage in our lives. Certainly, people debate, discuss, and consider it for years before they resort to it. It changes one's life permanently.

Hetherington, who studied "nearly 1,400 families and over 2,500 children, many followed for more than three decades," writes that "the end of marriage is usually brutally painful." But she also insists that 75–80 percent of those involved in time lead normal and happy lives. Some are happy from the beginning of the divorce, others take some years to recover from the pain, and some are lost and defeated for years (Hetherington and Kelly, 2002, pp. 10, 6–7).

Deciding to Divorce. Sometimes a couple arrives at that decision together, but usually one partner does first and then either tries to convince the other, or simply announces her or his decision to the other partner. In *Uncoupling: How Relationships Come Apart,* Diane Vaughan describes and discusses the process. Long before the physical separation, couples begin separating socially, "developing separate friends, experiences, and futures" (1986, p. xv).

"Uncoupling begins with a secret. One of the partners starts to feel uncomfortable in the relationship." We have made no decision to divorce, and our thoughts may be unarticulated. But "we walk around harboring and mulling over the secrets of our unhappiness." We may begin to complain openly to our partner, hoping to change him or her. In time, the complaints may be to convince the partner that the relationship cannot be saved and divorce is inevitable. We may then begin the transition to a new life. For example, many people read books on how to divorce and how to manage after divorce. We also need to start seeing ourselves as single again. People are often surprised when their partner leaves or announces the decision to leave. Over the years, couples "evolve a system of communication that suppresses rather than reveals information." "Concerted ignorance" develops (Vaughan, 1986, pp. 3, 6, 87–88).

The cover-up, to ourselves and our partner, eventually ends. Then begin open and usually angry discussions of the condition of the relationship and one partner's wish to end it. There may be attempts to save the relationship, including joint counseling. But usually there is no solution, and soon the couple separates. Thus begins a new life for both partners (and in 60 percent of divorces, for the children too).

Initial Problems. After the decision to divorce, made jointly or by one partner, they face a long list of practical decisions. "Who will move out of the marital residence? Will it need to be sold, and if so, how soon? . . . If the wife has not been employed outside the home during the marriage, from what sources will she derive financial support after the marriage is dissolved? If there are children, who will have primary responsibility for their care? What will be the division of financial responsibility for them?" (Schwartz and Kaslow, 1997, p. 28).

Divorce and Stress. In his review of the research literature of the 1980s and 1990s, Amato concluded "the divorced are worse off than the married in multiple ways." That includes health, standard of living, happiness, and more. One study concluded that divorced people in Britain had an "188% increase in the odds of depression." Acute illness, heart disease, suicide attempts, and alcoholism are more common among the divorced (Amato, 2000; see also Price and McKenry, 1988, pp. 59–60).

But some researchers argue that these differences between divorced and married people are relatively small. Also, as Amato says, researchers might find more positive consequences of divorce if only they looked for them (Amato, 2000; Hetherington and Kelly, 2002).

Stories of Divorce. Patchett begins the story of her divorce by revealing that divorce was on her mind even as she was getting ready for her wedding. "People ask me, if you knew it wasn't working, why did you marry him? And all I can say is, I didn't know how not to. I believed I was in too deep before the invitations were ever mailed, before the engagement. Maybe it was inexperience or maybe I was stupid. The relationship had a momentum that was taking us to this place, and I couldn't figure out how to stop it" (1995, p. 90).

A year after the wedding, she summoned up the strength to divorce. Many people were helpful and sympathetic, and she found a new job and a new apartment. But it was still a tough and distressing experience. "Sometimes I would spend half the morning in the shower because I couldn't remember if I'd already shampooed my hair and so I would wash it again and again. I would get so lost on the way to work some days that I had to pull the car over to the side of the road and take the map out of the glove compartment. I worked four miles from my house. When I woke up at 3:00 a.m., as I did every morning, I never once knew where I was" (Patchett, 1995, p. 90).

She read the people who complained that divorce had "become too easy. Waltz in, waltz out. Waltz in, maybe. . . . [Divorce is] grueling. I have never known anyone who went into marriage planning to get out, and I have never known anyone who got out simply. To leave you have to involve the courts. You have to sue the person you live with for your freedom. You have to disconnect your life from a life and face the sea alone. Never easy, blithe. Never" (Patchett, 1995, p. 98).

In 1992, I heard the stories of sixty-one divorced fathers. For many of them, the divorce became an opportunity to get closer to their children, to become parents for the first time. But "while noting the opportunities divorce provided, they were also sharply aware of the awful pain of divorce. For Robert Austin, divorce was 'probably a way to examine some of the issues you have carried through life,' but it was not an experience 'I would suggest to my worst enemy.' Quincy Waters was more graphic: 'I'd rather have gangrene'" (Liazos, 1997, p. 373). (Sherwood, 1997, and Taylor, 1997, each wrote a story of their divorce from each other.)

Relationships with Former Spouses. Especially when divorced people have children with former spouses, they will need to relate to each other. As we were ending our talk in 1992, one of the fathers told me, "it never ends."

Relationships vary from very friendly and cooperative to furious and fiery. In the mid-1980s, Ahrons studied ninety-eight couples and described four types of relationships. Twelve percent were Perfect Pals. They "enjoyed each other's company and tended to stay involved in each other's lives, phoning to share exciting news, for example." Thirty-eight percent were Cooperative Colleagues. Not as friendly as Perfect Pals, they still "managed to minimize potential conflicts, to have a moderate amount of interaction and to be mutually supportive of each other." Twenty-five percent were Angry Associates. Their "interactions were fraught with conflict. This groups was unable to untangle spousal and parental issues, thus setting the scene for fighting when they dealt with each other." Finally, 24 percent were Fiery Foes. They had little contact but fought bitterly when they did, and they "did not cooperate at all in parenting." The percentages and the types may not represent all divorced couples, but they indicate the great variety of post-divorce relationships (Stark, 1986, p. 55).

In Stacey's *Brave New Families,* Pam and Don divorced but stayed friends, partly for the benefit of their three children. Indeed, he was the photographer for her second wedding. Pam and Shirley (Don's new partner) became friends and together orchestrated gatherings of the four of them and the three children, found jobs and apartments for the children, and cooperated in other ways (Stacey, 1990).

A Reflection. Beyond the statistics and debates, beyond the accusations and justifications, divorce remains a painful, troublesome, and transforming experience. It is never easy. It becomes part of you identity and memory. And for many women and men, it is also an opportunity to expand and remake their lives. (See Hetherington and Kelly, 2002.)

Beliefs and Culture

Americans continue to hold ambivalent views and beliefs about divorce. We think people should strive harder to save their marriages; we argue that people turn to divorce too quickly; we fear that divorce harms the children and the community; but we also believe people should not stay in unhappy marriages, and we sympathize with friends and relatives who end their marriages.

In the divorce seminar I taught in the 1990s, every student interviewed two divorced people and reported to the class. In almost all cases, they said they understood the actions of and sympathized with those people. But at the beginning of the semester most students were convinced that people resort to divorce hastily. People worry about the high rate of divorce and "insist on the sanctity of the family," but they don't want their child to stay in "an obviously bad marriage—one where a spouse is abusive, an alcoholic, or a drug abuser, for example" (Rubin, 1994, p. 63).

What Americans Say about Divorce. A poll taken in 2000 exemplifies this ambivalence. When asked by phone, most of the 1,278 adult Americans said that divorce hurts children. To the question, "When parents get divorced, are children harmed?" they replied:

Almost always	42%
Frequently	22%
Sometimes	27%
Seldom	8%

(Kirn, 2000, p. 77)

But answers to two other questions show that most people do not disapprove of divorce. When asked if parents should stay in an unhappy marriage for the children's sake, 66 percent said not and 33 percent yes. Responses to another question show similar views. Sixty-six percent thought children are better off in "a divorce in which the parents are more happy," whereas 23 percent believed children are better of in "an unhappy marriage in which parents stay together mainly for the kids." Eleven percent were not sure (Kirn, 2000).

A review of five surveys in the 1980s and 1990s showed that most people in the United States approve of divorce, even when there are children (Thornton and Young-DeMarco, 2001, p. 119).

A Divorce Culture? Some writers maintain that we live in a "divorce culture," where divorce is almost an expectation.

> If you get the idea from the media, your therapist, or friends that staying in an unsatisfying marriage makes you a coward, or worse, a bad role model for your kids, you will have an even harder time believing that staying married makes sense. . . .
>
> The divorce culture thus sets in motion changes that affect even those spouses who don't split up. When people perceive their own divorce risk as high, they become afraid to invest in their own marriage; they hedge their bets, financially and emotionally. They think and act more like singles than spouses who have confidence in the institution of marriage. Divorce anxiety not only produces divorce, but it creates less happiness in marriage, even in those unions that do survive. Marriage can become just a piece of paper if you are always wondering in the back of your mind whether or not your partner might walk. (Waite and Gallagher, 2000, pp. 181, 184–185)

But the existence of divorce may instead, or, also, improve and save marriages. In "Wives' marital work in a culture of divorce," Hackstaff argues that some women use the threat of divorce to create egalitarian marriages and stay in them, instead of divorcing. (Hackstaff interviewed thirty-four spouses.) Women want to share marital work, and they threaten divorce if men do not. To make that threat credible "requires them to have financial independence, egalitarian ideals, and accessible divorce" (1998, p. 463). Hackstaff found that twenty-eight of the thirty-four spouses talked about "the need to work on marriage," that "spouses are 'working harder today'" to make marriages succeed (1998, pp. 462–463).

Stigma or Acceptance? The surveys I cited above show that divorce has been socially acceptable for some decades. Another sign of acceptance is the divorced people who commonly are elected to public office, when not long ago a divorce ended political aspirations. But Gerstel argued that in 1987 there was still some disapproval of divorced people. The divorced people she interviewed believed they were censured for their "misdeeds." They said they were excluded from social gatherings and people often avoided them (Gerstel, 1987).

Divorce Myths Ahrons believes we still hold many mistaken beliefs about divorce: (1) The rise of divorce means we do not value marriage. But almost everyone still marries, and there are signs that people are working harder to make good marriages. (2) "Divorce is a modern affliction." The history of divorce shows otherwise. (3) "Strict laws curb divorce." We'll see that this is not so. (4) "The longer your marriage lasts, the better it is." In fact, many couples stay in unhappy or miserable marriages. (5) Cohabitation makes divorce less likely. We saw in chapter 4 that it does not (Ahrons, 1994).

The Debate over No-Fault Divorce

We saw that over time legislatures have expanded the grounds for divorce. Abuse, desertion, and cruelty have almost always been reasons for ending marriages, as have adultery, alcoholism, and other actions. Also, even in the nineteenth century some laws essentially allowed people to end their unions because they were unhappy together—what we now call no-fault divorce. But always, until 1970, in every state one spouse was obligated to sue and blame (find fault with) the other.

No-fault was enacted in all states between 1970 and 1985. To some people, it brought sanity to divorce proceedings. People no longer needed to argue over or manufacture "faults." Honestly prevailed. Others, however, think it has been a disaster, especially for women. They argue that no-fault divorce gives people complete freedom to leave marriages. They need not discuss it with their spouses, they can leave simply because they are "unhappy." One writer called it "unchecked unilateral divorce." Opponents of no-fault fear that it has made it easier and more likely for people to leave their marriages. They think law can change behavior. If we make divorce easier, more people will turn to it. If we make it more difficult, we will send a message that we discourage divorce. Galston argues that in the same way laws against racial discrimination have over time changed "underlying racial attitudes," so will laws making divorce more difficult change attitudes about divorce (Galston, 2000, pp. 182–183).

In addition, opponents argue that under no-fault, women, fearing divorce may happen to them, must think of protecting themselves in case their husbands leave. Thus, they are more likely to pursue a career and job. They cannot choose what might be most beneficial for the entire family—mother, father, and children. They need to consider their own individual future. These critics state or imply that women would be more likely to stay home and care for the children and house if they were not so shaken by the fear of divorce (Parkman, 2000; Galston, 2000; Waite and Gallagher, 2000).

They ignore the history of divorce. Women, more than men, have seen divorce as a necessary escape from abusive and miserable marriages. Since the late 1700s, women have petitioned for 65–70 percent of divorces. If making divorce more difficult to obtain is meant to protect women from husbands who cavalierly leave them behind and deprive them of financial security, it cannot do so for most of them when mostly women leave marriages.

Has no-fault led to more divorces? Even Parkman, a dedicated opponent of present n fault laws, admits that divorce began its steep rise before no-fault appeared in California 1970, and later in other states. One of the steepest increases took place during the 196C Other decades, all before no-fault, show similar sharp increases in divorce. Parkman st thinks that no-fault had a "feedback effect." Others think it is at least "a factor affectir divorce" (Parkman, 2000, p. 93; Strong, and others, 2001, p. 511).

Parkman reviews studies that have asked whether the divorce rate has increased b cause of no-fault. Some conclude that it has not, others that it has. One study "determined th divorce rates would have been about 6 percent lower if states had not adopted no-fau divorce." Parkman concludes: "The more recent evidence lends some support to the arg ments that no-fault divorce has increased the divorce rate above the level than it otherwi would have reached" (2000, p. 99).

Ellman does not agree. "The divorce rate was 2.1 per 1,000 people in 1958, grew to 2 by 1968, and peaked at 5.3 in 1979. That is, the divorce rate began climbing more than decade before the no-fault movement began and peaked at about the time no-fault w adopted nationwide. Since then it declined, first to 5.0, where it held steady through 1986, ar more recently to 4.5 per 1,000—15 percent lower than in 1981. . . . A recent review conclud that the 'consensus among researchers and informed commentators' is that 'divorce law r forms had little or nothing to do' with the rising divorce rates of the 1960s and 1970s" (Ellma 2000, p. 192; see also endnote 23 on pp. 210–211 for a review and discussion of evidence c the effects of no-fault divorce).

In short, the divorce rate began to increase decades and centuries before no-fault a peared, and peaked just before and as most states enacted the law. And the rate stabilized ar even decreased during the 1980s and 1990s when no-fault was here.

Critics of no-fault propose a variety of changes in the law, which they think and hor will save some marriages from divorce. Galston thinks "unilateral" divorce should end; or spouse alone should not be allowed to end a marriage by arguing that the marriage h broken down. It should not be that "one spouse alone can decide unilaterally to get a divor without the consent or agreement of the other spouse." No-fault divorce—where neith spouse is accusing the other of misconduct—should be only by mutual consent (Weitzma 1985, p. 16; see also Galston, 2000, p. 185).

Parkman also opposes no-fault divorce without mutual consent. He would allow cu rent no-fault without mutual consent early in a marriage because at that point "a couple is st involved in an evaluation process" (he does not define "early"), but after that only mutu consent would suffice for no-fault divorce. Even under mutual consent, he would recommer counseling and a longer waiting period if there are children. And fault divorce should st exist to allow spouses to escape abusive marriages, for example (Parkman, 2000, pp. 18 192).

Louisiana (1997) and Arizona (1998) have changed their laws to make divorce mo difficult. Louisiana's "covenant marriage act" "gives couples planning on marrying in that sta a choice between two options: a standard marriage with the potential for a no-fault divor and a covenant marriage, which requires counseling before marriage and then only perm divorce based on fault grounds or on a lengthy separation. It would seem that couples ha not found covenant marriage to be an attractive alternative to no-fault, because only or percent of Louisiana newlyweds have chosen it" (Parkman, 2000, p. 10).

A common element of proposed divorce law reforms is a longer waiting period befo divorce is granted. Those proposing this change hope that if people are forced to wait long before they part, at least some will reconsider and stay in their marriages. Ellman doub longer waiting periods would save any marriages. At best, they would only postpone t inevitable, and would force couples to separate without divorce (as millions did in the pas Indeed, when couples truly want to end their marriage, longer waiting periods would on prevent them from starting their new lives. If we have shorter waiting periods for fault divorces and longer ones for no-fault divorces, we will only encourage couples to resort to the historical practice of manufacturing faults so they can end their marriages sooner. (See Ellman, 2000.)

WOMEN, MEN, AND DIVORCE

Historically, women have asked for 65–70 percent of divorces. In addition, many people have seen divorce as women's escape from abusive and destructive marriages. More recently, there has been an often-angry debate on whether divorce settlements and custody decisions for children favor women or men. Clearly, divorce is a gender issue.

Women's Experiences

When mothers divorce, they receive custody of the children in about 90 percent of the cases. Unless and until they remarry, they usually need to support themselves and their children at least partially, and start a new life as single parents. They face economic, parental, and social challenges.

In *Mothers and Divorce,* Arendell explored the lives of sixty middle-class divorced mothers in California. Their major problem was a sharp economic decline. Time, for themselves and with their children, was another struggle. Also, "in contrast to their expectations, most of these sixty women struggled for years to attain a satisfactory personal and social identity." One woman said: "What we're struggling with is who we are as women, aside from being mommy and wife or ex-wife. We don't know how to feel—or who we are—separate from these roles, or how to get that sense of self. I've been working a lot on who I am as a person, and it's just recently that I've even begun to think of myself as a potential mate" (1986, pp. 128–129).

Three-fourths of the women told Arendell that they had lost former friends. And forming new relationships with men was difficult for most of them, partly because they had children. But despite the harsh conditions of their lives, they concluded that their divorce had enabled them to find a life they preferred. "Keeping their families going, surviving economically and emotionally, had become a fundamental measure of success." The present looked good compared to "the unhappiness of the last months of marriage [and] the emotional chaos and identity crisis of the first months after divorce" (1986, pp. 148–149).

Men's Experiences

Nine years later, in *Fathers and Divorce,* Arendell wrote about the lives of seventy-five divorced fathers in New York State. She concluded that for sixty-six of them three themes dominated the stories they told her: "a rhetoric of rights and victimization, a belief in sex differences and male superiority, and a definition of the after-divorce family as a broken family." They "perceived themselves to be victimized and their rights were violated by the divorce. . . . [D]ivorce was understood as a battle—a 'war between the sexes,' in general, and with the former wife, in particular." In addition, "many men were inarticulate about their children. And much of what they did have to say about their offspring and their parental relationships was negative and conveyed detachment and disenchantment" (1995, pp. 45, 14, 142).

Two papers I wrote discuss my interviews with sixty-one divorced fathers (I should note that these sixty-one men, and the women and men Arendell interviewed, were not representative samples, were not necessarily typical of most divorced women and men of their times.) Most men changed after their divorce. Their gender shaped their lives before and after divorce. The control and even denial of emotions and feelings guided the divorces as it had their marriages. In the interviews they referred to pain, loneliness, and missing their children, but except for their children, they said relatively little about these issues. Nor does it seem that they explored their feelings while they experienced them. Thus we can begin to understand the data that show divorced men suffer much greater rates of illness than do divorced women. Left unspoken and unexplored, the sadness and pain and loneliness go underground.

Yet it is no contradiction to argue that divorce also became an opportunity for many, even most, of these men to begin changing their gender socialization. In time, most of them understood divorce as a moment to explore and to get in touch with their lives and histories, to be closer to their children, to pay attention to relationships and become better partners to new women. George Caldwell, the former macho military man who came to enjoy baking pies and who said his priority in life was his daughters, is a dramatic, but not unusual example of this change.

In *Divorce Talk: Women and Men Make Sense of Personal Relationships,* Riessman shows a clear difference in how women and men understood and talked about their divorces. Men hid their sadness; many appeared to feel no pain. In his story, Rick made no "reference to feeling hurt. Until the very end, there are no statements about loss, about missing the attachment of a spouse, or the routines of marriage." A common refrain is "'It's too hard to talk about or say a lot about.' For many men, emotions are hard to put into words" (1990, pp. 154, 156).

The men I talked with were also generally reluctant to say much about their emotions. They did refer to and talk about them, but most did so briefly and without showing much emotion as we talked, despite the many opportunities I offered them to do so. Only those very recently divorced, who missed their children or who were angry at their wives or the courts, showed sadness and some anger. They talked about the parenting arrangements, the new friends they made, the new women in their lives, and much else, but not about their emotions. In contrast, "Women have extensive vocabularies for conveying the experience of emotional distress. Unlike men . . . they have no difficulty talking about it at length (Riessman, 1990, p. 126).

Custody of Children

Many men, especially those in some men's groups, bitterly complain that courts usually favor women in awarding custody of the children. It may be that in some cases where divorced fathers were as good parents as, or even better than, the mothers, the courts did not give them fair consideration in awarding custody. But women receive custody most of the time *after* divorce because women still do most child care and housework *before* divorce (as we saw in the last chapter). Until most men share family work equally *while married,* they cannot fairly expect equal consideration for custody *at* divorce. The few men who do share cannot atone for most men's child-care omissions.

Economic Issues

Some people in the United States are poor and destitute, a very few are wealthy, but most are not affluent. Thus, when you divide into two households the income, property, and possessions that had been just adequate in one home, problems are inevitable. That is the major economic problem most separating couples face. It is only a few divorcing couples who fight over the division of considerable economic assets.

There are two major controversies in this area: (1) What does count as property? What is to be divided? (2) Are women or men (or both) the losers in this division?

Traditionally, a house, a car, and a bank account were the major material assets to be divided. Now (but only for some couples) "there are retirement benefits, stock benefits, non-cash compensation elements, deferred compensation." In short, there are *present holdings* and *future assets* (an attorney cited in Matchan, 1998, p. D5; for lists of each type, see Schwartz and Kaslow, 1997, pp. 103–104).

An example cited by many writers is the woman who works as a secretary to help put her husband through professional school (such as medical school), then leaves her job to raise their children as he begins his practice. Ten years later he leaves her and their two children for another woman. At one time, this couple would divide their present possessions and there the matter would end. But Weitzman (1985) and others have been arguing that when the marriage ends she should continue to receive part of his income, since she invested in his career by putting him through school and by staying home to raise their children. (I do not know how much court rulings have been following that logic; I do know that such cases are limited to upper-middle-class couples, and these days few women stay home as full-time housewives. Also, remember that women ask for most divorces.)

Whatever the division of material assets after divorce, divorced mothers' incomes rarely suffice to keep them in the same economic condition they enjoyed before divorce. To repeat, dividing the same income and possessions into two households automatically lowers the standard of living for everyone.

The controversy, however, has been over *how much women lose* and *how much men gain* economically after divorce. Weitzman began the debate when she wrote: "[W]hen income is compared to needs, divorced men experience an average 42 percent rise in their standard of living in the first year after the divorce, while divorced women (and their children) experience a 73 percent decline" Her study was based on "approximately 2,500 divorce cases drawn from court records between 1968 and 1977" in California (1985, pp. 323, xix).

The 42 percent and 73 percent figures were widely cited for years. After considerable debate among many people, even Weitzman agreed that her calculations were wrong. Today, the more commonly accepted calculations show that women's economic status falls 25–30 percent, and men's rises 10–15 percent, in the first year after divorce. (I have not seen studies of what happens five, ten, and more years after divorce.) But Braver, after taking into account taxes and tax exemptions for each person, visitation expenses by the father, health insurance costs paid by fathers, the expenses of setting up a new household, and other expenses, concluded that men were only 2 percent better off after divorce and women were only 1 percent worse off (Parkman, 2000, ch. 5; Galston, 2000, p. 180; Braver, 1998, ch. 4).

Hetherington concluded from her 30-year study that both women and men lose, "with the woman's economic resources declining by 30 percent and the man's 10 percent," adding that the gap is closing. A review of research published in the 1990s concluded that divorced women are "economically disadvantaged compared to divorced men or married women" (Hetherington and Kelly, 2002, p. 9; Amato, 2000, p. 1277).

I think that for some years after divorce, everyone's standard of living is reduced. In time, depending on whether they remarry, stay in the same job or get one with higher pay, and many other considerations, divorced people may live as well as they did before divorce, or even better. Generally, "the economic impact of divorce varies with the age of the parties, length of marriage, education, occupation, employment history, geographic locale, and socio-economic class" (Schwartz and Kaslow, 1997, p. 106).

WHY *DO* PEOPLE DIVORCE?

We have seen that people have given a wide variety of reasons, explanations, justifications, and rationales for ending their marriages. Sociologists, historians, and other writers have proposed their own explanations. Thousands of books and papers have been written on the causes of divorce, and more will be written.

Some Preliminary Observations

If you ask people why they divorced, they will offer specific and concrete accounts. For example, some women think that they changed and their husbands did not. Mundurucu men and women said they left their spouses because their husbands were lazy or had adulterous affairs. In various surveys through the years, people accused their spouses of drinking, adultery, physical and mental cruelty, sexual problems, non-support, desertion, in-law troubles, not sharing housework, financial problems, immaturity, untrustworthiness, incompatibility, unwillingness to communicate, growing apart, and many other sins of commission and omission. In 1987–1988, 129 mothers in the Philadelphia area said they had left their marriages because of "personal dissatisfaction," violence, heavy drinking, frequent absences from home, or "feelings of rejection and emotional pain" when they learned their husbands had been involved with other women (Price and McKenry, 1988, pp. 31–34; Kurz, 1995).

Few people, however, mention the social conditions and social changes that historians and sociologists offer as explanations. No one says, "I expected more out of marriage than people did in the nineteenth century," or, "we women are more able to support ourselves and are less likely to stay in unhappy marriages than our foremothers did." Many of the specific complaints people cite—adultery, cruelty, lack of communication, and non-support, for example—have existed in many American marriages since Colonial days. They were unlikely to lead women to divorce in the past, however. Marital expectations were different and women could not support themselves, so they stayed in the marriages of the same quality that many people now leave.

The divorce tales people tell, and the sociological explanations we offer, may differ from one society to another, from one historical period to another, and between regions in one society. Also, the real reasons people have and those sociologists propose may differ from the grounds that laws allow (as we have seen).

The Rise in Divorce

Some accounts and explanations for divorce are found in most times and places: adultery, cruelty, arguing and bickering, laziness, among others. Divorce is not unique to our time. It was and has been common in all societies outside peasant patriarchal ones. In U.S. history, the following gradual social changes have raised the divorce rate to its present levels. Similar social changes have created similar increases in other industrial societies.

Different Expectations of Marriage. Supporters and critics of divorce, and most sociologists and historians, agree that as the Colonial era ended and industrialization emerged in the United States women and men gradually began wanting and expecting more out of their marriages. *Great Expectations: Marriage and Divorce in Post-Victorian America* (May, 1980), *Divorce: An American Tradition* (Riley, 1991), and *The Divorce Culture* (Whitehead, 1997), among others, show that men and women were looking for happiness, communication, sexual pleasure, and personal growth in their marital relationships.

Because the expectations are high, intense, and important, people cannot stay in marriages they feel are empty and meaningless. Adultery and mental cruelty may be tolerated when the couple is an economic team in a small community, where each can find friendships and support in extended family and friends. They become less tolerable in the more isolated nuclear family; empty and meaningless marriages are more painful and impossible to maintain there.

This is the family shown in chapter 2, taken just before the wedding of the oldest daughter. At the time of this photo, the parents have been divorced for a year, yet just after this photo was taken they walked their daughter down the aisle together for her wedding. Despite the divorce, all enjoyed the celebration together.

Women's Growing Economic Independence. Fusako, the 54-year-old Japanese wife, decided to leave her husband. Thirty years of an unhappy marriage finally took their toll and she ran away from home. Unable to find a job to support herself, however, she returned to her marriage. Her search and failure summarize and symbolize U.S. and worldwide changes in women's lives. Japanese wives are becoming better educated and more independent, and they want "more personal happiness and fulfillment from their marriages" (Moshavi, 2000, p. A11).

Studies have shown that economically independent women are more likely to divorce. Fusako had no means to support herself. Neither did women in the nineteenth and most of the twentieth centuries. "Probably the main reason divorce rates have risen is that fewer women are economically trapped in the hell of a mutually exploitative marriage." In the past, "women had little choice but to remain with their husbands, no matter how ornery, obnoxious, overbearing, or cruel these men might be. Burdened with an exploitative man, a wife might threaten, cajole, argue, and run away occasionally, but fundamentally she was trapped" (Westhues, 1982, pp. 362–363).

I do not mean to diminish the economic problems women face today. Many are pushed down to poverty by divorce. But because they can find work, and because wages have risen, women who divorce now no longer face economic destitution. For example, whereas full-time working women averaged 60 percent of what full-time men earned in the 1950s, the average had risen to 76 percent by 2001. Women are able, and thus more likely, to escape miserable, abusive, cruel, and dangerous marriages. Changing gender roles require new reactions to unequal marriages.

Growing Social Acceptance of Divorce. Surveys, studies, and our experiences all show that divorce has steadily become more acceptable. People still find it regrettable, but they also see it as necessary, especially for friends and relatives enmeshed in unhappy and miserable marriages. This acceptance reflects the changes discussed in (1) and (2) here. No-fault divorce, a sign of the acceptance, arose because the law could not deny the social changes and the actions of millions of people.

Changing Society. Looking at U.S. and Western history over the past century and a half, Westhues concludes that divorce has also increased because couples engage in fewer common activities and have fewer common interests. He cites four specific changes: (1) Unlike farm families, modern couples rarely work together. Thus, they have fewer common bonds and experiences. (2) Many couples do not share common ethnic, religious, and social class backgrounds. (3) "Shared parental involvement" in raising children has declined. (4) The more years a couple spends together in common activity and in building a "common past" seems to decrease the chance of divorce. Sex and romance, he claims, do not suffice to create a long-lasting relationship (Westhues, 1982).

These changing conditions and values interact, they influence and are influenced by the others. Together, they have shaped how we think about marriage and divorce, and have made divorce a U.S. tradition and common experience. For us, as for the Native Americans before us, divorce is the mark of a free people who see no sense in staying in wretched and oppressive marriages. To undo divorce is to return to 1800. Would most of us want that? Even if we would, *could* we?

Other Conditions That May Contribute to Divorce

Housework. Hochschild thinks that husbands' unwillingness to share housework is a major cause of many divorces. "Men's resistance to sharing [housework] is by no means the only cause of divorce, but it is often an unacknowledged source of tension which underlies the others." In a 1966 study of 600 divorcing couples, "the second most common reason women cited for wanting divorce—after 'mental cruelty'—was 'neglect of home or children'" (1989, pp. 213–215).

And conversely, some women who saw other marriages break up over the husbands' refusal to share housework, decided to stop their struggles to convince their husbands to share. Fear of divorce forced them to stay in unequal marriages (1989, pp. 42–43, 86, 88).

Cohabitation. Some writers have argued that people who cohabit are more likely to divorce. In chapter 4, I reviewed the evidence presented for this claim and concluded it does not support such a conclusion. For example, the cohabitation rate has tripled from 1980 to 2000, while the divorce rate has remained stable and even declined somewhat during that same period.

Other Factors. Writers have discussed many other social conditions that may contribute to divorce: age (the younger the age at marriage, the higher the divorce rate); income; education; race; religion; remarriage; presence of children; and others. For example, "when family income drops by 25 percent, divorce rises by more than 10 percent" (cited in Rubin, 1994, p. 121). Also, in the 1980s, people marrying for the second time had a 25 percent higher rate of divorce than those marrying for the first time (Strong, and others, 2001, p. 509).

An Ethic of "Obligation to Self"?

While acknowledging higher expectations in marriage, changing gender roles, and the other causes most sociologists propose, some writers point to another social change as the major cause of divorce. They argue that Americans have come to value and be preoccupied with their own individual happiness over the social good of their children, families, and communities.

These writers do not want to abolish divorce. They admit that some marriages should end, but only for extreme cruelty, violence, and abuse. "Divorce is necessary in a society that believes in the ideal of affectionate marriage, and particularly in a society that seeks to protect women from brutality and violence in marriage." They believe, however, that marriages where people are merely "unhappy," where there is low conflict, can and should be saved. These are "good enough" marriages. Waite and Gallagher cite some statistics and studies that convince them that most unhappy marriages can, in time, become happy ones (Whitehead, 1997, p. 188; Waite and Gallagher, 2000, p. 148).

Whitehead thinks that an ethic of "expressive individualism" arose. "Its governing principle was that one's first obligation in the dissolution of marriage was to oneself." In the past, when considering divorce, people had also weighed the interests of "the other spouse, the children, relatives, and the larger society." No more. But "the parental role carries the obligation to sacrifice one's own interests and defer or even limit satisfactions in pursuit of children's well-being, and this makes it a role that runs contrary to the expressive ethic" (1997, pp. 66, 154).

In short, Whitehead argues, we cannot have total freedom in our actions. What we do affects others. Just as we understand that driving a car affects other people and the environment, and we pass laws to regulate how and where we can drive, so with divorce. Our decision to leave a marriage affects many others, and it must be regulated (1997, p. 188).

Waite and Gallagher also find that valuing individual happiness above all else has led to more divorce. For example, in 1962, 51 percent of young mothers saw divorce as the best solution to unhappy marriages. When interviewed again in 1977, 80 percent of these same women gave that answer. In a mid-1990s survey, only 17 percent of Americans agreed with the statement that parents should not divorce "even if they don't get along" (2000, p. 176; see ch. 13 of their book for a discussion of their view).

Is it true that millions of Americans end their marriages for their own selfish ends and ignore the harm they cause others, especially their children?

First, this is a general claim, one many people make. But when they do, they tend to exclude from it their divorced friends and relatives. In those cases, they know the pain people experience, they know how long people agonize before they leave their marriages. Divorce is not a selfish decision people make lightly.

Second, it is true that in everything we do we need to balance obligations to the community, to family, and to ourselves. Most people in all societies, at all times, strive to achieve that balance. For too long, however, for many women there was a great imbalance in their lives. Their own needs were minimized, ignored, and sacrificed for others. They were asked to endure long days, to cook and clean for husbands and children, to stay in empty or oppressive marriages, and to pay no attention to their own lives, all for the good of others. The various stages of the women's movement, from 1848 on, have sought to redress this imbalance in women's lives. Divorce gradually became one means for some women to find balance.

Third, critics of divorce seem to "admire people who perversely settle down into what sound like mockeries of marriage, yoking themselves to spouses whom they have ceased to love or respect. For them, marriage is primarily a social institution, designed for the efficient rearing of children, and for the transmission of values. Marriage is these things, of course; but it is also, and fundamentally, a sacrament between two people. Surely something is lost in a vision of marriage that is so willing to make do with the mere appearance of love between its protagonists, that seems to set so much store by the preservation of norms and forms and so little store by the heart. Not the therapeutic heart. The human heart" (Talbot, 1997, pp. 63–64).

Fourth, it was a generation of parents, many of whom stayed in "good enough" marriages in the 1950s and earlier, whose children later produced the high divorce rates of the 1970s. These baby-boomer children grew up in "the child-centered unions of the 1950s, when parents, especially Mom, sacrificed themselves on the altar of family values and suburban respectability. To today's anti-divorcers those may seem like 'good enough' marriages—husband and wife rubbing along for the sake of the children. The kids who lived with the silence and contempt said no thank you" (Pollitt, 2000, p. 82).

CHILDREN AND DIVORCE

At the core of the divorce debate are the children. Some writers argue passionately that whereas divorce may be liberating for adults, it damages the children for the rest of their lives. Others respond that, after initial sadness and problems, the great majority of the children lead normal lives. Both sides, and others, agree that divorce is a major experience that shapes children's and adults' lives.

How do children experience divorce?

Facing Parental Separation

Sadness, confusion, loss, anger, and fear of the future are common to most children when their parents first separate. For some others, there may also be a relief that there is an end to the intense conflict and violence that plagued their parents' relationship. These and other emotions vary depending on the age of the children, how much they are told and understand about the breakup, the new living arrangements, and whether one or both parents remain in their lives.

A Book of Divorce for Children. Much has been written about how, what, and when to tell children about the divorce. Perhaps the best guide remains *The Kids' Book of Divorce: By, for, and about Kids.* The book was organized and written by children in their early teens, all of whose parents had divorced. In addition to using their own experiences, they also interviewed other kids, parents, teachers, psychologists, and others (Rofes, 1981).

They write of fear, anger, and insecurity when their parents fight. They describe their parents' decision to separate, and how they learned about it.

> [It] can come suddenly, gradually, or after long discussions. Paul [14, said] "When my parents and I were eating dinner one evening they told me about their decision. Right out of the blue they said they were getting separated and dad was moving out tomorrow. I was horrified, since I had seen no signs leading up to this, and I resented them strongly for hiding so much from me." . . .
> Eleven-year-old Sue explains, "About four months ago I noticed when my parents were together that they seemed sort of cold and mean towards each other. That made me feel awkward and sad. It kept getting worse and I would ask them what was wrong, and they would say 'Mommy and Daddy just aren't getting along right now, dear' and leave it at that. I knew what separation and divorce were when two months later they discussed it with me." (Rofes, 1981, pp. 19–20).

They have definite ideas about when and how children should be told. "We would have much more respect for parents and their actions if they told their kids about the divorce as soon as they knew, rather than days later. . . . If there are several kids in the family it might be a good idea to tell them all together, even if there is a large age difference. This is because it would be hard for most of the kids we know to contain this information if they were told alone. Divorce is a hard secret to keep. . . . It is important for kids to be told truthfully about what is going on" (Rofes, 1981, pp. 23–24).

And they tell other kids, "When you get told about separation or divorce, don't think it's your fault. It isn't your fault, or your brother's or sister's. Both of your parents probably decided this themselves because of their own problems or fights they had" (Rofes, 1981, pp. 27–28). (See also Furstenberg and Cherlin, 1991, ch. 2, for a good discussion of the separation process and children's perception of it.)

Children's Drawings. Children often express their emotions and reflect their lives indirectly through drawings. Isaacs and Levin asked forty-one children of divorced parents, five to eleven years (average 8.3), to draw their families. They did so twice, during the first year of separation and then a year later. In the first-year set, children included their fathers, making them the same size as or larger than their mothers. A year later, most fathers were missing, smaller, or shown on a different plane or some distance apart from the rest of the family. Thus, "Children express their sense of the growing peripherality of their fathers." In the last 13 years, four of my students carried out similar projects, with similar results. Fathers were absent, smaller, to the side (Isaacs and Levin, 1984).

Adult Children's Memories. In her late twenties, Stephanie Staal, whose parents divorced when she was thirteen, wrote *The Love They Lost: Living with the Legacy of Our Parents' Divorce* (2000). She interviewed 120 people in their twenties to forties, and also included her own experiences, emotions, and memories. These 120 people were "a self-selected [sample] found through newspaper ads, postings on the Internet, and word of mouth," but they still "form a diverse sampling coming from a variety of ethnic, geographic, and social backgrounds and professions" (2000, p. 27).

An "overwhelming number . . . said they have never spoken of their parents' divorce, either to friends or within the family. Even in a culture where divorce is such a common experience, so many of our families didn't have the language to talk about divorce in a constructive way—either when it happened or years later" (Staal, pp. 34–35). (But it may be that people who had never talked about their parents' divorce were the most likely to take the opportunity to finally do so by answering Staal's ad.)

Thirty-two-year-old Timothy is thankful his parents divorced. "Had my parents not divorced, I would have turned out to be a complete, instead of a partial, basket case. No, seriously, it would have been a terrible thing for all parties involved if they had stayed together. So I'm glad this possible world did not become actual. Nasty divorces can be harmful to the children involved, but then so can unhappy marriages" (Staal, 2000, p. 8).

Staal herself, in an interview about her book, recalls an awful last year of her parents' marriage. "[My parents] tried to stick it out for an extra year. That year was horrible. . . . It's really devastating when your parents divorce. But it doesn't automatically mean that I wish my parents were still together. People who haven't gone through parental divorce don't really understand that" (in Kirn, 2000, p. 78).

Living Arrangements

Children wonder and worry about where they will live after their parents separate. That is a major disruption in their lives.

Long ago, children generally stayed with their fathers. "Until the end of the nineteenth century, children generally lived with their fathers after a divorce occurred. Fathers maintained rights over their children, who were considered part of their property. . . . As men increasingly worked outside the home, the household came to be seen as women's sphere. And it was seen as the responsibility of the wife to provide nurturing and emotional support for her husband and children. Mothers were deemed more fit to care for the children because of their supposedly superior moral and spiritual qualities." Since then, courts have been awarding custody to mothers about 90 percent of the time. Today, state laws are gender neutral on custody, and even as more fathers gain sole or joint custody (15–20 percent). Still children live primarily with their mothers after divorce, since mothers do most parenting before divorce (Furstenberg and Cherlin, 1991, p. 30; Coley, 2001, p. 745).

Custody Choices. There are four types.

1. *Legal custody by both parents.* It is stated as the first choice in many states and becoming more common. Major decisions about schooling, medical care, and upbringing in general are made equally by both parents. For example, either parent may give permission to operate on a child, sign permission slips for school trips, and so on.

Joint legal custody has two versions (a) Joint *physical* custody, where the children live equally in both homes, and (b) *primary* physical custody, where the children live mostly and mainly with one parent (usually the mother). In both cases, there is a wide variety of practices. Under joint physical custody, children may alternate weeks between the two homes; or, move every month, every two months, every year. Or, they may split the week evenly. A few people develop five-day cycles. Children spend every Monday and Tuesday with one parent, every Wednesday and Thursday with the other, and then alternate Friday, Saturday, and Sunday—thus, the 5–5 schedule.

There is also a variety of primary physical custody arrangements. A typical one has the children stay with the non-primary parent every Wednesday evening and overnight, every other weekend, and parts of school vacations and summers. Others vary from as little as one day a month to three days a week, which is almost equal time with both parents.

2. *Sole legal custody.* Once the most common type, it is legally and in practice less favored today. Under it, some children still spend time with their noncustodial parents; others see them rarely or never.

3. *Split custody.* Rarely, one parent takes one or more and the other parent takes the other child(ren). This is done when courts conclude that some of the children would benefit living with one parent and the others living with the other parent. Often, the mother takes the girls and the father the boys. Some people think it works well, and others warn that it "often has harmful effects on sibling bonds and should be entered into cautiously." Also, as they become teenagers, boys sometimes want to live with their fathers (Strong, and others, 2001, p. 530).

Fathers and Custody.. Since the 1980s, various fathers' groups have complained that courts are biased toward women when they decide the children's residence. Today, more fathers receive joint physical custody, or even primary custody, than did in the 1970s. Sixty-one fathers told me their custody stories when I advertised to interview divorced fathers in 1992. Remember that these men were not a representative sample of divorced fathers, and that they were more involved in their children's lives than most divorced fathers were.

1. *Absentee fathers.* Five of the men were absentee fathers from the very beginning of, or shortly after, the separation. For one of them, his teenage daughters had made the decision not to see him, and he hoped they would soon change their minds; in the meantime, he was talking with them periodically on the phone. For the other four, the circumstances and conditions of their lives at the time of divorce made the break with their children almost inevitable and they drifted out of each other's lives.

2. *Fathers with regular contact.* Twenty-seven fathers said that for most of the years since the divorce they had spent time with their children on some regular basis. It varied from a day once or twice a month (with or without an overnight stay), to every other weekend, to what amounted to two days a week, to about a third of the time.

For twelve of these fathers, the time with their children had decreased in the last two or so years before the interview. For some of them it was almost non-existent, for others sporadic. Most attributed the decrease to their children becoming teenagers and involved with part-time jobs, friends, school, and dating. Two other factors also contributed to the decline in time with their children. (1) The fathers had remarried and either they were now busy with their new families, or, for whatever reasons, the children felt uncomfortable and uneasy with their fathers in the new circumstances. (2) Some fathers or mothers had moved an hour or two away from the other parent, and the longer commute became an obstacle (or, excuse) to forego regular visitation.

3. *Fathers with joint physical custody.* For the five fathers in this group, it meant the children lived alternate months with each parent, or alternate weeks, or split weeks, or other

variations. In some cases the parents divided the time evenly, in others the children were with their mothers closer to 60 percent of the time. Despite the joint custody, three of the fathers had tense and occasionally angry relationships with their former wives. The other two described very cooperative and friendly relationships.

4. *Custodial fathers.* At the time of the interviews in 1992, or up to the time the children had reached the age of 18 some years before 1992, ten of the fathers had been the primary or sole custodial parent for all or most of the years since the separation. They came to that role through many routes, mostly because the mother was unable or unwilling to care for the children. For all these men, solo parenting began as very challenging and troubling. Most had done very little parenting before the divorce. In time, they learned and loved to parent their children. Part of the reason they volunteered to talk with me was to tell their "success stories" as parents.

The remaining ten fathers had had custodial arrangements and relationships with their children that fit none of the above categories. For some period after their separation, varying from one to four years, seven men had had one or more of their children live primarily with them. During other periods of their post-separation lives, they were typical "weekend fathers." And a few went through other periods when they hardly saw their children. (See Liazos, 1995, pp. 22–29, for more details and histories of some of the men.)

The Debate over Joint Physical Custody . Such custody works best when it is freely chosen by both parents, who had shared in raising the children before divorce, and who are friendly and committed to making it work for the children's benefit. It allows both parents to raise their children, gives them both some relief from parenting, and keeps alive the children's relationships with both parents.

It does require commitment and cooperation from both parents. (But in my study, three of the five fathers who had joint custody did not report friendly cooperation with the mothers.) Also, some children may consider it a burden not to have a home base. The children in *The Kids' Book of Divorce* seem not to have found joint custody a burden. And in a conversation with me in July 2001, one of those children, now 35, still thinks it worked well. She noted that her brother provided continuity because they were together as they moved from one home to another.

In their 1991 review of studies of custody, Furstenberg and Cherlin recommend that *legal* custody should be granted jointly to both parents, but courts should allow joint *physical* custody only when both parents want it. A 2002 review of 33 studies comparing 1,846 children in sole custody with 814 children in joint custody, and 251 children in two-parent families, concluded that children in joint custody are better adjusted than those living with only one parent. Children in "joint-custody arrangements had fewer behavioral and emotional problems, higher self-esteem and better family relationships and school performance compared with those in sole-custody situations" (Daw, 2002).

Child-Support Payments

From the earliest days of divorce, an ongoing problem and concern has been the financial ability of the custodial parent to raise the children. Riley thinks it was never addressed adequately. More recently, mothers, who have raised the children after most divorces, have faced financial hardships. In 1980, for example, alimony and child support provided only 8 percent of the income of "mother-headed families in which the mother is age twenty-five or over" (Riley, 1991; Arendell, 1986, p. 53).

In 1999, according to court agreements, 6,133,000 mothers and 658,000 fathers were to receive child-support payments from the other parent. For that year, 45 percent received the full amount, 29 percent partial, and 26 percent none. For mothers, it was 46 percent full, 29 percent partial, and 25 percent none. Mothers received an average payment of $3,844, and fathers $3,175. The average income for the year, including child support, was $24,983 for mothers and $39,047 for fathers. A number of studies concluded that most divorced fathers could afford to make higher payments than they do now (*Statistical Abstract,* 2002, p. 355; Wallerstein, 2003; Meyer and Bartfeld, 1996; Sorensen, 1997).

Braver argues that the above statistics exaggerate the number of *divorced* fathers who do not pay child support. "There are two conspicuous problems with the Census Bureau findings as well as the other survey findings I looked at. The first problem is that in many of the analyses the researchers *combined* divorced people with never-married people." The latter group includes a high proportion of poor teenage fathers, most of whom are unable to pay. Divorced fathers tend to be a "better-educated, higher-earning group" who are able to support their children after divorce, and "their payment history is more reliable than [that of] never-married fathers." The second problem is that the people who conduct the surveys of who pays tend to ask the custodial mothers only. Mothers, like fathers and all other people, "tend to slant their responses in a way that casts a positive light on themselves or people they like and that casts an unflattering light on those they don't like." Thus, Braver concludes that the percentage of divorced fathers who pay no or incomplete child support is lower than surveys indicate (1998, pp. 22–23).

Another study concluded that most fathers who pay no or little child support are unemployed or hold low-paying jobs. Other studies report that "significant amounts of paternal financial support, both cash and in-kind aid, may go unreported in formal systems." Some parents may be unwilling to report cash payments they receive to the U.S. Census Bureau, the agency that conducts surveys on child-support payments (Young, 2002b; Coley, 2001, pp. 744–745).

Federal and state laws passed in the 1980s and 1990s have improved both the rate of collection and the amounts collected. A 1996 federal law provided for, among other things, uniform interstate child-support laws and computerized statewide collections. "Child Support Enforcement offices are required to monitor payments to make sure they are made regularly and fully." And "Since January, 1994, support orders must include a provision for *wage withholding* unless both parents and the courts agree on another payment method." Probably as a result of the new laws, and new federal and state programs, in 1997 $13.4 billion in child-support payments were collected, $15.5 billion in 1998, and $19 billion in 2001 (Office of Child Support Enforcement, 1997, p. 4; *Statistical Abstract,* 2002, p. 355; Armas, 2000; Cimons, 1999).

Despite improvements, and even given the counting problems raised by Braver and others, many custodial parents receive little or no financial support from the other parent, and suffer economically. We could do much better. Many European societies do. All children are guaranteed a monthly amount paid to the custodial parent. Whatever the other parent cannot or will not pay, the government pays, thus making up the difference. The children are not victimized by parental inability or neglect (Schwartz and Kaslow, 1997, pp. 110–113; Furstenberg and Cherlin, 1991, ch. 3.) (See Whyte, 2000, part 3, for three papers with suggestions of ways to improve child-support payments.)

Divorced Fathers and Their Children

Public perceptions of divorced fathers, government campaigns to collect child-support payments from absentee fathers, studies and survey findings, and mass media stories all seem to indicate that many, perhaps most, divorced fathers neither support their children financially nor stay involved in their lives. A 1981 survey reported that 51.8 percent of divorced fathers had not seen their children even once in the previous year; 15.2 percent had seen them 1–11 times; 16.7 percent, 12–51 times; and 16.4 percent, at least 52 times. A 1988 survey reported less father absence. In the previous year, 18.2 percent had not seen their children at all; 13.6 percent, once; 22.1 percent, several times; 21.2 percent, 1–3 times a month; 12.4 percent, once a week; and 12.4 percent, several times a week. More recent surveys estimate that "a third of divorced fathers have no contact with their children" (Furstenberg and others, 1983; Seltzer, 1991; Coley, 2001, p. 744).

Braver thinks these surveys overreport fathers' absence from their children's lives, for two reasons. First, most surveys rely on answers from custodial mothers only; fathers were never asked. Second, the 1981 survey did not distinguish between divorced and never-married fathers. The 1988 survey did make the distinction, and found that "while 40 percent of the never-married fathers had no contact with their child in the past year, only 18 percent of divorced fathers had no contact" (Braver, 1998, p. 41).

In surveys Braver carried out, he found large differences between what mothers said and what fathers said. For example, mothers reported that their former husbands had an average of 4.2 days visiting the children in the last month, fathers reported 5.73 days. While fathers reported an average of the longest period of time without seeing the children of 9.13 days, mothers said it was 12.57 days. The point is not that one group is telling the truth and another is lying. We know from many studies that people are unreliable observers of situations where they are involved, so we cannot automatically believe the fathers or the mothers. But we cannot rely on the reports of only one group. When I asked Braver at a November 2001 conference what the true figures might be, he replied that we cannot tell, but we cannot accept as truth the reports of either group (1998, p. 44).

Even though we may never know how many divorced fathers disappear from their children's lives, and how frequently the others do see them, we do know that many fathers stay involved with their children. In my study of sixty-one divorced fathers (see above for summary), I concluded that whatever the custody arrangements, whatever the frequency of contact with their children, most of them believed they *were* their children's fathers. They had an emotional and social commitment to them. For most of them, there had been significant changes over time in their relationships with their children. They had struggled and worked to adjust to the growing up of their children, to their moving away, to the new marital status of one or both parents, and other changes. They had made and had changed a variety of arrangements to be with their children. Some went through periods of varying durations when they did not see their children very much. Through all these changes and difficulties, they asserted and felt that they had been their children's fathers. At the same time, while parenting became the primary focus in the lives of some of them after the divorce, it did not for most of them, even though they were involved and caring parents (Liazos, 1995, pp. 34–35).

But why are there some (or many) divorced fathers who are absent from or marginal to their children's lives? Some claim that it is too painful to leave their children after short visits or stays with them, and "a painful reminder of the life they left behind, triggering feelings of guilt or sadness." Others start new families, and their time, energy, and resources are devoted to them. Gradually, they disengage from their first children. Many fathers argue that their former wives make it difficult to see their children. Some move away and it is difficult to travel the long distances, for them or their children. Other fathers say that their teenage children are too busy with friends, school, part-time jobs, and dates (Cherlin, 1999, pp. 383–384; Dudley, 1991).

One father I interviewed had moved away and started a new family, and as his first children grew older they took the bus less often to see him, in time coming no more than twice a year. He thought that what may have happened was that "when I got divorced I started detaching from my children." It had taken him some years to reconcile himself to that reality. He saw his daughters as people he got along with when he saw them, and as an obligation (he was still paying child support). His relationship with them was more friendly, more "avuncular," rather than fatherly. There was resignation and sadness in his voice as he talked about his children.

Frank Furstenberg and Andrew Cherlin "have speculated that many fathers, when they were married, may have related to their children only indirectly, through their wives. They tend to see parenting and marriage as a package deal; when the wife is removed, they have difficulty connecting directly to their children" (Cherlin, 1999, p. 384).

There are probably fewer absentee fathers, and divorced fathers in general may be more involved, than the 1980s surveys report. Certainly most of the sixty-one fathers I met in 1992 were very much present in their children's lives. But even those of us very much committed to and engaged with our children's lives know that something is lost after divorce; full-time parenting of your children disappears forever.

Does Divorce Damage Children?

In the past twenty years, no one has shaped the public debate on children and divorce more than Judith Wallerstein and her associates at the Judith Wallerstein Center for the Family in Transition. She has interviewed a number of times the parents and 131 children of 60 families who divorced in 1971, in California. She is the lead author of three books on those families: *Surviving the Breakup: How Children and Parents Cope with Divorce* (1980, with Joan B. Kelly); *Second Chances: Men, Women, and Children a Decade after Divorce* (1990, with Sandra Blakeslee); and *The Unexpected Legacy of Divorce: A 25 Year Landmark Study* (2000, with Julia M. Lewis and Sandra Blakeslee). (Since in the second and third books "I" is used as the author's voice, I will henceforth refer only to Wallerstein.) Her research has received major media attention, including a cover story of her last book in *Time,* "What divorce does to kids" (Kirn, 2000). Wallerstein herself wrote that her research and the work of her center have "influenced public policy and the courts and informed the work of pediatricians, teachers, and the clergy" (2000, p. xxvii).

The major, repeated, and stressed argument and conclusion of her studies is that divorce has harmful emotional, social, and economic effects on children, which are surprising and unexpected. In *Second Chances,* Wallerstein reported that in the ten years since 1971, "the postdivorce years brought the following" for the children:

> The effects of divorce are often long-lasting. Children are especially affected because divorce occurs during their formative years. . . .
>
> For the children in our study, the postdivorce years brought the following:
>
> - Half saw their mother or father get a second divorce in the ten-year period after the first divorce.
> - Half grew up in families where parents stayed angry at each other.
> - One in four experienced a severe and enduring drop in their standard of living. . . .
> - Three in five felt rejected by at least one of the parents. . . .
> - Very few were helped financially with college education, even though they continued to visit their fathers regularly.
>
> Many of the children emerged in young adulthood as compassionate, courageous, and competent people. . . .
>
> In this study . . . almost half of the children entered adulthood as worried, underachieving, self-deprecating, and sometimes angry young men and women. . . .
>
> Finally . . . the cumulative effect of the failing marriage and divorce rose to a crescendo as each child entered young adulthood. . . . It was here that anxiety carried over from divorced family relationships threatened to bar the young people's ability to create new, enduring families of their own. (Wallerstein, 1990, pp. 297–300)

In 2000, *The Unexpected Legacy of Divorce* builds on that last sentence from 1990. Here Wallerstein claims that divorce brought deep and long-lasting damage in their lives. Shaken by their parents' divorce, they are weary of commitment and marriage. When they do marry, they idealize marriage and have unrealistic expectations. They grew up too fast, often feeling obligated to tend to their parents' and siblings' needs.

According to a summary in a *Time* story, "children take a long time to get over divorce. Indeed, its most harmful and profound effects tend to show up as the children reach maturity and struggle to form their own adult relationships. They're gunshy. The slightest conflict sends them running. Expecting disaster, they create disaster" (Kirn, 2000, p. 77).

Wallerstein asks Karen, one of the children: "So you were hesitating. Was it about Gavin or about marriage?" Karen responds: "About marriage. About being happy. You see, it's not all behind me. Part of me is always waiting for disaster to strike. I keep reminding myself that I'm doing this to myself, but the truth is that I live in dread that something bad will happen to me. Some terrible loss will change my life, and it only gets worse as things get better for me. Maybe that's the permanent result of my parents' divorce" (Wallerstein, 2000, p. xvi).

Wallerstein insists and repeats that divorce has a gradual, cumulative, and long-lasting effect. "Its impact increases over time and rises to a crescendo in adulthood. At each developmental stage divorce is experienced anew in different ways. In adulthood it affects personality, the ability to trust, expectations about relationships, and ability to cope with change" (2000, p. 298).

Like others, Wallerstein thinks parents should stay in "good enough" marriages. She thinks it's a myth that unhappy parents make for unhappy children. "Adult children of divorce are telling us loud and clear that their parents' anger at the time of the breakup is *not* what matters most. Unless there was violence or abuse or unremitting high conflict, they have dim memories of what transpired during this supposedly critical period." Children care mostly about parents who feed them, clothe them, pay attention to them, and provide for their other needs. A "lousy marriage . . . beats a great divorce," and children need their parents to stay together "for better or worse" (Wallerstein, 2000, p. xxv; Kirn, 2000, pp. 78–80). (See also Waite and Gallagher, 2000, pp. 144–147, and Galston, 2000.)

In closing the summary of Wallerstein's conclusions, I should note that at times she tones down her usually alarming comments about the effects of divorce on children. She says she is not against divorce. Also, "I don't know of any research, mine included, that says divorce is universally detrimental to children." She understands why parents leave "loveless marriages" and seek to find happiness in new ones. But the interests of the parents differ from those of the children. "Divorce can benefit adults while being detrimental to the needs of children" (2000, p. xxxiii).

Responses to Wallerstein. The sixty families Wallerstein chose to study were not a representative sample. They all lived in Marin County, California, in 1971. "These families were selected out of a much larger group of people who were referred to us by their family law attorneys on the basis of the parents' willingness to participate and using the criteria that all of the children had to be developmentally on track, never having been referred for emotional or developmental problems." In 1996, she interviewed 93 (71 percent) of the original 131 children, 38 men and 55 women. Clearly, they were volunteers from one county in California. She can no more generalize from that sample than can studies of divorced fathers with "convenience," volunteer samples (Wallerstein, 2000, p. 317; Liazos, 1995, 1997; Arendell, 1995).

There is another problem with her sample. "Although she screened out children who had seen a mental health professional, many of the parents had extensive psychiatric histories. Troubled families can produce troubled children, whether or not the parents divorce, so blaming the divorce and its aftermath for nearly all the problems Wallerstein saw among the children over 25 years may be an overstatement" (Cherlin, 2002, p. 443).

An even more serious problem may be Wallerstein's intense involvement with the children of the sixty families. Her words are revealing.

I have been following their lives in intimate detail, seeing them and both of their parents for many hours of interviews, at least every five years since 1971. (2000, p. xxvi)

Over the years, many of the children in this study have kept in touch with me. I've been invited to their weddings and attended several of them. Others send color photographs, including images of romantic weddings with all the trimmings. (2000, p. 315)

Our meeting had lasted three hours and both of us were spent emotionally. It was a sad, moving, gallant story, and Karen had told it vividly. Both of us cried as she spoke and both of us ended up smiling and thankful that she had ended on a note that was at least partly upbeat and hopeful. She was on her way to her wedding day. I'd been granted a great privilege to share her life.

As we embraced, I thanked Karen for her generosity and candor. I told her how impressed I was with her, how proud I was of all she'd done, and how much I hoped the years ahead would make up for her past sorrows. She invited me to stay in touch and offered to send me snapshots of their new home. (2000, p. xvii)

Such repeated and intense contact; such emotions from Wallerstein as shown in her crying during an interview; an investment of thirty years of her life—all these, and more, make it likely that she *elicited and created* many of the responses from the children. The process of participation over so many years, and their involvement in a famous study, "encourage them to see their lives" through Wallerstein's lens (Pollitt, 2000).

Wallerstein created ongoing bonds, ideas, and perceptions of their lives. Were they ever free not to judge their lives through her conclusions? By the time she interviewed them again in 1996, could they have avoided reading the two books about their lives, which came out in 1980 and 1989, or the many discussions of her research in newspapers, magazines, professional papers, other books, and television shows? As the years passed, as Wallerstein became more invested in the study, as the children filtered their experiences increasingly through her lenses, their responses and reflections of their lives become less credible.

Another long-standing criticism of Wallerstein's research has been the absence of a control group of children from non-divorced parents. (The "comparison" group she chose for the 25-year interviews is of limited use. They have not experienced the intense involvement the 131 children of the study did.)

Hetherington, in her thirty-year study of divorce, with a much larger sample and a control group, concluded that 25 percent of children from divorced families, versus 10 percent from non-divorced, showed "serious social, emotional, or psychological problems." At most we can say that children of divorce have a somewhat higher chance to experience problems, but the great majority lead normal lives. We do need to worry about that 15 percent difference, and we can and should develop programs to meet their economic and emotional needs. But we should not exaggerate the long-term effects of divorce on children. Hetherington reminds us that happy and competent children are raised in all types of families—divorced and non-divorced, single and two-parent, heterosexual and same-sex ones (Hetherington and Kelly, 2002, pp. 7, 12–16, 280).

Children of divorce do have problems. A major one is the mother's distracted attention because of "depression, anger, or economic pressures." Lower incomes force mothers to move, which disrupts children's lives. Lower income, relocation, and less parental attention do often follow divorce, but that is not inherent to divorce and not automatic. We can address these problems directly—for divorced and non-divorced families—as some European societies do, by providing more money and services to the parents and children. Trying to prevent or outlaw divorce, and blaming the divorcing parents for all their children's problems, is not helping anyone. Nor is it possible to prevent divorce, as history shows us (Coontz, 1997, pp. 101–104).

Robert Emery, who has done considerable research on children and divorce, says "For the most part, kids from divorced families are resilient. They bounce back from all the stresses. Some kids are at risk, but the majority are functioning well." And Paul Amato, whose research is cited by critics of divorce to support their views, does not seem to share their conclusions. "What most of the large-scale scientific research shows is that although growing up in a divorced family elevates the risk for certain kinds of problems, it by no means dooms children to having a terrible life. The fact of the matter is that most kids from divorced families do manage to overcome their problems and do have good lives." In his own review of 1990s research on the effects of divorce on children, Amato says that it shows "a small but consistent gap between children from divorced and two-parent families" in areas such as academic success, psychological adjustment, social competence, and long-term health (Kirn, 2000, pp. 77, 78; Amato, 2000, p. 1278).

One study supporting Amato's conclusion involved 568 college-age students. It found that although they were somewhat more likely to be pessimistic about their chances of having a good marriage, generally "children of divorce did not differ much from children of intact families on measures of depression or on their general sense of trust in other people." Also, "they are better off than children whose parents stay in conflict-ridden relationships" (Bass, 1990, summarizing the study).

A related finding has been that many of the post-divorce mental health problems children face may have been present before the divorce. Cherlin and others looked at the lives of some children during years long before the divorce, and then after the divorce. "Years before the breakup, three-year-old boys whose families eventually would disrupt were more likely to have been described as having behavioral problems than were three-year-old boys whose families would remain intact. . . . Much smaller differences were found among daughters." The family conflict that harms children after divorce "may precede the separation by many years." Others have made the same observation (Furstenberg and Cherlin, 1991, p. 64; see also Hetherington and Kelly, 2002, p. 279; Amato, 2000, pp. 1273, 1278).

Cherlin and his associates followed these children later in life to determine the long-term effects of divorce on them. "At age 33, the mental health of persons whose parents had divorced was somewhat worse, on average, than that of persons whose parents had stayed together. However, the majority of persons from divorced families were not showing signs of serious mental health problems. In addition, some of the differences in mental health between the two groups had been visible in childhood behavior problems at age 7, before any of the parents divorced. Some of the seeming effect of divorce at age 33, then, probably reflected long-term difficulties that would have occurred even without a divorce" (Cherlin, 2002, p. 443; Cherlin and others, 1998).

What are you to believe? Critics of divorce cite statistics and studies to show that divorce causes long-lasting damage in children. Other writers cite studies (sometimes the same studies that the critics do) showing that after initial problems most children of divorce do well in life, and many thrive. We read, on the one hand: "Correcting for predivorce conflict and income loss, divorce has an independent negative effect on . . . high school performance and dropout rates, college attendance and graduation, labor force attachment, crime, depression and other psychological disorders, suicide, out-of-wedlock birth, and the propensity to become divorced in turn" (Galston, 2000, p. 181).

But on the other hand, we are told: "Overall, the research literature on the effects of divorce on children suggests the following conclusions:

> Almost all children experience an initial period of intense emotional upset after their parents separate.
> Most resume normal development without serious problems within about two years after the separation.
> A minority of children experience some long-term problems as a result of the breakup that may persist into adulthood. (Cherlin, 2002, p. 445)

Cherlin's conclusions are supported by much research, foremost among them Hetherington's study (Hetherington and Kelly, 2002).

A major clue about what we believe is our interpretation of the statistics. If 30 percent of children of divorce say they have poor relationships with their mothers, and 16 percent of those from intact families say the same, it is true that children of divorced families have almost twice the rate. It is also true that the great majority of them—70 percent—do not have a poor relationship. Which statement is more significant? Which one do you believe (Whitehead, 1997, p. 161)? (Remember, also, that we do not know if conditions not related to divorce may contribute to the poor relationship.)

What *Do* Children of Divorce Need?

Children of divorce need primarily the same things as all children have always needed, and still need today: adults who love them and care for them; a home and enough family income for their material needs; good schools and friends.

To speak directly to their situation, children of divorce have four major needs. I base these on studies and reports I have read, the stories of the sixty-one divorced fathers I interviewed in 1992, and my experiences raising my daughters after my divorce.

1. *Financial security is first and foremost.* The evidence is overwhelming that most problems these children face are economic. Nations that have policies providing minimum incomes to *all* families do not have the delinquency, dropout rates, and other problems we have with children from single-parent and divorced families (Coontz, 1997, p. 151).

2. *Stability in their lives.* Parental divorce is a disruption, which is compounded if the children also change home, school, and friends. Everyone recommends that if at all possible the custodial parent and the children stay in the same home. Such stability was common among the Mundurucu, Iroquois, and other societies with divorce rates similar to ours.

3. *The presence of both parents.* Whatever the custodial arrangements, both parents should stay close to and spend time with the children. And as for all children everywhere, the more caring adults in their lives, the better their lives will be.

4. *No major conflicts between the parents.* Such conflicts should be avoided. As studies have shown, whether in marriage or after divorce, parental conflict makes children unhappy, and becomes an ongoing tension and distress in their lives (Sugarman, 2003; Amato, 2000).

Many other actions are possible. For example, since 1998, a Massachusetts law mandates workshops that teach divorced parents on "how to lessen the pain of divorce for children" seem to help many parents, and thus their children. Parents are urged not to belittle the other parent in front of the children, to be consistent and punctual on visits, and practice "age-appropriate honesty" (Taylor, 1999; other states have similar laws).

The American Academy of Matrimonial Lawyers wrote a booklet on "Stepping Back from Anger." Ann Landers reprinted ten of their recommendations. Here are a few:

- Never disparage your former spouse in front of your children.
- Reassure your children that they are loved and that the divorce is not their fault.
- Resist the temptation to let your children act as your caretakers.
- If you are the noncustodial parent, pay your child support. (Landers, 1999a, p. D3).

Children should get the last word on how divorce affects their lives.

And this is the final message of our book. We will not lie and tell you that divorce has no effect on kids. It causes you to feel many things and causes many changes in your life. You have to think of your family and your world differently. But there will come a day when things will settle down, when you will be able to look back without the intense pain you felt earlier. While divorce never ends, it grows easier to live with until you learn to fully accept the fact that, for better or worse, you have lived through one of the hardest times any child has to experience. And all of us feel stronger when it's finally a part of our past. (Eric Rofes, editor, 1981, *The Kids' Book of Divorce*, pp. 117–118)

(For other discussions on what children of divorce need, see Wallerstein, 1990, chs. 17 and 18; Skolnick, 1997; Buchanan, Maccoby, and Dornbush, 1996; Hines, 1997; Schwartz and Kaslow, 1997, ch. 7; Pedro-Carroll, 2001.)

LIFE AFTER DIVORCE

The closing lines from *The Kids' Book of Divorce* are hopeful. The loss, sadness, pain, and conflict gradually wane. The memories remain, but a new life also begins for the parents and the children.

"Divorce Is Never Good, but Good Can Come Out of It."

Almost all writing on divorce focuses on the negative aspects, on pain, loss, loneliness, regrets, and financial problems. Russ Horton, one of the sixty-one fathers who talked with me, and who spoke the words that provide the title for this section, is among some people who remind us that divorce also becomes an opportunity for gains.

In *Mothers and Divorce,* Arendell says that most of the women achieved "personal growth." "Despite their experiences with financial and social deprivations, nearly all of them expressed satisfaction with the personal growth they had accomplished. 'The best part has been finding myself—finding out that I'm a human being and capable of taking care of myself in situations that aren't pleasant. . . . I feel like, coming from where I was, I've accomplished so much.'. . . [T]hese women mentioned release from an unhappy marriage and its particular roles, new autonomy and independence, and success in managing to cope as a parent in changed circumstances" (1986, pp. 145–146).

Riessman found similar positive changes. The most mentioned benefit for women was "freedom from [the] subordination" they had endured in their marriages. They talked of liberation, control of their lives, and independence. The women also became more competent in managing their lives, in learning to fix things and controlling their own money. "My bills are paid every month. I've never bounced a check. I feel very good about myself." They also acquired new skills and new jobs, and many returned to school. Many spoke of "coming out of a shell" (1990, pp. 169, 173).

Men too made gains. Whereas "most men as a group tend to interpret their divorces less positively than women do . . . most men tend to manage to find positives in divorce. Like women, they define it as a 'growth process.'" For example, while women learned to fix things, many men learned to cook, shop, and arrange their homes (Riessman, 1990, pp. 183–184).

Most of the men I talked with also reported some growth and gains. For example, many talked about leaving empty marriages and discovering they can be closer to their children despite the divorce (and for the ten who were primary custodial parents, that they can raise them mostly alone). Whether they chose to leave their wives, as twenty-two did, or whether their wives made that decision, as thirty-two did, most men concluded that their divorce was a more positive than negative consequence. Six found it very positive, twenty-eight positive, fifteen both positive and negative, eleven negative, and one very negative.

When his wife left in 1983, Glen Duggan was very opposed to divorce. "It was devastating. . . . I felt like a complete failure. I was ashamed of getting divorced. I felt like I had failed at everything. I was embarrassed to tell people, I was embarrassed to see people. . . . I had nothing. . . . I felt bad because I knew divorce is no good for kids under any circumstances." But in 1992, admitting he would not have left his marriage, he joked. "I think I should thank my wife for divorcing me. . . . I'm a better person being divorced . . . [more] interesting and knowledgeable." He had met some "wonderful, wonderful people," had had great experiences, and had made friends he doubted he would have made had he stayed married. His greatest regret was that he did not have as much influence in raising his children as he wished he had.

For some of the fathers, of course, the divorce had been mostly an undesirable experience. And even those who concluded it had benefited them still felt sadness and loss. James Allen, separated in 1991 after twenty-two years of marriage, said that he was happier apart from his wife, but still felt "like part of me was torn away. Happy or not [my marriage] was very much part of me. Some of it was happy. There *were* good times. . . . She was part of my life and that's gone. . . . I lived with this woman for twenty-two years. How can it not be upsetting?" But to various degrees, most claimed and described new experiences, relationships, and insights that they interpreted as beneficial and helpful.

So, "divorce is never good, but good can [and often does] come out of it."

New Families

New relationships, new marriages, and new families are opportunities for a new life. Through cohabiting relationships, or marriages, or both, many women and men seek to rebuild their lives after divorce, seek to create new families for their children.

Overview and Statistics. Stepfamilies have always existed, but in the past parents' deaths usually created them. Today, people usually remarry after divorce. They enter second marriages for the same reasons they enter first ones: "Convenience, social pressure, love, companionship, support, and for some, pregnancy" (Schwartz and Kaslow, 1997, p. 386).

What is a stepfamily? Who counts as a member of one? Consider a scenario common to many people's lives. When Herb (a hypothetical divorced father) remarried, he "created a stepfamily that included his new wife, Alice, and her two children, June and Eddie. His own children, Mickey and Sally, lived with their mother but occasionally visited Herb and Alice's home. Does it then follow that Mickey and Sally, too, are part of a stepfamily? There is no rule for answering this question." A strict definition would only include children and adults who actually live in a household. But we can cast a wider net and include children who do not live in the household. For example, Mickey and Sally may visit occasionally, but if they were to stay with their father two to three days each week, it would make sense to include them. Consider people you know and explore your definition. How do we think of Herb's parents, for example. Are they June and Eddie's grandparents? We know that in similar cases they do act as grandparents (Furstenberg and Cherlin, 1991, p. 78).

Most divorced people remarry, although somewhat fewer of them do so now compared to the past. Recently, in over 40 percent of marriages every year at least one partner had been married before. By one estimate, stepfamilies will outnumber nuclear families by 2007. Of women divorced in the 1960s, 75 percent would eventually marry again; more recently, 67 percent would. For men, the decrease was from 80 to 75 percent. The decrease may in part be due to more people cohabiting instead of marrying, or cohabiting longer before they marry again. We do know that cohabitation increased dramatically in the 1980s and 1990s (Cherlin and Furstenberg, 1994, pp. 406–407; Schwartz and Scott, 2000, p. 382, 386).

The number of children living with both biological parents has been decreasing. In 1998, 68 percent did so, compared to 77 percent in 1980; 23 percent lived with the mother only (18 in 1980); 4 percent with the father only (2 percent in 1980); and 4 percent with neither parent (4 percent also in 1980). An estimated 25 percent of children born in the 1980s will live in a stepfamily before they reach adulthood. Like biological ones, stepfamilies average two children. About two-thirds of stepparents are stepfathers, since divorced women are far more likely to have custody of the children after divorce than men are (*Statistical Abstract,* 1999, p. 67; Cherlin and Furstenberg, 1994, p. 408; Mason, 2003).

Social Ambiguity. In most social situations, we know by tradition, or law, or both what we can expect of others and what they expect of us. For example, it is generally clear how children and parents, teachers and students, should behave with each other. These expectations also include how we address people in that setting. But what do children call their mother's new husband, their stepfather? There seems to be much less clarity of expectations and forms of address in stepfamilies. They face "unique problems for which there are not well worked out cultural solutions. Because Americans don't agree on how to conduct family relations within stepfamilies, cultural rules for stepfamilies to follow are vague or altogether lacking. Many stepparents find their responsibilities confusing, and many stepchildren are uncertain about what to expect from their stepparents" (Furstenberg and Cherlin, 1991, p. 77; see also Cherlin, 1978; Mason, 2003).

Stages in the Lives of Stepfamilies. When the marriage is the first one for both partners, people begin their relationship with only the two of them. Together, they develop understandings and expectations. Then, when they have children, they begin to build relationships and expectations with them. Stepfamilies differ. One or both of the partners bring children into the marriage, and the stepparent is new to the relationship. They need to proceed slowly.

In the first two years of a stepfamily there is usually some conflict, tension, and uncertainty. For example, the stepparent must build a relationship with the children who already have a relationship with their biological parent. Discipline can be a problem (see below). Most research shows that most *young* stepsons develop close relationships with their stepfathers. In time, compromises and understandings develop and stepfamilies exhibit the same range of family situations as biological ones (Bray and Kelly, 1998).

Discipline and Money Strains. Conflicts over money and discipline are common to most stepfamilies, especially in the early years. If, for example, a stepfather disciplines his stepchildren, he has no history and no established relationship to ease the tension, no assumed love and trust. Thus, it may be best to avoid discipline issues at the start. A long-term study of stepfamilies showed that "stepfathers . . . are most often disengaged and less authoritative as compared with nondivorced fathers" (Mason, 2003, p. 99).

Expectations may be unclear or different. For example, a stepfather may arrive home and find his wife "in the kitchen preparing dinner while her son is nearby reading a book. He may be inclined to ask the child to help out but is unsure how his wife will react to such a request. She may . . . feel angry because she believes that helping out isn't her son's role; or she may interpret her husband's request for participation as a criticism of her housework. Such a scene is less likely to occur in a nuclear family because the couple would have developed over time a common concept of how the family should operate" (Furstenberg and Cherlin, 1991, p. 84).

Money is another frequent problem. A stepfather who also pays child support to his biological children's mother may not have enough for two families. Also, if he feels guilty because he does not live with his biological children, he may buy them expensive gifts and give them money to assuage his guilt. His wife and stepchildren may resent such largesse, however. Also, income and lifestyle may differ between his new household and his children's household, possibly causing resentment and anger.

Strengths and Benefits of Stepfamilies. Stepfamilies often take a long time before they *feel* like families, and some may never develop that feeling. Family life can be confusing and tense. It may often be more difficult to be a stepparent than a biological one. As we saw, discipline and money can be problems.

But in time most stepfamily members develop positive emotions and experiences. Harmony follows conflict. Love grows. New relationships develop. A stepparent's parents may come to love the children and spend time with them. Children "grow up in well-functioning stepfamilies and have caring stepparents who provide affection, effective control and economic support" (Paul Amato, as cited in Mason, 2003, p. 99).

We could, as a society, support stepfamilies. They are here to stay, and it is better to embrace them than denounce them. We could slowly institutionalize them, begin creating clear roles, expectations, rights, and responsibilities. In law and daily life, stepparents could be allowed and expected to act like all other parents in financial obligations, custody rights, commitment, and related matters. (For opposing views on stepfamilies and policies toward them, see Popenoe, 1994, and Kurdek, 1994.)

Lastly, although stepfamilies are families, they cannot and should not live up to a nuclear family fantasy. Only disappointment awaits that fantasy. Children have parents and relatives in other families, parents have children in two or more families, new sets of grandparents arrive. We need to "develop a new set of expectations and behaviors" (Coontz, 1997, p. 108; see also Stacey, 1990, and Coleman, Ganong, and Fine, 2000).

CONCLUSION: THE MEANINGS OF DIVORCE

A decade later, I can still hear the words spoken by the sixty-one men in 1992.

"Divorce never ends."

"Divorce is never good, but good can come out of it."

"I'd rather have gangrene" than divorce.

I recall the awful emptiness I felt Sunday evenings after I drove my daughters back to their mother's home. And as I am surrounded by these words and memories, I cannot understand critics of divorce saying divorce is an easy and hasty escape, that anyone thinks of it as a road to idyllic personal growth and individual fulfillment.

Divorce is "anything but a whim." People spend "years working up to it" (Pollitt, 2000). Divorce is hard. Divorce is harsh. Divorce is painful. Divorce is costly—emotionally, socially, financially. Divorce is a "grueling affair" (Ann Patchett, 1995) and "an emptiness I didn't know existed" (Maureen Sherwood, 1997).

Divorce benefits many people, and it hurts some temporarily and others permanently. Hetherington tells us that divorce is brutally painful, but also that it is "a reasonable solution to an unhappy, acrimonious, destructive relationship," and 75–80 percent of divorced people "lead reasonably gratifying lives a few years after the divorce" (Hetherington and Kelly, 2002, pp. 279–280).

Divorce is part of the human condition, a tradition in America and most societies. For many women and men, it allows for an escape from violence, misery, oppression, and profound and intense unhappiness. It is often necessary.

But to say that divorce is a painful and hard experience does not mean we can blame divorce for juvenile delinquency, school failure, emotional troubles, and financial disasters. Most children of divorce survive and do well, and the majority of the problems many do have are caused by conditions that we can fix, primarily low income, if we stop blaming people and we really seek to help them.

In *Divorce: An American Tradition,* Riley describes conventions in the nineteenth and twentieth centuries that sought to make divorce difficult to obtain. They did not slow down divorce, nor will today's anti-divorce groups and conventions. They may save some marriages but they cannot undo history and culture. They seem to ignore the social, cultural, economic, gender, and other conditions that make divorce necessary and inevitable (Cobb, 1997; Leonard, 2001).

Recent history is instructive. People who argue that couples should stay in "good-enough" marriages may forget that the millions of men and women who divorced from the 1970s on *did* grow up in good-enough marriages during the "happy days" from the late 1940s to the early 1960s. Many saw their mothers suffocating in the suburban communities and homes.

Divorce is hard but societies have learned to adjust to it, as they have adjusted to so many other hard realities. Marriage and social stability can co-exist with divorce. Among the Kanuri, where "almost every marriage ends in divorce," people still place a "high value on marital stability and even perform a ritual at weddings to symbolize the desire of everyone that this particular marriage last" (Skolnick, 1996, p. 300; see also Goode, 1993).

We could focus on "good-enough divorces," when "Mom has enough money and Dad stays connected, when parents stay civil and don't bad-mouth each other, [and] kids do all right." We could commit ourselves to making such good divorces possible, instead of blaming divorced people, talking about "stigmatizing" them, and making divorce difficult to get. Most Americans have accepted the reality of divorce, and it's time for the Council on Families and its friends and allies to do the same (Pollitt, 2000).

Much could be done to make marriages better, and I have no objection to any voluntary programs and workshops to that end. I have no objections to programs and classes mandated by laws that stress "the welfare of the children must be the prime consideration of both parents" (Schwartz and Kaslow, 1997, pp. 34, 136–138).

But the most important action we can take to help couples, children, and families— married, divorced, single parent, remarried, same sex, grandparent, and others—is to provide them with a minimum standard of living and with community supports. Many problems are reduced or disappear when families are not stressed about whether they can afford decent homes, education, health care, and clothing.

13

Violence in Families

INTRODUCTION

Stories

Linda Logan. Linda Logan grew up in a respected middle-class family of five children, in a small northern New England town. She married young and she and her husband had two children. They were a happy and normal family. But after some years of marriage an experience triggered awful childhood memories, long repressed, that began to haunt her. She told her husband that between the ages of 5 and 15 she had been repeatedly raped by her father and a brother. Some family members believed Linda; others did not. Meanwhile, Linda, with her husband's loving support, went through years of therapy.

The name is fictional but the people and events are real. A high school friend I had not seen in years related it to me when we met. He is Linda's husband.

I heard the story some years ago, but Linda and her ordeal have stayed with me. I think of her every time we discuss violence in families in any of my courses. The story refuses to go away. It haunts me and always dismays and frightens me. If such long-lasting violence can happen in a respected family in a small town, could it be that violence (in various forms) exists in many, perhaps most, families? If so, what does this mean about families, about the love, protection, and nurturance we hope and expect to find in them?

Ignoring Violence in Families. While I was an undergraduate and graduate student in the 1960s, we never discussed violence in families in any of my classes. I began teaching in 1967, but it was not until the mid 1970s that sociology began to explore sexual assault, child abuse, incest, men battering women, and other forms of violence in families. Even though marital rape had been debated intensely for years in the nineteenth century (see below), it and other violence in families were ignored in the mid–twentieth century.

Donald Murray. In June 1994 Donald Murray revealed a sad family secret. He wrote in his *Boston Globe* column, "Over Sixty":

> Wife beating wasn't approved of in my family, but it existed. And nothing was done about it. It wasn't nice, but no one called the police when, at the Sunday dinner table after church, a husband ordered his wife upstairs; when he removed his belt as he followed her; when everyone at the dinner table heard the belt strike again, again, again. . . .
>
> The reason we kept this secret is because, at some level, we believed that the husband had a right—more than that, a duty—to maintain order in *his* house. . . .
>
> And where could a wife who married soon after high school, had only a limited education and no job skills go? There were few jobs for women. Women were married for life, were economically dependent and were duty bound. If they were beaten, the thinking went, they must not have served well. (Murray, 1994, pp. 49, 51)

A Poem. In 1986, Sharon Howell wrote a poem, "The Reasons . . . ?"

The Reasons . . . ?

He beat her, he told her because she was looking at another man. And he loved her so much, it made him fearful and crazy to think he might lose her. He told her he was sorry and that it wouldn't happen again, but, it did. Since the real reason he beat her was because . . . he could.

He beat her, he said because she was a poor housekeeper. And this reflected badly on him. And if she would just change her slovenly ways, he wouldn't have to beat her. But, the real reason he beat her was because . . . he could.

He beat her, he said because the children cried. And after working all day he felt she should be able to keep them quiet. And if she kept better control of them, beatings wouldn't be necessary. But, the real reason he beat her was because . . . he could.

He beat her, he told her because he was upset, things were going bad at work. And that she should understand that he was under great pressure. And further, if he didn't love her so much and want so much for her, he wouldn't beat her at all. But, the real reason he beat her was because . . . he could.

He beat her, he told her because she wasn't pretty anymore. And that she had let herself go. And the excuses went on–and–on. The dog died, the dish ran away with the spoon, the Red Sox lost the pennant. But, the real reason he beat her was because . . . he could.

The reason she took his beatings was because, at first, she loved him and believed he loved her. Then she believed that he beat her because he loved her. Then she believed that he beat her because she deserved to be beaten. She also let him beat her because she was used to living in fear. And finally, she let him beat her because she couldn't, wouldn't, why live if she believed, he would beat her, just because he could . . . ? (Howell, 1986, p. 29; used with permission of the publisher)

What Does It All Mean?

These stories trouble me. Violence should not exist in families. They suggest, however, that violence may be commonplace in families. Is it? *How* commonplace? And what are we to make of it, however common it may be? There are passionate and profound debates over these questions. I have no clear answer. I have been reading and contemplating stories, statistics, and studies for years. They baffle me, trouble me, scare me. Along the way and at the end of the chapter, I will offer my reflections and tentative conclusions.

For now, I need to note that whatever I say about the violence men commit in families, I do not mean to demonize men. I do not think men are inherently violent or evil. Men, like women, are caught in a society that normalizes violence in families, especially by men to control women. I will argue, however, that men also lose in these situations. They may gain control but they lose a loving family; they too pay a heavy price. Control does not mean happiness, and women and men both lose when men resort to violence.

Types of Violence

Since the early 1970s, when child abuse and violence against women were first raised as political and social problems, social scientists have also studied other forms of violence in families. There are now texts devoted entirely to "family violence." For example, the second edition of *Family Violence* devotes chapters to physical child abuse, child sexual abuse, child neglect, sibling abuse, ritualistic child abuse, spousal abuse, elder abuse, special populations (such as people with disabilities) and family violence, women and sexual violence, and stalking (Wallace, 1999). (For other texts on violence in families, see Sadler, 1996; Swisher, 1996; Barnett, Miller-Perrin, and Perrin, 1997.)

We have now added "neglect" to the study of violence in families. Other studies and books also explore emotional and psychic abuse. All of these types of abuse harm or destroy their victims. It is impossible, however, to discuss all of them adequately here. I will limit this chapter to a discussion of couple violence, most of which involves men hitting and hurting women.

VIOLENCE IN INTIMATE RELATIONSHIPS

Given our marriage ideals, how can we make sense of statements that women are more likely to be injured and killed by their lovers and husbands than by other people? Of the existence of over 2,000 U.S. shelters for battered women? Of the argument that some writers make that women are equally violent against men as men are against women? Is violence a rare, a sometime, or a common event in intimate relationships?

There are no definitive answers to any of these nagging and troublesome questions. I will discuss some research and writing on them, presenting differing perspectives, and I will offer some tentative conclusions. It may help you explore these questions and the implications they have for women, men, and marriages.

Cultural Perspectives

What do anthropologists tell us about violence in marriages? Some think it has existed in all societies, others argue that it was nearly absent in some and common in others. Martha Ward, in *A World Full of Women,* devotes a chapter to "A worldwide case: Wife beating and wife battering." She distinguishes between wife *beating* and wife *battering.* In wife beating, "a man deliberately [inflicts] physical pain on a woman within a male–female relationship or partnership. This is 'normal,' that is, expected in the customs of the culture. . . . Women do not like the beatings and would prefer to have husbands who did not beat them. But women are not always meek or passive; they often have strategies to defend themselves" (1999, pp. 235–236).

Wife battering is more injurious. It "goes beyond the physical reprimands that characterize wife beating. It includes the possibilities of severe injuries, maiming, and death. Battering is usually not acceptable to members of social groups; there are few or no cultural approvals or authorizations" (Ward, 1999, p. 236).

Ward concludes that the mistreatment of women is "universal," ranging from "mild physical rebuke to murder. In some societies, violence and mistreatment of women are extremely rare; in others it is a daily and predictable occurrence" (1999, p. 236; Ward is summarizing *Sanctions and Sanctuary: Cultural Perspectives on the Beating of Wives,* by Counts, Brown, and Campbell, 1991).

Ward also addresses a recent debate that there is symmetry in marital violence, that women commit as much violence as men do. Daniel Levinson addressed that issue in *Family Violence in Cross-Cultural Perspective* (1989). He studied ninety cultures found in the Human Relations Area File (a computerized source of ethnographic data of over 300 societies), and concluded that "husband beating was reported in 26.9 percent [of the cultures]; by contrast, wife beating occurred in 84.5 percent of the same groups. . . . [H]usband beating occurred in the majority of households in only 6.7 percent of those societies he sampled, and wife beating occurred in the majority of households in 48.7 percent of the groups." And wife battering was even more asymmetrical. "Men batter, kill, and maim women in domestic partnerships with far greater impunity than women do" (Ward summarizing Levinson, in Ward, 1999, pp. 238–239).

In a brief discussion, Kottak concludes that "although more prevalent in certain social settings than in others, family violence and domestic abuse of women are worldwide problems" (2000, p. 294).

In *Women and Men in Society,* O'Kelly and Carney show that violence is rare in some social settings and expected and accepted in others. In gathering-hunting societies, there is some fighting in marriages, instigated equally by men and women, but other people in the camp intervene quickly. Wife beating, however, is "uncommon" in these societies. Violence is more common in horticultural societies, and it is "often legitimized." But when women live near relatives who can provide protection, "it is less common or less extreme." But in some horticultural societies women are brutalized and victimized (1986, pp. 23, 55; see also Good, 1991).

Wife beating was also common in peasant (agrarian) societies, which were the most common type before the rise of industrialism. For example, during the early Middle Ages in Europe "husbands had the right to beat their wives." This was so too in pastoral societies. "Husbands usually have the right to mete out physical punishments to their wives whenever they deem it appropriate. Wife beating is common among pastoralists. But the man who exceeds the culturally acceptable standards of wife beating is likely to be the object of ridicule as one who prefers to fight women rather than men." Although the last sentence seeks to minimize wife beating, it also clearly tells us that it was acceptable (O'Kelly and Carney, 1986, pp. 109, 79).

Ward, Kottak, O'Kelly and Carney, and other anthropologists agree that wife beating was rare or non-existent under the following conditions:

1. Women have prominent and equal roles in economic and social life. They contribute equally to the material needs of their families and communities, for example, they gather or raise as much food as men (or more than men), and they share in deciding how those goods are to be used. In our terms, women make as much money as men do and they control its use.

2. Married couples are not isolated from the community. When married life is visible to relatives and neighbors, they are likely to intervene and stop men from beating their wives. When people who once lived in small, open camps move to more private and isolated nuclear family camps, wife abuse appears more often. Social isolation from kin and community removes watchful eyes that would step in and stop beatings (O'Kelly and Carney, 1986, p. 31).

History of Violence in the United States

As in much of the world, wife beating has always existed in the United States as have long struggles against it, including efforts to make it illegal. There are no statistics of any kind until recently, but court records and other historical documents reveal the existence of wife beating and battering.

The Puritans were aware of its existence because they made it illegal in 1641. But their emphasis on the sanctity of the family and patriarchal authority made the courts and the community reluctant to enforce the laws. Although male cruelty was a ground for divorce, women were rarely granted a divorce solely on that ground. Indeed, of the forty divorces granted in Massachusetts from 1639 to 1692, "not a single divorce was granted on the basis of 'cruelty' alone, the term for domestic violence at the time. Divorces that involved cruelty were always granted on the basis of some other factor as well, such as adultery or neglect." In later years, however, cruelty increasingly became a reason and a legal ground for divorce (M. Liazos, 1996, p. 26; Riley, 1991).

Awareness of and struggles against wife beating have varied, increasing at times and disappearing at others. For much of the nineteenth century, there was a strong movement to expose, make illegal, and stop wife beating and marital rape. But there was very little public discussion in the twentieth century before the 1960s. In the 1930s and 1940s people pretended it did not exist, or that it was funny (as Murray reveals in his column, above). West tells us that in Plainville around 1940, violence was the subject of folklore but it was rarely practiced, and only by people who did not "enjoy the community's respect" (M. Liazos, 1996; Hasday, 2000; West, 1945, p. 66).

In the 1950s, that era of family harmony, wife beating was acknowledged, at most, only as a joke. One *I Love Lucy* episode shows Ricky placing Lucy over his knees and spanking her on the buttocks. She had bought some furniture without his permission. Coontz thinks that this lack of media coverage may have protected people from the fear of social ills, such as wife beating. But she later notes that the denial of wife beating meant that victimized women had nowhere to escape (Coontz, 1997, pp. 39, 43). (It was only in the mid-1970s that the first shelters were founded. As I noted in the opening of this chapter, social sciences did not study and did not teach about violence in families until the late 1960s to early 1970s.)

Caplow and others, writing about families in Muncie, Indiana, in the late 1970s, acknowledge the existence of child abuse and wife abuse, but think their incidence was exaggerated. They argue that abuse had existed in the past but was not socially recognized (the Lynds do not mention abuse in their studies of Muncie in 1925 and 1935). Without offering any statistics, Caplow and others claim that wife abuse was gradually decreasing in 1970s Muncie, although awareness of it was increasing (1982, pp. 335–336).

In *Heroes of Their Own Lives: The Politics and History of Family Violence*, Gordon uses case records of social-work agencies in Massachusetts, from 1870 to the 1960s, to study violence in families. She concludes that it always existed but its visibility and our awareness and concern have varied. Visibility and concern increased during the 1960s because during that decade the civil rights, anti-war, student, women's, and other movements were questioning and challenging most institutions and traditions. "Born as a social problem in an era of a powerful women's rights movement, campaigns against child abuse and wife-beating have tended to lose momentum and support, even to disappear altogether, when feminist influence is in decline. In such periods family togetherness is often sought at the expense of individual rights and by ignoring intrafamily problems, rather than by exposing and attacking them" (Gordon, 1988, p. 26).

Struggles to Protect Battered Women in Massachusetts. Because for most of the twentieth century violence in families, and specifically wife beating, was invisible, we tend to think that it was always ignored. But a close study of laws and women's movements in Massachusetts history shows that during some historical periods wife beating and battering was the subject of heated debates and legislative struggles to outlaw it. Indeed, it has been legally prohibited during many periods, but laws were usually not enforced.

For example, these were some of the legal advances during the 1800s. "Abused wives who divorced their husbands had gained expanded property rights through the married women's property act. The laws on desertion were amended so that a battered wife could not be charged with desertion if she left her husband, indicating that it was her legal right to leave her batterer" (M. Liazos, 1996, p. 55).

Beginning in the late 1960s, violence against women became a political, social, and academic issue. The women's movement insisted that families, churches, schools, government bodies, and society at large pay attention. "Society" did not discover battered women; rather, *feminists and activists did,* and they helped and forced the rest of us to pay attention. They founded, supported, and ran the first shelters for battered women. In Massachusetts, for example, they worked for stricter laws to protect battered women, lobbied police and courts to enforce those laws, set up shelters, and gradually sought to increase public awareness (Schechter, 1982, p. 3; M. Liazos, 1996, ch. 7).

The history of laws and struggles in Massachusetts found in "The History of Legal Protection for Battered Women in Massachusetts," by Melissa Liazos, together with the overview of what anthropologists report about wife beating and battering, tell us that four conditions are necessary to prevent violence against women:

1. Laws prohibiting it
2. Enforcement of these laws

This photo was used in a recent campaign for a local initiative that would provide funds for certain non-profit organizations, including a shelter for battered women in Boulder, Colorado. (The initiative passed.) *(Used with permission of the Citizens for a Worthy Cause and DesRosiers Advertising)*

3. Economic, social, and political power for women so they can work to achieve the first two conditions.

4. "Public scrutiny of the private sphere." Women, men, and families must live in close communities, where they are not isolated from the eyes of family and neighbors (M. Liazos, 1996, p. 1).

How Much Violence? By Whom?

How serious and how frequent is violence between husbands and wives? Is it equal, or, are women the majority of victims? According to Ann Jones, "battery [against women] is [women's] greatest health problem, probably worse than breast cancer." She thinks "we never confront the enormity of this problem." On the other hand, Gelles thinks serious violence is not very common, and relatively few people are injured. Moreover, most of the time, even abusive parents and spouses love their children or spouses. Usually, "the family functions nonviolently (although the threat of physical violence and abuse tends to hang heavy in the air)" (Jones, 1994, p. 56; Gelles,1997, pp. 19–23). (That last qualifying sentence is significant. Violent actions affect victims long after they occur.)

Some Statistics. What *do* we count when we talk about marital violence? Shoves, kicks, punches, cuts, bruises, bleeding from such actions, injuries of various degrees, forced sex, use of knives, guns, and bats? How frequent must these acts be? Does one shove count? When you read surveys, look for what actions or observations were included. More inclusive definitions lead to larger numbers.

Considering only assaults that result in *injury,* Straus concluded that there are about 198,000 women assaulted each year, far less than the two million or more often cited as victims of "severe" assaults. Others offer higher numbers. Kurz examined various studies and surveys, and concluded that 10–20 percent of women are "beaten by a male intimate in a given year," and 25–50 percent are beaten at least once over their lifetime. Flowers cites the National Crime Victimization surveys from 1987 to 1991 (a period of five years) that "found 2.9 million women were the victims of violence by intimates, for an average of 572,032 victimizations per year." Other studies show that two million women are victimized every year, and many women never report the assaults they suffer (Straus, 1993, p. 52; Kurz, 2001, pp. 205–206; Flowers, 1994, p. 12).

A more recent story, while reporting that attacks between partners fell between 1993 and 1998, gives the following figures. Based on interviews with 300,000 households, the survey estimated there were 876,000 cases of abuse in 1998, compared to 1.1 million in 1993 (a reduction of 21 percent). The victimization rate by "intimate partners" was 9.8 per thousand for women in 1993 and 7.7 in 1998; 1.6 and 1.5 for men. The preceding survey was by telephone. A National Public Radio story raised the question whether women in abusive relationships would be able to tell the truth when they received the call, if their partners were in the room (Lichtblau, 2000; Morning Edition, May 18, 2000).

Violence against women exists throughout the world. Statistics compiled by the Center for Health and Gender Equity for Population Reports show that, over their lifetime, 13 percent of women in South Africa will suffer a physical assault by an intimate partner; 21 percent in Switzerland; 22 percent in the United States.; 28 percent in Nicaragua; 34 percent in Egypt; and 40 percent in India. "Abuse can run the gamut from hitting, slapping and kicking to sexual coercion to psychological control by intimidation and humiliation. Sometimes the physical symptoms last long beyond [when] the wounds have healed; some women live with irritable bowel syndrome and chronic pain syndrome. Others suffer with psychological problems such as depression or anxiety, or abuse alcohol and drugs" (Foreman, 2000).

A related debate is the extent of partner violence in various social classes, ethnic groups, and races. Some writers have concluded that it is higher among poor people and African Americans; it occurs in all classes, but the risk is greater is for poor people. Kurz too found that among the 129 women that she interviewed, those on welfare and with fewer resources experienced the most violence. She thinks, however, that it is possible they were more likely to turn to the police, given they had few other resources. In addition, men with higher incomes may have other means of control and resort to violence less often. Generally, then, poor women, white and black, may experience more violence, or, they are more likely to turn to official authorities, or they are less able to hide their situation (Gelles, 1997, p. 321; Kurz, 2001, pp. 211–212; Johnson and Ferraro, 2000, p. 953).

More recently, there has been research on violence in Asian families, other new immigrant families, and gay and lesbian couples. Little attention had been paid to them, and they may have been trying to hide the existence of violence in their midst (Campbell, Masaki, and Torres, 1997; Ferguson, 2001, readings 30, 11, and 32; English, 1993; Hill, 1999; Johnson and Ferraro, 2000).

Types of Violence. Most research and statistics on violence between intimate partners tend to include together very different actions and experiences. Johnson and Ferraro propose that we distinguish between four different types (2000).

1. *Common couple violence.* This refers to hitting, throwing objects, and similar actions by men and women "in the context of a specific argument." Unlike intimate terrorism (below) common couple violence does not cause injuries, and it is practiced equally by men and women.

2. *Intimate terrorism.* This involves serious injury, and it increases over time. Intimate terrorism is practiced mostly by men (in one study, 97 percent). It is part of a pattern of actions men use to control women. Recent research has shown that it also exists in same-sex couples.

3. *Violent resistance.* Battered partners, usually women, resort to violence to protect themselves from their batterers. Sometimes they kill them. (See "Women Who Kill" below.)

4. *Mutual violent control.* This is intimate terrorism practiced by both members of a couple. They both use violence to control the other (Johnson and Ferraro, 2000).

People who claim that women are as violent as men base their argument on research that does not distinguish between these four types. Women are equal perpetrators of common couple violence, but it is men who commit almost all intimate terrorism. Let us now explore the debate on gender symmetry in intimate violence.

Are Women as Violent as Men? After women began to expose and work to stop male violence in intimate relationships, at some point some writers began to argue that women were just as violent as men. They make two points: (1) "[W]omen's advocates exaggerate statistics on the number of women who suffer from domestic violence each year." (2) "[W]omen's abuse of men has been virtually ignored." There is sex symmetry in intimate violence; men and women engage in it in equal proportions and rates (Swisher, 1996, p. 8).

Historical data show that some women were taken to court by men for cruelty. Plymouth Plantation court records show that wives were accused of "abusive carriage . . . just about as often as husbands." Court records in some other counties in early Colonial Massachusetts contained "thirty-four notations of wife abuse, eleven instances of husband abuse, and two cases of mutual abuse." And "in the town of Ipswich . . . from 1650–1682, there were six recorded cases of wife abuse, four cases of husband abuse, and one case of mutual abuse" (Demos, 1970 p. 95; M. Liazos, 1996, p. 19). (At least some cases of husband abuse may have been instances of self-defense by abused wives; see below.)

Lately, media stories have focused on violence by women. Ann Landers reminded her readers that "husbands can suffer abuse too." A reader wrote: "I was an abused husband. During 10 years of marriage, starting on our honeymoon, my wife became more and more abusive, first verbally, then, physically. Years of counseling resulted in very little improvement. Every day, I lived in fear of her unprovoked attacks and storming rages. Finally, one night, my wife brutally beat me in front of our 7-year-old daughter. That was the night I decided I had had enough, and packed up and left." She replied: "You were brave to write, and thank you. Abused husbands are not as rare as you think. I have heard from several over the years and printed their letters" (Landers, 1999c, p. D8; for arguments that women are as abusive as men, see Cook, 1997; Pearson, 1997; Young, 1998, 2002c; Stockman, 2002b).

In 1995, Betsy Lucal wrote "The problem with 'battered husbands.'"In this paper she wonders why women's groups were successful in publicizing wife abuse and making it a "social problem," but men's groups have failed to convince sociologists and the public that physical assaults by wives are also a social problem. Her answer: Unlike women, men have been unable to build and sustain a social movement to lobby on behalf of men; "sustained media attention has been lacking"; and "if gender images make the identification and definition of battered wives easier, they make similar perceptions of battered husbands all the more difficult" (1995, p. 113).

Two comments. First, Lucal assumes that there is a large number of battered husbands, but makes no effort to prove that assumption. Second, of course, there *is* an organized men's movement: all the institutions men control, in politics, the court system, business, and the media. Recently, a character on a popular TV show complained, who looks out for the interests of middle-aged affluent men? "Congress," he was told. Lucal ignores the larger political and social context.

Two surveys, carried out in 1975 and 1985, have been the primary source of evidence for the conclusion that there is symmetry in violence between men and women. According to Straus, "The National Family Violence Surveys obtained data from nationally representative samples of 2,143 married and cohabiting couples in 1975 and 6,002 couples in 1985." Dobash and others go on to explain that "In each survey, the researchers interviewed either the wife or the husband (but not both) in each contacted household about how the couple settled their differences when they had a disagreement. The individual who was interviewed was presented with a list of eighteen 'acts' ranging from 'discussed an issue calmly' and 'cried' to 'threw something at him/her/you' and 'beat him/her/you up,' with the addition of 'choked him/her/you' in 1985" (Straus, 1993, p. 51; Dobash and others, 1992, p. 326).

Both the 1975 and 1985 surveys concluded that there was symmetry in violence. Some people complained that men were likely to underreport their violent acts, so the researchers then examined only the information provided by women. "The resulting overall rate for assaults by wives is 124 per 1,000 couples, compared to 122 per 1,000 for assaults by husbands *as reported by wives*. . . . The rate of minor assaults by wives was 78 per 1,000 couples, and the rate of minor assaults by husbands was 72 per 1,000. The severe assault rate was 46 per 1,000 couples for assaults by wives and 50 per 1,000 couples by husbands" (Straus, 1993, p. 51).

Such evidence may seem irrefutable. When women tell about their and their partners' actions, and they report similar rates of violence, can there be any doubt that there is symmetry? There is doubt. As Johnson and Ferraro show, there are very different types of violence. Most of what the surveys counted, which shows symmetry, were pushes and shoves, common couple violence. There is indeed a vast difference between a minor shove, or even a slap, and violent acts that injure and terrorize people.

Moreover, any

> respondent who acknowledges a single instance of having "pushed," "grabbed," "shoved," "slapped," *or* "hit or tried to hit" another person is deemed a perpetrator of "violence" by the researchers, regardless of the act's context, consequences, or meaning to the parties involved. Similarly, a single instance of having "kicked," "bit," "hit or tried to hit with an object," "beat up," "choked," "threatened with a knife or gun," or "used a knife or fired a gun" makes one a perpetrator of "severe violence."
>
> Consider a "slap." The word encompasses anything from a slap on the hand chastising a dinner companion for reaching for a bite of one's dessert to a tooth-loosening assault intended to punish, humiliate, and terrorize. (Dobash,and others, 1992, pp. 329–330)

For example, if after years of being battered and abused a wife hits her husband over the head with a bottle, we cannot simply count her as a violent spouse and ignore the long history of abuse she has suffered (Dobash and others, 1992, pp. 329–330).

We need to "assess the meanings, contexts, and consequences of . . . individual acts." The context often includes years of "economic deprivation, sexual abuse, intimidation, isolation, stalking, and terrorizing—all common elements of wife battering and all rarely perpetrated by women." Some battered women at some point strike back in self-defense and kill their abusive husbands. Can we ignore the history of abuse heaped upon them by their partners (Yllo, 1993, p. 613)?

Straus himself offers statistics that show vast inequality in violence that injures and maims. He summarizes research that shows "the injury adjusted rate for assaults by men is *seven times greater* than the rate of domestic assaults [resulting in injuries] by women." FBI data bear out that conclusion. The "number of women who kill their allegedly abusive partners has always been far lower than the number of abusive men who kill women—13 vs. 87 percent" (Straus, 1993, p. 52, emphasis added; Ranalli, 1999, p. B12).

There is more evidence for asymmetry. Records from hospital emergency rooms, assault cases "reported" to police, and spouses seeking to escape abuse, all contain mostly women's names. For example, 90–95 percent of assault victims in homes who call police are women. Various victimization surveys show that 80–90 percent of victims are women. A study based on a national sample concluded that "experiencing violence in the hands of a partner has significant adverse effects on a sense of personal control for women, but not for men . . . violence . . . is more detrimental to the self-perceptions and well-being of women than of men" (Umberson and others, 1998, p. 442; see also Dobash and others, 1992).

Above I cited the research that led Ward to conclude "the cross-cultural evidence simply does not support a claim of gender equality in beatings and batterings. . . . Men batter, kill, and maim women in domestic partnerships with a far greater impunity and frequency than women do." Evidence from many sources argues strongly against symmetry. Far more men attack and injure women than women do men (Ward, 1999, pp. 238–239).

Women Who Kill: Self-Defense? Some women do kill their husbands or lovers. As we saw, 13 percent of those who kill their partners are women. In 1994, there were "approximately 2,000 women serving prison time in the United States for defending themselves against a batterer" (Ferraro, 1997, p. 270).

Traditionally, if person A killed person B while person B was attacking them physically or with a weapon, person A could plead self-defense. Also traditionally, if a man regularly assaulted a woman but she killed him at a time when he was not assaulting her, she could not plead self-defense. Beginning in the 1970s, women's groups have sought to define and treat such killings as self-defense. They argued that a woman who is repeatedly beaten by her partner lives in fear for her life and feels trapped and unable to escape (this is often called the "battered-woman syndrome"). In desperation, feeling she will be killed but also feeling unable to leave because her husband will chase her down, and for other reasons, she may kill her husband. Such an argument of self-defense has prevailed in some courts cases and has been instituted in law in some states.

Gayle Henderson shot her husband in 1985. After four years of abuse, and after her husband James "punctured her eardrum, fractured her nose, tried to choke her and left her with multiple bruises" on Thanksgiving Day, she shot him in the head with his pistol. Her lawyer argued self-defense and the grand jury refused to charge her with murder (Sleeper, 1986).

Other women did not convince the courts that they were acting in self-defense. During her two years of marriage to Ken, from 1982 to 1984, "Donna was battered twenty-three times. . . . On the day of the killing, Ken returned home drunk, beat her, sexually assaulted her, and threatened to kill her. After a final assault in which he first choked her and then passed out, Donna obtained a gun and shot him. The trial court [in 1992 in California] refused to admit testimony regarding battered-woman syndrome and how it related to the requirement of imminence in self-defense. The jury convicted Mrs. Bechtel on first-degree murder, and she was sentenced to life imprisonment" (Wallace, 1999, p. 200; for more discussion of successful and unsuccessful arguments of self-defense, see pp. 198–202 in Wallace).

In 1994, Massachusetts passed a law that allowed women charged with killing their partners to "present both evidence of the abuse they had endured and expert testimony on the psychological damage it had caused." By 1999, this law had rarely been used, with only one case in all of Middlesex County. Fewer battered women are killing husbands, apparently, as "more shelters, tougher domestic violence laws, and better-trained police officers are heading off potentially deadly situations." Of the two cases tried under the new law, one woman who killed her abusive partner was not tried for murder, but the other was tried and found guilty. Some advocates for battered women "acknowledge that the [battered-woman] defense is sometimes misused" (Ranalli, 1999).

But Brownstein, who listened to the stories of women who killed their husbands, left wondering "why did you wait so long?" Many finally retaliated after the abusive husband had also begun to abuse the children (Brownstein, 2000, p. 86).

Shelley Bannister asserts passionately that women who are imprisoned for killing their abusive husbands are "political prisoners." They defend themselves from the abuse men inflict on them, from the controls of a patriarchal society. Whereas very few men are punished for the violence they commit against women, women who defend themselves are criminalized and imprisoned. In the same way that South Africans and others who fought or fight for their freedom are considered *political* prisoners when they are locked up, so should women who resist patriarchy and rebel against the abuse they suffer (Bannister, 1991).

Experiences of Violence, Control, and Terror

Profound human experiences are difficult to explain to those who do not share them. Violence in marriage probably is one such experience. Those of us who have not experienced it can only read about and try to understand the terror under which victims of abuse live.

Before I describe the development and stages of battery, let us first hear a few victims speaking about that experience (I present them chronologically).

In 1992, Elizabeth Murray was divorcing her husband Sean and was very carefully hiding from him. After suffering much abuse from him, she had had him arrested. "The weekend before the arrest had been particularly hellish, divorce records say. On July 12, he beat her three times in a day, 'He dragged me by the hair, pushed me to the floor, jumped at me with both feet and kicked me in the ribs, crotch, and stomach,' according to the affidavit she filed for the divorce." During their marriage, he controlled her life, "picking her up at work each night, forbidding her to lunch with fellow employees, spying on her at the office, and forbidding business trips." Even though she was very careful to avoid places where he might be, one day he saw her while she was picking up her mail from her former apartment, and he shot her to death (Rakowsky, 1992, p. 6).

Before she was killed by her husband in 1998, Elizabeth Holland described the violence. She wrote in an affidavit she filed: "In the last week, he knocked me down on the kitchen floor, telling me he was going to smash my face in, chased me through the house yelling and throwing things at me. He threw a glass at my head, shattering it, and overturned a table. All this occurred with Patrick [their son], age 8, in the immediate area" (in McNamara, 1998, p. B1).

Carla Flanagan finally escaped years of abuse and total control by her husband when she had him arrested in 1999. "She portrayed him as a cruel taskmaster. He would choose the cereal for their three children, 15, 11, and 8, she said. . . . The children, whom she said were repeatedly beaten with a shillelagh, table legs, and wooden and plastic baseball bats, could not sneeze or go to the bathroom without his permission. The family was virtually kept hostage, she said. . . . This summer, after two incidents in which she said her husband choked her until she became unconscious, she said she put the [escape] plan into action." He was arrested and they slowly created a normal life for themselves (Daniel, 1999, pp. B1, B5).

And in 2002, Dorothy Giunta-Cotter, after enduring years of abuse by her husband, "fled to Maine and moved into a safe home for battered women." In two months she moved back to Massachusetts and took out a restraining order against him. But even though he was arrested and brought to court, the court released him because the judge decided that there was not sufficient evidence to conclude he was a dangerous person. He soon broke into her home and shot her dead (Ellement and DeMarco, 2002).

The beatings and the deaths women suffer are the final stages of a long process of control and terror. These women experience "fear, shock, shame, anger, distrust, sadness, guilt, and helplessness." Some manage to escape by divorcing their husbands or leaving their partners. Of the 129 women Kurz interviewed, half were assaulted at least three times during their marriage. Their husbands also controlled their lives. "They most commonly reported that violence occurred when they attempted to act independently, for example, when they 'started to change' or when their ex-husbands found out that things did not go their way. Violence often occurred when dinner was late or when certain types of food were not available." The women left because of the control and the violence (Schechter, 1982, p. 18; Kurz, 2001, p. 209).

In "Battered women: Strategies for survival," Ferraro outlines five stages that battered women experience in their relationships with their abusers (1997).

1. *Ardor*. This is the dating and falling in love period. The two become bonded. Most women report no violence during this time. He wants her to spend all her time with him, but she sees this as romantic. She does not see his desire for "social exclusivity as oppressive or abusive." She cannot yet detect his controlling behavior (p. 261).

2. *Accommodation*. Violence begins. She learns to live with it, while trying to deflect, minimize, and stop it. Very few women leave after the first incident. They rationalize and even deny injury; some blame themselves, "I just can't learn to keep my mouth shut." In time, some do learn to keep their mouth shut to avoid giving him an excuse for hitting her. They see how rarely abusive men are punished, so they undertake an all-consuming strategy to please him to avoid violence. Others internalize his accusations (pp. 262–266).

3. *Ambivalence*. In time, they begin to realize the seriousness of their situation and their inability to change it. Often, there is a decrease in violence that leads to their ambivalence. Some move to protect themselves, at times fighting back. But "attempts to leave a violent man are dangerous; women are more likely to be killed while trying to leave a relationship than by trying to remain in it." Some go to shelters for battered women, but about half return because of "fear, continuing emotional involvement, desire to keep the family together, and lack of viable alternatives." In one study, "income and employment" were more likely to enable women to leave, rather than self-esteem. Of 85 women who were "unemployed, severely abused, and whose husbands earned over $10,000, 88 percent returned to their abusers after leaving a shelter" (pp. 267–268).

4. *Terror*. Women become convinced that it is more dangerous to leave than to stay (statistics show that it is true). They "perceive their abusers as possessing superhuman power to control and destroy them. Constant surveillance, threats, and punishments convince these women that the men they live with pose an omnipotent and omnipresent danger" (p. 268).

5. *Homicide*. At some point, feeling trapped and desperate, and having a realistic fear that they will be killed, some women kill their abusers (we saw examples previously). In 1994, there were about 2,000 women in prison for killing their batterers (pp. 269–270). (For a similar study of the "stages of engagement," see Dobash and Dobash, 1979.)

Battered women are unique victims because they live with their oppressors. In addition, the violence is very devastating because it happens in the social setting (home and family) where we hope and long for love, caring, trust, and security. Not only their bodies are violated; so are their expectations, dreams, and hopes for a loving family (Schechter, 1982, p. 19).

According to Jones, the result of the violence and control is not a psychological condition, it is not a "battered woman syndrome." "I would call it post-traumatic stress disorder. What happens is not peculiar to battered women. It you get beaten up enough and if your freedom of movement and autonomy are stripped from you bit by bit, you begin to suffer from post-traumatic stress disorder" in the same manner as hostages and prisoners of war (1994, p. 59).

Staying and Leaving

Some writers ask why women stay with violent men, given the experiences we just read.

The first answer is that many or most do leave. Some studies show that up to two-thirds eventually leave their abusive partners. According to one study, "after two and a half years, 43 percent of battered women had left their abusers and two-thirds of the women were living in non-violent situations." Many leave even at the cost of becoming homeless. Liebow learned that many of the homeless women living in shelters near Washington, D.C., in the late 1980s "came or were brought to the shelter to escape further beatings from their husbands" (Johnson and Ferraro, 2000, p. 956; Ferraro, 1997, p. 260; Liebow, 1993, p. 107).

Why do others stay? One reason is fear of injury and death. Women are most in danger for their lives when they leave their abusive partners. A second reason is lack of money and resources. They have no money and nowhere to go, and cannot find jobs to support themselves and their children. The more money and other resources women have, the more likely they are to leave (Horn, 1992).

Shelters

Before the 1970s, millions of women stayed with violent partners because there was nowhere to escape to. The founding and spreading of shelters offered women an alternative to staying. But since there is still a great shortage of shelters and of spaces in them, many women probably still stay because they have nowhere to go.

The women's movement of the late 1960s to early 1970s changed women's consciousness. As women talked with each other—as friends and in various consciousness-raising groups—they learned that they shared common problems and concerns. They realized that the problems were not individual and unique to them; other women shared them. That feminist movement, especially its anti-rape work, was the context of the battered-women's movement. Women began to understand male violence—whether by rape or physical assault—as a *social* problem. By talking with each other, each woman who was assaulted learned there were many others like her. Since the problem was social, the solution should be too. Women could not stop male violence as individuals alone. They needed to work together to help the thousands of women captive in violent relationships.

Thus arose the first shelters for battered women—conceived, organized, and run by women. Some entered the shelter movement through a feminist analysis of women as an oppressed group; some were victims of violence; and some were service-oriented professionals. Later, many religious and social-service groups and institutions set up and ran shelters, but it was the feminist movement and victims of violence that gave rise to shelters. They saw shelters as part of a larger movement for the liberation of and equality for women.

Setting up a shelter was an enormous undertaking. There were no models of how to do it, there was no money and no social support. Schechter describes those early days. "Living and working in a shelter implies crises for all involved. In addition to dealing with the overwhelming problems of shelter residents, staff had to face daily pressures. Since there was never enough money, women had to learn quickly how to write grant proposals, lobby, generate publicity, speak on radio and television, apply for loans and mortgages. They also had to learn how to organize staff and develop work procedures. At the same time that shelter work and its accomplishments were exhilarating, the strains were wearing. In the early years especially, worker 'burnout' was common, and some staff literally destroyed their health or personal lives" (1982, pp. 75–76).

But there were satisfactions and rewards also. It changed the lives of the staff and the women who found a haven. A founder of one shelter said: "What kept me going was that the shelter allowed the women's power to emerge. Listening to them was so moving. . . . The women's options often seem hopeless but their spirit rises above hopelessness and gives me hope" (In Schechter, 1982, p. 68).

Muncie, Indiana, a city of 80,000 in the 1970s, was part of the shelter movement. "Conversations with police officers and social workers in [Muncie] suggest that wife beating has been going on as long as they can remember but that only recently have wives called it to public attention." It was the feminist movement in the nation that gave voice to those wives. In 1977, the Muncie County Task Force on Battered Wives was created, and it recommended the establishment of a shelter. Called A Better Way, in 1979 alone it received about 1,900 calls from women with abusive husbands. "If the current rate continues [in 1980], the shelter will receive over 3,000 calls for assistance in 1980" (Caplow and others, 1982, pp. 134–135).

By 1992, there were about 1,400 shelters. In 2001, there were about 2,000 (an estimate from the National Coalition Against Domestic Violence, July 25, 2001). There were about forty in Massachusetts (an estimate from Jane Doe, Inc., the Massachusetts Coalition Against Sexual Assault and Domestic Violence, July 25, 2001). As large as these numbers may seem, these shelters often have no space for many women who need a place to stay. A study revealed that in 1998 in Massachusetts, "lack of space forced shelters to turn away nearly 12,000 women and children. . . . For every woman or child admitted to the shelters, at least three were shut out. . . . Massachusetts was not alone in facing a shelter shortage. Domestic-violence shelters in New York could take in only 6,000 of the 11,000 families seeking refuge in 1995. . . . In Oregon, similar shelters harbored just over 5,800 adults and children last year, but had to refuse more than 24,000" (Horn, 1992; Wong, 1999a, p. B1).

Many of the women for whom there is no room in battered-women shelters turn to shelters for the homeless (as we saw above), but those shelters are in known locations and offer less safety and security to the women. Indeed, in 1997 two women who fled to homeless shelters were found and killed by their partners.

The shelters have saved battered women, and women's lives. Ann Jones thinks they may have also saved some men's lives, whose wives would have killed them in self-defense if they had been unable to escape (the rate of women killing men has decreased). But she also looks forward to the day when we will no longer need them, the day violence will end. Now, "the shelters are kind of reverse jails for women" (1994, pp. 58–59).

And around 2000, as we discovered that people in same-sex couples also commit violence, and probably at the same rate people in heterosexual couples do, we also found out that there were no shelters for these victims. So supporters and victims created the first (and in 2003, the only) "safe house program" for gay men in the United States. Also, increased awareness of same-sex violence has meant that Boston hospitals started to "take gay domestic violence more seriously" (Mishra, 2002). (The story does not say if there are shelters or programs for abused lesbians.)

THE REASONS . . . ? BECAUSE HE COULD

Why do men assault and hurt the very people they love? Much of the previous discussion implies, hints, and even states explanations for wife beating and wife battering. First, I present a theory that makes sense to me, and then I discuss some other theories.

Isolation, Control, and Economic Dependence

After she explores wife beating and battering across history and cultures, Ward concludes that "anything that enhances personal autonomy, economic opportunities, or links to other women contributes to women's safety." In reverse, what contribute to violence are social isolation, male control in patriarchal societies, and women's economic dependence on men. Each of these conditions makes it more likely for women to be beaten, and it will be difficult for them to escape. When they exist together, they increase the chances for abuse (1999, p. 239).

Social Isolation. Ward thinks that "the most crucial factor in wife abuse is probably *social isolation.*" All anthropologists who have written on wife abuse agree that women who live in families and communities where other people know about and can intervene in family life are much less likely to be abused than are women who live in socially isolated (largely nuclear) families. When relatives and neighbors in extended families and small communities hear or witness abuse, they can intervene to stop it. When couples live without much community supervision, violence can arise. Studies that follow the development of abuse show that the men consciously isolate the women from friends and relatives (1999, p. 237).

Power and Control. Anthropological studies of wife beating and battering show that they are more likely to appear, and to be more serious, in patriarchal societies. Where men rule the institutions of the society—government, economy, and others—they also seek to rule the members of their families. Violence is a tool they use to control their partners. Study after study shows that men resort to violence when they wish to impose control over their wives, when they want them to behave in certain ways, when they are displeased by something their wives did. Indeed, violence tends to begin when women try to act independently, as Kurz found out in her study of 129 divorced women (Kurz, 2001, p. 209).

   Traditional folk stories from around the world (mostly from patriarchal societies) report and condone violence as a tool of male control. Violence is present in many stories about marriage. All kinds of men resort to it: "poor peasants, wealthy merchants, beggars, kings, landowners, educated mandarins, war heroes, and many others from Russia, China, Italy, Vietnam, England, and elsewhere are . . . abusers of women." Violence is a very effective tool:

> [M]en use physical force to demonstrate and protect their superiority and masculinity. . . .
>   Wives are in greatest danger when being critical, carping, disobedient, nagging, ambitious, and generally challenging to man's dominance. Many otherwise peaceful men may then use their greater strength as a weapon and prevail in a physical attack. There are two basic rationales: a husband needs to appear dominant; and a physical attack is usually available, if needed, to impose and maintain this dominance (Ucko, 1995, pp. 36, 38–39)

   In his interviews with abusive men, Ptacek shows that violence was a conscious and planned tool to control their wives. It was "more indicative of a deliberate strategy than an inability to control one's emotions." The transcripts of the interviews reveal that the men "were motivated by a desire to silence their partners; to punish them for their failure as 'good wives'; and to achieve and maintain dominance over these women. Their objectives were accomplished, according to the men: The women fell silent; they were taught a lesson; and they were shown who was in control of the relationship and to what length the batterer would go in maintaining control" (1988, pp. 629, 628). (See also Robb, 1992.)

   Abusive men and some social scientists offer justifications and rationalizations (such as some men's inability to control their emotions; see below), but control and domination are the issue. The examples above make that clear. Men want meals cooked a certain way; wives who are obedient to their every wish; wives who will not challenge them and will not grow. Control is the goal and violence is one of many tools some men use to attain it. For other men, "verbal abuse, withholding affection, or withdrawing resources may suffice" (Schechter, 1982, p. 219; see also Kurz, 2001, p. 212).

Economic Dependence. Anthropologists have found that when women are economically independent they are beaten much less or not at all (see earlier discussion). Much U.S. evidence leads to the same conclusion. Women are much more likely to stay in abusive relationships, and men are more likely to abuse them, when women cannot support themselves. In her study of 129 divorced mothers, Kurz found that women with few resources, especially those on welfare, experienced more violence than other women, 71 percent of them, in contrast to the 50 percent for the entire group (2001, p. 211).

Horn summarizes research that shows women are more likely to leave abusive relationships if they have money and other resources, and to stay in them if they do not. "If a woman has a job that can support her and her children, and has transportation, child-support payments, and other financial resources, she is more likely to make a final break" (1992, p. 21).

We have seen in the chapters on gender and the economy that despite considerable progress, women continue to earn less money than men and to be segregated in lower-paying jobs. To some degree, money is a resource that confers power. It allows men to feel entitled to control their wives and to dictate their wishes.

Other Explanations

There have been many other attempts to explain why men beat and batter their wives. Abusive men themselves offer their accounts or excuses. Alcohol and drug abuse, unemployment, stress at work, the violence in American culture, the personalities of the abusive men and the abused women, are only some explanations offered through the years. (See Kurz, 2001, pp. 206–208; Wallace, 1999, pp. 180–184; Ptacek, 1988).

Men's unemployment and other work problems are often cited as major causes of violence against women. Men without jobs are angry and frustrated. Without their provider role—the major aspect of their identity—they feel lost and hopeless. In this condition, they blindly strike at their wives. The men Faludi talked with had "lost their compass in the world. They had lost or were losing jobs, homes, cars, families." The only time they felt in control was when they beat their wives. Studies claim that men who are unemployed and or working part-time are twice as likely to beat their partners. Rubin says that the combination of unemployment and alcohol "is a potentially deadly one that exponentially increases the likelihood that a man will act out his anger on the bodies of his wife and children" (Faludi, 1999, p. 9; Horn, 1992; Rubin, 1994, p. 118).

No doubt unemployment is very stressful. It causes economic hardships and worries. It does assault men's sense of themselves. But why do men take out their frustrations on their partners? They do not cause their frustration. Why not attack other men, the companies that laid them off, the government that will not guarantee them a job? Why do they displace their anger on their wives? Why do they mostly assault their wives?

Alcohol and drug abuse is often cited as a cause of male violence against their partners. Men deny responsibility for their actions by blaming their "loss of control" on alcohol. One study asked 256 women, who went to emergency rooms because of injuries inflicted on them by their partners, about the habits and lives of their partners. The authors concluded that women had "more than three times the risk of domestic violence when husbands or male partners abuse alcohol or drugs, go in and out of jobs, or break up with the women." One of the authors told the reporter that the study offered "the strongest evidence so far that links alcohol abuse by the male partner with domestic violence." Another study made a similar connection between drug and alcohol abuse with male violence (Ptacek, 1988; Associated Press, 1999d).

An association and statistical correlation is not a cause, however. It is true that men who batter their partners tend to abuse alcohol and drugs. But that abuse is not the major cause of their violent actions. Most men with drug and alcohol problems do not batter. Also, we know from studies of other cultures that in those places alcohol abuse is not associated with violence; it does not give permission and an excuse to men to hit others. There is something in U.S. culture that permits men to deny responsibility for their actions by blaming alcohol for hitting women. Very few drunken men hit the police, their bosses, and their friends. Why hit their wives? (Jacobson and Gottman, 1998; Gelles, 1997).

Others blame the socialization and personality of the men. They cite their feelings of insecurity and inadequacy, dependency, poor impulse control, poorly developed egos, deprived childhood, and abuse they received as children. Johnson and Ferraro, however, show in detail that the argument that fathers pass on violent behavior to their sons is not supported by the statistical evidence (2000, p. 958).

Let us look at poor impulse control. Two psychologists who studied 201 married couples over eight years concluded that while there are a few people with biological and psychological conditions that make their behavior uncontrollable, "in the vast majority of cases, battering is a choice in the same sense that all other voluntary actions are" (Jacobson and Gottman, 1998, p. 479; see also Ptacek, 1988).

Abusive men tend to "lose control" when they wish to dominate their wives. They do not lose control in other social situations. They are not violent criminals. A study of New York City abusers found that 90 percent of them did not have criminal records. In Ptacek's study, seventeen of the eighteen men blamed alcohol, drugs, and frustrations for their violent acts. But only five of them were also violent outside the family. So, why *do* men "lose control" with their female partners (Flowers, 1994, p. 13; Ptacek, 1988, p. 624)?

Violent men seek to excuse and justify their behavior by focusing on alcohol, provocation by their wives, loss of job, and numerous other external conditions. They minimize the hurt they cause and deny responsibility and injury. These are rationalizations and excuses. So, why do men beat and batter their partners? Not because their partners irritate or provoke them. "Common sense tells us that all people who know each other intimately irritate each other: irritation does not cause violence; it is an excuse offered by a man who believes he has the authority and right to beat a woman" (Schechter, 1982, p. 24; see also Ptacek, 1988).

Men Beat Their Wives and Partners Because They Can

Men beat their wives because they seek control over them. Because the male-dominated culture has traditionally assumed men are in control. Because men are in control of the economy and other institutions still. Violence is "a conscious strategy used by men to control women and maintain the system of gender inequality" (Aulette, 1994, p. 326). This system benefits men. Violence is one of a number of means they use to perpetuate it.

Johnson and Ferraro largely agree with this explanation of violence, but they remind us that people in same-sex couples also use violence to control their partners, as do some women against their male partners. They suggest that violence, as a strategy for power and control, may apply to many situations and relationships. Men using violence to control women is one variety (Johnson and Ferraro, 2000).

WHAT SHOULD WE DO?

Violence has harmful emotional, social, and economic consequences for women. Automatically, it also harms men, children, families, communities, and the entire society. Men can only exist in relationships, families, workplaces, and communities *with* women. If women's lives are damaged, so are men's. We need to erase violence from our lives.

But how can we end something so old and pervasive? We need to do many things. But as we do them, our focus should remain on the root causes, on the gendered nature of violence. It dictates what we must do: eliminate male domination and patriarchy, create gender equality, and provide women with the resources (money, jobs, etc.) they need to achieve autonomy.

Progress Made

We must first acknowledge that some progress has been made. Women's groups and victims have exposed and revealed the sad secret. We can no longer pretend. In the 1970s, feminists and victims struggled and sacrificed to create safe places for battered women, and thus began the shelter movement. Shelters may indeed be jails in reverse, and there are not enough of them, but millions of women over the years have found a safe place to escape and begin a new life. Now we need to fund more of them, for all women who need them for as long as we need them.

There are now clear laws against violence at home. They are not always enforced by the police and the courts, but there is considerable enforcement. Increasingly, more women speak out, report the violence, seek assistance from police, courts, shelters, women's organizations. There is some evidence that the violence may be decreasing. (See earlier discussion of data presented in Lichtblau, 2000).

Years of organizing and sustained political work led to the 1994 passage by Congress of the Violence Against Women Act. The act provided $1.5 billion for "education, hot lines, battered women's shelters, and increased prosecutions." It may be partly responsible for reducing violence against women. There are "hot lines" everywhere—telephone numbers for abused women who want advice, information about resources, someone to listen to them (Lichtblau, 2000; Kurz, 2001, p. 205).

Without shelters, hot lines, laws against violence, and the awareness we now have, it must have been painfully lonely for abused women in the 1960s and before. Ignorance of abuse may have enabled some people to feel safe, but it made it hell for the millions of women who endured abuse silent and alone. We cannot forget how far we have come.

An Anthropologist's View

Martha Ward thinks that we can increase women's safety if we promote their "personal autonomy, economic opportunities, or links to other women." Preceding and following discussions expand on her recommendation (1999, p. 239).

Jane Doe, Inc.

Judith Beals is executive director of Jane Doe, Inc., the Massachusetts Coalition against Sexual Assault and Domestic Violence. The organization raises funds for shelters and related activities. After Beals reminds us that "while 85 percent of the violence is directed against women, men are victims, too," she offers four suggestions. (1) Prevent abuse by focusing on the root causes of violence in families: "inequality, sexism, racism, classism, heterosexism, and other abuses of power and privilege." (2) Strengthen and support the shelters and the work they do. They need more money, in part to pay living wages to the people who work in them. (3) Control and re-educate batterers better than we now do. (4) Study each family killing more intensively, and use that knowledge to prevent more killings (Beals, 2000).

Autonomy and Gender Equality

Ward and Beals both make wise suggestions. They can be fully realized only if we work toward a society of true autonomy and equality for men *and* women. Patriarchy in all its forms must end.

We can begin with marriage and the marriage ceremony. As now practiced, it gives men a sense of entitlement and superiority. "The ritual with which most marriages begin still reflects the problem. When a man's bride comes to him off the arm of her father, the subliminal message is that property is being exchanged between males. When a woman surrenders her own name to take her husband's, the subliminal message is that she will subordinate her identity to his." In 2001, 90 percent of brides still took their husbands' names (Carroll, 1992, p. 15; Wen, 2001b).

The marriage ceremony and women changing their name are powerful symbols of male control and domination. They reflect traditional male ownership of fields, houses, property, jobs, and money. These possessions enabled men to exercise control over women, who could not provide for themselves. We have begun to undo the total male control of economic resources, but more needs to be done. Women find it difficult to leave violent relationships because they cannot support themselves and their children. All women, and specifically those fleeing violence, need affordable housing, income supports, jobs, free health care, child care, clothing, food, utility assistance, and more. They need these specific services and goods when they leave; they need income and jobs in the long run to support themselves. More important, they need economic independence *before they marry* so they will enter marriage as equal partners. That may not end violence totally and immediately, but it will make it less likely, partly because men will know women can afford to leave controlling and abusive relationships (Ferraro, 1997, pp. 270–271; Schechter, 1982, p. 238; Horn, 1992; Baum, 2000).

Men against Violence

Women and men must and can come together to create the economy and society where all people have the opportunity for jobs and incomes that will allow them to be equal partners. Men can also work to end violence in intimate relationships. Some men's groups are doing so. Some men's organizations are counseling violent men to overcome their controlling actions and habits. (Counseling and therapy probably help only some men; see below.) In Massachusetts and some other places, men organize and publicly take "a stand against domestic violence and sexual assault and are encouraging other men to do likewise." In Gloucester, during a town parade watched by about 25,000 people, "86 men—bankers, clergymen, and artists, too—turned up to march. They called their ad hoc group Gloucester Men against Domestic Abuse. . . . A few hecklers took verbal shots at the group . . . but not many." They carried on their cause through discussions in bars, homes, and other places (Kahn, 2000, pp. D1, D8).

Some clergy have organized to educate themselves and others about domestic abuse, and to work against it. Traditionally, clergy were inclined to try to "repair an abusive relationship" and save a marriage. Now "the first priority is to protect the victim." To that end, ten Massachusetts Christian and Jewish congregations organized the Safe Havens Project. It aims to "train clergy on how to talk to the victims as well as abusers; require clergy members to write sermons on the issue; and help congregations host workshops and distribute relevant literature, among other things." In a similar vein, all doctors, nurses, and other health-care providers should ask about domestic abuse if they see physical signs that may be evidence of it (Ribadeneira, 1998; Foreman, 2000).

Legal Strategies

Violent assault against domestic partners is a crime in all fifty states. That has been a significant step in reducing violence. Enforcement remains a problem, however. Some police departments make no or poor response when women call them; others operate effectively and do respond. One issue is what police should do when they arrive on the scene but the victim refuses to file charges against the attacker, despite the evidence of abuse. In some states, police are required to make an arrest irrespective of the victim's wishes. Ann Jones says we need to be firm and consistent in arresting, prosecuting, and sentencing batterers. Police, prosecutors, and judges should work together to give a clear message that violence is a crime and will not be tolerated (Jones, 1994).

Some cities and counties have established comprehensive programs to stop violence. As early as 1978, the Norfolk County (Massachusetts) District Attorney's office created a unit that "aimed to improve police and judicial responses . . . integrating the services provided by the DA's office, the courts, the police, other community agencies, and . . . battered women's shelters and advocates themselves. The program emphasizes access to legal protection for women and prosecution for batterers. Daily briefings are held for battered women on their rights, and there are two psychologists who work with the domestic violence unit to conduct support groups, individual counseling, and court advocacy efforts on behalf of these women. The office follows up police reports of family violence incidents with letters and phone calls to the victims" (M. Liazos, 1996, p. 91).

In October 2000, a Boston district court, with a grant of $1.9 million from the U.S. Department of Justice, created a "new court session dedicated solely to domestic violence cases . . . the court [will] provide a kind of one-stop shopping, offering services for victims and defendants. The court will hear all domestic violence cases from beginning to end, bringing specially trained prosecutors, probation officers, investigators, and victims' advocates together with victims and offering everything from special translators to shelter referrals and even emergency economic aid" (Latour, 2000, p. B2).

The Limits of Therapy

Sometime in the late 1980s, I invited a speaker from EMERGE, a group that counsels men who abuse their wives, to one of my classes. His major advice to my female students was that if they were ever assaulted by their partner, to leave immediately. Don't stay around hoping you'll change him, he told them. Very few abusive men change.

But there is a debate on the likelihood of reforming violent men. Jacobson and Gottman say there is little evidence that therapy changes them. To think that it does is dangerous and gives a false sense of security. While "many men decrease their level of violence over time, few of them stop completely. And when they do stop, the emotional abuse usually continues." Indeed, over the first two years of their study, 93 percent continued the abuse, although the degree of it "dropped substantially" in 54 percent of the cases. But after the initial assaults have terrorized the victims, there is less need to use violence to control them (Jacobson and Gottman, 1998, p. 480; Ebbert, 1998a).

Other researchers and counselors of abusive men are less pessimistic. They think treatment programs are more effective than Jacobson and Gottman think. EMERGE is one program that works with about 300 abusive men a week. Its director thinks that even though about half of the men do not complete the program, and "a quarter to a third of its graduates revert to battering . . . abusers often succeed after repeated attempts at rehabilitation" (Ebbert, 1998a; for a court program that "counsels men named in restraining orders," see Wilmsen, 2002).

Therapy may and does help some men. It cannot be the major part of the solution, however, because most men who abuse are not psychologically disturbed. As we saw above, violence is a conscious attempt to control women. We need to change the social conditions that encourage and allow men to dominate through violence.

Some Practical Advice

What do you do if a friend tells you she is being abused? Jones suggests you do three things: tell her that you know how difficult it is for her; tell her you will help, but only if you really mean it; and help her find available resources like shelters, legal aid, and so on (Jones, 1994).

Foreman cites some very concrete steps that women can take to protect themselves. Safety manuals "advise . . . that a battered woman tell one or more neighbors about the violence so they can call 911 if they hear or see a disturbance in the woman's home. During an argument, a woman should walk into a room that she can leave easily. Staying away from rooms, such as the kitchen, where there are items that could be used as weapons, is also a good idea. Having a bag packed with spare keys, money, documents and clothes and keeping it at the home of a friend or relative also makes sense" (2000, p. C4).

Self magazine provided a list of "60 ways to stop domestic violence." They range from broad suggestions like building more shelters, funding a national hot line for victims to call for information and referral, and funding more research on domestic violence, to very concrete suggestions like requiring telephone companies to print hot line numbers on the front cover of the phone book, creating a national computer registry of men under restraining orders, and even holding a benefit to raise money for shelters. The list is comprehensive and challenging (*Self* Magazine, 1994).

This list of things to do, long as it may seem, barely touches the range of issues, programs, and suggestions to end violence in intimate relationships. Much must and can be done. The guiding principle in all we do is the search for gender equality, since gender inequality is the basic cause of male violence and control.

CONCLUSION

I find it troubling and painful to write about violence in families. I keep thinking of Linda Logan's life. I can't comprehend the wounds, scars, and even death people (mostly men) inflict on people (mostly women) they love. As I end this chapter, the studies and statistics and examples do not suffice to explain violence. As much as I do believe the theory that violence is a tool men use to control their partners in male-dominated societies, at some deeper level it does not satisfy me. For at the same time, these men do love their wives, they depend on them, they raise their children. How can they assault them? Even as I do very much believe the theory of violence as male control, how can we explain the cases of women battering men? These cases are many times fewer than those of men battering women, but they do exist, at least a few thousand a year in the United States. How can we explain them? And how do we explain violence in same-sex relationships?

I am also troubled by the debate of what we count as violence and how we count it. By counting shoves and slaps, do we exaggerate violence? But isn't a slap hurtful and damaging? Is it possible that there is much more violence—from slaps to cuts to knifings—than the victims can ever feel safe to report? And what about the relationships where the physical assaults have ended, but the memory, the fear, and the terror remain? Can they be counted as non-violent relationships?

These and more questions trouble me. They will not go away. The most disturbing suspicion of all is the possibility that some type of violence exists in most families. If we take child abuse, elder abuse, sexual violence, violence between partners, and all the others I mention early in this chapter, can it be that one or more of them have visited most families? Sometimes I'm certain the answer is yes; at other times I find it impossible to believe. Can violence co-exist with love, caring, and protection? If so, where are the family joys? Perhaps people who escape abuse are seeking these family joys.

14

Closing Reflections and Parting Comments

Writing this book has been a long journey for me, both personally and professionally. It began in May 1999, a month after my mother died, and it is now August 2003. In that time, much has happened in my family. Both my daughters were married, as was a niece. Nephews and nieces had children. And just three weeks ago, most of our extended family had a family gathering in our ancestral village of Longo, Albania (that part of Albania is populated by ethnic Greeks and borders Greece). We came together from Greece, the United States and Albania. The memory and the emotions are very much with me as I write this.

In our family you can see all the changes, joys, and conflicts I present in this book, but the importance we all attach to our family brought us all together for a few days. So let me close the book with a brief discussion of both the changes and the significance families have in all our lives. I will also mention some uncertainties and ambivalence about families that still trouble me, and I will close with a toast and a wish.

RECENT AND ONGOING CHANGES

Same-Sex Marriages

As we saw in chapters 1 and 4, same-sex marriage has come to Holland, Belgium, and Canada. The United States and other countries are likely to join them soon. A Dutch acquaintance tells me that most Dutch people have accepted same-sex marriage and there has been no social upheaval because of it.

Divorce

As we saw in chapter 12, divorce has a long history in the United States. It has been the subject of much concern, debate, and controversy. It peaked in the 1960s and 1970s, but it has stabilized and even declined slightly since then. Divorces per 1,000 population were 2.2 in 1960, 3.5 in 1970, 5.3 in 1981 (the highest point), 4.7 in 1990, and 4.2 in 2000. Thus, while there has been a significant increase in divorce, it has slowed down, and most people still marry (*Statistical Abstract,* 2002, p. 59).

Working Mothers

The number of working married mothers with children under 6 has increased steadily since the 1950s. From about 12 percent in 1950, it grew to 30 percent in 1970, 60 percent in 1990, and came to a high of 63.7 percent in 1998. It decreased slightly to 62.5 percent in 2001. These numbers show a long, strong, and steady trend of more mothers working that may have reached a plateau. It may be that now some more mothers of young children will stay home

Again, we see the family from chapter 2, but everyone is not in this photo. One daughter is spending the holiday with her partner's family, and the father is spending the holiday with his new partner's family. Yet the father's parents are celebrating with the family as well as are a cousin and her husband. This family has been directly affected by all of the changes summarized in this chapter, yet it endures with much love and caring for each other.

with them a few more years than most young mothers have been doing. It will take some years before we can tell if this reversal becomes a trend, and what it may indicate (*Statistical Abstract*, 1977, p. 392; 2002, p. 373).

We have discussed other family developments that show both important changes and strong commitment to families and family relationships. Here are a few examples. Women all over the world are having fewer children, in many countries so few that populations are declining, but most women all over the world are having at least one child. People are getting married later, are staying married for shorter periods, and some are cohabiting instead of marrying, but the vast majority of women and men very much want intimate and romantic ties with another person. Family members are less likely to live near relatives and they see each other less often than in past times, but they insist that family ties and relatives are very meaningful to them. And as much as hospitals, nursing homes, assisted living facilities, and other institutions are taking over caregiving, family members still provide much or most caregiving.

You could think of many more examples. All indicate that profound changes have taken and are taking place in our family lives, but also that family relationships are vital and irreplaceable in our lives.

PERSPECTIVES ON FAMILIES

This summary and the entire book clearly argue that families may be changing and often troubled, but they are also important and enduring in our lives (see ch. 3). However, I encourage you to examine this perspective critically. Reflect carefully on the studies and statistics I present, consider other evidence you have gathered, read other studies, and include your own and others' experiences with your families. You may find that none of the three perspectives in chapter 3 describes your present view on the condition of families today. Also, as you go through life your view may change. Your own family history and social conditions that you encounter may alter how you think about the state of families in the United States and the world.

My perspective has certainly changed. When I began teaching this course in 1980, and for some years after, I thought that families had been declining and deteriorating for decades and centuries and were continuing to do so. But gradually, as I read more studies and as I taught the course more times, I came to the perspective I present in this book.

But if you read the book very carefully, you may have noticed that in some places I still see a long-term decline in the strength and importance of families. For example, sometimes I think that when people say in polls that their families are the most important part of their lives, they are expressing more of a wish than a reality.

My ambivalence is most obvious in chapter 7, on kin and community. The images of family and community among the people of East London, the Abkhasians, the Mangione family of Mount Allegro, and others, are powerful symbols of strong extended family ties that are rare today. The daily visits between adult children and their parents found in East London and Boston's West End in the 1950s, for example, overpower the data on monthly family contacts described in Muncie, Indiana, in the 1970s, and in other places today. Try as I may, I cannot convince myself that the frequency, strength, and importance of family ties and contacts today even approximate those of the earlier families discussed in chapter 7.

This ambivalence on the strength of families today may be seen in other places in the book. It represents my own struggle to make sense of the condition of my own family, immediate and extended, and of families in general. For example, our recent family gathering in Longo made vivid for me the many relatives I have. There were thirty of us, with ten more missing, all of us the children, grandchildren, great-grandchildren, and spouses of children and grandchildren of my parents, Georgia and Theodoros Liazos. I delighted in holding my grandniece Georgia Zokos, four months old, named after my mother. There are also many cousins and their families, many of whom I met during this trip. But such gatherings are rare, and when we are not together, all we have is at most weekly phone calls. We are close emotionally and we care for each other, but geography separates us and we are not part of each other's daily lives. So I ask myself, what is the larger reality, the love we feel, or the absence of frequent association?

SOME IMPORTANT REMINDERS

In addition to the concluding thoughts above, I would like to close with reminders of some of the major themes and arguments of this book.

1. Conflicts, troubles, and changes have been the mark and destiny of families in all societies throughout history. They are also for us today. But just as present, to some degree in all families, are joys and good times.

2. Economic, political, and social conditions, and changes in these conditions, have always shaped the life and history of families all over the world. For example, poverty in the past and the closing and moving of factories today forced people to migrate for jobs, and we saw in chapter 8 how migration shapes families. For me, my own migration is a daily reminder of this reality.

3. We cannot understand families today without a solid understanding of the history of families. This history has many stages. There was not just one type of family in the "good old days." For example, the lives of children in Colonial families were vastly different from those in 1950s families. Colonial children worked alongside their parents and learned reading and farming from them; children in the 1950s went to schools and other institutions to learn reading and job skills.

4. There has been a wide variety of families throughout history, across cultures, and in the United States today. The nuclear family of father, mother, and children has been just one

of many types people have created for their times and places. I hope that the examples I include in this book have made this reality clear. So when we see different family arrangements in the United States today we should not be surprised or upset. Family changes and family diversity have always been present.

5. Often, we allow our wish of how we think families *should be* to influence our understanding of how families *have been and are*. I hope my comments just above will help you avoid this confusion. But I also know that it is very difficult for people to agree on what the history of families has been, or on what the condition of families is today (see chapters 2 and 3). For there has been an intense debate about what has happened and what is happening to American families, indeed, about what a family is, and about the negative or positive nature of recent changes.

6. Even though I often question whether what people say is what they really mean, there is no doubt that in most people there is an intense belief, desire, and commitment to the family as the most important experience and reality in their lives. In anonymous surveys my students write in the first class, and in family histories they pass in at the end of the semester, they insist that this is true for them. Is it so for you and people you know? What other evidence, in addition to the surveys I cite in earlier chapters, is there to help us understand how important families are in our lives?

7. Family changes don't happen by themselves. Decisions made by governments, economic institutions, various groups, families, and individuals bring about these changes. In various groups and settings, we can take collective social actions and seek collective solutions to bring about the family changes we need and want. History is filled with examples, and I have mentioned some. The struggle for gender equality is an outstanding example. As I show in chapter 9, as individuals and in groups, women, and some men, have worked to create equal marriages. From that history I conclude that we cannot overcome the constraints of gender roles without a long and continuous struggle. The same principle applies to the work necessary to have and to make more family time. All kinds of groups must work to change government and corporation policies so that people are allowed and encouraged to devote more time to their families.

So I close with the following wish.

A TOAST AND A WISH: MORE FAMILY TIME

At both my daughters' weddings (August 2000 and August 2002), I was privileged to offer a toast. I reprint it below, and I offer it to all of you, whatever your age, family situation, and relationship. I encourage you to work with others to fashion a society that gives people family time.

I hope and I wish you will always have time in your life—
time for each other;
time for your children;
time for your family;
time for your friends and community.

The most precious gift you have given me is the slow and relaxing times I have spent with you as you were growing up, especially the camping trips and the soft ice cream we ate two to three times a day, the evening picnics at the beach listening to the waves and baseball games, and watching the fireflies and the stars at night.

Time is all we have in life, and it is my greatest wish that you will always make time and have time for each other.

References

Abel, Emily. 1989. "The ambiguities of social support." In Hansen and Garey, 1998, pp. 557–573.

Adler, Marina. 1997. "Social change and declines in marriage and fertility in Eastern Germany." *Journal of Marriage and the Family,* 59:1, February, pp. 37–48.

Ahrons, Constance. 1994. *The Good Divorce.* New York: Harper/Collins. Part reprinted in Susan Ferguson, ed., 2001. *Shifting the Center* (2nd ed.). Mountain View, CA: Mayfield, pp. 355–367.

Albelda, Randy. 1999. "What welfare reform has wrought." *Dollars and Sense,* January/February, pp. 15–17.

Aldous, Joan; Gail M. Mulligan; Thoroddur Bjarnason. 1998. "Fathering over time: What makes the difference." *Journal of Marriage and the Family,* 60:4, November, pp. 809–820.

Amato, Paul R. 1994. "The implications of research findings on children in stepfamilies." In Alan Book, and Judy Dunn, eds. 1994. *Stepfamilies: Who Benefits? Who Does Not?* New Jersey: Erlbaum.

Amato, Paul R. 2000. "The consequences of divorce for adults and children." *Journal of Marriage and the Family,* 62:4, November, pp. 1269–1287.

Andersen, Margaret L. 2000. *Thinking about Women* (5th ed.). Boston: Allyn and Bacon.

Anderson, Kristin L. 1997. "Gender status and domestic violence." *Journal of Marriage and the Family,* 59:3, August, pp. 655–669.

Aquilino, William. 1996. "The life course of children born to unmarried mothers." *Journal of Marriage and the Family,* 58:2, May, pp. 293–310.

Arendell, Terry. 1986. *Mothers and Divorce.* Berkeley, CA: California.

Arendell, Terry. 1995. *Fathers and Divorce.* Thousand Oaks, CA: Sage.

Arendell, Terry. 2000. "Conceiving and investigating motherhood: The decade's scholarship." *Journal of Marriage and the Family* 62:4, November, pp. 1192–1207.

Aries, Philippe. 1962. *Centuries of Childhood.* New York: Vintage.

Armas, Genaro. 2000. "Study finds many lack support." *Boston Globe,* October 14, p. A6.

Armas, Genaro. 2001. "Single-parent households more common globally." *Boston Globe,* November 21, p. A6.

Armas, Genaro. 2002. "Marriage rate rises with education." *Boston Globe,* February 8, p. A16.

Arnold, David. 1987. "Repeal of 1784 cohabitation ban makes couples law-abiding again." *Boston Globe,* May 9, p. 17.

Aschenbrenner, Joyce. 1975. *Lifelines: Black Families in Chicago.* New York: Holt, Rinehart, and Winston.

Associated Press. 1997. "N.J. settlement will allow homosexual couples to adopt." *Boston Globe,* December 18, p. A8.

Associated Press. 1998. "U.S. sees 25% rise over 3 years in number of single fathers." *Boston Globe,* December 11, p. A21.

Associated Press. 1999a. "Study ties high divorce rate to premarital cohabitation." *Boston Globe,* February 3, p. A3.

Associated Press. 1999b. "Parents of many poor children work, welfare researchers say." *Boston Globe,* February 25, p. A12.

Associated Press. 1999c. "N.H. law repeals ban on gay adoptions." *Boston Globe,* May 4, p. B5.

Associated Press. 1999d. "Domestic abuse by men is linked to alcohol use." *Boston Globe,* December 16, p. A8.

Ataiyero, Kayce T. 1999. "Women down on marriage, study finds." *Boston Globe,* July 15, pp. B1, B6.

Aulette, Judy. 1994. *Changing Families.* Belmont, CA: Wadsworth.

Aulette, Judy. 2002. *Changing American Families.* Boston: Allyn and Bacon.

Auster, Carol J. 1996. *The Sociology of Work.* Thousand Oaks, CA: Pine Forge.

Babson, Jennifer. 1999. "Higher rents squeezing city neighborhoods." *Boston Globe,* May 13, pp. D1, D5.

Bacdayan, Albert S. 1977. "Mechanistic cooperation and sexual equality among the Western Bontoc." In Alice Schleget, ed. 1977. *Sexual Stratification.* New York: Columbia, pp. 271–291.

Bader, Eleanor. 1999. "Cohousing." *Dollars and Sense,* January/February, pp. 22–25.

Bailey, Marci. 1997. "Minding the children without breaking bank." *Boston Globe,* July 21, pp. B5, B6.

Balalova, Jeanne, and Philip N. Cohen. 2002. "Premarital cohabitation and housework." *Journal of Marriage and the Family,* 64:3, August, pp. 743–755.

Ball, Deborah. 1997. "The small Italian family." *Boston Globe,* June 4, p. A2.

Bane, Mary Jo. 1976. *Here to Stay: American Families in the Twentieth Century.* New York: Basic.

Bannister, Shelley A. 1991. "The criminalization of women fighting against male abuse." *Humanity and Society,* 15:4, November, pp. 400–416.

Barnes, Annie S. 2000. *Everyday Racism.* Naperville, IL: Sourcebooks.

Barnett, Olga; Cindy L. Miller-Perrin; Robin D. Perrin. 1997. *Family Violence across the Lifespan.* Thousand Oaks, CA: Sage.

Barnett, Rosalind Chait, and Janet Sibley Hyde. 2001. "Women, men, work, and family." *American Psychologist,* 56:10, October, pp. 781–796.

Barnett, Rosalind Chait, and Caryl Rivers. 1996. *She Works, He Works: How Two-Income Families Are Happier, Healthier, and Better Off.* New York: HarperCollins.

Barnett, Rosalind Chait, and Caryl Rivers. 2000. "Mommy gap is widening." *Boston Globe,* May 13, p. A19.

Barnett, Rosalind Chait, and Caryl Rivers. 2002. "The 'epidemic' of childlessness." *Boston Globe,* April 27, p. A11.

Barrow, Virginia M. 1996. *Aging, the Individual, and Society* (6th ed.). Minneapolis: West.

Barry, Ellen. 2002. "After day care controversy, psychologists play nice." *Boston Globe,* September 3, pp. E1, E3.

Barry, Skip. 1998. "City families face housing squeeze." *Dollars and Sense,* January/February, pp. 32–36.

Basch, Norma. 1999. *Framing American Divorce.* Berkeley, CA: California.

Bass, Alison. 1988. "Living together: Bad omen for marriage." *Boston Globe,* January 18, pp. 33, 35.

Bass, Alison. 1990. "Children of divorce pessimistic." *Boston Globe,* November 19, p. 37.

Baum, Anna. 2000. "Taking control." *Dollars and Sense,* January/February, pp. 10–11, 38–40.

Baxandall, Rosalyn. 1976. "Who shall care for our children?" In Jerome Skolnick and Elliott Currie, eds. 1976. *Crisis in American Institutions* (3rd ed.). Boston: Little, Brown.

Beals, Judith E. 2000. "Domestic violence is rising; we need to act." *Boston Globe,* October 5, p. A27.

Bell, Inge, and Bernard McGrane. 1999. *This Book Is Not Required* (rev. ed.). Thousand Oaks, CA: Pine Forge.

Belsky, Jay. 1990. "Parental and nonparental child care and children's socioemotional development." *Journal of Marriage and the Family,* 52:4, November, pp. 885–903.

Benet, Sula. 1974. *The Abkhasians.* New York: Holt, Rinehart, and Winston.

Bengston, Vern L. 2001. "Beyond the nuclear family: The increasing importance of multigenerational bonds." *Journal of Marriage and the Family,* 63:1, February, pp. 1–16.

Bennett, William. 1996. "Homosexual marriage is not a very good idea." *Boston Globe,* June 5, p. 15.

Benokraitis, Nijole V. 1996, 1999, 2002. *Marriages and Families* (2nd, 3rd, and 4th eds.). Upper Saddle River, NJ: Prentice Hall.

Benokraitis, Nijole V., ed. 2000. *Feuds about Families: Conservative, Centrist, Liberal, and Feminist Perspectives.* Upper Saddle River, NJ: Prentice Hall.

Benokraitis, Nijole V., ed. 2002. *Contemporary Ethnic Families in the United States.* Upper Saddle River, NJ: Prentice Hall.

Bergen, R.K. 1996. *Wife Rape.* Thousand Oaks, CA: Sage.

Bergmann, Barbara. 1998. "Watch out for 'family friendly' policies." *Dollars and Sense,* January/February, pp. 10–11.

Bergmann, Barbara. 2000. "Deciding who's poor." *Dollars and Sense,* March/April, pp. 36–38, 45.

Bernard, Jessie. 1972. "The two marriages." In Karen V. Hansen and Anita Ilta Garey, eds., 1998. *Families in the U.S.: Kinship and Domestic Politics.* Philadelphia: Temple, pp. 449–457.

Bernard, Jessie. 1981. "The good-provider role." *American Psychologist,* 36:1, January, pp. 1–12. In James Henslin, ed. 1992. *Marriage and Family in a Changing Society* (4th ed.). New York: Free Press, pp. 275–285.

Bernard, Thomas J. 1992. *The Cycle of Juvenile Justice.* New York: Oxford.

Bidwell, Lee D. Miller, and Brenda J. Vander Mey. 2000. *Sociology of the Family.* Boston: Allyn and Bacon.

Billingsley, Andrew. 1992. *Climbing Jacob's Ladder: The Enduring Legacy of African-American Families.* New York: Simon and Schuster.

Bird, Gloria, and Keith Melville. 1994. *Families and Intimate Relationships.* New York: McGraw-Hill.

Blankenhorn, David. 1995. *Fatherless America: Confronting Our Most Urgent Social Problems.* New York: Basic.

Blanton, Kimberly. 2000. "25% of Mass. families struggling." *Boston Globe,* January 13, pp. C1, C5.

Blau, Francine. 1976. "Women in the labor force." In Jerome Skolnick and Elliott Curie, eds. 1976. *Crisis in American Institutions.* Boston: Little, Brown, pp. 215–230.

Blood, Robert O., and Donald M. Wolfe. 1960. *Husbands and Wives.* New York: Free Press.

Blum, Jeffrey, and Judith E. Smith. 1972. *Nothing Left to Lose.* Boston: Beacon.

Boldt, Megan. 2003. "N.D. rejects effort to repeal cohabitation law." *Boston Globe,* April 6, p. A10.

Bonilla-Silva, Eduardo. 2003. *Racism without Racists.* Lanham, MD: Rowman & Littlefield.

Bortner, M.A. 1988. *Delinquency and Justice.* New York: McGraw Hill.

Boston Globe. 1998. "In memoriam." December 31, p. A18.

Boston Globe. 1999a. "Ignorance about domestic violence" (editorial). *Boston Globe,* February 12, p. A24.

Boston Globe. 1999b. "In memoriam." December 30, p. A22.

Bradbury, Thomas N.; Frank D. Fincham; Steven R.H. Beach. 2000. "Research on the nature and determinants of marital satisfaction: A decade in review." *Journal of Marriage and the Family,* 62:4, November, pp. 964–980.

Braver, Sanford L. 1998. *Divorced Dads: Shattering the Myths.* New York: Tarcher/Putnam.

Braverman, Harry. 1974. *Labor and Monopoly Capital.* New York: Monthly Review.

Bray, James, and John Kelly. 1998. *Stepfamilies: Love, Marriage and Parenting in the First Decade.* New York: Broadway.

Brennan, Tricia, and Chuck Collins. 1998. "Cooperating kids (and parents too)." *Dollars and Sense,* January/February, p. 8.

Brenner, Harvey. 1973. *Mental Illness and the Economy.* Cambridge, MA: Harvard.

Brenner, Johanna. 1998. "On gender and class in U.S. labor history." *Monthly Review,* 50:6, November, pp. 1–15.

Breslow, Marc. 1998. "How people spend their money." *Dollars and Sense,* January/February, pp. 14–18.

Brown, Susan L., and Alan Booth. 1996. "Cohabitation versus marriage." *Journal of Marriage and the Family,* 58:3, August, pp. 668–678.

Brownstein, Henry H. 2000. *The Social Reality of Violence and Violent Crime.* Boston: Allyn and Bacon.

Bryjak, George J., and Michael P. Soroka. 1997. *Sociology* (3rd ed.). Boston: Allyn and Bacon.

Buchanan, Christy M.; Eleanor E. Maccoby; Sanford M. Dornbush. 1996. *Adolescents after Divorce.* Cambridge, MA: Harvard.

Burke, Phyllis. 1993. *Family Values: A Lesbian Mother's Fight for Her Son.* New York: Vintage.

Burke, Phyllis. 1996. *Gender Shock: Exploding the Myths of Male and Female.* New York: Anchor.

Cadwallader, Mervyn. 1966. "Marriage as a wretched institution." *Atlantic Monthly,* November.

Calhoun, Craig; Donald Light; Suzanne Keller. 1997. *Sociology* (7th ed.). New York: McGraw-Hill.

Campbell, Doris Williams; Beckie Masaki; Sara Torres. 1997. "Domestic violence in African American, Asian American, and Latino communities." In Benokraitis, ed., 2002, pp. 289–298.

Campbell, Jacquelyn; Paul Miller; Mary Caldwell. 1994. "Relationship status of battered women over time." *Journal of Family Violence.* 9:2, pp.99–111.

Campbell, Meg. 1999. *Solo Crossing.* New York: Midmarch Arts.

Caplow, Theodore; Howard M. Bahr; Bruce A. Chadwick; Reuben Hill; Margaret Holmes Williamson. 1982. *Middletown Families: Fifty Years of Change and Continuity.* Minneapolis: Minnesota.

Caplow, Theodore; Louis Hicks; Ben J. Wattenberg. 2001. *The First Measured Century.* Washington, DC: AEI.

Capps, Reilly. 2002. "Family Week gives P-town new slant on the 'gay lifestyle.'"*Boston Globe,* August 15, pp. H1, H7.

Carroll, James. 1992. "Learning from a woman's murder." *Boston Globe,* December 22, p. 15.

Center for the Study of Social Policy. 1984. "The 'flip-side' of black families headed by women: The economic status of black men." In Staples, 1991, pp. 117–123.

Cerullo, Margaret, and Phyllis Ewen. 1982. "Having a good time: The American family goes camping." *Radical America,* 16:1–2, January–April, pp. 13–44.

Chafetz, Gary. 1992. "Cambridge ordinance extends benefits to city workers' partners." *Boston Globe,* September 15, pp. 21, 26.

Chafetz, Janet Salman. 1997. "'I need a (traditional) wife!': Employment-family conflicts." In Dana Dunn, ed. 1997. *Workplace/Women's Place.* Los Angeles: Roxbury, pp. 116–123.

Chambliss, William J. 1994. "Policing the ghetto underclass." *Social Problems,* 41:2, pp. 177–194.

Chavez, Leo R. 1992. *Shadowed Lives: Undocumented Immigrants in American Society.* Fort Worth, TX: Harcourt Brace.

Chavez, Paul. 2002. "Cal. legislates paid family leave." *Boston Globe,* September 24, p. A3

Cherlin, Andrew. 1978. "Remarriage as an incomplete institution." *American Journal of Sociology,* 84:3, pp. 634–650.

Cherlin, Andrew. 1999, 2002. *Public and Private Families* (2nd and 3rd eds.). New York: McGraw-Hill.

Cherlin, Andrew, and Frank Furstenberg. 1992. *The New American Grandparent.* Cambridge, MA: Harvard.

Cherlin, Andrew, and Frank Furstenberg, Jr. 1994. "Stepfamilies in the United States: A reconsideration." *Annual Review of Sociology,* v. 20.

Cherlin, Andrew; P. Lindsay Chase-Lansdale; Christine McRae. 1998. "Effects of parental divorce on mental health throughout the life course." *American Sociological Review,* 63:2, April, pp. 239–249.

Chevan, Albert. 1996. "As cheaply as one: Cohabitation in the older generation." *Journal of Marriage and the Family,* 58:3, August, pp. 656–667.

Chinas, Beverly Newbold. 1992. *The Isthmus Zapotecs: A Matrifocal Culture in Mexico* (2nd ed.). Fort Worth, TX: Harcourt Brace Jovanovich.

Chinas, Beverly Newbold. 1993. *La Zandunga: Of Fieldwork and Friendship in Southern Mexico.* Prospect Heights, IL: Waveland.

Chinlund, Christine. 2002. "Announcing gay unions." *Boston Globe,* July 29, p. A11.

Chira, Susan. 1996. "Study says babies in child care keep secure bonds to mothers." *New York Times,* April 21.

Christensen, Bryce J. 1988. "The costly retreat from marriage." *The Public Interest,* Spring, pp. 59–66.

Christian Coalition. 1995. *Contract with the American Family.* Chesapeake, VA: Christian Coalition.

Cimons, Marlene. 1999. "Measures target deadbeat parents." *Boston Globe,* January 1, p. A3.

Cobb, Nathan. 1996. "Adult children of divorce." *Boston Globe,* April 15, pp. 34, 36.

Cobb, Nathan. 1997. "Divorce backlash." *Boston Globe,* June 19, pp. E1, E4.

Cobb, Nathan. 2000. "Times of their lives." *Boston Globe,* June 20, pp. D1, D8–11.

Coleman, Marilyn; Lawrence Ganong; Mark Fine. 2000. "Reinvestigating remarriage: Another decade of progress." *Journal of Marriage and the Family,* 62:4, November, pp. 1288–1307.

Coles, Robert. 1976. *Migrants, Sharecroppers, Mountaineers.* Boston: Atlantic Monthly.

Coles, Robert. 1977. "The children of affluence." *Atlantic Monthly,* September, pp. 52–66.

Coley, Rebekah Levine. 2001. "(In)visible men: Emerging research on low-income, umarried, and minority fathers." *American Psychologist,* 56:9, September, pp. 743–753.

Collins, Chuck, and Felice Yeskel. 2000. *Economic Apartheid in America.* New York: New Press.

Collins, Randall, and Scott Coltrane. 1995. *Sociology of Marriage and the Family* (4th ed.). Chicago: Nelson-Hall.

Coltrane, Scott. 1996. *Family Man.* New York: Oxford.

Coltrane, Scott, and Michele Adams. 2001. "Men, Women, and Housework." In Dana Vannoy, ed. 2001. *Gender Mosaics.* Los Angeles: Roxbury, pp. 145–154.

Connell, Noreen. 1998. "Understanding schools: Why money matters." *Dollars and Sense,* March/April, pp. 14–17, 39.

Conniff, Dorothy. 1988. "What's best for the child?" *Progressive,* November, pp. 21–23.

Cook, Philip. 1997. *Abused Men: The Hidden Side of Domestic Violence.* Westport, CT: Praeger.

Coontz, Stephanie. 1992. *The Way We Never Were: American Families and the Nostalgia Trap.* New York: Basic.

Coontz, Stephanie. 1997. *The Way We Really Are: Coming to Terms with America's Changing Families.* New York: Basic.

Coontz, Stephanie. 2000. "Historical perspectives in family studies." *Journal of Marriage and the Family,* 62:2, May, pp. 283–297.

Cordima, Jacquelyn. 1998. "The 1950s weren't paradise for everyone." *Boston Globe,* December 15, p. A13.

Cose, Ellis. 2003. "The black gender gap." *Newsweek,* March 3, pp. 46–51.

Cott, Nancy. 1978. "Divorce and the changing status of women in eighteenth-century Massachusetts." In Michael Gordon, ed. 1978. *The American Family in Social-Historical Perspective.* New York: St. Martin's.

Council on Families in America. 1996. "Marriage in America: A report to the nation." In David Popenoe, and others, eds. 1996. *Promises to Keep.* Lanham, MD: Rowman and Littlefield.

Counts, Dorothy; Judith Brown; Jacquelyn Campbell, eds. 1991. *Sanctions and Sanctuary: Cultural Perspectives on the Beating of Wives.* Boulder, CO: Westview.

Coverman, Shelley. 1989. "Women's work is never done." In Jo Freeman, ed., 1989. *Women: A Feminist Perspective* (4th ed.). Mountain View, CA: Mayfield, pp. 356–370.

Cowan, Philip A., and Carolyn Pape Cowan. 2002. "No point in promoting bad marriages." *Boston Globe,* May 12, p. E8.

Cowan, Philip, and Carolyn Pape Cowan. 2003. "New families: Modern couples as new pioneers." In Mason, Skolnick, and Sugarman, 2003, pp. 196–219.

Cox, Frank D. 1999. *Human Intimacy* (8th ed.). Belmont, CA: Wadsworth.

Cready, Cynthia M.; Mark A. Fossett; K. Jill Kiecolt. 1997. "Mate availability and African American family structure in the U.S. metropolitan South, 1960–1990." *Journal of Marriage and the Family,* 59:1, February, pp. 192–203.

Crittenden, Ann. 2001. *The Price of Motherhood.* New York: Holt.

Cronan, Sheila. 1971. *Notes from the Third Year: Women's Liberation.* New York.

Cuber, John F., and Peggy B. Harroff. 1965. *Sex and the Significant Americans.* Baltimore, MD: Penguin.

Curtin, Sharon. 1972. *Nobody Ever Died of Old Age.* Boston: Atlantic Little, Brown.

Dahlberg, Frances, ed. 1981. *Woman the Gatherer.* New Haven, CT: Yale.

Daly, Kerry J. 2001. "Deconstructing family time: From ideology to lived experience." *Journal of Marriage and the Family,* 63:2, May, pp. 283–294.

Daniel, Mac. 1999. "'Every day was a war,' wife says." *Boston Globe,* September 25, pp. B1, B5.

Daniels, Matthew E. 1998. *The Crisis of Family Decline in Massachusetts.* Newton, MA: Massachusetts Family Institute.

Davis, Angela. 1981. *Women, Race, and Class.* New York: Random House.

Davis, William. 2000. "Grand central." *Boston Globe,* April 6, pp. F1, F8.

Daw, J. 2002. "Joint custody might be best option for children, study says." *Monitor on Psychology,* June, p. 16.

Dedman, Bill. 2002. "Proportion of married Americans drops slightly in new census." *Boston Globe,* June 5, p. A6.

Degler, Carl. 1974. "What ought to be and what was: Women's sexuality in the nineteenth century." *American Historical Review,* 79, December, pp. 1467–1490. In Michael Gordon, ed. 1978. *The American Family in Social-Historical Perspective.* New York: St. Martin's, pp. 403–425.

Degler, Carl. 1980. *At Odds: Women and the Family in America from the Revolution to the Present.* New York: Oxford.

Demo, David. 1992. "Parent-child relations: Assessing recent changes." *Journal of Marriage and the Family,* 54:1, February, pp. 104–117.

Demos, John. 1970. *A Little Commonwealth: Family Life in Plymouth Colony.* New York: Oxford.

Demos, John. 1975. "The American family in past time." In Arlene Skolnick, and Jerome Skolnick, eds. 1977. *Family in Transition* (2nd ed.). Boston: Little, Brown.

Demos, John. 1986. "Child abuse in context: An historian's perspective." In Hansen and Garey, 1998, pp. 651–667.

Deutsch, Anthony. 2000. "Same-sex marriage measure passes in Netherlands." *Boston Globe,* Sept. 13, p. A2.

Deutsch, Francine. 1999. *Halving It All.* Cambridge, MA: Harvard.

DeVault, Marjorie L. 1991. "Constructing the family." In Arlene Skolnick and Jerome Skolnick, eds. 1997. *Family in Transition* (9th ed.). New York: Longman, pp. 58–69.

di Leonardo, Micaela. 1987. "The female world of cards and holidays: Women, families, and the work of kinship." In Hansen and Garey, 1998, pp. 440–453.

Dobash, R.E., and R. Dobash. 1979. *Violence against Wives.* New York: Free Press.

Dobash, Russell P.; R. Emerson Dobash; Margo Wilson; Martin Daly. 1992. "The myth of sexual symmetry in marital violence." *Social Problems,* 39:1, February, pp. 71–92. Reprinted in Benokraitis, ed., 2000, pp. 325–333.

Doten, Patti. 1996. "Why mothers can't win." *Boston Globe,* July 18, pp. 29, 31.

Douglass, Frederick. 1855. *My Bondage and My Freedom.* New York: Dover, 1969.

Downs, James F. 1972. *The Navajo.* New York: Holt, Rinehart, and Winston.

Dubin, Murray. 1995. "Balancing act." *Boston Globe,* May 11, pp. 1, 12.

Dudley, James R. 1991. "Increasing our understanding of divorced fathers who have infrequent contacts with their children." *Family Relations,* 40, July, pp. 279–285.

Dwyer, Ryle. 1999. "Spare us from the moral code of our intolerant past." *The Examiner* [Cork City, Ireland], January 6, p. 10.

Ebbert, Stephanie. 1998a. "Few batterers are treatable, study suggests." *Boston Globe,* May 11, pp. C1, C2.

Ebbert, Stephanie. 1998b. "Domestic violence reports on rise." *Boston Globe,* October 23, pp. B1, B7.

Ebbert, Stephanie. 1999. "Housing crunch in Boston hits the middle class." *Boston Globe,* January 18, pp. A1, A12.

Edin, Kathryn. 2000. "Few good men: Why poor mothers stay single." *American Prospect,* 11:4, January 3. Reprinted in Arlene Skolnick and Jerome Skolnick, eds., 2003. *Family in Transition* (12th ed.). Boston: Allyn and Bacon, pp. 161–170.

Edin, Kathryn, and Laura Fein. 1997. *Making Halves Meet: How Single Mothers Survive Welfare and Low-Wage Work.* New York: Russell Sage.

Ehrenreich, Barbara. 2001. *Nickel and Dimed: On (Not) Getting By in America.* New York: Metropolitan.

Elkin, Frederick, and Gerald Handel. 1989. *The Child and Society* (5th ed.). New York: Random House.

Elkind, David. 1998. *All Grown Up and No Place to Go.* Reading, MA: Addison-Wesley.

Ellement, John, and Peter DeMarco. 2002. "System failed slain woman." *Boston Globe,* March 29, p. B5.

Ellman, Ira Mark. 2000. "The misguided movement to revive fault divorce." In Whyte, 2000, pp. 189–210.

Elsner, Alan. 2002. "Data reflect many abandoned teens." *Boston Globe,* February 7, p. A9.

Ember, Carol, and Melvin Ember. 1999. *Cultural Anthropology* (9th ed.). Upper Saddle River, NJ: Prentice Hall.

English, Bella. 1987. "Abuse knows no status." *Boston Globe,* November 30, p. 19.

English, Bella. 1993. "Asian women breaking a code." *Boston Globe,* June 21, p. 13.

English, Bella. 2001. "On the block." *Boston Globe,* July 15, pp. E1, E6.

Erikson, Kai T. 1976. *Everything in Its Path.* New York: Simon and Schuster.

Ettelbrick, Paula. 1989. "Since when is marriage a path to liberation?" *Out/look: National Lesbian and Gay Quarterly,* Fall, pp.14–17. In Hansen and Garey, 1998, pp. 481–485.

Ewen, Elizabeth. 1985. *Immigrant Women in the Land of Dollars.* New York: Monthly Review.

Fallows, Marjorie. 1979. *Irish Americans.* Englewood Cliffs, NJ: Prentice Hall.

Faludi, Susan. 1999. *Stiffed: The Betrayal of the American Man.* New York: Morrow.

Farley, John. 2000. *Minority Relations* (4th ed.). Upper Saddle River, NJ: Prentice Hall.

Farley, Reynolds, and Walter Allen. 1987. *The Color Line and the Quality of Life in America.* New York: Russell Sage.

Farrell, Betty. 1999. *Family.* Boulder, CO: Westview.

Feagin, Joe R., and Clairece Booker Feagin. 1999. *Race and Ethnic Relations* (6th ed.). Upper Saddle River, NJ: Prentice Hall.

Feagin, Joe R., and Karyn D. McKinney. 2003. *The Many Costs of Racism.* Lanham, MD: Rowman and Littlefield.

Fenton, Gail McClelland. 1997. "No time for spiders." *Sanctuary,* May/June, pp. 6–7.

Ferguson, Susan J., ed. 2001. *Shifting the Center: Understanding Contemporary Families.* Mountain View, CA: Mayfield.

Ferrante, Joan. 1995, 1998, 2000. *Sociology* (2nd, 3rd and 4th eds.). Belmont, CA: Wadsworth.

Ferrante, Joan, and Prince Browne, Jr., eds. 2001. *The Social Construction of Race and Ethnicity in the United States.* Upper Saddle River, NJ: Prentice Hall.

Ferraro, Kathleen J. 1997. "Battered women: Strategies for survival." In Andrew Cherlin, ed. 2001. *Public and Private Families* (2nd ed.). New York: McGraw Hill, pp. 260–273.

Figart, Deborah, and Ellen Mutari. 1998. "It's about time: Will Europe solve the work/family dilemma?" *Dollars and Sense,* January/February, pp. 27–31.

Filipov, David. 2001. "Armenia's exodus widows." *Boston Globe,* March 30, pp. A1, A28.

Finnegan, William. 1998. *Cold New World.* New York: Random House.

Firth, Raymond. 1936. *We, The Tikopia: Kinship in Primitive Polynesia.* Boston: Beacon.

Fitzgerald, Susan. 2001. "Study links child care to aggression." *Boston Globe,* April 19, p. A3.

Fletcher, Michael. 1999. "Marriage not in blissful state, study says." *Boston Globe,* July 2, p. A11.

Flowers, R. Barri. 1994. "The problem of domestic violence is widespread." In Swisher, 1996.

Ford, Bob. 1994. "Stealing the children." Watertown Press [Massachusetts], January 27, p. 6.

Foreman, Judy. 1993. "Parents—they just keep on giving." *Boston Globe,* May 31, pp. 25–26.

Foreman, Judy. 1994. "Skipping a generation." *Boston Globe,* September 10, p. 3.

Foreman, Judy. 1998. "Making a place for nursing mothers." *Boston Globe,* January 5, pp. C1, C4.

Foreman, Judy. 2000. "Out of the shadow." *Boston Globe,* March 21, pp. C1, C4.

Fox, Greer Litton, and Velma McBride Murry. 2000. "Gender and families: Feminist perspectives and family research." *Journal of Marriage and the Family,* 62:4, November, pp. 1160–1172.

Frank, Ellen. 1998a. "Haven from home?" *Dollars and Sense,* January/February, pp. 38k–39.

Frank, Ellen. 1998b. "It takes a community." *Dollars and Sense,* January/February, pp. 12–13.

Franklin, Donna. 1997. *Ensuring Inequality: The Structural Transformation of the African-American Family.* New York: Oxford.

Fredriksen-Goldsen, Karen I., and Andrew E. Scharlach. 2001. *Families and Work: New Directions in the Twenty-First Century.* New York: Oxford.

Friedl, Ernestine. 1962. *Vasilika: A Village in Modern Greece.* New York: Holt, Rinehart, and Winston.

Friedland, William H., and Dorothy Nelkin. 1971. *Migrant.* New York: Holt, Rinehart, and Winston.

Furstenberg, Frank, and Andrew Cherlin. 1991. *Divided Families: What Happens to Children When Parents Part.* Cambridge, MA: Harvard.

Furstenberg, Frank; Christine W. Nord; James L. Peterson; Nicholas Zill. 1983. "The life course of children of divorce: Marital disruption and parental contact." *American Sociological Review,* 48:5, October, pp. 656–668.

Gallagher, Sally K., and Naomi Gerstel. 2001. "Connections and constraints: The effects of children on caregiving." *Journal of Marriage and the Family,* 63:1, February, pp. 265–275.

Gallagher, Thomas. 1982. *Paddy's Lament: Ireland 1846–1847.* New York: Harcourt Brace Jovanovich.

Gallardo, Eduardo. 2002. "Divorce proposal is dividing Chileans." *Boston Globe,* January 2, p. A8.

Galston, William A. 2000. "The law of marriage and divorce: Options for reform." In Whyte, 2000, pp. 179–187.

Gans, Herbert J. 1962, 1982. *The Urban Villagers.* New York: Free Press.

Garson, Barbara. 1975. *All the Livelong Day.* New York: Penguin.

Gates, Henry Luis, Jr. 1994. *Colored People: A Memoir.* New York: Knopf.

Gelles, Richard J. 1997. *Intimate Violence in Families* (3rd ed.). Thousand Oaks, CA: Sage. Part reprinted in Benokraitis, 2000, pp. 318–324.

Gerson, Kathleen. 1993. *No Man's Land.* New York: Basic.

Gerson, Kathleen. 1998. "Gender and the future of the family." In Vannoy and Dubeck, 1998, pp. 11–21.

Gerstel, Naomi. 1987. "Divorce and stigma." *Social Problems,* 34:2, April, pp. 172–186.

Gerstel, Naomi, and Harriet Gross. 1984. *Commuter Marriage: A Study in Work and Family.* New York: Guilford.

Gerstel, Naomi, and Harriet Gross. 1995. "Gender and families in the United States: The reality of economic dependence." In Jo Freeman, ed. 1995. *Women: A Feminist Perspective* (5th ed.). Mountain View, CA: Mayfield.

Gilbert, Dennis. 1998. *The American Class Structure* (5th ed.). Belmont, CA: Wadsworth.

Giele, Janet. 1996. "Decline of the family: Conservative, liberal, and feminist views." In David Popenoe and others, eds. 1996. *Promises to Keep.* Lanham, MD: Rowman and Littlefield.

Gillis, John R. 1985. *For Better, For Worse: British Marriages, 1600 to the Present.* New York: Oxford.

Glass, Jennifer. 1998. "Gender liberation, economic squeeze, or fear of strangers: Why fathers provide infant care in dual-career couples." *Journal of Marriage and the Family,* 60:4, November, pp. 821–834.

Glenn, Norval D. 1992. "What does family mean?" *American Demographics,* 14:6.

Glenn D., Norval. 1997. *Closed Hearts, Closed Minds: The Textbook Story of Marriage.* New York: Institute for American Values.

Goldscheider, Frances K., and Linda J. Waite. 1991. *New Families, No Families?* Berkeley, CA: California.

Goldstein, Amy. 2000. "In domestic shift, many wives have become family breadwinners." *Boston Globe,* February 29, p. A3.

Gomstyn, Alice. 2002. "220,000 children in state are latchkey kids, survey finds." *Boston Globe,* January 23, p. B8.

Gonzales, Juan L. 1998. *Racial and Ethnic Families in America* (3rd ed.). Dubuque, Iowa: Kendall/Hunt.

Good, Jeffrey. 2000. "Gays ponder breadth of a Vt. 'civil union.'" *Boston Globe,* April 27, pp. A1, A31.

Good, Kenneth. 1991. *Into the Heart.* New York: HarperCollins.

Goode, WIlliam J. 1993. *World Changes in Divorce Patterns.* New Haven: Yale.

Good Tracks, Jim G. 1973. "Native American non-interference." *Social Work,* 18:6, November, pp. 30–35.

Goodman, Ellen. 1996. "The latest parent trap." *Boston Globe,* May 16, p. 25.

Goodman, Ellen. 2000. "Kids, divorce, and the myth." *Boston Globe,* September, p. A17.

Gordon, Linda. 1988. *Heroes of Their Own Lives: The Politics and History of Family Violence.* New York: Penguin.

Gordon, Suzanne. 1991. "When parents come home." *Boston Globe,* November 1, pp. 61–62.

Gosselin, Peter. 1997. "Arlie H. aghast as conservatives embrace her book liberals bash it." *Boston Globe,* May 28, pp. F1, F8.

Gottman, John. 1994. *Why Marriages Succeed or Fail.* New York: Simon and Schuster.

Graff, E. J. 1998. "The inevitability of same-sex marriage." *Boston Globe,* February 12, p. A27.

Graff, E. J. 1999a. "Making marriage partners equal." *Boston Globe,* February, p. A25.

Graff, E. J. 1999b. "Marriage à la mode." *Boston Sunday Globe Magazine,* June 13, pp. 6–13.

Graff, E. J. 1999c. *What Is Marriage For?* Boston: Beacon.

Graff, E. J. 1999d. "Justifying our love." *Village Voice,* June 29, pp. 74, 77.

Graff, E. J. 1999e. "Same-sex spouses in Canada." *Nation,* July 12, pp. 23–24.

Graff, E. J. 2003. Private communication.

Graham, Renee. 1998. "Entertaining 'herstory' of housework." *Boston Globe,* May 22, p. D10.

Grant, Julia. 1998. *Raising Baby by the Book.* New Haven, CT: Yale.

Greenhouse, Steven. 1993. "If the French can do it, why can't we?" *New York Times Magazine,* November 14, pp. 59–62.

Griffin, John Howard. 1961. *Black Like Me.* New York: Signet.

Griffiths, Lyndsey. 2000. "Hardships plague women worldwide, UN report says." *Boston Globe,* September 21, p. A14.

Grossfeld, Stan. 1999. "The new 'homeless.'" *Boston Globe,* May 17, pp. A1, A10–11.

Guendelman, Sylvia. 2003. "Immigrant families." In Mason, Skolnick, and Sugarman, 2003, pp. 244–264.

Gullo, Karen. 2000. "Parents juggle more day-care options." *Boston Globe,* March 8, p. A4.

Gutman, Herbert G. 1976. *The Black Family in Slavery and Freedom: 1750–1925.* New York: Vintage.

Gwaltney, John Langston. 1993. *Drylongso: A Self-Portrait of Black America.* New York: New Press.

Hackstaff, Karla B. 1998. "Wives' marital work in a culture of divorce." In Hansen and Garey, 1998, pp. 459–473.

Hagedorn, John M. 1988. *People and Folks: Gangs, Crime and the Underclass in a Rustbelt City.* Chicago: Lake View.

Hamer, Jennifer, and Kathleen Marchioro. 2002. "Becoming custodial dads: Exploring parenting among low-income and working-class African American Fathers." *Journal of Marriage and the Family,* 64:1, February, pp. 116–129.

Hammond, Dorothy, and Alta Jablow. 1976. *Women in Cultures of the World.* Menlo Park, CA: Cummings.

Hansen, Karen V. 1994. "Masculinity, caregiving, and men's friendship in antebellum New England." In Hansen and Garey, 1998, pp. 575–585.

Hansen, Karen V., and Anita Ilta Garey, eds. 1998. *Families in the U.S.: Kinship and Domestic Politics.* Philadephia: Temple.

Harder, Blaine. 2001. "Bible belt couples 'put asunder' more, despite efforts." *New York Times,* May 21, p. A14.

Hareven, Tamara. 1982. "American families in transition." In Arlene Skolnick and Jerome Skolnick, eds. 1983. *Family in Transition* (4th ed.). Boston: Little, Brown, pp. 73–91.

Hareven, Tamara. 2000. *Families, History, and Social Change.* Boulder, CO: Westview.

Harris, Phyllis Brandy, and Joyce Bichler. 1997. *Men Giving Care: Reflections of Husbands and Sons.* New York: Garland.

Hart, Jordana. 2000a. "Child care costs forcing reliance on unlicensed." *Boston Globe,* March 22, pp. B1, B4.

Hart, Jordana. 2000b. "Statistics say abuse hits close to home." *Boston Globe,* May 30, pp. B1, B8.

Hartmann, Heidi. 2002. "Interview with Ruth Conniff." *Progressive,* August, pp. 29–33.

Harvey, Brett. 1993. *The Fifties: A Women's Oral History.* New York: Harper/Collins.

Harvey, David. 1993. *Potter Addition: Poverty, Family, and Kinship in a Heartland Community.* New York: Aldine de Gruyter.

Hasday, Jill Elaine. 2000. *Contest and Consent: A Legal History of Marital Rape.* University of Chicago Law School, Occasional Paper 41 (May).

Hatchett, Shirley. 1991. "Women and Men." In James Jackson, ed. 1991. *Life in Black America.* Newbury Park, CA: Sage, pp. 84–104.

Hawkins, Alan, and E. Jeffrey Hill. 1998. Book review of Hochschild, 1997, and Robinson and Godbey, 1997. *Journal of Marriage and the Family,* 60:1, February, pp. 260–262.

Hays, Sharon. 1996. *The Cultural Contradictions of Motherhood.* New Haven, CT: Yale.

Hays, Sharon. 2003. *Flat Broke with Children: Women in the Age of Welfare Reform.* New York: Oxford.

Hecker, Ann Prince. 1997. "Terrors of the tube." *Sanctuary,* May/June, pp. 8–9.

Helburn, Suzanne, and Barbara Bergmann. 2002. *Childcare: The Way Out.* New York: Palgrave.

Henry, Jules. 1941. *Jungle People.* New York: Vintage, 1964.

Henslin, James R. 1992. "Why so much divorce?" In James Henslin, ed. 1992. *Marriage and Family in a Changing Society.* New York: Free Press, pp. 389–396.

Henslin, James R. 1998, 2002, 2004. *Essentials of Sociology* (2nd, 4th, and 5th eds.). Boston: Allyn and Bacon.

Hertz, Rosanna. 1986. *More Equal than Others.* Berkeley, CA: California.

Hesse-Biber, Sharlene, and Greg Lee Carter. 2000. *Working Women in America: Split Dreams.* New York: Oxford.

Hetherington, E. Mavis, and John Kelly. 2002. *For Better, for Worse: Divorce Reconsidered.* New York: Norton.

Hewlett, Sylvia Ann; Nancy Rankin; Cornell West, eds. 2002. *Taking Parenting Public: The Case for a New Social Movement.* Lanham, MD: Rowman & Littlefield.

Hightower, Jim. 2003. "CEOs pay themselves $7,452 an hour (on average)." *The Hightower Lowdown,* June, pp. 1–4.

Hill, Robert. 1999. *The Strengths of African American Families.* Lanham, MD: University Press of America.

Hines, Alice M. 1997. "Divorce-related transitions, adolescent development, and the role of the parent-child relationship." *Journal of Marriage and the Family,* 59:2, May, pp. 375–388.

Hochschild, Arlie Russell. 1989. *The Second Shift: Working Parents and the Revolution at Home.* New York: Viking.

Hochschild, Arlie Russell. 1995. "Ideals of care." In Hansen and Garey, 1998, pp. 527–538.

Hochschild, Arlie Russell. 1996. "The emotional geography of work and family life." In Amy S. Wharton, ed. 1998. *Working in America.* Mountain View, CA: Mayfield, p. 422–433.

Hochschild, Arlie Russell. 1997, 2000. *The Time Bind: When Work Becomes Home and Home Becomes Work.* New York: Henry Holt.

Hoebel, E. Adamson. 1960. *The Cheyennes.* New York: Holt, Rinehart, and Winston.

Hofferth, Sandra L., and John F. Sandberg. 2001. "How American children spend their time." *Journal of Marriage and the Family,* 63:2, May, pp. 295–208.

Horn, Patricia. 1992. "Beating back the revolution: Domestic violence's economic toll on women." *Dollars and Sense,* December, pp. 12–13, 21–22.

Horsfield, Margaret. 1998. *Biting the Dust: The Joys of Housework.* New York: St. Martin's.

Horton, James Oliver, and Lois E. Horton. 1997. *In Hope of Liberty: Culture, Community, and Protest among Northern Free Blacks, 1700–1860.* New York: Oxford.

Horwitz, Allan V.; Helen Raskin White; Sandra-Howell-White. 1996. "Becoming married and mental health." *Journal of Marriage and the Family,* 58:4, November, pp. 895–907.

Houseknecht, Sharon, and Jaya Sastry. 1996. "Family 'decline' and child well-being." *Journal of Marriage and the Family,* 58:3, August, pp. 726–739.

Howell, Sharon. 1986. "The reasons . . . ?" *Radical America,* 20:1, p. 29.

Hutchinson, Earl Ofari. 1992. *Black Fatherhood: The Guide to Male Parenting.* Los Angeles: IMPACT!

Ingoldsby, Bron B. 1995. "Mate selection and marriage." In Bron Ingoldsby and Suzanna Smith, eds. 1995. *Families in Multicultural Perspective.* New York: Guilford, pp. 143–151.

Isaacs, Marla Beth, and Irene Raskow Levin. 1984. "Who's in my family? A longitudinal study of drawings of children of divorce." *Journal of Divorce,* 7:4, Summer, pp. 1–21.

Jackson, Derrick. 1996. "The double standard on drug crimes." *Boston Globe,* August 23, p. A19.

Jackson, Maggie. 2003. "Family issue blurs gender roles." *Boston Globe,* January 5, pp. H1, H7.

Jacobs, Harriet. 1861. *Incidents in the Life of a Slave Girl.* In Henry Louis Gates, Jr., ed. 1987. *The Classic Slave Narratives.* New York: New American Library.

Jacobs, Ruth. 1993. *Be an Outrageous Older Woman.* Manchester, CT: KIT.

Jacobs, Ruth. 1996. *Women Who Touched My Life.* Manchester, CT: KIT.

Jacobs, Sally. 1992. "More gay men hearing the call of fatherhood." *Boston Globe,* September 28, pp. 1, 5.

Jacobson, Neil, and John M. Gottman. 1998. *When Men Batter Women*. New York: Simon and Schuster.

Jesser, Clinton J. 1996. *Fierce and Tender Men*. Westport, CT: Praeger.

Jesuit Relations. 1896–1901. *The Jesuit Relations and Allied Documents*. Cleveland: Burrows Brothers.

Johnson, Michael P., and Kathleen J. Ferraro. 2000. "Research on domestic violence in the 1990s: Making distinctions." *Journal of Marriage and the Family*, 62:4, November, pp. 948–963.

Jolivet, Muriel. 1997. *Japan: The Childless Society*. New York: Routledge.

Jones, Ann. 1994 "Where do we go from here?" *Ms*, September/October, pp. 56–63.

Jones, Charles; Lorne Tepperman; Susannah J. Wilson. 1995. *The Futures of the Family*. Englewood Cliffs, NJ: Prentice Hall.

Jones, Jacqueline. 1985. *Labor of Love, Labor of Sorrow*. New York: Basic.

Joslin, Daphne, ed. 2001. *Invisible Caregivers: Older Adults Raising Children in the Wake of HIV/AIDS*. New York: Columbia.

Jurkowitz, Mark. 2002. "A Times policy on gay unions stirs press waters." *Boston Globe*, August 28, pp. D1, D6.

Kahn, Joseph P. 1995. "Happily ever after." *Boston Globe*, May 29, pp. 31, 34.

Kahn, Joseph P. 2000. "Strong, not silent." *Boston Globe*, April 27, pp. D1, D8.

Kain, Edward. 1990. *The Myth of Family Decline*. Lexington, MA: Lexington.

Kamen, Paula. 2000. *Her Way: Young Women Remake the Sexual Revolution*. New York: New York University. Part reprinted in Arlene Skolnick and Jerome Skolnick, eds. 2003. *Family in Transition* (12 ed.). Boston: Allyn and Bacon, pp. 152–161.

Kantrowitz, Barbara, and Pat Wingert. 1999. "The science of a good marriage." *Newsweek*, April 19, pp. 51–57.

Kantrowitz, Barbara, and Pat Wingert. 2001. "Unmarried, with children." *Newsweek*, May 28, pp. 46–55.

Katz, Jackson, and Sut Jhally. 1999. "Missing the mark." *Boston Globe*, May 2, pp. E1, E5.

Kerbo, Harold R. 2000, 2003. *Inequality* (4th and 5th eds.). New York: McGraw Hill.

Kiecolt, K. Jill. 2003. "Satisfaction with work and family life: No evidence of a cultural reversal." *Journal of Marriage and the Family*, 65:1, February, pp. 23–35.

Kimmel, Michael, and Michael A. Messner, eds. 1995. *Men's Lives* (3rd ed.). Boston: Allyn and Bacon.

King, Valerie. 2003. "The legacy of a grandparent's divorce." *Journal of Marriage and the Family*, 65:1, February, pp. 170–183.

Kirn, Walter. 2000. "Should you stay together for the kids?" *Time*, September 25, pp. 74–82.

Kiser, Jane. 1998. "Behind the scenes at a 'family friendly' workplace." *Dollars and Sense*, January/February, pp. 19–21.

Klagsbrun, Frances. 1985. *Married People: Staying Together in the Age of Divorce*. New York: Bantam.

Kleiman, D. 1990. "Even in the frenzy of the 90s, dinner time is still family time." *New York Times*, December 5, pp. A1, C6. Reprinted in Bird and Melville, 1994, pp. 282–283.

Knight, Robert. 1994. "How domestic partnerships and 'gay marriage' threaten the family." *Insight*, June.

Knox, Richard. 1999. "Health risk tied to stress of caregiving is measured." *Boston Globe*, December 15, p. A3.

Kobrin, Frances. 1976. "The fall in household size and the rise of the primary individual in the United States." In Michael Gordon, ed., 1978. *The American Family in Social-Historical Perspective* (2nd ed.). New York: St. Martin's, pp. 69–81.

Komarovsky, Mira. 1962. *Blue-Collar Marriage*. New York: Random House.

Kong, Deborah. 2002. "Asian assisted living seen as break with tradition." *Boston Globe*, January 2, p. A16.

Kong, Dolores. 1999a. "Study says working mothers don't cause children harm." *Boston Globe*, March 1, pp. A1, B4.

Kong, Dolores. 1999b. "Housing crisis causing health risks, study finds." *Boston Globe*, April 8, p. A4.

Kotlowitz, Alex. 1991. *There Are No Children Here*. New York: Doubleday.

Kottak, Conrad Phillip. 1999. *Mirror for Humanity* (2nd ed.). New York: McGraw Hill.

Kottak, Conrad Phillip. 2000. *Cultural Anthropology* (8th ed.). New York: McGraw Hill.

Kozol, Jonathan. 1988. *Rachel and Her Children*. New York: Crown.

Kozol, Jonathan. 1991. *Savage Inequalities*. New York: Harper.

Kozol, Jonathan. 1995. *Amazing Grace: The Lives of Children and the Conscience of a Nation*. New York: Crown.

Kurdek, Lawrence A. 1994. "Remarriage and stepfamilies are not inherently problematic." In Alan Booth and Judy Dunn, eds. 1994. *Stepfamilies: Who Benefits? Who Does Not?* New Jersey: Erlbaum.

Kurz, Demie. 1995. *For Richer, for Poorer: Mothers Confront Divorce.* New York: Routledge, pp. 46–62. In Benokraitis, ed., 2002, pp. 345–353.

Kurz, Demie. 2001. "Violence against women by intimate partners." In Dana Vannoy, ed. 2001. *Gender Mosaics.* Los Angeles: Roxbury.

Lakshmanan, Indira. 1995a. "Windows on children's worlds." *Boston Globe,* June 5, pp. 1, 6.

Lakshmanan, Indira. 1995b. "Under poverty's burden." *Boston Globe,* June 6, pp. 1, 10.

Lakshmanan, Indira. 1996. "Hawaii abuse prevention may catch on in Mass." *Boston Globe,* April 14, pp. 1, 24.

Lamanna, Mary Ann and Agnes Riedmann. 2000. *Marriages and Families* (7th ed.). Belmont, CA: Wadsworth.

Landau, Saul. 2002. "The end of the maquila era." *Progressive,* September, pp. 24–26.

Landers, Ann. 1987. "What she has endured as a battered wife." *Boston Globe,* April 3, p. 27.

Landers, Ann. 1997. "The joys (?) of parenthood." *Boston Globe,* January 8, p. D5.

Landers, Ann. 1999a. "Ten ways to shield kids from pain of divorce." *Boston Globe,* February 3, p. D3.

Landers, Ann. 1999b. "Divorced dad says kids are worth the struggle." *Boston Globe,* February 6, p. G7.

Landers, Ann. 1999c. "Husbands can suffer abuse too." *Boston Globe,* December 2, p. D8.

Landis, Judson R. 1995. *Sociology* (9th ed.). Belmont, CA: Wadsworth.

Landry, Bart. 2000. *Black Working Wives: Pioneers of the American Family Revolution.* Berkeley: California.

LaRossa, Ralph. 1988. "The culture and conduct of fatherhood." *Family Relations,* 37:4, pp. 451–457.

Latour, Francie. 2000. "A strategy to fight domestic violence." *Boston Globe,* September 8, p. B2.

Lauer, Jeanette, and Robert Lauer. 1985. "Marriages made to last." *Psychology Today,* June, pp. 22–26.

Leacock, Eleanor Burke. 1981. *Myths of Male Dominance.* New York: Monthly Review.

Lee, Dorothy. 1959. *Freedom and Culture.* Prospect Heights, IL: Waveland, 1987.

Lee, Gary R.; Chuck W. Peck; Raymond T. Coward. 1998. "Race differences in filial responsibility expectations among older parents." *Journal of Marriage and the Family,* 60:2, May, pp. 404–412.

Lee, Richard. 1993. *The Dobe Ju/'hoansi* (2nd ed.). Fort Worth, TX: Harcourt Brace.

LeMasters, E. E., and John DeFrain. 1989. *Parents in Contemporary America* (5th ed.). Belmont, CA: Wadsworth.

Leonard, Mary. 1999. "Labor and women push for equal pay for equivalent labor." *Boston Globe,* February 25, pp. A1, A22.

Leonard, Mary. 2001. "Rising industry works to keep marriages going." *Boston Globe,* June 25, pp. A1, A4.

Lerner, Gerda. 1979. "The lady and the mill girl." In Nancy F. Cott and Elizabeth Pleck, eds. 1979. *A Heritage of Her Own.* New York: Simon and Schuster, pp. 182–196.

LeVine, Robert, and Merry White. 1987. "The social transformation of childhood." In Jane Lancaster, and others, eds. 1987. *Parenting across the Life Span.* New York: Social Science Research Council.

Levinson, Daniel. 1989. *Family Violence in Cross-Cultural Perspectives.* Newbury Park, CA: Sage.

Lewis, Diane. 1998. "Even on top, women seen earning less than men." *Boston Globe,* November 10, pp. D1, D15.

Lewis, Diane. 1999a. "Women's gains tied to jump in incomes." *Boston Globe,* March 17, pp. A1, A17.

Lewis, Diane. 1999b. "Equality on the homefront." *Boston Sunday Globe,* June 13, p. F4.

Lewis, Diane. 1999c. "Many shifts in modern workweek." *Boston Globe,* July 6, pp. A1, A6.

Lewis, Diane. 1999d. "Fathers with their companies in tow, make a move toward the homestead." *Boston Globe,* August 8, pp. F1, F4.

Lewis, Diane. 2000. "Women lawyers' exodus." *Boston Globe,* December 4, pp. A1, C8.

Lewis, Diane. 2003a. "Leave law on brink of change." *Boston Globe,* February 9, pp. G1, G5.

Lewis, Diane. 2003b. "In hard times, bitter divorces." *Boston Globe,* May 29, pp. E1, E6.

Ley, Camara. 1954. *The Dark Child.* New York: Farrar, Straus, and Giroux.

Liazos, Alex. 1982. *People First: An Introduction to Social Problems.* Boston: Allyn and Bacon.

Liazos, Alex. 1986. *Before Patriarchy: Social and Gender Equality.* Unpublished manuscript.

Liazos, Alex. 1989. *Sociology: A Liberating Perspective* (2nd ed.). Boston: Allyn and Bacon.

Liazos, Alex. 1990. *Watertown Sun,* May 30, 1990.

Liazos, Alex. 1991. "Childcare and time to be parents." *Humanity and Society,* 15:3 (August), pp. 291–303.

Liazos, Alex. 1995. "Fathers still: Parenting after divorce." *Humanity and Society,* 19:3, August, pp. 19–36.

Liazos, Alex. 1997. "Grieving and growing: Experiences of divorced fathers." *Humanity and Society,* 21:4, November, pp. 353–376.

Liazos, Melissa. 1996. *The History of Legal Protection for Battered Women in Massachusetts.* Senior Thesis, Radcliffe College.

Lichtblau, Eric. 2000. "Attacks between partners fall." *Boston Globe,* May 18, p. A3.

Lieblich, Julia. 2000. "Episcopalians take no stand on gay unions." *Boston Globe,* February 14, p. A3.

Liebow, Elliot. 1993. *Tell Them Who I Am: The Lives of Homeless Women.* New York: Penguin.

Lindberg, Laura Duberstein. 1996. "Women's decisions about breastfeeding and maternal employment." *Journal of Marriage and the Family,* 58:1, February, pp. 239–251.

Logan, John, and Glenna D. Spitze. 1996. *Family Ties.* Philadelphia: Temple.

Logan, Sadye. 2001. *The Black Family: Strengths, Self-Help, and Positive Change* (2nd ed.). Boulder, CO: Westview.

Longcope, Kay. 1992. "Gay parenthood comes of age." *Boston Globe,* December 17, pp. 38, 42.

Louie, Miriam Ching. 2001. *Sweatshop Warriors: Immigrant Women Take On the Global Factory.* Cambridge, MA: South End.

Loven, Jennifer. 2001. "Survey finds teenagers place high value on family ties." *Boston Globe,* August 8, p. A4.

Lucal, Betsy. 1995. "The problem with 'battered husbands.'" *Deviant Behavior,* 16:2, pp. 95–112.

Ludtke, Melissa. 1997. *On Our Own: Unmarried Motherhood in America.* New York: Random House.

Lynd, Robert S., and Helen Merrell Lynd. 1929. *Middletown: A Study in Modern American Culture.* New York: Harcourt, Brace, and World.

Lynd, Robert S., and Helen Merrell Lynd. 1937. *Middletown in Transition.* New York: Harcourt, Brace, and World.

Macionis, John. 1999. *Sociology* (7th ed.). Upper Saddle River, NJ: Prentice Hall.

MacLeod, Jay. 1995. *Ain't No Makin' It.* Boulder, CO: Westview.

MacQuarrie, Brian. 2000a. "Vt. house approves bill allowing same-sex unions." *Boston Globe,* April 26, pp. A1, A18.

MacQuarrie, Brian. 2000b. "Some in Vt. bristle at civil unions." *Boston Globe,* April 28, pp. B1, B6.

Mainardi, Pat. 1970. "The politics of housework." In Donald Scott and Bernard Wishy, eds. 1982. *America's Families: A Documentary History.* New York: Harper, pp. 515–520.

Mangione, Jerre. 1942. *Mount Allegro: A Memoir of Italian American Life.* New York: Columbia, 1981.

Mangione, Jerre, and Ben Morreale. 1992. La Storia: Five Centuries of the Italian American Experience. New York: HarperCollins.

Manning, Wendy D., and Daniel T. Lichter. 1996. "Parental cohabitation and children's economic well-being." *Journal of Marriage and the Family,* 58:4, November, pp. 998–1010.

Mantsios, Gregory. 1994. "Class in America: Myths and Realities." In Paula S. Rothenberg, ed. 1994. *Race, Class, and Gender in the United States* (3rd ed.). New York: St. Martin's, pp. 131–143.

Marks, Stephen. 2000. "Teasing out the lessons of the 1960s: Family diversity and family privilege." *Journal of Marriage and the Family,* 62:3, August, pp. 609–622.

Marsiglio, William; Paul Amato; Randal D. Day; Michael E. Lamb. 2000. "Scholarship on fatherhood in the 1990s and beyond." *Journal of Marriage and the Family,* 62:4, November, pp. 1173–1191.

Mashberg, Tom. 1993. "More mothers unwed, unwistful." *Boston Globe,* July 15, pp. 1, 23.

Mason, Mary Ann. 2003. "The modern American stepfamily." In Mason, Skolnick,, and Sugarman, 2003, pp. 96–116.

Mason, Mary Ann; Arlene Skolnick; Stephen D. Sugarman, eds. 2003. *All Our Families.* New York: Oxford.

Matchan, Linda. 1995a. "Hectic on the homefront." *Boston Globe,* June 4, pp. 1, 30.

Matchan, Linda. 1995b. "Someone to look up to." Boston Globe, June 7, pp. 1, 12.

Matchan, Linda. 1998. "The militant divorcee." *Boston Globe,* December 15, pp. D1, D5.

Matchan, Linda. 2000. "Love lost, life found." *Boston Globe,* January 3, pp. C1, C5.

Mauer, Marc, and Tracy Huling. 1995. *Young Black Americans and the CJS: Five Years Later.* The Sentencing Project.

Mauldon, Jane. 2003. "Families started by teenagers." In Mason, Skolnick, and Sugarman, 2003, pp. 40–65.

May, Elaine Tyler. 1980. *Great Expectations: Marriage and Divorce in Post-Victorian America.* Chicago: Chicago.

May, Martha. 1985. "Bread before roses." In Hansen and Garey, 1998, pp. 143–155.

Mayer, Susan. 1997. *What Money Can't Buy.* Cambridge, MA: Harvard.

McCaffrey, Shannon. 2000. "Bull market leaving poorest far behind, report says." *Boston Globe,* January 18, p. A4.

McGrory, Brian. 1999. "Alienation finds a future on the Web." *Boston Globe,* July 16, p. B1.

McLanahan, Sara. 1994. "The consequences of single motherhood." *American Prospect,* Summer, pp. 48–58.

McLanahan, Sara S., and Gary Sandefur. 1994. *Growing Up with a Single Parent.* Cambridge: Harvard.

McNair, Jean. 1996. "Lesbian in Virginia abandons 3–year custody battle for son." *Boston Globe,* August 16, p. 3.

McNall, Scott, and Sally Allen McNall. 1983. *Plains Families: Exploring Sociology through Social History.* New York: St. Martin's.

McNamara, Eileen. 1998. "Battered wives let down by laws." *Boston Globe,* October 17, p. B1.

McQueen, Anjetta. 2000. "After school, many children on own." *Boston Globe,* September 11, p. A3.

Mead, Margaret. 1935. *Sex and Temperament in Three Primitive Societies.* New York: Morrow.

Meckler, Laura. 1998. "Health gap still exists between races." *Boston Globe,* November 27, p. A3.

Meckler, Laura. 1999. "Millions above poverty line had financial woes, study finds." *Boston Globe,* July 9, p. A13.

Meckler, Laura. 2002. "Marriage promotion invites unease." *Boston Globe,* April 16, p. A16.

Meiksins, Peter. 1998. "Confronting the time bind: Work, family, and capitalism." *Monthly Review,* 49:9, February, pp. 1–13.

Meiksins, Peter, and Peter Whalley. 2002. *Putting Work in Its Place: A Quiet Revolution.* Ithaca, NY: Cornell.

Meltz, Barbara. 1990. "The magic of grandparent relationships." *Boston Globe,* February 13, pp. 57, 61.

Meltz, Barbara. 1996. "Nurturing nature: Stay-at-home dads help erase stereotypes." *Boston Globe,* June 13, pp. 85, 89.

Meltz, Barbara. 2002. "Bed sharing is more common than you think." *Boston Globe,* November 21, p. H3.

Melville, Keith. 1980. *Marriage and Family Today* (2nd ed.). New York: Random House.

Merrill, Deborah. 1997. *Caring for Elderly Parents: Juggling Work, Family, and Caregiving in Middle and Working Class Families.* Westport, CT: Auburn House.

Messenger, John C. 1969. *Inis Beag: Isle of Ireland.* New York: Holt, Rinehart, and Winston.

Meyer, Daniel R., and Judi Bartfeld. 1996. "Compliance with child support orders in divorce cases." *Journal of Marriage and the Family,* 58:1, February, pp. 201–212.

Meyer, Madonna Harrington, ed. 2000. *Care Work: Gender, Labor, and the Welfare State.* New York: Routledge.

Miller, John. 2000. "A rising tide fails to lift all boats." *Dollars and Sense,* May/June, p. 42.

Milligan, Susan. 2003. "Gay civil unions find support in Democratic field." *Boston Globe,* April 26, pp. A1, A4.

Mintz, Stephen, and Susan Kellogg. 1988. *Domestic Revolutions: A Social History of American Life.* New York: Free Press.

Mishra, Raja. 2002. "A need for shelter." *Boston Globe,* December 18, pp. A1, A36.

Mitchell, John H. 1997. "Forgiven trespasses." *Sanctuary,* May/June, p. 2.

Moberg, David. 1999. "Most young workers have missed out on the boom." *Boston Globe,* October 16, p. A21.

Money, John, and Anke A. Ehrhardt. 1972. *Man and Woman, Boy and Girl.* Baltimore: Johns Hopkins.

Moody, Kim, and Simone Sagovac. 1995. *Time Out: The Case for a Shorter Work Week.* Detroit: Labor Notes.

Morning Edition. 2000. National Public Radio, May 18.

Moshavi, Sharon. 2000. "Japan's older wives learn to leave." *Boston Globe,* February 26, pp. A1, A11.

Moynihan, Daniel Patrick. 1965. *The Negro Family: The Case for National Action.* Washington, DC: Government Printing Office. In Lee Rainwater and William Yancey, eds. 1967. *The Moynihan Report and the Politics of Controversy.* Cambridge, MA: MIT.

Mulroy, Elizabeth. 1995. *The New Uprooted: Single Mothers in Urban Life.* Westport, CT: Auburn House.

Murphy, Yolanda, and Robert Murphy. 1985. *Women of the Forest* (2nd ed.). New York: Columbia.

Murray, Donald M. 1992. "The good ol' days that never were." *Boston Globe,* September 8, pp. 53, 55.

Murray, Donald M. 1994. "A sad secret revealed." *Boston Globe* , June 21, pp. 49, 51.

Murray, Donald M. 1999. "Comfortable silence gilds their golden years." *Boston Globe,* May 8, p. C3.

Mutari, Ellen, and Deborah M. Figart. 2001. "Finland experiments with the six-hour day." *Dollars and Sense,* September–October, pp. 32–35, 44.

Nanda, Serena, and Richard Warms. 1998. *Cultural Anthropology* (6th ed.). Belmont, CA: Wadworth.

Neft, Naomi, and Ann Levine. 1997. *Where Women Stand.* New York: Random.

Negri, Gloria. 1999. "Love is still young for couples who spent their lives together." *Boston Globe,* October 16, p. B3.

Newman, David. 1999. *Sociology* (3rd ed.). Thousand Oaks, CA: Pine Forge.

Newman, Katherine. 1993. *Declining Fortunes.* New York: Basic.

Newman, Katherine. 1996. "Working hard, working poor." *Nation,* July29/August 5, pp. 20–23.

Newman, Katherine. 1999. *No Shame in My Game: The Working Poor in the Inner City.* New York: Knopf. Portion reprinted in Andrew Cherlin, ed. 2001. *Public and Private Families* (2nd ed.). New York: McGraw-Hill, pp. 113–126.

Newsinger, John. 1996. "The great Irish famine." *Monthly Review,* 47:1, April, pp. 11–19.

Nock, Steven L. 1998. *Marriage in Men's Lives.* New York: Oxford.

Oakley, Ann. 1974. *Woman's Work: The Housewife, Past and Present.* New York: Vintage.

Oakley, Ann. 1975. *The Sociology of Housework.* New York: Pantheon. Parts reprinted in Arlene Skolnick and Jerome Skolnick, eds. 1977. *Family in Transition* (2nd ed.). Boston: Little, Brown, pp. 186–192.

Oakley, Ann. 1981. *Subject Women.* New York: Pantheon.

Office of Child Support Enforcement. 1997. *Handbook on Child Support Enforcement.* Washington, DC: U.S. Department of Health and Human Services.

O'Grady, Laura. 1998. "Who says mothers can 'choose' to stay home?" *Boston Globe,* June 27, p. A14.

O'Kelly, Charlotte, and Larry Carney. 1986. *Women and Men in Society* (2nd ed.). Belmont, CA: Wadsworth.

Overholser, Geneva. 2001. "Burdens of the work-and-motherhood mix." *Boston Globe,* March 22, p. A21.

Palmer, Randall. 1999. "Canadian family ruling favors gays." *Boston Globe,* May 21, p. A8.

Pardo, Mary. 1990. "Mexican American women grassroots community activists: 'Mothers of East Los Angeles.'" In Hansen and Garey, 1998, pp. 250–262.

Parkman, Allen M. 2000. *Good Intentions Gone Awry: No-Fault Divorce and the American Family.* Lanham, MD: Rowman and Littlefield.

Parrillo, Vincent. 2000. *Strangers to These Shores* (6th ed.). Boston: Allyn and Bacon.

Parry, Wayne. 2002. "New Jersey City eliminates barriers to family life." *Ridgewood News* [New Jersey], March 28, p. A2.

Patchett, Ann. 1995. "Breaking a vow." *Vogue,* April, pp. 89–90, 98.

Patterson, Charlotte J. 2000. "Family relationships of lesbians and gay men." *Journal of Marriage and the Family,* 62:4, November, pp. 1052–1069.

Paulson, Michael. 2000. "Reform rabbis agree to allow same-sex marriages." *Boston Globe,* March 30, p. A3.

Pearson, Patricia. 1997. *When She Was Bad: Violent Women and the Myth of Innocence.* New York: Viking.

Pedro-Carroll, JoAnne. 2001. "The promotion of wellness in children and families." *American Psychologist,* November, pp. 993–1004.

Perry-Jenkins, Maureen; Rena L. Repetti; Ann C. Crouter. 2000."Work and family in the 1990s." *Journal of Marriage and the Family,* 62:4, November, pp. 981–998.

Pertman, Adam. 2000. "Well-being of children improves, study says." *Boston Globe,* June 20, pp. B1, B5.

Pfeiffer, Sacha. 1999. "Ruling affirms 'de facto' parents." *Boston Globe,* June 30, pp. B1, B6.

Phillips, Frank. 2003. "Support for gay marriage." *Boston Globe,* April 8, pp. A1, A7.

Pierce, Christine. 1995. "Gay marriage." *Journal of Social Philosophy,* 26:2, Fall.

Piercy, Kathleen. 1998. "Theorizing about family caregiving." *Journal of Marriage and the Family,* 60:1 February, pp. 109–118.

Pitcoff, Winton. 2000. "No place to call home." *Dollars and Sense,* March/April, pp. 24–25, 45–47.

Pleck, Joseph H. 1987. "American fathering in historical perspective." In Hansen and Garey, 1998, pp 351–361.

Pogrebin, Letty Cottin. 1983. *Family Politics: Love and Power on an Intimate Frontier.* New York: McGraw-Hill.

Pollitt, Katha. 1993. "Bothered and Bewildered." *New York Times,* July 22.

Pollitt, Katha. 2000. "Is divorce getting a bum rap?" *Time,* September 25, p. 82.

Polsgrove, Carol. 1988. "One mother's search for child care." *Progressive,* November, pp. 16–20.

Popenoe, David. 1994. "The evolution of marriage and the problem of stepfamilies: A biosocial perspective." In Alan Booth and Judy Dunn, eds. 1994. *Stepfamilies: Who Benefits? Who Does Not?* New Jersey: Erlbaum.

Popenoe, David. 1996. *Life Without Father.* New York: Free Press.

Popenoe, David. 1999. "Can the nuclear family be revived?" *Society,* 36, July/August, pp. 28–30.

Portman, Adam. 2000. "Well-being of children improves, study says." *Boston Globe,* June 20, pp. B1, B5.

Presser, Harriet. 1998. "Toward a 23 hour economy." In Vannoy and Dubeck, 1998, pp. 39–47.

Price, Sharon, and Patrick McKenry. 1988. *Divorce.* Newbury Park, CA: Sage.

Pryor, Jan, and Bryan Rogers. 2001. *Children in Changing Families: Life After Parental Separation.* Malden, MA: Blackwell.

Ptacek, James. 1988. "Why do men batter their wives?" In Hansen and Garey, 1998, pp. 619–633.

Quinn, Shannon, and Leslie Cintron. 2000. "If technology makes our lives easier, why are we so stressed out?" *Boston Globe,* September 9, p. A15.

Raabe, Phyllis Hutton. 1998. "Being a part-time manager: One way to combine family and career." In Vannoy and Dubeck, 1998, pp. 81–91.

Radina, M. Elise. 2001. "Cultural values and caregiving." In Marilyn Coleman and Lawrence Ganong, eds. 2003. *Points and Counterpoints.* Los Angeles: Roxbury, pp. 265–271.

Rakowsky, Judy. 1992. "Nightmare ends in death, as husband had threatened." *Boston Globe,* December 17, pp. 1, 6.

Ranalli, Ralph. 1999. "Few use 'battered woman' defense." *Boston Globe,* November 1, pp. B1, B12.

Rank, Mark Robert. 1994. *Living on the Edge: The Realities of Welfare in America.* New York: Columbia. Parts reprinted in Mark Robert Rank and Edward Kain, eds. 1995. *Diversity and Change in Families.* Englewood Cliffs, NJ: Prentice Hall.

Rankin, Nancy. 2002a. "Introduction." In Hewlett, Rankin, and West, 2002, pp. 1–9.

Rankin, Nancy. 2002b. "Fixing social insecurity: A proposal to finance parenthood." In Hewlett, Rankin, and West, 2002, pp. 265–271.

Rauch, Jonathan. 2002. "The marrying kind." *Atlantic Monthly,* May, p. 24.

Reich, Robert. 2000. "Taming consumption." *Boston Globe,* April 26, p. A23.

Retsinas, Nicholas. 1999. "In urban housing, the poor lose again . . ." *Boston Globe,* July 12, p. A9.

Reuters. 1998. "NYC extends same rights to unwed." *Boston Globe,* June 25, p. A8.

Reuters. 2002. "Iranian panel OKs divorce rights bill." *Boston Globe,* December 2, p. A4.

Ribadeneira, Diego. 1998. "Program seeks to educate clergy on domestic violence." *Boston Globe,* November 21, pp. B1, B8.

Riessman, Catherine Kohler. 1990. *Divorce Talk: Women and Men Make Sense of Personal Relationships.* New Brunswick, NJ: Rutgers.

Riley, Glenda. 1991. *Divorce: An American Tradition.* New York: Oxford.

Riley, Lisa A., and Jennifer E. Glass. 2002. "You can't always get what you want—infant care preferences and use among employed mothers." *Journal of Marriage and the Family,* 64:2, February, pp. 2–15.

Risman, Barbara J., and Danette Johnson-Sumerford. 1998. "Doing it fairly: A study of postgender marriages." *Journal of Marriage and the Family,* 60:1, February, pp. 23–40.

Rivers, Caryl. 1999. "What good old days?" *Boston Globe,* April 12, p. A13.

Robb, Christina. 1992. "Escaping abuse." *Boston Globe,* May 11, pp. 30, 33.

Robertson, Tatsha. 1999a. "'Invisible homeless' seen as growing trend." *Boston Globe,* May 11, pp. B1, B5.

Robertson, Tatsha. 1999b. "A hand in marriage." *Boston Globe,* May 24, pp. B1, B12.

Robinson, John P., and Geoffrey Godbey. 1997. *Time for Life.* University Park, PA: Pennsylvania.

Rodriguez, Cindy. 1998. "A breathtaking epidemic." *Boston Globe,* November 21, pp. B1, B4.

Rodriguez, Cindy. 2001a. "Migration's disruption of children weighed." *Boston Globe,* June 29, p. A3.

Rodriguez, Cindy. 2001b. "Many more fill the roles of single fathers." *Boston Globe,* July 10, pp. A1, B4.

Rodriguez, Cindy. 2002a. "Baby makes 2." *Boston Globe,* October 17, pp. B1, B6.

Rodriguez, Cindy. 2002b. "Immigration boom continues." *Boston Globe,* November 27, p. A3.

Rofes, Eric, ed. 1981. *The Kids' Book of Divorce.* New York: Vintage.

Roschelle, Anne R. 1997. *No More Kin: Exploring Race, Class, and Gender in Family Networks.* Thousand Oaks, CA: Sage.

Rosenberg, Ronald. 1999. "Women find balance in biotech workplace." *Boston Globe,* December 8, pp. D1, D17.

Rosencrance, Linda. 1996. "Book touts positive aspects of two-income homes." *Watertown Press* [Massachusetts], June 27, p. 9.

Ross, Emma. 2003. "Single-parent homes studied." *Boston Globe,* January 24, p. A8.

Rothman, Robert A. 1998. *Working.* Upper Saddle River, NJ: Prentice Hall.

Rubenstein, William, ed. 1993. *Lesbians, Gay Men, and the Law*. New York: New Press.

Rubin, Gayle. "The traffic in women: Notes on the political economy of sex." In Rayna Reiter, ed. 1975. *Toward an Anthropology of Women*. New York: Monthly Review, pp. 157–210.

Rubin, Lillian B. 1976. *Worlds of Pain: Life in the Working-Class Family*. New York: Basic.

Rubin, Lillian B. 1983. *Intimate Strangers*. New York: Harper and Row.

Rubin, Lillian B. 1994. *Families on the Fault Line*. New York: Harper/Collins.

Russakof, Dale. 2000. "States reject Clinton attempt at paid parental leave." *Boston Globe,* August 2, p. A3.

Russell, James W. 1997. "Mexico's rising inequality." *Monthly Review,* 49:7, December, pp. 28–33.

Saad, Lydia. 1995. "Children, hard working taking their toll on baby boomers." *The Gallup Poll Monthly,* April, pp. 21–24.

Sadker, Myra, and David Sadker. 1994. *Failing at Fairness: How Our Schools Cheat Girls*. New York: Simon and Schuster.

Sadler, A.E., ed. 1996. *Family Violence*. San Diego, CA: Greenhaven.

Salmon, Jacqueline. 2000. "Study says time mothers spend with children has not changed." *Boston Globe,* March 28, p. A3.

Sanders, Bernie. 2000. "Falling behind in boom times." *Boston Globe,* February 12, p. A15.

Schechter, Susan. 1982. *Women and Male Violence*. Boston: South End.

Schein, Muriel. 1971. "Only on Sundays." *Natural History,* April.

Schiller, Nina Glick. 1993. "The invisible women: Caregiving and AIDS." In Hansen and Garey, 1998, pp. 487–512.

Schoenborn, Charlotte A., and Barbara Foley Wilson. 1998. "Are married people healthier?" Paper presented at the American Public Health Association meeting, Boston, MA, November 15.

Schor, Juliet. 1991. *The Overworked American*. New York: Basic.

Schor, Juliet. 1999. *The Overspent American*. New York: HarperPerennial.

Schor, Juliet. 2002. "Time crunch among American parents." In Hewlett, Rankin, and West, 2002, pp. 83–102.

Schultz, Emily, and Robert Lavenda. 2001. *Cultural Anthropology* (5th ed.). Mountain View, CA: Mayfield.

Schwartz, Lita Linzer, and Florence W. Kaslow. 1997. *Painful Partings: Divorce and Its Aftermath*. New York: Wiley.

Schwartz, Mary Ann, and Barbara Marliene Scott. 1994, 2000. *Marriages and Families* (1st and 3rd eds). Englewood Cliffs, NJ: Prentice-Hall.

Schwartz, Pepper. 1994a. *Love between Equals: How Peer Marriage Really Works*. New York: Free Press.

Schwartz, Pepper. 1994b. "Peer marriage." *The Family Therapy Networker,* September/October, pp. 57–61.

Scott, Donald, and Bernard Wishy, eds. 1982. *America's Families: A Documentary History*. New York: Harper and Row.

Scott, Elizabeth. 2000. "Marriage as a precommitment." In Whyte, 2000, pp. 161–178.

Seccombe, Karen. 2000. "Families in poverty in the 1990s." *Journal of Marriage and the Family,* 62:4, November, pp. 1094–1113.

Seccombe, Karen. 2002. "'Beating the odds' versus 'changing the odds': Poverty, resilience, and family policy." *Journal of Marriage and the Family,* 64:2, May, pp. 384–394.

Seccombe, Karen; Delores James; Kimberly Battle Walters. 1998. "'They think you ain't much of nothing': The social construction of the welfare mother." *Journal of Marriage and the Family,* 60:4, November, pp. 849–865.

Seelow, David. 1999. "Fathers—from heroes to villains." *Choice,* June, 1741–1749.

Sege, Irene. 1989. "Cohabitation, while the trend, is not marriage insurance." *Boston Globe,* July 3, pp. 1, 6.

Sege, Irene. 1999. "Tables are turned at family mealtime." *Boston Globe,* August 31, pp. A1, A12.

Self Magazine. 1994. "60 ways to stop domestic violence." November, pp. 172–175, 185.

Seltzer, Judith. 1991. "Relationship between fathers and children who live apart." *Journal of Marriage and the Family,* 53:1, February, pp. 79–101.

Seltzer, Judith. 2000. "Families formed outside of marriage." *Journal of Marriage and the Family,* 62:4, November, pp. 1247–1268.

Sernau, Scott. 1997. *Critical Choices*. Los Angeles: Roxbury.

Shanklin, Eugenia. 1994. *Anthropology and Race*. Belmont, CA: Wadsworth.

Sharff, Jagna W. 1998. *King Kong on 4th Street*. Boulder, CO: Westview.

Shea, Lois. 1998. "Same-sex marriage hopes go north." *Boston Globe,* November 17, pp. B7, B8.

Sheehan, Susan. 1995. "Ain't no middle class." *The New Yorker,* December 11, pp. 82–92. In Andrew Cherlin, ed. 1999. *Public and Private Families.* New York: McGraw Hill, pp. 85–93.

Sherrill, Susan Leigh. 2002. "Night of family time strikes a nerve across the nation." *Ridgewood News* [New Jersey], March 29, pp. A4, A5.

Sherwood, Maureen. 1997. "An emptiness I didn't know existed." *Esquire,* May, pp. 60–61.

Shostak, Marjorie. 1981. *Nisa: The Life and Words of a !Kung Woman.* New York: Vintage.

Shostak, Marjorie. 2000. *Return to Nisa.* Cambridge, MA: Harvard.

Skocpol, Theda. 2002. "What it will take to build a family-friendly America." In Hewett, Rankin, and West, 2002, fall pp. 219–233.

Skolnick, Arlene. 1991. *Embattled Paradise.* New York: Basic.

Skolnick, Arlene. 1992, 1996. *The Intimate Environment* (5th and 6th eds.). New York: Harper.

Skolnick, Arlene. 1997. "Family values: The sequel." *American Prospect,* May–June, pp. 86–94.

Skolnick, Arlene, and Stacey Rosencratz. 1994. "The new crusade for the old family." *American Prospect,* Summer, pp. 59–65.

Sleeper, Peter. 1986. "No indictment for abused wife." *Boston Globe,* January 1, p. 19.

Slone, Verna Mae. 1979. *What My Heart Wants to Tell.* New York: Harper Perennial.

Small, Meredith. 1998. *Our Babies, Ourselves.* New York: Anchor.

Snow, David, and Leon Anderson. 1993. *Down on Their Luck.* Berkeley, CA: California.

Sobel, David. 1997. "Take back the afternoon." *Sanctuary,* May/June, pp. 10–13.

Sorensen, Elaine. 1997. "A national profile of nonresident fathers and their ability to pay child support." *Journal of Marriage and the Family,* 59:4, November, pp. 785–797.

Staal, Stephanie. 2000. *The Love They Lost: Living with the Legacy of Our Parents' Divorce.* New York: Delacorte.

Stacey, Judith. 1990. *Brave New Families.* New York: Basic.

Stacey, Judith. 1996. *In the Name of the Family.* Boston: Beacon.

Stacey, Judith. 2003. "Gay and lesbian families: Queer like us." In Mason, Skolnick, and Sugarman, eds., 2003, pp. 144–169.

Stack, Carol. 1974. *All Our Kin.* New York: Basic.

Stack, Carol. 1996. *Call to Home.* New York: Basic.

Stack, Steven and J. Ross Eshleman. 1998. "Marital status and happiness: A 17–nation study." *Journal of Marriage and the Family,* 60:2, May, pp. 527–536.

Staples, Robert, ed. 1991. *The Black Family: Essays and Studies* (4th ed.). Belmont, CA: Wadsworth.

Stark, Elizabeth. 1986. "Friends through it all." *Psychology Today,* May, pp. 54–60.

Statistical Abstract of the United States. 1977, 1979, 1982–1983, 1987, 1998, 1999, 2002. Published yearly. Washington, DC: U.S. Census Bureau.

Steil, Janice M. 1997. *Marital Equality: Its Relationship to the Well-Being of Husbands and Wives.* Thousand Oaks, CA: Sage.

Stein, Maurice. 1960. *The Eclipse of Community.* New York: Harper and Row.

Steinhorn, Leonard, and Barbara Diggs-Brown. 2000. *By the Color of Our Skin.* New York: Plume.

Stier, Haya, and Marta Tienda. 1993. "Are men marginal to the family? Insights from Chicago's inner city." In Ann Vail, ed., 1999. *Taking Sides: Family and Personal Relationships* (4th ed.). Guilford, CT: Dushkin, pp. 193–200.

Stockman, Farah. 2002a. "Unmarried vie for equal rights." *Boston Globe,* June 30, pp. B1, B6.

Stockman, Farah. 2002b. "A search for equality." *Boston Globe,* October 28, pp. B1, B6.

Stoddard, Thomas B. 1989. "Why gay people should seek the right to marry." *Out/Look: National Lesbian and Gay Quarterly,* Fall. In Hansen and Garey, 1998, pp. 475–479.

Stone, Lawrence. 1977. *The Family, Sex, and Marriage in England,* 1500–1800. New York: Harper and Row.

Straus, Murray A. 1993. "Domestic violence is a problem for men." In Swisher, 1996.

Strong, Bryan; Christine DeVault; Barbara S. Sayad. 1998. *The Marriage and Family Experience* (7th ed.). Belmont, CA: Wadsworth.

Strong, Bryan; Christine DeVault; Barbara W. Sayad; Theodore F. Cohen. 2001. *The Marriage and Family Experience* (8th ed.). Belmont, CA: Wadsworth.

Sudarkasa, Niara. 1988. "Interpreting the African heritage of Afro-American family organization." In Hansen and Garey, 1998, pp. 91–104.

Sugarman, Stephen D. 2003. "Single-parent families." In Mason, Skolnick, and Sugarman, 2003, pp. 14–39.

Swisher, Karin L., ed. 1996. *Domestic Violence.* San Diego, CA: Greenhaven.

Takaki, Ronald. 1993. *A Different Mirror.* Boston: Little, Brown.

Talbot, Margaret. 1997. "Love, American style." *New Republic,* April 14. In Henry L. Tischler, ed., 2001. *Marriage and Family Issues.* Upper Saddle River, NJ: Prentice Hall, pp. 59–63.

Tanner, Lindsey. 2002. "Doctors back rights of gays to adopt." *Boston Globe,* February 4, p. A2.

Tasker, Fiona, and Susan Golombok. 1997. *Growing Up in a Lesbian Family.* New York: Guilford.

Tauchert, Tom. 2002. "Village to host evening for families." *Ridgewood News* [New Jersey], March 22, pp. A1, A10.

Taylor, Jerry. 1999. "Classes lessen pain of divorce for children." *Boston Globe (Northwest Weekly),* March 21, pp. 1, 7.

Taylor, John. 1997. "Divorce is good for you." *Esquire,* May, pp. 52–59.

Taylor, Ronald L., ed. 2002. *Minority Families in the United States* (3rd ed.). Upper Saddle River, NJ: Prentice Hall.

Terkel, Studs. 1970. *Hard Times: An Oral History of the Great Depression.* New York: Pantheon.

Terkel, Studs. 1974. *Working.* New York: Avon.

Teyber, Edward, and Charles Hoffman. 1987. "Missing fathers." *Psychology Today,* April, pp. 36–39.

Thorne, Barrie, with Marilyn Yalom, eds. 1982. *Rethinking the Family: Some Feminist Questions.* New York: Longman.

Thornton, Arland, and Linda Young-DeMarco. 2001. "Four decades of trend in attitudes toward family issues in the United States: The 1960s through the 1990s." *Journal of Marriage and the Family,* 63:4, November, pp. 1009–1037.

Townsend, Nicholas. 1998. "Fathers and sons: Men's experiences and the reproduction of fatherhood." In Hansen and Garey, 1998, pp. 363–376.

Treas, Judith. 1995. "Older Americans in the 1990s and Beyond." *Population Bulletin,* 50:2, May.

Trigger, Bruce G. 1990. *The Huron: Farmers of the North* (2nd ed.). Fort Worth, TX: Holt, Rinehart, and Winston.

Truehart, Charles. 1999. "France gives rights to unwed couples." *Boston Globe,* October 14, p. A4.

Tucker, M. Belinda, and Claudia Mitchell-Kernan, eds. 1995. *The Decline of Marriage among African Americans.* New York: Russell Sage.

Turnbull, Colin M. 1961. *The Forest People.* New York: Simon and Schuster.

Turnbull, Colin M. 1983. *The Human Cycle.* New York: Simon and Schuster.

Ucko, Lenora Greenbaum. 1995. *Endangered Spouses.* Lanham, MD: University Press of America.

U.S. Census Bureau. 1998. *Money Income in the United States, 1998.* Washington, DC: U.S. Government Printing Office.

U.S. Census Bureau. 1999. *Current Population Reports,.*Washington, DC: U.S. Government Printing Office, pp. 60–206.

Uhlenberg, Peter. 1996. "Mortality decline in the twentieth century and supply of kin over the life course." In Hansen and Garey, 1998, pp. 69–77.

Ulrich, Laurel Thatcher. 1987. "Housewife and gadder: Themes of self-sufficiency and community in eighteenth century New England." In Hansen and Garey, 1998, pp. 241–250.

Umberson, Debra; Kristin Anderson; Jennifer Glick; Adam Shapiro. 1998. "Domestic violence, personal control, and gender." *Journal of Marriage and the Family,* 60:2, May, pp. 442–452.

Van Ausdale, Debra, and Joe R. Feagin. 2001. *The First R: How Children Learn Race and Racism.* Lanham, MD: Rowman and Littlefield.

van Dam, Laura. 1997. "Wild in the streets." *Sanctuary,* May/June, pp. 3–5.

Vannoy, Dana, ed. 2001. *Gender Mosaics.* Los Angeles: Roxbury.

Vannoy, Dana, and Paula Dubeck, eds. 1998. *Challenges for Work and Family in the Twenty-First Century.* New York: Aldine de Gruyter.

Vaughan, Diane. 1986. *Uncoupling: How Relationships Come Apart.* New York: Oxford.

Veevers, Jean. 1980. *Childless by Choice.* Scarborough, Ontario: Butterworth.

Vissing, Yvonne. 2002. *Women without Children: Nurturing Lives.* New Brunswick, NJ: Rutgers.

Voydanoff, Patricia. 1984. *Work and Family.* Palo Alto, CA: Mayfield.

Voydanoff, Patricia. 1987. *Work and Family Life.* Newbury Park, CA: Sage.

Wagner, David. 1993. *Checkerboard Square: Culture and Resistance in a Homeless Community.* Boulder, CO: Westview.

Waite, Linda J., and Maggie Gallagher. 2000. *The Case for Marriage.* New York: Doubleday.

Walker, Alexis. 1996. "Couples watching television: Gender, power, and the remote control." *Journal of Marriage and the Family,* 58:4, November, pp. 813–823.

Walker, Samuel; Cassia Spohn; Miriam DeLone. 2000. *The Color of Justice* (2nd ed.). Belmont, CA: Wadsworth.

Wallace, Harvey. 1999. *Family Violence* (2nd ed.). Boston: Allyn and Bacon.

Wallace-Wells, Benjamin. 2000. "More working families seek food aid, study says." *Boston Globe,* January 21, p. B2.

Wallen, Jacqueline. 2002. *Balancing Work and Family: The Role of the Workplace.* Boston: Allyn and Bacon.

Wallerstein, Judith. 1995. *The Good Marriage: How and Why Love Lasts.* Boston: Houghton Mifflin.

Wallerstein, Judith. 2003. "Children of divorce." In Mason, Skolnick, and Sugarman, 2003, pp. 66–95.

Wallerstein, Judith, and Sandra Blakeslee. 1990. *Second Chances: Men, Women, and Children a Decade after Divorce.* New York: Tichnor and Fields.

Wallerstein, Judith, and Joan B. Kelly. 1980. *Surviving the Breakup: How Children and Parents Cope with Divorce.* New York: Basic.

Wallerstein, Judith; Julia Lewis; Sandra Blakeslee. 2000. *The Unexpected Legacy of Divorce.* New York: Hyperion.

Walsh, Joan. 1986. "Family ties: Feminism's new frontier." *Progressive,* September, pp. 21–23.

Walshok, Mary Lindenstein. 1981. *Blue-Collar Women: Pioneers on the Male Frontier.* Garden City, NY: Anchor.

Ward, Martha C. 1999. *A World Full of Women* (2nd ed.). Boston: Allyn And Bacon.

Warner, W. Lloyd. 1963. *Yankee City.* New Haven, CT: Yale.

Washington Post. 1994. "Quality often poor in 'family' day care, survey asserts." *Boston Globe,* April 4, p. 3.

Washington Post. 1996. "Delaying for better or worse: Rise in marriage age put to economic shifts." *Boston Globe,* March 13, p. 3.

Watson, Roy E.L. 1983. "Premarital cohabitation vs. traditional courtship." *Family Relations,* January.

Wattenberg, Ben. 1985. *The Good News Is the Bad News Is Wrong.* New York: Simon and Schuster.

Way, Niobe, and Helena Stauber. 1996. "Are absent fathers really absent?" In Bonnie J. Ross Leadlater and Niobe Way, eds. 1996. *Urban Girls: Resisting Stereotypes, Creating Identities.* New York: New York University.

Weiss, Joanna. 2001. "The breast-feeding brigade." *Boston Globe,* April 18, pp. C1, C10.

Weitoft, Gunilla R.; Anders Hjern; Bengt Haglund; Mans Rosen. 2003. "Mortality, severe morbidity, and injury living with single parents in Sweden: A population-based study." *The Lancet,* 361 (January 25), pp. 289–295.

Weitzman, Lenore. 1981. *The Marriage Contract.* New York: Free Press.

Weitzman, Lenore. 1985. *The Divorce Revolution.* New York: Free Press.

Welter, Barbara. 1966. "The cult of true womanhood: 1820–1860." *American Quarterly,* 18:2, Summer, pp. 151–174.

Weltner, Linda. 1999. "Mothers deserve help, not blame." *Boston Globe,* May 6, p. E2.

Weltner, Linda. 2000. "What computer games can't teach." *Boston Globe,* May 11, p. H2.

Wen, Patricia. 2000. "Researchers worrying as teens grow up online." *Boston Globe,* Aprl 21, pp. A1, A26.

Wen, Patricia. 2001a. "In science, love now has a reality check." *Boston Globe,* February 14, pp. A1, A24.

Wen, Patricia. 2001b. "Tradition, in name only." Boston Globe, March 17, pp. A1, A12.

Wen, Patricia. 2002a. "Good fathers? It figures." *Boston Globe,* August 12, pp. A1, A4.

Wen, Patricia. 2002b. "A couple's work." *Boston Globe,* November 9, pp. B1, B3.

Wen, Patricia. 2002c. "Cohabitors' pacts tie legal knot for unwed." *Boston Globe,* December 16, pp. A1, A16.

West, James. 1945. *Plainville, USA.* New York: Columbia.

Westhues, Kenneth. 1982. *First Sociology.* New York: McGraw–Hill.

Weston, Kath. 1991. *Families We Choose.* New York: Columbia.

White, Lynn, and Stacy J. Rogers. 2000. "Economic circumstances and family outcomes." *Journal of Marriage and the Family,* 62:4, November, pp. 1035–1051.

Whitehead, Barbara Dafoe. 1993. "Dan Quayle was right." *Atlantic Monthly,* April, pp. 47–84.

Whitehead, Barbara Dafoe. 1997. *The Divorce Culture.* New York: Knopf.

Whitehead, Barbara Dafoe, and David Popenoe. 2002. "Marriage makes a comeback." *Boston Globe,* May 12, p. E8.

Whyte, Martin King, ed. 2000. *Marriage in America: A Communitarian Perspective.* Lanham, MD: Rowman and Littlefield.

Williams, Eric. 1944. *Capitalism and Slavery.* New York: Capricorn , 1966.

Willie, Charles. 1981. *A New Look at Black Families* (2nd ed.). Bayside, NY: General Hall.

Wilmsen, Peter. 2002. "Changing focus." *Boston Globe,* April 12, pp. B1, B12.

Wilmsen, Steven. 1999. "Law and the disorder it can bring to family life." *Boston Globe,* June 24, pp. D1, D7.

Wilson, William J. 1996. *When Work Disappears: The World of the New Urban Poor.* New York: Knopf.

Winfield, Liz. 1996. "Why can't we marry?" *Boston Globe,* June 5, p. 15.

Wong, Dolores Sue. 1999a. "Shelters for battered women found lacking." *Boston Globe,* May 10, pp. B1, B8.

Wong, Dolores Sue. 1999b. "Single fathers embrace role, fight stereotype." *Boston Globe,* July 5, pp. A1, A16.

Wright, James D.; Beth A. Rubin; Joel A. Devine. 1998. *Beside the Golden Door: Policy, Politics, and the Homeless.* New York: Aldine de Gruyter.

Wright, Richard. 1945. *Black Boy.* New York: Harper Perennial, 1966.

Yeung, W. Jean; John F. Sandberg; Pamela E. Davis-Dean; Sandra L. Hofferth. 2001. "Children's time with fathers in intact families." *Journal of Marriage and the Family,* 63:1, February, pp. 136–154.

Yllo, Kersti. 1993. "Through a feminist lens: Gender, power, and violence." In Hansen and Garey, 1998, pp. 609–618.

Young, Cathy. 1998. "Domestic violations." In Henry Tischler, ed. 2001. *Debating Points: Marriage and Family Issues.* Upper Saddle River, NJ: Prentice Hall.

Young, Cathy. 2002a. "Is there an upside to divorce?" *Boston Globe,* January 23, p. A15.

Young, Cathy. 2002b. "New look at 'deadbeat' dads." *Boston Globe,* February 11, p. A15.

Young, Cathy. 2002c. "Recognizing men abused by women." *Boston Globe,* November 11, p. A17.

Young, Michael, and Peter Willmott. 1957. *Family and Kinship in East London.* Baltimore: Penguin.

Zelizer, Viviana A. 1985. *Pricing the Priceless Child: The Changing Social Value of Children.* New York: Basic.

Zinn, Maxine Baca, and D. Stanley Eitzen. 1996, 1999. *Diversity in Families* (4th, and 5th eds.). New York: Longman.

Zitner, Aaron. 1992. "'Subfamily' a growing phenomenon." *Boston Globe West Weekly,* October 14, pp. 1, 4.

Zuckoff, Mitchell. 1988. "Abuse not high risk in day care." *Boston Globe,* March 22, p. 82.

Zweig, Michael. 2000. *The Working-Class Majority.* Ithaca, NY: Cornell.

Index

Abkhasian people, of Georgia
　Republic, 119–120, 125
absent(ee) fathers, 39, 43, 71, 95–98,
　248, 252
abuse, domestic. *See* violence, in
　families
achievement orientation, of African
　American families, 191
acquired immune deficiency
　syndrome (AIDS), 110, 129
adolescence, historical perspective
　on, 21
adoptions, in lesbian and gay
　families, 5
adultery, 6
African American families, 5, 28;
　achievement and work orientation
　of, 190–191; caregiving in, 110–
　113; class structure of, 191(table);
　divorce and, 233; economic and
　social statistics on, 186–188, 190;
　enslavement and "freedom" of,
　29–33; flexible family roles in,
　191–193; focus on positive by,
　190; gender roles in, 192–193;
　grandparenting in, 128; income
　and employment of, 186–188; in
　poverty, 187, 188, 194; kinship in,
　122, 123, 125, 180, 193–194;
　migration of, out of South, 145–
　146, 147; parents and children in,
　82–84; sharing and nonsharing of
　housework in, 219; strengths of,
　186, 190–194; struggles of, 186–
　189
AIDS. *See* acquired immune
　deficiency syndrome
Aid to Families with Dependent
　Children (AFDC), 183
Ain't No Makin' It (McLeod), 93,
　154–155, 184–185
alcohol abuse: unemployment and,
　156; wife abuse and, 277–278
All Our Kin (Stack), 82–83, 125, 157,
　180
alternate shift couples, 174, 183,
　201–202
alternative insemination, 100
Alternatives to Marriage Project, 65
Amazing Grace (Kozol), 93
American Enterprise Institute, 37
American Indians. *See* Native
　Americans
American wakes," 141–142

apartheid, 139
Arapesh people, of New Guinea, 80
Arnaz, Desi, 28
assisted conception, 4
"assisted living" facilities, 111
asthma, 92, 188
Aulette, Judy, 45
automation, rise of, 150
autonomy, 280

backsliding, 176
Back to the Future (film), 25–26
Ball, Lucille, 28
battered men, 270. *See also* husband
　abuse
battered women, 266–267;
　experiences of, 272–274; practical
　advice to, 282; shelters for, 28, 45,
　266, 273, 274–275, 279, 281;
　violence committed by, 270–272,
　273. *See also* wife abuse
Be an Outrageous Older Woman
　(Jacobs), 124
Bethnal Green, East London, 118–
　119, 127, 131–132
bilateral descent, 11
birth rates, 14, 154, 188
Bishop family, 5, 10, 83, 123, 147–
　148
*Biting the Dust: The Joys of
　Housework* (Horsfield), 216
Black Boy (Wright), 33
Black Like Me (Griffin), 33
Blankenhorn, David, 39
Blue-Collar Marriage (Komarovsky),
　181
*Blue-Collar Women: Pioneers on the
　Male Frontier* (Walshok), 162
bonding, of parents and children,
　79–80
Bracero program (1942–1964), 143
*Brave New Families: Stories of
　Domestic Upheaval in Late
　Twentieth Century America*
　(Stacey), 41, 45, 48, 60, 235
breast-feeding, 81–82
Bush, George W., 61

*Call to Home: African Americans
　Reclaim the Rural South* (Stack), 5,
　10, 74, 83–84, 110–113, 125, 146,
　148, 157, 180
capitalism, rise of, 20, 138, 195

caregiving, to elders, 109–113, 116,
　124; class differences in, 180;
　crisis in, 111; experiences of, 112–
　113; historical perspective on,
　109; solutions of, 111–112; stress
　of, 113; today, 109–110
Center for Health and Gender Equity
　for Population Reports, 268
"chain migration," 147
"Changing Families," course on, 35,
　71, 125, 207
Changing Families (Aulette), 45, 71
child abuse, 114, 156, 263, 266, 272
child care, 42, 82, 83, 85, 88–90;
　alternate shift couples and, 174;
　earnings gap and, 168; family-
　work imbalance and, 201–202;
　farming out of, 176; by
　grandparents, 128; historical
　perspective on, 88, 169; sharing
　vs. nonsharing of, 54, 109, 163,
　165, 169–173, 193, 197, 198, 201,
　203, 210, 216–217, 219, 223, 244;
　two-worker families and, 206;
　working women and, 173–174.
　See also childrearing
child custody, 101, 240, 247–249
childhood: class divisions and, 178–
　180; concerns about decline of,
　86–87; historical perspective on,
　16, 21–22, 84; joys of, 71–76
child labor laws, 19, 21, 84
childlessness, 74–75
childrearing: communal, 78;
　concerns about devaluation of,
　87–88; cultural differences in, 76–
　78; historical perspective on, 84,
　85. *See also* child care
children: in African American
　families, 43, 92–93, 179–180; co-
　sleeping of, 80; day care and, 88,
　89(table), 90–91, 161, 173, 174,
　185, 213–214; divorce and, 234,
　235, 236, 246–257; fatherless, 39,
　43, 71, 95–98, 248, 252; feeding
　of, 81–82; gender identities of,
　160; parents and, 71–102; in
　poverty, 92–93, 151; raising, 87–
　88; reasons for having, 73–76;
　speedup of family lives and, 208–
　209; today, 85–93; touching
　(holding) of, 80–81
child support payments, 249–250,
　259

Chinese immigrants, 142–143, 256
Christian Coalition, 37, 38, 43
Civil Rights movement, 28–29
civil unions, 1, 66–67
clan, defined, 10
class(es), 178–185, 191(table);
childhood and, 178–180; daily
living and, 183–184; defined, 177–
178; extended families and, 180–
181; gender roles and, 182–183;
marriage and, 178, 181–183;
primacy of, 184–185
class endogamy, 178
Clinton, Bill, 37, 67
*Closed Hearts, Closed Minds: The
Textbook Story of Marriage*
(Glenn), 40, 61
cohabitation, 62–65, 98; defined, 62;
and divorce, 64–65, 244, 258;
legal aspects of, 65; normalization
of, 63–64; reasons for, 64; sharing
of housework and, 219–220; types
of, 62–63
cohousing, 135–136
Colonial period; caregiving in, 116;
childrearing in, 84; communities
in, 132; divorce in, 226; family life
in, 12–13, 14–16, 20, 22, 285;
gender identities in, 162, 163;
marriages in, 52
communal childrearing, 78
communities, 116–118, 130–137,
209; affordable housing and, 157;
historical perspective on, 132–134;
in societies outside United States,
130–132; today, 134–136
companionate families, 22
companionate marriages, 22, 52, 53,
55, 182
comparable worth, 168
Conference on Families, 8
conflicts, family, 9
consumption, reduced, 211
"Contract with the American Family:
A Bold Plan to Strengthen the
Family and Restore Common-
Sense Values" (Christian
Coalition), 38
control issues, in family violence,
269, 272–274, 276–277, 281, 282.
See also power inequalities,
violence and
co-sleeping, 80
Council on Families in America, 37,
38, 39, 40, 43, 47, 61, 62, 64, 224,
229, 261
couple violence, 269
crime, juvenile, 13, 95, 96
"Crisis of Family Decline in
Massachusetts, The" (Christian
Coalition), 38–39
Cult of True Womanhood, 18, 19
"culture of poverty," 184, 185
custody, of children, 101, 240, 247–
249

"Dan Quayle Was Right"
(Whitehead), 40

day care, 88, 89(table), 90–91, 161,
173, 174, 185, 213–214
death and dying, historical
perspective on, 125
decline of families. *See* family
decline, concerns about
delinquency, juvenile, 71
descent group, defined, 10–11
discipline, in stepfamilies, 259
discrimination, racial, 186, 187, 189, 194
divorce, 9, 35, 41, 43, 47, 56, 57, 59,
94, 189, 204, 224–261; by
alternative shift couples, 202; as
American tradition, 226–231;
beliefs about, 236–237; benefits
of, 257–258; causes and
explanations of, 229–230; child
custody and, 247–249; child
support payments and, 249–250,
259; cohabitation and, 64–65, 244,
258; conflicts over housework
and, 54, 220, 244; deciding to,
234; economic issues in, 154, 184,
240–241, 243; effects of, on
children, 95–96, 252–257;
experiences of, 226, 233–235;
extended life spans and, 20;
father-child relationship after,
250–252; and former spouses,
relationships with, 235;
grandparenting and, 128; grounds
for, 228–229, 265; historical
perspective on, 13, 14, 18, 24, 26,
52, 53, 225, 226–231, 237;
individual happiness and, 24, 244,
245; job loss and, 167; legal
aspects of, 228–229; life after,
257–260; marital expectations and,
242; meanings of, 227, 260–261;
men's experiences of, 235, 239–
240; in modern industrial
societies, 226; myths about, 237;
needs of children after, 256–257;
new families after, 251, 258–260;
no-fault, 229, 231, 237–239, 243;
"obligation to self" and, 39, 244–
245; ongoing debate about, 227–
228; in pre-industrial societies,
225; reasons for, 226, 228–229,
241–245; recent and ongoing
changes involving, 283;
relationships with former spouses
and, 235; rise in, 242–244; social
acceptance of, 237, 243; statistics
on, 51, 61, 188, 231–233,
232(table), 238; stories of, 234–
235; stress and, 234; threat of, as
source of power, 172; universality
of, 225–226, 233; women's
experiences of, 235, 239; work-
family imbalance and, 201
Divorce: An American Tradition
(Riley), 226, 242, 260
"divorce culture," 39, 54, 236–237
"divorce mills," 227
*Divorce Talk: Women and Men Make
Sense of Personal Relationships*
(Riessman), 240

Dix, Dorothy, 24
domestic partner laws, 67, 68–69
domestic violence. *See* violence,
families
Donna Reed Show, The (TV show
10, 25
donor insemination, 4
Douglass, Frederick, 30
drug use and abuse, 186–187, 19
277–278
*Drylongso: A Self-Portrait of Blac
America* (Gwaltney), 191

earnings, 150–151, 152. *See also*
income
Eclipse of Community, The (Stein
133
Economic Apartheid in America
(Collins and Yeskel), 158
economic conditions: class divis
and, 177–185, 190; consequen
for families, 153–158; historica
perspective on, 149–153. *See a*
poverty
economic dependence, 276, 277
economic independence, 243
Edgar, Jim, 37
education, gender differences in,
167–168, 168(table)
Efe people, of Central Africa, 80
egalitarian marriages, 56, 171, 17
219
Ehrenreich, Barbara, 22
eight-hour day, 9
elders: caregiving to, 109–113, 1
124, 180; living arrangements o
124–125
emancipation, African American
families after, 32
EMERGE (therapy for abusive me
281
employment. *See* work
endogamy, class, 178
enslaved Africans, 140–141
equality, 56, 170. *See also* sharing
nonsharing, of child care and
housework
estrangement, familial, 115
Etzioni, Amitai, 37, 41
"expressive individualism," 245
extended families, 29, 31, 41–42,
107, 116–130, 136, 224, 283; cl
divisions and, 180–181; define
10; grandparenting and, 126–1
193; historical perspective on,
120–122. *See also* kinship

Failing at Fairness (Sadker and
Sadker), 161
families: class divisions and, 177–
185; communities and, 130–13
difficulties in study of, 46–49;
feminist perspectives on, 43–4
49; gender and, 159–176;
historical perspective on, 12–3
285–286; kinship and, 116–130
living in, 103–115; migration a
138–149; new, after divorce, 25

158–260; violence in, 262–282. *See also individual types of families*
Families on the Fault Line (Rubin), 202, 218
family, defined, 7–9
Family and Kinship in East London (Young and Willmott), 6, 125, 180
family decline: concerns about, 13–14, 37–40, 43, 47, 285; myth of, 40–41
family feuds, 108
"family friendly" policies, at worksite, 212–213, 214
family gatherings, 106–107
family incomes, 151–152, 187(table)
family leaves, 9, 209, 212
family meals, 103–106
"family nights," 87
Family Politics (Pogrebin), 8
Family Protection Act, 38
family secrets and facades, 48–49
Family Ties (Logan and Spitze), 74
family time, hope for more, 286
family traditions, 107
Family Values: A Lesbian Mother's Fight for Her Son (Burke), 4
family violence. *See* violence, in families
Family Violence (Wallace), 263
Family Violence in Cross-Cultural Perspective (Levinson), 264
family wage, 18, 197
family-work imbalance, 42, 163, 172–173, 199, 201–203; solutions to, 200, 206, 209–215
famine, migration and, 139, 141
farming families, 12–13, 19
farming out, of family chores and responsibilities, 222
fatherhood, historical perspective on, 85, 169
Father Knows Best (TV show), 10, 25
Fatherless America (Blankenhorn), 71
fathers: absent(ee), 39, 43, 71, 95–98, 248, 252; as caregivers, 5, 16, 163; custodial, 248, 249; divorced, and their children, 250–252, 257; "good provider" role and, 163–167; single, 200; work-family imbalance and, 42, 163, 172–173
Fathers and Divorce (Arendell), 239
feeding, of children, 81–82
feminist perspective(s), 18, 28, 85; on domestic violence, 60; on families, 43–45, 49; on marriage, 42, 60; on power inequalities, 43–44, 60
flextime, 206, 209, 212, 214
food preparation, 24, 103–106
Forest People, The (Turnbull), 78
Frazier, E. Franklin, 32
friendship, between husbands and wives, 55, 182
front porch, disappearance of, 134
Full Faith and Credit clause, 67

gangs, unemployment and, 190

gathering-hunting societies: childrearing in, 81; communities in, 130, 138; divorce in, 225; extended families in, 118; gender identities in, 160; household tasks in, 215; marital conflict in, 264–265
gay parents, 100–101
gender, 159–176; child care and, 169–174, 175, 176; class divisions and, 182–183; divorce and, 239–240; historical perspective on, 162–163; housework and, 169, 172, 197–198, 215–223; income and, 167–168; vs. sex, 159–160; work and, 162–163, 167, 196–197; violence and, 269–272
gender equality, 280, 282, 285
gender identities. *See* gender roles
gender roles, 17, 159, 161–162, 192–193, 196, 230, 243, 244, 286
Good News Is the Bad News Is Wrong, The (Wattenberg), 41
"good enough" marriages, 245, 253, 260
"good old days," 20, 43, 46–48, 285
"good provider" role, 18, 163–167, 175
grandchildren, 126, 127, 129–130
GrandFamilies House, 129
grandparents: generational ties and, 129; historical perspective on, 127–128; one-parent families and, 99; today, 128
Great Depression, 26
Greater Boston Interfaith Organization, 157
Great Expectations: Marriage and Divorce in Post-Victorian America (May), 242
"guest workers," 139–140

Halving It All: How Equally Shared Parenting Works (Deutsch), 169–170, 172, 176
Hard Times: An Oral History of the Great Depression (Terkel), 26
health, marriage and, 57–58
health care reform, 158, 185, 211–212
Here to Stay: American Families in the Twentieth Century (Bane), 41
Heroes of Their Own Lives: The Politics and History of Family Violence (Gordon), 266
He Works, She Works: How Two-Income Families Are Happy, Healthy, and Thriving (Barnett and Rivers), 153
"History of Legal Protection for Battered Women in Massachusetts, The" (M. Liazos), 266–167
"homelands," in South Africa, 139
homeless families, 113–115, 178, 212, 274, 275
housewives, 17
housework, 9, 173–174, 215–223; alternate shift couples and, 174;

economic decisions involved in, 217, 220–222; farming out of, 176, 222; historical perspective on, 169, 215–217; job loss and, 166; power inequality and, 217, 221–222; sharing vs. nonsharing of, 54, 109, 162, 163, 169–173, 193, 197, 198, 201, 203, 210, 215–223; socialization and, 162, 163, 217, 220; statistics on, 218–220, 219(table); today, 217–220; two-worker families and, 206
housing costs, 152–153, 156, 157, 212
Human Cycle, The (Turnbull), 77
husband abuse, 264, 269
Husbands and Wives (Blood and Wolfe), 58–59

illness: divorce and, 240; marriage and, 57–58
I Love Lucy (TV show), 28, 29, 265–266
immigrant women workers, 145
income: class differences in, 177–178; family, in 2000, 187(table); gender differences in, 168; inequalities in, 151–152, 158; insufficient, for family support, 198
individual happiness, divorce and, 24, 244, 245
individualism, 19, 230, 244–245
industrialism, 132–133, 195, 229; childhood and, 84; families under, 12, 14, 17–20; gender identities and, 162, 163; "good provider" role and, 164, 196; migration and, 140
In Hope of Liberty: Culture, Community, and Protest among Northern Free Blacks, 1700-1860 (Horton and Horton), 32
In the Name of the Family (Stacey), 41–42
Intimate Strangers (Rubin), 165
intimate terrorism, 269
Irish immigrants, 141–142
Iroquois people, 11, 256
isolation, wife abuse and, 276

Jane Doe, Inc., 279–280
job security, declining, 150–151. *See also* unemployment
joint custody, legal vs. physical, 248, 249
Judith Wallerstein Center for the Family in Transition, 252
Ju/'hoansi people, 11, 80, 81, 118, 120, 127, 159, 215
juvenile courts, 21, 84
juvenile crime and delinquency, 13, 71, 95, 96

Kanuri people, in Africa, 225, 261
Kids' Book of Divorce: By, for, and about Kids (Rofes), 246, 249, 256, 257

Kinsey, Alfred, 41
kinship, 5, 21, 25, 116–130, 157,
 285; in African American families,
 193–194; in East London in 1950s,
 118–119; elders and, 123–125; in
 gathering-hunting societies, 118;
 historical perspective on, 120–122;
 in Longo, Albania, 136–137;
 today, 125, 134–136; working-
 class families and, 180–181. *See
 also* extended families
"kin work," 108–109, 216
!Kung people, 11, 118. *See also*
 Ju/ 'hoansi people

labor force participation: by blacks
 vs. whites, 191(table); by men vs.
 women, 162–163, 165, 169,
 191(table), 196–198, 206; by wives
 with husband present, 167(table)
Landers, Ann, 256, 269
La Storia (Mangione and Morreale),
 146
latchkey children, 13, 42
layoffs, "good provider" role and,
 166–167, 202
lead poisoning, 179–180
Leave It to Beaver (TV show), 10,
 13–14, 25, 26, 27, 28, 29
lesbian parents, 4–5, 100–101
life spans, 20–21
Life Without Father (Popenoe), 39,
 71
*Little Commonwealth, A: Family Life
 in Plymouth Colony* (Demos), 2,
 20
living arrangements, after divorce,
 247–249
"living simply," 211, 222, 223
Longo, Albania, 73, 116–118, 125–
 126, 130, 136–137, 283, 285
love, 259, 285; romantic, 16, 18, 22,
 24
*Love They Lost, The: Living with the
 Legacy of Our Parents' Divorce*
 (Staal), 247

male dominance, ideology of, 163
male-provider families, 200. *See also*
 "good provider" role
marriage(s), 50–62, 70; benefits of,
 57–58; class differences in, 181–
 182, 183; companionate, 22, 52,
 53, 55, 182; concerns about
 decline in, 61–62; divorces per
 (ratio), 231–232; economic
 conditions and, 154, 192;
 egalitarian, 56, 171, 172, 219;
 equality and sharing in, 175–176;
 feminist critiques of, 60; good,
 characteristics of, 54–57; "good
 enough," 245, 253, 260; high
 expectations of, 242; historical
 perspective on, 22–23, 24, 26,
 41, 52–53; over time, 58–60;
 peer, 55–56; reasons for, 50;
 recent and ongoing changes
 involving, 284; research on, 53–

54; same-sex, 1, 7, 9, 34, 51,
 66–67, 68, 69–70, 101, 283; in
 slave families, 29–31; statistics
 on, 51–52, 51(table); under
 industrialism, 18; work-family
 imbalance and, 201–202
*Marriage in America: A Report to the
 Nation* (Council on Families), 39,
 61
matriarchy, 11, 189
"matrifocal" household, 30
matrilineal descent, 11
Mbuti people, of Zaire, 77–78, 118,
 130–131, 163
meals, cooking and eating, 103–106
mental illness, 156
micro-world vs. macro-world, 46
Middletown (Lynd and Lynd), 23, 95
Middletown Families (Caplow and
 others), 25, 40, 60
Middletown in Transition (Lynd and
 Lynd), 23
*Migrants, Sharecroppers,
 Mountaineers* (Coles), 93
migration, 138–149, 158, 195;
 debates on effects of, 146–148;
 poverty and, 139, 140, 142, 143,
 144, 145, 146, 147, 149, 158, 285;
 reflections about, 148–149; return
 rates of migrants and, 148; to
 United States, 140–145; within
 United States, 145–146
minimum wage, 150, 158
"modern" families (of 1800s), 17–18
modified extended families, defined,
 10
money strains, in stepfamilies, 259
Montagnai people, of St. Lawrence
 Valley, 78
Moral Majority, 37, 38
"moral mother," 173
motherhood, historical perspective
 on, 85
mothers: in Colonial times, 15–16;
 kinship work done by, 108–109;
 in nineteenth century, 24; single,
 43, 98, 99–100, 155, 201, 219; in
 slavery, 31; working, 13, 35, 41,
 89, 96, 105, 106, 153, 165, 168,
 173–174, 197, 201, 283–284
Mothers and Divorce (Arendell), 239,
 257
Mount Allegro (Mangione), 3, 10,
 106, 125
movies, 24
Moyers, Bill, 186
multigenerational bonds, 126
Muncie, Indiana: decline of
 communities in, 133; "good
 provider" role in, 164; historical
 trends in, 23–25; housework in,
 216, 218, 219(table); kinship in,
 121–122; marriages in, 60–61;
 shelter movement and, 275; wife
 abuse in, 266, 275
Mundurucu people, of Amazon, 76–
 77, 131, 159, 225, 226, 256
mutual violent control, 269

Myth of Family Decline, The (Kain),
 41

National Alliance for Caregiving, 11(
National Coalition Against Domestic
 Violence, 275
National Crime Victimization
 surveys, 268
National Family Violence Surveys,
 270
National Organization for Women,
 37
National Women's Conference, 44
Native Americans, 11, 145, 225, 230,
 256
Negro Family, The (Moynihan), 189
*Nickeled and Dimed: On (Not)
 Getting By in America*
 (Ehrenreich), 184
1950s, 25–29, 46, 47, 153, 223, 285
Nobody Ever Died of Old Age
 (Curtin), 127
no-earner families, 201
no-fault divorce, 229, 231, 237–239,
 243
*No Man's Land: Men's Changing
 Commitments to Family and Work*
 (Gerson), 171
Northern free blacks, 32–33
nuclear families, 2, 7, 29, 33, 116,
 285–286; defined, 10; as "normal"
 and universal, 48; sense of
 community and, 133, 134–135; vs
 stepfamilies, 258, 260
nursing, of babies. *See* breast-
 feeding
nursing homes, 111

"obligation to self," divorce and, 39,
 244–245
one-earner families, 152, 201
one-parent families, 98–100, 201
*Our Babies, Ourselves: How Biology
 and Culture Shape the Way We
 Parent* (Small), 78
Overspent American, The (Schor), 21(
Ozzie and Harriet (TV show), 25

parenthood, 71–102; after divorce,
 235; historical perspective on, 76–
 78, 84–85; joys of, 71–76; sharing
 of, 169–174, 175, 176
parents: blaming, 93–95; caregiving
 to, 109–113; gay and lesbian, 100-
 101
patriarchy, 11, 15, 280
patrilineal descent, 11
peer marriages, 55–56
People and Folks (Hagedorn), 190
Plymouth Colony, 2–3
Plymouth Plantation, 12, 14, 109,
 120
Pogrebin, Letty Cottin, 8, 44, 49, 54
political conditions, migration and,
 138, 139, 140, 142–143, 149
"Politics of Housework, The"
 (Ainardi), 215
Pollitt, Katha, 20

Popenoe, David, 39
post-traumatic stress disorder, in battered women, 274
potato famine, in Ireland, 141
poverty, 92(table), 179, 183–185; absent fathers and, 95, 96; African American families in, 187, 188, 194; children in, 43, 92–93, 179–180; "culture" of, 184; extended families and, 180; migration and, 139, 140, 142, 143, 144, 145, 146, 147, 149, 158, 285; single motherhood and, 155; violence in families and, 268–269; wage insufficiency and, 151
power inequalities: changing, through earning potential, 171–172, 183, 221; feminist perspective on, 43–44, 60; housework and, 171, 217, 221–222; violence and, 156, 276–277, 278
premarital sex, 14, 16
private family, rise of, 22
Promise Keepers, 8
provider role. See "good provider" role
public housing, 153

racism, 145, 186, 189, 190
Reagan, Ronald, 8, 38
reciprocal aid, 180–181
rent and renters, 153, 156
repressed sexuality, myth of, 19
return migration, 148
romance and romantic love, historical perspective on, 16, 18, 22, 24

Safe Havens Project, 280
"safe house program," for gay men, 275
same-sex couples, 1, 2, 23, 34, 51, 65–70, 98; rights and benefits for, 67, 68–69; violence between, 275, 278
same-sex marriages, 1, 7, 9, 34, 51, 66–67, 101; countries allowing, 68; debates on, 69–70; recent and ongoing changes involving, 283; struggle for, 66–67
same-sex unions, 67–68. See also civil unions
Sanctions and Sanctuary: Cultural Perspectives on the Beating of Wives (Counts, Brown, and Campbell), 264
Sanders, Bernie, 157–158
Savage Inequalities (Kozol), 93
schooling, mandatory, 84
secondary gains, 172
Second Chances: Men, Women, and Children a Decade after Divorce (Wallerstein and Blakeslee), 252
Second Shift, The: Working Parents and the Revolution at Home (Hochschild), 54, 172, 173, 174, 197, 203, 217, 220
"second shift," 215, 220
secrets, family. See family secrets and facades

separation, of parents, 246–247. See also divorce
sex, gender vs., 159
sexual relations: marriage and, 52, 55, 56; premarital, 14, 16
"shacking up," 62
Shadowed Lives: Undocumented Immigrants in American Society (Chavez), 143
sharecropping, 33
sharing vs. nonsharing, of child care and housework, 54, 109, 162, 163, 169–173, 193, 197, 198, 201, 203, 210, 215–223, 244
shelters, for battered women, 28, 45, 266, 273, 274–275, 279, 281
sibling relationships, 123
SIDS. See sudden infant death syndrome
"silicon syndrome," 42
"simple living," 211, 222, 223
single-earner families, 152, 201
single-parent families, 43, 98–100, 189, 192, 197, 200, 201, 208, 219
slaves and slavery, 14, 29–31, 138, 140–141, 186, 189, 191
sleeping, with parents. See co-sleeping
social class. See class(es)
social isolation, wife abuse and, 276
socialization, 159, 160–162, 240, 278. See also gender roles
social security, 9
Sociology of Housework, The (Oakley), 216
sole legal custody, 248, 249
Solo Crossing (Campbell), 224
speedup, of family lives, 208
split custody, 248
Stacey, Judith, 45, 49
standard of living, after divorce, 241
"Stealing the Children" (Ford), 165
stepfamilies, 258–260
"Stepping Back from Anger" (American Academy of Matrimonial Lawyers), 256
Stiffed: The Betrayal of the American Man (Faludi), 166
storytelling, 106–107
Stratis, Sofia, 116–118, 126, 136
Strengths of African American Families, The (Hill), 190
stress: caregiving and, 113; divorce and, 234
sudden infant death syndrome (SIDS), 80
suicide, 156, 234
supportive detachment, toward children, 94
Surviving the Breakup: How Children and Parents Cope with Divorce (Wallerstein and Kelly), 252

tax reform, 158
teenagers: homeless, 114; and parents, conflicts with, 21; pregnancy among, 192

television, fictional families on, 10, 13–14, 25, 26, 27, 28, 29, 265–266
Terkel, Studs, 26, 198
There Are No Children Here (Kotlowitz), 93, 180
Tikopia people, of Polynesia, 6–7, 77, 93, 127, 196
Time Bind, The: When Work Becomes Home and Home Becomes Work (Hochschild), 54, 71, 87, 105, 107, 173, 197, 202, 203, 205, 207–208
Torn, Rip, 195
touching (holding), of children, 80–81
traditions, family, 107
True Womanhood, Cult of, 18, 19
two-earner (two-worker) families, 200–201, 203, 204, 206

Uncoupling: How Relationships Come Apart (Vaughan), 234
unemployment, 149, 156, 166, 186, 190, 202–203, 277
Unexpected Legacy of Divorce, The (Wallerstein, Lewis, and Blakeslee), 252, 253
unions, 149–150, 200
United for a Fair Economy, 158
Urban Villagers (Gans), 180
U.S. Census Bureau, 7, 70

violence, in families, 9, 262–282; control issues in, 269, 272–274, 276–277, 281, 282; cultural perspectives on, 264–265; economic dependence and, 277; experiences of, related by victims, 272–274; gender differences in, 269–272; historical perspective on, 265–267; legal strategies for responding to, 280–281; men against, 280; limits of therapy for, 281; power issues in, 156, 276–277, 278; practical advice for stopping, 282; reasons and explanations for, 275–278; as self-defense, questions about, 271–272; solutions to, 278–282; statistics on, 268–269; types of, 263–264, 269; unemployment and, 156, 277
Violence Against Women Act, 279
violent resistance, 269

wages, 150–151. See also income
Wallerstein, Judith, 39
Walsh, Joan, 44–45, 49
Way We Never Were, The (Coontz), 13
Way We Really Are, The (Coontz), 71
welfare, families on, 183, 184
Western Bontoc people, in Philippines, 160
We, The Tikopia: Kinship in Primitive Polynesia (Firth), 6
What My Heart Wants to Tell (Slone), 3, 104, 133

Whitehead, Barbara Dafoe, 39
wife abuse, 262–263, 264, 265, 266.
  See also battered women
"Wives' Marital Work in a Culture of
  Divorce" (Hackstaff), 54
Women and Men in Society (O'Kelly
  and Carney), 264
Women's Educational and Industrial
  Union, 152
women's movement, 196, 245, 266,
  274. *See also* feminist
  perspective(s)
"women's work," 87, 169, 217
work: concerns about reversal of

home and, 203–206; daily living
  and, 207–209; employment status
  of parents and, 200(table); and
  family, interactions between, 198–
  203; hours spent at, 206–207, 210–
  211, 214, 222; nature of, 195–196;
  negative spillover from, 201–203.
  See also labor force participation
workaholism, 42, 47
"Work and Its Meaning" (Rubin), 202
work-family imbalance: 42, 163,
  172–173, 199, 201–203; solutions
  to, 200, 206, 209–215
work force. *See* labor force
  participation

working-class families, 177, 178,
  180–181, 183–184, 185, 190, 216,
working mothers, 13, 35, 41, 153,
  165, 173–174, 197, 201; child-c
  arrangements for children of, 8
  meal preparation and, 105, 106
  recent and ongoing changes
  involving, 283–284; wages earn
  by, 96, 168
World Full of Women, A (Ward),
Worlds of Pain (Rubin), 165, 180,
  182, 202, 218

About the Author

Alex Liazos is professor of sociology at Regis College in Weston, Massachusetts, and the author of two other texts in sociology: *People First: An Introduction to Social Problems* and *Sociology: A Liberating Perspective*. He has also written several papers, one of which, "The Poverty of the Sociology of Deviance: Nuts, Sluts, and Preverts" (1972) has been reprinted in over twenty volumes of collected readings.

Liazos lives in Watertown, Massachusetts, where he was elected to the Watertown Town Council for three terms. He is active in groups working for affordable housing, peace, the environment, the rights of people with disabilities, and other social-justice causes. His hobbies include riding his bicycle on the paths along the Charles River and participating in a group that produces folk music concerts.